THE 1993
INFORMATION PLEASE®
ENVIRONMENTAL ALMANAC

COMPILED BY

World Resources Institute

HOUGHTON MIFFLIN COMPANY BOSTON & NEW YORK 1993

Editor in Chief Allen Hammond
Managing Editor Terry Stutzman Mast
Senior Editor Cheryl Simon Silver
Production Coordinator Marilyn M. Powell

Production Staff
James R. Mangani, map and graphics production
Eric Rodenburg, map and data production
Dale Hopper, editorial assistant
Kim Anderson, data entry
Susan Kunhardt, copy editing
Michael K. Hayes, proofreading

Principal Contributors: Beryl Benderly, Russell Clemings, Kathleen Courrier, Pamela S. Cubberly, Catherine McMullen, Gregory Mock, Steve Nadis, Thomas Prugh, Kathleen Rude, Cheryl Simon Silver, Elizabeth Stark, Karen Dorn Steele.

Photo credits: p. 8, United Nations Photo Library; p. 32, Library of Congress *U.S. News & World Report* collection; p. 126, Library of Congress Farm Security Administration collection; p. 300, rice planting in Bangladesh, The World Bank.

ISBN (Cloth): 0-395-63767-8
ISBN (Paper): 0-395-63766-X
ISSN: 1057-8293

Comments and suggestions from readers are invited. Because of the many letters received, however, it is not possible to respond personally to every correspondent. Nevertheless, all letters are welcome and each will be carefully considered. Address all correspondence to Houghton Mifflin Company, 2 Park Street, Boston, Massachusetts 02108.

Information Please is a registered trademark of Houghton Mifflin Company.
Printed in the United States of America

WP Pa   BP Hbd 10 9 8 7 6 5 4 3 2 1

STATE OF THE PLANET 8

The United Nations Conference on Environment and Development drew leaders and environmental activists from nearly 200 countries to Rio de Janeiro in June 1992. What was accomplished there? What wasn't? Where do we go from here?

CLOSE TO HOME 32

What are the most critical environmental issues affecting our daily lives and lifestyles? How can we as individuals and as concerned citizen groups help to bring about change in government policy and environmental practice?

TABLE OF CONTENTS

A NATIONAL VIEW — 126

Toxic residues of the Cold War nuclear buildup, losses of native animals, plants, and natural places, the struggle over timber cutting in prime forest habitat. . . . Have the demands we place on our national environment taken us beyond the point of no return?

Scientists see the stratosphere above and the soil below losing their abilities to protect and support our ever-expanding global population. What are the main environmental concerns of 143 countries?

TABLE OF CONTENTS

ACKNOWLEDGEMENTS

Special thanks: The editors and writers gratefully acknowledge these institutions, publications, and individuals for contributing data, information, and advice.

Highlights of the Year: Adapted by permission from *Greenwire: The Daily Executive Briefing on the Environment*, © APN, Philip Shabecoff, executive publisher. For more information, contact Donald Tighe, *Greenwire*, 782 N. Washington Street, Falls Church, VA 22046. (703) 237-5130. Cheryl Simon Silver adapted the material. Deborah Estes and Robert Livernash contributed to the adaptation of topical news items within chapters.

Wastes: Allen Blakely, National Solid Wastes Management Association; Jonathan V.L. Kiser, Integrated Waste Services Association; Jim Glenn, *BioCycle: Journal of Waste Recycling*.

Energy: Tom Welch, Energy Information Administration, U.S. Dept. of Energy; Cynthia Mitchell, consulting economist; Peter Gray, Friends of the Earth; Eric Hirst, Oak Ridge National Laboratory; John Morrill, American Council for an Energy-Efficient Economy; Robin Roy, Office of Technology Assessment; Rick Tempchin, Edison Electric Institute; John Rudd, Freshwater Institute; Mike Foley, National Association of Regulatory Commissioners (reviewer).

Transportation: James J. MacKenzie, World Resources Institute.

Air Pollution: Ray Wassel, National Academy of Sciences.

Grassroots Activities: Lynn Bock, Environmental Support Center; Martha Schumacher, Institute for Conservation Leadership; Donna Carroll, Gwich'in Steering Committee; the writers of grassroots entries, and the other individuals who contributed networking ideas; Benjamin A. Goldman, "Grass-roots Organizations," in *The Truth About Where You Live: An Atlas on Toxins and Mortality* (Times Books, Random House, 1991).

Cleaning up after the Cold War: Don Provost, Washington Dept. of Ecology; Jim Thomas, Hanford Education League; Bob Alvarez, U.S. Senate Governmental Affairs Committee.

Wildlife: Pegi Dover, World Wildlife Fund-Canada; Doug Inkley, National Wildlife Federation; Michael O'Connell, World Wildlife Fund; Bob Pacific, U.S. Fish and Wildlife Service; Bruce Peterjohn, Patuxent Wildlife Research Center; Katherine Ransel, American Rivers; Michael Sutton, TRAFFIC(USA), World Wildlife Fund.

Wetlands and Forests: Tom Yocom, U.S. Environmental Protection Agency; Larry Tuttle, The Wilderness Society; Richard Rice, Conservation International; Douglas MacCleery, USDA Forest Service.

Industry: Doug Blanke, Minnesota Attorney General's Office; Charles McGlashan, Deloitte & Touche. The credit line on page 194 should read: From Frances Cairncross, *Costing the Earth: The Challenge for Governments, the Opportunities for Business*. (Boston, Harvard Business School Press, 1992), pp. 317–318. © 1992 by Frances Cairncross. Reprinted by permission of the publisher.

State and Province Comparisons and Profiles: Carolyn Clarke, proofreader; Paul Rump and Maureen Copley, State of the Environment Reporting; Kirk Hamilton, Hélène Trepanier, and Craig Gaston, Statistics Canada.

Ozone Depletion: Michael J. Kurylo, Upper Air Atmospheric Research, NASA; Joel Levy and Reva Rubenstein, Global Change Division, U.S. Environmental Protection Agency; Owen B. Toon, NASA-Ames; Edward Browell, NASA-Langley; Joe Waters, Jet Propulsion Laboratory.

Land Degradation: Kevin C. Burke, Lunar and Planetary Institute.

Country Comparisons and Profiles: Beryl L. Benderly, profile revision writer; Linnaea Schroeer, proofreader; Mieke van der Wansem, country reports for UNCED; Dirk Bryant and Norbert Henninger, data assistance; former Soviet Union data: John Dunlop, Ward Kingkade, Center for International Research, U.S. Bureau of the Census; R. Roberts, William Seltzer, United Nations Statistical Division; Francesco Pariboni, Statistics Division, Food and Agriculture Organization of the United Nations; in-country reviews were received from: China, India, Israel, Malaysia, Nepal, Saudi Arabia, Singapore, Brazil, Peru, Suriname, Zimbabwe, Hungary, Trinidad and Tobago.

Index: Julie Phillips, indexer.

Technical Service: EPI, Rockville, MD. Vincent Llewellyn, backup desktop production

State of the Planet

In 1992, the Earth Summit focused world attention on the environment.

After nearly two years of preparatory work, more than 170 nations sent delegations to the Earth Summit—the United Nations Conference on Environment and Development held in Rio de Janeiro, Brazil, last June. Also present were representatives of thousands of nongovernmental organizations, many major industrial corporations, and nearly 9,000 members of the media. Some 118 heads of state—the largest such gathering of leaders ever—attended the final ceremonies.

The conference's drawing power and the expansive news coverage aptly illustrated that, with the demise of the Cold War, environmental issues are now at the center of the world's pressing problems. Global warming, ozone depletion, the destruction of the world's forests, the accelerating extinction of species and resulting loss in biodiversity, the pollution of air and water, the improper disposal of toxic wastes—all these have become familiar headlines.

Yet as the Rio conference proved, the world is still divided. Leaders of developing countries in the southern hemisphere insisted at Rio that environmental protection alone was not enough. They argued that agreements about global environmental issues must also include measures for the economic development that many of them so badly need. Moreover, they asserted, the rich countries of the North must assist poor countries in their struggle to develop if the environment is to be protected. As Brazilian President Collor de Mello, host of the conference, put it, "You can't have an environmentally healthy planet in a world that is socially unjust." The

---

State of the Planet News
Washington, D.C., 8/1/92—*In an internal assessment of the Rio Earth Summit, EPA Administrator William K. Reilly conceded that the Bush administration had assigned a low priority to negotiations on forest protection, dragged its feet on signing a global warming treaty, and committed few resources to the conference. "No doubt this contributed to the negative feelings toward the United States," Reilly wrote. U.S. positions at the conference came under intense criticism from industrial and developing countries alike.*

North acknowledged the connection between environment and development in many of the conference documents, and some industrial countries did commit themselves to increased monetary aid. But the North refused to commit to specific steps to reduce their own industrial pollution, while pressing the developing countries of the South to protect forests and wildlife. The debate was heated at times, and the angry polarization between nations of the North and South was a vivid reminder of the risk of a new and very different kind of cold war—one between rich and poor.

Beyond the North-South tension, however, the Rio conference made the larger point that protecting the environment and promoting economic growth are not opposed to each other but rather are ultimately inseparable actions. This complementarity of environmental and economic goals was clearly a new idea to some of the governments represented at Rio. At the core of this idea is a fusion of environmentalism and economics into a potent, if still fuzzy, concept called sustainable development.

In essence, sustainable development means economic growth that we can live with and that future generations can live with too. It means growth that improves human welfare but does not squander the resources of the planet nor undermine the biological systems on which life depends. Sustainable development essentially requires human societies to take into account the long-range consequences of their actions. The concept is thus not easy to translate into specific actions that individuals or governments can grapple with. It is nonetheless important: sustainable development may well become the basis of a rethinking of economic principles and national accounting systems. And as the environmental consequences of "business as usual" become ever more apparent, sustainable development may even become the organizing principle of the 21st century.

But apart from beginning the education of governments and their leaders in such new ideas, what did Rio accomplish? The initial press coverage spanned the spectrum, from success to failure. Now, some months after the delegates have departed from Rio's conference halls, restaurants, and beaches, it is possible to gauge a little more carefully the likely consequences of what was debated there.

The Fruits of Rio

The Earth Summit produced two new international treaties on climate and on biodiversity, a statement on forests, the Rio Declaration, and an action plan for sustainable development known as Agenda 21. In addition, the meeting produced a consensus that negotiations should begin for a treaty to curb the trend in which once-productive lands are increasingly turning into deserts. Countries also established a watchdog commission to monitor progress on the pledges made at Rio.

The Climate Treaty. The United Nations Framework Convention on Climate Change sets out broad principles rather than establishing legal obligations. It requires countries to use their "best efforts" to reduce emissions of climate-altering greenhouse gases and mentions a target of stabilizing emissions at 1990 levels. At the insistence of the United States, however, it does not commit signatories to any timetable for meeting such targets. Nor does it require industrialized countries to share technology for controlling greenhouse emissions with developing countries. Nonetheless, the treaty establishes in international law the principle that nations must take into account the global environmental consequences of their economic and technological decisions, particularly in energy matters.

Furthermore, the treaty commitments can be hardened by subsequent agreements, for which the organization groundwork is already prepared under the terms of the Convention. This is in fact exactly what happened to an earlier international agreement on ozone-destroying gases. Following

discovery of the Antarctic ozone hole, the Montreal Protocol to Control Substances That Deplete the Ozone Layer in 1987 added specific obligations to an initially vague framework treaty, the Vienna Convention. These commitments were subsequently increased to accelerate the phaseout of these gases.

One commentator described the climate treaty as having "the potential of forcing governments to change domestic policies to a greater degree than any [existing] international agreement." It was signed by all industrial nations and many developing nations, more than 160 at summer's end.

The Biodiversity Treaty. The United Nations Convention on Biological Diversity calls for the development of national strategies for the conservation and sustainable use of biological diversity, including the establishment of lists of species to be preserved. But like the climate treaty, it does not set any deadlines or other hard-and-fast legal obligations. Nor does it set clear obligations for sharing the fruits of genetic engineering between countries that exploit genetic knowledge and countries in which the valuable genes are discovered or for protecting the intellectual property rights represented by genetic innovations, although some of these issues are expected to be worked out in additional negotiations. The treaty was signed by all industrial nations except the United States and by most developing countries, more than 150 in all.

The Forest Agreement. Hopes for a treaty intended to preserve the world's forests foundered on disagreements between North and South. Developing countries, lead by India and Malaysia, insisted that forests are subject only to the sovereign decisions of the nations in which they occur—and thus that their uses and their management could not be subject to an international treaty. Developing nations also point out that the industrial countries of the North long ago cut down many of their forests, converting vast areas to farmland or other uses that helped to enrich those countries; the developing nations insist on the right to do the same with their forests, if they so choose. Developed countries tried to negotiate principles that would put some moral pressure on countries to preserve their forests or to manage them sustainably, but the final document, a Statement of Agreement on Forest Principles, does more to legitimize existing practices (Malaysia is the world's largest exporter of tropical timber) than to protect forests.

The Rio Declaration. This 27-point statement commits countries that sign it to pursue sustainable development and to work toward eradicating poverty. It is not legally binding, but may turn out to have significant moral and political force—as did the Helsinki declaration on human rights—if public opinion solidifies on these issues. Among the new principles it enunciates are the "special responsibility" of developed countries for global environmental restoration because of their technological and financial capabilities and their major contribution to pollution and resource consumption.

Agenda 21. This massive 800-page document contains recommendations designed to guide countries toward sustainable development and protection of the global environment. The recommendations are nonbinding but nonetheless contain a number of constructive ideas and provisions, including development by each country of national strategies for sustainable development; adoption of community-based approaches to sustainable development with decentralized decisionmaking on management of natural resources and reform of land ownership to give rural and indigenous people title over or rights to land; actions to improve the status and participation of women in sustainable development activities in developing countries; removal of subsidies that conflict with sustainable development; and adoption of pollution taxes and other economic incentives. However, the document does not commit rich countries to increase their financial aid to poor countries in amounts that would help implement some of these recommendations, although some individual countries did make pledges of additional aid.

Commission on Sustainable Development. This new United Nations commission is intended to ensure effective follow-up to the Earth Summit and to report on progress in implementing Agenda 21.

Measured against many prior attempts to forge global treaties and agreements, the Earth Summit was an unprecedented success—especially given the North-South split, the requirement that all agreements be achieved by consensus, the diverse and difficult subject matter, and the short, two-year cycle of negotiations. The language of the new agreements and declarations is in many respects revolutionary, laying the framework for global action on two key environmental topics and committing governments to principles that have the potential to fundamentally alter present economic and social patterns.

The Earth Summit established another precedent as well. By allowing nongovernmental groups into the preparatory process, the conference exposed the negotiations to the pressures of public opinion. Thousands of representatives of such groups—representing many different aspects of the public at large—debated, persuaded, and often educated the delegates. It may well be impossible for international diplomacy ever to fully retreat behind closed doors again, at least on issues that so directly concern large segments of the public; if so, the world's peoples will have gained a more direct voice in global decision-making.

Yet the crucial test will be whether the commitments made in Rio are kept—whether the bold words lead to actions in the months and years ahead. That in turn will depend on the political will of the world's leaders and, perhaps equally, on continued attention by the media and continued pressure from nongovernmental groups and from citizens around the world.

An Environmental Challenge

So how is the United States doing with regard to environmental concerns? The United States can point to much progress in cleaning up specific sources of air and water pollution over the past 20 years. It has arguably the world's best system of national and state parks and an extensive network of national forests, wilderness areas, and nature preserves. It is a leader in climate research, in many other areas of environmental science, and in the development of many new, more efficient, and cleaner technologies.

Yet it is not hard to point to many areas in which the United States is clearly not on a sustainable path. It is the world's largest user of fossil fuels—coal, oil, and natural gas—and is consequently the world's largest source of the climate-altering gases that contrib-

ute to global warming: 22 percent of global carbon dioxide emissions, 18 percent of all greenhouse gases taken together. On a per capita basis, U.S. residents have a potential impact on global warming eight times that of the world average and nearly twice that of Japan. Combustion of fossil fuels is also the cause of most urban air pollution and of the acid rain that damages monuments, mountain lakes, soils, and vegetation. Using energy more effi-

> **State of the Planet News**
> Mexico City, 6/16/02—At a press conference called to sign a debt-for-nature swap, Mexican President Carlos Salinas de Gortari said that the best way to resolve environmental problems is through expanded trade and through opening markets to developing economies, not through more donations or foreign aid. Nonetheless, he announced that Latin American nations will compete for their share of the expanded development aid called for by the Earth Summit.

ciently and accelerating development of other energy sources could make a major difference over time. Imposing carbon or pollution taxes would accelerate a transition to more sustainable energy sources.

Historically, the United States has subsidized development and exploitation of natural resources. That made sense a century ago, when such policies were established. Now such subsidies are coming under increasing scrutiny; elimination of subsidies, it is increasingly argued, would help to ensure wiser and more efficient use of such resources.

The United States subsidizes cutting of timber in the national forests, for example, just as many developing countries subsidize logging or clearing of tropical forests. An added source of controversy is the cutting of old-growth forests, especially in the Pacific Northwest. Such forests take longer than 200 years to fully regenerate, far longer than current harvesting cycles. Thus, current practices are far from sustainable, since they cannot preserve these forests—and the species that live in them—as stable ecosystems that can be appreciated by future generations. The existence of such practices was a source of considerable embarrassment to the United States at the Earth Summit, since the Bush administration was proposing that developing countries adopt policies to preserve their forests for future generations.

Agriculture is another natural resource-based industry that is heavily subsidized through direct support

---

State of the Planet News

London, 5/31/92—The Economist *describes population growth as "The Question Rio Forgets."* The article argues that population growth is a root cause, along with poverty, of much of the environmental degradation in the developing world. The issue is extremely controversial, with the Catholic Church arguing that population growth only seldom causes environmental problems, while some developing countries view population growth as less important to global sustainability than high consumption patterns in industrial countries.

---

payments, price supports, and protection from competition. The amounts of taxpayer dollars involved in these subsidies are large: an estimated $17 billion to $22 billion per year. Agriculture is also the largest and possibly the most damaging source of water pollution in the United States. Intensive use of pesticides and fertilizers leads to runoff, to contamination of some underground water supplies, to pesticide residues in some fish, to overfertilization of estuaries, and frequently to disruption of freshwater and coastal ecosystems.

The United States also subsidizes livestock production on federally owned rangelands and the supply of irrigation water in many parts of the western United States. This circumstance leads to inefficient and often inappropriate use and is consequently a major contributor to overgrazing, to salinization of soils, and to the shortage of water for urban areas in some parts of California.

Quite apart from subsidies, some uses of natural resources are so heavy that the resource may disappear or be permanently degraded. In some parts of the country, water is being pumped from underground aquifers at rates far higher than it can be replenished. With such unsustainable practices, some major aquifers will be pumped dry in a generation, leaving farms and cities that now depend on such aquifers without adequate water supplies. Carelessly disposed of toxic wastes are leaking into and contaminating still other aquifers. Overfishing—a problem in most major marine fisheries off U.S. coasts—is another instance of using a resource too hard. New restrictions were placed on the Pacific Northwest salmon catch in 1992 in an attempt to preserve that fishery from collapse.

Perhaps the greatest challenge to the United States, however, is to demonstrate global leadership in dealing with the issues raised by the Earth Summit. Developing countries, hard pressed to meet basic human needs and develop industrial economies, have neither the economic resources, the trained personnel, nor the inclination to pioneer sustainable development. They argue that the rich countries must lead and must first demonstrate at home what they would preach abroad.

A second imperative is to form effective international partnerships for sustainable development. If we want tropical forests preserved and poor people lifted out of poverty, then the industrial countries will have to help. The analogy is often made to the Marshall Plan initiated by the United States after World War II. Then, the United States provided massive aid to help the countries of western Europe, devastated by war, rebuild their infrastructures and restart their economies. The impetus for this aid was not wholly altruistic—it created huge markets for American goods and strong democracies that could resist the Communist threat. In the same way, it can be argued that it is in the direct self-interest of the industrial countries of the North to aid the development of the South on the scale of the Marshall Plan. The opportunities and needs are many: financial aid, support for family planning policies and services that can help limit population growth, technical assistance, sharing of cleaner, more efficient technologies, and others.

A Global View

The Secretary General of the Earth Summit, Canadian Maurice Strong, summed up the hope of the Rio conference this way: "The people of our planet, especially the young and the generations which follow them, will hold us accountable for what we do or fail to do in Rio. Earth is the only home we have; its fate is literally in our hands." It is a sentiment that applies also to the follow-up from Rio and to the actions of individuals and governments in every country in coming years. That is where the editors hope this Almanac can play a modest role, in providing you, its readers, with information that will allow you to form your own judgments and take your own actions on environmental issues.

State of the Planet was written by Allen Hammond, editor-in-chief of the 1993 Information Please Environmental Almanac.

Highlights of the Year

A Calendar of Environmental Events

October 1991

1 Big Three automakers agree to reduce dumping of toxics into the Great Lakes. The cuts are voluntary, and the manufacturers can find the most cost-effective way to make the cuts.

1 Interior Secretary Manuel Lujan Jr. summons high-level White House cabinet members and presidential advisors, the so-called "God squad," to consider whether to exempt the endangered northern spotted owl from protection. The exemption would open the door for more federal timber harvests in OR.

1 People for the Ethical Treatment of Animals protests use of animals in auto safety tests. GM dealerships were boycotted in 20 states as part of PETA's "Heartbreak of America" campaign.

2 Federal government proposes that all children be tested for lead exposure by age 2. Policy shift is tied to growing evidence that low levels of lead contamination can impair mental development.

2 U.S. and Canada set goal of "zero discharge" of dangerous chemicals into Lake Superior.

2 Exxon Corp. announces national program to collect and recycle used motor oil. Exxon and Mobil are the first two oil companies to accept used oil at their service stations.

3 Excessive pesticide use is common in Philadelphia schools, according to studies by Public Citizen's Congress Watch and Citizen Action of Pennsylvania. Warnings for teachers and students are inadequate, investigators found.

3 Sulfuric acid should remain on the list of chemicals that must be reported in the Toxics Release Inventory, charges the Environmental Defense Fund. The group blasted an EPA proposal to remove the chemical from the list.

3 Kraft General Foods is using recycled plastic—polyethylene terephthalate, or PET—in its 24-ounce salad dressing bottles. This is the first use of recycled plastic in food containers other than soft drink bottles.

4 The Dept. of Energy will ship nuclear waste to federal lands in NM, even though Congress has not authorized the move. The waste will reside in the Waste Isolation Pilot Plant in salt caverns nearly half a mile underground.

4 West Virginia Gov. Gaston Caperton reverses the position he took in April 1991 when he granted an exemption from an executive order banning new landfills. Caperton now opposes a landfill proposed for McDowell Co.

5 Midwest industries legally dumped 7 million gallons of oil and grease and 89,000 pounds of lead into the Great Lakes in 1990, a General Accounting Office study reports.

8 Federal government cuts maximum lead exposure levels by more than half, to 10 micrograms of lead per deciliter of blood. The move is based on findings that as many as one in six U.S. children have absorbed dangerous levels of lead.

8 Ford Motor Co. plans to produce 2,500 1993 Taurus sedans that will run on either gas or methanol and 100 electric 1993 Ecostar minivans. Ford will use the vehicles to test-market alternatively powered vehicles.

8 Forest Service agrees to swap 202 acres of its land and $30,000 for 302 acres of pasture in Texas's Sam Houston National Forest. Sierra Club charges U.S. is trading healthy forestland for degraded pasture. Forest Service concedes loss of timber, but says the deal helps government land consolidation.

9 EPA Administrator William Reilly chides the National Parks and Conservation Association for giving President Bush a "D+," noting, "I would hope they would raise this to a 'C'."

9 Exxon Corp. will pay $1 billion in state and federal civil and criminal fines related to the Exxon *Valdez* oil spill in 1989. A federal judge in Anchorage approved the settlement. Environmentalists say the fines will neither cover cleanup costs nor encourage oil company efforts to avoid future spills. The *L.A. Times* reports that the true cost of environmental damage to Prince William Sound stemming from the Exxon *Valdez* spill may reach $15 billion, according to unpublished studies by state and federal researchers.

9   Three environmental groups sue the Fish and Wildlife Service for failing to protect the razorback sucker, a fish native to the Colorado Basin. The groups charge that failure to list the fish as an endangered species violates the Endangered Species Act.

9   Dept. of Energy halts nuclear waste shipments to NM, avoiding a showdown with Congress and the state.

9   Environmental testing laboratory, Enviro-Analysts, Inc., of Racine, WI, is found guilty of submitting false reports on the industrial waste of its corporate clients.

9   Sierra Club Legal Defense Fund warns FL water board that it will sue unless the board limits its groundwater withdrawal.

10   Bank of the West (BOTW) and The Nature Conservancy (TNC) of California announce that half of the $7 fee for a new BOTW Conservancy checking account will go to TNC to fund northern CA projects.

10   Satellite passing over Antarctica measured the lowest stratospheric ozone level on record, NASA reports.

11   New laws give CA sweeping powers to improve both safety of rail transport of toxic materials and state emergency response. The legislation follows the Southern Pacific rail accident that poured the toxic pesticide metam sodium into the upper Sacramento River in July 1991.

11   Two hundred citizen groups, businesses, and government officials launch campaign to promote energy efficiency and renewable energy sources.

12   EPA will investigate a Brevard County, FL, neighborhood with high rate of Hodgkin's disease. The area is near a suspected toxic dump for the South Patrick Air Force Base.

13   Environment Canada adds North American black bear to its endangered species list in response to Asian demand for internal organs for use in folk remedies.

13   Oil well fires in Kuwait could be extinguished by the end of 1991, much sooner than early projections. More than 600 of the 700 runaway fires are under control.

13   Plastic six-pack rings are being revamped by maker, Illinois Tool Works. The company is responding to a ME solid waste law that bans the use of standard rings because they are hazardous to wildlife.

14   Overflowing landfills in Dade County, FL, are two months away from shutdown, officials report.

15   Tennessee buys land from failed savings and loan at bargain prices. The state Wildlife Resources agency will use the land to enhance wildlife preservation efforts.

15   Police arrest 35 environmental activists who jumped the fence at a construction site for the nation's largest hazardous waste incinerator. More than 300 protested OH governor's failure to reconsider operating permit for the Cleveland plant.

16   Dow Chemical Co. creates board of outside advisors with environmental backgrounds to help formulate Dow's environmental policy.

16   A 45-mile stretch of Sacramento River, CA, ecosystem may not recover from 1991 pesticide spill for up to 50 years, state study finds.

16   Kodak receives U.S. patent for an improved method of recycling PET polyesters.

20   Georgia's plants and animals are slowly disappearing, an ongoing biological survey reveals. Midway through the first review since 1974 of the state's list of protected species, 230 plants and animals are recommended for protection, up from the 80 now protected by GA.

21   Five states, along with health and environmental organizations, file suit against federal government to force stronger ground-level ozone standards.

21   Decline in numbers of North American songbirds may be caused by fragmentation of their northern habitats, researchers suggest, based on a 10-year study of two bird species in NH. Other experts say the decline is more closely tied to destruction of tropical forests where the birds winter.

22   Federal appeals court throws out EPA ban on importing, making, or using asbestos. Ruling opens way for continued use of asbestos.

24   Texas Water Commission considering imposing pumping limits on the Edwards Aquifer asks U.S. judge to help balance human costs and costs to endangered species. Environmentalists object, saying move violates Endangered Species Act.

25   State and federal judges urge Congress to set up a national fund, financed by asbestos producers, to compensate victims of exposure.

25　New Jersey's new energy policy will stress conservation over new production capacity. The plan to cut consumption 25 percent in 10 years will save $4.5 billion a year.

25　Missouri's Dept. of Natural Resources wants to add 90,000 acres to the state's park system to help preserve the parks from environmental threats.

26　Public health officials warn Oakland and Berkeley, CA, residents returning to their fire-damaged homes that surviving containers of paints, solvents, and other substances may contain hazardous, high-pressure fumes.

26　Women living in areas with high concentrations of suspended dust face a 37 percent higher risk of developing cancer than women who live in less polluted areas. Loma Linda researchers studied 6,000 women for 10 years.

29　Nine eastern states agree to adopt California's strict auto emissions standards.

30　Smog caused by commuter traffic leads EPA to add four suburban counties to the official Washington, D.C., smog zone. Some of the counties were considered rural only 10 years ago.

30　EPA proposes first rules for reducing acid rain. The rules follow the 1990 Clean Air Act Amendments, which aim to halve emissions of sulfur dioxide by the year 2000.

30　Fund for Animals plans to sue U.S. Fish and Wildlife Service for delaying its decision on whether the FL black bear is an endangered species.

30　All-natural lawn care products company acquires rights to an insecticide, azadirachtin, made from seeds of the neem tree. Ringer Corp. will market the compound as Neem.

31　U.S. Navy plans to conduct 30 underwater explosives tests in the Florida Keys near or inside the Florida Keys National Marine Sanctuary. Results will provide data on mine clearing in the Persian Gulf.

31　Effluent from nearly one third of Canada's paper mills may be harmful to the environment, Canadian scientists report. The government will classify the total effluent from chlorine-using mills as toxic, rather than regulating single contaminants as it had in the past.

November 1991

1　Texas extends ban on harvesting oysters in Galveston Bay because of bacterial contamination from sewage systems, storm water runoff pollution, and other sources.

1　Flight attendants, current and former, file class-action suit against a group of tobacco companies. The seven plaintiffs claim they contracted cancer, heart disease, and respiratory illnesses because of exposure to smoke from passenger's cigarettes.

1　Detroit fails to keep poisonous metals and chemicals out of sewer system, two environmental groups charge.

2　Fifty to 70 percent of wetlands could lose their protected status under a new definition proposed by the Bush Administration, government field testing shows.

3　Land in IA set aside for a nuclear power plant will be used instead to re-create a native prairie ecosystem. The U.S. Fish and Wildlife Service will plow prime farmland, clearing the site for plants that thrived there in the mid-1800s.

3　Children suffering from height deficiencies related to moderate levels of pre- or postnatal lead exposure may be able to "catch up" if exposure is reduced, a U. of Cincinnati researcher finds.

4　Newly discovered chemical reactions convert sand into chemical compounds that may be used in making substances including plastics and ceramics, U. of Washington scientists report in the journal *Nature*.

4　Household hazardous waste will be collected through a pilot project planned by the IL EPA. The agency is looking for communities to cosponsor the long-term program.

5　Delaware wants Pennsylvania to clean up its streams. Wilmington, DE, and surrounding New Castle Co. draw 70 percent of their public water supplies from sources that come first through Pennsylvania's Chester Co.

6　Wichita, KS, funds cleanup of Superfund site itself so that redevelopment scheme could proceed. City planners were discouraged by Superfund's record of delay and by mounting costs at another site nearby.

6　Malfunction in a new sulfur recovery unit at Ashland Oil's refining complex in Catlettsburg, KY, spreads sulfur powder over Kenova, WV.

7　Auto industry urges states to slow plans to adopt tougher antipollution standards now required for cars sold in CA.

7　Radon levels in one of every five MD homes exceed EPA-recommended levels, survey finds.

9   Ozone layer over the Northern Hemisphere thinning faster than expected. Team of atmospheric researchers launches mission to learn whether an ozone "hole" is forming over north pole.

11   Uncontrolled burning of used oil in residential and industrial boilers is the largest single source of airborne lead emissions in U.S., industry and environmental groups report. They say lead in used oil is "virtually unregulated" by the federal government.

13   Many well-known manufacturers allow too much lead in dinnerware, suit alleges. The Environmental Defense Fund and the CA Attorney General take action against 10 major producers. Industry reps say lead exposure is "infinitesimal."

13   Sears, Roebuck and Co. and its suppliers announce they will reduce the volume of packaging of goods sold at Sears by 25 percent by 1994.

13   Duval Co. becomes the first FL county to meet the state goal for recycling 30 percent of its garbage.

14   Pan Am, joining 40 other airlines, agrees to stop shipments of birds caught in the wild.

14   Oklahoma citizens oppose imports of out-of-state industrial wastes and sludge.

15   Home Depot retail chain discontinues sale of lead solder in its plumbing departments nationwide.

15   Vice President Quayle's Council on Competitiveness is working to weaken the Clean Air Act Amendments of 1990 through "wantonly illegal activities," Rep. Henry Waxman (D-Calif.) charges on the one-year anniversary of President Bush signing the law.

15   Snake River sockeye salmon is added to the endangered species list, the National Marine Fisheries Service confirms.

18   Comeback of the CA gray whale prompts the National Oceanic and Atmospheric Administration to propose removing it from the Endangered Species list.

19   High-tech $38 million sterilization plant in Dacono, CO, begins to accept bins of medical waste from Front Range, CO, and Boulder Co. The waste is sterilized in a steam-filled autoclave.

19   Environmental deterioration of the 430-mile Sierra Nevada mountain range prompts officials and experts to meet to consider how to protect the range as a "single ecosystem."

20   Environmental groups accuse timber firms of destroying Pacific yew trees in the process of logging other trees. The yew bark is used to make taxol, a promising cancer drug.

20   Council on Economic Priorities publishes reports on the environmental records, including pollution prevention and cleanup, of 35 major corporations. One hundred reports are planned.

20   House of Representatives passes CA Desert Protection Act, the largest land protection bill in the continental U.S. Landmark bill would expand federal protection for 7.1 million acres. Bill goes to Senate.

21   Air pollution in the smoggiest U.S. cities dropped 10 percent during the past decade, EPA reports. Still, 74 million people live in cities that fail to meet federal clean air standards.

22   Certification standards for facial and toilet tissue products are issued by Green Seal group.

22   Stabilizing emissions of methane at present levels over the next century could reduce global warming by about 25 percent, scientists write in the journal *Nature*.

23   California air board adopts strict gasoline reformulation plan. Gas will be 30 percent cleaner and 12 to 17 cents per gallon more expensive by March 1996.

23   Ozone-mapping device built by U.S. is launched on board a Soviet satellite. The device supplements another Total Ozone Mapping Spectrometer aboard the NIMBUS-7 satellite, which is expected to run out of power within two years.

27   Congress agrees on $151 billion transportation bill, setting a new course that encourages use of mass transit, and gives states more choice in how to spend federal transportation money.

27   *Exxon Valdez* oil spill in 1989 killed 350,000 to 390,000 seabirds, the General Accounting Office tells Congress.

December 1991

3   Striped bass fishermen involved in six-year-old suit against General Electric Co. charge that GE knew discharges containing PCBs could harm the now-contaminated NY fishing grounds.

3   New metal hydride battery may improve range and reduce recharge time for electric vehicles, engineers at Energy Conversion Device's Ovonic Battery Division report.

4   Louisiana's largest criminal environmental investigation begins as state police examine who is responsible for illegal storage of 200,000 gallons of acids, pesticides, and solvents.

5 Petland pet store franchises will no longer buy wild-caught parrots.

5 Only 10 of 650 tribal leaders approached have expressed interest in receiving a federal study grant to explore using their lands as possible sites for a nuclear waste storage facility.

5 Canadian paper mills must eliminate production of dioxins and furans by 1996, but new regulations do not limit highly toxic organochlorines, critics charge.

6 Global emissions of carbon dioxide fell in 1990, despite oil field fires in Kuwait, Worldwatch Institute reports.

6 Two Houston energy companies form joint venture to build at least five compressed natural gas fueling stations in Houston in 1992.

7 Mercury found in Lake Champlain sediments may indicate widespread contamination, researchers studying toxics warn.

9 Specific environmental claims on products inspire more buyer confidence than certification by consumer groups Green Seal or Green Cross, survey finds.

9 First step of larger effort to learn how spill of toxic metam sodium affected health of Dunsmuir, CA, residents begins as health department receives $30,000 federal grant for survey.

9 Connecticut can reduce its air pollution in the short term through strategies more cost effective than California's low-emission-vehicle program, CT environmental commissioner says.

10 Which remaining habitats are most critical to long-term survival of migratory songbirds? The Nature Conservancy organizes major new study.

10 Mega-technologies won't reverse the threat to the ozone layer, scientists warn. Best solution, they say, is to "stop putting CFCs into the atmosphere."

11 Endangered wild salmon in the Columbia and Snake rivers will be protected by a partial plan adopted by the Northwest Power Planning Council. Sierra Club says plan is inadequate.

11 First U.S. food irradiation plant granted license in FL. The process kills bacteria and insects on food.

11 Citizens submit petition of right-to-know law to OH State General Assembly. Law would require consumer warnings on privately produced products that contain any of 458 toxic chemicals.

11 Coalition of ranchers, miners, and loggers meets in Idaho Falls, ID, to plan fight against environmentalists.

12 Price tag for cleaning up U.S. hazardous waste sites could be $750 billion over the next 30 years, U. of Tennessee researchers estimate.

12 Borrowers should disclose any possible contamination of sites they own, Canadian Bankers Association urges. They would like new legislation that would also "clarify" lender liability laws.

12 Northern Hemisphere warming recorded appears to be occurring at night, NOAA scientists say. Average low temperatures rose 1.5° F over the last 40 years; average highs stayed about the same.

13 South Pacific Ocean may be absorbing less carbon dioxide than scientists presumed, NOAA researchers report. About half of the CO_2 emitted by human activity was thought to go into the oceans, especially in the Southern Hemisphere, but high levels of the gas were not found in that area at the times studied.

13 Walt Disney Co., bowing to objections from environmentalists, abandons plans to build a giant resort in Long Beach, CA.

14 Developers give 220 acres to Anne Arundel County, MD, for use as a limited-access park and wilderness preserve, and will build 3,000 homes on the rest of the 830-acre plot.

15 Efforts to control ground-level ozone may be "misdirected." They place too much emphasis on control of volatile organic compounds and too little on nitrogen oxides, a National Academy of Sciences panel reports.

15 Coral reef at FL Keys may die in only 10 years if present rate of decline continues.

16 Greenway supporters want to create ribbons of protected space along the Potomac River in MD, VA, WV, and DC. The protected open space would allow wildlife to travel an unbroken path between habitats.

16 New York sues EPA for allowing other states to "dispose of toxic chemical waste in the state of New York without New York's permission."

16 Fish in Tensas River in LA contain unsafe concentrations of EPA-banned pesticides DDT and toxaphene. State health department may restrict fishing in area.

17 Zebra mussel that has been so disruptive to the ecology of the Great Lakes may be headed to the Chesapeake Bay, scientists fear.

17 Park Service issues plan to diminish commercialization in Yosemite Valley.

18 Eggshells of bald eagles nesting near the lower Columbia River contain dioxin, U.S. Fish and Wildlife Service discovers. Toxin may be a sign that the environmental health of the waterway is deteriorating.

18 Town of Oyster Bay, Long Island, cancels incinerator contract.

18 Immense land tract (126 sq. mi.) in the heart of the Ozarks acquired for conservation purposes. The Nature Conservancy and the MO Dept. of Conservation bought the land from Kerr-McGee Corp.

18 World grain harvest is 86 million tons, or nearly 5 percent less in 1991 than in 1990, Worldwatch Institute reports. Fall in production was concentrated in the former Soviet Union and in the U.S.

January 1992

3 Texas's Nature Conservancy purchases an 18,552-acre ranch, which includes the state's largest waterfall. The ranch will be used to study how business and recreational uses affect nature.

6 Lack of national standards for green labeling and advertising are causing companies to back away from green ads because their claims are challenged by government and consumer groups, Better Business Bureau officer says.

6 Button batteries used in cameras, watches, hearing aids, and calculators will be recycled through a new program in Michigan's Eaton and Barry counties. The program is designed to help keep heavy metals out of landfills.

7 Electromagnetic radiation from power lines and a nearby electrical substation caused her brain tumor, a 19-year-old woman from Guilford, CT, alleges in a suit against two CT utility companies.

7 Greenhouse effect of nitrogen oxides in aircraft exhaust fumes is 30 times greater than the effect of an equivalent amount of the gases emitted at the Earth's surface, U.K. researchers report in the journal *Nature*.

8 Polluted floodwaters gush into coastal bay systems, fouling more than 80 percent of Texas's most productive oyster reefs.

10 Personal and household goods will be regulated by California's Air Resources Board as the state steps up efforts to tackle its persistent air pollution.

10 Recyclable materials would be banned from disposal at landfills, according to a bill endorsed by Gov. Evan Bayh and the IN House Environmental Affairs Committee. The state's goal is to reduce solid waste 35 percent by 1995 and 50 percent by 2000.

10 Northern Telecom bans CFCs from its manufacturing processes.

13 West Warwick, RI, will sell compost made from sewage sludge the town used to landfill at a cost of $1,000 per day. The compost is made from sludge and wood ash.

13 New coal treatment process increases heat value of coal prevalent in MT and WY from 8,600 to 11,700 Btus and sulfur content by 40 percent. The "syncoal," developed by Entech, may provide an alternative for coal-burning utilities in the Midwest as they try to comply with Clean Air Act requirements for reducing sulfur dioxide emissions.

15 New Jersey becomes the first state in which all electric utilities have joined "Green Lights," EPA's program to encourage voluntary installation of energy-efficient lighting.

16 Sulfate emissions and ozone depletion mask the effects of global warming in the Northern Hemisphere, a U.N. climate panel reports.

17 Newly discovered, and pale, coral species may mean that studies on global warming and coral bleaching must be reconsidered, researchers find.

18 Pentagon cleanup of all bases contaminated by hazardous wastes will begin by the year 2000. Estimated cost is $25 billion.

19 Federal government agrees to buy 3,125 alternatively fueled vehicles from Chrysler and GM.

22 Green Seal proposes environmental standards for water-efficient fixtures. Products that meet the standards for certification earn the right to use the Green Seal ecolabel.

22 Reynolds Metals Co. extends its aluminum recycling programs to half of the U.S.

23 Florida's environmental secretary calls for a moratorium on new municipal trash incinerators to help curb mercury poisoning in the Everglades and other state wetlands.

23 American Reclaiming Corp. closes down Houston's only recycling plant for recovered plastic because of a "collapsing market."

24 A House subcommittee approves legislation to turn the Rocky Mountain Arsenal into a national wildlife refuge.

28 Environmental groups threaten to sue the U.S. Fish and Wildlife Service, charging that it should be investigating why numbers of two duck species, Alaska's spectacled and Steller's eider, are decreasing rapidly.

28 Docktor Pet Centers, the largest U.S. pet store chain, will no longer sell wild-caught parrots.

28 Numbers of bald eagles at NM wintering sites dropped 40 percent since 1990, survey reveals.

31 Waste Management, Inc., sues to force 150 insurers to share the cost of cleaning up Superfund sites for which the company is responsible because of land acquisition.

31 Kansas's chief engineer orders severe irrigation cutbacks near Great Bend so that more water can reach Cheyenne Bottoms, one of the most important wetlands in the Western Hemisphere.

February 1992

2 Toxic releases in GA fell 17 percent between 1989 and 1990. Of the 100 million pounds of toxic chemicals reported released, nearly three fourths was discharged into the air.

4 Republicans on an IN Senate committee amend proposed bill that banned throwing away recyclable materials.

4 Scientists detect highest levels of ozone-destroying compounds ever measured over Canada. Conditions for ozone destruction are far worse than expected.

4 Campbell County High School (KY) students organize rally to protest plans for a 7-mile pipeline to discharge salty wastewater into Licking River. Up to 300 protestors join in.

4 Religious and environmental groups join forces to urge California's governor and legislature to take steps to stabilize population growth. The loose coalition says the state absorbs 59,000 new residents each month.

5 Only $9.6 million of Exxon Corp.'s first $90 million settlement payment for the *Exxon Valdez* oil spill will go toward restoration. The bulk will be spent to reimburse the government for legal and scientific expenses.

6 Sewage line ruptures in San Diego, spilling 180 million gallons of partially treated sewage into the ocean per day.

8 Human error is the most recurrent problem at the nuclear power plants in the Nuclear Regulatory Commission's Region I, which includes PA and NJ, official says.

8 Increased levels of ultraviolet radiation reaching the Earth as the ozone layer thins may weaken immunities, thus causing an increase in certain infectious diseases, according to a new U.N. report.

10 Half of climate scientists polled worldwide believe the greenhouse effect could reach a point at which global warming could not be stopped, Greenpeace International reports. Thirteen percent said a "runaway" greenhouse effect is likely; 32 percent said it is possible.

11 The World Resources Institute, the World Conservation Union, and the United Nations Environment Program unveil plan for combating the global loss of biodiversity at a meeting in Caracas, Venezuela.

11 Indiana cannot ban out-of-state trash. Federal appellate judge rules that the ban would violate U.S. Constitution's interstate commerce clause.

11 White House steps up phaseout of ozone-depleting chemicals. Plans to end production of the chemicals by 1995 follow NASA findings of ozone depletion over parts of North America.

12 Health authorities close nearly 100 miles of southern CA coastline following massive sewage spills.

12 Concentrations of CFCs in the atmosphere increased at a significantly slower rate in 1991, says Sherwood Rowland, collaborator on the discovery connecting ozone depletion and CFCs.

12 Rocket leaking nerve gas discovered at Lexington-Bluegrass Army depot. None of the deadly gas escaped, Army spokesperson says.

12 No cancer-causing pollution found in Brevard County, FL, EPA reports as it concludes investigation of mysteriously high number of cancer cases in one neighborhood.

13 EPA cancels some uses of EBDC, a class of fungicides used on nearly every U.S.-grown vegetable and fruit crop. The fungicide is banned for use on 11 food crops, but it can be used on 45 others.

13 Southern California's heaviest winter storms of the century raise hopes that drought will end in California's central coast area.

13 Austin, TX, introduces its "Green Builder" program designed to encourage environmentally sound home building.

14 Indiana may drop off EPA's list of cities violating federal ozone standards because ozone levels have remained below federal standards for three years in a row.

17 Asbestos trial begins in Baltimore as 8,600 plaintiffs sue 14 companies for millions of dollars in damages.

17 Spectacled eider will go on threatened species list, and Steller's eider will be studied more closely, U.S. Fish and Wildlife Service says. Retired agency biologist petitioned to put both sea ducks on the Endangered Species list.

18 Texas radioactive waste board moves quickly to acquire west TX ranch for use as site of low-level nuclear waste dump.

18 Officials from two UT counties reject idea of creating a national park in the Escalante River canyons. County residents instead propose making the canyons a national conservation area, which would allow continuation of existing land uses.

19 Needles from Pacific yews yield taxol, a promising cancer drug, researchers at the U. of Mississippi find. Previously, taxol could be extracted only from the bark, and the process killed the tree.

19 Gas station owners in Philadelphia and Pittsburgh say state regulations requiring them to install expensive vapor control equipment could drive them out of business.

19 Seventy percent of U.S. endangered species will be more vulnerable if rapid global warming occurs, World Wildlife Fund reports.

19 HCFCs should not be considered a "safe" alternative to CFCs, Institute for Energy and Environmental Research warns. In a study based on data from DuPont, the group concludes that HCFCs are three to five times more dangerous than industry and the government claim.

20 U.S. Senate passes national energy strategy, 94-4. Provisions to allow drilling in the Arctic National Wildlife Refuge are not included in the final version.

21 EPA, environmental groups, oil companies, and the U. of Maryland join forces to create a "halon bank" where existing stocks of halon-

1301 fire-protection chemicals can be recycled to users who lack ozone-safe alternatives.

21 Chrysler Corp. recalls 141,000 cars that exceed federal hydrocarbon and carbon monoxide emission limits.

21 Loggers in Vancouver ask a local school board to pull a children's book from an elementary school library. *Maxine's Tree*, is about a girl who adopts a tree in the Carmanah Valley as she tries to save the forest from clear-cutting.

24 Canadian government and auto industry representatives sign agreement that will set standards for exhaust emissions, similar to those set out in the U.S. Clean Air Act, that will be the most rigorous in the world.

24 Known radiation releases from eastern ID nuclear engineering laboratory expose workers and their families living nearby to excessive doses of radiation, General Accounting Office reports.

25 President Bush unveils plan for tackling pollution along the U.S.-Mexico border.

27 Although dolphins drown in "purse" seine nets used to catch tuna, no practical alternative exists, four-year study by the National Academy of Sciences concludes. National Research Council says dolphin deaths can best be reduced by better training for boat captains.

27 U.S. Supreme Court hears oral argument in case to determine whether SC oceanfront property owner who was denied right to build on the land should be compensated.

27 Sulfur in coal can be removed by a new process before coal is burned. U. of Cincinnati researchers say their process is less expensive to operate than existing systems.

27 Seafood contamination is widespread, first federal inspection of U.S. seafood processing facilities shows. Microbiological contamination, decomposition, or filth showed in 20 percent of the samples analyzed.

27 Operators of Yankee Rowe nuclear power plant decide the plant will stay closed permanently. The plant was taken off line last year because of safety concerns.

March 1992

1 Toxic PCBs may be converted into tiny diamonds useful in industrial applications through a process developed by U. of Minnesota engineer.

1 Only 32 of 139 priority CA toxic waste sites are "clean," but $100 million budgeted in the early 1980s for cleanup is already spent.

2   Thirty to 40 percent of the world's tropical rainforests disappeared between 1950 and 1990, National Research Council reports.

2   Pollutants dumped into Detroit River may be causing deaths of bald eagle hatchlings along Lake Erie, National Wildlife Federation spokesperson says.

3   Music industry will phase out the long-box package for compact discs.

3   Workers in Boston prepare to dig up 3,200 cubic feet of soil contaminated by oil and PCBs in preparation for the first phase of the "Big Dig" and Boston Harbor Tunnel construction.

3   Baltimore is a nuclear-free zone, City Council decides. Approval implies closer regulation of transportation of nuclear materials through the city and bans disposal of radioactive waste within city limits.

6   California air quality board approves market in pollution credits.

6   Cleanup efforts begin to pay off for dirtiest part of Tampa Bay, FL. Levels of chlorophyll, a key indicator of pollution, are half what they were 10 years ago in certain areas, but mud remains toxic.

6   Ultraviolet ray warnings should be issued during weather reports in high skin cancer areas such as Australia and Hawaii, two U. of Hawaii scientists urge.

6   Scientists at a Russian research center will work on ways to use nuclear fusion to produce energy. The U.S. Dept. of Energy will pay 116 researchers at Moscow's Hurchatov Institute $65 a month each.

6   Federal Michigan Scenic Rivers Act, signed by President Bush, protects 1,000 miles of 25 river segments in MI from development.

9   Dept. of Energy and West Virginia U. join forces to develop low-cost technique for retrofitting gas-powered cars to run on natural gas.

10   Boston Edison agrees to cut pollution from a South Boston generating plant by converting from oil to natural gas by 1995.

11   Chrysler, Ford, and GM form partnership to promote and develop technology for recycling materials from scrap motor vehicles.

11   Eleven Northeast states adopt two-stage plan for curbing nitrogen oxide emissions from coal-burning power plants.

12   Cost estimates for incinerating post-Cold War stockpiles of chemical weapons jump again, to $7.5 billion to $8 billion.

12   Timber-related employment in the Pacific Northwest will continue to decline whether or not the habitat of the spotted owl is protected, new report by the American Forestry Association concludes.

12   Appellate Court sets key precedent by ordering sweeping environmental review of the last large tracts of undeveloped pine forest on Long Island. If upheld, environmentalists say, the suit could spur comprehensive planning in other areas that, like the L.I. Pine Barrens, are environmentally sensitive.

13   Water managers in FL approve Everglades cleanup plan that allows $395 million over the next decade to reduce the amount of agricultural pollution flowing into the area.

14   U.S. Fish and Wildlife Service decides diversion of water to farmers in California's Klamath Basin will not threaten two rare species of fish, the short-nosed and Lost River suckers, after all.

14   Galveston Bay National Estuary Program (TX) establishes centralized hotline so people can report pollution incidents. (1-800-3-OUR BAY)

15   Sabal palm, Florida's state tree, is dying along the Gulf of Mexico coastline. Researchers suspect that saltwater, rising in response to a warmer climate, is drowning the palms' root systems.

16   State of AK runs half-page ads in several major newspapers linking jobs to the opening of the Arctic National Wildlife Refuge for oil drilling.

16   Puerto Rico may ban coal burning in power plants. A bill being weighed by the Senate would also kill existing plans for building coal-fired power plants. Puerto Rico burns no coal, but coal producers worry that legislation could be copied elsewhere.

17   Head of Chatsworth, CA, company indicted by a federal grand jury for illegally shipping more than a ton of hazardous waste to Pakistan. If convicted on all charges, Tariq Ahmad of Reno, NV, could be fined $3.75 million and be sentenced to 78 years in prison.

17   Union of Concerned Scientists protests rule proposed by the Nuclear Regulatory Commission that it says would extend licenses of nuclear power plants despite age, safety, environmental, or economic considerations.

17 Florida developers race to build medical waste incinerator before governor signs moratorium.

17 Radon levels in nearly every drinking-water well in NH exceed federal standards for safety, state water supply engineer says.

18 Rubber manufacturer in Odessa, TX, may close rather than comply with court settlement. Ruling requires Dynagen to spend millions on equipment to cut releases of carcinogens.

19 Bush Administration announces "cash for clunkers" plan that would allow companies to buy old, polluting cars and remove them from the road in exchange for credits toward meeting requirements for reducing emissions.

19 Oil companies opposing California's strict new requirements for reformulated gasoline seek statewide referendum on whether cleaner air is worth higher gas prices.

19 Cloudburst flushes so much toxic material from an abandoned CA mine that the U.S. Bureau of Reclamation has to dilute the waste with enough water to supply 250,000 households for a year. The mine has been on the Superfund list since 1983.

19 Operators of the *Santa Clara*, which dropped 441 drums of arsenic trioxide off NJ coast, agree to help with cleanup.

19 Vulcan Chemicals, based in Wichita, KS, will build a $9 million plant to recycle hydrochloric acid and turn it into road salt.

19 Mexico steps up diplomatic efforts to block U.S. construction of radioactive waste dumps in the U.S.-Mexico border zone.

20 Pollution passing from RI sewage plants into rivers and Narragansett Bay declined by 13.8 percent last year, state officials report.

22 Ski resorts in New England rely increasingly on machines that produce artificial snow. Winters in the past decade have been warm and snow-poor. Environmentalists and sportsmen say snowmaking threatens the region's rivers and streams, drawing down already low water levels.

22 Marchers rally at U.S.-Mexican border to protest proposed hazardous waste landfills in the border region.

22 Florida's Save the Manatee Club will take its parent group, the FL Audubon Society, to court. The 30,000-member club wants to split off, taking its logo and assets, but FL Audubon opposes the move.

24 President Bush lists a treaty on climate change as one of his top priorities for the Rio Earth Summit (UNCED) in June.

24 Up to 40,000 plant species may become extinct by 2050, the U.N. reports. Authors blame population growth, farming techniques, and habitat destruction for the loss of diversity.

24 Automobile emissions testing, the first mandatory annual test in Canada, will begin in the Vancouver area at the end of the summer.

25 Sewage treatment plant in St. Louis Co., MO, collects methane emitted by decomposing sewage sludge and converts it into electricity. Plant now generates 85 percent of its own electricity.

26 Rockwell International agrees to pay $18.5 million fine for pollution at Rocky Flats nuclear weapons compound. Fine believed to be second largest criminal environmental fine in U.S. history.

26 Coca-Cola Food donates 55,000 acres of tropical forest in Belize to The Nature Conservancy. The land will be used to expand the Rio Bravo Conservation and Management Area.

27 East Coast lags West Coast for first time in output of oysters, mussels, scallops, and clams, NOAA reports. Poor water quality, overfishing, and disease are blamed.

27 Numbers of aluminum cans recycled in U.S. increased 3 percent last year, but the percentage of cans recycled dropped from 63.6 percent in 1990 to 62.4 percent in 1991, the Aluminum Association reports.

27 PSI Energy, Inc. (IN), says it will need a 18 percent rate hike in the next eight years to pay for the $1.34 billion cost of complying with federal clean air laws.

28 New York cancels talks on state contract for electricity from Canada's controversial Great Whale hydropower project. NY Gov. Mario Cuomo says it would be cheaper for the state to rely on energy conservation to increase power supply.

29 Water rationing ends in Southern CA as drought abates, ending longest period of mandatory conservation in local history.

29 PCBs may be related to development of breast cancer, U. of Michigan researcher reports.

29 Sports fishermen pressure state to lift ban on fishing on part of the Hudson River in upstate NY. Ban was imposed because of PCB contamination.

30 Glidden Co. launches Spred 2000. The odorless paint does not contain petroleum-based solvents or emit volatile organic compounds.

30 Ten Northeast states develop strategy for reducing emissions of greenhouse gases and preparing for potential climate change and sea-level rise.

April 1992

1 First New York City laundromat with environmental theme opens. Ecowash uses biodegradable laundry detergents for its dropoff loads and machines that use less water than standard washers.

1 The red sea urchin faces extinction in the face of overharvesting to meet steady demand from Japan, the CA Dept. of Fish and Game warns. Last year, the urchin brought revenues of $30 million to CA fishermen.

2 EPA issues proposed rules for use of reformulated, clean-burning fuels in nine U.S. cities with the worst ozone pollution.

3 Eight Northeast states agree on extensive controls of nitrogen oxide emissions from power plants. Goal is to halve utility emissions of NOx.

3 Indiana U. plans to sell MS cattle ranch to a firm planning to build a hazardous waste incinerator. Opponents charge irresponsibility and environmental racism because the 6,027-acre ranch is in Noxubee County, MS, which is predominantly black.

5 Cruise ships in AK waters emit so much smoke that scenic views are being obscured.

5 Idaho may recommend Kootenai River white sturgeon for Endangered Species list.

7 Waste management is one of the fastest growing and most profitable industries of the decade, International Labor Organization reports.

7 Sen. Timothy Wirth (D-Colo.) decides not to seek reelection to a second term. Wirth, a leading Senate environmentalist, says he is "frustrated by a governmental logjam."

7 Nonstick, nonpolluting alternative to Teflon is announced by Dow Chemical Co. The new materials, hybrids of commercial plastics and Teflon, could be available within a year.

8 Modest gains in automobile fuel efficiency can be made without sacrificing a substantial degree of safety, a National Academy of Sciences research committee concludes. Improved mileage would cost about $500 to $2,500 per car.

8 The Columbia and Snake river system tops conservation group American Rivers annual list of North America's most endangered rivers. The system flows through ID, OR, and WA.

8 Scientists tell Senate panel that children of women who eat Great Lakes fish contaminated by chemicals are more prone to birth defects. Fishing industry counters that the fish are the cleanest they have been in years.

9 More than 45,300 sites nationwide may be contaminated with radioactive waste, a study commissioned by the EPA reports. CO, with 7,060, leads the states in numbers of contaminated sites.

10 St. Louis salvage company pleads guilty to storing PCBs illegally and agrees to pay for the cleanup. The firm will also replace a $55,000 testing device to replace the one broken because contamination levels were so high—more than 800 times the safe level.

12 Federal panel sets strict limits on the Pacific Ocean salmon fishing season.

12 Maryland will tax gas-guzzling cars, while fuel-efficient cars earn tax credit.

13 Poll of 600 registered voters taken for *The Oregonian* finds that sentiment shifted significantly toward job protection and away from owl protection in the two years since the last poll.

15 Activist Jeremy Rifkin and a coalition of environmental groups announce media campaign to reduce U.S. beef consumption.

15 Cape Cod group says that nitrogen-rich effluent from proposed Boston Harbor sewage outfall tunnel could trigger larger than normal algae blooms in the bay, and "substantially" increase the risk of toxic red tides.

17 Snake River chinook salmon is threatened, government declares. Recovery plan will likely include increased flows in the Columbia River, prohibition of recreational boating, and smaller salmon harvests.

18 Low and early snowmelt runoff in Columbia River Basin reduces flow of Snake River, making it harder for threatened Snake River salmon to move quickly from spawning grounds to the ocean.

19 At least 11 towns in ME reject stronger shoreland zoning ordinances mandated by the state. Property rights activists call moves to preserve forestlands and scenic coastal areas a massive land grab conspiracy by the environmental movement.

20   Texas highway department's new name, TX Dept. of Transportation, reflects its new mission to balance highway construction and maintenance with environmental protection.

20   Faber-Castell unveils the American EcoWriter, a pencil made of recycled newspaper and cardboard fibers.

21   Florida environmentalists call recently ended legislative session the worst in 20 years.

22   Numbers of spotted owls in WA forests rebounds, but officials say the threatened species still needs protection.

22   Shrimp catches in the Gulf of Mexico have increased since turtle excluder devices (TEDs) were mandated in 1989. Environmentalists say this proves the TEDs, designed to protect sea turtles from shrimp nets, do not hurt the shrimp industry; shrimpers say good catches are tied to favorable weather conditions.

22   Total U.S. costs for pollution control increased from $26 billion in 1972 to $85 billion in 1987 (1986 dollars), the National Association of Manufacturers reports, based on EPA figures. Numbers are projected to reach about $160 billion by 2000.

23   Indiana Gov. Evan Bayh announces plans for first Governors' Conference on the Environment.

24   Most of the money spent by insurance companies on Superfund sites has gone toward legal battles, a Rand Corp. study finds. The money would have been enough to clean up 15 Superfund sites a year. Only 21 percent of Superfund money spent by industry goes to lawyers.

24   Federal government sues FL company to prevent it from importing into the U.S. luxury cars that do not meet U.S. emissions standards.

24   Greenpeace protestors crash annual shareholders' meeting of DuPont Canada Inc. to demand that DuPont stop producing ozone-destroying chemicals.

25   Survey of 600 Tampa-area residents finds most would be willing to pay up to $100 more in taxes to clean up the Tampa Bay.

26   Parks and trails at NY parks and historic sites will be renovated over the next 10 years with $300 million from park revenue.

27   Bush Administration says annual U.S. output of carbon dioxide can be reduced by 125 million to 200 million metric tons by the year 2000. The reductions would stem from actions, such as use of natural gas, taken for other reasons.

27   U. of Texas seeks investors to commercialize a new method of cleaning up oil spills. The method uses tiny beads of sand coated with titanium dioxide to break oil down into components easily digested by microbes.

27   Missouri acquires title to the town of Times Beach. When cleanup of the dioxin-tainted ghost town concludes, the state may convert the town into a park.

28   National Marine Fisheries Service proposes that shrimpers be required to use turtle excluder devices year round.

28   Cohoes, NY, votes to help the Norlite Corp. pay for $22.3 million worth of equipment, most of which will be used to control pollution, at the company's local plant. The plant makes lightweight building material and burns hazardous waste as fuel.

29   Iowa researchers document a dramatic drop in numbers of rural water wells contaminated with nitrates at levels that exceed federal standards for safety. Improvements could be tied to 1988 and 1989 drought conditions, which encouraged better water management, and also to better use of chemicals.

30   President Bush extends his 90-day moratorium on all new regulations another four months.

May 1992

1   Unseasonably high temperatures in the Arctic prevented a hole from forming in the ozone layer over the north pole this year, NOAA reports.

I   Soot and smoke from thousands of fires set by rioters foul Los Angeles's already-polluted air.

1   High bacteria levels in the Cuyahoga River (OH) threaten the health of people using the river for recreational purposes around Cleveland and Akron. The hazard is greatest after heavy rainfalls, report says.

2   The Forest Service allows too much logging in the Cherokee National Forest in east TN, suit by TN conservation groups charges.

4   The main culprit in the acid rain problem may be nitric acids, not sulfuric acid as commonly thought, USGS hydrogeologist says. He and other acid rain researchers say forest management practices should be reconsidered.

5   Nearly four out of five RI residents would pay more in income taxes or user fees to finance efforts to clean up the Narragansett Bay, survey finds.

5 The deaths of some 80 golden eagles and 490 birds of prey at Altamont Pass, CA, may have been caused when they flew into the electricity-generating windmills, a two-year survey by the CA Energy Commission reveals.

6 In an Arm & Hammer poll, 54 percent of fifth and sixth graders say they are afraid environmental problems will never be solved.

6 Parents' purchase decisions are swayed by environmental information they get from their children, a survey by Environmental Research Associates shows.

6 Bush Administration is widely criticized for its role in weakening the global warming treaty to be presented at the UNCED Earth Summit.

7 Blood of modern humans contains up to 1,000 times more lead than that of their ancestors, whose blood contained the natural level of the toxic metal, scientists report in the *New England Journal of Medicine*.

8 No more raw sewage from Victoria and Vancouver Island, BC, will flow into the Strait of Juan de Fuca, pledges BC Premier Mike Harcourt. The cities have been dumping 15 million gallons a day.

8 Capt. Joseph Hazelwood will teach students at the State U. of New York Maritime College how to stand watch on the bridge. Hazelwood was the skipper at the helm of the *Exxon Valdez* at the time of the oil spill.

9 Supporters and opponents of geothermal energy development clash at eight-hour-long hearing in HI.

9 Black bear hunting can continue, FL Game and Fresh Water Fish Commission decides. An estimated 400 to 1,500 black bears remain in FL. About 60 were killed by hunters last year.

10 Michigan's drinking water is threatened by contamination from animal wastes and excessive use of fertilizers, Clean Water Action reports.

10 Texas doctor who treats victims of petroleum-related poisonings says he is treating six patients suffering from exposure to oil during cleanup of the *Exxon Valdez* spill and to the toxic agents used in the cleanup. William Rea says he expects "hundreds" more patients from the spill.

12 Cars converted to run on propane show significant increases in emissions, CA Air Resources Board finds. The board suspects cars converted to run on natural gas may also emit high levels of pollutants.

12 Ecoterrorists target ranchers who graze their livestock on public lands in AZ, CA, and NV, Rep. James Hansen (R-Utah) tells House panel.

12 Environmental impact of proposed high-speed rail system to link four TX cities is considered at public meeting in Bryan.

14 Bush Administration introduces alternative recovery plan for the northern spotted owl. Plan emphasizes preservation of logging jobs over species protection.

14 Environmental audit ordered by Indianapolis mayor Stephen Goldsmith reveals problems that could cost up to $1.3 billion to correct.

14 More than 5,000 people on the big island of HI rally in support of geothermal development on the island.

14 Anhauser-Busch announces thinner and narrower lids for its canned beers. New lids use less aluminum and could save the compny about $12 million a year.

15 Sixty-one percent of 808 AZ adults polled by the *Arizona Republic* say they would be willing to pay between 2 and 4 cents more per gallon for gasoline to cover installation of vapor-recovery systems that would reduce fumes at service stations.

15 Newport, IN, building that houses 4 million pounds of VX nerve agent, a deadly chemical weapon, could not withstand a tornado or earthquake, Army study reveals. IN governor wants it moved.

17 President Bush approves moves to nullify key Clean Air Act regulations that require industry to notify the public about operations changes and increases in pollutant releases and to participate in a 45-day review process.

19 Environmental groups accuse U.S. of trying to weaken biodiversity treaty to be signed at the UNCED Earth Summit. Government objects to provisions that would adversely affect the U.S. biotechnology industry.

19 Adirondack National Park (NY) marks its 100th anniversary amid controversy about development and protection.

20 World nuclear energy generating capacity dropped for the first time in 1991, a survey by several environmental watch groups reports.

20 Millions of asthma and respiratory disease sufferers rely on portable medicine inhalers that use CFCs as propellant. American Lung Association asks for a treaty exemption to allow use of the devices.

22 AR judge orders five boxcars containing 50 tons of New York City trash to be sent back to Brooklyn.

22 EPA will analyze Rio Grande water in search of a link between the river and neural tube birth defects in Cameron Co., TX. Since 1989, at least 30 babies whose mothers lived within 2.4 miles of the Rio Grande were born with fatal anencephaly (without most of their brains).

22 First fuel cell designed for commercial application uses natural gas to produce electricity. Southern CA Gas Co. displays the model, which will produce power for the South Coast Air Quality Management District in Diamond Bar, CA.

23 State legislators in NY introduce bill that would lead to development of strategy for limiting New York's emissions of greenhouse gases.

23 Farmers could drain millions of acres of wetlands under a draft USDA proposal that would exempt farmers from a 1990 law that bars federal subsidies to those who drain or alter wetlands "in bad faith."

26 Genetically engineered food needs no more regulation than naturally grown foods, FDA rules. Gene-altered foods may reach stores in 1993.

26 Boston Pops and conductor John Williams release *Green Album* to contribute to the environmental awareness of listeners.

27 Two British Columbia industries pollute air and water, causing abnormally high rates of illness in Northport, a rural WA community near the Canadian border, residents claim. Northport residents want a thorough scientific investigation.

27 More than 300 people go to Texaco's Fairfax, VA, oil storage facility to demand its closure. They blame leaking tanks for huge underground spill.

28 Despite uncertainty about the processes involved in global warming, a U.N. intergovernmental panel reaffirms its earlier conclusion that an average increase in temperature of 1.5 and 3.5 °C is likely over the next 100 years.

28 Texas Low-Level Radioactive Authority votes to build state's first low-level radioactive waste dump on a 16,000-acre ranch 90 miles southeast of El Paso.

29 U.S. Fish and Wildlife Service holds hearing in Tucson, AZ, to consider reintroducing the Mexican gray wolf into the wild. There are 53 in captivity and an estimated 10 to 100 in the wild in Mexico.

28 U.S. industry cut its releases of toxic chemicals by 11 percent from 1989 to 1990, EPA reports based on the latest Toxics Release Inventory.

June 1992

1 Biodiversity treaty presented at the UNCED Earth Summit is "fundamentally flawed," State Dept. says, and U.S. will not sign.

1 Proclaiming a major advance in electric lighting, a CA firm announces its newly developed E-lamp. The bulbs use radio waves instead of a filament to produce light.

1 Federal judge fines Rockwell International Corp. $18.5 million for environmental crimes committed at Rocky Flats nuclear weapons plant near Golden, CO. Sierra Club and others say the U.S. Dept. of Energy, which owns the plant, should also be held accountable for violating environmental laws.

2 U.S. Supreme Court limits states' right to close their borders to out-of-state wastes.

2 Costs of closing Yankee Rowe nuclear plant in western MA is now $247 million, double an earlier estimate, owners say.

3 The UNCED Earth Summit opens in Rio de Janeiro.

3 International carbon dioxide market could limit global emissions of the greenhouse gas and should be created, Chicago Board of Trade director Richard Sandor says.

4 U.S. Forest Service announces "ecosystem management" plan for national forests that could reduce clear-cutting by up to 70 percent.

4 About 600 wildlife species are accepted candidates for listing as endangered or threatened, but official designation probably is unlikely until the year 2006 or later, two-year General Accounting Office study finds. GAO attributes delays to the low priority Interior and Commerce Depts. attach to implementation of the Endangered Species Act.

7 Approval of President Bush's handling of environmental matters is 36 percent, a 26 percent drop since a year ago, ABC poll shows.

8 Major apparel marketer is first to devote entire line to clothing made with organic cotton and nontoxic dyes. VF Corp. markets Wrangler and Lee jeans.

8 Canada may take action under international law to protect Atlantic fish stocks, Canadian fisheries and ocean minister warns.

9 PCBs and pesticide by-products are linked for the first time to breast cancer in humans in study by CT toxicologists.

11 Recent satellite pictures show great damage to U.S. forests, NASA scientists report. Clear-cutting in the evergreen forests in the Pacific Northwest is so extensive the forests could lose their ability to support a diversity of species, the scientists say.

12 "The day of the open checkbook is over," President Bush says at the UNCED Earth Summit, referring to his refusal to sign treaties that harm America's economic interests.

12 Nuclear Regulatory Commission approves Long Island Power Authority plans to decommission and destroy the $5.5 billion Shoreham nuclear power plant.

12 U.S. Supreme Court rules that citizens or groups cannot sue the government unless they can demonstrate personal and immediate harm from a government action affecting the environment. Ruling means that Endangered Species Act does not apply to U.S.-funded projects overseas.

15 Forest Service and Bureau of Land Management overestimate reforestation efforts in the Pacific Northwest, causing exaggerated logging quotas that cannot be sustained, House committee reports.

15 Group of companies and government agencies in CA form Calstart, a consortium to develop technology for electric-powered vehicles.

15 Louisiana released greater quantities of toxic chemicals into the water than any other state, eight times more than the next highest discharger, the state of WA. Discharges reported are part of EPA's Toxics Release Inventory.

17 Maryland must rescind its new gas-guzzler automobile tax, under orders from National Highway Traffic Safety Administration. MD was the first state to pass such a law.

17 Thirty-one of 50 top U.S. industrial corporations have executives directly responsible for environmental affairs, compared with 25 in 1990, Arthur D. Little survey shows.

17 Maine Conservation Corps receives $638,000 federal grant to set up conservation and service corps programs for economically and educationally disadvantaged youths.

18 Twenty-two percent of registered voters likely to vote in November's election say they have previously chosen candidates based on their environmental records, according to Times Mirror Magazines poll.

19 Six major computer companies have joined EPA's new Energy Star Computers Program, designed to encourage development of more energy-efficient personal computers. EPA estimates the new machines could save individuals and businesses up to $1 billion a year in electricity costs.

19 Photovoltaic cell that could "make solar power cheaper and more widespread" will be in commercial production within a year, Texas Instruments announces.

21 Seven governors want clean air protections geared toward the Grand Canyon extended to 15 other western wilderness areas and national parks.

21 Some owners of hillside property near Los Altos Hills, CA, object to an open space tax that will preserve 280 acres of undeveloped land nearby.

22 Canada has achieved 84 percent of its targeted reductions for sulfur dioxide emissions, Canadian officials report.

22 Electromagnetic fields emitted by overhead power lines can be dramatically reduced by stringing the wires over one another, rather than parallel. The fields can be eliminated by burying the cables underground, according to a consultant's report to the RI Public Utilities Commission.

23 EPA begins test of power plant technology that uses lime stored in silos to reduce sulfur dioxide emissions. If the experimental process is successful, it would be cheaper than using scrubbers to reduce SO_2 emissions.

23 Two thousand acres of farmland in New York's Hudson Valley will be permanently protected, David and Margaret Rockefeller decide. The farm will be the largest single agricultural tract ever preserved in NY.

24 Coalition of 30 environmental, labor, and government organizations say they will back congressional attempt to shut down Vice President Quayle's Council on Competitiveness. Council is trying to loosen many key environmental regulations, citing economic concerns.

25 House Appropriations Committee votes to cut off congressional spending for the President's Council on Competitiveness.

26 Save the Manatee Club can proclaim its independence from the FL Audubon Society, circuit court judge rules.

26 AZ rancher loses 84 cattle because they were grazing on federal lands without a permit. Bureau of Land Management seized and auctioned the livestock.

27 Pentagon's $25 billion plan to clean up its 17,500 toxic waste dumps is scientifically unsound and may subject the public to extremely grave health risks, National Research Council panel finds.

28 Big Three automakers pool resources and talent to find ways to reduce auto emissions.

28 For the last time, New York City's processed sewage sludge heads for sea. Congress banned ocean dumping four years ago; today is federal deadline.

30 Selective harvesting rather than clear-cut logging might not stop forests' decline, scientists warn.

30 Old Town Trolley Tours of Washington, DC, converts its vehicles to use propane instead of gas. Goal is to reduce air pollution and damage to national monuments.

30 GM launches program to test 50 ethanol-fueled cars for use in IL and WI state fleets.

July 1992

1 IBM stops using CFCs at its San Jose plant (CA) as the company moves toward total phaseout by 1994. Five years ago, IBM was the nation's biggest discharger of CFCs.

1 Alcoa Aluminum Co. of America unit sells $7.5 million of air pollution credits to Ohio Edison Co., the biggest such transaction since the allowance trading program was set up under the Clean Air Act.

1 Clean Air Act provisions requiring companies that service air conditioning and refrigerator units to "capture and recycle" CFCs are effective today. Until now, the ozone-destroying gases were vented into the air.

2 Community Alert Network in Contra Costa Co., CA, says the county's computerized phone alert system failed to notify 5,000 North Richmond residents of a possible emergency at a nearby Chevron refinery because a recently fired employee had sabotaged the system.

2 Texas must find new sources of water as population increases, state comptroller says. Eighty percent of the state's potential reservoir sites have already been built.

3 Canada imposes two-year ban on cod fishing off much of Newfoundland. Many fishermen say they will ignore the ban because they cannot live on the $225 per week interim stipend offered by the government.

3 Diazinon, a lawn-care pesticide, is suspected in a spate of bird kills around the state of VA.

4 Iowa resident and his 12-year-old son begin a round-the-world voyage in a boat powered by soybean oil. They want to promote soybean oil as an alternative to diesel fuel.

5 Three drinking-water wells near El Paso, TX, are found to be contaminated with human waste. Health officials watch for cholera bacteria.

6 Tractor trailers that deliver ingredients used at Domino's Pizza outlets now carry do-it-yourself kits for highway oil spills.

7 Volcanic debris from the 1991 eruption of Mt. Pinatubo in the Philippines has cooled the Earth, confounding efforts to detect global warming, NOAA scientists say.

8 California's South Coast Air Quality Management District recommends shifting emphasis so that drivers rather than business bear the main economic burden of fighting smog.

9 Federal appeals court rejects EPA policy that allows use of cancer-causing chemicals on food if the risk they pose is minimal. Court upholds 1958 law that bans all carcinogenic food additives.

9 Twenty electric utilities offer $30 million prize to first company that builds a refrigerator that uses no CFCs and 25 to 50 percent less electricity than 1993 federal standards mandate.

9 Democratic presidential nominee Bill Clinton chooses Sen. Al Gore (TN), a known environmentalist, as his running mate.

10 *Exxon Valdez* Capt. Joseph Hazelwood is immune from prosecution because he reported the spill to the Coast Guard, AK Court of Appeals rules, overturning his misdemeanor conviction.

11 Michigan Dept. of Transportation may re-route a 21.5-mile-long, multi-million dollar freeway to save habitat of Mitchell's satyr, a tiny butterfly on the Endangered Species list.

13 Jury in nation's largest asbestos trial finds six companies negligent and liable for failing to warn workers that exposure to asbestos poses health hazards.

14 U.S. will no longer produce plutonium and enriched uranium for use in nuclear weapons, Bush Administration announces.

16 Tests show that 29 Chicago suburbs have too much lead in their drinking water supplies, under a new federal standard.

Close To Home

Environmental issues affect us first where we live, In our homes and communities.

How can you take on an environmental problem that threatens your health or your community? In this section, the stories of how 12 local grassroots groups did just that can give you hints. Does your local electric utility support conservation? How effectively it does probably depends on whether your state regulates utilties in an environmentally enlightened manner—see our State Energy Report Card on Utility Planning in the energy chapter.

In which part of the country do we drive the most fuel-efficient—and the least efficient—vehicles? See the rank-ings of state fuel efficiency in the transportation chapter.

This section also provides information to help you address many other environmental questions. What kind of homes are most likely to have high levels of lead in drinking water? How much waste do we generate, and how much worse is our trash problem getting? Which kind of air pollution has proved most difficult to reduce? Which uses more water, a bath or a load of laundry? Which is a "better" beverage container in terms of the amount of energy required in manufacturing energy, a refillable glass bottle or a recycled aluminum can? Which 10 U.S. rivers are most endangered? How does perfume and after-shave pollute the air? How should you get rid of hazardous household waste? What are the best environmental books?

How has the California drought inspired new approaches to water conservation? Is burning trash to generate energy a safe form of recycling? What percent of our rivers are now clean enough for swimming and fishing? Which states discharge the most industrial toxic waste to public sewers? Did the $2 billion we spent on bottled drinking water really provide any additional safety?

Water

A thirsty nation responds to the two greatest challenges to our water resources: pollution and insufficient supply.

Although water is more necessary to human survival than anything but air, humans throughout history have been drawn to arid climates. Many early civilizations, such as Egypt and Sumeria, were established in deserts or semideserts. Today, California, a modern equivalent of those desert cultures, is relearning ancient lessons as well. California's experience in the past few years reminds us that events or conditions that interrupt water supply can cause severe hardships that reverberate through human social and agricultural systems.

In California, the population mushroomed in the last 20 years from 20 million to 30 million people, making it the nation's most populous state. Yet annual rainfall throughout the state is relatively low, ranging from less than 10 inches in San Diego and Bakersfield to about 14 inches in Los Angeles and 20 inches in San Francisco, compared with 33 inches in Chicago and 44 inches in New York. For the past six winters, precipitation in California has been far below these averages, ranging from 61 to 90 percent of normal statewide. As a result, California has cut back its water use—no small feat for a state whose per capita household water use is the nation's ninth highest.

In anticipation of the next drought, several California coastal communities with inadequate local water supplies are developing systems that can remove salt from sea water. A study last year by the Metropolitan Water District of Southern California showed, however, that desalting sea water would cost five times as much as treating sewage for reuse.

For most jurisdictions, conservation is a better bet, and they are stretching water supplies instead of trying to increase them. Thus, in late 1991, 63 water suppliers representing most of the state's urban areas signed a conservation agreement with a dozen environmental groups. The agreement may become a model for the nation. It requires water utilities to adopt 16 sweeping "best management practices" for urban water conservation, ranging from offering rebates on low-flush toilets to providing free water audits to the biggest users.

The drought also encouraged unprecedented efforts at water marketing. In both 1991 and 1992, the state

---

Water News

Sacramento, 4/92—*Spurred by a six-year drought, California officials this month proposed a change to the Uniform Plumbing Code to permit the use of reclaimed (or "gray") water in single-family homes. If the International Association of Plumbing and Mechanical Officials approves the change late in 1992, it would become part of official building regulations. This would likely result in wider use of gray water in 22 states that use the Uniform Code. Most existing codes prohibit or severely restrict its use.*

Department of Water Resources set up a water bank, acting as a broker to buy water from suppliers with surpluses and sell it to those with shortages.

Some cities took steps to reuse wastewater from their sewage treatment systems. The centrally planned community of Irvine in Orange County has installed parallel plumbing systems in four new high-rise office buildings to use reclaimed water for uses such as flushing toilets. In one building, 78 percent of the water used is reclaimed sewage.

Californians are not alone in altering their means of supplying and using water. Cities everywhere are finding that reuse, recycling, and conservation are the most cost-effective methods of developing new water supplies for growing populations in water-short areas. But just as popular culture often takes root in California before migrating east, California's response to drought bears watching, as conservation and market-driven mechanisms for allocating scarce supplies take precedence over new construction.

Water Use and Treatment

The United States uses about 338 billion gallons of fresh water per day for all uses, or about 1,400 gallons per capita, more water than any other industrialized country. About 10 percent of that water is used for public tap water supplies, 11 percent is used by industry, 38 percent is used to cool electric power-generating plants, and 41 percent is used for irrigated agriculture. Almost all the water for public use is treated and disinfected to standards set under the Safe Drinking Water Act Amendments of 1986 by the U.S. Environmental Protection Agency (EPA).

Costs of treatment and disinfection vary widely. Some western cities that use groundwater from protected deep aquifers are not required to disinfect it. In other cities, heavy treatment is often required. More treatment results in higher costs for tap water.

Many cities add chlorine to their water to kill bacteria and remove objectionable odors and color. While chlorine is effective, it also reacts with dissolved organic matter to form chemicals such as chloroform and trihalomethanes, which have caused cancer in laboratory animals.

One response to the high cost of treating, disinfecting, and delivering safe drinking water to the consumer is to reduce consumption. Ways to do this include avoiding use of drinking-quality water for non-drinking uses and reusing water at home.

On average, about 84 percent of the water used in a home goes down the drain and into a sewage or septic sys

tem. Some of this water contains human wastes and is unusable for health reasons.

Growing numbers of cities, especially on the coasts, however, are trying to find ways to reuse some of their sewage effluent for purposes that do not require highly treated and disinfected water. In Cape Coral, Florida, a city of 78,000 people, reclaimed wastewater will soon be piped through separate water lines for use by homeowners for lawn watering. In Los Angeles, wetlands maintained in the Sepulveda Dam Recreation Area are irrigated with treated wastewater from a nearby treatment plant.

Some water—contaminated only by soaps and similar substances, or wholly untainted—could be reused for outdoor watering, for instance. However, local health and building codes usually prohibit the creation of water

Gray Water

When you fill your bathtub, you use 36 gallons of water. When you do your laundry, you use 35 to 50 gallons. Shaving takes a gallon if you work from a full basin; 5 to 10 if you just let the water run.

Add all that together, and you've got enough "gray water" to irrigate every tree, shrub, and flower bed in the average yard. Even if you take only the simplest step and reroute your washing machine drain hose into a barrel for reuse, you can substantially reduce outdoor freshwater use. Yet most local plumbing codes forbid installing gray-water systems.

The reason is simple: Gray water may contain dangerous bacteria or other microorganisms. If you have a cold, the water you use to brush your teeth, for example, may contain the virus that made you sick.

Nevertheless, some water-short local governments do allow the use of gray water, with some precautions. One of those is Santa Barbara County, California.

Officials there offer several tips for safe use of gray water.

● Don't drink it.

● Don't use it where it could mix with drinking water.

● Don't use it to irrigate a plant that might be eaten or that, like a tomato plant, produces fruit that might be eaten.

● Don't use sprinklers to apply it, and don't let it puddle.

● Never use any water that has come into contact with human feces or food.

● Do not use gray water to irrigate acid-loving plants, such as azaleas.

● Do give your gray-watered plants an occasional drink of fresh water to flush away harmful minerals and other contaminants.

systems for using this so-called "gray water." (See box, Gray Water.)

Pinpointing Pollution Sources

When the Clean Water Act became law in 1972, it focused on the most visible and repugnant sources of water pollution—human sewage outfalls, bilious discharges of industrial wastes, and other "point sources," so called because they can be traced to a single point and controlled.

Thanks largely to more than $75 billion spent over the past two decades on building and upgrading sewage treatment plants and to additional billions spent by manufacturers and private industry, many point sources are now under control.

From 1972 to 1982, the amount of biochemical oxygen demand (the amount of oxygen needed by bacteria to break down a specific amount of organic matter) declined by 46 percent at municipal sewage treatment plants and by at least 71 percent in industrial discharges. This indicates that the Clean Water Act's lofty goals of making the nation's waters safe for fishing and swimming are being achieved, at least in a majority of cases. In 1990, states surveyed 656,804 miles of rivers and streams for fishability and found that 80 percent met that standard. They also surveyed 586,386 miles for swimmability and found that 75 percent qualified. (See table, Where Can We Fish and Swim?)

Irrigation-Related Pollution

In its natural condition, most of the western half of the United States is a desert. Today, however, states like Texas, Arizona, and California are agricultural giants, thanks to the 20th-century miracle of modern irrigation.

Although irrigation dates to early Nile civilizations, the modern era began in the late 1840s in British India, when civil engineers applied their skills to the ancient art. As a result, one third of the world's crops are now produced on irrigated land.

This spectacular bounty is now under siege by one of its side effects: a buildup of salt and toxic trace elements in the soils and waters of irrigated regions.

Scientists at the U.S. Department of Agriculture's United States Salinity Laboratory, which studies this problem, estimate that salinization costs American farmers more than $5 billion per year in reduced crop yields.

Globally, the Worldwatch Institute estimates that one quarter of the world's irrigated land—roughly 150 million acres—is threatened with destruction by salinization and related problems.

In addition, in many arid regions, water can dissolve toxic trace elements from soils in irrigated farm fields. The resulting contaminated groundwater may later emerge on the surface, or be drained off via ditches or buried, perforated pipelines. Drainage water from a California irrigation project, contaminated with the element selenium, caused widespread deaths and deformities in ducks and other waterfowl at the Kesterson National Wildlife Refuge in the early 1980s. Subsequent studies have uncovered similar problems near projects in Nevada, Utah, Wyoming, Arizona, Montana, Colorado, and Kansas.

For farmers and water managers, combating these problems often means developing greater sophistication in applying water to the land. Scientists at the salinity laboratory and elsewhere have developed new techniques, such as drip irrigation, that permit farmers to control water with far greater precision than before. These techniques minimize over-irrigation, reducing the amount of contaminated groundwater that must be drained away and disposed of.

Where Can We Fish and Swim?
(river miles testing clean enough, by state, 1990)

State	River Miles Tested for Fishing	Number of Miles Fishable	River Miles Tested for Swimming	Number of Miles Swimmable
Alabama	11,857	8,703	11,857	8,703
Arizona	5,296	662	5,296	1,810
Arkansas	11,310	9,426	11,310	9,236
California	11,448	9,069	10,463	7,947
Colorado	28,770	28,105	31,377	9,062
Connecticut	893	664	893	679
Delaware	643	498	643	98
Florida	7,950	6,750	7,950	6,750
Georgia	20,000	19,395	0	NA
Hawaii	349	349	349	349
Illinois	13,123	11,476	4,525	1,144
Indiana	4,994	2,986	2,304	138
Iowa	7,155	90	7,155	158
Kansas	12,079	8,838	11,042	627
Kentucky	9,339	6,914	3,595	1,481
Louisiana	8,535	6,510	8,535	5,670
Maine	31,672	31,282	31,672	31,506
Maryland	17,000	15,618	17,000	16,998
Massachusetts	1,623	1,061	1,624	682
Michigan	36,350	35,632	36,350	36,086
Minnesota	6,079	2,292	5,021	2,045
Mississippi	15,839	8,023	15,839	13,086
Missouri	21,063	11,216	21,069	5,370
Montana	51,212	38,474	51,211	46,096
Nebraska	7,330	5,131	12,011	1,035
Nevada	1,559	793	1,574	735
New Hampshire	1,347	1,294	1,390	859
New Jersey	1,719	1,315	592	91
New Mexico	3,117	2,851	3,117	3,117
New York	70,000	69,300	70,000	69,200
North Carolina	37,293	23,820	37,293	23,820
North Dakota	9,204	8,548	9,204	8,489
Ohio	7,688	2,524	0	NA
Oklahoma	3,778	2,161	3,633	2,148
Oregon	27,739	26,197	27,739	26,773
Pennsylvania	23,832	19,137	23,832	19,137
Rhode Island	626	512	626	512
South Carolina	3,594	3,230	3,430	2,010
South Dakota	3,964	3,085	802	396
Tennessee	11,081	10,857	11,081	10,420
Texas	16,203	16,044	16,203	14,435
Utah	11,779	1,303	4,320	120
Vermont	5,266	4,468	5,265	4,854
Virginia	10,809	8,862	10,809	8,862
Washington	5,141	2,070	4,928	3,441
West Virginia	19,818	17,969	19,812	18,415
Wisconsin	13,302	8,272	13,192	8,235
Wyoming	19,437	19,430	947	947

Source: U.S. Environmental Protection Agency, *National Water Quality Inventory: 1990 Report to Congress* (March, 1992), Table 1-4, p. 14.
Note: NA = not available.

Top 10 States for Toxic Discharges to Surface Water

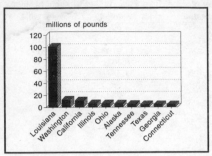

millions of pounds

Source: U.S. Environmental Protection Agency (EPA), *1990 Toxics Release Inventory: Public Data Release* (EPA, Washington, D.C., May 1992), Table 4, p. 23.

Nevertheless, that leaves 129,000 surveyed river miles unsafe for fishing and 149,000 unsafe for swimming. The reason they are not safe, in many cases, is something that was largely overlooked in the original Clean Water Act—pollution by nonpoint sources, or sources that cannot be traced to any single discharge.

The first coordinated assault on these pollution sources began in 1987, with a congressional amendment to the Clean Water Act. Since then, 44 states have received EPA approval for nonpoint source management programs as the law provides. Nonpoint sources covered by these management programs include runoff from streets and lawns; erosion from disturbed hillsides; and agricultural pesticides, fertilizers, and manures.

Because of its scattered, ill-defined sources, nonpoint pollution can be difficult to control, but its effects can be seen in water bodies across the continent. Fertilizers and animal wastes can wash from farmland and suburban lawns into streams and lakes, where the high nutrient loads create oxygen-depleting algal blooms.

In the Everglades—the "river of grass" that covers the interior of southern Florida—the use of fertilizer on sugar cane fields near Lake Okeechobee has produced high levels of nitrogen and phosphorus in the 221-square-mile Loxahatchee National Wildlife Refuge. The resulting algal blooms steal oxygen away from fish and other aquatic wildlife. These nutrients also promote heavy cattail growth, which crowds out native sawgrass and fundamentally alters the unique Everglades ecology. The fast-growing cattails drop

Water News

Baltimore, 12/18/91—*An EPA study of the Chesapeake Bay suggests that air pollution will have to be significantly cut and that New York, Delaware, and West Virginia will have to be enlisted in the cleanup campaign if water quality is to be restored. According to the study, air pollution accounts for nearly 30 percent of the nitrogen entering the estuary, and these three states are responsible for approximately 15 percent of the Bay's nutrients.*

leaves, which decay and form an ooze that further degrades water quality.

Pesticides, if used improperly or under unusual geological conditions, can contaminate groundwater. On eastern Long Island, 23 percent of 330 wells surveyed contained aldicarb, a highly toxic pesticide once used on the region's potato fields, at levels exceeding state health guidelines.

Other nonpoint pollution sources are as varied as human activity. Oils and toxic metals from vehicles wash into lakes and streams, and industrial toxic chemicals reach groundwater if spilled or disposed of improperly. Landfills for household and hazardous wastes can leach toxic liquids into underlying groundwater.

And acid rain—created by sulfur and nitrogen oxide air emissions—can destroy sensitive lakes. In New Hampshire, for example, a recent survey showed that 85 percent of the state's lakes have difficulty buffering the effects of acid rain, and half have unsatisfactory acid levels during winter.

Water from the Tap

Given all these potential sources of pollution, how safe is the average homeowner's drinking water? In general, if it is tap water from a public utility, the answer is probably "very safe," but with a few caveats.

Under 1986 amendments to the 1974 Safe Drinking Water Act, EPA requires public water suppliers to test for dozens of chemical and bacterial pollutants and to notify their customers if their water violates these standards.

The requirements apply to systems serving 15 or more connections or 25 or more people. The 1986 amendments also banned use of lead pipe or lead-containing solder in public water systems, and required suppliers to educate their users about potential sources of lead and its health effects.

Under the law, EPA sets two standards for each pollutant. The first is called a Maximum Contaminant Level Goal (MCLG). It must be set at a level that is not expected to cause any adverse health effects over a lifetime of exposure, and that level must include a margin of safety. There is no penalty for water systems that violate this standard, however.

The second standard is called a Maximum Contaminant Level (MCL) and is a legally enforceable standard. By law, EPA must set the MCL at a level as close as possible to the MCLG, lim-

Top 10 States for Toxic Discharges to Public Sewers

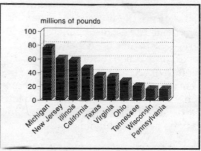

millions of pounds

Michigan, New Jersey, Illinois, California, Texas, Virginia, Ohio, Tennessee, Wisconsin, Pennsylvania

Source: U.S. Public Research Interest Group, National Environmental Law Center, as cited in *Greenwire: The Daily Executive Briefing on the Environment*, Vol. 1, No. 131 (1991), item 6.

ited only by cost and technology. In most cases, but not all, the MCL is less stringent than the MCLG. To review EPA's drinking water standards, request the booklet, *Is Your Drinking Water Safe?*, by calling EPA's Drinking Water Hotline (800) 426-4791; (202) 382-5533 for residents of Alaska and Washington, D.C.

Of all the potential contaminants regulated by the EPA, only two, bacteria and nitrate, pose an immediate health threat if their MCLs are exceeded. High nitrate levels are a serious threat to children between six months and one year of age. Those chemicals can react with oxygen-carrying hemoglobin in the blood to cause an anemic condition known as "blue baby syndrome." Water with nitrate levels exceeding the MCL of 10 milligrams per liter (10 parts per million) should not be given to infants under any circumstances.

Bacteria, measured as total coliform bacteria, can signify that a water system has been contaminated by human or animal feces. As with nitrates, high levels of coliform may pose an immediate health threat.

Although coliform bacteria are not always harmful in themselves, they can indicate the presence of other bacteria that may cause cholera, dysentery, gastroenteritis, hepatitis, typhoid fever, and other serious illnesses. Although exceeding the standard on occasion does not trigger enforcement action, systems that exceed the standard more than 5 percent of the time may be declared in violation.

Of the other potential drinking water contaminants, lead is especially worrisome because it can enter a system long after the water has left the treatment plant. (See box, Lead in Drinking Water.)

In general, drinking water quality in the United States and Canada is far better than that in most countries, especially in areas served by a large public water system. However, water from small systems serving fewer than 15 customers, or from private wells, may

Lead in Drinking Water

Unlike most drinking water contaminants, lead most often enters the water after it leaves the treatment plant, leaching from lead plumbing or from lead-based solder in copper plumbing systems.

The likelihood that a home's drinking water contains high lead levels is greatest in two types of homes:

● Homes built before 1930 with plumbing made of lead, a dull-gray metal soft enough to be scratched easily with a house key. Some older cities also have lead in the water distribution systems, most often in the service connection between the water main and the home.

● Homes with copper plumbing joined by lead-based solder, when the home is relatively new, the water is soft and corrosive, the home has brass fittings on its plumbing fixtures, or the water frequently sits in the pipes for several hours.

Small amounts of lead cannot be seen, smelled, or tasted in water. The only certain way to detect its presence is through testing, which costs from $20 to $100. Local utilities or county health departments can perform tests or provide names of qualified laboratories.

Homeowners can take several steps to reduce their lead exposure. First, hot water leaches lead faster than cold water, so water from the "hot" faucet should not be used for drinking or cooking.

Second, because lead levels may be higher in water that has been in contact with plumbing for long periods, it may be a good idea to flush the cold water line by leaving the faucet on until all water that has been sitting in pipes inside the house is flushed out—this may take several minutes. This practice may not be possible in large buildings.

Lead levels can also be reduced by replacing plumbing that contains lead, by installing a calcite filter on the water line to reduce corrosion, or by using a reverse-osmosis or distillation device to treat water used for drinking or cooking. One can also switch to bottled water for cooking and drinking.

Current U.S. Environmental Protection Agency (EPA) drinking water standards call for lead levels no higher than 50 micrograms per liter (50 parts per billion [ppb]). EPA has proposed a requirement that public water utilities that test their water and find more than 15 ppb take steps to reduce lead levels and educate their customers about reducing their lead exposure. In addition, the 1986 Safe Drinking Water Act Amendments prohibited the use of lead in new public water systems or plumbing systems.

Home Water Treatment Devices

Home water treatment devices are installed for two reasons: to purify contaminated water, and to correct purely aesthetic problems with the water such as taste, odor, color, or hardness. In either case, it is first essential to determine what impurities must be removed.

Water systems that serve 15 or more connections must notify their customers if their water violates standards. These notices specify the contaminants involved and include ways, if any exist, to correct or avoid the problem. Utilities will also provide, upon request, test results for hardness and other aesthetic qualities. For private well owners, testing is usually at the individual's expense.

Public systems users may want to test at home for three contaminants—lead, coliform bacteria, and nitrates—that can enter water after it leaves the treatment plant. (See box, Drinking Water Testing.)

The U.S. Federal Trade Commission says that free in-home water tests, often offered by people selling treatment units, do not contain enough detail to fully gauge drinking water quality.

Also, potential buyers should be wary of claims that a treatment device has the approval of the U.S. Environmental Protection Agency (EPA). While EPA registers treatment devices, it does not test or approve them.

Once the type of contamination is known, the correct treatment device can be identified. Many devices require professional installation, and all require periodic maintenance to remain effective.

The most common types of devices are:

- **Physical filters**, which remove particles such as grit, sediment, dirt, and rust. They cannot, however, remove disease-causing organisms.

- **Activated carbon filters**, which remove many organic chemical contaminants and some inorganic chemicals, such as chlorine. They do not remove other inorganic chemicals such as salts or metals, and if they are not properly maintained, they can serve as breeding grounds for disease-causing organisms.

- **Reverse osmosis units**, which remove most inorganic chemicals, such as salts, leads and other metals, nitrates, and asbestos. They do not remove disease-causing organisms, and they waste four gallons of water for every gallon they produce.

- **Distillation units**, which remove most dissolved solids, such as salts, minerals, and metals. They may not remove some organic chemicals, and their energy use is high.

- **Ultraviolet disinfection units**, which kill bacteria and viruses. They do not remove chemical pollutants and may not be effective against spores and cysts.

be at greater risk of contamination. Since the Safe Drinking Water Act regulations do not apply to such sources—no effective method for federal testing of these water supplies has been developed—EPA suggests that users of these water systems have their water tested regularly by local laboratories. (See boxes, Home Water Treatment Devices and Drinking Water Testing.)

Dams and Diversions

A century ago, the Colorado River was a raging torrent that tossed like driftwood the heavy boats used by John Wesley Powell, the first explorer to navigate the river through the Grand Canyon. Today, restrained by dams, the Colorado is a docile series of glassy pools from its Wyoming and Colorado headwaters to the Mexican state of

Bottled Water

In 1990, Americans bought more than 2 billion gallons of bottled water. They spent $2.2 billion and consumed an average of eight gallons each. Did they waste their money?

The answer probably depends on their reasons for buying bottled water. Some people buy bottled water because they object to the taste, smell, or color of their tap water. Those people probably got their money's worth.

Others, however, believe that drinking tap water is unhealthy, and that bottled water is significantly better. While that may be true in cases where local pollution problems make tap water unsafe to drink, in general there is no assurance that bottled water is superior.

Most bottled water is regulated by the federal Food and Drug Administration (FDA), which requires that the products meet all federal drinking water standards, be clean and safe for human consumption, and be processed and distributed under sanitary conditions.

Some states, such as California, Pennsylvania, and Florida, have adopted stricter standards. Bottlers that sell their products in only one state are regulated by state health authorities, not the FDA.

Mineral waters, club sodas, seltzers, and other waters that are consumed as beverages are not required to meet bottled water standards. In fact, a selling point for many mineral waters is their high content of calcium and other minerals, which would put them in violation of the federal drinking water standards if they applied. Most such waters list their mineral content on their labels. People who are limiting their sodium intake for health reasons should be careful about drinking mineral waters, which may be high in sodium. Bottled waters may have the same problem.

One important way in which many bottled waters differ from most tap waters is in the way they are disinfected. Most tap water suppliers use chlorine, which can leave an aftertaste. In contrast, most bottlers use ozone, which disinfects but does not leave an aftertaste.

How Much Bottled Water Do We Drink?
(national per capita consumption, 1985–90)

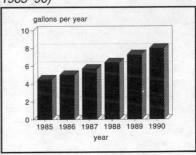

Source: *Beverage Marketing*, The U.S. Bottled Water Marketing & Packaging Report, 1991.

Sonora, where it dribbles to a stop several miles short of its former mouth.

Like the Colorado, every other major U.S. river is now in harness, for irrigation, hydroelectric power, flood control, or a combination of these purposes. The economic benefits of these existing dams and reservoirs are undeniable. The works of one federal agency alone, the U.S. Bureau of Reclamation, produce an estimated annual benefit of $9.6 billion in crop revenues and $648 million in electrical power, plus $29 million in tax revenues and related economic activity.

At the same time, however, most of these projects have caused severe environmental damage. Because the Colorado River no longer carries water to its former mouth in Mexico, the Colorado delta, a verdant wetland that naturalist Aldo Leopold called "this milk-and-

Drinking Water Testing

About 15 percent of Americans—40 million people—rely on private wells, springs, or cisterns for their water. Unlike users of public water systems, these people often must gauge their water's safety for themselves.

The U.S. Environmental Protection Agency (EPA) recommends that owners of private wells have their water tested annually for nitrates and coliform bacteria. If the water's taste, odor, or color changes, or if there are heavy rains, more frequent coliform testing is recommended.

High levels of coliform may indicate that human or animal wastes have contaminated the well with disease-causing viruses, bacteria, or protozoa. High nitrate levels are caused by fertilizers or human or animal wastes, and can cause a blood disorder known as "blue baby syndrome" in young children. The syndrome is caused by a lack of oxygen in the blood.

The EPA also recommends that well owners have their primary kitchen tap tested for lead and radon at least once. Lead can damage the brain, kidneys, and liver, while radon has been linked to human lung cancer.

For other contaminants, the EPA recommends testing if the well is near land that may be contaminated. For example, if a neighboring farmer uses certain pesticides, then testing for those chemicals may be advised to determine whether they have infiltrated the well water.

Local health departments usually can help with coliform testing. State drinking water programs, usually located in the state health or environmental department, can help in locating laboratories that are certified to do other tests. So can EPA's Safe Drinking Water Hotline, which is open from 8:30 AM to 4:30 PM, EST, at (800) 426-4791 or (202) 382-5533.

---

honey wilderness," is now a dried, shrunken remnant of its former self, fed only by a trickle of salty drainage from an upstream irrigation project.

Salmon populations in the Pacific Northwest have declined from more than 10 million to fewer than 3 million since Grand Coulee and more than 100 other dams were erected on the region's principal river system, the Columbia, and its main tributary, the Snake. Today, the U.S. Army Corps of Engineers is manipulating water levels in some of those reservoirs in a desperate attempt to sweep young salmon out to sea before they starve or are eaten by larger predators.

Moreover, the inflation of construction costs and a sharp reduction in available federal funding has made dam building more of a burden to state and local governments. When first authorized in 1965, Auburn Dam, on the American River near Sacramento, would have cost $485 million. The federal government would have paid a large share of the cost, and would have made a no-interest loan of the rest.

Today, the same dam would cost an estimated $2.1 billion—and the federal contribution would be much smaller. Instead of paying 100 percent of the portion attributable to flood control, for example, the federal government is now willing to pay only 75 percent. A coalition of local governments is struggling to raise enough money—$700 million—to build a scaled-down version of the dam, without the irrigation or hydroelectric power features of the 1965 version.

How the dam-building equation has changed is demonstrated by the fate of Two Forks Dam, a project that the Denver Water Department proposed to build on the South Platte

River, about 25 miles from downtown Denver. Even 20 years ago, the chances of such a dam being seriously challenged for environmental concerns would have been minimal. This time, however, the Clean Water Act came into play, and in March 1990, the dam was vetoed by the EPA, which cited unacceptable and avoidable losses of riverine wildlife habitat.

Restoring Water Habitats

Environmental groups are attempting to win back some of what was lost when many existing dams were built. American Rivers, a Washington, D.C.-based river conservation organization, is leading an effort to win environmental concessions during the current relicensing of hydroelectric power dams regulated by the Federal Energy Regulatory Commission (FERC), which is scheduled to review 231 existing hydroelectric dams on 105 rivers in 24 states by the end of 1993. Among the group's goals is to improve fish habitat by increasing stream flows below such dams, and to force installation of fish ladders and other devices to assist migration. (See table, Rivers at Risk.)

The dams regulated by FERC are mostly small ones that were built solely for hydropower. Larger dams on rivers like the Columbia and Colorado are regulated differently because they provide irrigation or other services in addition to hydroelectric power.

Four competing bills were making their way through Congress in 1992 to restructure operations of one of the nation's oldest and largest irrigation projects, the Central Valley Project in California. To varying degrees, each of the bills would divert some water from existing uses—mainly irrigated agriculture—to restore shrunken rivers and wetlands. Seeing the handwriting on the wall, farmers banded together and wrote a bill of their own that would shift a smaller amount of water to en-

Rivers at Risk

Endangered Rivers of 1992

1. Columbia and Snake River system (Northwest)
2. Alsek and Tatshenshini River system (Alaska and British Columbia)
3. Great Whale River (Quebec)
4. Everglades (Florida)
5. American River (California)
6. Colorado River (Arizona)
7. Mississippi River (Midwest)
8. Penobscot River (Maine)
9. Beaverkill and Willowemoc River system (New York)
10. Blackfoot River (Montana)

Threatened Rivers of 1992

11. Animas River (Colorado)
12. Clavey River (California)
13. Elwha River (Washington)
14. Gunnison River (Washington)
15. Illinois River (Oregon)
16. Klamath River (Oregon)
17. New River (North Carolina)
18. Ohio River (Ohio, Pennsylvania, and West Virginia)
19. Ouachita River (Arkansas and Louisiana)
20. Passaic River (New Jersey)
21. Rio Conchos (Chihuahua, Mexico, and Rio Grande, Texas)
22. Savannah River (Georgia)
23. Susquehanna River (Pennsylvania)
24. Verde River (Arizona)
25. Virgin River (Arizona, Nevada, and Utah)

Source: American Rivers, 1992.
Note: Each of these 25 rivers faces damage from dams, water diversions, mining, dredging, land development, and/or pollution.

vironmental uses. As of August 1992, the outcome was still uncertain.

Also in California, a series of court decisions dating to the late 1970s has forced Los Angeles to reduce its diversions from a series of shrinking desert lakes east of the Sierra Nevada. The largest of these, Mono Lake, is a unique saline lake with towering calcium carbonate formations called "tufa."

The state Supreme Court forced Los Angeles to restore some of the lake's inflows by invoking a concept rooted in ancient Roman law to formulate what it called the "public trust doctrine." This doctrine holds that the waters of the state are owned jointly by all of the people and may be reallocated to suit shifting public interests. As a result of later court decisions arising from this doctrine, Los Angeles has been ordered to restore flows in four nearby

> **Water News**
> Washington, D.C., 11/20/91—Atrazine, a herbicide suspected of causing cancer, was found in 146 Mississippi River samples taken by the U.S. Geological Survey. In 27 percent of the samples, levels exceeded those allowed by the EPA for drinking water. Installing water filtering systems to remove the atrazine could cost millions, according to the Natural Resources Defense Council.

rivers to protect fish, and to release enough water from its aqueducts to maintain the lake's present level.

In Florida, Congress is considering a bill to undo the Army Corps of Engineers' 1960s-era channelization of the Kissimmee River, the primary stream feeding Lake Okeechobee at the northern end of the endangered Everglades. When the once-meandering 103-mile stream was channelized into a 56-mile

canal, 43,000 acres of wetlands were dried up, and waterfowl populations dropped by 90 percent. Now, conservationists and Senator Bob Graham (D-Fla.), backed by the state government and the local water management district, are trying to persuade the federal government to restore the Kissimmee to its natural state.

And in Arizona, an environmental study scheduled to be completed this year is considering the operation of the hydroelectric power plant at Glen Canyon Dam, on the Colorado River just above the Grand Canyon. In the past, the U.S. Bureau of Reclamation changed the river's flow frequently and rapidly to generate power for periods of peak demand. That caused heavy erosion on sand bars and beaches downstream, within Grand Canyon National Park. The study is expected to result in new operating rules for the dam and power plant.

International Dam Building

For all the change in the U.S. dam-building business, little has changed in many other countries. Some of the largest, potentially most environmentally damaging water projects are now in the planning stages in Canada, Mexico, China, Chile, and Viet Nam.

In Quebec, a province-owned utility called Hydro-Quebec has built a series of hydroelectric dams since 1971 on rivers that empty into James Bay in northern Quebec. These dams produce, in all, almost 30,000 megawatts of electricity, as much as 30 nuclear power reactors. The resulting power provides most of the province's needs, including those of its pulp and paper mills, with enough left over to sell 6 percent of its output to neighboring provinces and the northeastern United States.

Now, Hydro-Quebec is proposing to dam the Great Whale River and generate another 3,000 megawatts, much of it intended for sale in the United States. Native Cree Indians are fighting the project, saying it will destroy their ability to support themselves through fishing, hunting, and trapping. In February 1992, the International Water Tribunal in The Netherlands, an unofficial body of water development experts, said that the project should be halted until an environmental review can be done.

Other nations are planning similarly ambitious projects. In Chile, the government plans to spend more than $3 billion to build six hydroelectric dams on one of the nation's largest rivers, the Bio-Bio, flooding 52,000 acres. In Viet Nam, the new Hoa Binh Dam, the largest in Southeast Asia, cost $1 billion to build, displaced 50,000 people, and produces 1,900 megawatts of power. India is planning a series of 30 dams on the Narmada River. Thailand and Laos are planning a $2.7 billion project on the Mekong River. Mexico wants to build two dams on the Usumacinta River on the Guatemalan border. Environmentalists say the Mexican dams would damage the largest surviving rainforest in North America, the Lacandon rainforest, which is fed by the river.

For sheer magnitude, however, none of these projects can match China's proposed Three Gorges project, which passed by a 2-1 margin in April 1992 by the national legislature, in a rare break from its usual rubber-stamp unanimity. The 600-foot-high dam, the world's largest hydroelectric power dam, would create a 370-mile-long lake on the Yangtze River. It would flood 60,000 acres of farmland, along with nearly 800 factories and existing power stations, and displace an estimated 1.2 million people, including two cities of 100,000 apiece.

Each of these projects is driven by one imperative: to produce more electrical power in order to raise the national standard of living to a level comparable to that of nations—like the United States—that already have their dams in place. Whether these nations will make the same mistakes that ours has made along the way remains an open question.

This chapter was written by Russell Clemings, a writer in Fresno, California.

Wastes

Slow markets for recyclables and ever-increasing waste output by citizens are prompting discussion and ideas for more effective waste management.

The recession has made times tough for many Americans—even trash collectors. In the past year, news stories have told us that when money is tight, people hold onto their belongings and throw out less trash destined for the landfill. In the spring of 1992, commercial waste managers felt the squeeze from industry as well, as industrial waste output was down. The incineration of Superfund hazardous waste was curtailed, and Chemical Waste Management, Inc., of Oakbrook, Illinois, reported that 1991 profits fell 42 percent from those in 1990.

Because of an economic slowdown in Asia, the American Paper Institute reported a 1991 decline in wastepaper exports to South Korea, Taiwan, and Japan. Exports that had increased between 1986 and 1988 were leveled off by the pervasive recession, and the Institute expected U.S. exports not to increase again at least until after 1995.

But a decrease in waste destined for landfilling, export, or burning has had a positive effect—for recyclers. According to a May 1992 report in the *Journal of Commerce*, the buyers of recyclable materials benefited from price

How Much Waste Do We Generate?
(1960 to 1990)

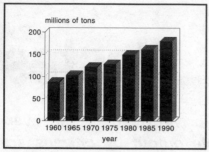

millions of tons

Source: U.S. Environmental Protection Agency (EPA), *Characterization of Municipal Solid Wastes in the United States: 1990 Update* (Office of EPA, Solid Waste and Emergency Response, June 1990), Table 1, p. 10.
Note: Data for 1990 reflect the most recent year (1988) for which EPA has national information.

decreases in 1991 as the average price for used newspaper went from $20 to $5 a ton. Recycling of old newspaper reached a record 6.6 million tons, an increase of 90 percent since 1983. The American Paper Institute indicated that the building of several new mills to process the old papers and the creation of a greater variety of recycled products contributed to a total collection of 31.1 million tons of recycled paper—including newspapers, cardboard, and office paper.

Unfortunately, the recessionary slowdown for some waste managers probably does not reflect a long-term change of habit by the typical U.S. citizen. Nationwide, the physical reality of our mounting trash continues to present a challenge, and the costs of managing community wastes are rising quickly, adding stress to already tight city budgets. In 1991, for example, municipal waste collection, processing, and disposal ran anywhere from $59 to $194 per ton in the United States. By 1996, one waste management consultant estimates that the cost will have risen to $128 to $219 per ton.

Waste Output

The amount of solid waste that the average U.S. resident produces is well over one half ton a year, according to the U.S. Environmental Protection Agency (EPA). That means every individual from Hawaii to Maine is producing roughly 4 pounds of trash today. Predictions are that by the year 2000, the per capita rate will reach 4.4 pounds per day, and the rate for the country as a whole will reach 216 million tons a year. That tops the 1988 figure (approximately 180 million tons) by 10 percent. (See chart, How Much Waste Do We Generate? and table, How Our Per Capita Garbage Is Changing.)

Environment Canada reports that waste output by Canadian citizens has increased as much as 25 percent in the last 10 years. In 1989, Canadian cities generated approximately 33 million tons (30 million metric tons) of waste, and the average output was 3.96 pounds (1.8 kilograms) per person per day. The same year, a study of residential waste output in Ontario suggested that paper and paperboard made up almost 40 percent of the total, and food and plant waste was a close second at just over 30 percent.

Between 1970 and 1986, the U.S. population increased by 18 percent, but its trash output increased by 25 percent. The growth in per capita solid waste output was a hefty 30 percent. Still, it is important to note that these municipal solid wastes make up only 1 percent of the total solid waste created annually in the United States. Industry produces nearly twice as much hazardous waste and 42 times as much solid waste. Thirty-nine percent of U.S. solid waste results from mining and utility wastes, among others. (See chart, U.S. Solid Waste and Its Sources.) A discussion of manufacturers' contributions to waste is included in the "Industry" chapter.

Even though citizens of the United States and Canada generate twice as much garbage per person as individuals in other industrialized countries, the problem that North Americans face in finding ways to deal with the garbage is not unique. On the contrary, the predicament has established itself around the world. At least 60 percent of the countries submitting national reports to a preparatory United Nations meeting preceding last summer's Earth Summit conference in Brazil said that solid wastes were among their biggest environmental concerns. The reports frequently cited problems concerning agricultural chemicals, quantities of household waste, and in-

U.S. Solid Waste and Its Sources
(output per year)

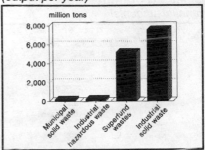

Source: Council on Environmental Quality, *United States of America National Report* (prepared for the United Nations Conference on Environment & Development, 1992), Exhibit 6h.1, p. 333.
Note: Superfund (Resource Conservation and Recovery Act) wastes include discards from oil and gas operations (1.5 billion tons), mining (3.6 billion tons), cement kiln dust (4 million tons), and electric utility wastes (85 million tons).

dustrial and toxic wastes. (See chart, Municipal Waste Generation in Selected Countries.)

How Our Per Capita Garbage Is Changing
(in pounds per day, with projections to 2000)

Waste Materials	1960	1970	1980	1990	1995	2000
Total nonfood product wastes	**1.65**	**2.26**	**2.57**	**2.94**	**3.18**	**3.38**
Paper and paperboard	0.91	1.19	1.32	1.60	1.80	1.96
Glass	0.20	0.34	0.36	0.28	0.23	0.21
Metals	0.32	0.38	0.35	0.34	0.34	0.35
Plastics	0.01	0.08	0.19	0.32	0.39	0.43
Rubber and leather	0.06	0.09	0.10	0.10	0.10	0.11
Textiles	0.05	0.05	0.06	0.09	0.09	0.09
Wood	0.09	0.11	0.12	0.14	0.16	0.17
Other	0.00	0.02	0.07	0.07	0.06	0.06
Other wastes						
Food wastes		0.37	0.34	0.32	0.29	0.28	0.27
Yard wastes	0.61	0.62	0.66	0.70	0.70	0.70
Miscellaneous inorganic wastes	0.04	0.05	0.05	0.06	0.06	0.06
Total waste generated	**2.66**	**3.27**	**3.61**	**4.00**	**4.21**	**4.41**

Source: U.S. Environmental Protection Agency, *Characterization of Municipal Solid Wastes in the United States: 1990 Update* (Office of EPA, Solid Waste and Emergency Response, June 1990), Table 29, p. 61, and Table 41, p. 79.
Note: Data for 1990 reflect the most recent year (1988) for which EPA has national information.

Municipal Waste Generation in Selected Countries
(annual amounts)

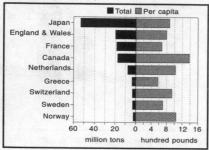

Source: *World Resources 1992–93* (Oxford University Press, New York, 1992), Table 21.4, p. 319. **Note:** Data are for 1989 except for The Netherlands and Japan (1989) and Sweden (1985).

In the United States, the EPA has established a priority list of methods for managing solid wastes. (See box, EPA's Waste Management Hierarchy.) Ideally, says EPA, the United States as a whole should aim for recycling 25 percent of municipal wastes by 1995. Some states have already surpassed

> **Wastes News**
> New Orleans, 8/11/92—*A federal appeals court has ruled that a law banning the importation of hazardous waste from foreign countries is unconstitutional because it infringes on Congress's power to regulate interstate commerce. The law was challenged by a hazardous waste landfill operator in Carlyss, Louisiana, who wanted to import waste from maquiladora factories in Mexico.*

that percentage goal by carrying out aggressive recycling and waste reduction programs. However, *BioCycle* magazine put the overall 1991 U.S. recycling rate at just 14 percent.

Some states have acted on the idea that when fees for garbage pickup are low, citizens are encouraged to be wasteful. As a result, communities like Seattle have found that an effective incentive for changing waste patterns is to charge families more when they put more than one trash container out at the curb. Seattle ranks third in the amount of overall municipal waste recycling, after Honolulu and Newark, New Jersey (see "Green Metro Areas" chapter.) But, in Seattle's case, collecting so much waste for recycling has created other problems, such as creating backlogs of some collected materials. (See box, Seattle Residents Recycle 45 Percent.) Overall, Washington takes the lead over other states by recycling 34 percent of its municipal solid waste.

The states, which are responsible for dealing with their own wastes, have instituted a variety of recycling goals. (See tables, U.S. Solid Waste Output and Management, by State, and State Goals for Recycling.)

Industry Critiques the Hierarchy

Some managers in the solid waste industry—made up of landfill operators, trash collectors, sorters and haulers, and incinerator and waste-to-energy plant operators, to name a few—argue that when communities take the EPA's hierarchy to heart, they miss seeing the larger picture.

The waste-to-energy combustion industry, for example, represented by the Integrated Waste Services Association (IWSA) in Washington, D.C., says that EPA's suggestion to in all cases do x before y only increases the frustration of cities trying to resolve waste management problems. Jonathan Kiser, director of waste services programs at IWSA, says "We will always need landfills, even after combustion, and after

EPA's Waste Management Hierarchy

The U.S. Environmental Protection Agency has established the following list as a goal for dealing with solid waste.

- **Reduce** waste by preventing its creation.

- **Recycle** and **compost** as much waste as possible.

- **Incinerate** waste or **treat** it in other ways to reduce its volume.

- **Landfilling** waste is last in the list of options.

recycling—to handle those by-products for which there are no reuses."

What the waste-to-energy industry promotes is that communities be allowed to choose the type of waste management options that meet their individual needs—to mix and match. As waste output fluctuates and the components and quantities of municipal solid waste change with the times, municipalities need to be ready with several available options for managing their wastes. Many in the industry promote waste-to-energy combustion (converting heat from burning trash into usable electricity) as one form of recycling.

At the Center for the Study of American Business in St. Louis, staff members have said that "the present bias toward recycling" is not cost-effective. Rather than being an "environmentally benign" process, as some might believe, recycling creates its own pollution as it consumes energy and requires chemical additives and water and sludge treatment. The big national push for recycling is based on "misconceptions" about other waste management options, including landfilling

They, too, urge communities to take an "integrated approach" to waste management by combining methods to best suit their needs.

Because the common neighborhood reaction to some of these other options, especially the building of new trash-burning facilities, has been strongly negative in recent years, IWSA is working hard to change the public's fears about the health and environmental hazards of newer combustion facilities that employ monitored environmental safeguards.

Seattle Residents Recycle 45 Percent

In 1991–92, Seattle residents contributed 45 percent of their household waste for recycling, a rate that ranks among the top in the country.

The city's no-nonsense waste collection scheme is partly responsible. If residents want to throw out more in a week than one 20-gallon bin can hold, they are charged extra. In 1991, fees for the first waste container ran $10.70 per month. Additional bins cost extra. As a result, waste management officials there have seen a significant drop in the amount of waste residents destined for the landfill. Eighty-nine percent of the people who use curbside garbage pickup set out just one can a week. Sixty-six percent of the residents pay just $2.00 per month to have their yard waste picked up. Pickup of recyclable items is free.

While the strategy to cut down on garbage destined for the landfill has worked well, waste officials admit that the sluggish market for recyclables has created bottlenecks of collected materials. Mixed waste paper, for example, now costs the city $10 per ton to get rid of, when it used to be able to sell it for $10 per ton. City officials and local business consultants are working to create new markets for the used goods.

U.S. Solid Waste Output and Management, by State
(1991)

State	Waste Generated (tons/year)	Recycled (%)	Incinerated (%)	Landfilled (%)
Alabama[a]	4,500,000	8	3	89
Alaska	500,000	6	15	79
Arizona[b]	2,900,000	5	0	95
Arkansas[c]	2,000,000	5	7	88
California[a]	45,000,000	17	2	81
Colorado[a]	2,400,000	16	0	84
Connecticut	2,900,000	15	65	20
Delaware	750,000	8	20	72
Florida	18,700,000	21	17	62
Georgia	4,400,000	5	4	91
Hawaii[a]	1,300,000	4	42	54
Idaho[b]	850,000	8	2	90
Illinois	14,600,000	12	2	86
Indiana[c]	5,700,000	8	17	75
Iowa[a]	2,300,000	10	2	88
Kansas	2,400,000	5	0	95
Kentucky	3,500,000	10	0	90
Louisiana	3,500,000	10	0	90
Maine	950,000	17	45	38
Maryland[c]	5,100,000	10	17	73
Massachusetts[b]	6,800,000	29	47	24
Michigan[d]	11,700,000	25	19	56
Minnesota[c]	4,400,000	31	25	39
Mississippi	1,400,000	8	3	89
Missouri[b]	7,500,000	10	0	90
Montana[b]	600,000	6	1	93
Nebraska	1,300,000	10	0	90
Nevada	1,000,000	10	0	90

Wastes News
Louisville, Kentucky, 2/20/92—Operators of *a hazardous waste incinerator in Calvert County, Kentucky, have unknowingly burned radioactive waste from Department of Energy (DOE) uranium enrichment plants. The DOE recently acknowledged that its standards for labeling such waste are inadequate and that it could not ensure that radwaste is not shipped to commercial facilities. Officials at the uranium plants said that wastes sent to Calvert County had only "trace" radiation and posed no threats to area workers.*

Newspaper articles and casual discussions of trash-burning plants tend to refer to all such facilities as "incinerators" when in fact relatively few of those still exist. (See box, The Burning Issue.) Despite public concerns about burning trash, a number of states are choosing to increase the amount of waste they send to combustors to be burned. While the pace of planning and building these facilities varies from region to region, the reasons for their construction are based largely on one factor. As city-owned landfill space runs out and states increasingly

U.S. Solid Waste Output and Management, by State (cont.)
(1991)

State	Waste Generated (tons/year)	Recycled (%)	Incinerated (%)	Landfilled (%)
New Hampshire[e]	1,100,000	5	23	72
New Jersey	7,100,000	30	17	53
New Mexico[e]	1,500,000	5	0	95
New York	22,000,000	14	13	73
North Carolina[b]	6,000,000	17	4	79
North Dakota	400,000	10	0	90
Ohio[a]	15,700,000	3	8	89
Oklahoma[e]	3,000,000	10	10	80
Oregon	3,300,000	21	6	73
Pennsylvania	9,500,000	10	25	65
Rhode Island	1,200,000	15	0	85
South Carolina	4,000,000	5	7	88
South Dakota[e]	800,000	10	0	90
Tennessee[c]	5,000,000	2	9	89
Texas[b]	18,000,000	10	1	89
Utah	1,200,000	10	10	80
Vermont	390,000	20	8	72
Virginia	9,000,000	10	10	80
Washington	5,100,000	34	7	59
West Virginia	1,700,000	10	0	90
Wisconsin	3,400,000	17	3	80
Wyoming[b]	320,000	3	0	97
Total	**280,675,000**	**14**	**10**	**76**

Source: *BioCycle* (Vol. 33, No. 4), April 1992, Table 1, p. 47.
Notes: Waste generated data represent commercial, residential, and institutional waste, unless otherwise noted. a. Commercial, residential, institutional, industrial, sewage sludge, construction and demolition debris. b. Commercial, residential, institutional, construction and demolition. c. Commercial, residential, institutional, some industrial. d. Commercial, residential, institutional, Industrial. e. Commercial, residential, institutional, industrial, construction and demolition.

refuse to take other localities' trash for landfilling, cities are doing what they feel they must do to handle their own daily volumes of trash.

One source claims that the total trash-burning capacity in the United States increased about 21 percent from the end of 1990 to the end of 1991. Among the states with the highest capacity for burning waste are Massachusetts (9,700 tons per day) and Pennsylvania (7,300 tons per day). In one year, Pennsylvania went from three to six combustors and increased the percentage of municipal solid waste it burns from 17 to 25 percent.

Waste Reduction

Reducing solid wastes requires cutting back the number and volume of discarded products. Manufacturers can change product content and packaging. Those that take the problem of hazardous waste disposal seriously can also work to reduce the content of toxins and harsh chemicals in their products. Consumers can help cut trash by changing what they buy.

Consumers can reduce household waste by buying high-quality, long-lasting items that can be repaired, in-

The Burning Issue

The public knows them as "incinerators." The waste management industry uses the term "combustors." What are they referring to? What follows are descriptions of a number of types of facilities that burn municipal trash, but in different mixes and for different results.

Incinerators, as such, do just what we have always thought they do. Mixed trash goes in, unsorted, and is burned. The resulting ash typically is landfilled. According to the industry, just 37 of these basic incinerators are still in operation in the United States, and they process 2.1 million tons of municipal solid waste a year.

Mass burn incinerators, or **mass burn combustors,** are one of three systems for burning waste in which the heat generated from the burning material is converted into usable electricity. Mixed garbage burns in a single combustion chamber where the temperature reaches 2,000° F. The by-products are ash, which is typically sent to a landfill, and combustion gases. As the hot gases rise from the burning waste, they heat water held in tubes around the combustion chamber. The boiling water is used to generate steam and/or electricity. The gases pass through a spray dryer and a fabric air filter to remove contaminants before they are released from a stack into the air.

Modular combustion systems typically have two combustion chambers, a lower one for the burning of mixed trash and an upper one for the heating of gases. A burner in the second, or higher, chamber heats gases at least momentarily to 1,800° F to destroy dioxins. As in mass burn systems, the gases are put through air filters before they are released. In modular units, energy is recovered with a heat recovery steam generator. These incinerator units are called "modular" because the newer versions can be built from prefabricated units. They are often much smaller than mass burn plants.

Refuse-derived fuel combustors burn presorted waste and convert the resulting heat into energy. Bulky wastes, such as appliances, are removed in the "tipping area," where trucks dump the mixed garbage. The remaining waste travels on a system of conveyor belts, through a series of magnets, screens, and other devices that shred and separate the trash. The best burning material, or that which generates the most amount of heat, is saved for combustion, and the remainder is either landfilled or recycled. Often, the waste saved for burning is mixed with coal or another hot-burning fuel to produce energy.

Of the last three types of combustors, called waste-to-energy (WTE) plants by the industry, 140 were in operation in the United States in August 1992. Of those, 64 were mass burn, 49 were modular, and 27 were refuse-derived fuel (RDF) plants. In all, they typically consumed 80,100 tons of waste per day and generated the annual equivalent of 16.4 million megawatts of usable power. The Integrated Wastes Services Association equates that to the electricity supplied by 30 million barrels of oil (or 19 supertankers the size of the *Exxon Valdez*).

In combustion systems employing the most modern techniques and environmental controls, only garbage that cannot be reused, recycled, or composted is burned; air contaminant systems filter out pollutants; and ash is transported in covered, leak-proof containers and disposed of in landfills designed and monitored exclusively for ash. Such "state-of-the-art" systems most likely reflect more the ideal than the reality among existing combustors. This ideal is further defined by IN-FORM, a nonprofit environmental research group, in a study of 15 mass burn and RDF plants of varying age, size, design, and emissions control systems.

The study found that only one plant of the 15 studied achieved the emission levels set by the group for six primary air

The Burning Issue (continued)

pollutants (dioxins and furans, particulates, carbon monoxide, sulfur dioxide, hydrogen chloride, and nitrogen oxides). Six plants did not meet any. Only two employed the safest ash management techniques.

While the WTE industry credits the report for supplying communities with a helpful guide to understanding how waste-to-energy plants work, how to finance them, and how to manage ash wastes, it questions the group's authority to set its own "state-of-the-art" emissions standards. A reviewer for the National Solid Wastes Management Association wrote that INFORM's standards "are far more stringent than EPA's New Source Performance Standards," which deal more with emissions levels that are consistently achievable with new technology.

Both groups would likely agree, however, that achieving the best benefits from waste combustion includes designing a plant well, operating it under closely monitored practices, ensuring that employees are thoroughly trained, handling ash carefully, and keeping tabs on a plant's effects on the environment. Most important, according to INFORM, is the work that takes place before burning: "maximum source reduction and maximum recycling within the community before incineration is considered."

Studies by both camps—the WTE industry and groups like INFORM who seek solutions to environmental concerns related to waste management issues—call for further research and improvement of combustion technology and emissions controls. INFORM notes that communities concerned about air emissions, toxic components of ash, and plant odors deserve standardized information on existing incinerators and combustors in order to make intelligent comparisons and decisions. The group suggests an annual inventory of emissions—including lead, mercury, volatile organic compounds, and the six air pollutants mentioned above—that would define categories and output. Such a report might take a form similiar to that of the U.S. Environmental Protection Agency's Toxics Release Inventory for industrial releases (see "Industry" chapter).

For More Information

To find out more about waste-to-energy systems, write to the Integrated Waste Services Association at 1133 21st Street, Suite 205, Washington, DC 20036. To buy a copy of INFORM's report, *Burning Garbage in the U.S.: Practice vs. State of the Art*, by Marjorie Clarke, Maarten de Kadt, and David Saphire, write to INFORM, Inc., 381 Park Avenue South, New York, NY 10016.

stead of buying short-lived "disposable" alternatives. The consumer typically pays a much higher price per unit for such convenience items.

Disposable packaging and containers take up a great deal of landfill space. According to the most recent EPA figures, packaging makes up 31.6 percent (56.8 million tons per year) of U.S. solid waste. Of the total container and packaging waste, plastic materials make up 12.8 percent. Ahead of plastics in terms of volume are paper and cardboard (51 percent) and glass containers (23 percent).

Many advocates of waste reduction use the term *precycling*. That concept refers to a consumer making environmentally sound choices at the point of purchase. It includes avoiding products with extra packaging (for example, canned or boxed vegetables instead of fresh, unbagged, or bulk items) or products made to satisfy only short-term needs (such as disposable razors and non-refillable pens). Con-

The Top 12 States for Recycling
(1991)

percentage of municipal waste

(Bar chart showing states from highest to lowest: Washington, Minnesota, New Jersey, Massachusetts, Michigan, Florida, Oregon, Vermont, California, Maine, North Carolina, Wisconsin)

Source: Adapted from *BioCycle* (Vol. 33, No. 5), May 1992, Table 1, p. 30.

sumer choices can go a long way to influence what manufacturers make, while also preventing some trash from ever entering the waste stream.

In one step toward responding to consumer concern about waste in the entertainment field, the Recording Industry Association of America announced that by April 1993, compact disks will no longer be packaged in the "long box," a cardboard container at least twice as long as the disk itself. Instead, CDs will for the most part be enclosed only in shrink wrap.

Reusing a product can be one of the simplest approaches to reducing solid

State Goals for Recycling
(includes yard waste composting)

State	Recycling[a] Goal (%)	Target Year	State	Recycling Goal (%)[a]	Target Year
Alabama	25	1991	Nebraska	25	NA
Arkansas	40	2000	Nevada	25	1994
California	50	2000	New Hampshire	40	2000
Connecticut	25	1991	New Jersey	25[d]	1990
Delaware	21	2000	New Mexico	50	2000
Florida	30	1995	New York	60	2000
Georgia	25	1996	North Carolina	25	1993
Hawaii	50	2000	North Dakota	40	2000
Illinois	25	2000	Ohio	25	1994
Indiana	50	2000	Oregon	50	2000
Iowa	50	2000	Pennsylvania	25	1997
Kentucky	25	1997	Rhode Island	15	1993
Louisiana	25	1992	South Carolina	30	1997
Maine	50	1994	South Dakota	50	2005
Maryland	20[b]	1994	Tennessee	25	1996
Massachusetts	25	2000	Texas	40	1994
Michigan	20–30	2005	Vermont	40	2000
Minnesota	30[c]	1996	Virginia	25	1995
Mississippi	25	1996	Washington	50	1995
Missouri	40	1998	West Virginia	50	2010
Montana	25	1996			

Source: *BioCycle* (Vol. 33, No. 5), May 1992, Table 1, p. 30.
Notes: a. Includes yard waste composting. b. Fifteen percent goal for counties with less than 100,000 residents; 20 percent goal for counties over 100,000 residents. c. Thirty percent goal in Minnesota, but 45 percent goal in the seven-county Minneapolis-St. Paul area. d. Does not include leaf composting as part of the goal. In 1990, a solid waste management task force recommended a 60 percent recycling goal, although it is not currently mandated by law.
NA = not available.

waste. Maine has set an effective example by reusing toll cards on its highways. Cards handed over at the exit booth are returned to their starting points and used again. The state has found that each year it can avoid having to print 26 million new cards, a savings of $100,000.

A four-county recycling program in western Iowa has been able to make money by selling worn-out clothing and other textiles to a company that makes wiping cloths. Clothing that is wearable does not end up in the rag bag, either, but is sold to make money for local workshops for handicapped adults.

Recycling's Many Forms

The country's burden of managing solid waste would be lessened if citizens could cut back the amount of materials they throw away. Recycling is a significant way to:

- keep large amounts of solid wastes out of landfills, prolonging the lives of the landfills, and saving the cost of waste disposal;

- conserve resources, avoiding the high costs of extracting virgin materials through mining, tapping, cutting down trees, and the like;

- save energy, since the manufacturing of secondary (recycled) glass, steel, and aluminum products and some plastic bottles uses considerably less energy and creates fewer pollutants than does primary manufacturing.

The number of curbside recycling programs across the United States rose to 3,955 in 1991, a 40 percent increase from the number of programs in 1990 and a 250 percent increase since 1989. These figures cover recycling efforts serving 71 million people. (See graph,

The Top 12 States for Yard Waste Composting
(1991)

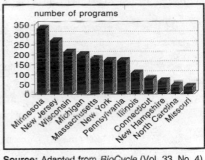

number of programs

Source: Adapted from *BioCycle* (Vol. 33, No. 4), April 1992, Table 4, p. 54.
Note: The total number of programs in the country is 2,201.

The Top 12 States for Recycling.) Despite the fact that new state laws added 300 mandatory programs in 1991, volunteer recycling programs outnumber mandatory ones 1,569 to 1,376. All states but three engage in curbside programs. Currently, Wyoming and Alaska have no curbside pickup recycling programs. Delaware does not have any either, but has a system of drop-off sites.

Once recyclables have been collected, materials recovery facilities (MRFs) fill the gap between the users and the reusers. MRFs are the sending-out point for recyclables that go to other markets for reprocessing. In 1991, the United States had 191 working MRFs, 19 under construction, and 59 in the planning stages.

Besides tackling the recycling of cans, bottles, and plastics, a number of states have increased their goals for recycling yard waste: lawn clippings, leaves, and twigs. Yard waste makes up 31.6 million tons of the country's municipal solid waste. As cities become more aware of the amount of

Getting Rid of Household Hazardous Wastes

This is a sampling of the types of products containing chemicals that, when disposed of improperly, can add toxins to our waste stream and water systems.

Product	Hazardous components	Disposal
Plastics	Organic chlorine compounds, organic solvents	Recycle when possible
Pesticides	Organic chlorine compounds, organic phosphate compounds	Use all/share; store for hazardous waste collection
Medicines	Organic solvents and residues, traces of heavy metals	Small amounts down drain
Paints	Heavy metals, pigments, solvents, organic residues	Share, recycle; store for hazardous waste collection
Oil, gasoline; other petroleum products	Oil, phenols and other organic compounds, heavy metals, ammonia, salt acids, caustics	Recycle at approved facility; take to hazardous waste collection site
Metals	Heavy metals, organic solvents, pigments, abrasives plating salts, oils, phenols	Recycle
Leather	Heavy metals, organic solvents	Reuse; give away
Textiles	Heavy metals, dyes, organic chlorine compounds, solvents	Reuse; give away
Auto batteries	Sulfuric acid, lead	Take to service station or reclamation center
Household batteries	Mercury, zinc, silver, lithium, cadmium	Take to reclamation center or battery store that collects them; keep safely at home until community collection is organized

For more information on the safe disposal of specific products, contact your city or county waste department or the U.S. Environmental Protection Agency, toll free (800) 424-9346. One private firm providing such information is the Environmental Hazards Management Institute, 10 Newmarket Road, P.O. Box 932, Durham, NH 03824; (603) 868-1496, or (800) 446-5256.

space these wastes take up in municipal landfills, bans on landfilling yard waste have increased by 56 percent, and city-run composting programs are becoming more prevalent. A number of municipalities are also encouraging their residents to compost lawn and food waste at home. (See graph, The Top 12 States for Yard Waste Composting.) In 1991, 2,201 cities were set up to compost yard waste. That number reflects an increase of 800 programs over 1990 data.

An EPA study estimates that 13.2 million tons of food wastes are produced in our cities every year. In order to study the most cost-effective ways to dispose of food scraps, the Seattle Solid Waste Utility did a study. Starting with the fact that some 30,000 tons of commercial food waste is sent to Seattle's landfills each year and 14,000 tons of commercial food waste is treated in its municipal water system, the Utility compared the cost of landfilling food scraps over grinding them in garbage disposals and then treating the water. Their results showed that treating food wastes in the municipal water system cost approximately 80 percent more than the cost of landfilling them. Just having access to a food disposal, the utility said, is a deterrent to separating food wastes for composting.

Kick-Starting Recycling Markets

In response to a glut of materials in some recycling markets and increased prices for collection, a growing number of states are aiming to keep recyclables from piling up in warehouses by instituting laws that require percentages of some products to be made up of recycled components. Another common tactic is that of directing the state government itself to use recycled products. Illinois, for example, requires any state-funded building weatherization project to use recycled cellulose. West Virginia aims for government paper purchases by the end of 1993 to include 20 percent recycled content. That amount will increase to 40 percent at the end of 1995.

The sometimes frustrating realities of gearing up and maintaining an ambitious recycling project have been felt by the country's most populous metropolitan area: New York City. A 1989 law aimed for recycling 2,100 tons of the 17,000 tons of daily residential waste by April 1992. Two months before the deadline, however, city officials discussed repealing the law in favor of one that expanded the collection of recyclables much more slowly. "Because of a combination of union regulations, citizen confusion and resistance, and low prices for the recy-

cled material," stated *The New York Times*, "the law . . . is proving much more expensive than the city expected."

States are also learning that simply setting a certain goal for recycling or waste reduction will not necessarily make it happen. Steady funds are needed to keep the programs going. As a result, some states have placed surcharges on landfill tipping fees (see Landfills for the 1990s, below) or special purchase fees on hard-to-reuse materials (such as tires) that have given them the necessary financial leverage to fund a variety of recycling and composting programs. By banning compostable material from landfills and collecting it separately from other solid wastes, a number of municipalities have been able to benefit by either selling the cured product or simply avoiding landfill fees. A leaf-composting

Wastes News
Toronto, 8/14/92—A recent survey offers evidence that Canadians are enthusiastic recyclers. Of 13,000 households, half of which use recycling containers for paper, glass, and metal, nearly seven out of eight reported using recycling services. Forty-five percent regularly buy paper products with recycled content.

program set up in Quincy, Massachusetts, in response to such a law has reportedly saved the community more than $200,000 for landfilling.

In addition to taxing wastes disposed of in landfills, states are increasing the pressure on manufacturers and product service centers to take back the items—such as appliances and battery ies—that they sell as a way of encouraging appropriate disposal and recycling of components. Germany has taken an especially aggressive approach to requiring manufacturers to deal with their own excess packaging (see box, Germany Forces Industry to Recycle Packaging).

Other recycling efforts by communities and businesses have seen encouraging results in the past year. More than 17,000 of the country's 31,000 supermarkets collected plastic grocery bags for recycling in 1991. A community-run flea market in Huron County, Ohio, was set up next to the county landfill as a way of reusing items destined for the dump.

On a larger scale, in 1992 approximately 40 newspaper de-inking plants were in the planning stages across the United States and Canada, since the ink must be removed before recycling can take place. Large paper companies

Germany Forces Industry to Recycle Packaging

Manufacturers in Germany have their hands full—of empty packages. In a situation forced upon them by a new national law, product manufacturers must now create ways to reuse the material that makes up their packages, whether it be glass, plastic, paperboard, aluminum—or whatever. As the amount and variety of returned material creates an interesting challenge for recyclers, the mandate appears to have spurred the creative juices of manufacturers and recyclers alike. And in a country that ranks highest among European nations for output of municipal waste (824.1 pounds per capita in 1987), new solutions to reducing solid wastes are welcome.

The law has come into effect in several steps. In December 1991 it required that all manufacturers take back and recycle packaging materials used for transporting products to stores. By April 1, manufacturers were required to collect and recycle all product sales packaging (such as the box that contains and displays a product). On January 1, 1993, the law will require packages, such as the vegetable cans and foil or plastic wrappers around the actual contents, to be recycled.

Faced with a dispute over which manufacturers would carry what burden of the management of the law, industries created a new company, Duales System Deutschland (DSD), to carry out the details. DSD charges packagers a fee for each product. Those that pay a fee are entitled to print the System's "Green Dot" recycling symbol on their package. DSD has also required each industrial sector to commit to process the collected recyclables according to the law. With the Green Dot as a guide, consumers deposit the recyclables into bins distributed for home use. Every four weeks, the bins are collected by independent contractors and then sorted by material for recycling.

While the system appears to be working relatively well among consumers, complaints among some manufacturers are taking a while to die out. Real problems exist, especially where technologies for processing certain collected materials have not even been developed. Until solutions are found, some materials pile up.

The new law has sparked heated debate and criticism from outside Germany's borders as well. Industries in the European Community and around the world accuse the new system of being a barrier to trade.

But the law's effect on the amount and kinds of new packaging is worth noting. According to *Tomorrow* magazine, "Secondary sales packaging is already disappearing from German store shelves, as is plastic transparent packaging."

Manufacturers are trying a number of new approaches to getting their products to consumers. In one example, Seib Folien, manufacturer of plastic bags for trash and freezer use, now folds its bags so that all it takes to keep them together is a single rubber band. As a result, the company has cut back its packaging waste from 15,435 to 1,764 pounds (7,000 to 800 kilograms) per 500,000 bags.

needing a reliable source for recycled paper were pitching in financially to see that a regional plant to handle 60,000 tons a year was built.

While some reports reflect discouragement at a slow market for the purchase of recyclables, the incentives being taken by states, communities, and individuals should prove helpful in the long run. Other waste experts, predicting that it is just a matter of time for recycling markets to take off, suggest that consumers have a critical part to play in maintaining a consistent demand for recycled products.

Landfills for the 1990s

There is an interesting trend afoot regarding the use of American landfills. While their numbers have steadily decreased over the past two decades (the total dropped from 8,000 operating in 1988 to 5,812 at the end of 1991), their average size has increased. Pennsylvania, for example, had 72 landfills for municipal waste in 1989 and a projected remaining life of 5 years. In 1991, it had only 44 landfills, but had increased its estimated remaining capacity to 15 years.

New EPA regulations for landfills scheduled for October 1993 are projected to seriously affect the number of operable landfills. The requirements include installing plastic and clay liners, collecting and treating systems for liquids that leach out the bottom of the landfill, monitoring groundwater and surface water for harmful chemicals, and monitoring the landfill surface for escaping methane gas.

The new regulations will force landfill operators to either upgrade their systems or close operations. Predicting an inability to improve the environmental situation of its 75 landfills, Mississippi expects to close 60. Kansas

Average Landfill Tipping Fees, by Region
(1988 and 1990)

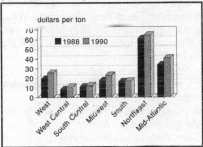

Source: Susan K. Sheets and Edward W. Repa, National Solid Wastes Management Association, *1990 Landfill Tipping Fee Survey* (NSWMA, Washington, D.C., 1991) Figure 1, p. 7.
Note: States are organized as follows: West—WA, OR, ID, CA, NV; West Central—MT, ND, SD, WY, NE, UT, CO, KS; South Central—AZ, NM, OK, TX, AR, LA; Midwest—MN, WI, IA, IL, MI, MO, IN, OH; South—KY, TN, NC, SC, MS, AL, GA, FL; Northeast—ME, NH, VT, MA, CT, RI, NY; Mid-Atlantic—PA, NJ, DE, MD, VA, WV. Alaska and Hawaii are not included.

expects to lose up to 28 years of its current 30-year projected capacity.

One national outcome of the new regulations, according to the National Solid Wastes Management Association (NSWMA), is that an increase in the number of corporate-run landfills will be unavoidable, since those are the only groups that could afford to build and run them. Estimated costs of building and maintaining a landfill that adheres to the new EPA regulations run near $125 million, with up to 55 percent of that amount going for taxes, insurance, and the like.

Landfill tipping fees are already on the rise: the overall trend reflected a 17 percent increase in average costs in just two years, from 1988 to 1990. In 1991, tipping fees per ton ranged from $0 to $200. (The average is $26.50 per ton.)

(See graph, Average Landfill Tipping Fees, by Region.) In general, according to NSWMA, high fees, such as those in the Northeast and mid-Atlantic states, reflect a higher level of environmental protection. Landfills in the west central and south central states generally have the lowest percentage of landfills with protective features.

Fees also reflect the amount of space left in a particular landfill—less room means a higher price. Overall, the Northeast has only 3.8 years left in existing landfills. Higher fees are also charged by landfills that have to pay an additional state-enforced levy. On average, however, the typical U.S. landfill in 1990 covered 173 acres, buried 1,308 tons of waste a day, and was expected to last another 14.2 years. A 1991 *BioCycle* magazine survey placed the range of years remaining for U.S. landfills between 3 (Georgia) and 50 (Oregon).

There is a bright spot regarding landfilled wastes, however, that can primarily be attributed to recycling efforts. Between 1989 and 1992, the amount of U.S. municipal solid waste sent to landfills decreased by 8 percent, from 84 to 76 percent of the total. During the same period, recycling increased from 9 to 14 percent.

Finding New Solutions

Our nation's historical waste "solution" becomes more and more a thing of the past as the total number of operable landfills continues to decrease significantly. But new technologies in waste management, combustion, and recycling, with stricter environmental regulations and more creative incentives for sparking the purchase and reuse of materials, should help the nation reach critical goals. Reduce, reuse, and recycle continue to be the operative words when making—or avoiding the creation of—trash.

Writer Terry Stutzman Mast is managing editor of the 1993 Information Please Environmental Almanac.

Energy

After years of boosting production and charging users more, the U.S. utility industry is being reprogrammed to save electricity—and to encourage its customers to do the same.

A quiet revolution is taking place in the way U.S. electric utilities plan for the future. At its heart is a paradox: Utilities can make money by encouraging and even helping consumers to use less electricity.

This upending of traditional policy works because utilities that aggressively pursue conservation and efficiency programs can often avoid the enormous costs of building new power plants—costs that would be passed on to consumers as higher electricity rates. Among the results, consumers get part of the savings, so their rates rise less

rapidly than they would have otherwise. Utilities keep the rest of the savings as a return on their investment in energy efficiency—their own and, more importantly, their customers'. Overall, the economy becomes more energy efficient and more competitive, and the environment benefits from less energy-related pollution.

Although this transformation has gone virtually unnoticed by most consumers and the general media, it is difficult to exaggerate its profundity. A system that for decades had responded to rising demand by automatically producing more power is being reprogrammed to conserve it.

Although only 5 percent of the world's people live in the United States, the nation accounts for 25 percent of world energy consumption and has long been regarded as backward in terms of energy policy. Now, however, the United States is blazing the path. Japan and other industrialized nations routinely praised as models of energy efficiency are studying the successes of American utilities in promoting energy conservation.

An important change in outlook is driving the transformation as the high costs of our thirst for energy are becoming clearer. Americans increasingly see *saving* energy, rather than forever making, buying, and using more of it, as

Energy News
Washington, D.C., 2/17/92—*An alkaline battery with no mercury added is being test marketed in Indiana and Texas by the Eveready Battery Co.* Advertising Age *reports that the battery has 90 to 92 percent of the life of similar Energizer batteries. Six states have passed laws requiring that all batteries be free of added mercury by 1996.*

crucial to environmental progress and a strong economy.

Moreover, conservation is no longer equated with deprivation. Even cautious observers say there is an enormous amount of energy that can theoretically be "mined" by promoting efficiency and conservation without lowering the quality of life. The utility industry's own research group, the Electric Power Research Institute (EPRI), estimates that making maximum use of available technologies could save up to 44 percent of projected electricity use in the year 2000.

Managing Demand

In the past, utility planning usually meant focusing on supply and finding the cheapest way to add generating capacity (new power plants). Traditional regulatory policy rewarded utilities for selling more electricity, penalized them for saving it, and offered them no incentives to encourage conservation or efficiency.

But the 1970s radically altered the planning environment. Energy shocks such as the oil embargoes and declining supplies of coal and oil drove fuel prices up sharply. The costs of new plants soared because of high interest rates and longer construction times. Environmental and safety worries made it difficult to site new power plants, and building them saddled utilities with heavy financial risks. For the first time in years, utilities were forced to ask regulators for dramatically higher rates.

These rate increases aroused ratepayers and consumer activists and stimulated new thinking about energy use. Was more energy the only ticket to further economic growth? Must supply always increase to meet rising demand? Why were utilities allowed to make money only by selling power? Suppose they could make money by saving it instead?

Multiple Options

The answers to these questions helped spawn a new, more broadly based philosophy of energy planning in which new power plants are only one of many options for meeting rising demand. Planners studied the energy and economic trends of the 1970s and 1980s and saw that economic growth does not necessarily depend on parallel growth in energy consumption. They also realized that demand could be cut

Utility Conservation Programs: Two Success Stories

One of the nation's largest utilities, Southern California Edison, first began encouraging its customers to use less electricity in 1978, when it offered incentives for installing more efficient equipment. This pioneering effort has paid off, saving billions of kilowatt-hours of electricity and allowing the utility to reduce its generating capacity needs by the equivalent of several new plants. Edison estimates that the savings in generated power through 1991 have prevented emissions of 29,000 tons of nitrogen oxides, 24,000 tons of sulfur dioxide, and nearly 18 million tons of carbon dioxide.

Edison's multifaceted conservation programs include energy audits; incentives to builders of energy-efficient houses; incentives for industrial and residential customers to upgrade their air conditioners, refrigerators, lighting, heat pumps, and other hardware; direct assistance to low-income customers; technical consulting services to businesses and industry; and many others.

Wisconsin Electric, a much smaller utility, began its Smart Money Energy Program in 1987 and already has cut energy demand by about 4 percent. Wisconsin Electric picks up part of customers' bills for efficient new air conditioners, refrigerators, water heaters, shower heads, lighting, and dehumidifiers. By paying customers who turn in old refrigerators, freezers, and room air conditioners, the utility retires inefficient units and is able to collect and recycle the units' chlorofluorocarbon coolants. Customers can also save energy and money by letting the utility partially restrict energy use during times of heavy demand through the use of timers or radio-control devices on water heaters and dehumidifiers.

Wisconsin Electric believes that the Smart Money program, by avoiding combustion of nearly half a million tons of coal, has prevented emissions of 6,150 tons of sulfur dioxide, 2,150 tons of nitrogen oxides, and almost 1 million tons of carbon dioxide through 1991.

through conservation, especially if regulations were changed to make it financially attractive for utilities. The integrated resource planning (IRP) approach to utility regulation requires utilities to evaluate, integrate, and implement—demand reducing and supply-enhancing resources based upon the primary criterion of minimizing total costs. This allows utilities many choices besides new power plants, such as buying excess power from elsewhere or improving power transmission and distribution.

Among the most widely used and important options are programs to manage demand and to improve the efficiency of energy use. These programs take many forms (see box, Utility Conservation Programs: Two Success Stories), but the key to their success is that regulators have changed the rules to allow utilities to recover investments in conservation, just as they have always done for new plants. Because the average cost of energy efficiency improvements is half or less the cost of building and running new power plants, the rates utilities charge their customers can rise more slowly than they otherwise would; consumers with higher-efficiency equipment, partially or completely financed by the utility, save money because they use less energy. In short, everybody wins.

The integrated planning philosophy and regulations that encourage utilities to invest in their customers' energy efficiency are increasingly common, although not all states have yet adopted them. By a conservative estimate, 11 states have adopted IRP and

A State Energy Report Card on Utility Planning

The State Report Card assesses states's status in building integrated resource planning (IRP) into existing utility regulatory systems. IRP requires electric utilities to evaluate, integrate, and implement—in order of cost-effectiveness—demand-reducing and supply-enhancing resources based upon the primary criterion of minimizing total costs. The rating system considers not only the status of states's efforts in implementing IRP, but also the relative effectiveness of the IRP process in mitigating costly power plant construction, enhancing consumer energy-efficiency savings through utility help, minimizing customer power bills and utility revenue requirements, requiring consideration of additional environmental factors, and expanding IRP to regulated gas utilities.

The report card gives an "F" for those states that have made little or no progress in implementing IRP or achieving its desired results; a "D" for states just getting under way in either IRP implementation or achievements; a "C" for states with limited success in IRP implementation and/or achievements; a "B" for states with moderate success in IRP implementation and/or achievements; and an "A" for states that have implemented IRP and/or are achieving many of its desired results.

Source: Cynthia Mitchell, consulting economist, Reno, Nevada.
Note: Nebraska is not included in this state-based assessment, because its utilities are all run by municipalities.

State Energy Report Card

(1991 data)

State	Grade	State	Grade	State	Grade
California	A	Missouri	B	Arizona	D
Maine	A	North Carolina	B	Delaware	D
Massachusetts	A	South Carolina	B	Indiana	D
Nevada	A	Utah	B	Kansas	D
New Hampshire	A	Connecticut	C	Kentucky	D
New York	A	Florida	C	New Mexico	D
Oregon	A	Illinois	C	North Dakota	D
Rhode Island	A	Louisiana	C	Alabama	F
Vermont	A	Minnesota	C	Alaska	F
Washington	A	Montana	C	Idaho	F
Wisconsin	A	New Jersey	C	Michigan	F
Colorado	B	Ohio	C	Mississippi	F
District of Columbia	B	Pennsylvania	C	Oklahoma	F
Georgia	B	Texas	C	South Dakota	F
Hawaii	B	Virginia	C	Tennessee	F
Iowa	B	Wyoming	C	West Virginia	F
Maryland	B	Arkansas	D		

are achieving many of its desired results, and another 10 are close. (See box, A State Energy Report Card on Utility Planning.) In addition, at least 23 states and the District of Columbia have laws or regulations allowing utilities to earn additional revenue from successful utility-sponsored energy efficiency programs. More than 500 utilities offer programs that range from simple informational services, such as including energy-saving tips in monthly bills, to supplying energy audits of homes and businesses and helping customers finance energy improvements. Utilities spend more than $1.2 billion a year on demand-management programs.

Experts seem to disagree only about how much, not whether, energy is being saved. In the best programs, as many as 70 percent of customers participate, reducing their energy use by as much as 30 percent.

Benefits of Conservation

By EPRI's conservative estimates, conservation programs will reduce peak summer demand for electricity at least

---

Conserving the Energy in Objects

When you walk into a dark room and flip on the light switch, you tap energy to deliver a service—illumination. While the switch is on, the energy is turned into light. When you turn it off, the light and the energy are gone forever.

But energy also goes into objects. To make an aluminum soda can, for example, energy is spent to mine bauxite ore, separate out the impurities, and shape it into sheets and then into cans. The can "stores," or embodies, this energy.

If the can is thrown away when empty, the energy is discarded with it. Recycling saves money and energy because it takes 65 percent less energy to recycle the can than to make another from scratch (see

chart). Other kinds of containers, especially refillable glass bottles, are even more economical to reuse or recycle.

Tapping products' embodied energy is thus a major option for conservation, and beverage containers are only one of many possibilities. Researchers at Argonne National Laboratory in Argonne, Illinois, for example, have developed a process to remove the zinc coating from galvanized steel, which is used in a variety of products, including auto and truck bodies and highway guardrails. The process could enable reuse of millions of tons of scrap metal every year, saving about 70 percent of the energy (per ton) required to make new steel.

Energy Consumption to Make a 12-Ounce Beverage Container

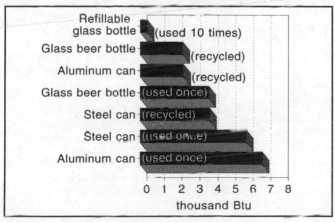

Source: Argonne National Laboratory.

How Energy Use Is Measured

Barrel = 42 gallons of petroleum oil. Each barrel of petroleum motor gasoline produces 5.25 million Btus; each gallon produces 12,500 Btus.

Btu (British Thermal Unit) = the standardized measure for the amount of heat produced from various types of energy. One Btu is the approximate energy equivalent of one burning wooden match tip.

Cubic feet (cu. ft.) = used to measure capacities of dry natural gas. One cubic foot of dry natural gas produces approximately 1,031 Btus of energy.

Kilowatt (kW) = a measure of electrical power. A motor requiring 1 kW operating for 1 hour would consume 1 kilowatt-hour (see below). Kilowatts can also be a measure of electrical generation capacity. A small windmill may have a capacity of 2 kW and a large coal-fired plant may have a capacity of 1,000 kW. One megawatt (MW) is the equivalent of 1,000,000 watts.

Kilowatt-hour (kWh) = used to measure electricity use. One kWh is the amount of electricity that an operating 100-watt light bulb would consume in 10 hours. It is equivalent to 3,411 Btus.

Quad = 1,000,000,000,000,000 (one quadrillion) Btus of energy. One quad equals 171.5 million barrels of oil.

Short ton = 2,000 pounds. Used to measure capacities of coal.

Therm = Another measure of natural gas. One therm is equal to 100,000 Btus and is roughly equivalent to the energy in 97 cu. ft. of natural gas.

Source: Adapted from Energy Information Administration, *Annual Energy Review 1988.*

World Primary Energy Consumption
(quadrillion Btu, 1991)

North America	863.1
USA	780.8
Canada	82.3
Latin America	161.3
Western Europe	553.8
Former Soviet Union & Central Europe	642.8
Middle East	94.6
Africa	87.1
Asia & Oceania	720.2
World	**3,123.0**

Source: *BP Statistical Review of World Energy* (British Petroleum, London, June 1992), p. 34.

grams will spread to additional states and utilities, because of concern about the environment, a combination of pressure and incentives from regulators, and the persistent difficulty of financing and finding sites for new power plants and transmission lines. The 1990 Clean Air Act Amendments will help too, since they included incentives for utilities and regulators that pursue conservation programs. (See "Air Pollution" chapter.) Finally, with more experience and improved incentives, utilities will undoubtedly get better at running the programs and will realize bigger paybacks from them.

Environmental Impacts

Abundant energy that has fueled prosperity in industrialized nations brings curses as well as blessings. The combined production, distribution, and consumption of energy is the greatest single source of stress on the environment. It also poses threats to human health.

Generating energy by burning coal, oil, and natural gas produces carbon dioxide, the gas responsible for about

6.7 percent in the year 2000, and perhaps as much as 14.5 percent. Total consumption could decline by as much as 9.8 percent.

Furthermore, these estimates do not consider the likelihood that the pro-

half of the buildup of greenhouse gases in the atmosphere—thus increasing the risk of climate change. (See "Greenhouse Warming" chapter.) Nitrogen oxides (NOx) and sulfur dioxide (SO2), also created by burning fossil fuels, are the precursors to acid rain and other forms of acid deposition; NOx also helps to form smog. Together, these emissions harm wildlife and wildlife habitat, lakes, rivers, soils, crops, materials, and buildings. Human health also suffers, because SO2 and smog can damage lung tissue and cause respiratory disease.

Even before burning, the extraction of coal, oil, and gas causes environmental damage. Oil spills from tankers and offshore drilling platforms pollute coastal and marine environments. Mining can destroy or displace farmland and wildlife habitats, pollute groundwater, and change groundwater characteristics and flow patterns. The solid wastes left over from mining are a source of air and water pollution. In all, the cost of environmental damage from fossil fuel use has been estimated at $100 billion per year in the United States alone.

Other conventional forms of energy generation pose their own problems. Nuclear power plants are expensive, consume large amounts of cooling water, and create nuclear wastes. Even hydroelectric power, the biggest source of renewable energy in the United States and often regarded as one of the cleanest, requires flooding vast areas of land and building dams that sometimes prevent fish from reaching spawning ar-

eas. (See "Wildlife" chapter.)

The United States and Canada together are the heaviest users of energy in the world, accounting for 27.6 percent of global energy consumption. (See table, World Primary Energy Consumption.) This is the annual equivalent of 2.4 billion tons of oil. The World Energy Consumption Per Capita table tells the story another way: U.S. and Canadian consumers use nearly twice as much energy per capita as do people who live in Central Europe and seven or eight times as much as do people in developing countries.

Sources and Uses

The energy consumed in the United States, about 85 quadrillion Btus (quads) per year (see box, How Energy Use Is Measured), comes from many sources. According to the U.S. Energy Information Agency (EIA), petroleum accounts for about 40 percent, natural gas 23 percent, coal 22 percent, and nuclear power 7 percent. Other

World Energy Consumption Per Capita
(1971–1991)

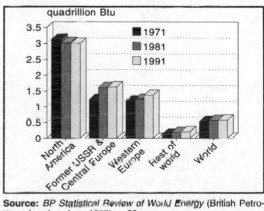

Source: *BP Statistical Review of World Energy* (British Petroleum, London, June 1992), p. 36.

World Fuel Reserves
(projected reserve to production ratio, 1991)

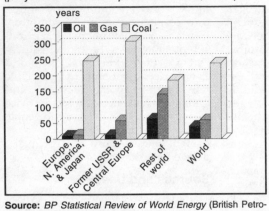

Source: *BP Statistical Review of World Energy* (British Petroleum, London, June 1992), p. 36.

freezers use a lot of energy, but so do some unexpected items, such as waterbed heaters and color television sets.

Industry, which includes manufacturing, agriculture, mining, and construction, uses about 39 percent of the end-use total. More than two thirds of industry's energy consumption goes for heat and power to run equipment. About 30 percent, in the form of petroleum and natural gas, is used as raw materials to make plastics, chemicals, and fertilizers.

sources, including power from hydroelectric facilities and energy from other renewables, account for 8 percent. About 17 percent of the energy used in the United States is imported.

A startling amount of this energy is simply lost as a result of fundamental limits to the efficiency of power plants and other equipment. Engineering advances are improving efficiency, but nearly one quarter of the total still disappears in electrical generation and distribution losses.

The remainder, the energy that is actually delivered to the point of use, is called the end-use total. Thirty-four percent of it goes for transportation. (See "Transportation" chapter.) Houses and apartments use 16 percent, while commercial establishments consume about 10 percent. Most of the energy used in residential and commercial buildings goes for lighting, space heating and cooling, water heating, and running household appliances and office equipment. In homes, major appliances such as refrigerators and

Trends and Projections

Total U.S. energy consumption has increased an average of 1.1 percent every year since 1970. The oil crises of the 1970s led to major improvements in energy efficiency, which has increased overall by 25 percent. This allowed the economy to grow about 2.5 percent per year, while energy demand remained fairly flat.

In 1985, however, stable oil prices and supplies helped ease the pressure to improve efficiency, and the rate of improvement began to drop off sharply. From 1985 to 1988, energy use rose 8 percent, with more than half of the increased supply coming from petroleum. The demand for energy, especially for coal and oil, is expected to continue rising.

Reserves of these fossil fuels are relatively large. At current rates of production, more than 40 years' supply of recoverable oil remains worldwide and more is being discovered. U.S. and Canadian oil reserves would only last about 10 years at current production rates, but the two countries still have enough coal to last 262 years. China and the states of the former Soviet Union also have huge coal reserves. (See chart, World Fuel Reserves.)

Even if coal and oil remain cheap, it may not be wise to fully tap these sources of energy. Burning any fossil fuel releases carbon dioxide, the most important greenhouse gas. Using the world's remaining reserves of fossil fuels would more than quadruple carbon dioxide (CO_2) levels in the atmosphere and almost certainly raise average global temperatures, perhaps disastrously. (See "Greenhouse Warming" chapter.)

Reinventing the Bulb

Efforts to cut the amount of energy consumed by lighting may receive a big boost when a new kind of light bulb becomes available in 1993. The new bulb, called the E-Lamp (electronic lamp), uses high-frequency radio waves to generate light. Standard incandescent bulbs use a filament.

The bulb is expected to produce light for at least 20,000 hours, whereas an incandescent bulb lasts only 750 to 1,000 hours. A 100-watt standard bulb costs about 30 cents a week to buy and operate for four hours a day, but a 25-watt E-Lamp would provide the same light for only 9 cents a week. The new bulbs initially will cost about the same—$12 to $15 each—as the compact fluorescent bulbs introduced several years ago, but E-lamps will last longer because there is no electrode to burn out. The new bulb also is smaller, its developers claim, and can be used in any indoor or outdoor fixture.

The E-Lamp was developed by Intersource Technologies, with backing from American Electric Power, the nation's second-largest electric utility.

Green Lights: A Businesslike Look at Efficiency

The U.S. Environmental Protection Agency (EPA) estimates that lighting accounts for nearly one quarter of all U.S. electricity use, of which as much as 90 percent is used for business and other commercial uses. The EPA believes that using energy-efficient lighting where it paid for itself in reduced electric bills would cut the national demand for electrical power by 10 percent and reduce annual emissions of carbon dioxide by 232 million tons—an amount equal to the emissions of 42 million autos.

This is the thinking behind EPA's Green Lights program, which was launched in 1991 to promote voluntary lighting efficiency improvements by corporations and state and local governments. Participants agree to survey all their facilities and install (where profitable) new, more efficient lighting within five years. In return, EPA provides technical support that helps participants conduct their surveys, locate sources of efficient lighting, and identify sources for financial assistance, including utility incentive programs.

Green Lights has grown rapidly. By June 1991, 73 corporate and government "partners" had signed up. A year later, that number had more than tripled to 276, including at least seven state governments and a number of Fortune 500 companies. Green Lights "allies," which are lighting manufacturers, service providers, or utilities, also agree to upgrade their lighting as well as help EPA with the technical support programs. There were 271 allies in June 1992.

Conserving energy reduces CO_2 output. So does improving the efficiency of generating technologies that use fossil fuels, by squeezing out more energy for every unit of CO_2 emitted. The best way to cut CO_2 emissions, of

Alternative Energy Sources

A major theme of the energy debate is the need for and feasibility of a shift away from fossil fuels and nuclear power to other, more environmentally benign sources. Here, in brief, are the prospects of several alternatives.

Solar photovoltaic cells. Photovoltaic (PV) cells convert sunlight directly into electric current. They have been used for many years for small, limited applications. PV power is not very efficient and is therefore expensive (20 to 30 cents per kilowatt-hour [kWh] versus 4 to 6 cents/kWh for electricity from conventional sources). Maximum efficiencies have improved to 30 percent, however, and continued progress could make PV cells competitive by 2010. If cost-effectiveness were ignored, PV cells could theoretically supply much more power than they do today; even at 15 percent efficiency, all U.S. energy needs could be met by covering a bit more than 1 percent of the land area of the lower 48 states with PV-cell arrays. The lack of efficient means of storing electricity also limits its PV-cell applications at present; conversion into hydrogen, a clean-burning fuel, is being explored for the future.

Wind energy. The 16,000 existing wind generators in the United States already supply more than 2 billion kWh of power every year, at an average cost of 8 cents per kWh. Total capacity is now over 1,600 megawatts. Most wind generators are in California, but the untapped wind potential of several midwestern and western states is vastly larger. Some forecasters predict that technology improvements over the next two decades will reduce generating costs to 3.5 cents per kWh, even for some less-than-ideal sites. Because wind "farms" can often be used for ranching or other purposes at the same time, good sites can be extremely profitable.

Fuel cells. Fuel cells, which convert fuel to power electrochemically rather than by combustion, were invented in 1839 but thus far have found only a few minor applications, such as power sources for spacecraft. Recently, however, fuel cells' advantages—they are clean, flexible, quiet, compact, and upwards of 60 percent efficient—have spurred development of commercial-scale units that can be built easily on urban sites close to demand. A 2-megawatt pilot plant using the most promising technology, the molten carbonate fuel cell, is being tested in California. The Electric Power Research Institute estimates that the potential market for this kind of plant is at least 14,000 megawatts. Experiments aimed at developing fuel cells that could power automobiles are also under way.

Biomass. According to the U.S. Energy Information Agency, biomass (materials from biological sources that can be burned for energy or used to make fuels such as ethanol and methanol) accounted for 3.3 percent of U.S. energy consumption, or about 2.8 quads, in 1990. Most of the energy is used in the pulp, paper, and lumber industries. Ninety-eight percent came from burning wood and municipal waste, the rest from ethanol. The roughly 140 existing municipal waste-to-energy plants burn about 17 percent of all municipal solid waste (mainly to reduce waste volume prior to landfilling), and 90 percent of the power generated is sold to utilities. The long-term potential of biomass is substantial; the U.S. Department of Energy estimates that biomass will supply 55 quads by the year 2000. Development of biomass-generation schemes involving fast-growing trees could help bring costs down to 4 cents per kWh.

Geothermal. Underground heat can be tapped and used directly for space heating or to generate electricity. Geothermal plants currently generate about 2,800 megawatts of power in the United States, but 23,000 megawatts are available to be developed by current technologies.

course, is to convert to technologies that do not rely on fossil fuels at all. (See box, Alternative Energy Sources.)

Whether this will happen in the United States probably depends on the energy policies we choose. Without a change in direction, total energy use and consumption of fossil fuels will continue to increase. As a result, so will energy-related pollution.

But some experts believe a very different future is possible with only modest changes in government policy to encourage more rapid adoption of cost-effective efficiency technologies. An analysis by the Union of Concerned Scientists and three other environmental groups argues that such a policy would reduce total energy consumption, cut fossil fuel use and expand the use of renewable energy, and improve efficiency by 40 percent by 2010.

Not only would emissions of CO_2, SO_2, and NOx decline under this conservative scenario, but consumers would also save a lot of money. An investment of $1.2 trillion over the next 40 years would save $3.1 trillion in energy costs—a net gain of $1.9 trillion. Bigger investments would save even more.

Energy and the Consumer

Households are major energy users, accounting for 16 percent of total U.S. consumption. According to the most recent EIA data, America's 90.5 million households spent nearly $98 billion on energy in 1987, an average of about $1,080 per household. These figures do not include expenditures for transportation, although these make up a substantial portion of each household's energy use and expense. The average U.S. household operates 1.8 vehicles. Americans drove more than 1.5 trillion

vehicle-miles in 1988, burning 82.4 billion gallons of fuel at a cost of over $81 billion.

Space heating accounted for about 54 percent of all U.S. household energy use. Appliances (including lighting) accounted for 23 percent, water heating

for 18 percent, and air conditioning for 5 percent. Total energy used for space heating has been declining for several years, although expenditures have risen. Consumption in the other categories is generally up, especially electricity for air conditioning. American houses and appliances still use one fifth to one third more energy in heating, lighting, and so on than do those in the more efficient industrialized countries.

Such needless inefficiency puts a heavy load on natural systems. The United States is responsible for about 20 percent of all manmade CO_2 emissions, or about 44,000 pounds per person per year. Residences account for 18 percent of those emissions.

Getting in Gear

It may help to think of energy improvements as an investment. For example, according to the *Consumer Guide to Home Energy Savings*, published by the American Council for an Energy-Efficient Economy, replacing a heating

Energy Consumption by Household Appliances and Products

Household Product	Homes with Appliances (%)	Typical Energy Consumption (kWh/yr)
Aquarium/terrarium	5–15	200–1,000
Auto block heater	2–6	150–800
Black & white television	50–60	10–100
Bottled water dispenser	1–2	200–400
Ceiling fan	10–25	10–150
Clock	100	17–50
Clothes washer	73	103
Coffee maker	30–50	20–300
Color television	96–99	75–1,000
Computer	10–20	25–400
Crankcase heater	25–35	100–400
Dehumidifier	10–13	200–1,000
Dishwasher	43.1	165
Electric blanket	25–35	75–200
Electric clothes dryer	51	993
Electric mower	5–8	5–50
Electric range/oven	56.8	650
Freezer (frost-free)	11.7	1,820
Furnace fan	45–60	300–1,500
Garbage disposer	40–50	20–50
Grow lights & accessories	2–5	200–1,500
Humidifier	8–15	20–1,500
Instant hot water	0.5–2	100–400
Iron	20–40	20–150
Pipe & gutter heater	2–5	30–500
Pool pump	4–6	500–4,000
Refrigerator (frost-free)	67.3	1,591
Spa/hot tub (electric)	1–2	1,500–4,000
Sump/sewage pump	10–20	20–200
Toaster/toaster oven	90–100	25–120
VCR	60–70	10–70
Ventilation fan	30–60	2–70
Waterbed heater	12–20	500–2,000
Well pump	5–20	200–800
Whole-house fan	8–10	20–500
Window fan	5–15	5–100

Source: Leo Rainer, Steve Greenberg, and Alan Meier, Lawrence Berkeley Laboratory.

system that is 65 percent efficient with one that is 90 percent efficient will save $27 for every $100 spent on fuel. This kind of improvement can save a typical household so much money on fuel costs that the return on investment can easily be two or three times the interest paid by a savings account or certificate of deposit.

Passive measures can also yield dramatic reductions in energy consumption. Investments in strategically placed trees, vines, and shrubs can slash air-conditioning costs, for example. In one Florida experiment, careful shielding of a test house with trees and shrubs cut requirements for hot-day air-conditioning in half.

Consumers shopping for new appliances should consider buying energy misers. Different appliances have vastly different energy appetites. (See table, Energy Consumption by Household Appliances and Products.) Giving in to the lure of a cheap, low-efficiency appliance means paying more in the long run because of its higher operating costs.

Finding an energy-efficient appliance has been made easier in some cases by a federal law requiring EnergyGuide labels (Energuide in Canada)

Home Energy Checklist for Action

To Do Today

● Turn down your water heater's thermostat to 120 degrees.

● Clean or replace filters for the furnace, air conditioner, and heat pump.

● Survey your incandescent lights to see if they can be replaced with compact fluorescent bulbs, which can save three quarters of the electricity used by incandescents. The best targets are 60 watt to 100-watt bulbs used several hours a day. Make sure the fixtures will accept the compact fluorescents, which are 6 to 9 inches long.

To Do This Week

● Visit the hardware store and buy a water heater blanket, low-flow shower heads, faucet aerators, and compact fluorescent bulbs as needed.

● Rope-caulk very leaky windows.

● Assess your heating and cooling systems. Determine if replacements are justified, or if you should retrofit them to make them work more efficiently.

To Do This Month

● Collect your utility bills, separating gas and electric. Target the biggest bill for energy-conservation remedies.

● Check your attic or crawl space for insulation.

● Insulate hot water pipes and ducts wherever they run through unheated areas.

● Seal the biggest air leaks in your house. The worst leaks are usually utility cutthroughs for pipes, gaps around chimneys, recessed lights in insulated ceilings, and unfinished spaces behind cupboards and closets.

● Consider hiring an energy auditor, or see if your utility offers audits.

● Install a clock thermostat to cut back on heating and air conditioning when you are away or asleep.

To Do This Year

● Insulate your attic and have cellulose blown into uninsulated walls.

● Replace aging, inefficient appliances. It is generally a good investment, even if the old one is not worn out.

● Upgrade leaky windows.

● Reduce your air conditioning costs by planting trees and shrubs around the house, especially on the west side.

Source: Adapted from *Consumer Guide to Home Energy Savings*, American Council for an Energy-Efficient Economy, Washington, D.C./Berkeley, California, 1991.

Energy Efficiency in the Federal Government

The federal government is the nation's largest single energy consumer, accounting for 2.3 percent of the total and spending nearly $9.9 billion for energy purchases in 1990.

Because of its economic and policy clout and its ability to set an example, the government can strongly influence energy-related behavior. Its own conservation record, however, is mixed. Total energy consumption by the government has declined since 1985, but only by 0.5 percent.

A 1991 U.S. Office of Technology Assessment report pointed out the room for improvement. The good news is that progress is being made, with more attention and money devoted to efficiency. For example, the Defense Logistics Agency, which supplies lamps to all defense agencies, recently compiled a catalog of en-

ergy-efficient light bulbs, a simple but significant move to encourage purchasing. And the General Services Administration, the government's housekeeper, has made highly efficient, electronically ballasted fluorescent lamps its "default" choice for new lighting in existing buildings.

In April 1991, President Bush signed an executive order requiring, by the year 2000, a 20 percent improvement in the energy efficiency of federal buildings and industrial facilities over 1985 levels. The order also requires a 10 percent reduction from 1991 levels in federal motor vehicle fuel use by 1995.

Although federal conservation-related spending declined from $297 million in 1981 to less than $50 million in 1990, it is now rising again, with about $100 million appropriated in 1991.

on new appliances. Drawing on data from standardized government tests, the labels estimate the appliance's yearly operating cost and compare it with those of other appliances of the same type. Labels on air conditioners and heat pumps state the efficiency rating rather than the operating cost. The higher the number, the better.

Consumers can contact their local utilities to ask if they offer rebates or other incentives for the purchase of efficient furnaces, ovens, refrigerators, air conditioners, compact fluorescent light bulbs, or other appliances.

Finally, consumer activists interested in promoting utility conservation

at the policy level can learn about their state's regulatory stance by calling the state utility ratepayer advocate's office. Most states have them, although they go by different names. If in doubt, contact the National Association of State Utility Consumer Advocates (NASUCA) in Washington, D.C., at (202) 727-3908. NASUCA also publishes a helpful booklet, the *Least-Cost Utility Planning Consumer Participation Manual*, that explains the ins and outs of regulation.

This chapter was written by Thomas Prugh, a freelancer based in Silver Spring, Maryland.

Transportation

New kinds of communities and less polluting autos, fuels, and transit systems are emerging as we rethink our reliance on cars.

Any discussion of transportation in North America must begin with the automobile. The discussion often ends there, too, which points to a critical weakness in today's transportation systems: lack of diversity. More than 80 percent of the total miles traveled in the United States are by automobile. The dominance of a single mode of transportation, and the dearth of viable alternatives, has helped to create to a host of social, economic, and environmental problems.

It is something of a paradox. On the one hand, cars have raised living standards around the world, offering mobility previously undreamed of. On the other hand, as the population of motor vehicles grows exponentially, the hoped-for advantages quickly evaporate. Today there are about 190 million motor vehicles in the United States and more than 550 million worldwide. Commuters trapped on congested thoroughfares day after day are not thinking about the unprecedented mobility made possible by cars. When chronic urban smog and global environmental threats are factored into the equation, one might reasonably argue that cars have diminished, rather than enhanced, our quality of life.

New Roads, More Problems

The problems are complex, as are any solutions that have a chance of succeeding. America's auto dependence is, among other things, a huge economic drain. Two thirds of the oil consumed in the United States is devoted to transportation, with half the total consumed by motor vehicles. In 1990, more than 40 percent of that oil was imported, accounting for 60 percent of the nation's trade deficit. About half the space in American cities, including roads, parking lots, driveways, garages, gas stations, and car washes, is devoted to motor vehicles. Air pollution from these vehicles is another headache, often literally. In greater Los Angeles, for instance, emissions from 8 million cars and trucks generate 70 to 80 percent of the area's noxious fumes.

The ill effects are not confined to a particular region. Nitrogen oxide emissions from cars on city streets, carried by the winds, contribute to ozone pollution (smog) and acid rain in rural areas. (See "Air Pollution" chapter.) There are also global impacts. Motor vehicles worldwide produce about 14 percent of the carbon dioxide added to the atmosphere from fossil fuel combustion, plus about 28 percent of the chlorofluorocarbons—chemicals that both add to greenhouse warming and deplete the ozone layer.

Traffic congestion, the inevitable by-product of too many cars, is another vexing problem. In 1989, according to the U.S. Department of Transportation (DOT), congestion on interstate highways caused 8 billion hours in delays and tens of billions of dollars in wasted fuel and lost productivity. By the year 2000, the DOT estimates, these delays on the nation's highways could increase fourfold.

It is largely a matter of numbers. In most countries, more people are driving more cars more miles than ever before. In the United States, more than 2 trillion miles are traveled by motor vehicles each year—nearly twice the 1970 total. This increase in "vehicle-miles traveled" has largely offset gains in efficiency and pollution control, while making traffic problems all but insoluble.

Laying down more roads is not the answer to traffic congestion and pollution, although it has been advanced as such for decades. New roads encourage more driving, which adds to pollution and urban sprawl.

A more enlightened response must come on several levels. First, an arsenal of policy tools must be unleashed to combat congestion. The second involves improved urban mass transit systems, along with the long-range urban planning necessary to make them work. Finally, technology, much of which is available today, can be used to make cars cleaner and more efficient.

U.S. Vehicle Use
(annual vehicle miles traveled)

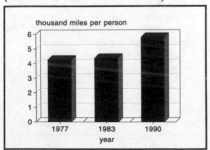

Source: U.S. Department of Transportation, *Highway Statistics 1990* (U.S. G.P.O., Washington, 1991), Summary Statistics, p. 211.

Automobiles can be developed that use fuels that produce low emissions or none at all.

All other things being equal, doubling the fuel economy of new U.S. cars from today's average of 27.5 miles per gallon (mpg) to 55 mpg would cut per-car fuel consumption and carbon dioxide output in half.

Is that kind of change realistic? Some cars on the market today, such as the Geo Metro and Honda Civic VX, already get about 55 mpg, but many people want or need a vehicle bigger than a subcompact.

Prototype vehicles show that it is possible to achieve 100 mpg or more. The catch is that these "concept cars" often use expensive materials and are not readily suited to mass production. Nevertheless, engine modifications, lightweight materials, and streamlined designs offer ample opportunities for improvement.

Cutting Vehicle Pollution

Efforts to cut vehicle pollution, meanwhile, are proceeding on several fronts. About 60 percent of the pollutants from a typical car trip are given off in the first few minutes, before the catalytic converter heats up. Electrical devices that bring the converter to its operating temperature within a few seconds are being tested. The evaporation of gasoline vapors that escape during refueling at service stations is another major contributor to smog. In March 1992, accordingly, President Bush ordered service stations in most states to fit gas pump nozzles with vapor collectors that prevent fumes from escaping.

Parallel efforts are under way to make gasoline cleaner. The lead content of gasoline has steadily declined since the 1970s; the use of this additive will be banned entirely by 1995 or 1996. The U.S. Environmental Protection

Notes from Underground

After a decade of environmental reviews and political wrangling, construction has finally begun on the "Big Dig," Boston's $5 billion highway project that will complete the largest remaining segment of the interstate highway system. Thirteen million cubic yards of earth will be dug up to add a third harbor tunnel and bury the Central Artery that now runs through the city.

One objective is to reduce congestion on the elevated artery, where traffic on the average workday exceeds design capacity from 6 AM to 8 PM. Each year, drivers stuck in Boston highway bottlenecks waste an estimated 250 million hours and 300 million gallons of gas. Everyone agrees that during the 10-odd years of construction, traffic will get worse before it gets better. Yet some experts predict that the third harbor tunnel will be as packed as the existing two tunnels are now on the day it opens. While the expanded Central

Artery will be able to handle more vehicles than the present highway, new developments planned for downtown Boston and nearby areas are expected to generate tens of thousands of new vehicle trips a day by 1995. Without specific measures to discourage driving, postconstruction gridlock could rival today's.

A lawsuit filed by the Conservation Law Foundation was rescinded on March 13, 1992, when state transportation officials agreed to ease congestion by expanding mass transit and imposing tougher parking limits. "The only way this project works well is if you keep people from using it," says Andrew Hamilton of the Conservation Law Foundation. "Otherwise, the project will just serve as a springboard for more pollution and more congestion. In essence, all we'll be doing is spending $5 billion to move a traffic jam underwater and underground."

Canadian Energy Use in Transportation, 1988

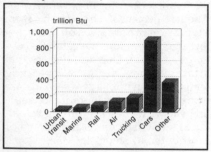

trillion Btu

Source: Statistics Canada, *Human Activity and the Environment, 1991* (Ottawa, 1991), Table 3.1.2.3, p. 57.

Agency (EPA) set limits in 1992 on the volatility (the tendency to evaporate) of gasoline sold during the summer, when smog is most likely to form. Oil companies, meanwhile, are developing cleaner-burning fuel mixtures. By the middle of the decade, increasing quantities of this reformulated gas will be sold in California and the Northeast.

Another strategy is to find fuels to replace gasoline altogether. Some air quality benefits may be secured through the use of compressed natural gas, ethanol, or methanol, but only two presently known "energy carriers"—electricity and hydrogen—offer the prospect of mobility without the usual by-products of greenhouse gases or other pollutants.

Standards adopted by California, New York, and Massachusetts will require that "zero-emission" vehicles make up 2 percent of the cars sold in 1998 and 10 percent of those sold in 2003. Ten other eastern states and the District of Columbia (D.C.) are considering adopting these standards.

The regulations should give zero-emission vehicles a big push, because these 13 states and D.C. account for almost one third of the new cars sold in the United States. Chrysler began limited production of electric minivans for testing in 1992. A Swedish company, Clean Air Transport, hopes to put 10,000 hybrid gas-electric cars on sale in greater Los Angeles by 1995. GM, meanwhile, has vowed to have its all-electric Impact ready by the middle of the decade.

Electric cars do not give off any exhaust, although they run on electricity generated by power plants that usually do pollute. Even so, it is preferable from an environmental standpoint to run cars on conventionally generated electricity than on gasoline. However, there is scarcely any pollution at all if the electricity that charges the auto battery comes from the sun.

> **Transportation News**
> Austin, 5/5/92—*The Texas Air Control Board has created a toll-free line, 1-800-453-SMOG, so that people can report the license number, model, and location of any vehicle emitting extraordinary amounts of exhaust. Owners of the vehicles are not fined or penalized but are sent letters asking that the vehicle be repaired. This effort to clean up the air will cost the state about $50,000 a year.*

In 1991, Solectria, a company based in Waltham, Massachusetts, started selling its battery-powered, solar-electric car, the Force, for approximately $25,000. The car can travel 80 to 135 miles on a single charge from a standard electrical socket; rooftop solar panels provide for eight additional miles of driving each day if the car has been out in the sun. Experimental Solectria models that are not yet on the market can travel 25 to 30 miles a day, equivalent to about 10,000 miles a year, strictly on sunlight.

Getting a Charge Out of Parking

Strict clean air regulations effective in 1998 will introduce droves of electric cars to California and the Northeast. The greatest pollution reductions will occur if at least some of the electricity needed to operate these vehicles comes from sunlight, rather than from conventional power plants. Part of the answer may be to install solar rechargers at parking lots.

The "solar carport," the first such U.S. facility, was to begin operation in 1992 at the South Coast Air Quality Management District headquarters in Diamond Bar, California. A 3,000-square foot array of solar cells will be mounted above a section of the headquarters parking lot. Initially, five spaces will be equipped with plugs that feed electricity produced by the solar cells directly to the car batteries. Excess electricity will feed back to the normal power grid.

Planners hope that this small-scale demonstration, built by Southern California Edison, will spur the deployment of similar structures at shopping centers and office parks. Such carports will provide a convenient way for people to recharge their cars, while quelling concerns about having enough power to get back home. In this way, recharge stations extend the range and usability of electric cars.

An estimated 200,000 electric vehicles will be on the road in California by the year 2000. Much of the electricity for those vehicles could be generated from solar panels that use only a small fraction of the space already available at California business and shopping center parking lots.

Battery and Hydrogen Power

With the advent of a better battery, solar-electric cars could achieve a more respectable range. Fortunately, there have been some recent promising developments in battery technology. In May 1992 the U.S. Advanced Battery Consortium, a joint funding program between the U.S. Department of Energy and the auto and electric industries, awarded $18.5 million to the Ovonic Battery Company of Troy, Michigan, to further develop its nickel metal hydride battery for electric vehicle use. Compared with lead-acid batteries, nickel metal hydride batteries offer the promise of faster recharge, extended range, no toxic components, and a long life (100,000 miles).

Hydrogen vehicles are somewhat less advanced than their electric counterparts but face similar obstacles. One is that on-board fuel storage systems, like batteries, tend to be considerably bulkier and heavier than gasoline tanks, which restricts vehicle range. The second challenge is that there is no infrastructure for hydrogen distribution and refueling comparable to that for gasoline. These barriers have not kept hydrogen prototypes off the roads. In fact, a fleet of about 20 Mercedes-Benz test vehicles has already logged more than half a million miles.

Hydrogen is most simply made by passing an electric current through water, a process called electrolysis. Internal combustion engines can be modified to run on pure hydrogen, but "fuel cells" are clearly the cleanest and most efficient way to go. Fuel cells electrochemically combine hydrogen and oxygen from the air to create electricity, with water vapor the only appreciable by-product. At 60 percent efficiency, they are roughly three times more efficient than combustion engines, which means that a hydrogen car powered by a fuel cell can travel about three times farther than a hydrogen car with a more conventional engine. The drawback is that present fuel cells are expensive, and practical experience with them in vehicles is essentially nil. However, a Florida-based company, U.S. FuelCells Manufacturing, Inc., has set out to develop a hydrogen fuel cell-powered car capable of meeting the 1998 zero-emission requirement.

Although hydrogen cars are expected to produce low or no emissions, they are only as clean as the method used to produce hydrogen in the first place. Projects under way in Germany and Saudi Arabia and at the University of California at Riverside will soon demonstrate solar production of hydrogen for vehicles as well as for other applications.

Assuming that affordable, nonpolluting electric or hydrogen cars can be mass produced, the question remains: How will they be able to move freely on city streets that are approaching a state of perpetual gridlock? Although high-tech solutions such as automated, electronic highways can theoretically

State Fuel Efficiency Ranking, 1990
(average miles traveled per gallon of fuel consumed)

State	Fuel Efficiency Ranking	Average Miles Per Gallon	State	Fuel Efficiency Ranking	Average Miles Per Gallon
Hawaii	1	19.74	Florida	26	15.76
Vermont	2	17.71	New Mexico	27	15.74
New Hampshire	3	17.65	Oklahoma	28	15.70
Arizona	4	17.51	Oregon	29	15.69
Wisconsin	5	17.43	New York	30	15.65
District of Columbia	6	17.36	Colorado	31	15.64
			New Jersey	32	15.56
Massachusetts	7	17.29	Pennsylvania	33	15.45
Connecticut	8	17.24	Mississippi	34	15.43
California	8	17.24	Ohio	35	15.22
Maryland	10	16.95	Missouri	35	15.22
Virginia	11	16.89	South Carolina	37	15.06
Michigan	12	16.80	Tennessee	37	15.06
Rhode Island	13	16.79	West Virginia	39	14.87
Washington	14	16.75	Kansas	40	14.77
Louisiana	15	16.63	Montana	41	14.55
Maine	16	16.49	Kentucky	42	14.39
Georgia	17	16.38	South Dakota	43	14.26
Delaware	18	16.37	Nebraska	44	13.75
Minnesota	19	16.29	North Dakota	45	13.32
Utah	20	16.23	Illinois	46	13.24
Idaho	21	15.86	Iowa	47	13.23
North Carolina	22	15.83	Nevada	48	13.14
Indiana	23	15.82	Arkansas	49	12.86
Texas	24	15.80	Wyoming	50	12.08
Alabama	25	15.77	Alaska	51	11.23

Source: Adapted from U.S. Department of Transportation, *Highway Statistics 1990* (U.S. G.P.O., Washington, D.C., 1991), Table MF-21, p. 5, and Table VM-2, p. 193.
Note: Ranks represent how many miles were traveled per gallon of gasoline and gasohol consumed in the state in 1990.

increase the capacity of our roads, a better strategy might be to put fewer cars on the road. This goal is best achieved by encouraging car and van pools, high-occupancy vehicle lanes, and developing policies that will make parking more expensive and less available. At the same time, traffic planners and lawmakers are exploring transit alternatives attractive enough to lure people out of their cars, at least temporarily.

Encouraging Mass Transit

The 1991 Surface Transportation Act is a step in the right direction. The bill, which authorizes $151 billion for highways and public transportation over the next six years, gives states much more latitude in deciding how to spend the federal funds. However, just because states have more discretion in this area does not necessarily mean they will assign a higher priority to transit projects. Nor will expanded transit systems automatically solve regional transportation problems unless they are carefully designed to meet public needs.

In Moscow, for example, 8 million people ride the subway each day, more than any other subway system in the world. Because few people own cars, nearly everyone in Greater Moscow relies on the trains to get from place to place. The subway is the true lifeline of the city, and its ongoing growth is inextricably tied to new commercial and residential development.

In Toronto, similarly, more than three fourths of the downtown commuters get to work via public transportation. The reason is simple: Zoning practices that cluster apartments, office buildings, and retail stores around subway stops have made rapid rail more convenient than driving.

Officials in the San Jose, California, area had a similar goal. While building a 21-mile aboveground light rail (trolley) network, they put transit stops close to shopping centers and office buildings and placed parking lots farther away. The strategy appears to have paid off. More people ride the system after five years of operation than were originally forecast. If the trolley were not in place, most of its passengers would be driving cars instead.

Comparable success is hoped for the Blue Line, Los Angeles's $870 million light rail system, which began op-

---

Transportation News

New York, 11/4/91—A nationwide survey by Commuter Transportation Services shows that the number of commuters in carpools is down from 33 percent in 1980 to 22 percent today. Surveys by New York transportation agencies show that carpool commuters are even fewer in the New York area: 85 to 90 percent of commuters drive to work by themselves.

---

erating in 1990. The 22-mile track, linking Long Beach with downtown Los Angeles, is the first component of Metrorail, a proposed $5 billion, 150-mile light rail and subway network. It remains to be seen whether rail transit can perform well in a city defined by auto-induced sprawl. If ridership on the Blue Line and subsequent legs does not meet expectations, regional officials may be forced to scale back their ambitious plans.

Servicing the Suburbs

The painful reality is that mass transit may not be the universal solution. No one has yet devised a system that can economically service low-density suburbs, an ever-expanding segment of the country that owes its existence to the automobile. Even in densely populated regions where rail systems make sense, trains become an inherently rigid mode of transport once tracks are laid. The proposed Personal Rapid Transit system in metropolitan Chicago, however, will feature small cars, carry no more than five passengers, and run on narrow guideways. The fully automated, computerized system will take people directly to their destinations, bypassing intermediate stops. If prototype testing proves successful over the next two years, an experimental system will be built in one of Chicago's suburbs. Proponents of personal rapid transit claim the technology could lead to the restructuring of cities.

San Francisco architect Peter Calthorpe has already begun the restructuring task. He was recently asked by Sacramento County to draft zoning codes that put mass transit and pedestrian travel at the center of all new county developments. Calthorpe's planned communities revolve around "pedestrian pockets"—dense clusters of stores, offices, and restaurants—linked by mass transit and within walking distance of homes. Construction is under way on one such project, Laguna West, which will house 8,000 people. Calthorpe has drafted plans for a 175,000-person community, Sutter Bay, which would be connected to Sacramento by light rail.

The Miami-based team of Andres Duany and Elizabeth Plater-Zyberk has designed dozens of new towns throughout the country. Residents of "neo-traditional" towns like Seaside, Florida, can reach most places in town by foot or bike. Alternatively, they can comfortably travel by bus or train. "Neo-traditional towns offer a choice,"

Duany says. "Yes, you can drive, but you can also walk."

Broadening Public Options

The element of choice is the key to loosening gridlock's grip on the nation. For decades, transportation policy in the United States has been primarily limited to pouring concrete for new roads. A more diversified strategy, emphasizing a host of options, is desperately needed. We can no longer afford to design cities only to accommodate cars; the environmental, aesthetic, and psychological costs are just too high.

Designing cities for people, on the other hand, will take a shift in attitude, as well as some courage and creativity. Officials in Portland, Oregon, for instance, took money earmarked for a planned segment of interstate highway and used it to build a light rail system that opened in 1986. Since then, pollution in the city has dropped, and businesses along the rail line are thriving. More people now walk in the downtown area because the surroundings are more congenial. A waterfront park stands where the canceled freeway was supposed to go.

As Portland has shown, transportation planning works best when it is broadly defined. It is not enough simply to find ways to get people from one place to another. Through revised zoning ordinances and controlled development, we also have to bring those places we travel among—homes, offices, schools, and stores—closer together so that people can realistically contemplate leaving their cars behind, or maybe do without them altogether.

Science writer Steven Nadis, of Cambridge, Massachusetts, is coauthor of Car Trouble *(with James J. MacKenzie, by Beacon Press, Boston, forthcoming).*

Air Pollution

New laws, technologies, and market tools are stepping up the fight for clean air.

Twenty-five years ago, the air of the United States was so degraded by human activity that the health of the people and the environment were compromised. Spurred by the Clean Air Act legislation passed in 1970, the United States began to clamp down on emissions from factories, power plants, and cars. Utilities gradually reduced (or lofted higher into the atmosphere) the sulfur dioxide emitted from their smokestacks. Automakers installed catalytic converters to cut pollutant emissions and developed ways to boost fuel efficiency. Petroleum refiners removed lead from gasoline.

Gradually, the skies became cleaner, but not clean enough. In 1990, Congress passed sweeping amendments to the Clean Air Act. The effects are just beginning to be felt, but their long-term impact is likely to be significant. In California, even more drastic measures are being tried to clean up that state's smoggy skies. Change is afoot—from the technologies with which factories monitor their emissions, to the new market systems that allow companies to barter pollution credits, to the reformulation of products we use to scent our bodies and clean our homes.

What Is Air Pollution?

Suspended particulates are actual pieces of ash or smoke, soot, dust, and liquid droplets released to the air by the burning of fuel, industrial processes, agricultural practices, or a number of natural processes. Larger particles tend to settle out of the air fairly quickly, but smaller particles can remain aloft for a long time; when inhaled, they can lodge in the lungs and contribute to respiratory disease.

Smog forms when nitrogen oxides (NOx) produced by burning fuel and volatile organic compounds (VOCs) escape to the atmosphere. The sources of VOCs include unburned hydrocarbons from automobile fuel tanks, other chemicals from a wide variety of commercial establishments and factories, and natural sources such as trees. In the atmosphere, these chemicals react or combine to form a mixture of up to 100 different compounds in the presence of sunlight and heat. The result is the hazy, dirty brown air we know as smog.

The most important constituent of smog is ozone, a gas that is toxic on contact to most living organisms and is often the cause of eye irritation and respiratory problems. Ozone is also toxic to many plants. It damages leaves and slows growth, and is thought to reduce potential crop yields in the United States by 5 to 10 percent.

Sulfur dioxide (SO_2) is a gas released when sulfur-containing fuels such as coal and oil are burned; sulfur dioxide can cause respiratory problems. In the atmosphere sulfur dioxide is also converted to acid and thus becomes a major source of acid rain.

Acid rain (or other forms of acid precipitation) forms when sulfur dioxide or nitrogen oxides combine with water droplets in the atmosphere to form highly corrosive acids. Over time, acid precipitation can increase the acidity of lakes, streams, and soils to the point that they change local

Top 10 States for Air Emissions of Toxics, 1990

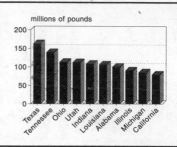

Source: U.S. Environmental Protection Agency, *1990 Toxics Release Inventory: Public Data Release* (U.S. G.P.O., Washington, D.C., May 1992), Table 4, p. 23.

ecosystems. Acid rain can also contribute to forest damage.

Carbon monoxide (CO) is released when fuel doesn't burn completely. The gas has no odor and is a poison; once inhaled, it interferes with the body's ability to absorb oxygen and causes drowsiness, headache, and even death, especially in those suffering from heart disease or respiratory problems. Cars and trucks are the main source of carbon monoxide.

Toxic air pollutants include a wide variety of cancer-causing and other chemicals hazardous to human health. Toxics are released to the air during manufacturing processes. Refineries, chemical plants, and dry cleaning establishments are frequent sources. Toxics are also produced by cars that burn leaded gasoline. The volume of toxics emitted is very small compared to other forms of air pollution. But their impact on the environment and on human health is still a cause for concern, especially for those who live in the immediate vicinity of such emissions or who are exposed to spills of toxic chemicals.

The Struggle for Cleaner Air

Concentrations of nearly all of the six major air pollutants (see box, What Is Air Pollution?) for which the U.S. Environmental Protection Agency (EPA) has set air quality standards have dropped significantly nationwide since 1970, and especially since 1980. The EPA reports that emissions of lead dropped an impressive 97 percent, accompanied by decreases in emissions of particulates, sulfur dioxide, carbon monoxide, and ozone. (See graphs, U.S. Air Pollution Trends, 1970–90). Levels of only one of the pollutants—nitrogen dioxide—did not improve, but increased 6 percent as a result of increased fuel combustion.

Despite widespread progress, in 1990, at least 74 million people lived in areas that still exceeded at least one air quality standard. According to the EPA, as many as 140 million people may have lived in areas that had ozone levels, or smog, in excess of national standards during that year. Other airborne toxic substances also pollute urban areas and may cause cancer or

other serious health effects. The recent clean-air legislation includes provisions to cut emissions of nearly 200

toxic substances by 90 percent within a decade.

It is too soon to detect changes in air quality or emissions as a result of the Clean Air Act Amendments, or to know with any accuracy how much their implementation will cost—or save. But nationwide, adjustments in legislation, technology, and corporate and personal behavior are reinvigorating the struggle against air pollution and the health and environmental effects it causes.

The War on Smog

On sunny summer days, many urban areas are swathed in the spongy brown air known as smog. Unlike other pollutants, ground-level ozone, the primary constituent of smog, forms in the atmosphere through chemical reactions between volatile organic compounds (VOCs) and nitrogen oxides (NOx) in the presence of sunlight. Ozone contributes to and aggravates respiratory problems, damages trees and crops, and contributes to global warming.

According to a 1991 U.S. National Academy of Sciences (NAS) report, *Rethinking the Ozone Problem in Urban and Regional Air Pollution*, many scientists believe that unlike stratospheric ozone concentrations (see "Ozone Depletion" chapter), which are declining, concentrations of ground-level ozone are increasing over large regions of the United States. An NAS committee examined why 20 years of efforts to meet air quality standards for ozone have largely failed. One reason, the committee concluded, is that the EPA has not sufficiently verified separate emissions of VOCs and NOx but has relied instead on measurements of the ground-level ozone that forms when these two gases interact. As a result, some ozone

> **Air Pollution News**
> Salt Lake City, 1/26/92—Utah's well-populated valleys are mired in gray particulate pollution in the winter months. The problem is especially bad in the Provo-Orem area, ranked as one of the five worst cities in the country for particulate pollution. The bad air is afflicting sensitive breathers and in some cases is even life-threatening; one doctor claims about 50 Utah County residents die each year because of air pollution.

U.S. Air Pollution Trends, 1970–90

Sulfur Dioxide Emissions

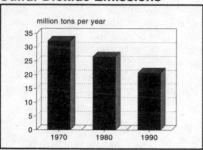

million tons per year

Nitrogen Oxides Emissions

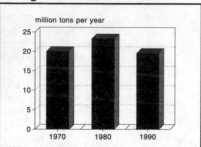

million tons per year

Carbon Monoxide Emissions

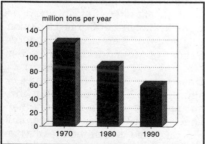

million tons per year

Source: U.S. Environmental Protection Agency (EPA), *National Air Quality and Emissions Trends Report, 1990* (EPA, Research Triangle Park, N.C., November 1991).

control programs may have been misdirected. The panel found, for instance, that automobile emissions of reactive organic compounds are two to four times greater than EPA estimates. This would mean that emissions controls mandated in past years have been less effective than believed in bringing down total VOC levels. The report also notes that plants and trees are known to emit organic compounds which, in the presence of NOx generated by human activity, boost ozone concentrations. Because most VOC inventories have not accounted for this natural, uncontrollable source, ozone control strategies have been less effective than expected.

These conclusions may lead regulators to readjust their thinking. In the past, ozone reduction strategies have assumed a certain balance between VOCs and NOx, so that it was thought to be more effective to control VOCs than NOx. Now, in areas where VOC levels are substantially higher than previously assumed, control efforts may need to focus on NOx.

California, particularly the Los Angeles Basin, which is known for its frequent ozone alerts, is leading the war on ozone. In the basin, geography that prevents dirty air from dissipating, growing numbers of cars and people, and frequent sunny days give rise to a noxious layer of smog. Three days out of five, the basin exceeds at least one federal air quality standard.

These problems have prompted California to adopt the nation's most aggressive smog control measures, and peak ozone levels have dropped sharply in recent years. But the basin's pollution will continue to grow. In the next 20 years, an additional 6 million people—and their cars, energy-using appliances, and hydrocarbon-laden consumer products—are expected to join the 12 million already there.

In 1989, an ambitious and costly plan to combat California's regional pollution took force. The plan targets obvious polluters such as utilities and heavy industry. It also singles out commuters, small businesses such as furniture refinishers, auto body shops, and dry cleaners, and a range of household items that contribute a surprisingly hefty load of fumes. (See box, How Perfume Pollutes.)

Cars, too, must meet stringent emissions requirements. These regulations will force automakers who want a share of the lucrative California market to develop new smog-control technologies, such as fuel combustion and propulsion systems. The California rules to control motor vehicle emissions, adopted in 1990, spell out a four-step timetable for introduction of cleaner-running cars. The last stage, introduction of zero-emission autos powered by electricity rather than fuel combustion, begins in 1998. By 2003, 10 percent of new cars sold in California must be zero-emission autos. (See "Transportation" chapter.)

The first response to the standards came early: In May 1992, Ford showrooms in California featured two 1993 models that met the first stage of the state's demanding timetable for low-emission vehicles—four years ahead of schedule. Ford cut emissions by adapting existing catalytic converter technology, enlarging the device and moving it closer to the engine. The new converter also heats up more quickly, reducing the quantities of noxious fumes that form when a car is started.

The urgency with which California is trying to clean up its air is inspiring more stringent laws in the rest of the nation, too. New York and Massachu-

U.S. Air Pollution Trends, 1970–90

Total Particulates

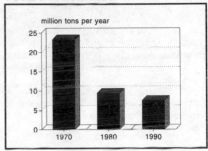

Volatile Organic Compounds

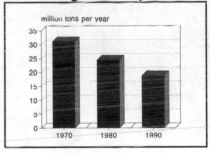

Lead Emissions

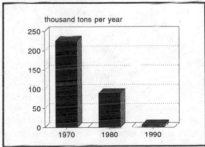

Source: U.S. Environmental Protection Agency (EPA), *National Air Quality and Emissions Trends Report, 1990* (EPA, Research Triangle Park, N.C., November 1991).

How Perfume Pollutes

That bottle of after-shave you gave Dad is harmless enough—until he splashes it on. When the alcohol evaporates, it eventually meets up with sunlight, where it reacts with nitrogen oxides and helps produce smog. It is difficult to imagine how a splash or two can cause much harm, but when the action is performed by millions of people in some regions each day, the effects add up.

In California, where 30 million people splash, spray, and clean their homes on a regular basis, emissions of volatile organic compounds (VOCs) from consumer products like spray starch, charcoal lighter fluid, automotive brake cleaner, and disinfectant make up 10 percent of the total nonvehicular VOC emissions, or about 200 tons a day. As emissions from cars, factories, and utilities decrease in response to stringent control measures, the proportion of pollutants from consumer products will grow.

Now, a company that wishes to sell its after-shave—or consumer products in neary a dozen categories (see table, Limits on Volatile Organic Compounds in Consumer Products)—in California must meet new rules controlling the ingredients. Toilet waters, colognes, and perfumes that pre-date the regulations can remain as they are, but fragrances introduced after 1984 must pass the new standards. Combined with similar reformulation standards adopted in the last several years for 17 other types of products, the rules will cut California's emissions of smog-forming hydrocarbons by 60 tons a day, equal to the pollution output of 7.5 million new 1991 model cars.

The Air Resources Board in California says that nearly half of the more than 2,600 consumer products covered by the new rules already meet the requirements. The cost to the consumer product industry is likely to be passed on to consumers, who will at least get a greater percentage of the real product, and less pollutant, as more products are water-based or as solid forms are substituted for aerosols.

This regulatory foray into vanities and broom closets is likely to affect the rest of the nation, because other smog-choked jurisdictions often follow California's lead when it comes to mending air-polluting ways. New York has already adopted some of California's standards that reduce VOCs emitted from consumer products, and other states are likely to follow.

Limits on Volatile Organic Compounds in Consumer Products
(allowable percent by weight, 1995)

Product Category	Allowable Percent
Aerosols	
Cooking sprays	18
Automotive brake cleaners	50
Carburetor choke cleaners	75
Charcoal lighter materials	
Disinfectants	60
Dusting aids	
Aerosol	35
All other forms	7
Fabric protectants	75
Hand dishwashing detergents	2
Household adhesives	
Aerosol	75
All other forms	10
Insecticides	
Crawling bug	40
Flea and tick	20
Flying bug	30
Foggers	40
Lawn and garden	20
Wasp and hornet	40
All others	20

Source: California Environmental Protection Agency, Air Resources Board, 1991.

Canadian Air Pollution Trends, 1979–89
(annual averages for four pollutants)

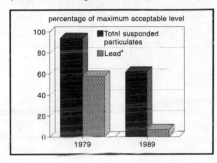

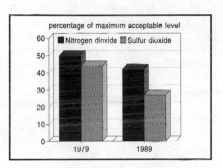

Source: Adapted from T. Furmanczyk, Environment Canada, in Government of Canada, *The State of Canada's Environment 1991* (Minister of Supply and Services, Ottawa, 1991), Figure 2.5, p. 2-12.
Note: Because no maximum pollutant level has been established for lead, the annual averages shown here were indexed by setting the 1974 value at 100.

setts have adopted California's motor vehicle emissions standards. Ten other eastern states and the District of Columbia have expressed support for the program but have not yet agreed to implement the standards.

Automakers are not being asked to shoulder the entire burden of cleaning up the air. In a ruling that is likely to transform the practices of petroleum refiners, the Clean Air Act Amendments require that reformulated, cleaner-burning fuels be sold by 1995 in nine U.S. cities with the worst ozone pollution problems. The ruling applies to Baltimore, Chicago, Hartford, Houston, Los Angeles, Milwaukee, New York, Philadelphia, and San Diego.

These nine cities together consume about 20 percent of the motor fuel used in the United States each year. The EPA estimates that if all areas with ozone pollution problems participated, reformulated gasoline could make up 55 percent of the motor fuel sold in the United States. Reformulated gas is expected to reduce VOCs and toxic pollutants by 15 percent from 1990 levels

and by 25 percent by the year 2000. Some northeastern and mid-Atlantic states have already notified the EPA

Air Pollution News
Cleveland, 8/4/92—*Federal and local officials have shut down a lead-smelting operation that exceeded national air quality standards for lead pollution by 2,600 percent—the worst in Ohio and possibly the worst in the nation. The Ohio EPA ordered Masters Metals Inc. to immediately shut down its lead-smelting operations because of air pollution violations. The city of Cleveland took similar action in a local court.*

that they intend to adopt or expand the reformulated fuel program in 1995. These states are Connecticut, Delaware, Maine, Maryland, Massachusetts, New Hampshire, New Jersey, New York, Pennsylvania, Rhode Island, and Virginia.

Utilities, too, are on the brink of radical changes. Ozone, as well as VOCs and NOx, is transported by wind, so that the ozone created in one part of an industrial corridor such as the Northeast can cause and add to pollution problems in another. The Clean Air Act Amendments of 1990 call for regional solutions to this problem. As one response, eight northeastern states have banded together to impose controls on electric generating stations that will cut emissions of nitrogen oxides by half. About 60 percent of NOx in the region comes from cars and trucks, and another 20 percent comes from utility boilers.

A Market for Pollution

One revolutionary effect of the Clean Air Act Amendments is creation of a free-market trading system for pollution allowances. In adopting the amendments, Congress mandated that emissions of sulfur dioxide, the main

> **Air Pollution News**
> Washington, D.C., 8/7/92—Atmospheric pollution apparently is the cause of rising concentrations of mercury in some remote lakes, according to a study published in the journal Science. The study examined sediments from seven lakes in Minnesota and Wisconsin. It found that yearly deposition of atmospheric mercury had increased from 3.7 to 12.5 micrograms per square meter since 1850.

cause of acid rain, be cut in half by the year 2000, and requested that a market system be instituted. To get things started, Congress identified 110 electric utilities and assigned to each a number of pollution "allowances" based on its history of fuel use. Each allowance represents 1 ton of sulfur dioxide. Plants whose emissions exceed their allowances can make up the difference by buying allowances—in effect, the right to pollute—at market rates from utilities that pollute less than they are allowed.

Economists and environmentalists have been promoting such a market-based alternative to old-style "command-and-control" environmental regulation for years. The market will increase options available to plants deciding how to meet tough pollution standards. Some will choose to invest in new equipment and cleaner technologies and to seek the most cost-effective ways to reduce pollution. They hope to help pay for their investments by selling their unused pollution allowances to plants for which the costs of meeting the new rules are higher than the costs of buying someone else's pollution credits. As electric utilities, and eventually other sources of air pollution such as smog, trade their allocations there should be less air pollution, and at a lower cost.

The system's first takers emerged in May 1992, when the Tennessee Valley Authority (TVA) announced that it had purchased from Wisconsin Power and Light the right to emit 10,000 tons of sulfur dioxide. These two utilities, hundreds of miles apart, were the first to disclose a trade under the new market system. In effect, the trade gives the TVA a cushion as it moves to cut sulfur dioxide emissions by 800,000 tons by 1995 through pollution control technologies and cleaner fuels.

In the area of pollution credits, California has again mounted an ambitious regional effort to combat its unique pollution woes. The system is similar to the federal market but more extensive, initially covering 2,700 of the largest polluters. While some companies envision savings, others fear great costs. Regional air quality regulators claim that the market will save money: A recent study found that the program would reduce costs to industry in 1994 by 65 percent compared with the costs projected under 1992 regulations, a savings of $429 million.

Monitoring to verify compliance remains a challenge, as state and federal regulators seek better ways to measure emissions. A new approach being tested in California may hold promise for application in the rest of the country as well. Smokestacks and other major sources of pollution will be wired with sensors or other devices that can measure emissions—mostly NOx and reactive organic gases—around the clock. If successful, the new regulatory system will cut record-keeping costs for factories and other sources of air pollution, as well as spur innovation in the air quality monitoring industry.

Global Air Pollution

Cleanup efforts in Canada, Japan, and European nations also have caused a substantial decline in levels of particulates and lead. The use of catalytic converters in automobiles has reduced emissions of carbon monoxide (CO),

Indoor Air Pollution

As harmful as outdoor air pollution is, the air we breathe indoors—at home, at work, in the car—may pose an even greater threat to our health. With no winds to disperse them, the chief indoor contaminants—chemicals used in consumer and building products and the by-products of smoking, cooking, and poorly vented furnaces—can build up. The move toward more airtight, energy-efficient houses aggravates the problem. Concentrations of some toxic and cancer-causing pollutants are up to 100 times greater indoors than out.

The health risks are magnified because people spend 80–90 percent of their time indoors. In 1990, the U.S. Environmental Protection Agency (EPA) placed indoor pollution at the top of a list of 18 sources of environmental health risk in terms of the numbers of cancers caused in the general U.S. population. Health threats include carcinogens from cigarette smoke, which contains carbon monoxide, aldehydes, and a variety of carcinogens such as benzene. Gas appliances and unvented kerosene heaters contribute as well because they are a primary source of indoor nitrogen dioxide, which irritates lungs. Building materials give off formaldehyde, a probable carcinogen. The cost of health problems caused by indoor pollution is estimated in the tens of billions of dollars each year in the United States alone. Yet exposure to indoor pollutants is largely unregulated.

Homes and buildings in developing countries are also polluted, but the sources and concentrations are different. In developing nations, most indoor pollutants come from everyday activities such as cooking and heating with fuels such as coal or biomass—wood, crop wastes, or dung. The World Health Organization (WHO) estimates that as many as two thirds of the world's peoples burn these fuels, often in stoves with little or no ventilation. When WHO studied the problem in rural Kenya, average particulate levels in houses where wood or crop residues were used for cooking were more than 20 times higher than WHO says is safe. Levels of aromatic hydrocarbons such as benzene, many of which have been identified as carcinogenic, were also very high.

Exposure levels this high can cause health problems such as chronic lung and heart diseases, cancer, and acute respiratory infections, especially in children. An estimated 400 million–500 million people in the developing world, mostly infants, women, and the elderly, are exposed to these risks. In response, developing countries and aid agencies are focusing on converting to cleaner fuels and properly vented stoves and heaters.

NOx, and VOCs. These devices are widely used in the United States, Japan, and Canada, but are just beginning to come into use in Europe.

Emissions of sulfur dioxide have declined in most industrial countries, but in many cases the use of very tall smokestacks has served to simply transport the pollutants to another region downwind. For example, U.S. emissions of SO_2 and NOx in the Midwest and Northeast account for about half of the acid rain falling on eastern Canada. Much of the acid precipitation falling on Scandinavian countries comes from Britain, Eastern Europe, and the former Soviet Union. Acid deposition can severely affect ecosystems on land and in water and can corrode stone and metal building materials and monuments.

Despite some improvements in industrialized countries, many developing countries face rapidly worsening air quality in their major cities and are only beginning to combat it. Mexico City, for example, has had several pollution episodes so severe that the government temporarily closed factories and schools. Experts fear that global emissions of SO_2 and NOx—key components of crop- and soil-damaging acid deposition—are likely to increase as energy demands in developing countries continue to rise. The number of vehicles in use around the world is also expected to double to 1 billion in the next 40 years, adding to pollution pressures. Much of this growth will take place in developing countries, where the automobile population is expected to increase by more than 200 percent by the end of the century.

Air pollution's assault on ecosystems and human health can be reversed, but the task demands strong popular and political will and, perhaps most importantly, financial resources. There are encouraging signs, however. More industries are accepting the notion that reducing emissions can lead to greater efficiency and profits. (See "Industry" chapter.) Policymakers are exploring creative uses of market forces. France, for example, was the first nation to impose a direct pollution tax, which requires emitters to pay per unit of pollution discharged. A free market in pollution credits, such as that adopted in the United States in 1990, has been discussed in Europe. The cleanup will also require the use of technical options such as switching to cleaner-burning fuels and new combustion technologies that reduce NOx emissions from coal-fired installations. Energy planners are also turning to conservation, one of the most efficient and least expensive tools for reducing emissions from stationary sources such as power plants.

This chapter was written by Cheryl Simon Silver, a Maryland-based writer and senior editor of the 1993 Information Please Environmental Almanac.

Grassroots Activities

You may or may not find them in your local Yellow Pages, but grassroots environmental groups are out there—and they are gaining in effectiveness.

Frank Carsner's years of involvement with the Toxic Victims Association grew from the severe health problems he suffers from his former work as an industrial truck painter. The group formed a decade ago after Carsner, of Portland, Oregon, and three other painters spoke up about being given no training or protective equipment for their job, which involved coating 28 to 30 trucks a day with harmful petro-chemical-derived paints. Over the years, as his health has allowed, Carsner has provided research, peer support, congressional testimony, and counsel to victims of similar situations in connection with National Toxic Action in Boston. Currently, Carsner is fighting a plan for aerial spraying of neighborhoods with pesticides.

Grassroots groups are formed by individuals who, out of frustration with a problem caused (or not being solved) by a government, business, or industry, decide to pool their efforts and voices to make a change. *One Person's Impact*, a newsletter published in Westborough, Massachusetts, by a group of the same name, says that what motivates people to get involved in environmental issues is "a direct threat to the health and well-being of their own personal environments." When the issue "becomes personalized, . . . primal energies surface."

The concerns held by grassroots groups in North America today often center around issues of environmental compromise or threats to physical health—proposed development in a long-established wilderness area or the siting of a toxic waste incinerator are two examples—but they are linked with other, equally serious issues. Some groups have formed to point out racial injustices or lack of consideration for generations-old cultures and traditions. Even leaders of these grassroots groups that started with exclusively "social" concerns admit they soon run into environmental links. The natural environment, pure or tainted, is the foundation for our work, our food, our shelter, our recreation.

Threats to Culture and Health

In one example of grassroots response to a threat to lifestyle, the 7,000 Gwich'in people in 17 remote communities in northeastern Alaska and northwestern Canada have undertaken an aggressive lobbying and publicity campaign. Their fight is against the federal government's proposal to drill for oil on the Arctic National Wildlife Refuge (ANWR). The Gwich'in claim that drilling would disrupt migrations and calving of the Porcupine caribou herd on which their culture depends for food, clothing, tools, and spiritual sustenance.

Ten years of efforts to make their voices heard in the government debate on the drilling proposal spurred the entire Gwich'in nation to come together in 1988 for the first time in a century. One result of that historic meeting was the formation of an eight-member Gwich'in Steering Committee. The Committee maintains an active voice for environmental protection of the entire ANWR ecosystem.

In a Kokomo, Indiana, campaign still in its early stages, Helen Cleaver began by knocking on her neighbors' doors, a petition in hand. Her concern was pollution from an oil recycling and scrap metal plant in her neighborhood, where residents are mainly elderly and living on low incomes. As she collected some 130 signatures and talked with people, she realized that she was not alone in her concern. "They all complained of ill health, bronchitis, pneumonia," Cleaver said. They were tired of the fumes, dust, and "oily residue" that settles in their homes, on their clothes, and in their hair. At this stage, Cleaver's biggest question is, "How can we raise money for attorney fees?"

Without the counsel of individuals or groups that have trod the path before them, how *do* new groups move toward finding solutions?

Martha Kostuch concentrates her efforts on fighting the placement of dams on wild rivers in western Canada. Fledgling groups in her region often turn to her to help get the ball rolling. Kostuch leads a four- to five-hour workshop, taking small groups through a step-by-step process that defines their concerns. At the end of the session, each group summarizes its problem, its potential solutions, and the action plan it has determined to set in place.

Kostuch uses methods with other groups that have survived testing in grassroots efforts of her own. That same approach is used on a larger scale within new groups that have formed specifically to offer training and consultation to grassroots groups across the continent.

Training Grassroots Leaders

At the nonprofit Institute for Conservation Leadership (ICL) in Washington, D.C., Executive Director Ed Easton says his group's mission is to empower individuals and train them to develop additional leadership skills. His own grassroots involvement in environmental issues began when he joined a group for a canoe trip in North Carolina. Such social connections, he said, "bind people together." Easton then volunteered with the North Carolina chapter of the Sierra Club. He organized a leadership conference for people in other groups who shared his lack of connectedness. "Our country is full of tiny environmental organizations staggering around with no direction," he said. "It's one of the things that cripples efforts."

The aim of ICL is to define and refine local- and state-level grassroots activists' efforts. Between January 1991 and June 1992, approximately 1,000 people participated in institute training sessions that included a seven-day Individual Leadership Training. Weekend sessions included training for executive directors and sessions on how to develop an active board of directors, how to recruit and encourage volunteer leaders, how to get a statewide or issue-related network working effectively, and how to conduct effective meetings and develop committees.

Help with Fundo

In a similar vein, the Environmental Support Center (ESC), formed in 1990, tries to help local, state, and regional nonprofit grassroots groups in the United States achieve their goals more effectively. This aim includes helping groups find pro bono legal advice, get technical or scientific help, raise funds,

procure office equipment, and improve their relations with state and national groups. In its first year, ESC helped more than 100 groups.

For example, in 1992, ESC screened applicant groups for the placement of 100 personal computers donated by Apple Computer, Inc. Recipient groups were required to be nonprofit grassroots groups that represent low-income or minority communities.

When a group asks for special help, ESC contracts experts to meet with them and then subsidizes the cost of training and technical sessions by 50 to 80 percent, up to $1,500 per year for each group. Both ESC and the Institute for Conservation Leadership are nonprofit groups and rely on grant funds, service contracts, and donations.

Regional Groups Give Support

In many cases, environmental groups have organized themselves into networks spanning several states in order to field a wider range of issues. Executive Director Michael Schechtman and others at the Northern Rockies Action Group (NRAG) in Helena, Montana, offer on-site consulting and training workshops in Montana, Idaho, and Wyoming. NRAG counsels groups about long-range planning and helps activists recruit staff and volunteers to help them better achieve their goals.

In Guelph, Ontario, Tom Klein Beernink directs the Ontario Environment Network, which works to keep approximately 570 member groups informed of one another's activities and issues. "We provide the structure for occasional caucuses on issues like forestry, land use, and waste reduction," said Joseph Jolley, a volunteer. When so many groups "band together," he said, "it's an effective way of reinforcing our concerns."

The Citizen's Clearinghouse for Hazardous Waste (CCHW) is one example of a broad effort that grew out of a specific local issue. From 1978 to 1980, Lois Gibbs, a resident of Niagara Falls, New York, was president of the Love Canal Homeowners Association. After learning her neighborhood was built near more than 20,000 tons of toxic waste, Gibbs led the homeowners group to success in their demands to be relocated. She was overwhelmed with calls from residents across the country requesting help in fighting similar problems in their towns.

Since 1981, when the group was founded, Gibbs and her staff have helped at least 7,500 U.S. and Canadian groups organize, strategize, and get training. CCHW links local groups fighting similar issues, so that people can move from a NIMBY (Not in My Backyard) perspective to one of "NIABY (Not in *Anyone's* Backyard)."

Probing Further

If your grassroots activist group needs help in planning long-range strategies and organizing for action, several organizations are ready to provide it. The following list is by no means complete, but it can help you get started.

The Advocacy Institute, 1730 Rhode Island Avenue, N.W., Washington, DC 20036, (202) 659-8475. (A center for training, counseling, and support of citizen and professional public interest activists in the United States and abroad.)

Citizen's Clearinghouse for Hazardous Waste, P.O. Box 6806, Falls Church, VA 22040, (703) 237-2249. (As a "center for environmental justice," CCHW helps local groups organize to fight pollution related to waste management and contamination issues.)

CONCERN, Inc., 1794 Columbia Road, N.W., Washington, DC 20009, (202) 328-8160. (A source of environmental information for individuals and groups pursuing safe solutions to problems that threaten the environment and public health.)

Environmental Support Center, 1731 Connecticut Avenue, N.W., Suite 200, Washington, DC 20009, (202) 328-7813. (Supports the organizational and long-range planning and funding needs of regional, state, and local environmental groups.)

Institute for Conservation Leadership, 2000 P Street, N.W., Suite 413, Washington, DC 20036, (202) 466-3330. (Provides research to and training of grassroots leaders to help them reach their goals more effectively.)

Institute for Local Self-Reliance, 2425 18th Street, N.W., Washington, DC 20009, (202) 232-4108. (Works with urban residents to develop environmentally sound forms of consumption and production.)

U.S. Public Interest Research Group, 215 Pennsylvania Avenue, S.E., Washington, DC 20003, (202) 546-9707. (This national office represents 25 state-based PIRGs as it lobbies to change legislation for the benefit of the environment and consumer protection.)

Groups Tell Their Own Stories

In the following pages, 12 grassroots groups in the United States and Canada describe themselves and their goals and strategies. Some of these groups have realized their goals and are maintaining education programs in the area of concern. Others have moved on to new issues. One thing all have in common—their successes result from the cooperation of many committed people over the course of many years.

ALASKA

Susitna Valley Association

There we were; eight people in the back room of an air taxi service with a big problem. The state had just revealed a plan for an extensive timber sale in the heart of the Susitna Valley across Cook Inlet from Anchorage.

The Susitna Valley is a vast 2-million-acre river delta stretching from Anchorage to Mt. McKinley. The boreal forests of the delta, interspersed with wetlands, provide some of Alaska's most valuable fish, animal, and bird habitats. It is a remote area, accessed by boat, plane, snow machine, dog sled, skis, and hiking trails.

Consisting of almost all public land, the valley has become an integral part of the lifestyle that many of the 250,000 Anchorage residents came to Alaska to experience. It serves as a highly valued wilderness escape for residents and tourists alike, while also supporting the subsistence lifestyle of a number of small, remote communities.

Therefore, when the state proposed to cut roads deep into the valley and log the forests, people representing a wide diversity of interests and concerns were quick to respond. The problem the eight of us had was deciding how to organize the response for the greatest possible effect, and to prevent duplication of efforts. We decided one coalition organization should be formed. The coalition would serve as an identifiable "spokes-organization" for the Susitna Valley timber issue, assuring that all forest values, not merely timber, were fairly and equally considered in the state's planning process.

Since the coalition would bring together a number of groups that sometimes found themselves at odds with each other, our first task was to establish ground rules. We had to be sure our focus was strictly limited to the issues at hand—that the area of common ground was clearly defined and understood.

In addition, since it was important to provide evidence of strong grassroots support from large numbers of people, we made membership simple and informal. We charged no dues, choosing instead to rely on periodic appeals for donations. The strategy resulted in an effective and congenial coalition of 4,400 individual members and 69 organizations!

A core group, representative of the various interests, was set up to make decisions and carry on organizational business. The group prepared a purpose-and platform statement that was direct in scope, and we adhered to it. We had a prepared agenda for each meeting to help keep us from straying into controversial territory. But we also made a point of having fun.

The coalition was highly successful. After four years of effort, we successfully negotiated the Susitna Forestry Guidelines that recognize the values we set out to protect. In the process, we significantly raised the state's awareness of both the environmental and recreational values of the Susitna Valley. The proposed timber sale was dropped.

—Loisann Reeder

Loisann Reeder, President
Susitna Valley Association
9000 Slalom Drive
Anchorage, AK 99516
(907) 346-1943

NEVADA

Citizen Alert Water Campaign

In 1975, when the federal government identified Nevada as the recipient of the nation's first high-level nuclear waste dump, Citizen Alert was started by two women who toured the state asking residents, "Does high-level nuclear waste concern you?" Today, Citizen Alert has over 3,000 members, and our issues have expanded to include concerns over the military's use of land and airspace, nuclear weapons testing, hazardous waste storage, Native American land rights, and groundwater protection.

In recent years, water has emerged as a critical issue. In October 1989, the Las Vegas Valley Water District (LVVWD) filed applications to appropriate all the available groundwater in the three neighboring rural counties for importation to Las Vegas. Ranchers and residents of small towns in the affected counties quickly identified the threat, remembering how the fertile Owens Valley in California was pumped dry to create the urban sprawl of Los Angeles. Nevada law allows for formal protest of water applications. However, the rural people and their local government leaders clearly felt outgunned by their politically and financially powerful urban adversary.

Citizen Alert jumped into the fray, condemning the "water grab" and calling on our members to file protests. We then met with ranchers, county leaders, environmental groups, and Indian tribes, to develop a plan to coordinate protesters' efforts, share information, and help as many people as possible file protests.

In Las Vegas, where we circulated a petition and fact sheet on the water grab, we found many who supported our cause. Many residents believe the city should reduce water demand rather than commit to a multi-billion-dollar pipeline project.

As a result of the combined efforts of Citizen Alert and the counties, tribes, and organizations, the State Engineer was flooded with 3,600 protests. Thanks to the unprecedented number of filings and the wide range of concerns raised by the protesters, the hearings on the applications continue to be delayed. Meanwhile, the LVVWD has decided to drop 20 percent of the water applications. These were located in environmentally sensitive areas.

In the urban area, we have raised the issue of conservation as a cost-effective alternative to importing water. But changing the way Las Vegas views water issues is a large part of the battle. The city's rapid growth threatens to exhaust its supply of water from the Colorado River. Still, Las Vegas has taken no steps to moderate growth and has adopted only minimal water conservation programs.

Citizen Alert will continue to fight the water grab, mobilizing activists for the upcoming hearings and demanding accountability from city officials to balance growth with a sustainable water policy.

—Louis Benezet, Chris Brown

Louis Benezet, Water Coordinator
Citizen Alert
P.O. Box 1681
Las Vegas, NV 89125
(702) 648-8982
Fax (702) 646-0471

ALBERTA

Friends of the Oldman River

Ours is a story of a grassroots group taking on big government. Our fight is for the Oldman, the Crowsnest, and the Castle rivers and against the dam built by the government of Alberta at their junction in southwestern Alberta.

In 1978, when it began, the provincial government claimed that farmers needed irrigation water and downstream communities needed a secure water supply. They were challenged by the Environment Council of Alberta, which said that an onstream dam was not required then or in the foreseeable future. Critics of the dam believe it is part of a scheme that includes plans to export water to the United States.

These are the last wild rivers in southern Alberta. The Crowsnest is an internationally recognized fishery. The Oldman, edged with cottonwood forests—one of the most endangered prairie ecosystems—is the "Sacred River" to the Blackfoot Indians. The area to be flooded is also treasured for its archeological significance.

Friends of the Oldman River (FOR) formed in August of 1987, when 17 persons met to develop an action plan for saving the rivers. FOR has grown to over 500 individual and many organizational members representing thousands of people. Organizational tasks—incorporating FOR, selling memberships, and raising funds— have been time consuming. We sponsored Alberta's largest outdoor environmental rally, featuring musicians, well-known speakers, and native leaders. That event did much to increase public awareness.

Perhaps FOR's most far-reaching successes have been our legal battles over licensing of the dam. Most recently, FOR forced the federal government to appoint an independent panel to conduct an environmental assessment of the dam.

In one case, the Supreme Court ruled that the federal and provincial governments share responsibility for environmental protection and that the Federal Environmental Assessment Process is valid and legally binding. This is the most important environmental legal decision in Canada so far.

In May 1992, the Federal Environmental Assessment Panel for the Oldman Dam recommended that its low-level diversion tunnels be opened to allow unimpeded flow of the river. While the Canadian government rejected the recommendation to decommission the dam, it adopted 22 other suggestions aimed at reducing the dam's impacts.

Even though the Oldman Dam has been built, a great deal has been accomplished. Public awareness and the establishment of these legal precedents will make it much harder to ignore the environment in the future. Other major dam proposals in Alberta have been put on indefinite hold. More emphasis is now being placed on water conservation. And the Friends of the Oldman River are still hopeful that the dam will be decommissioned and the three rivers allowed to run free once again.

—Martha Kostuch

Martha Kostuch
Friends of the Oldman River
Box 288
Rocky Mountain House, AB T0M 1T0
(403) 845-4667

WYOMING

Lander Recycling Center

Until the fall of 1989, the residents of Lander (pop. 7,000) and Fremont County (pop. 33,000), Wyoming, had no drop-off recycling center where residents could take recyclable materials. Concerned citizens asked the Wyoming Outdoor Council (WOC) to help organize a volunteer committee to address this issue.

The issue of waste reduction and recycling was a new one for WOC, a 501(c)(3) nonprofit grassroots organization founded in 1967. Typically, our group works at the grassroots level on statewide environmental issues such as timbering, land management, habitat conservation, and environmental education. WOC also helps maintain an informal conservation network of state environmental groups.

But in the fall of 1989, the Lander recycling committee and the WOC jointly opened the town's first recycling center, an unenclosed drop-off center located on donated city land. The facility was unstaffed, but it was maintained by a private businessman who collected and sold the materials. WOC's office handled the coordination and all volunteer efforts. After a short time, this arrangement failed, and WOC and the volunteers closed down the site.

Thanks to continuing support from the WOC, ongoing volunteer efforts, and various grants, the new Lander Recycling Center (LRC) opened its doors in May 1990. The LRC now diverts an average of 11 tons monthly away from the local landfill.

WOC's goal was not to assume the responsibility of managing the facility, but rather one of public education and support for new initiatives. As use of the LRC by the citizens continued to grow, it went beyond the capabilities of the staff of approximately 15 volunteers. WOC was called on more and more for financial and managerial support. In December 1991, WOC decided to reduce its support of the center and help to find a new long-term solution for managing the LRC.

Numerous presentations were given to city and county public officials, the Solid Waste District, and civic groups, demonstrating the huge success of the program. After a difficult time during which some feared the center would be closed altogether, another nonprofit organization stepped forward with the intention of taking over the program and using the opportunity to employ its clients. This new organization intends not only to keep the facility open, but also to expand the center's hours of operation and types of materials collected.

—Dot Vali

Dot Vali
Waste Education Program Director
Wyoming Outdoor Council
201 Main Street
Lander, WY 82520
(307) 332-7031

NEW MEXICO

The SouthWest Organizing Project

The SouthWest Organizing Project (SWOP) is a multiracial, multi-issue, community-based organization in Albuquerque, New Mexico. Our members work throughout the state to respond to the environmental consequences of local and federal government decisions to place heavy industry, toxic dumping sites, waste incineration plants, and military bases close to our low-income communities in rural and urban areas. For African-American, Asian-American, Native American, and Latino people, environmental activism is an extension of our work for social and racial justice.

SWOP turned 10 years old in 1992. We began working on environmental issues a few years ago, when we surveyed a community in Albuquerque's inner city. We asked residents to identify their major community concerns. They complained of a lack of city response to their neighborhood and to the health impacts of emissions from a nearby particle board manufacturer.

That company had for years spewed contaminated sawdust into the neighborhood. The weight of heavy trucks carrying the raw sawdust on local streets had begun to crack the walls of the centuries-old houses. The plant was noisy, and the soil and groundwater were contaminated from improperly disposed chemicals. Dangerous levels of formaldehyde, benzene, and toluene were routinely used in production; health problems such as skin rashes, breathing disorders, and liver problems plagued the community.

City officials and plant management often insulted residents who complained; they argued that the plant provided needed jobs and was not violating existing environmental laws. But with pressure from an organized community, the company was forced to invest $3 million to clean up its act. Company officials have said they are glad they have replaced outmoded and no longer legal equipment

SWOP learned from that experience that we must identify our issues: from our perspective, this situation was one of environmental racism. We also learned that we can win—in many cases against enormous odds—if we are organized. Then we analyzed toxic contamination in communities of color and saw that race, poverty, and the environment are interlocking issues.

What does this mean? Surely it means that other communities are at risk from toxic poisoning. Field workers are not surviving to middle age. The poisoning of uranium miners only hinted at the land's devastation in the wake of tailings spills. These are only a few of many overwhelming examples.

Much of the mainstream environmental movement, as well as national government policies, overlooks the special concerns of communities like ours. But we see the growth of peoples' organizations whose leadership comes from the affected communities—locally, nationally, and internationally.

—Jeanne Gauna

Jeanne Gauna, Co-Director
SouthWest Organizing Project
211 10th Street, S.W.
Albuquerque, NM 87102
(505) 247-8832
Fax (505) 247-9972

MINNESOTA

Friends of the Boundary Waters Wilderness

The Friends of the Boundary Waters Wilderness is a Minnesota-based environmental organization focused on the protection and enhancement of the wilderness character of the Boundary Waters Canoe Area (BWCA) Wilderness in northeastern Minnesota's Superior National Forest and the larger, international Quetico-Superior ecosystem in which it lies. The Quetico-Superior ecosystem includes the 1.1-million-acre BWCA Wilderness, Ontario's 1.2-million-acre Quetico Provincial Park (a wilderness-class park adjacent to the BWCA along the border), and Minnesota's 219,000-acre Voyageurs National Park.

When federal legislation was proposed in 1976 to dismantle the BWCA as a wilderness, the Friends formed in response.

The BWCA is the only lakeland wilderness and the most heavily visited site in the National Wilderness Preservation System. Over 1,000 clean lakes are connected with streams and rivers in the BWCA, set amid forests of pine, spruce, birch, and aspen. It is the largest wilderness and contains the largest block of virgin forest east of the Rockies.

The Friends currently have about 3,000 members from around the nation who provide financial support, letters, and phone calls on key issues at critical times. The organization relies upon dozens of active volunteers and board members and has 2.5 staff positions.

Contributions of the Friends include:

- Passage by Congress of the 1978 BWCA Wilderness Act.

- Passage of state acid rain legislation in the early 1980s and subsequent adoption of the strongest acid rain standards in the world.

- Protection for the federally threatened eastern timber wolf through litigation to block hunting and a precedent-setting road-density agreement.

- Removal of military jets above the BWCA Wilderness through litigation against the U.S. Air Force and Air National Guard.

- Defeat of proposals to open Quetico Provincial Park to development.

- Federal funding for land acquisition purchases in and near the BWCA Wilderness.

- Advocacy with the U.S. Forest Service to ensure full implementation and enforcement of wilderness laws and regulations.

- Opposition to mining along the edges of the BWCA and Quetico.

—Kevin Proescholdt

Kevin Proescholdt, Executive Director
Friends of the Boundary
Waters Wilderness
1313 Fifth Street, S.E., Suite 329
Minneapolis, MN 55414
(612) 379-3835

ONTARIO

Earthroots

Earthroots (previously the Temagami Wilderness Society) has been involved in grassroots environmental activism since 1986.

Earthroots sees that our environmental problems are neither simple nor easily solved. The two main areas we focus on, the Temagami pine forest and the public use of water from James Bay, are both highly complex issues. Because of the diversity of concerns involved in environmentalism, Earthroots uses a variety of political strategies—direct action, lobbying, research, education, and networking.

Our actions can be as dramatic as mobilizing hundreds of people to blockade a logging road, as we did in 1989 on the Red Squirrel Road in Temagami to prevent the logging of the largest old-growth pine forest in the world. Most of our direct actions are less intense and involve targeting specific individuals on public occasions in order to force our concerns to be taken up.

While actions of this sort have had an enormous impact, less dramatic actions such as producing counterresearch on logging practices, mining, or the effects of hydroelectric dams also have a great impact, provided that such research is always undertaken in concert with a clear political strategy for its use. For this reason we visit over 100 schools and universities every year as part of a public-education program designed not simply to distribute information, but to tell people how they can get involved in grassroots environmentalism.

Lobbying in the traditional sense (something that is outside of the financial abilities of most small groups) remains a powerful tool. We have developed rather untraditional methods that are in keeping with our activist nature and budget. For instance, once we built a massive chainsaw and mounted it on the top of a truck equipped with a loudspeaker blaring a recording of a chainsaw. The truck followed the Ontario Premier (then David Peterson) to protest his decision to allow logging in Temagami. In the same manner, we went to Ottawa on Earth Day 1991 and delivered a mercury-poisoned fish from James Bay to Prime Minister Brian Mulroney to help pressure the government into stopping construction of the James Bay II dam.

All of these strategies involve some degree of networking. Our involvement with any number of other social advocacy groups has proved to be one of the best tools we have for building support for our concerns. It also allows us to be actively involved in other areas where people are struggling to make a better world. Ultimately, we at Earthroots feel that it is only through cooperation of this sort that social change will come about.

—**Rikk Salamat**

Rikk Salamat, Coordinator
Earthroots
401 Richmond Street, Suite 251
Toronto, ON M5V 3A8
(416) 599-0152
Fax (416) 340-2429

ALABAMA

Alabamians for a Clean Environment

In early 1983, I was like most people in the rural South. The environment here was in no danger, I thought. I was naive and completely trusting of those in authority.

In 1977, a new industry was started in north Sumter County, Alabama, by several men, including the son-in-law of Governor George Wallace. The company got the only waste disposal permit in the state and was sold to Chemical Waste Management, Inc. (CWM), of Illinois in 1978.

Local citizens were curious about the site but were reassured by the company and the regulatory agencies that there was no cause for alarm. They said the "stuff" there was only paint and glue. In reality, the country's largest toxic waste facility had moved in, and Sumter County would soon become the nation's dumping ground for the most dangerous wastes known.

In 1983, CWM expanded and announced a plan to construct a hazardous waste incinerator. It was at this point that seven of us formed Alabamians for a Clean Environment (ACE) to gather information and educate the public about the site.

We were totally unprepared for the opposition that confronted us. The issue was complex and political, and we found that we needed expert technical advice. We held public meetings, produced a newsletter, and began fundraising efforts. We secured an environmental attorney to help prepare us to fight the proposed incinerator, which was to be the largest in burning capacity ever built.

Geological documentation revealed the site to be full of faults and cracks. The site was also over three major aquifers. The wastes, including military production and Superfund site cleanup waste, came from 48 states and several foreign countries. It contained deadly poisons, acids, corrosive materials, and explosives.

To stop the construction, we held a statewide campaign that included regular protests. Finally, in 1989, the U.S. Environmental Protection Agency announced that the permit to build the incinerator would be withdrawn. We were pleased for a short time—until CWM stated that it would build an incinerator with a new design. We are now involved in another battle.

The data we collected about the site and its impact were helpful to other communities across the nation. Alternatives to dumping and burning waste are available, and we are pushing industries to reduce and recycle.

My work these past 11 years has been both rewarding and devastating. I often reminisce about the old days, when my life was simpler, but I would not trade anything for the understanding I have gained. Each of us can make a difference, and each voice is significant.

—Kaye Kiker

Alabamians for a Clean Environment
P.O. Box 177
York, AL 36925
(205) 392-7443

GEORGIA

Friends of the Environment

Friends of the Environment (Friends) was organized to oppose the state of Georgia's attempt to locate a large hazardous waste incinerator and storage facility in Taylor County. In addition to defeating the proposed incinerator, Friends is attempting to change the state's policy from the construction of more hazardous waste dumps to one of hazardous waste reduction.

Although Friends is a relatively small grassroots group of about 100 citizens, much has been accomplished in its short history. At a 1988 leadership training course sponsored by Citizen's Clearinghouse for Hazardous Wastes, Inc., members of the group received invaluable assistance from Lois Gibbs (a former resident of Love Canal, New York, and founder of the Clearinghouse) and others.

In 1990, Friends helped draft and pass the Georgia Hazardous Waste Reduction Planning Amendment to the Georgia Hazardous Waste Management Act. This important legislation requires all large-quantity generators of hazardous waste in Georgia to audit their production processes and submit hazardous waste reduction plans to the Georgia Environmental Protection Division. The plans are to be updated regularly.

Friends and its allies across the state and the country have made a difference. Aided by Greenpeace, we marched 100 miles to rally at the state capitol. The citizens held candlelight vigils in 10° F weather at the Governor's Mansion and staged many rallies and nonviolent protests with the help of other groups such as Eco-Action. Friends of the Environment has also brought national waste experts to Georgia to share their expertise.

In 1991, as a result of public outcry and outrage over the proposed Taylor County incinerator, Georgia's new governor, Zell Miller, introduced and signed legislation that reconstituted the Georgia Hazardous Waste Management Authority.

The authority's focus was changed to hazardous waste reduction, and the makeup of the authority now includes academics, environmentalists, and business representatives. In addition, the authority is reconsidering its decision to locate an incinerator in Taylor County.

Friends of the Environment has proven that a small, determined group of grassroots activists can make a difference in the way the hazardous waste issue is addressed in Georgia.

—**Louise Love**

Debbie Buckner
Friends of the Environment
Route 1, Box 76
Junction City, GA 31812
(706) 269-3630

NEW YORK

The Adirondack Council

The Adirondack Council is dedicated to protecting the natural character of the Adirondack Park in northern New York. An 18,000-member not-for-profit organization, the Council was founded in 1975. Sixteen full-time staff members work with a privately contributed budget of $1.4 million from the Council's headquarters in Elizabethtown and an office near the state capitol in Albany.

Unlike other state parks, Adirondack Park is a mixture of public and private lands woven into a 6-million-acre patchwork larger than the state of Vermont. It is the largest park in the lower 48 states and one of the oldest, founded on May 20, 1892. The public lands, about 42 percent of the Park, are protected under the New York State Constitution. On the private lands that make up the remaining 58 percent, 130,000 permanent residents make their homes. These private lands are subject to a wide variety of pressures.

Many of the threats to the Park that the Council finds itself fighting involve making moral appeals to policymakers. In order to gain the clout it needs to overcome New York's often exclusive focus on urban issues, the Council goes beyond the Park's borders in asking for help from members. The Council's membership, a mere 0.1 percent of the state's population, is kept well informed. When important policies or legislation is debated, at least 1,500 members can regularly be counted upon to write letters, make phone calls, and visit their state legislators.

The Council also represents the Adirondack interests of the Natural Resources Defense Council, the Wilderness Society, and the National Parks and Conservation Association. It receives no money from these national groups, but occasionally calls upon these groups' 800,000 members to help put pressure on public officials to protect the Park.

By showing state and local officials that people within their own districts are watching their actions, the Council has won significant gains over the past 17 years in protecting forest and farmlands, controlling air and water pollution, halting harmful pesticide use, altering low-level military jet training patterns, preserving wildlife habitat, reintroducing once-native wildlife species, preserving biological diversity, increasing recreational opportunities, and minimizing the damage caused by heavy tourism.

—John Sheehan

John Sheehan, Communications Director
Adirondack Council
P.O. Box D-2
Elizabethtown, NY 12932
(800) 842-PARK

NEW JERSEY

The Baykeeper Program

The Baykeeper Program is run by the American Littoral Society, a nonprofit national environmental organization with headquarters on Sandy Hook, New Jersey. The main focus of the Baykeeper Program is maintaining and monitoring the environmental well-being of the New York-New Jersey Harbor.

One man, Andrew Willner, is the Baykeeper. Andy, his staff, and volunteers act as environmental watchdogs and advocates for the ecological health of the harbor and its tributaries.

One of our most important tools is the Citizen Water Quality Monitoring Program. Currently, we have 24 sites around the harbor in both states. Every other week volunteers test water at their sites for dissolved oxygen, acidity, salt content, cloudiness, temperature, water depth, and silting. Volunteers also make notes of tide and weather conditions, algae growth, aquatic vegetation, floating debris, wildlife, and any other activities they feel may be significant. Their test results provide useful data on the normal water conditions. Abnormal test results may indicate potentially hazardous events. In many cases we have found that the presence of testing teams helps to make other people us-

ing the waters around the sites more aware of the local environment and the issues that affect it.

More than 80 volunteers currently test harbor waters at the various sites. They include high school and junior high school student groups, an urban canoe club, local civic and environmental groups, and concerned individuals. This year the Baykeeper plans to increase the number of testing sites to 40, thereby filling site gaps around the harbor and venturing farther upstream on many of the tributaries.

As a result of the success of the Citizen Water Quality Monitoring Program, the Baykeeper is in the process of establishing a compliance monitoring program for the same waters. This new program would help local, state, and federal agencies respond to and monitor pollution events, prosecute polluters, and identify possible problem areas to stop pollution before it can happen.

—Dennis Reynolds

The Baykeeper
American Littoral Society
Sandy Hook
Highlands, NJ 07732
(000) 291-0055

NEWFOUNDLAND

Quidi Vidi Rennie's River Renewal

This is the story of a group of concerned individuals who cared enough about their local environment to work together to right a wrong. Almost 10 years ago, local biologists (some of whom are world-renowned experts on river systems) described the waterways of the capital city of St. John's, Newfoundland, as "rivers treated like sewers." With some foresight, Mayor Shannie Duff arranged a meeting of special-interest groups and individuals who wanted to protect and enhance the area around Quidi Vidi Lake and the Rennie's River, its main waterway through the heart of the city.

As a result of that meeting, the Quidi Vidi Rennie's River Development Foundation was established in 1984. A registered, volunteer charitable organization, it is made up of a coalition of interest groups and professional associations working to take a sensitive, creative, and aggressive approach to the enhancement of the city's freshwater resources and associated open spaces.

In 1986, the Foundation completed a master plan that became the blueprint for development and restoration activities along the Rennie's River waterway and around Quidi Vidi Lake. The Foundation's goal is to implement the plan over a 10-year period. This multi-million-dollar project, funded by federal, provincial, and municipal governments, corporate donations, and contributions from a great number of individuals, has been recognized both locally and nationally.

The Foundation has successfully completed a range of projects:

- A fish ladder at the outlet of Quidi Vidi Lake was built to permit the passage of migratory fish species.

- Approximately 3 km (1.26 mi.) of walking trails were laid along the banks of Rennie's River and around Quidi Vidi Lake.

- Aquatic, semiaquatic, and riparian habitats have been enhanced for fish and birds.

- Channelized and culverted streams have been restored.

- Educational and interpretive programs are being offered through the new Newfoundland Freshwater Resource Centre.

The Centre is the main component of the master plan. It houses the only public fluvarium in North America as well as a variety of aquaria and displays. The fluvarium itself comprises nine large viewing windows that allow visitors to observe the natural, underwater world of Nagle's Hill Brook. In 1991, its first full year of operation, the Centre received over 55,000 visitors from around the world.

The work of the Foundation is an ongoing demonstration of just how much can be accomplished with cooperation.

—Mavis J. Higgs

Mavis J. Higgs, Development Officer
Quidi Vidi Rennie's River Development
Foundation
Box 5, Nagle's Place, Pippy Park
St. John's, NF A1B 2Z7
(709) 754-3474
Fax (709) 754-5947

50 of the Best Books on the Earth

If you want to know more and think harder about the environment than watching TV nature programming allows, or if you want to build an environmental library, start with the books listed here. Many are classics, and the rest are among the best of their kind. Some treat such big questions as whether people have a right to subdue nature, while others, more technical, set out to show, say, the relative merits of landfilling versus garbage incineration. A few are out of print, but they are well worth a trip to a library or a good used bookstore.

Classics

1. *Only One Earth: The Care and Maintenance of a Small Planet*
Barbara Ward and René Dubos
Norton, 1972

This must be the liveliest and most moving book ever inspired by a conference (in this case, the United Nations Conference on the Human Environment, held in Stockholm in 1972). It may even be the best environmental book ever written by more than one person. Its premise is that the two worlds we occupy—"the biosphere of [our] inheritance, and the technosphere of [our] creation"—are on a collision course. Showing how science has both improved and undermined life on the planet, how economic growth can spawn economic hardship, and how nationalism interferes with attempts to create a world community committed to egalitarian and ecological principles, political economist Ward and microbiologist Dubos made the arguments for "one earth" with greater passion, eloquence, and understanding than anyone else before or since.

2. *Silent Spring*
Rachel Carson
Houghton Mifflin, 1962 (reissued 1987)

Rachel Carson's 1962 breakthrough book on pesticide abuse can't be blamed for setting the shrill emotional tone of the ensuing debate over the use of agricultural chemicals, though it definitely did set the agenda. *Silent Spring* is a model of careful reasoning, good science, and the slow accretion of detail to make a point—basically, that misapplied pesticides are really biocides, wiping out whole ecosystems. Recently reissued, the book has been variously credited with sparking the creation of the U.S. Environmental Protection Agency, broadening the base of the environmental movement, spawning a new class of environmentally alert books, inspiring a generation of women to take up field science, and, not least, getting most applications of DDT banned in this country.

3. *The Closing Circle*
Barry Commoner
Knopf, 1971 (out of print)

Barry Commoner introduced Americans to ecology. The budding science had many practitioners two decades ago, but Commoner was the first to explain in a conversational voice how the laws of ecology worked. Everything is connected to everything else, he demonstrated, everything must go somewhere, nature knows best, and there is no free lunch. Commoner was also among the first to note that, from an environmental standpoint, the kind of economic growth matters more than the quantity, and that technology choices are what mainly determine pollution levels. (Now convinced that U.S. environmental regulation has failed, Commoner revisits many of the issues raised in *The Closing Circle* in *Making Peace with the Planet*, Pantheon, 1990.)

4. *A Sand County Almanac*
Aldo Leopold
Oxford, 1949 (reissued 1989)

At once a work of philosophy, ecology, and first-rate literature, *A Sand County Almanac* reads like music. The first movement is a bright celebration of nature as experienced on a used-up prairie farm that Leopold is nursing back to life. The second is a more somber lament on what is lost as civilization "advances." The third, a political march, consists of clear and shrewd proposals for reeducating ourselves about the needs of and for wildlife and wildlands. Published posthumously, the volume contains the now-famous essay "Thinking Like a Mountain" and the even more famous "Golden Rule of Ecology"—"A thing is right when it tends to preserve the integrity, stability, and beauty of the biotic community" and "wrong when it tends otherwise."

5. *The Machine in the Garden: Technology and the Pastoral Ideal in America*
Leo Marx
Oxford University Press, 1964

Combing American literature and sorting through images of the United States in European letters, Leo Marx examines the dualism embedded in our culture. On the one hand is the myth and reality of "America as nature's garden, a new paradise of abundance." On the other is the 200-year-old American love affair with technology, the more sophisticated the better. As the title implies, wilderness is still the context of the American dream, however divorced the dream has become from daily life.

6. *Gaia: A New Look at Life on Earth*
J.E. Lovelock
Oxford University Press, 1975

The biosphere, far more than the sum of its parts, functions as a single organism. So wrote independent British scientist J.E. Lovelock in 1975, rocking the scientific establishment. His hypothesis is that what keeps our planet a fit place for life are interactions between living and inorganic matter. We disturb the complex system of organisms, air, oceans, and land surface at our own peril: The system can always adjust, but people may not be so adaptable. (Often misunderstood, Lovelock answered his critics in *The Ages of Gaia: A Biography of Our Living Earth*, Oxford, 1982.)

7. *Small is Beautiful: Economics as if People Mattered*
E.F. Schumacher
Harper & Row, 1975

A renegade economist who once headed up the British Coal Board, E.F. Schumacher was the spiritual head of the "appropriate technology" movement that began in the 1970s, and this book was its catechism. In it, Schumacher held up Buddhist teachings against the doctrines of modern economics and found the latter wanting. He preached community self-sufficiency, the need to give organizations a human face by keeping them small, and the virtues of manageable, decentralized technologies. He also bid us to measure progress in terms of peace and well-being as well as material prosperity.

8. *The Desert Year*
Joseph Wood Krutch
Viking, 1951 (current edition: University of Arizona Press, 1985)

This record of how a Connecticut Yankee came to understand and then love a landscape that once meant less to him than "a pot on the windowsill or a goldfish on the desk" charts a subtle conversion experience. By returning again and again to the raw and then-unpopulated West and, finally, by transplanting himself there, Krutch discovered—and beautifully conveyed—the all-important difference "between looking at something and living with it."

9. *Roadless Areas*
Paul Brooks
Knopf, 1942 (Ballantine Paperback, 1971) (out of print)

This trip log and nature guide covers the off-road journeys of Paul and Susie Brooks starting in the early 1940s. Punctuated by digressions on, say, the historical importance of fire, canoe-handling techniques, or the composition of the forest's understory, these tales of quiet adventures are set in a time before national parks had become crowded and camping gear had become another manifestation of conspicuous consumption and high technology. But there is no way to date the voice that tells us that "the measure of our maturity is our willingness not to control every inch of our environment."

10. *The Limits to Growth*
Donella Meadows and colleagues
Universe, 1974

Perhaps the most controversial environmental book ever published, *The Limits to Growth* sold over 4 million copies worldwide and ignited a still-simmering debate inside as well as outside the environmental community. Using then-sophisticated computer modeling techniques, the 30 or so researchers who contributed to this book tried to plot how such trends as rapid population growth, increased pollution, agricultural development, and growing energy and minerals use would interact and influence the human prospect. The news was all bad—economic and social collapse seemed imminent—but luckily, some of the assumptions proved wrong. Still, many were basically correct. The book forced people to recognize the possibility of natural limits, and it legitimized computer modeling in environmental forecasting. The *Limits* scenarios have recently been refined and more data added. (See *Beyond the Limits*, Universe, 1992. Again, the team's findings are scary, but the authors insist that trend need not be destiny.)

11. *The Population Bomb*
Paul R. Ehrlich
Ballantine Books, 1968

Paul Ehrlich deserves credit for making millions of college students and other Americans aware in the late 1960s that accelerating population growth could offset or undo even the most heroic efforts to protect the environment. With alarmist statements and prophecies—meat would soon become a staple for the rich only, and India's economy and society were about to fall—Ehrlich preached the neo-Malthusian notion that human demands on natural resources were growing at unsustainable rates. Although Ehrlich's gravest predictions never materialized, mainly because he slighted technology's role in boosting agricultural yields, he introduced an important antidote to the inebriating idea that nature knows no bounds in the service of its most intelligent carnivore. (For a seasoned update of Ehrlich's ideas, see *The Population Explosion* by Paul R. and Anne H. Ehrlich, S & S Trade, 1990.)

12. *Turtle Island*
Gary Snyder
New Directions, 1974

Turtle Island is what North America was called in many Native American creation myths. Gary Snyder gave the same name to this Pulitzer Prize-winning book of poems about ancient peoples, cowboy bars, animals, demons, the "great mother," the "great family," affluence, nuclear power, child-rearing, and the call of the wild. His hope is that "Anglos, Black people, Chicanos, and others beached up on these shores" could "hark again to [their shared] roots, to see our ancient solidarity, and then to the work of being together on Turtle Island." A curious amalgam of fact lists, myth, chants, environmental position statements, parables, and free verse, Turtle Island anticipated the current debates on biodiversity and cultural diversity. In the poetry, Snyder comes at nature's hard truths in a language all his own and yet somehow handed down.

Overviews and Anthologies

13. *Sustaining the Earth: The Story of the Environmental Movement—Its Past Efforts and Future Challenges*
John Young
Harvard University Press, 1991

No single-author environmental book of recent years has been more ambitious than Young's. With a firm grasp of environmental politics on three continents (North America, Australia, and Europe), expertise on the aboriginal peoples of Southeast Asia, and a perceptive take on what separates the Third World from the First, Young makes the case that environmentalism as we know it is about to die and a new post environmentalism to rise Phoenixlike from its ashes. His main point—hard to dispute after the Earth Summit in Rio in 1992—is that environmental goals can no longer be pursued apart from social justice, cultural diversity, family and communitarian values, and respect for life in all its forms.

14. *Man and the Natural World*
Keith Thomas
Pantheon, 1983

With the claim that "it is impossible to disentangle what the people of the past thought about plants and animals from what they thought about themselves," Thomas opens a fascinating inquiry into how the English (and, by extension, all Westerners) have treated plants and animals over the last several centuries. He traces a gradual expansion of care and respect that brought cats and dogs indoors and raised gardening to an art. The underlying message is that the triumph of aesthetic values and humanist belief over practical concerns may be one of the biggest steps people on both sides of both oceans in a hemisphere have taken toward survival with dignity.

15. *Eco-Science: Population, Resources, and Environment*
Paul Ehrlich, Anne Ehrlich, and John Holdren
W.H. Freeman, 1970 (out of print)

This 1,051-page text on what Paul Ehrlich was later to call "the machinery of nature" is the closest thing to an owner's manual for the planet ever published. (The irony, of course, is that the more you understand about Earth's complex dynamics and systems, the harder it becomes to imagine humankind taking the driver's seat.) The book covers natural processes and human well-being, population and renewable resources, energy and materials, the sources and costs of environmental disruption, and the environmental choices we now face. No doubt the recent explosion of scientific knowledge makes updating this tell-all compendium a headache, but it's a pity that *Eco-Science* has slipped out of print.

16. *The Arrogance of Humanism*
David Ehrenfeld
Oxford University Press, 1978

Biologist David Ehrenfeld detests the myth that our species is equipped to somehow "run" nature. Citing technological failures and crushing mistakes of judgment, Ehrenfeld claims that "our arrogance about what we think we know and what we think we can do has made it impossible for us to accept or deal any longer with the unknowable and undoable." Against humanist doctrine, Ehrenfeld proposes the Noah Principle: " All species and communities should be conserved because they exist and because this existence itself is but the present expression of a continuing historical process of immense antiquity and majesty." Provocative and curmudgeonly, this book anticipated the "deep ecology" movement and gave powerful ammunition to those afraid of where technology is taking us.

17. *This Incomparable Lande: A Book of American Nature Writing*
Thomas J. Lyon, editor
Houghton Mifflin, 1989

You may wonder why certain American authors were left out of this anthology, but not why any of the 21 picked survived the cuts. The passages selected span four centuries and represent a cross section of the best natural history and philosophy, field guides, tales of adventure and exotic places, and pastoral writing. Most of these excerpts can be found elsewhere, but not without digging, and Lyon's long critical essay on the history of U.S. nature writing—seen as a long struggle with an "awakening of perception to an ecological way of seeing"—will no doubt be anthologized itself.

18. *The Norton Book of Nature Writing*
Robert Finch and John Elder
Norton, 1990

Like other Norton guides to literature, this one is a single-volume library. Its 921 pages cover virtually all the major American nature writers of the 18th and 19th centuries and an easily defended group of the best in this century—right up to Terry Tempest Williams (born 1955). The biographical and historical notes supplied by the two editors, themselves front-ranking nature writers, give shape to what would otherwise be an embarrassment of riches. This unequaled volume is for the bedside, not the beach.

19. The Rights of Nature
Roderick Frazier Nash
University of Wisconsin, 1989

In the American mind, nature isn't what it used to be—or so argues Nash in this crisp intellectual history of changing attitudes toward the world apart from human beings and machines. In the tradition of American liberalism, "rights" are slowly being extended to other species, bodies of water, even trees. Don't scoff, says Nash: just 150 years ago abolitionists had to press the case that slaves had rights, and women were "enfranchised" only during this century. Now it's the spotted owl's rights that are on the line—a turn of events perhaps set in motion in 1215 when the Magna Carta was signed.

20. Our Country, the Planet
Shridrath Ramphal
Island Press, 1992

Revisiting the issues raised in Only One Earth 20 years ago, Ramphal reaffirms the essential wisdom of the earlier book and tracks the demographic, economic, and social changes that make sustainable development both more necessary and more difficult than ever to achieve. To him, the questions at the heart of our environmental future and the human prospect are how much policymakers and individuals will be influenced by notions of sustainability, how the great divide between the rich of the North and the poor of the South will be addressed, and how much "global governance" nations will abide. As necessary as political change is, says Ramphal, shared ethical norms and new ways of seeing the role and purpose of human life are even more important.

21. Remaking Society: Pathways to a Green Future
Murray Bookchin
South End Press, 1990

A class warrior, feminist, and vigorous opponent of nationalism and racism, Murray Bookchin makes the case in Remaking Society that our environmental ills stem from injustice and inequality, and that they won't disappear until we deal with the root causes. Step one, says Bookchin, is looking to history. In ancient Athens, revolutionary France, and the late 1960s in the United States, Bookchin finds models for the various building blocks of an ecologically sound democracy.

22. Sisters of the Earth
Lorraine Anderson, editor
Vintage, 1991

The bits and pieces in this collection of women's writings on nature were skillfully mined from two centuries of American women's diaries, stories, poems, trip logs, and essays. Anderson wasn't looking for any particular themes or viewpoints—only good reading—so the "sisters" range from backyard gardeners to adventurers, scientists to poets, angry young women to wise old ones. But if the contributors defy generalizations, the editor does hazard one: the women these disparate writers speak for are more likely than most men to accept nature "as is."

23. Earth in the Balance: Ecology and the Human Spirit
Albert Gore, Jr.
Houghton Mifflin, 1992

The product of years of immersion in environmental politics and of a midlife soul-searching brought on in part by his son's brush with death, Earth in the Balance is a brave attempt to reconcile economic and political realities with the needs for a planetary rescue operation and for spiritual recovery from recent dog-eat-dog decades. Senator Gore succeeds brilliantly, inviting hope that the popular debate over these issues will not only come alive but also reach new heights. Among the Democratic senator from Tennessee's most interesting ideas are those for a Strategic Environmental Initiative and a Global Marshall plan.

24. *At Odds with Progress*
Bret Wallach
University of Arizona Press, 1991

Bret Wallach is an astute historian of some of the United States' most important and interesting environmental battles. And history has taught him that, however compelling arguments based on economics, social welfare, or ecology may be in conflicts over land use, most conservation success stories can be traced back to an arational decision based on nothing more—or less—than some person's or group's deep love of a place. His tales and travels range from the mountains of Tennessee and the potato fields of Maine to the grasslands of North Dakota and the Columbia River basin in Washington State.

Environmental Economics & Politics

25. *Ecology and the Politics of Scarcity Revisited*
William Ophuls and A. Stephan Boyan, Jr.
W.H. Freeman, 1992

In this update of a work (*The Politics of Scarcity*) that influenced many of the environmental movement's leaders in the 1970s, Ophuls and Boyan review ecosystem stresses and set forth the depressing hypothesis that the scarcities that inevitably flow from population growth and heavy consumption of natural resources by the rich threaten liberal democracy. With the frontier exhausted, Ophuls and Boyan contend, individual liberty will have to be restricted for the sake of the common good unless dramatic social changes—very roughly outlined in the book—occur well before scarcities hit full force. Their critique of the current crisis in government is more powerful than their vision of a new society, but, as Thomas Lovejoy writes in the fore-

word to the new edition, Ophuls and Boyan pose life-and-death questions.

26. *Costing the Earth*
Frances Cairncross
Harvard Business School Press, 1992

This primer on the recently arranged marriage of environmental protection and economics clues governments and corporations in on how to beat the high costs of going green. Cairncross shows how polluting less and stretching energy farther is in everyone's interest, including industry's, and makes a convincing case that taxes and various other "market mechanisms" are both more efficient and more effective than regulation at getting industry to do more than meet minimum environmental standards.

27. *The Politics of the Solar Age: Alternatives to Economics*
Hazel Henderson
Anchor Books, 1981 (reissued in 1988 by Knowledge Systems)

This sassy critique of how conventional economics and economists have helped bring on the environmental crisis poses interesting questions that are still inching into the mainstream debate over how we use energy and natural resources. Henderson was an early critic of the method that economists use to calculate gross national product—not separating sound investments from waste or expenditures on junk—and the treatment of efficiency as an end in itself rather than a means to social goals. The costs of business as usual, Henderson claims, are unemployment, the widening gap between the haves and the have-nots, stresses on families and communities, and a heavy public tab for environmental cleanup.

28. *Home Economics*
Wendell Berry
North Point Press, 1987

If we Americans were really materialistic, surmises Wendell Berry, we would treat both natural resources and the products made from them much more carefully than we do. No, says Berry, the problem is that we don't respect the material world enough. In Home Economics, Berry blames our national obsession with consumption and price for environmental degradation and holds up the small-time farmer as the exemplar of a way of life in which what is taken from the Earth is returned to it measure for measure. Berry has been called romantic, moralistic, and out of sync with his times, but rural and family values have no more eloquent defender.

29. For the Common Good: Redirecting the Economy Toward Community, the Environment, and a Sustainable Future
Herman E. Daly and John B. Cobb, Jr.
Beacon Press, 1989

If decade after decade of economic growth is at the bottom of environmental stress, is there any alternative besides depression and decline? Yes, say economist Herman Daly and theologian John Cobb, but not without radical social reforms and new world views. The beginning, these maverick scholars contend, is rethinking the role of economics in relation to the common good. In particular, the market—great at allocating goods and services but not at promoting social justice, participatory democracy, or sustainable economic development—must be kept in its place. To reach these broader goals, Daly and Cobb propose revamping universities, restricting trade and making communities more self-reliant, measuring progress with a Physical Quality of Life Index as well as the gross national product, and attaching religious importance to questions of social and environmental justice. Theirs is a grand, if sketchy, plan of the sort that politicians rarely come up with and bureaucrats never do.

Nature and Natural Resources

30. Biophilia: The Human Bond with Other Species
Edward O. Wilson
Harvard University Press, 1984

The world's leading authority on ants and a Pulitzer Prize winner to boot, E.O. Wilson wrote Biophilia to give the uninitiated a sense of the passion and blessed drudgery that is the professional field biologist's lot. The book is also a celebration of the diversity of life—most of it still unknown to science and much of it disappearing fast in the wake of economic development and habitat loss. Wilson bets his reputation that the "one process now going on that will take millions of years to correct is the loss of [genes and species] . . . the folly our descendants are least likely to forgive us."

31. Soft Energy Paths
Amory Lovins
Harper Colophon Books, 1977 (out of print)

The sworn enemy of "supply side" energy analysts, a hero of the environmental movement, and a high-level consultant to the utility industry, Amory Lovins has brought humor, flashes of brilliance, and, above all, astonishing statistics to the most pressing energy questions of our time. In Soft Energy Paths, he challenged the conventional wisdom about how much energy the U.S. economy really needs (far less than usually imagined) and about how to get it (in large measure, from local renewable sources and from energy conservation) Using a nuclear reactor to generate power for most uses, Lovins has quipped, is like "using a chain saw to cut butter."

32. Cadillac Desert
Marc Reisner
Penguin, 1986

Water wars—whether between two groups of farmers, agricultural areas and cities, two government agencies, or neighboring states—have been a shaping force in the rise of the American West. In Cadillac Desert, Marc Reisner, the foremost historian of these conflicts, vividly brings to life the greed, graft, pipe dreams, and bureaucratic empire-building that drives them and that could pave the way to dusty death for the heavily populated arid western states.

33. *In the Rainforest: Report from a Strange, Beautiful, Imperiled World*
Catherine Caufield
University of Chicago Press, 1986

In the Rainforest is the record of Catherine Caufield's journey into the Brazilian rainforest and her conquest of the scientific literature on tropical biology. Rich and opinionated, the book captures the uniqueness of the rainforest ecosystem and the irony of the political and economic forces that are destroying it. In passionate language, she unveils the contradictions of the Amazon, especially its great fecundity and the fragility of the resource base when disturbed by road-building, uncontrolled logging, and livestock grazing.

34. *The Frail Ocean*
Wesley Marx
Coward McCann, 1967 (out of print)

An early work of environmental consciousness-raising often compared to Rachel Carson's *Silent Spring*, *The Frail Ocean* put an end to the convenient notion that the oceans could absorb pollution and provide seafood endlessly. Marx graphically put such ecological upsets as the massive *Torrey Canyon* oil spill in England, red tide in southern California, and whaling in the northern Pacific into long-term perspective. He also took a devoted teacher's delight in introducing readers to the underwater realm of life. (For an update, see Marx's sequel: *The Frail Ocean: A Blueprint for Change in the 1990s and Beyond*, Globe Pequot, 1991.)

35. *The Changing Atmosphere*
John Firor
Yale University Press, 1990

John Firor is in the inner circle of scientists puzzling out the probability and likely impacts of global climate change. Like the white-suited figure who emerges spotless from a pie fight, he is one authority who rose above the fray in the late 1980s and early 1990s—when scientific reputations were being made or lost on the basis of what amounted to long-term weather forecasting—by sticking to the facts and interpreting them with caution and experience. His short, balanced book on acid rain, ozone depletion, and global warming is thus a powerful wake-up call for remaining skeptics. Firor elegantly demonstrates how unlikely it is that nature will snap back given the current level of atmospheric assault and roughs out an energy program that, if combined with population stabilization and forest protection, would preserve the atmospheric "skin" that stands between us and deadly heat and ultraviolet radiation.

36. *The Fate of the Forest: Developers, Destroyers, and Defenders of the Amazon*
Alexander Cockburn and Susanna Hecht
Verso, 1990

Why is the Amazonian rainforest in blazes and tatters? Cockburn and Hecht say that the current sad state of affairs has been generations in the works—the unsurprising outcome of the rubber boom that began in the mid-1850s, the form of elite capitalism that developed in Brazil after World War II, and, more recently, national indebtedness. The authors call for a "socialist ecology" to save Amazonia, but not without first treating readers to a rhythmically rendered political and economic history of the region.

37. *Pilgrim at Tinker Creek*
Annie Dillard
Harper & Row, 1974 (reissued 1988)

Nature writing at its most vivid and intense, *Pilgrim at Tinker Creek* depicts, even obsesses over, Earth's fecundity and the millions of life-and-death relationships that make up an ecosystem. Watching the seasons pass on a creekside patch of land in southern Virginia, Dillard muses brilliantly on the engaging complexity of life in its many warring yet interdependent forms. Her goal seems to be learning how to see the natural world unblinkered, and her angle of vision shifts constantly, ranging from that of an insect to that of God—a narrative dance every bit as interesting as the subject matter itself.

38. *The Moon by Whalelight*
Diane Ackerman
Random House, 1991

Ackerman's love of places where few people have set foot and of the wildlife that lives in such places is matched only by her sense of adventure. She tags along after scientists to bat caves, Antarctic penguin rookeries, alligator-infested swamps, and whale hangouts, recording the strange habits of researchers and researched alike and waxing lyrical on the rituals of survival. For Ackerman, life on Earth is nothing if not a feast of the senses, especially touch.

39. *Arctic Dreams: Imagination and Desire in a Northern Landscape*
Barry Lopez
Scribner, 1986

Perhaps the most self-conscious of nature writers, Barry Lopez describes not only exotic landscapes that few of us will ever see, but also humanity's growing alienation from the rest of creation—the result of innate human willfulness as much as bad environmental decisions. Likening the Eskimos to the shell-shocked victims of the first atomic explosions, Lopez says that "the sophisticated, ironic voice of civilization insists that their insights are only trivial, but they are not." A sense of loss pervades this lyrical work because Lopez's voice itself is sophisticated and ironic. Only in the masterful concluding passages does he break free of his own conditioning and his fear that there is no going back, not even for an occasional miraculous moment.

40. *Desert Solitaire*
Edward Abbey
Touchstone, 1970

Not for nothing did his friends call Edward Abbey "Cactus Ed." This account of a spring-to-fall season as a park ranger in Arches National Monument in Utah shows his prickly intelligence in perfect form. Whether ranting about the evils of roads and tourists, taking outrageously unfair potshots at the elderly and the handicapped (who, Abbey contended, had no business demanding special access to pristine places best seen on foot), or making the federal government look silly, Abbey manages to offend, amuse, and, surprisingly often, catch the emperor naked. Even though his work is distinguished by an antisocial (and antifeminist) streak, Abbey never for a moment forgets his audience: his sense of humor and his finely honed style are at least as distinctive as his ideas about wilderness, anarchy, and the American West.

Reports and References

41. *World Resources 1992–93*
World Resources Institute (in collaboration with the U.N. Environment Programme and the U.N. Development Programme)
Oxford University Press, 1992 (most recent volume)

Many of the people who put together the almanac in your hand were at the time moonlighting from their day-in, day-out jobs: producing *World Resources*, a daunting tome that appears every other year in print (and on diskette for computer buffs). This world-famous reference work is a compendium of essays on hot environmental topics, assessments of environmental conditions and trends, and hundreds of tables and charts on everything from energy consumption to livestock populations and the availability of contraceptives. Each volume stresses a timely theme—sustainable development and the Earth Summit in the 1992–93 edition. Writing in the *Washington Post* in 1992, T.H. Watkins of the Wilderness Society noted *World Resources'* extraordinary breadth, depth, and *weight* and urged the president to use the 3.5-pound book to "beat some sense" into his Washington advisors. (Nothing of the sort happened.)

42. *The Home Planet*
Kevin W. Kelley, editor
Addison Wesley, 1988

This collection of oversized color photographs of Earth as seen from space momen-

Six Environmental Books for Kids

Children remember best what they can see, touch, hear, and smell. However, when the issue concerns the wonders of and threats to Earth's tropical rainforests, for example, a book written and illustrated especially for them can be the next best experience to being there.

Recent children's books on the environment appeal to a child's inborn curiosity about the world's variety of living things. In many cases, fantasy helps to draw a child into a story and relate the ultimate message. And as the messages have become more socially aware, the illustration in children's books has also become more detailed—even highly sophisticated—as children have proven themselves to be critical and appreciative readers. Books for older readers, such as Susan Sharpe's *The Waterman's Boy* below, enhance young people's natural inquisitiveness by encouraging them to get involved and take action to protect natural places.

Even as international government leaders are finding they must be bound by a global responsibility to protecting the world's natural systems, the current generation of environmental books for children has found a way to approach culturally diverse themes, as well. An increasing number of titles are bringing the stories of indigenous peoples from North America and around the world to the laps of America's children.

What follows is a mere sampling from some of the best that current children's literature has to offer.

The Great Kapok Tree,
Lynne Cherry
Gulliver Books, 1990

When an ax-slinging man falls asleep during a break from work, the many creatures who live in and around the giant tree he is hacking away at one by one whisper the rainforest's secrets in his ear. Sound science and richly textured illustrations set each other off perfectly in this award-winning book. (Ages: 4–8)

Crow and Weasel
Barry Lopez
North Point, 1990

This spirit quest by two "braves" rendered as animals with the hearts and minds of men leads to encounters with the unknown and results in a deep understanding of nature and human needs and obligations. Beautifully illustrated by Tom Pohrt.
(Ages: 6–adult)

---

tarily robs onlookers of speech. Against the obdurate blackness of space, the planet looks like the shared vision of an artist and an engineer. No words are needed, but quotations by the astronauts who have seen these life-changing views firsthand are included for the terminally printbound. (The general drift is that getting a little distance is humbling.) If you don't have a coffee table, buy one for this book.

43. *State of the World*
Worldwatch Institute
Norton, 1992 (most recent volume)

The release of Worldwatch's annual report on the state of the environment is a midwinter rite in Washington, usually falling some weeks before Ground Hog Day. Every year since 1984, Lester Brown and his staff have tracked environmental trends and problems

Six Environmental Books for Kids (continued)

Waterman's Boy
Susan Sharpe
Bradbury Press, 1990

In this well-wrought mystery (reissued in 1991 as *Trouble at Marsh Harbor* by Puffin Books), a young boy explores the Chesapeake Bay, a fascinating ecosystem that turns out to be the scene of a crime against nature.
(Ages: 8–10)

Just a Dream
Chris Van Allsburg
Houghton Mifflin, 1990

A boy's dream of a polluted, treeless, and garbage-filled future inspires him to mend his ways in this imaginative picture book by the author/illustrator of the best-selling *Polar Express*.
(Ages: 4–adult)

One Day in the Tropical Rain Forest
Jean Craighead George
illustrated by Gary Allen
Crowell, 1990

When bulldozers arrive to raze his rainforest home, Tepui's roundabout way of trying to save it only deepens his appreciation for the forest's biological diversity. (Other books in George's naturalist series cover a day in the desert, the woods, the prairie, and the alpine tundra.)
(Ages: 9–12)

Brother Eagle, Sister Sky
Penguin, 1992

Paintings by Susan Jeffers make this version of Chief Seattle's famous tribute to the Earth a visual and emotional experience.
(Ages: 5–adult)

---

that they think bear watching—population growth, food supplies, the conversion of agricultural land, etc.—and point out the policy mistakes that will keep humanity from achieving a "sustainable" future. Often, the best essays cover topics that most people wouldn't automatically consider environmental—cigarette smoking, say, or the hidden costs of a weapons buildup.

44. *The Global 2000 Report*
Gerald Barney and colleagues
U.S. Government Printing Office, 1980
(reissued in 1991 by Seven Locks Press)

The most far-reaching attempt yet by the U.S. Government (in this case, the Council on Environmental Quality and the State Department) to peer into the environmental future, this grim report and its 1,000 pages of technical annexes concluded that the world of 2000 would be more crowded, more polluted, and less stable ecologically and more vulnerable to disruption "than it

was in 1980." The rest of the world, especially Germany and Japan, took *Global 2000* more seriously than the United States did—too bad, since its general conclusions seem right on target now and its framework could be dusted off and used again.

45. *Our Common Future*
World Commission on Environment and Development
Oxford University Press, 1987

The final report of the World Commission on Environment and Development, *Our Common Future* is at once a highly negotiated document and an easy-to-read bestseller (over 500,000 copies are in print in some 20 languages) The book reflects the collected wisdom of the 23 blue-ribbon commissioners, thousands of citizen activists and local bureaucrats who grabbed the mikes during three years of hearings held around the world, and a gaggle of experts who worked with the commission to outline what governments must do to restore environmental health to the planet, stabilize global population, and stimulate economic growth, especially in poor countries. Even the report's critics agree that it weaves an impressive number of politically realistic proposals into a coherent plan for sustainable development—defined here as "development that meets the needs of the present without compromising the ability of future generations to meet their own needs." (For a progress report on meeting the goals set forth in *Our Common Future*, take a look at Linda Starke's *Signs of Hope: Working Towards Our Common Future*, Oxford University Press, 1990.)

46. The Earth as Transformed by Human Action: Global and Regional Changes in the Biosphere over the Past 300 Years
William C. Clark and colleagues, eds.
Cambridge University Press, 1990

The revised proceedings of a symposium held in 1987 and the sequel to another encyclopedic work (*Man's Role in Changing the Face of the Earth* (University of Chicago Press, 1956), *Earth Transformed* is a long, scholarly, and sometimes difficult work on how the human presence has changed the planet. But a serious reader's patience is rewarded here, and the book's conclusions that plant life and soils are in danger, with the atmosphere, water, and other resources not much better for wear, register indelibly—so heavy is the weight of fact and analysis. Reading this book of essays straight through would qualify as an act of environmental martyrdom, but do make sure your library has it and visit it there.

Lifestyles

47. The Simple Act of Planting a Tree
TreePeople with Andy Lipkis and Katie Lipkis
Jeremy P. Tarcher Books, 1990

Billed as a "citizen forester's guide," this workbook on how to get urban forestry projects off the ground is based on the TreePeople's tree-planting experiences since the organization's founding in 1973. A million trees later, the group—headed by Andy Lipkis, who began his career as a modern-day Johnny Appleseed while still in high school—knows just as much about community organizing and fund-raising as about how, where, when, and why to plant trees, and it's all here, including supply lists, scheduling forms, and tips on everything from getting permits to monitoring costs.

48. Muddling Toward Frugality
Warren Johnson
Sierra Club Books, 1978

Looking ahead to what he believes are inevitable scarcities, Warren Johnson claims that the future will doubtless find us both poorer and richer. We will certainly travel and buy less, for instance, but we will also live in healthier communities with a higher tolerance for individual needs. If the 1980s cast doubt on Johnson's provocative 1960s-ish ideas, the 1990s invite us to revisit this underground classic.

49. Fifty Simple Things You Can Do to Save the Earth
The Earth Works Group, 1989

Thanks no doubt to the media blitz leading up to Earth Day, this self-published book was the number one bestseller in 1990, topping the charts with 1,305,713 copies. It spawned a "Fifty Simple Things" industry (later books were for kids, businesses, and diehards who wanted to do 50 more things) and carved out a market niche for other "green lifestyle" books (notably, Diane MacEachern's *Save the Planet*, Jeffrey Hollender's *How to Make the World a Better Place*, John Elkington, Julia Hailes, and Joel Makower's *The Green Consumer*, and Heloise's *Hints for a Healthy Planet*). Offering sound advice culled from various environmental organizations, the book may have contributed to the mistaken notion that recycling and low-flow toilets will save the world. But it also dealt a one-two punch to the politically deadening belief that all environmental problems are beyond the control of ordinary people.

50. *Rubbish: The Archeology of Garbage*
William Rathje and Cullen Murphy
HarperCollins, 1992

This witty probe into what goes down in the dump turns up surprising facts (the middle class goes for name-brand foods, while rich folks buy generic and house brands), busts myths (per capita, people aren't creating more garbage than they did decades ago, just different types), and delivers the straight scoop on such burning issues as waste-to-energy operations and incineration. A major finding is that paper and construction and demolition debris (not fast-food containers and disposable diapers) make up the menacing bulk of what Americans throw out. The book, basically the annals of the work of the Garbage Project at the University of Arizona, ends with "10 commandments," including, "Don't think of our garbage problems in terms of a crisis," "Buy recycled and recyclable products," and "Be willing to pay for garbage disposal."

Kathleen Courrier is publications director of World Resources Institute, a book columnist for Sierra magazine, and series editor of Beacon Press/WRI Guides to the Environment.

A National View

Of states, provinces, cities, and of the country as a whole.

How much does your state spend on keeping drinking water clean or maintaining natural resources? Are those expenditures high or low compared to those of other states? Which state spends the most on managing wastes and conserving energy? Residents of which state drive more miles per person than any other? Which Canadian province is most efficient in its use of energy?

Of the major U.S. metropolitan areas, which have the best environmental conditions—from clean air and safe drinking water to low toxic pollution—

and most enlightened policies an practices—from recycling of wastes the pricing of energy to extensive u of mass transportation?

For the nation as a whole, how mar endangered species are there, and the number growing or shrinking? F what types of wildlife are U.S. impo from other countries the greates mammals (including furs), reptiles (cluding skins), birds, or orname tropical fish?

In what states has contaminatio the environment with radioactive terials produced by the U.S. gov

weapons factories been
nsive? Why is this little-
em described by some ob-
serious that the cleanup
ore than $100 billion and
, as 40 years?

dustrial releases of toxic
increasing or decreasing?
o industries account for the
ortion of these pollutants?

What can company managers do to improve their environmental policies?

What can citizens themselves do to improve their local environmental conditions or solve problems in their communities?

This section contains answers to such questions and takes a national view of environmental issues and conditions.

y
is
or
ts
—
n-
tal

of
na-
rn-

Cleaning up after the Cold War

Secrecy, haste, and disregard for public health all contributed to the piecemeal nuclear catastrophe that is one of the nation's most serious and least known environmental problems.

Although the Cold War is over, another battle involving America's nuclear weapons is merely in the planning stages. It concerns dangerous and poorly contained radioactive and chemical wastes, hundreds of square miles of often highly contaminated soil and groundwater, and the health of communities and ecosystems neighboring government nuclear weapons facilities—and, in some instances, downwind or downriver from them—in 12 states stretching from Washington to Florida. It amounts to the world's most serious instance of radio-active contamination outside of the former Soviet Union.

Such widespread contamination and the huge stockpile of yet-to-be-disposed-of wastes represents the hidden environmental cost of the Cold War and the nuclear arms race it engendered. Yet the damage accumulated gradually, not as a result of a single accident, and it went largely unnoticed for years. Secrecy, ignorance, haste, poor management, disregard for public health—all contributed to this piecemeal nuclear catastrophe. The end result is one of the nation's most seri-

Types of Radioactive Waste

High-level waste: The highly radioactive waste material that results from the reprocessing of spent nuclear fuel, including liquid waste produced directly in reprocessing and any solid waste derived from the liquid that contains a combination of transuranic waste and fission products in concentrations requiring permanent isolation. High-level wastes generate large amounts of heat as radioactive components decay.

Transuranic waste: These wastes are formed as a product of weapons-related activities and nuclear power generation. They contain low concentrations of radioactive elements heavier than uranium. Transuranics, including plutonium, do not generate troublesome quantities of heat. But unlike low-level wastes, transuranics have uncommonly long half-lives and must be isolated from the environment for many thousands of years. Since 1981, the U.S. Department of Energy has

defined this waste as materials containing 100 nanocuries (nano = one billionth) per gram of transuranic elements.

Low-level waste: Radioactive waste not classified as high-level waste, transuranic waste, or spent nuclear fuel. Nuclear byproducts from research may be classified as low-level waste if they contain less than 100 nanocuries per gram of transuranic elements.

Hazardous waste: Nonradioactive waste that is designated hazardous to people or the environment under the Resource Conservation and Recovery Act (RCRA) and U.S. Environmental Protection Agency regulations. Examples of these wastes present at the nuclear weapons production sites include chromium, PCBs (polychlorinated biphenyls), and cyanide.

Mixed waste: Waste containing both radioactive and hazardous components as defined by the Atomic Energy Act and RCRA, respectively.

ous and least known environmental problems.

Cleaning up contaminated areas and dealing with wastes may take 40 years, according to government estimates—nearly as long as the Cold War itself. Estimates of cleanup costs are huge, more than $100 billion, and may rise further, eating up some of the elusive "peace dividend."

Only in the past few years has the immensity of the problem become apparent, now that the production of nuclear weapons has virtually ceased. Yet the full scope of the environmental damage and of the cleanup efforts required is still unknown. In addition, disclosure of the pollution and the public health risks have triggered bitter legal battles pitting states and local communities against the federal government. On April 21, 1992, the U.S.

Supreme Court ruled that the federal government does not have to pay punitive fines for violating its own water pollution and hazardous waste laws at the weapons sites. But Congress may pass legislation that would strip away that immunity.

Stockpiling Wastes

The problem began during the secrecy and haste of the World War II Manhattan Project that built the atomic bomb and expanded during the Cold War years. To produce the plutonium, uranium, and tritium needed for nuclear weapons, the government built a vast industrial complex that sprawled clear across the country, from Florida to the Pacific Northwest. But these facilities produced far more waste than weapons. For every pound of plutonium, for example, the huge Hanford facility in the state of Washington also produced approximately 170 gallons of dangerous high-level radioactive liquid waste and 27,500 gallons of less dangerous but still radioactive low-level wastes. (See box, Types of Radioactive Waste.)

As early as 1948, in secret memoranda to the Atomic Energy Commission in Washington, D.C., some government officials expressed their concerns about the growing volumes of radioactive wastes contained in what were intended to be only interim storage facilities. But after the Soviet Union exploded its first atomic bomb in 1949, ending America's short-lived monopoly, the weapons program shifted into high gear. Waste problems were considered secondary, and national security restrictions shielded the weapons sites and their practices from public scrutiny. During a major expansion of the weapons complex during the 1950s, the volume of wastes grew dramatically.

For nearly four decades, the weapons bureaucracy was largely self-regulating, rebuffing oversight from states in which labs and production sites were located. Secrecy was maintained under the national security provisions of the Atomic Energy Act, passed after World War II to establish civilian control of nuclear weapons.

As the nation enacted new environmental laws in the 1970s, a double standard evolved. The Atomic Energy Act continued to exempt the weapons complex from regulations on waste treatment and toxic emissions that governed private industry and many other federal agencies. But in recent years, the U.S. Department of Energy (DOE), which now manages the nuclear weapons complex, has come under increasing pressure from the states where the facilities are located and from lawsuits

by environmental citizen groups. As a result, DOE has been forced to acknowledge that it is subject to regulation by the U.S. Environmental Protection Agency (EPA) and is covered under federal Superfund legislation. DOE must also answer to the states, under

> **Cold War Cleanup News**
> London, 1/31/92—The International Disarmament Corporation, a company that will specialize in the dismantling of Soviet nuclear weapons systems, has been formed by Lockheed, Olin, and the McDermott International subsidiary Babcock & Wilcox. The Financial Times reports the group will offer its service to the four commonwealth states that lack the expertise to dismantle former Soviet weapons.

the Resource Conservation and Recovery Act (RCRA), a federal law governing mixed radioactive and chemical wastes.

Despite such regulations, huge volumes of dangerously radioactive wastes are still stored throughout the nation under "interim" conditions. The challenge now is to place the wastes in safer, more permanent storage places that protect public health and the environment and, where possible, to clean up contaminated areas.

In addition, attention is turning to the long-term environmental and health threats that nuclear weapons wastes pose to people living in the vicinity of the government reservations. The hazard comes not only from millions of gallons of wastes that are still to be disposed of but also from seriously contaminated soil, groundwater, and surface water. At many facilities, radioactive and chemical contaminants also have been released into the air or into nearby rivers, increasing health risks to those living downwind or downriver. Several federal studies are under way to assess the damage already done to human health.

Where They Built the Bombs

The nuclear weapons complex consists of 14 weapons research, production, testing, and assembly facilities in 12 states. In addition, there are two proposed storage facilities for nuclear wastes, including the wastes from the weapons complex. (See map, U.S. Nuclear Weapons Sites; see also boxes, Nuclear Materials Production Sites, Warhead Production Sites, Weapons Research Sites, and Weapons Testing Site.) These government nuclear weapons reservations occupy more than 3,350 square miles and employ over 100,000 people.

The weapons complex includes:

- Weapons research and development at the Los Alamos National Laboratory in Los Alamos, New Mexico; Sandia National Laboratory in Albuquerque, New Mexico; and Lawrence Livermore National Laboratory in Livermore, California.

- Nuclear materials production (plutonium and tritium) at the Hanford Plant in Hanford, Washington, and the Savannah River Site near Aiken, South Carolina; uranium processing at the Fernald Materials Production Center near Cincinnati, Ohio, and the Idaho National Engineering Laboratory near Idaho Falls, Idaho.

- Warhead production at the Rocky Flats Plant in the suburbs of Denver, Colorado; the Y-12 plant in Oak Ridge, Tennessee; the Mound Plant in Miamisburg, Ohio; the Pinellas Plant near St. Petersburg, Florida; the Kansas City Plant in Kansas

City, Missouri; and the Pantex Plant near Amarillo, Texas.

- Weapons testing at the Nevada Test Site, near Las Vegas, Nevada.

- Nuclear waste storage at the new Waste Isolation Pilot Project (WIPP) near Carlsbad, New Mexico, where DOE wants to bury some of the wastes to test the safety of long-term geological disposal, and at the proposed Yucca Mountain national waste repository, in the southwest corner of the Nevada Test Site.

A Plan of Attack

The production sites no longer make weapons material, although a reactor to produce tritium is being kept on standby at the Savannah River plant. For the most part, work has been shifted to cleanup. Since 1989, DOE has produced Five-Year Plans to guide cleanup. Site characterization programs—efforts to describe the problems and map the spread of contamination—are under way and will continue for another four or five years.

The EPA and state environmental agencies have also assumed a role in weapons site cleanup, broadening opportunity for citizen participation. As of June 1992, nine of the weapons sites were proposed for, or listed on, the National Priorities List for cleanup action under the Superfund law. All 14 sites are subject to regulation under RCRA. In the DOE's most recent Five-Year Plans, almost two thirds of the agency's current and future funding is dedicated to waste operations and cleanup. DOE has separate programs for the storage and disposal of the three main types of radioactive waste, including high-level, transuranic, and low-level wastes. DOE also is working

U.S. Nuclear Weapons Sites

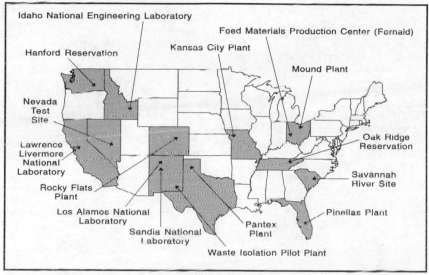

Idaho National Engineering Laboratory

Feed Materials Production Center (Fernald)

Kansas City Plant

Hanford Reservation

Mound Plant

Nevada Test Site

Oak Ridge Reservation

Lawrence Livermore National Laboratory

Savannah River Site

Rocky Flats Plant

Los Alamos National Laboratory

Pinellas Plant

Sandia National Laboratory

Pantex Plant

Waste Isolation Pilot Plant

Source: U.S. Congress, Office of Technology Assessment, *Complex Cleanup: The Environmental Legacy of Nuclear Weapons Production* (U.S. G.P.O., Washington, D.C., 1991), p. 16.

with EPA and the states to manage hazardous chemical waste and mixed wastes, which contain both radioactive and chemical components.

The cleanup problems that DOE has identified as especially difficult include leaking and unstable single-shell tanks containing high-level waste at the Hanford site in Washington; plutonium in the soil at Rocky Flats, Colorado; silos containing waste from uranium processing at the Fernald Feed Materials site in Ohio; buried transuranic waste at the Idaho National Engineering Laboratory; and groundwater contamination at almost every site.

The DOE's long-term plans call for shipping high-level and transuranic wastes from the weapons sites where they are now stored to two repositories. Congress has directed DOE to

study a site at Yucca Mountain, Nevada, to determine its suitability for a deep geological repository for used nuclear fuel from commercial reactors and for high-level waste from the weapons plants. Under the DOE plan, high-level waste would be shipped there and stored for thousands of years. Many Nevada elected officials and citizen activists oppose the project, saying the site is unsafe.

In addition, Congress in 1980 authorized construction of the Waste Isolation Pilot Plant near Carlsbad, New Mexico, to test the safe disposal of transuranic wastes from U.S. defense programs. The repository is expected to cost $700 million when complete; operating costs are estimated at $2.5 billion over 25 years. The DOE plans call for shipping millions of cubic feet of transuranic wastes to WIPP from the

Nuclear Materials Production Sites

Hanford Plant

Location: Hanford, Washington
Size: 360,000 acres
Status: A Superfund site. All plutonium production facilities are shut down. May 1989 "tri-party" agreement between U.S. Department of Energy (DOE), U.S. Environmental Protection Agency (EPA), and the state of Washington directs cleanup. Some small cleanups accomplished; site studies in progress for major work at 1,400 waste sites and four groundwater contamination plumes (a pollutant trail).
Problems: High-level liquid and semi-solid wastes containing radiation and chemicals are stored in 177 tanks. Some 66 of 149 older tanks have been identified as leakers or potential leakers. Potentially explosive hydrogen gas generated in some tanks is a major concern. Two hundred square miles of groundwater are contaminated. DOE admitted in 1990 that airborne releases of iodine 131 from Hanford in the 1940s were large enough to cause health risks to nearby residents.

Savannah River

Location: near Aiken, South Carolina
Size: 192,000 acres
Status: A Superfund site. South Carolina and federal agencies are negotiating a cleanup agreement. When operating, Savannah River produces tritium; in the past, it also has produced plutonium.
Problems: Aging production reactors were shut down in 1988 for safety reasons. DOE is pumping industrial solvents out of an aquifer beneath the site. Studies of major contamination sites are under way. Ten of 51 large steel tanks containing high-level nuclear wastes have developed leaks. Tank and transfer pipe leaks have contaminated thousands of cubic feet of soil. Groundwater is contaminated with tritium, and potentially cancer-causing industrial solvents have seeped into the Tuscaloosa Aquifer.

Idaho National Engineering Laboratory

Location: near Idaho Falls, Idaho
Size: 570,000 acres
Status: A Superfund site. The lab reprocesses naval reactor fuel to recover uranium. Has 61 percent of the nation's transuranic wastes stored in 55-gallon drums. Site studies to direct cleanup planned through 1995, when actual cleanup will begin.
Problems: Contaminants in unlined burial trenches have migrated into the soil, with plutonium detected in a clay layer about 110 feet below the site. Also, hazardous chemicals have been found in groundwater at about 600 feet. DOE has identified three major sources of groundwater contamination: carbon tetrachloride and trichloroethylene from past disposal practices and radiation from reactor operations. A 40-square-mile plume of tritium has been identified beneath the reservation, but it is barely detectable at the site boundary.

Fernald

Location: near Cincinnati, Ohio
Size: 128 acres
Status: A Superfund site. Uranium ingots, rods, and tubes for weapons production facilities were manufactured here. Focus at site has shifted to cleanup. Sitewide investigation of contamination problems is under way. Some groundwater cleanup has started. U.S. Centers for Disease Control plans a study of uranium dust contamination in nearby communities.
Problems: Soil, surface water, and groundwater have been contaminated by a variety of radioactive and hazardous chemicals. Uranium dust in stacks, vents, and a landfill has blown into areas surrounding the site. Contaminated groundwater is migrating off-site toward an important source of drinking water, the Great Miami Aquifer.

sites around the country where these wastes are now stored in 55-gallon drums. But the facility has experienced a series of delays and, as of June 1992, is not yet open.

Most of the nation's high-level waste is stored in huge underground tanks at Savannah River and Hanford. Together, these two sites hold more than 96 percent of the high-level waste by volume and 92 percent of the radio activity; Idaho has the remainder. (See chart, Volume of High-Level Nuclear Waste.) DOE plans to separate these wastes, remove some less radioactive components, and turn the most dangerously radioactive materials into glasslike solids in a process called vitrification. The vitrified wastes would be stored in the Yucca Mountain repository. Plans call for mixing the low-level portion of these tank wastes with cement and burying it in large concrete vaults at Savannah River and Hanford.

Each weapons site also generated large volumes of low-level and hazardous wastes. The waste was typically disposed of in unlined shallow trenches, as was the case at the Hanford, Savannah River, Idaho, Oak Ridge, and Los Alamos sites and the Nevada Test Site. Alternatively, it was shipped away for burial, as was the practice at the Pinella site in Florida and the Mound and Fernald sites in Ohio. These practices are still followed at facilities that are still operating. Nonradioactive hazardous wastes at most sites are shipped to a commercial facility for treatment and disposal.

Leaking Tanks and Deliberate Dumping

Nowhere is the complexity of the cleanup challenge greater than at Hanford, the nation's most contaminated site. The cost of cleanup at this site

Volume of High-Level Nuclear Waste
(by site, 1988)

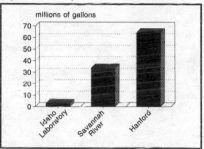

millions of gallons

Source: U.S. Congress, Office of Technology Assessment, *Complex Cleanup: The Environmental Legacy of Nuclear Weapons Production* (U.S. G.P.O., Washington, D.C., 1991), p. 46.

alone is expected to be at least $57 billion—one third to one half of the current total national estimate.

This remote nuclear reservation in southeast Washington state was the site of the world's first full-scale nuclear reactor, which produced plutonium for the bomb dropped on Nagasaki on August 9, 1945. Over half the wastes generated by the nation's nuclear weapons production program are at Hanford.

Production of new plutonium stopped at Hanford in 1987 when N Reactor, the nation's largest weapons reactor, was shut down because of safety concerns and a declining need for plutonium. Now, even recycling of scrap plutonium for nuclear weapons has ceased. This activity would resume only if officials determine that plutonium recycling has a place in Hanford's cleanup plan.

In May 1989, Washington state officials, DOE, and EPA signed an agreement to clean up the Hanford reservation within 30 years—by 2019.

Warhead Production Sites

Rocky Flats

Location: suburbs of Denver, Colorado

Size: 6,550 acres

Status: A Superfund site. Colorado and federal agencies have a cleanup agreement. The plant produced plutonium and beryllium components for weapons, but most production work has shut down, and focus has shifted to cleanup.

Problems: Contaminated groundwater from Rocky Flats may affect drinking water supplies in the Denver suburbs. A series of accidents, spills, and fires at the facility, beginning in the 1950s, has contaminated the area with plutonium and other hazardous elements. Urban sprawl in the Denver area has brought people much closer to the plant than in the 1950s; the majority live downwind.

Mound Plant

Location: Miamisburg, Ohio

Size: 192 acres

Status: A Superfund site. Manufactures small, high-explosive components and radioisotope batteries for bombs. The U.S. Department of Energy (DOE) plans to stop weapons work and shift emphasis to cleanup by 1995 or 1996. Site study, with cooperation of the U.S. Environmental Protection Agency and the state of Ohio, may take eight to nine years. A 12-year-old environmental impact statement is being revised. Cleanup will take about 20 years.

Problems: Groundwater contamination has been found both on- and off-site. Studies note the most serious threat to human health is from contaminated groundwater in a sole-source aquifer. A groundwater monitoring program is tracking the contamination, which is still below maximum allowable levels. Surface water contamination also has been detected on- and off-site, and DOE has taken some steps to prevent its spread. Contaminated soils have also been discovered, but the full scope of the problem has not yet been determined.

Pinellas Plant

Location: St. Petersburg, Florida

Size: 128 acres

Status: Makes neutron triggers for weapons using tritium from Savannah River. DOE plans to halt this work in late 1995 or early 1996 and shift jobs to cleanup. The site does not have Superfund status, but a study identified 14 contaminated areas. No exposure or risk estimates have been conducted.

Problems: Groundwater contamination has been found close to the surface, and studies are under way to determine whether a deeper aquifer, a major regional source of drinking water, has been affected. Discharges at Pinellas include tritium, lead, chromium, and other toxic metals.

Shortly thereafter, DOE also issued its first blueprint for the 30-year national cleanup plan. James Watkins, DOE secretary, said the agency would conduct an open cleanup process allowing public input and would test several new technologies to reduce the cost of cleanup.

Hanford's cleanup problems include leaks in old tanks containing deadly high-level wastes; soil contaminated by highly radioactive liquids that were dumped into unlined trenches or pits; radioactive tritium that has leached from contaminated soil into underground waters and is already entering the Columbia River, a major regional waterway on the eastern boundary of the nuclear reservation; and aging production reactors and chemical reprocessing plants that must be decommissioned in a way that will shield their toxic contents from people and from the Columbia.

In addition, there is the problem of estimating the damage to human

Warhead Production Sites (continued)

Kansas City Plant

Location: Kansas City, Missouri

Size: 320 acres

Status: Manufactures electronic and mechanical weapons components. This facility may play a prominent role in DOE's plans for a smaller, reconfigured weapons complex.

Problems: The entire site is located within an area subject to periodic floods. Hazardous, nonradioactive contaminants have been detected in groundwater, and DOE has installed a "pump-and-treat" system to stop further migration of the contaminated waters. More than 100 groundwater monitoring wells have been drilled. High concentrations of toxic chemicals have been found in a former streambed adjacent to the site.

Soil contaminated with uranium, cadmium, lead, and toxic chemicals has been found on the site. A community outreach program has been established to address concerns of local residents.

Pantex Plant

Location: Amarillo, Texas

Size: 8,960 acres

Status: The final assembly point for U.S. nuclear weapons, Pantex also fabricates larger high-explosive parts and recycles older warheads. With the end of the Cold War, the plant will be active in weapons disassembly. Pantex is not a Superfund site; instead, cleanup is proceeding under federal Resource Conservation and Recovery Act laws.

Problems: Radioactive and chemical contamination has been found in surface ponds, landfills, storage areas, and buildings. No exposure or risk estimates have been concluded. Detailed hydrological studies are planned. Gasoline contamination has been detected in localized water zones below the site. Water and sediments in ditches that drain from the weapons production areas are believed to be contaminated with radioactive materials and chemicals; assessments are under way.

health from past releases of radiation and, perhaps, of compensating the affected individuals.

In the 1940s and 1950s, activities at Hanford exposed thousands of people in communities downwind of the site to large airborne releases of a radioactive form of iodine known as iodine 131. This form of iodine is readily taken into the body, where it accumulates in the thyroid gland and can cause cancer.

The federal government did not declassify and release reports that documented the extent of the area contaminated by these releases until 1986, and did not admit that the doses were large enough to cause significant health risks until 1990.

Many different types of chemicals also were used at Hanford to process nuclear fuels. Of those released into the environment, the greatest concern focuses on such toxic metals as lead, mercury, and cadmium and such chemicals as cyanide, carbon tetrachloride, and a number of chlorinated hydrocarbons. Some of the chemicals eventually break down into harmless materials, but the metals remain dangerous indefinitely.

In the early days of the weapons program, engineers responsible for waste disposal thought radioactive liquids could be safely poured into the ground. Their assumption was that Hanford's arid soils would trap the radiation high above the water table. But this assumption proved incorrect in many cases, especially when the wastes contained certain chemicals as well. Today, the groundwater beneath some 200 square miles of the Hanford site is radioactively contaminated.

Weapons Research Sites

Oak Ridge National Laboratory

Location: Oak Ridge, Tennessee
Size: 58,000 acres
Status: Until recently, the Y-12 plant at Oak Ridge manufactured nuclear weapons components from enriched and depleted uranium and other materials and also recycled retired or obsolete weapons. Today, the plant no longer produces nuclear weapons components. It will continue to dismantle retired weapons and will maintain a capability to produce new weapons components.
Problems: Primarily low-level solid radioactive wastes and mixed wastes were stored in trenches and a landfill. Tritium, cesium 137, and hazardous chemicals have been found in water in the trenches; some contaminants have migrated into groundwater. Radioactive cesium 137 released from Oak Ridge has been found in the sediment of a Tennessee Valley Authority reservoir used for fishing and swimming. Also, more than 1 million pounds of mercury is unaccounted for; much of it has been deposited in the sediment of a creek that traverses the city of Oak Ridge.

Lawrence Livermore National Laboratory

Location: Livermore, California
Size: 7,680 acres
Status: A Superfund site. The U.S. Department of Energy (DOE), U.S. Environmental Protection Agency (EPA), and the state of California have signed a cleanup agreement for this weapons research and development plant. A public-risk assessment addressing soil and groundwater contamination was released in May 1990.
Problems: Soil and groundwater are contaminated with hydrocarbons, some of which has spread beyond the facility boundaries. Gasoline, lead, and chromium have been detected in groundwater, and about 20 local drinking water supply wells have been closed. Water is being treated at two pilot decontamination facilities. Sediments and soils are also being studied.

Los Alamos National Laboratory

Location: Los Alamos, New Mexico
Size: 48,000 acres
Status: A weapons research and development site. A sitewide environmental impact statement was issued in 1979, and annual environmental surveillance reports have been issued since 1980.
Problems: Some shallow wells in canyons contain minimal contamination, but no contamination of the primary aquifer has been found. EPA is studying 15 canyons to determine whether sediments are contaminated, and DOE will be required to study subsurface soils.

When the groundwater contamination was initially discovered in 1945, Hanford officials estimated that it would take 50 years for the contaminated water to reach the Columbia River. That estimate also turned out to be incorrect; within two years it had been revised downward to between 1 and 10 years.

Since 1944, according to a recent DOE estimate, enough water and liquid wastes have been pumped directly into the ground to raise the water table under the Hanford site by 75 feet.

Wastewater containing radioactive materials and hazardous chemicals from cooling systems at old Hanford facilities continues to be dumped into the soil at 33 Hanford locations. DOE plans to discontinue this practice by June 1995.

Scientists are still studying the best way to deal with the dangerous wastes stored at Hanford in 149 old single-shell tanks and 28 newer, double-shell tanks. Immediately after World War II, a now-obsolete processing method produced tremendous quantities of these liquid wastes. Later refinements in processing reduced the volume of wastes but raised their radioactive content. Decay of radioactive materials within these wastes produces tremendous amounts of heat. Chemicals, including nitrates and ferrocyanide, were added to the wastes in an effort to make them less corrosive but served to increase the risk of explosion. A recent DOE study estimated that the tanks contain 208 million curies of radiation, some of it in long-lived forms such as strontium 90, cesium 137, uranium, and plutonium.

Because there was a critical shortage of tanks during the arms buildup of the 1950s, some tank wastes containing high levels of radiation were deliberately discarded into the soil. Hanford managers let high-level wastes "cascade" from tank to tank for lack of storage space. They added chemicals to precipitate out some of the radiation, creating a sludge that settled to the bottom. The remaining liquid was pumped off to a trench or to an unlined open pit known as a crib.

The most highly concentrated chemical and radioactive wastes ever discharged to the ground at Hanford were called "scavenged" wastes. These were produced when liquids from an early processing method were mined, or scavenged, to recover valuable uranium; the remaining wastes were ex-

Disposal Methods Used for Radioactive Wastes

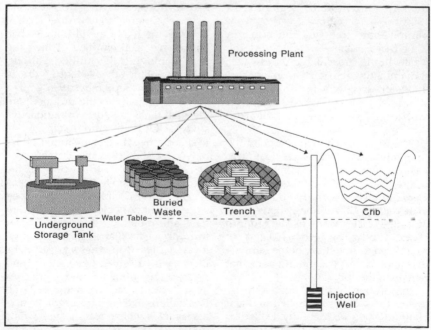

Source: Adapted from U.S. Congress, Office of Technology Assessment, *Complex Cleanup: The Environmental Legacy of Nuclear Weapons Production* (Washington, D.C., February, 1991), p. 25.

Weapons Testing Site

Nevada Test Site
Location: near Las Vegas, Nevada
Size: 864,000 acres
Status: Nuclear weapons have been tested in aboveground and subterranean explosions since the 1950s. There is radioactive and chemical contamination in soil, surface water, groundwater, and sediments. Negotiations are under way between the U.S. Department of Energy (DOE) and the U.S. Environmental Protection Agency (EPA) for a Superfund cleanup.

DOE is studying a site at Yucca Mountain, which straddles the southwest boundary of the Nevada Test Site, for a deep underground repository for commercial spent reactor fuel and high-level weapons wastes. The 1,400-acre reposi-

tory site would occupy both Nevada Test Site property and adjacent land owned by the federal Bureau of Land Management and the U.S. Air Force. DOE's current projections indicate 2010 as the earliest date the repository would open.

Problems: Groundwater contamination has been discovered on the test site, but its full extent is unknown. DOE plans to drill a series of wells over the next decade to measure the contamination. Soil contamination, including 3,000 acres of soil contaminated with plutonium from weapons tests, is believed to be a hazard to the environment and to human health. DOE has taken interim steps to fence off the contaminated bomb craters and other areas and to post warnings.

tremely concentrated. Beginning in 1954, these concentrated wastes were pumped into trenches and cribs; in some cases, cribs were filled until the waste liquids reached groundwater, contaminating it to such an extent that the water exceeded safe drinking water standards. (See diagram, Disposal Methods Used for Radioactive Wastes.)

The EPA, which is in charge of the contaminated soil and water cleanup at Hanford, has begun sampling soil sites where wastes intended for tank storage were dumped. According to EPA estimates, about 127 million gallons of radioactive wastes were discharged into Hanford soils. The agency has not yet completed its inventory of the radioactive and chemical contaminants that remain in the soil.

In addition to these deliberate releases, the older, single-shell tanks at Hanford have accidentally leaked at least 750,000 gallons of wastes into the ground. In 1979, to reduce the chance of future leaks, Hanford managers began to transfer liquids from the old single-shell tanks to new double-shell tanks. Some 105 of the 149 single-shell tanks have been emptied of their liquids, removing 3.5 million gallons. Pumping of the other 44 tanks is due to be finished by September 1996.

What remains in the pumped single-shell tanks is a form of radioactive sludge. DOE is still studying this waste to determine whether it should be removed or stabilized inside the tanks. Developing a plan to dispose of the sludge is expected to take 5 to 10 years.

The newer double-shell tanks used since 1970 have not leaked, but the contents still must be turned into a safer form of waste. Plans call for the low-level wastes from these tanks to be mixed with a cementlike material and poured into underground vaults. At least 44 vaults, each containing 1.4 million gallons of the mixture, will be necessary. DOE began testing such vaults in 1988 and plans to fill 14 more by 1996. The vaults will occupy large areas and require long-term monitoring.

High-level radioactive wastes from double-shell tanks will be poured into stainless steel canisters at the Hanford Waste Vitrification Plant and made into glass. The canisters will be stored at Hanford until they can be shipped to the proposed national waste repository at Yucca Mountain, Nevada.

Meanwhile, tank wastes must be monitored carefully. DOE has been criticized for mismanaging these wastes by several oversight groups, including the agency's own "Tiger Teams," organized by DOE Secretary James Watkins; the U.S. National Academy of Sciences; and the U.S. Of-

> **Cold War Cleanup News**
> Fernald, Ohio, 3/27/92—*Property owners within two miles of the former Fernald uranium processing plant will receive a $73 million settlement from the U.S. Department of Energy (DOE) in compensation for a decline in property value as a result of contamination. DOE estimates that it will take $10 billion and 20 years to complete the radioactive waste cleanup at the site.*

fice of Technology Assessment, the investigative arm of Congress. These groups identified about two dozen important safety issues, including the buildup of potentially explosive hydrogen gas in some of the Hanford tanks and the presence of the chemical ferrocyanide, which increases explosion hazards.

Aging Reactors and Tritium Leaks

The Savannah River Site in South Carolina also presents many cleanup challenges. About 34 million gallons of high-level waste stored in underground tanks await vitrification at a new Defense Waste Processing Facility

under construction there. A waste storage building also has been constructed to store 2,300 canisters of the glass logs that DOE hopes eventually to ship to the proposed Yucca Mountain repository. The low-level portion of these wastes will be pro-cessed in a new Saltstone Manufacturing and Waste Facility at Savannah River and then permanently stored in aboveground concrete vaults on the site.

DOE also plans to keep K Reactor, an old Savannah River production reactor, on standby to produce tritium, the perishable gas used in nuclear warheads. Safety concerns forced the shutdown of Savannah River's tritium reactors in 1988, but DOE restarted the K Reactor to prove it can work safely and then put it on standby while planning for a new replacement reactor.

An accident at Savannah River in December 1991 leaked tritium into the Savannah River, further straining relations between DOE and members of the local community.

Plutonium Pollution

The Rocky Flats Nuclear Munitions Plant near Denver, Colorado, was built in 1951 at the beginning of the government's hydrogen bomb program. Rocky Flats's mission was to manufacture the plutonium fission bombs that trigger thermonuclear warheads. Plutonium, one of the most toxic and long-lived radioactive elements, is at the core of the problems at Rocky Flats.

Spills, accidents, and fires at Rocky Flats have contaminated workers and the surrounding area with plutonium. About 1.4 million people live within 50 miles of the Rocky Flats facility, and when the wind blows, plutonium is distributed over the area.

In 1957, a major fire broke out in filters over the containment devices

Investigating the Health Effects of the Cold War

To address public concerns about health and safety, the federal government is conducting new studies at some of the nuclear weapons production sites. Only a handful of studies of community health impacts of weapons programs have ever been conducted by the U.S. Department of Energy (DOE), and they all have been in response to pressure from citizen groups.

At Hanford, two of the most ambitious and scientifically sophisticated studies ever conducted at a DOE site are under way: the Hanford Environmental Dose Reconstruction Project, funded by DOE, and the Hanford Thyroid Disease Study, a project of the U.S. Centers for Disease Control and the Fred Hutchinson Cancer Research Center in Seattle, Washington. Both studies were requested by officials of the state of Washington, Native American tribes living nearby, and concerned citizens.

The dose study is an effort to reconstruct the possible exposures of people living near Hanford during the Cold War. The first phase of the study indicated that as many as 13,000 children living near Hanford in the late 1940s may have received up to 70 rads of radiation by drinking milk contaminated with iodine 131. Today, U.S. Environmental Protection Agency guidelines call for withholding milk and fresh fruits and vegetables when thyroid doses of 1.5 to 15 rads are anticipated.

For the thyroid study, researchers at the Fred Hutchinson Cancer Research Center in Seattle will compare the health of a group of unexposed people with that of a group who lived downwind of Hanford and were children or teenagers at the time of the heaviest exposures.

Officials at the Idaho National Engineering Laboratory also have planned a dose reconstruction study. This study has been criticized by citizens and Idaho officials because until recently it excluded public participation and did not include all of the facility's historic emissions.

A 1983 pilot study of mercury contamination problems around the Oak Ridge Reservation was conducted by the Centers for Disease Control at the request of Tennessee health officials because of concerns about mercury contamination. The project concluded that people living near the site in the 1980s were not overexposed, but it did support a fishing ban in a nearby creek that had been sought by state authorities and opposed by DOE.

While these studies have begun to give a more precise assessment of the health risks from radioactive waste operations and storage, the U.S. Office of Technology Assessment has called for much more aggressive investigation of public health concerns by independent environmental health professionals.

---

used to prevent plutonium from leaving the plant. The filters had not been changed in four years, and when firefighters turned on the ventilation system, the fire spread. Plant officials did not know how much plutonium escaped. When smokestack monitors were turned on seven days after the fire, they showed that emissions contained radioactivity levels 16,000 times greater than those permitted by safety standards. Soil samples also showed high levels of radioactivity. However, Rocky Flats officials did not inform

state health officials or warn local residents of the accident or the releases of plutonium.

In 1979, leaders of the Colorado Medical Society called for the plant to be relocated. Many protests and demonstrations were held at the gates of the facility. Early in 1989, citing public opposition, DOE released a plan to phase out Rocky Flats by 2010 and closed most of the plant for safety and environmental repairs.

In June 1989, Rocky Flats was raided by agents from the EPA and the Federal

Bureau of Investigation, who sought documents that would establish criminal violations of environmental laws. The raid led to the largest fines ever collected against a weapons contractor. In March 1992, Rockwell International Corporation, the former contractor for the site, pleaded guilty to illegally disposing of radioactive wastes and agreed to pay $18.5 million in fines.

Storing Mixed Wastes

Rocky Flats, Hanford, Savannah River, and other large sites store large volumes of mixed wastes that also contain hazardous wastes subject to RCRA. Under 1984 amendments to RCRA, mixed wastes cannot be buried in the ground unless EPA grants disposers an exemption.

In January 1990, DOE reported to EPA that it had no national facilities to treat these mixed wastes. EPA agreed there was a critical shortage of treatment facilities and granted DOE a two-year extension of RCRA land disposal deadlines, until May 1992. DOE hopes eventually to ship such wastes to the still-unfinished WIPP facility in New Mexico for burial.

Health Threats to Nearby Communities

The DOE says contamination at its nuclear sites poses no immediate threat to surrounding communities. But the Office of Technology Assessment (OTA), the analytical branch of Congress, has challenged this assertion. The OTA asserts that DOE does not have a complete inventory of all its environmental releases, cannot precisely say where they went, and is just beginning health studies intended to estimate the doses of radiation to which members of the public were exposed at a few sites. In addition, OTA says the DOE's conclu-

sions are flawed because health problems would appear gradually, not immediately, and would involve not cancer deaths but more subtle effects, including genetic mutations and reproductive problems.

Public distrust of DOE is very high. Until recently, the agency and its predecessors, the Energy Research and

> **Cold War Cleanup News**
> Lamar County, Mississippi, 12/4/92—A U.S. Department of Energy study will look at the causes of death of Lamar County residents between 1980 and 1990 to try to determine whether underground nuclear detonations in the 1960s could have harmed people near the site. The U.S. Environmental Protection Agency contends that no radioactivity contamination has been detected off site.

Development Administration and the Atomic Energy Commission, avoided notifying the public about deliberate waste releases and withheld news of accidents on the grounds of national security.

Many of the toxic and radioactive contaminants released from these sites are clearly dangerous to public health if absorbed in sufficient quantities. Radiation, in sufficient doses, causes cancer in humans. Many of the heavy metals used in weapons work also are potent threats to human health: lead causes nerve damage and birth defects, mercury can damage the central nervous system, and chromium is a potent carcinogen. (See box, Investigating the Health Effects of the Cold War.) Despite these potential dangers to human health, there are very few scientific studies that establish the doses of toxic materials to which the public around the weapons plants may have been exposed.

Cleanup Agreements, Decrees, or Consort Orders at Nuclear Weapon Sites

Site	Participants	Date of Signing
Fernald	DOE, EPA	July 1986
	DOE, state	December 1988
	DOE, state	December 1988
Hanford	DOE, state	May 1989
Idaho National Engineering Lab	DOE, EPA	July 1987
Kansas City Plant	DOE, EPA	June 1989
Lawrence Livermore National Laboratory	DOE, EPA, state	November 1988
Los Alamos National Laboratory	DOE, state	Under negotiation
Mound Plant	DOE, EPA	Under negotiation
	DOE, state	Under negotiation
	DOE, state	Under negotiation
Nevada Test Site	DOE, EPA, state	Under negotiation
	DOE, state	Under negotiation
Oak Ridge Reservation	DOE, EPA	Under negotiation
	DOE, EPA, state	1983
Rocky Flats Plant	DOE, EPA, state	July 1986
	DOE, state	June 1989
	DOE, EPA, state	December 1989
Savannah River Site	DOE, state	February 1989
	DOE, EPA	July 1987
	DOE, state	May 1988
	DOE, EPA, state	Under negotiation

Source: U.S. Congress, Office of Technology Assessment, *Complex Cleanup: The Environmental Legacy of Nuclear Weapons Production* (U.S. G.P.O., Washington, D.C., 1991).

Lawsuits and Liability Questions

Lawsuits involving several sites, including Hanford, Rocky Flats, and the Fernald site in Ohio, have been filed on behalf of "downwinders"—people living near the facilities who claim their health, crops, and neighborhoods were damaged by exposure to radiation and toxic chemicals.

Under federal law, the government weapons program is largely immune from lawsuits. Others who have sued the government have lost, including people living in small towns downwind from the Nevada Test Site who contracted leukemia after they were exposed to fallout from bomb tests and Native Americans working in uranium mines who later developed lung cancer. Congress passed legislation to compensate these groups as well as some others.

Recently, lawsuits against DOE and its private contractors have been filed by people who lived near Hanford in the 1940s and 1950s, the years of heaviest releases of iodine 131 and other radioactive materials from Hanford's reprocessing plants. In July 1990, after the first phase of a Hanford study on radiation releases was made public, Energy Secretary James Watkins admitted that the Cold War-era releases of iodine 131 from Hanford were large enough to be a health risk to people living nearby at the time of the releases.

How Much Will the Cleanup Cost?

Since the full scope of the environmental problems at the nuclear weapons sites is still unknown, estimates of the cleanup costs are still uncertain. But the total cost is certain to be huge. A Five-Year Plan issued by the U.S. Department of Energy (DOE) calls for expenditures of more than $30 billion for fiscal years 1992 through 1996. According to an authoritative report from the congressional Office of Technology Assessment, however, such expenditures "represent only the discovery phase of a program that could require hundreds of billions of dollars to complete."

What is certain is that environmental cleanup and restoration will absorb an increasingly large fraction of the DOE budget and that current cleanup expenditures are certain to rise.

The DOE Cleanup Budget

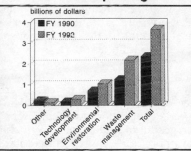

Source: U.S. Congress, Office of Technology Assessment, *Complex Cleanup: The Environmental Legacy of Nuclear Weapons Production* (U.S. G.P.O., Washington, D.C., 1991) p. 56.

Colorado health officials have negotiated an agreement with DOE and EPA to conduct health studies around Rocky Flats once the site's environmental pollution problems have been characterized. Idaho has signed a similar "agreement in principle" to conduct health studies.

At the Fernald Feed Materials Production Center near Cincinnati, Ohio, metallic uranium ingots, rods, and tubes had been manufactured since the 1950s. In the mid-1980s, after learning that their communities had been contaminated by airborne uranium dust and by radiation in groundwater, nearby residents filed suit against the plant operators. The suit was settled for $73 million in 1989. The U.S. Centers for Disease Control in Atlanta, Georgia, plans a dose reconstruction study of uranium emissions from Fernald.

Cleanup Costs and Timing

As DOE plans the costly cleanup program, Congress, environmental groups, and citizen activists are pointing out problem areas. DOE needs to use its budget effectively in an era of huge federal budget deficits, and elected officials do not want the agency to repeat problems with the Superfund, where little real cleanup has been achieved despite years of costly studies. (See box, How Much Will the Cleanup Cost?)

Budget constraints may make it impossible to remove all contaminants from groundwater and completely clean deeply buried soils, and many sites may never be returned to a condition adequate for unrestricted public access.

One debate concerns the proposed $1.6 billion Hanford Vitrification Plant. DOE wants to move ahead with construction of a full-scale plant, but the Office of Technology Assessment and some environmental groups say it might be prudent instead to build a pilot plant to make sure the technology will work.

There are political problems as well. DOE faces substantial opposition in Nevada and New Mexico to its two waste repository projects and a resulting backlash among western governors, who are reluctant to accept more defense wastes for "interim" storage when the future of the two permanent repositories is uncertain.

Transuranic waste from Rocky Flats, the Mound Plant in Ohio, and other sites, for example, have for years been shipped to the Idaho National Engineering Laboratory for "temporary" storage. But in September 1989, Idaho Governor Cecil Andrus closed state borders to additional wastes. Threatened with federal lawsuits, Andrus later dropped his opposition, and Idaho once again began accepting defense wastes from out of state.

Even if no additional waste is moved across state borders for temporary storage, it will take 20 years for waste now stored at the weapons site to be trucked to the new WIPP. DOE's deadlines to open both the WIPP and the Nevada repositories have repeatedly slipped. The WIPP was originally supposed to open in 1988, and DOE now says Yucca Mountain will not be ready until at least 2010 and probably 2015.

These delays mean that periods of temporary storage of wastes at the weapons production sites could be much longer than the public has been led to believe. Until safe long-term storage is achieved, DOE will be faced with the increasingly unpopular necessity of storing radioactive materials at the weapons sites for long periods.

In addition, DOE also faces questions about worker safety during cleanup activities. Thousands of workers could be exposed to potentially harmful substances during environmental sampling, cleanup of soil and groundwater, and decontamination and decommissioning of buildings and reactors.

Existing laws do not address all the contamination at the weapons sites. For instance, there are no federal standards for allowable limits of radiation in soil—a major problem at many sites, including Hanford, Savannah River, Rocky Flats, and the Idaho site. Proposed guidelines for contamination of soil by transuranics were issued by EPA in 1979 and then withdrawn. EPA now estimates it will be 5 to 10 years before new guidelines are issued.

With these and other uncertainties, the Office of Technology Assessment has told Congress that DOE's stated goal of cleaning up all the nuclear weapons sites within 30 years is unrealistic. This environmental legacy of the Cold War will live on for at least another generation.

Author Karen Dorn Steele is on leave from the Spokesman-Review *newspaper in Spokane, Washington, to write a book on nuclear waste issues, with the aid of a grant from the Mac-Arthur Foundation.*

Ecotourism

Rising interest in nature vacations has mixed results for host countries and the resources they promote.

Eager to experience nature firsthand, more and more tourists are abandoning traditional "fun in the sun" vacations for treks into the Himalayas, bird watching in the Central American rainforest, and archaeological digs in the American Southwest. This growing trend of traveling to relatively remote and unspoiled areas without the usual vacation luxuries and trappings has come to be called nature travel, or ecotourism.

Even closer to home, many of the millions of visitors to U.S. national parks come to see natural splendors and wildlife or to experience nature firsthand. The national parks have become so popular and the visitors so numerous—especially at some parks—that they threaten the very environmental qualities and the sense of contact with nature that draw tourists from the United States and from other countries. (See table, Most Visited U.S. National Parks, 1990.)

In part because of this crowding, perhaps, increasing numbers of Americans are going abroad as ecotourists. Some of this travel is due to enormous growth in the overall travel industry

Most Visited U.S. National Parks, 1990

National Park	Number of Visits
Great Smoky Mountains (Tennessee)	8,151,769
Grand Canyon (Arizona)	3,776,685
Yosemite (California)	3,124,939
Yellowstone (Wyoming)	2,823,872
Olympic (Washington)	2,794,903
Rocky Mountain (Colorado)	2,647,323
Zion (California)	2,102,400
Glacier (Montana)	1,986,737
Mammoth Cave (Kentucky)	1,924,538
Shenandoah (Virginia)	1,771,780

Source: U.S. Department of the Interior, National Park Service, Socio-Economic Studies Division, Denver, February 1991.

during the past decade, but demand for educational and nature-oriented tours, and travel to exotic locations is clearly on the rise.

A World Wildlife Fund (WWF) survey of nearly 500 travelers to Costa Rica, Mexico, Belize, Ecuador, and the Dominican Republic found that 46 percent came specifically to visit protected wilderness areas. Ecotourism has become a phenomenon significant enough to merit its own organization. The Ecotourism Society, based in Alexandria, Virginia, is dedicated to "conserving natural environments and sustaining the well-being of local people through responsible travel."

Responsible ecotravel ranges from actually participating in scientific research to visiting a natural site in an environmentally sound way. A good ecotourist, while appreciating the glories of nature, does nothing to impinge upon or compromise it. The traveler also contributes something to the place visited, whether through his or her own labors or through economic benefits to local inhabitants.

Bird watching and wildlife observing are far and away the most popular activities for nature tourists. Kenya, with its grand and impressive animals, has long been one of the most popular destinations. More than 30 percent of Kenya's foreign exchange is from tourism, more than from exports of either coffee or tea.

In recent years Central and South American countries also have been attracting increasing numbers of tourists. Costa Rica and Ecuador are now two of the most popular wildlife destinations. Although they lack the allure of elephants and lions, Central and South America offer such diverse and exotic attractions as the iguanas and the blue-footed boobies of the Galápagos, the brilliantly plumed quetzals of Costa Rica, and elusive jaguars. Besides these famous animals, the rainforests of Central and South America contain the most diverse vegetation in the world. (See table, Popular International Destinations and Activities.)

Why are travelers abandoning their flip-flops and piña coladas for hiking boots and water bottles? Many people have become bored with spending two weeks sitting on the beach or by the pool. They want adventure, discovery, and stimulation. At the same time, many seek respite from the crowding and fast pace of their daily existence and are searching for destinations offering unspoiled scenery and a chance to rediscover nature.

Beyond these reasons is increasing concern for the environment and recognition that many unique natural environments are vanishing. Many travelers want to become part of an ecological solution, not problem, and they see ecotourism as a painless and enjoyable way to give something back to the natural environment.

Popular International Destinations and Activities
(for U.S.-based tour operators)

Activity	Percentage of Operators Involved	Destinations In Order of Preference
Trekking/hiking	72	Nepal Kenya Tanzania China
Bird watching	66	Kenya Mexico Costa Rica Tanzania
Nature photography	66	Kenya Tanzania
Wildlife safaris	63	Kenya Tanzania Nepal
Camping	60	Kenya Tanzania
Mountain climbing	41	Nepal Kenya Tanzania
Fishing	38	Costa Rica
River rafting/ canoeing/ kayaking	34	Nepal Puerto Rico
Botanical study	31	Mexico Puerto Rico

Source: Karen A. Ziffer, *Ecotourism: The Uneasy Alliance* (Conservation International, Ernst Young, Fall 1989), Exhibit 11, n.p.
Note: Other nature-oriented activities promoted by U.S.-based ecotourism guides include archaeological study, deep sea activities, spelunking, boat trips to uninhabited islands, orchid study, butterfly watching, and four-wheel-drive excursions.

The Economics of Ecotravel

For the host countries, which are almost universally less developed and poorer than the home countries of their visitors, ecotourism offers the potential for high economic benefit. Estimates of the amount of money generated by ecotourism run as high as $30 billion a year—although the amount kept by the host countries varies tremendously, as we shall see. Nature travelers generally have plenty of money to spend and, according to a WWF study, are more willing to spend than other tourists.

By offering an economic incentive for preserving natural areas, ecotourism provides developing countries with an alternative to the logging and slash and-burn farming that result in deforestation and destruction of natural ecosystems. The profits generated from viewing wildlife are economic justification for protecting species that might not be guarded otherwise. A study of Amboseli National Park in Kenya determined that each lion there was worth $27,000 and each elephant herd worth $610,000 in tourist revenue per year. Tourism in the Galápagos

> **Ecotourism News**
> Kigali, Rwanda, 4/29/92—*Mrithi, a 400-pound male mountain gorilla seen in the film* Gorillas in the Mist *and by thousands of Western tourists to the country, has been found shot to death. The gorilla apparently was shot by accident by either a Rwandan soldier or a rebel. Sporadic fighting in and around the forest habitat of the gorillas has been continuing since early 1991.*

now brings Ecuador as much as $180 million a year.

One of the most dramatic examples of the environmental benefit of ecotourism is in Rwanda, where tourism is largely responsible for saving that nation's gorillas from extinction. The gorilla was threatened by both poachers and local farmers, whose land-clearing practices were destroying the gorilla's natural habitat. Rwanda's Parc des Volcans, created by Dian Fossey as a wildlife preserve, has become an international attraction and the third largest source of foreign exchange for Rwanda. Revenues from the $170-a-day fee that visitors pay to enter the park have allowed the government to create antipoaching patrols and employ local farmers as park guides and guards.

But ecotourism is not a free lunch. It takes a tremendous amount of planning and organization to attract enough tourists to make money and still maintain the unspoiled nature of wildlands. Revenues from tourism are also unpredictable, with seasonal ebbs and flows. Worse, simply opening the doors to tourists without foresight can easily destroy the natural resources many developing countries are seeking to promote.

Stresses to Nature and Natives

Once a protected area becomes a tourist attraction, the environment is threatened. Kenya's Amboseli Park, for instance, receives more than 200,000 visitors a year, many of them day trippers from Nairobi who drive frantically around the park trying to see the "big five" animals (elephant, lion, leopard, cape buffalo, and rhinoceros) in just a few hours. At times, a virtual swarm of jeeps and buses surrounds a handful of animals, while cameras click and video cameras buzz. The number of cheetahs in Amboseli has declined to fewer than eight; these streamlined cats have changed their hunting patterns from dawn and dusk

Annapurna National Park

Those who crossed the mountains of Nepal were once a rare subset of world travelers. Then, in the 1970s and 1980s, trekking in the Himalayas became a popular and accessible activity among the young and robust. Before 1965, fewer than 10,000 tourists visited Nepal each year. By 1987, the number had risen to 240,080.

Unfortunately, in their quest for adventure, trekkers have damaged this fragile mountain environment. The demand for firewood, the main source of fuel among the sky-high lodges where tourists stay, soared as increasing numbers of travelers required hot meals and baths. According to the World Wildlife Fund, the demand for fuel and building material by lodge operators and trekking groups pushed back the timberline by several hundred feet. Entire ridges that were recently covered with rhododendron now are barren.

Careless trekkers have ventured off the trails, destroying vegetation, and have created their own trails of discarded tin cans and packaging. Exotic animals such as hog deer, tahr (a wild goat), and goral (a type of goat antelope) are being hunted in increasing numbers. And deforestation is destroying the natural habitat of the rare snow leopard and the red panda.

To combat the destruction, Nepal created the Annapurna Conservation Area Project in 1986. This grassroots organization encourages villagers to take greater responsibility for their environment. One of the project's goals is to train lodge owners in environmentally sound methods of hotel management, such as using fuel-efficient water heaters instead of burning timber. Solar panels have been erected in a few areas for this purpose. The project's members are further countering deforestation by providing free seedlings for volunteers to plant.

The thousands of trekkers whose visits are responsible for the cycle of destruction have also been targeted. One of the project's most significant steps was to ban wood burning by trekkers and require them to use kerosene stoves instead. The switch to kerosene may save more than 3,500 pounds of wood per day.

to the middle of the day to avoid the hordes of tourists.

Tens of thousands of visitors to the Galápagos are threatening the ecosystem in a variety of ways. About 100 new plant species have been introduced to the islands, threatening to kill off indigenous ones. Animals such as the sea lion and the albatross have exhibited behavioral changes since the dramatic rise in tourism.

Beyond the threats to wildlife is the threat to local cultures and people. Some critics argue that Westerners corrupt remote and primitive societies merely through their presence by creating the desire for the kind of materialistic wealth more common to industrialized countries. Others claim that even when travelers come with the noblest of intentions—to help indigenous cultures solve their problems—they actually contribute to what has been called neo-colonialism, the imposition of Western values on cultures and practices in developing countries.

More directly, local people may be displaced when an area is designated a protected area for tourist travel. Even if residents are not told to leave, they may be forced out as the influx of tour-

International Tourist Arrivals, 1990
(by world region)

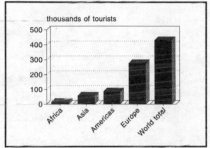

Source: World Tourism Organization, as cited in World Conservation Monitoring Centre, *Global Biodiversity: Status of the Earth's Living Resources*, Brian Groombridge, ed. (Chapman & Hall, London, 1992), Table 27.3, p. 414.

ists drives up the cost of living. The reverse can be just as damaging: Nationals from throughout the country may flock to a popular new tourist area in an attempt to get their share of the newfound wealth. In the Galápagos, for example, the islands' population has tripled in the past decade.

Unfortunately, many local inhabitants never see the money generated by

---

The National Audubon Society's Travel Ethics for Environmentally Responsible Travel

1. Wildlife and their habitats must not be disturbed.
2. Audubon tourism to natural areas will be sustainable.
3. Waste disposal must have neither environmental nor aesthetic impacts.
4. The experience a tourist gains in traveling with Audubon must enrich his or her appreciation of nature, conservation, and the environment.
5. Audubon tours must strengthen the conservation effort and enhance the natural integrity of places visited.
6. Traffic in products that threaten wildlife and plant populations must not occur.
7. The sensibilities of other cultures must be respected.

Source: Reprinted with permission of the National Audubon Society.

A Sampling of Ecotours

All sorts of groups offer vacations with ecological themes: universities, for-profit travel companies, nonprofit environmental organizations, and hiking and nature societies. Some groups, such as The Nature Conservancy, require you to join before taking a trip. Many of the trips are priced to include a tax-deductible contribution to some type of conservation effort. If you do volunteer work, part or all of the trip's cost may be tax deductible.

A recent report from Conservation International estimates that more than 5,000 tour operators are involved with nature or adventure travel. Plenty of travel companies with no experience are jumping on the ecotourism bandwagon, so the prefix "eco" in a group or company name does not necessarily mean much. (See box, How to Choose an Ecotour.) Here is a sampling of groups with good track records.

Earthwatch
680 Mount Auburn Street
Box 403-N
Watertown, MA 02272
(800) 776-0188

International Expeditions
1 Environs Park
Helena, AL 35080
(800) 633-4734

Journeys International
4011 Jackson Road
Ann Arbor, MI 48103
(800) 255-8735

Mountain Travel/Sobek
6420 Fairmount Avenue
El Cerrito, CA 94530
(800) 227-2384

National Audubon Society
Travel Programs
950 Third Avenue
New York, NY 10022
(212) 546-9140

The Nature Conservancy
1815 North Lynn Street
Arlington, VA 22209
(703) 841-5300

Oceanic Society Expeditions
Ft. Mason Center, Bldg. E
San Francisco, CA 94123
(415) 441-1106

Overseas Adventure Travel
349 Broadway
Cambridge, MA 02139
(800) 221-0814

Sierra Club Outing Department
730 Polk Street
San Francisco, CA 94109
(415) 923-5630

Smithsonian Research
Expedition Program
490 L'Enfant Plaza, S.W.
Suite 4210
Washington, DC 20560
(202) 287-3210

University Research
Expeditions Program
University of California
2223 Fulton Street
Berkeley, CA 94720
(510) 642-6586

Victor Emanuel Nature Tours
P.O. Box 33008
Austin, TX 78764
(800) 328-8368

Wilderness Travel
801 Allston Way
Berkeley, CA 94710
(800) 247-6700

World Wildlife Fund
Membership Travel Program
1250 24th Street, N.W.
Washington, DC 20037
(202) 293-4800

nature tourism in their area. If the region in which a natural attraction is located is sparsely developed, the country may end up importing the goods and services required to support the tourist trade. This means that all too often, the profits leak back to the industrialized world through the tour operators, the airlines, and other sources of necessary services and goods.

The World Bank has estimated that 55 percent of gross tourism revenues to the developing world actually accrue to developed countries. In some areas, the leakage is even worse. For instance, one study found that less than 10 cents of every tourist dollar spent in the popular Annapurna region of Nepal stays there. More of these dollars can be kept within the host country if parks and businesses use local goods and services as much as possible, and if development related to tourism, such as lodging and food service, is based on local materials, cuisine, and foodstuffs and on the expertise of local villagers. To succeed, the three links in the ecotourism chain— the host nation, tour operators, and the tourists themselves —must all work to protect the wilderness and local cultures.

Seeking a Balance

Many nations are trying to follow the examples of a few countries that have learned how to satisfy tourists while maintaining the environment and stoking the economy. Costa Rica, for example, has devoted over 12 percent of its land to national parks and deliberately manages for protection of biodiversity, as well as for tourism. Managers of the Great Barrier Reef, a 1,243-mile-long coral reef ecosystem off the northeastern coast of Australia, provide another example in which careful planning for a variety of uses has paid off.

The Great Barrier Reef Marine Park Authority, based in Canberra, Australia, is set up to respond to a number of interest groups and the environmental pressures to the reef that they represent. The Authority is advised by a consultative committee made up of representatives from groups with a vested interest in the reef and the surrounding ocean waters: fishermen, politicians, tour guides, aborigines, scientists, and conservationists. Special zones, established to keep different uses separate from one another, have so far worked well. The Marine Park

---

How to Choose an Ecotour

Choosing a reliable and responsible tour operator is one of the most important decisions you can make when planning an environmentally oriented trip. Questions to ask include:

● How large is the tour, and what is the ratio of tourists to tour guides?

● Are the guides local? Do they speak the language of the country being visited? Are any of the guides trained naturalists?

● How long has the company been in operation? How long has it been taking tourists to your destination? Will the company provide references?

● Does the company seek to reduce the environmental impact of tourists? What form of transportation will you be using? How will garbage be disposed?

● Does the tour respect local customs and culture?

● Will you be staying in modest lodgings or in big hotels? Can the tour operator ensure that some of your money will benefit the local community?

● Is part of your fee contributed to a local conservation project?

Sources: The Ecotourism Society and Conservation International.

How Important Are the Issues Facing U.S. National Parks?
(opinion poll)

Issue	Percent Citing as Major Issue
Preserving wildlife	91
Reintroducing native and endangered species	76
Visitor safety	75
Threats from commercial developers	74
Need for park maintenance	69
Attracting a quality park work force	62
Quality visitor facilities and services	57

Source: Research & Forecasts, Inc., *Citibank MasterCard and Visa Report on Our National Parks: Preserving a Priceless Heritage*, 1991, p. 27.
Note: The poll reflects the responses of 1,006 adults asked to rate increasingly complex issues faced by the National Park Service regarding park management and protection.

Authority's power to enforce the zoning uses even takes precedence over most state and federal legislation that might conflict with park goals.

Developing countries are coming to realize they must have a long-term plan that incorporates the interests and participation of local populations. According to an extensive report by WWF, ecotourism can become a tool for conservation and rural development only if local people are directly involved and directly benefit.

By encouraging travelers to use local guides, patronize local hotels and restaurants, and fly on national airlines, host countries keep more of their tourist money. To increase revenues and control visitor capacity, many countries are considering raising entrance fees to parks and reserves, which are generally very low.

Tour operators can do their part to protect local cultures and environments by promoting trips that follow sound ecological principles and by helping travelers understand and appreciate the culture and nature of the place they are visiting. Ethical guidelines developed by the National Audubon Society for all trips under its sponsorship have become a standard for the field. (See box, The National Audubon Society's Travel Ethics for Environmentally Responsible Travel.) The best ecotour operators not only advocate treading lightly but also donate a portion of their profits to protect the sites they visit. For instance, International Expeditions, based in Helena, Alabama, sponsors rainforest workshops for ecotravelers at Peru's Amazon Biosphere Reserve. The proceeds help support biological research, con-

Ecotourism News
Yellowstone National Park, Wyo., 8/3/92—*Development pressures are threatening Yellowstone National Park on several fronts. To the north, 165,000 acres of privately held timberland inside Gallatin National Forest are being sold to an Oregon firm and may be logged or otherwise developed. To the northeast just a few miles outside the park, a proposal to open a major gold mine could affect water quality inside the park. Even inside the park, Yellowstone's very popularity—a record 3 million people were expected in 1992—may adversely affect Yellowstone's grizzly bear population.*

servation, and education at the Amazon Center for Environmental Education and Research.

A key component of responsible travel is choosing a tour operator who is sensitive to the environment. But individuals must assume responsibility too. To get the most out of a trip—and leave the smallest footprint on the site's environment—tourists should learn as much about the ecology and ethnology of their destinations as possible before they depart. While visiting preserves and parks, they should follow basic rules such as staying on designated trails, not disturbing animals to get a great picture, and not bribing guides to bend the rules.

Tourism in U.S. National Parks

For many people, traveling abroad to experience nature is not a practical option. Nor is it necessary. The U.S. National Park system is among the largest and best maintained in the world, regularly attracting millions of foreign visitors. National forests offer even more opportunities for hiking, mountain climbing, and camping. Other uses of the national forests such as mining, logging, and cattle grazing are, in fact, coming under increasing pressure, and not just from environmentalists. In the region near Yellowstone and Grand

Trends in Park Visits for Recreation
(U.S. National Parks)

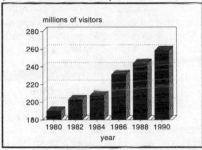

Source: U.S. Department of the Interior, *National Park Service Statistical Abstract 1990*, Socio-Economic Studies, Denver, n.d.

Teton national parks, for example, tourism and recreational development based on the quality and beauty of the environment are increasingly being viewed by both economic planners and local residents as a more profitable direction for the region's economic future than cattle ranching.

How You Can Help Our National Parks

Beyond sorting trash into recycling bins, there are several ways park visitors can help sustain the fragile park ecosystems. Here are some tips:

● Try not to visit during the peak season. Parks are far less crowded in May or September. Consider visiting one of the lesser known but no less spectacular parks such as Bighorn Canyon Recreational Area in Montana.

● Try to minimize driving. Slow down, and don't try to see everything.

● Use only designated campgrounds.

● Use biodegradable soap.

● Don't litter—pack out what you pack in.

● Use toilets when possible. Otherwise, bury your waste.

● Don't touch artifacts or remove branches or plants from the park.

● Don't feed, touch, annoy, or get too close to animals.

But there can be too much of a good thing. During the peak vacation months of July and August, the traffic trying to enter popular parks such as Yellowstone and Yosemite resembles the city gridlock many travelers are attempting to escape. More than 250 million people visited national parks in 1990, about 20 percent more than a decade ago. (See graph, Trends in Park Visits for Recreation.) This huge volume of visitors leaves behind an equally impressive volume of garbage. People stray from the trails, harass the animals, and blare music from their radios. Fumes from their cars and recreational vehicles permeate the air.

As environmental concerns gain importance among Americans, more people are saying that preserving the natural beauty of our parklands is a higher priority to them than recreational pursuits, according to a recent survey on the park system by the National Park Foundation. Survey respondents said the top two issues facing the National Park Service should be preserving wildlife and reintroducing native and endangered species of plants and animals. (See table, How Important Are the Issues Facing U.S. National Parks?)

One way park officials have responded to environmental pressure has been to step up recycling programs to handle the garbage that campers leave behind. Recycling is being heavily promoted in most of the major parks, including the Grand Canyon, Acadia, the Great Smoky Mountains, Yosemite, Mount Rainier, and the National Mall in Washington, D.C. More than 220 tons of plastic, glass, aluminum, and other products were recycled by the parks in 1991. Aside from reducing waste, the products made from recycled materials have provided the parks with needed benches, picnic tables, and trail markers.

For More Information

The following books may be available in libraries, or they can be ordered from your local bookstore.

Eco Vacations: Enjoy Yourself and Save the Earth, by Evelyn Kaye, Blue Penguin Publications, 1991.

Environmental Vacations: Volunteer Projects to Save the Planet, 2nd ed., by Stephanie Ocko, John Muir, 1992.

Volunteer Vacations, 3rd ed., by Bill McMillon, Chicago Review Press, 1991.

Ecotourism: The Potentials & Pitfalls, 2 vols. by Elizabeth Boo, World Wildlife Fund, 1990.

EarthTrips: A Guide to Nature Travel on a Fragile Planet, by Dwight Holing, Conservation International, Living Planet Press, 1991.

This chapter was written by Elizabeth Stark, a writer based in Washington, D.C.

Wildlife

Debate over the role of the Endangered Species Act has polarized the supporters of habitat preservation and those with economic concerns. Is there a middle ground?

In the two decades since it was enacted, the Endangered Species Act (ESA), the centerpiece of U.S. wildlife law, has rarely been amended by Congress. In 1992, however, a range of economic interests united to force major changes in the highly popular law as Congress prepared to debate its reauthorization. Conservationists rallied in defense.

The emotionally charged debate focused public attention on a fundamental question: As people and economic activity fill every corner of the landscape, how much biological diversity can or should be preserved? The ESA prohibits hunting, harassment, collection, or capture of any species determined to be endangered or threatened and requires the U.S. Fish and Wildlife Service (FWS) to start programs to recover each species listed. All federal agencies must ensure that their actions, including those on federal lands considered critical habitat, do not harm any plant or animal species listed as threatened or endangered.

Critics charge that trying to save all endangered species ends up saving none. Since 1973, fewer than 20 species have had their status improved from endangered to threatened or been removed from the list. (See table, Delisted U.S. Species.)

ESA opponents believe the Act goes too far, blocking economic progress, trampling on property rights, and jeopardizing livelihoods. On the Gulf Coast, shrimp fishermen protest federally required turtle excluder devices, saying the costly equipment—which allows endangered sea turtles to escape from shrimp nets—reduces their catch. California real estate developers vie for the commercially valuable coastal habitat of the small, blue-gray bird called the California gnatcatcher, which has been proposed for listing as endangered.

In the past, listings of species rarely affected more than a specific activity or project. Recently, however, the ESA

> **Wildlife News**
> Boston, 3/18/92—*An environmental lawsuit forcing the government to develop a plan to restore depleted stocks of cod, haddock and flounder off New England has fishermen up in arms. The plan would force fishermen to stop fishing several months a year and to use larger-mesh nets so that younger fish could escape. Fishermen in towns like New Bedford, Massachusetts, protested that the plan would have a devastating effect on the industry.*

has begun to affect entire regions, notably the Northwest. Loggers there fear major job losses from reduced timber cuts in publicly owned old-growth forests that harbor the threatened northern spotted owl and along rivers where endangered and threatened salmon run. Farmers, industrialists, and fishermen worry how efforts to restore salmon runs will cost their businesses. (See box, Can Salmon Be Restored to Western Rivers?) Should preservation of a single species slow or stop economic activities that provide jobs and other benefits to thousands of people?

Backers dispute that the ESA hinders economic activity. A World Wildlife Fund study shows that only 18 out of 2,000 projects or activities evaluated by the FWS from 1986 to 1991 for impacts on endangered species were blocked or withdrawn. In fact, the ESA permits landowners to work out "habitat conservation plans" that permit development while protecting listed species. The Northwest has lost more timber jobs to the automation of timber

Delisted U.S. Species
(through 1991)

Species Name	Reason for Delisting
Butterfly, Bahama swallowtail	Original data in error
Cactus, purple-spined hedgehog	Original data in error
Cisco, longjaw (fish)	Extinct
Dove, Palau	Recovered
Duck, Mexican	Original data in error
Fantail, Palau (bird)	Recovered
Gambusia, Amistad (fish)	Extinct
Milk-vetch, Rydberg (plant)	Recovered
Owl, Palau	Recovered
Pupfish, Tecopa	Extinct
Pearly mussel, Sampson's	Extinct
Pelican, brown	Recovered (Southeast population)
Pike, blue	Extinct
Sparrow, dusky seaside	Extinct
Sparrow, Santa Barbara song	Extinct
Treefrog, Pine Barrens	Original data in error

Source: U.S. Fish and Wildlife Service, as cited in General Accounting Office, *Endangered Species Act Report* (GAO/RCED-92-131BR, Washington, D.C.), p. 38.

cutting and milling, increased exports of raw logs, and a shift of the industry to the U.S. Southeast than it will from the listing of the spotted owl. Shrimpers in the Gulf of Mexico, required to use turtle excluder devices during 1990 and 1991, caught more pounds of shrimp per day fished than in the previous three years, when the devices were not required.

ESA supporters present a very different picture of the Act's goals. In the last 200 years, the United States has lost half its wetlands, 90 percent of its northwestern old-growth forests, and 99 percent of its tallgrass prairie. Possibly as many as 490 species of native plants and animals vanished as a result, and another 9,000 species of U.S. plants and animals are now at risk. (See graph, Threatened and Endangered U.S. Wildlife Species.)

The ESA has dramatically slowed the rate of extinction. Sixty U.S. endangered species are now increasing in number or expanding their ranges, including species once reduced to a few individuals, such as the whooping crane, red wolf, and black-footed ferret. Many other species have stabilized.

Progress has come cheaply, supporters maintain. The FWS budget for endangered species in 1991—$39 million—equaled government spending for just 1 mile of urban interstate.

Preventive Medicine

For good or ill, the ESA is the one legal mechanism in the United States that can force communities to balance conservation with development. Whether the ESA should play this role is hotly disputed. Both sides would probably agree that waiting until species become endangered makes their recovery difficult and economic impacts on communities more severe.

Threatened and Endangered U.S. Wildlife Species
(1974–91)

Source: U.S. Fish and Wildlife Service, unpublished data.

Ideally, the ESA should serve as an "emergency room" for species on the decline, but only if we also practice preventive medicine, say conservationists, by helping healthy populations of wildlife before they get in trouble. The United States, however, currently spends most of its wildlife dollars to manage game and endangered species, shortchanging the 85 to 90 percent of all species still in good shape. In 1986, state agencies spent 20 times more on management of game species than on nongame species.

Traditionally, nations have protected a cross section of wildlife by setting aside habitat in reserves and parks. In the United States, the National Wildlife Refuge System—470 refuges from the frigid Alaskan coast to tropical Puerto Rico—protects more than 90 million acres.

Yet, in many eyes, the demand for recreation and other uses is jeopardizing that system. Water sports, such as jet skiing, may have driven away the last colony of frigate birds from the Key West National Wildlife Refuge in Florida. Oil and gas operations may harm endangered whooping cranes in Texas's Aransas National Wildlife Refuge. Recent battles over wildlife refuges range from leasing refuge land for an Alabama golf course to congressional debate on opening 2,300 square miles of the Alaska National Wildlife Refuge to oil drilling.

Refuges 2003

Mirroring debate on the ESA last year were public comments on "Refuges 2003"—a U.S. effort to establish clearer priorities for the refuge system. Thousands of citizens, responding to a number of FWS-presented options, registered opinions that varied from encouraging stricter wildlife preservation to increasing recreational and commercial use.

The aims of the refuge system have greatly broadened over time—from sanctuaries for nesting birds, waterfowl, and big game to recreation areas for hunting, boating, and hiking, to sources of minerals and oil and critical habitat for endangered species.

According to a 1989 General Accounting Office study, nearly 60 percent of national wildlife refuges allow activities harmful to wildlife and habitat, including military bombing runs, logging, off-road vehicle use, jet skiing, and mining. Outside factors, such as oil spills, air and water pollution, wandering livestock, weeds, and introduced species, can be equally damaging.

Most refuges no longer safeguard wildlife, said a 1992 Defenders of Wildlife study. It recommended that ref-

---

Can Salmon Be Restored to Western Rivers?

Flowing from British Columbia, Montana, and Idaho through Washington to the Pacific, the Columbia River system once hosted impressive runs of 10 million to 16 million salmon annually. By the late 1970s, hydroelectric dams, logging, and pollution had reduced this figure to 2.5 million. As many as 106 populations of western salmon have been extirpated and others are now at risk. The Snake River, the Columbia's largest tributary, now carries no more than 10,000 salmon to the sea each year. The 1991 and 1992 listings of the Snake River sockeye salmon and the Snake River chinook salmon under the Endangered Species Act have, nonetheless, upset many people in the Northwest, since recovery efforts will affect a heavily resource-dependent economy.

Salmon-related industries alone produce $1 billion in personal income every year and 60,000 jobs for citizens in the Northwest. Dams have made it possible for agriculture, industry, and residents to enjoy cheap hydroelectric power and irrigation water.

But dams slow the migration of young fish to the sea, increasing predation and throwing off their metamorphosis into saltwater fish. Logging silts up salmon spawning grounds and clears rivers of fallen trees that provide fish with hiding and resting places.

A recovery program would probably reduce the allowable Pacific salmon catch. Increased spring water releases to speed young salmon more quickly to the sea would reduce water and electricity for irrigation and industry, already hit by drought. The timber industry, also under pressure from listing of the northern spotted owl, will probably have to restrict cuts along rivers.

The upcoming relicensing of numerous dams in the Northwest and across the country (see "Water" chapter) will provide conservationists an opportunity to push for increased passage around dams for ocean-bound fish and even removal of dams that no longer produce enough power to justify the damage caused to river ecology.

Top 10 States for Fishing and Hunting Licenses
Fishing (FY 1991)   *Hunting (FY 1991)*

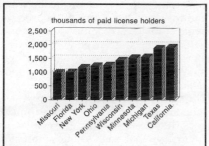

Source: U.S. Fish and Wildlife Service, Division of Federal Aid, 1992.

uges focus on protecting the biological diversity of endemic species, a position that angers recreationists who do not want to be locked out of natural areas. Of all the refuges in the system, 262 allow hunting as "compatible with the purposes of the refuge." According to FWS, as many as half a million animals are killed by hunters every year on wildlife refuges.

Hunters, who responded in force to the options presented during the Refuges 2003 comment period, defend their role in helping to manage refuge animal populations. In addition, hunting groups argue that their sport, which raised $350 million from taxes on hunting and fishing equipment in 1992, has historically generated substantial financial and political support for wildlife conservation. (See table, Hunting in U.S. Wildlife Refuges.)

The final document for Refuges 2003 is expected to be published by the end of 1993. U.S. FWS claims it will attempt to take these differing opinions on the best use of refuges into account.

Planning for Open Spaces

While the future of the U.S. wildlife refuges is debated, a movement to pre-serve habitat and open space at a local level is growing. Communities and groups are creating "greenways" and other protected areas that safeguard habitat and species.

With limited funding—often a mix of federal, state, local, and private money—local agencies and citizens are using private land trusts, tax incentives to landowners to limit development on

Hunting in U.S. Wildlife Refuges

Number of Refuges open to:

Hunting	244
Trapping	89
Fishing	268

(Total acreage available is 85 million)

Annual Hunter Visits to Refuges for:

Migratory birds (ducks, geese, swans, doves, cranes, etc.)	303,497
Upland game (rabbit, hare, squirrel, opossum, fox, raccoon, bobcat, turkey, quail, partridge, pheasant, etc.)	201,209
Big game (deer, moose, elk, caribou, bear, antelope, mountain goat, coyote, etc.)	232,727

Sources: U.S. Fish and Wildlife Service data, 1989, and the Humane Society of the United States, 1989.

Protecting Nature and Business in Texas

Deep in the heart of Texas lies a surprisingly spectacular area of wooded canyons, forested hills, and limestone caves, harboring significant endangered wildlife—from bald eagles to goldencheeked warblers to Texas salamanders. In all, 70 species of endangered plants and animals depend on this hill country.

But the region also supports 2.5 million Texans, including the residents of San Antonio and Austin, a fact that might have spurred conservationists to seek protection of some of these wildlands in traditional parks and reserves.

In one of the nation's more novel conservation projects, however, The Nature Conservancy (TNC) is working with public agencies and private groups in the region to integrate human activities with nature. TNC has identified significant areas of biological diversity and is taking three approaches to protect them.

● *Core wilderness areas.* TNC is working to create four to six large protected areas and has already purchased the first, north of Del Rio.

● *Ecologically sound ranching.* TNC is working wth owners of large ranches to incorporate ecological principles in managing their land while still turning a profit, for example, through nature tourism. These ranchlands could form "buffers" of habitat near wilderness areas.

● *Urban wildlife habitat.* Austin area governments, environmentalists, and developers have invited TNC to help carve out 60,000 acres of habitat in the metropolitan area for endangered species preserves around which development can occur.

overlooked natural areas and link existing parks.

Often, these arrangements gain the cooperation of developers, businesses, and residents, who can in the process avoid costly legal disputes over endangered species, earn good publicity, and, in the case of residential development, end up with more attractive and salable property.

Open space benefits communities economically. Scenery and recreational opportunities attract investment from companies that wish to offer employees a livable environment. Encouraging more compact development of housing and public buildings also decreases the cost of such utilities as water and sewers. When open spaces are left in newly developed communities, residents can enjoy their natural beauty as well as the essential "services" they provide, such as groundwater supplies and flood control.

Knowledge Is Power

An invaluable tool in these efforts to preserve natural spaces is The Nature Conservancy's Natural Heritage Program, an ambitious effort to compile an inventory of the location and status of rare species of plants and animals throughout the United States and most of the Western Hemisphere. With just a phone call to The Nature Conservancy (TNC), communities, developers, and landowners may be able to direct development away from vulnerable local species and habitats.

A wide range of land managers might use TNC's database—the Army Corps of Engineers, about to dredge and fill a wetland, for example, or the Department of Transportation while determining the route of a proposed roadway. In fact, this extensive inventory, which is continually expanded

their property, purchase of development rights rather than complete ownership, and other means to protect

and updated, gives any agency, group, or person the opportunity to consider the impact of projects or activities on biological diversity. Doing so early can prevent the eleventh-hour conflicts over the ESA headlined so frequently this past year.

Some suggest, in fact, that the United States needs to replace its current patchwork of wildlife laws and practices with a comprehensive strategy to promote biological diversity based on a full assessment of the nation's plant and animal life. This type of program could authorize federal agencies to *prevent* species from becoming threatened or endangered by re-

versing policies that encourage resource misuse, such as agricultural water subsidies, or by encouraging community and state planning for species conservation. For several years, Congress has considered a bill, the National Biodiversity Strategy Act, that proposes such a program, but so far the idea has made little headway.

Wildlife Update—International

At home and abroad in 1992, economics was central to the debate over wildlife. At several international forums, delegates discussed how much to limit trade in wild animals and plants in the interest of preserving species.

Signs of Trouble?

Just as miners carried canaries into mine shafts to warn of dangerous gases, scientists watch declines in so-called indicator species to watch for warnings as to the declining health of ecosystems.

In recent years, scientists have recorded widespread declines in the numbers of migratory songbirds in the Western Hemisphere and of wild mushrooms in Europe. Other scientists have noted the loss of frog and other amphibian species worldwide. These widespread trends alarm scientists, because they may signal serious regional or global environmental degradation.

Scientists attribute the decline of songbirds to loss of habitat—particularly forests—throughout their range, from Canada to Central America and northern South America. The Breeding Bird Survey, conducted each year since 1966 by the U.S. Fish and Wildlife Service, has revealed serious declines in forest-dwelling birds, such as the wood thrush, rose-breasted grosbeak, yellow-billed and black-billed cuckoo, Tennessee warbler, worm-eating warbler, and ovenbird.

European mushrooms are not simply being overharvested. Both edible and ined-

ible species in every kind of forest are suffering, causing some scientists to blame the effects of air pollution. The situation points to the ecological decline of forests, whose health is closely linked with that of fungi populations.

Declines in frog populations—a worldwide trend discovered when scientists began sharing 20 years of anecdotal evidence—are more puzzling. Some species are disappearing in certain areas and doing well in others. Others seem totally unaffected. Among many species in trouble are Costa Rica's golden toad (which may already be extinct), Australia's gastric brooding frog, Oregon's Cascades frog, and California's red-legged frog.

Scientists blame multiple factors, including acid rain, heavy metal and pesticide contamination of ponds and other surface waters, habitat change brought on by deforestation, and unusual weather brought on by global warming, as well as human predation in some regions. In France, thousands of tons of frog legs imported from Bangladesh and Indonesia are consumed each year.

Canada Moves to Protect Biological Diversity

To date, only 3.4 percent of Canada's territory is protected, including a limited range of habitats. But in recent years, strong public support for protecting Canada's diversity of animals and plants has bolstered government and private efforts to conserve biological diversity.

The Green Plan

In 1990, the government of Canada released *Canada's Green Plan*, which, among other items, committed the nation to protecting a full 12 percent of its lands and waters by the year 2000, in part by completing the national parks system, and to maintaining and enhancing the health and diversity of plant and animal life.

Specifically, by 1996, five new national parks and three new marine parks will be created and a national strategy to increase wildlife research, law enforcement, and habitat conservation will be launched.

A Wildlife Policy for Canada

In 1990, wildlife ministers from all Canadian provinces pledged to implement a comprehensive policy on wildlife that requires maintaining and restoring ecological processes and biological diversity, as well as ensuring that all uses of wildlife are sustainable.

Endangered Spaces Campaign

Spurring the government's effort to protect biological diversity is a broad, citizen-based fund-raising and lobbying effort called the Endangered Spaces Campaign, which has catalyzed the largest coalition of Canadian conservation interests ever. Over 350,000 citizens and 225 organizations have endorsed its centerpiece, The Canadian Wilderness Charter. The charter targets the year 2000 for federal, provincial, and territorial governments to protect representative habitats.

Proposed Wildlife Legislation

The proposed Wild Animal and Plant Protection Act, introduced to Parliament in 1991, "would augment federal controls over the import, export, and interprovincial transport of wild animals and plants; stiffen penalties for poaching and illegal trade in domestic and foreign wildlife; and improve enforcement mechanisms."

In 1991, legislators introduced two pieces of legislation in Parliament to increase legal protection for endangered species, to date covered only through Canada's participation in the Convention on International Trade in Endangered Species (CITES).

- The Endangered Species and Biological Diversity Act would ensure the protection and restoration of biological diversity and protect endangered ecosystems and species in Canada.

- The Endangered and Threatened Species Act would empower the provinces to protect and rehabilitate critical habitat for endangered species, but would not address trade in these species.

African elephant. Trade in elephant ivory and habitat loss have diminished African elephant numbers from 2.5 million in 1970 to around 609,000 today. Ivory trade was banned by the Convention on International Trade in Endangered Species (CITES) in 1989, collapsing the market for ivory and reducing elephant poaching by an estimated 80 percent in most of Africa.

At the 1992 meeting of CITES delegates, several southern African nations proposed relaxing CITES protection for their healthy elephant populations. Selling ivory and meat from elephants culled from growing herds, these delegates said, would raise funds for conservation and for people living near protected areas. CITES delegates rejected the idea, however, fearing that allowing any ivory trade at all would spur renewed poaching.

African rhinoceros. Poaching for rhino horn, which is used in traditional medicine and as an aphrodisiac, has critically endangered African rhinos. Zimbabwe proposed at the CITES meeting to cut off and sell the horns of remaining rhinos to avert further poaching and finance conservation. But delegates to CITES rejected this idea also, saying a legal rhino horn market would only increase poaching.

Atlantic bluefin tuna. This magnificent fish grows to 12 feet in length and can speed across the ocean in 50 days. The bluefin tuna is so prized by commercial and sport fishermen that its populations have plummeted by more than 90 percent in the last 20 years. Conservationists pushed for listing of the Atlantic bluefin tuna on CITES, a proposal sponsored by Sweden and opposed by the United States and Japan. Delegates did not institute a ban, opting instead for a conservation plan to be implemented by other international bodies.

Black bear. Of the eight bear species worldwide, the populations of six are declining. Booming Asian demand for bear parts—gall bladders, claws, and paws—caused conservationists to seek increased CITES protection of the next logical target—American black bears. These are still abundant and can earn hunters as much as $10,000 each. Often, poachers of other bear species would claim the parts they were trading were from an American black bear, because trade permits for the U.S. species were not required. But CITES delegates voted to list the American black bear in Appendix II, to reflect the need for some regulation. (See box, Protecting Wildlife through Law.) As a result, permits are now required.

U.S. Wildlife Imports
(typical year)

Wildlife	Imports (number & value)
Primates	16,000–18,000 live animals (mostly for research) Declared value: $2 million–2.5 million
Furs	6 million skins Declared value: $800 million
Ivory	Trade banned in 1989 (Prior years: 5 million–6 million carved products, 5,000 raw ivory tusks) Declared value: $25 million–30 million
Birds	800,000 live (about 250,000 parrots) Declared value: $15 million
Reptiles	1.2 million live, 1.5 million skins, 30 million manufactured products Declared value: $300 million
Ornamental fish	125 million live animals Declared value: $25 million–30 million
Shells	12 million–15 million raw shells, 50 million manufactured products Declared value: $12 million–13 million
Corals	1,000–1,500 tons of raw corals, 2 million–3 million manufactured products Declared value: $5 million–6 million

Source: U.S. Fish and Wildlife Service, Office of Management Authority, as cited in *United States of America National Report*, United Nations Conference on Environment & Development (Council on Environmental Quality, 1992), p. 108.

Whales. Populations of great whales, many harvested to dangerously low levels for the commercial trade, were given a reprieve in 1985, when the International Whaling Commission (IWC) imposed a moratorium on killing whales. A loophole, however, allowed Japan to kill up to 330 minke whales annually for "scientific" studies, which many believe cover up continued commercial whaling. Pro-whaling nations, mostly Japan, Iceland, and Norway, have fought the ban on whaling for years.

Although most whale species have shown no signs of recovery from earlier hunting, the IWC may soon lift the moratorium on hunting of the relatively more plentiful minke whale. The possibility of renewed commercial whaling has led the French government to propose a whale sanctuary for the entire southern ocean surrounding Antarctica. To date, only the Indian Ocean has been declared off limits to whale hunting.

Wildlife News

Dover, Delaware, 8/17/92—*Record numbers of white-tailed deer are wreaking havoc with crops and ornamental plants in Delaware. In an effort to control the problem, the state doubled the number of hunting permits offered for the 1991–92 season to 2,000, according to a state wildlife official. Approximately 1,900 were sold. The same number of permits will be offered for the 1992–93 season, and new regulations will allow each hunter to take two deer instead of just one.*

Wildlife Update—United States

Not all news about sensitive species is bad, however. Some efforts to protect U.S. species are paying off. The following nine species have benefited from serious protection efforts.

American alligator. Hunting and loss of habitat in Florida, Louisiana, and Texas had pushed the American alligator to near-extinction when it was listed as endangered in 1967. A 20-year crackdown on alligator hunting led to

its full recovery. The alligator remains listed as threatened only because it can be confused with another endangered species, the American crocodile.

Antioch Dunes evening primrose. One of more than 250 endangered plants protected by the ESA, this large, white primrose is found only in California's Antioch Dunes, which have been damaged by sand mining, industrial development, invasion by weeds, and illegal off-road vehicle activity. Although the Antioch Dunes evening primrose remains endangered, protection and restoration of part of its habitat have helped the species rebound.

Bald eagle. Already declining from habitat loss and shooting, bald eagle populations took a nosedive in the 1940s, because the pesticide DDT caused the birds to lay thin-shelled eggs. Listed as endangered in 1967, this eagle has recovered in many parts of its range, thanks to federal, state, and private protective measures and a ban on DDT. The status of the species may soon be upgraded to threatened.

Black-footed ferret. Black-footed ferrets, never a common species, were once found throughout the Great Plains. Campaigns to kill off the ferrets' chief prey, prairie dogs, devastated ferret populations, as did exposure to canine distemper and loss of prairie habitat. Listed as endangered in 1967, all remaining wild ferrets were captured in 1987 for captive breeding. In 1991, more than 50 ferrets were returned to the wild in Wyoming.

California condor. The condor, North America's largest bird, once soared in western skies from British Columbia to Baja California. Listed as endangered in 1967, the bird that Native Americans called "thunderbird" had so declined by 1987 that biologists removed those left in the wild for captive breeding. In

Protecting Wildlife through Law

The following laws were designed to protect wildlife and habitat in the United States or Canada.

United States

The Lacey Act, 1900. Outlaws interstate export or import of wildlife harvested or possessed against the laws of the state.

Migratory Bird Treaty Act, 1918. Prohibits hunting or injury to wild birds moving between the United States, Britain, and Mexico.

Migratory Bird Conservation Act, 1929. Authorized purchase of new areas for waterfowl refuges.

Migratory Bird Hunting Stamp Act, 1934. Requires hunters over age 16 to buy a $1 federal waterfowl stamp before hunting migratory waterfowl.

The Pittman-Robertson Act, 1937. Raises money for state wildlife conservation programs from excise taxes on rifles, shotguns, ammunition, and archery equipment.

Marine Mammal Protection Act, 1972. Bans the killing and importing of whales and nearly all marine mammals. The moratorium can be waived after determining the current status of the species and the likely impact of proposed hunting.

Endangered Species Act, 1973. Gives federal protection to species determined to be threatened with or in danger of extinction.

Fish Conservation and Management Act, 1976. Restricts foreign fishing in U.S. territorial waters. Established eight regional fishery management councils to determine which fisheries require conservation and management.

Canada

Canada Wildlife Act. Authorizes the Minister of Environment to foster wildlife and habitat conservation in Canada through various means, to protect endangered species, and to procure and manage public lands for wildlife-related programs.

National Parks Act, 1919. Regulates the use and acquisition of lands, the use of resources and facilities in the parks, fire prevention, and public safety. Protects flora, fauna, soil, waters, fossils, natural features, air quality, and cultural, historical, and archaeological resources in the parks.

Migratory Birds Convention Act, 1917. Implements a 1916 convention between Canada and the United States protecting migratory birds, including game, non-game, and insectivorous species.

Game Export Act. Requires export permits for possessing game killed in another province and exporting dead game to another province or outside of Canada.

Fisheries Act, 1868. Places control, protection, and management of all fisheries, both inland and marine, with the federal government.

Continued on next page

a controlled environment, the biologists eventually increased the birds' population to 52. In 1992, two captive-bred condor chicks were released in the 84-square-mile Sespe Condor Sanctuary of Los Padres National Forest, north of Los Angeles. Many naturalists fear, however, that so much of the condor's habitat has been destroyed that the birds may never be able to live in the wild again.

Gray whale. In 1992, the California gray whale became the first endangered marine mammal to be reclassified as threatened. In 1946, the species was believed to number only about 2,000. Since its listing in 1970, gray whale numbers have swelled to 21,000. Migrating in near-shore waters from the Bering Sea to Baja California, they remain exposed to industrial, recreational, and other human activities. The

Protecting Wildlife through Law *(continued)*

Relevant International Programs: Land Treaties

Convention on International Trade in Endangered Species of Wild Fauna and Flora (CITES). Regulates international trade and transit of certain animals and plants, their parts, and resulting products. Species listed in Appendix I are considered rare and endangered, and their commercial trade is generally prohibited. Appendix II species, not currently endangered, may be overexploited if their trade is not regulated.

International Convention for the Regulation of Whaling, 1946. Regulates the whaling industry through quotas and through open and closed seasons, decided upon by the International Whaling Commission (IWC). Canada has withdrawn its membership in the IWC but generally follows its regulations.

North American Waterfowl Management Plan, 1986. A 15-year cooperative effort between the United States and Canada to restore sufficient wetland habitat to reestablish and maintain waterfowl populations at 1970 levels—a breeding population of 62 million and a fall flight of 100 million ducks. Provides for acquisition of key habitat as well as a program to encourage farmers to manage retired land for wildfowl.

Marine Mammal Commission has recommended continued protection under the ESA.

Grizzly bear. Grizzly bear habitat once extended the length of the Rocky Mountains from Alaska to Mexico. But human migration westward and systematic killing of grizzlies as a threat to livestock and people have reduced the species's southernmost range to Washington, Idaho, Montana, and Wyoming. Listed in 1975 as threatened in the lower 48 states, grizzly bear populations are now reported stable as a result of conservation efforts in six specific areas in the Rocky Mountains.

Red wolf. Southeastern states once harbored the wide-ranging red wolf. Long regarded as a pest even by the federal government, which spent $10 million between 1915 and 1942 on its eradication, the red wolf found protection under the ESA in 1967. The last wild red wolves were captured in the 1970s for captive breeding. In 1991, red wolves were reintroduced into the Great Smokies National Park.

Whooping crane. The whooping crane is North America's tallest bird and one of its most endangered. Conversion of its nesting and wintering habitats to farmland and other uses diminished the species's once-abundant flocks. In 1941, only 16 of the birds migrated to wintering grounds in Texas. Listed for protection in 1967, whooping cranes have slowly increased in number to 150 birds, thanks to captive breeding efforts, refuge establishment, and other measures.

The author, Pamela Cubberly, lives in Silver Spring, Maryland.

Wetlands and Forests

Spotted owls, a technical manual, and a sluggish economy ignite the U.S. debate about the nation's wetlands and forests.

In 1992, U.S. politicians, environmentalists, private industries, and concerned citizens engaged in heated debates over uses and misuses of wetlands and forests. At issue were the economic and environmental concerns surrounding these ecosystems. On one hand, some people argued that unabated cutting of forests and draining of wetlands are critical to maintaining the nation's economic health; on the other hand, some claimed that the environmental contributions of these natural systems justify their protection, even if it means loss of jobs.

While these arguments are nothing new, the debate has been heavily influenced by a lingering economic recession and an administration inclined to loosen or rewrite environmental regulations in a way most favorable to business interests. Thus, forests are being harvested and bulldozed so heavily that certain kinds of North American forest may disappear. And the long-standing practice of draining and filling wetlands received a substantial boost from a Bush administration proposal to change the very definition of a wetland.

Attitudes of pro-business interests toward these two major types of ecosystems could not differ more. Forests are highly valued for their timber and for the jobs they provide; wetlands, especially seasonal ones, are often viewed as worthless, swampy obstacles to development. Yet to an environ-

> **Wetlands News**
> Boston, 11/2/91—*More than 100 beach homes, damaged by a coastal storm last week, cannot be rebuilt. New, stricter state and federal laws now bar owners from rebuilding in coastal wetlands when the damage is more than 50 percent of the homes' value, and if septic and water systems have been affected.*

mentalist, both are richly productive areas, extremely valuable to people and the environment. They provide habitat for wildlife and plants; improve water quality; store floodwaters; sustain renewable resources such as timber, fish, and shellfish; and provide a wide range of recreational, educational, and scientific opportunities. Often, these resources are exploited for short-term gains rather than managed for long-term productivity. Such shortsighted practices have already claimed more than half the United States' wetlands and most of its virgin forests.

Wetlands—Critical Ecosystems

There is no "typical" wetland. Wetlands can be forested floodplain swamps, cattail-lined marshes, or shallow potholes. They can extend for miles or cover less than an acre. Some stay wet year-round, others dry out after a few months, and some stay dry for years before filling again with water.

Wetlands offer a diversity of benefits. They provide habitat for as many as 600 wildlife species and 5,000 plant species. At least 45 percent of the nation's listed endangered animals and 26 percent of the listed endangered plants survive only in wetlands or rely on them during a part of the year. Approximately two thirds of the major U.S. commercial fishes depend on estuaries and salt marshes for nursery or spawning grounds.

Throughout their yearly migrations, millions of waterfowl, shorebirds, and other birds rest, feed, and seek shelter on a diverse network of wetland complexes covering North and South America, from Latin America and Mexico, across the United States, through Canada, and up to Alaska and the Arctic Circle.

Wetlands have been called "nature's kidneys" for their ability to filter out contaminants. Wetlands collect sediments that, in excess, would pollute rivers and streams, and wetland plants absorb certain nutrients and other contaminants. In fact, wetlands do such a good job at improving water quality that small towns and some industries are building treatment systems that use wetland plants to clean their wastewater.

Wetlands provide other environmental benefits as well. When ocean storms batter the shoreline, coastal wetlands help protect the mainland, buffering it against damaging waves and flooding. River wetlands act as storage for excess water and buffer against destruction by floods. Wetlands also can recharge the groundwater and help control soil erosion. People frequent wetlands for recreation from hunting and fishing to bird-watching and canoeing.

While each wetland type may serve general functions, such as the flood control exerted by bottomland hard-

State Ranking of Wetland Losses
(in the last 200 years)

State	Acres Lost	Percent Lost	State	Acres Lost	Percent Lost
Florida	9,286,713	46	Nebraska	1,005,000	35
Texas	8,387,288	52	Colorado	1,000,000	50
Louisiana	7,410,300	46	South Dakota	955,100	35
Arkansas	7,085,000	72	Oregon	868,100	38
Illinois	6,957,500	85	Virginia	774,387	42
Minnesota	6,370,000	42	Wyoming	750,000	38
Mississippi	5,805,000	59	Pennsylvania	627,986	56
Michigan	5,616,600	50	New Jersey	584,040	39
North Carolina	5,400,000	49	Connecticut	497,500	74
Indiana	4,849,367	87	Idaho	491,300	56
California	4,546,000	91	Washington	412,000	31
Ohio	4,517,200	90	Kansas	405,600	48
Wisconsin	4,468,608	46	Arizona	331,000	36
Missouri	4,201,000	87	Montana	306,700	27
Alabama	3,783,800	50	Delaware	256,785	54
Iowa	3,578,100	89	Nevada	251,000	52
North Dakota	2,437,500	49	Utah	244,000	30
Oklahoma	1,892,900	67	New Mexico	238,100	33
South Carolina	1,755,000	27	Massachusetts	229,514	28
Georgia	1,545,000	23	Alaska	200,000	0.1
New York	1,537,000	60	Vermont	121,000	35
Kentucky	1,266,000	81	Rhode Island	37,536	37
Maine	1,260,800	20	West Virginia	32,000	24
Maryland	1,210,000	73	New Hampshire	20,000	9
Tennessee	1,150,000	59	Hawaii	7,000	12

Source: T.E. Dahl, *Wetland Losses in United States 1780's to 1980's*, U.S. Department of Interior, 1990.

wood swamps, every wetland is unique. The only way to determine the specific combination of benefits any particular wetland offers is to evaluate it individually.

What We Have Lost

The United States has lost more than half of its wetlands in the past 200 years. Today, only 104 million acres of wetlands remain in the lower 48 states, covering 5 percent of the land surface. While the rate of wetland destruction has slowed over the last 20 years, the United States still loses 290,000 acres of freshwater and coastal wetlands every year. California has lost the greatest portion of its wetlands (91 percent). Florida, however, at 9.3 million acres, has lost the largest acreage. (See table, State Ranking of Wetland Losses.)

Canada contains about 24 percent of the world's wetlands—nearly 314 million acres (127 million hectares), covering 14 percent of the country. (See graph, Canadian Wetlands, by Province.) Canada has lost 49.4 million acres (20 million hectares), or 14 percent of its original wetlands. Up to 65 percent of coastal salt marshes in the Atlantic region, 70 percent of all wetlands in southern Ontario, and 71 percent of wetlands in prairie agricultural areas have been filled in or converted to

Louisiana's Coastal Wetlands

Along the Gulf Coast, more than 4 million acres of coastal marshes buffer uplands from the sea. Most of these marshes are in Louisiana, stretching along the entire length of the state, where they form the largest continuous wetland system in the lower 48 states. Louisiana's coastal wetlands are an important component of Gulf Coast ecology, and they foster regional industries including commercial fisheries and the thriving fur trade. Yet human activities and natural causes are making the wetlands disappear so fast that all of Louisiana's wetlands—the entire southern part of the state—could be destroyed in little over 100 years.

The value of these coastal marshes lies in their vast productivity as well as in their size. The Gulf Coast waters spawn the nation's largest fishery, and nearly all commercial fish and shellfish caught there spend some part of their lives in coastal marshes.

Ducks, geese, and other water birds also find these marshes attractive, especially during the winter months, when more than two thirds of the entire Mississippi Flyway waterfowl population seeks refuge here. Furbearers, including muskrat, mink, nutria, otter, and raccoon, thrive in Gulf Coast wetlands. As a result, more fur is harvested here than from any other area in the United States. This high productivity is tied directly to the diversity of wetland habitats that make up the coastal marsh system—freshwater, intermediate, brackish, and saline marshes.

Up to 50 square miles (32,000 acres) of these valuable coastal wetlands in the Gulf are being lost every year. This translates to 88 acres of marsh each day that are converted to open water.

Loss of Sediments

Louisiana's wetlands used to be sustained by the Mississippi River, which picks up 265 million tons of sediment each year. These sediments were deposited at the river's mouth, continuously re-creating coastal wetlands. Before humans interfered, the sediments over time built twice as many acres of wetlands as were lost to erosive wave action, hurricanes, subsidence, and other natural events.

The problem is, Mississippi sediments do not stop here anymore. The river has been deepened for navigation and is lined with levees that prevent the escape of most floodwaters. Sediments and fresh water are trapped in the channel, and instead of feeding the surrounding wetlands, they are dumped over the edge of the continen-

other uses. An estimated 75 percent of all wetlands in southern occupied portions of Canada have been lost.

Historically, agriculture has been responsible for over 85 percent of the wetland losses in both the United States and Canada. A recent U.S. Fish and Wildlife Service report found that from the 1970s to the 1980s, 54 percent of the decline was caused by agriculture and 5 percent by urban expansion. For the remaining 41 percent, areas were drained and cleared of vegetation, but had not yet been converted to either agriculture or urban use.

Redefining Wetlands

Concern for wetlands protection continues to grow as people learn about the many benefits these valuable ecosystems provide and about their continued destruction. In 1989, even President George Bush called for a national policy of "no net loss of wetlands," a pledge that has been a rallying cry for conservationists. It also became a political problem for the Bush administration, which was being pressured by those who benefit financially from the conversion or destruc-

Louisiana's Coastal Wetlands (continued)

tal shelf. Without the deposition of sediments, the Mississippi Delta has already lost 51 percent of its wetlands to the sea.

Attempts are being made at the mouth of the Mississippi to save some of these sediments from burial at sea. At several locations on the east side of the river, water is being diverted out of the main canal into open water bays that historically were vegetated marshes. These diversions deposit sediments that are beginning to build back some wetlands.

There is one place in the Gulf where the natural creation of coastal marshes is still allowed—the mouth of the Atchafalaya River, just west of the Mississippi. Geologists predict that by the year 2030, most of this delta will be transformed from shallow water to 40,000 acres of emergent marsh and thousands of acres of productive mudflats. Unfortunately, this buildup cannot keep pace with the accelerated loss along the rest of the coast.

Saltwater Intrusion

The coastal marshes are crisscrossed by an extensive network of artificial channels that are used for navigation and oil and gas exploration. Unfortunately, more than commerce floats into the marshes via these straight, deep pathways. Saltwater in-

trudes from the Gulf, killing plants found in freshwater and brackish marshes and eventually reducing these wetlands to open, unproductive water.

Resource managers do not have clear answers for dealing with saltwater intrusion, so they are working with various techniques, including freshwater diversions and levees.

Three freshwater diversion projects are planned that would channel water from the Mississippi River and flush it into adjacent wetlands that historically were fresh or intermediate marshes. These diversions are intended to push saltwater back and re-create the full complex of all four marsh types.

Levees are used as protective barriers to keep saltwater out of designated marshes. Water-control structures in these levees can allow for the yearly migration of saltwater fish and shellfish that use coastal marshes as nurseries before they return to the sea as adults.

Levees built along both sides of canals act to keep saltwater in the channels. However, levees are often poorly maintained and breaks in these barriers are common, allowing saltwater to flow freely into the wetlands. Repairing such breaks is important but rarely done.

tion of wetlands. As time passed, the administration shifted away from its original pledge of no net loss.

One of the most controversial moves supported by the Bush administration was an effort to restrict the types of wetlands covered under federal laws and programs. To accomplish this, as of mid-1992 the administration was attempting to rewrite the scientific manual that helps trained personnel identify wetland types in the field and define their boundaries.

Such changes are opposed by many experts. After independent extensive

field tests, scientists representing federal and state governments, environmental groups, and wetland owners found that the redefinition would eliminate one third to one half the nation's wetlands from federal oversight and protection.

The wetlands most likely to be eliminated are temporary and seasonal ones, including prairie potholes, floodplain wetlands, bottomland hardwood swamps, playas, and vernal pools. These types are often wrongly identified as dry land by casual observers. Their wet-dry cycle is critical for plant

Canadian Wetlands, by Province
(acreage and percent of national total)

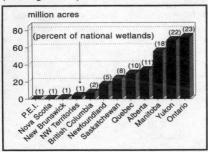

Source: Energy, Mines, and Resources Canada, as cited in Statistics Canada, *Human Activity and the Environment 1991* (Minister of Industry, Science, and Technology, Ottawa, Ontario, 1991), Table 4.1.4.2, p. 161.

germination and growth, which maintains the wetland's productivity. Depending on the amount of annual precipitation, some wetlands may stay dry for many months or even a number of consecutive years.

The common misperception is that a small wetland that dries up every year provides fewer benefits than does a large one that rarely goes dry. In reality, temporary and seasonal wetlands provide benefits that permanent wetlands cannot. (See box, Wetlands Aren't Always Wet.) Their exclusion from the federal wetlands definition could exacerbate river flooding, increase flood damage, and jeopardize many wildlife species. In particular, 78 threatened or endangered mammal and plant species rely on wetlands that would be disqualified under the new definition.

About 74 percent of U.S. wetlands are privately owned. To a large extent, the conservation of wetlands is dependent on the actions of private landowners. Federal and state governments, as well as nonprofit organizations, offer technical assistance, cost sharing, educational, and other incentive programs to encourage landowners to conserve and restore wetlands on their properties.

Wetland Regulations

There are no federal laws that prohibit the draining, filling, or converting of wetlands. Those on the books regulate only certain activities. The main one—the Section 404 permit program under the Clean Water Act (CWA)—is designed to minimize impacts to wetlands, lakes, and rivers by regulating the dumping of solid materials into them. Anyone intending to dump dredged or fill material into these water bodies must obtain a permit from the U.S. Army Corps of Engineers. The Corps can deny a permit if it does not comply with certain CWA guidelines.

Some landowners say that Section 404 unduly restricts what they can do with their land. Yet less than 5 percent of the permits submitted for wetlands conversion are denied each year. Also, the Corps permits the filling of any wetlands smaller than 10 acres. For these and other reasons, many conservationists feel that Section 404 does not adequately protect wetlands.

Before issuing a permit, the Corps usually requires an applicant to compensate for the wetland loss they will cause by restoring or creating wetlands at another site. Scientists are able to successfully restore some types of degraded wetlands. However, wetlands creation—constructing a wetland where none naturally exists—is a new technology and does not always produce viable wetland ecosystems to replace those destroyed. (See box, Can We Create a Wetland?)

Wetlands Aren't Always Wet

Temporary and seasonal wetlands, such as prairie potholes and bottomland hardwood swamps, do not contain water year-round. They undergo a wet-dry cycle that is essential to their ecology and to their abilities to provide valuable wildlife habitat, floodwater storage, and other important functions.

Prairie potholes in the Great Plains are shallow basins that fill with water in the spring (when weather conditions cooperate) and then often dry up before fall. Even though some are as small as 20 feet across, potholes are invaluable in breeding season to waterfowl and other water birds.

Since they are small and shallow, potholes are warmed quickly by the early spring sun. Soon they teem with invertebrates that ducks and other water birds can easily reach. Invertebrates provide an essential source of protein for egg-laying ducks. Larger, deeper marshes do not produce invertebrates early enough or in sufficient quantities to fulfill the nutritional requirements of nesting hens.

The productivity of temporary and seasonal potholes is maintained by the wet-dry cycle. During the dry times, certain plants are able to start growing in the wetland. When the water returns, older plants that have died will decompose quickly, releasing nutrients into the system. These nutrients feed the algae, which in turn feed invertebrates.

The invertebrates found in these types of wetlands are specially adapted to the wet-dry cycle. They reproduce quickly and profusely when water is present. Also, most fish and other aquatic predators that would feed on invertebrates cannot survive in potholes because these wetlands dry out regularly. This lack of fish leaves more invertebrates for waterfowl and other water birds.

Bottomland hardwood swamps found in river floodplains in the South and Southeast look like regular forests for half of the year. But these forested wetlands are adapted to absorb floodwaters from early winter through spring, when the rivers overflow their banks. This first-rate flood control provides a buffer for towns and cities downstream.

When the river's flow and local rains drop off during summer, most parts of the swamp dry up. The diverse assemblage of plants and animals found in hardwood swamps are adapted to this seasonal wet-dry cycle.

Most parts of the swamp dry up in the summer when the river's flow and local rains drop off. At this time, trees, vines, and other plants thrive in the swamp. They produce leaves, seeds, fruits, and nuts that provide food for a variety of animals, including waterfowl, songbirds, wild turkey, deer, squirrels, and raccoons.

With the coming of autumn, ripe acorns fall to the ground and become food for wood ducks, wintering mallards, turkey, and other animals.

Within several weeks after winter floodwaters start to cover the forest floor, a host of aquatic invertebrates that have been dormant emerge and reproduce. Invertebrates eaten by fish, reptiles, amphibians, and birds form the basis for the food chain in bottomland hardwood swamps.

Aquatic invertebrates feed on fallen leaves, eventually breaking them down into basic nutrients that plants need for growth. These nutrients, however, sustain more than just the swamp. Many of them are flushed downstream to nourish life in the river itself and the richly productive estuaries on the coast.

As winter wanes and spring approaches, the cycle begins again with trees and plants in bloom, deriving nourishment from the nutrients released the winter before. Since the forested wetland dries out in the summer, it will once again be ready to absorb and control next winter's floodwaters.

When reviewing permits, the Corps must first determine if wetland loss can be avoided or minimized. It can allow mitigation by restoration or creation only as a last resort. Critics say that the Corps often ignores the first two steps to the detriment of natural wetlands. (See box, When Someone Wants to Change a Wetland: What You Can Do.)

The future of the Section 404 program rests in Congress, where members are debating proposed bills that will either strengthen or weaken wetlands protection under the program.

Forests—or Timberland?

At the time of white settlement, approximately 1.1 billion acres of forest thrived in the United States, covering 49 percent of the landscape. While some Native American tribes did cut trees for wood or to create farmland, large-scale clearing of forests accompanied the exploding population growth

---

Can We Create a Wetland?

As the nation's wetland inventory dwindles, a new practice is emerging that some claim may help to replenish one of nature's essential systems. Wetland creation is the process of building a wetland on an upland site or in an area that historically did not support wetlands. Despite its relative infancy, wetland creation is being promoted as tried-and-true technology and is used to justify the filling and draining of natural systems. While conservationists support detailed research in this field, they emphasize that trading natural wetlands for created ones is not an equal exchange.

Wetland creation should not be confused with restoration, which repairs the damage done to altered wetlands. In general, restoration efforts have a higher success rate than do creation projects. As usual, it is easier to fix something that is broken than to create something from scratch.

The problem is that the technology and expertise do not exist to replicate all aspects of natural wetland systems. Scientists do not understand enough about how wetlands work and how they adapt to changes over time. Such information is essential to successful wetland creation. Nonetheless, the federal government increasingly allows developers to destroy natural wetlands if they promise to create wetlands to replace them.

Based on existing data, scientists can approximate some types of marshes and can create certain wetland functions, such as floodwater storage or habitat for waterfowl. Other functions and combinations of qualities are extremely difficult or impossible to re-create. These include groundwater recharge, habitat for endangered species, and biological diversity.

Creating wetlands can be expensive. Building a marsh can cost anywhere from $3,000 to $70,000 per acre. This does not include the cost of buying the land.

So far, most wetland creation projects have focused on two wetland types: coastal wetlands along the Atlantic seaboard, and marshes built on dredged material along major rivers and coastlines. Assessments of existing created systems indicate that 50 percent of them fail. "Success" usually indicates that plants become established and continue to grow for three to five years over most of the wetland area.

Vegetation is the easiest and most economical indicator to measure because it is readily visible. Such measures of success, however, do not verify that a project is functioning properly as an ecosystem or that it will persist over time. To evaluate success more accurately, scientists would have to monitor numerous factors for at least 10 to 20 years, which is expensive and time-consuming. Instead, the federal government holds a developer responsible for created wetlands for no more than five years. If the wetland fails after that, no one is liable and the nation loses yet another marsh.

When Someone Wants to Change a Wetland: What You Can Do

1. Permit application

Anyone intending to dump dredged or fill material into wetlands must apply for a permit from the U.S. Army Corps of Engineers (Corps).

2. Corps issues public notice

The public notice will give you a brief description of the proposed activity, its location, potential environmental impacts, a deadline for receiving written comments, and the address for the agency receiving those comments.

3. Comment period

Application is reviewed by the Corps and other interested federal and state agencies, organizations, and individuals. The normal comment period is 30 days. You may request an extension if necessary to gather information and prepare your statement.

4. Public hearing

Normally the Corps does not hold a public hearing on a permit; citizens need to request that one be held. The Corps will use the testimony presented at the hearing in its permit review.

5. Corps evaluates application

The Corps evaluates the permit application based on guidelines listed to comply with the Clean Water Act.

6. Environmental assessment and statement of finding

For every permit issued, the Corps prepares a statement of finding that explains why the permit was granted. This document is public information and can provide data that will help you monitor permit compliance or reevaluate a permit.

7. Permit issued or denied

7a. Monitoring for compliance

Neither the Corps nor the U.S. Environmental Protection Agency (EPA) has enough staff to monitor compliance of permits issued. You can help these agencies by monitoring permitted activities yourself and reporting any potential violations. The Corps prints a report of 404 permits issued; you can get on this mailing list.

7b. EPA veto authority

EPA does have the authority to veto a permit to which it objects. This veto authority is referred to as a "Section 401(c)" action. Your input and community support can be very helpful in convincing EPA to exercise its veto authority.

Who to Call

U.S. Army Corps of Engineers, Chief, Regulatory Branch, Washington, D.C., (202) 272-0199. This office can direct you to the closest division office. Or call the EPA, Wetlands Division, Washington, D.C., (202) 260-1915.

Source: Kathleen Rude, "You Can Make a Difference," *Ducks Unlimited*, September/October 1990, p. 28.

of new Americans and their need for farmland and pasture. From the 1600s to 1920, 370 million acres of forests (34 percent) were cleared, leaving 730 million acres today.

While the acreage of U.S. forests has not changed since the 1920s, most of these wooded areas have, at some time, been altered by logging. Only 10 to 15 percent of today's forests have never been cut. In the 1920s, harvesting of trees on private and public lands exceeded tree growth by 200 percent. Today, annual tree growth (22.5 billion cubic feet) is greater than harvest (16.4 billion cubic feet).

Who Owns the Timberland?
(1987 and projection to 2000)

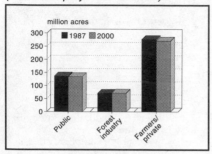

Source: U.S. Department of Agriculture, Forest Service, *An Analysis of the Timber Situation in the United States: 1989–2040*, Table 70, p. 111.

The U.S. Forest Service classifies 66 percent of the nation's forestland (483 million acres) as timberland—forests productive enough to grow commercially valuable trees. Timberland can legally be harvested. Seventy-two percent of U.S. timberland is privately owned, and these areas produce 79 percent of all commercially cut timber. The federal government owns 20 percent of the timberland (primarily in national forests), which contributes 13 percent of the annual harvest. The rest is owned by states, counties, and Native Americans. A little over 5 percent of all productive forestland is federally protected in wilderness areas or national parks and cannot be logged.

While logging on private lands has always been commonplace, the cutting of trees on federal lands was insignificant before World War II. The post-war housing boom and the heavy logging of private forests resulted in a substantial increase in commercial timber harvest on national forestlands. In recent years, controversy has arisen over the management of federal forestlands. Much of the criticism is directed at the

Forest Service, which oversees 88 percent of the federal forests (85.2 million acres).

Questioning Federal Management

The U.S. Forest Service has a mandate to manage its forests for multiple uses, including timber harvest, recreation, wildlife habitat, wilderness, watershed protection, and range management. The Forest Service has come under fire for placing timber harvest above all other uses of national forests. Critics both inside the service and out claim that its primary management concern is "getting the cut out," even if it jeopardizes endangered species, water quality, or the forest ecosystem itself. Forest Service employees reportedly have been fired, transferred, or forced to retire for refusing to sell as much timber as the administration indicated or for questioning timber sales because of the damage such sales would cause to endangered species or archaeological sites.

The Forest Service's annual budget is based in part on the gross receipts from timber sales. The more trees it sells, the larger the budget it receives. Such an arrangement encourages large-scale harvesting, and has even led the Forest Service to sell timber at a loss from more than half of its national forests. On those tracts the Service spent more money providing access, such as new roads, to these sites than it made from the sale of trees. While the Forest Service is adopting new policies to improve this situation, critics claim that its accounting practices mask even larger losses. For fiscal year 1991, the Forest Service reported net revenues of $171 million from timber sales. The Wilderness Society (TWS) refutes that number, claiming that the Service actually lost $12.5 million. In addition, TWS reports that the Service wasted $271 million of taxpayer money that year selling timber below cost from 96 of the 120 national forests. Had the Service confined its timber sales to only the remaining 24 forests, it would have netted $336 million, and fewer forests would have been clearcut.

Old-Growth Forests

The forests in the Pacific Northwest harbor some of the oldest and largest plants on the continent. Giant sequoia trees can live more than 3,500 years and stand 300 feet tall. Equal in height, a Douglas fir can command a girth of 50 feet and live to be 1,000. (See box, Defining Old Growth.)

On national forests in Oregon, Washington, and California, between 3.8 million and 4.3 million acres of old growth remain. This represents about one sixth of the forests that once covered up to 25 million acres of the region. About one quarter of the old growth in the Pacific Northwest is classified as wilderness and is protected from logging. On a national scale, the Forest Service estimates that less than 7 percent of U.S. forests can be classified as old growth.

In the Canadian province of British Columbia, 138 million acres (55.9 mil-

---

Defining Old Growth

From a traditional forester's view, old-growth stands are those where the overall increase in wood production has reached its peak. This definition was important as a reflection of the maximum amount of timber that could be harvested.

Today, however, people define old growth more broadly, and include some distinctive features. Old-growth stands contain significant numbers of large, live, old trees. And "old" is defined for the given tree species—150 years for white pine trees and 3,000 years for bristlecone pines. The presence of large snags, or dead standing trees, is also critical to the definition. Generally, but not necessarily, old growth is virgin terrain that has never been harvested. The Wilderness Society defines "classic" old growth as "containing at least eight big trees per acre exceeding 300 years in age or measuring more than 40 inches in diameter at breast height."

An old-growth ecosystem is a place of dynamic interactions, where species are dependent on one another. When a towering Douglas fir dies, perhaps from disease, it remains a critical component of the system. For decades, the hollow snag remains standing, offering animals a place to live and a source of food. Pileated woodpeckers excavate holes in search of grubs and ants. These insects, in turn, begin the process of decomposing the wood, gradually releasing the stored nutrients and energy back into the ecosystem. Raptors use the snag as a lookout post. Cavity-nesting species such as the flying squirrel might move in. As the snag decays, it attracts more insects, which are food for other wildlife.

In time, the upright snag topples to the ground. As it grows soft and moist, amphibians take up residence. Nitrogen-fixing bacteria inoculate the log, and mycorrhizal fungi penetrate it. Soon, the log is an ideal habitat for young seedlings. The growing trees use the energy stored for so long in the massive tree. Even as the tree breaks apart from rot, it continues to provide services to the ecosystem. Pieces may roll into a nearby stream, creating a small debris dam. This creates a new habitat for aquatic species; it also traps sediment and improves water quality. In time, aquatic insects attack the log and it decays to formlessness. All evidence of the tree is gone, but the ecosystem is perpetuated by its substance.

Cancer Drug from the Forest

Among the treasures tucked away in the old-growth forests of the Pacific Northwest is taxol, a cancer-battling chemical newly discovered in the bark of the Pacific yew. Until recently, the yews, slow-growing trees that thrive in the shadows of giant fir and redwoods, were viewed as trash trees by loggers.

Now, however, the taxol these trees produce holds great promise for women afflicted with ovarian cancer, and may be effective against breast and lung cancer. The drug may cause remissions in some patients whose cancers have not responded to other treatments. It is already priced at $600 per gram. While taxol does not cure cancer, it may enable tens of thousands of cancer patients to live longer and with less pain.

Taxol is still being researched and is not yet available to the general public. Yet by 1992, scientists were expressing dual concerns—one on behalf of cancer patients, and one on behalf of the trees.

First, would there be enough taxol to meet demand, or would desperate patients be forced to beg for the drug? The Pacific yews could not furnish sufficient drug for even the 12,000 to 13,000 American women who die each year of ovarian cancer. If taxol also proves effective in treating other kinds of cancers, demand could skyrocket.

Second, would poaching for yew bark (already a problem in Washington and Oregon) further jeopardize the Pacific yews, which are already threatened by continued clearcutting of old-growth forests? Up to 30 pounds of yew bark is needed to produce just 1 gram of taxol, and a mature yew produces at most 20 pounds of bark. The National Cancer Institute estimates that the need for taxol will soon reach 300 kilograms per year, which translates into 7.5 million pounds of bark and more than 400,000 trees annually. The current inventory of Pacific yews cannot meet this demand on a sustained basis.

Before either concern came to fruition, the taxol story took an unexpected and happy twist. *The New York Times* (6/21/92) reported on a new process that makes taxol from a compound that can be extracted from needles on branches clipped from yews. In addition to Pacific yews, counterparts abundant in Europe and Asia will be used. The drug company, Bristol-Myers-Squibb, will modify the core compound, converting it into taxol. In less than five years, no bark will be required. At the same time, taxol acquired a competitor, a compound called taxotere patented by Rhone-Poulenc Rorer. Taxotere is produced through the same basic method but uses a slightly different side chain in altering the core molecule.

lion hectares) of mature forests still stand. Most is in public ownership. Since the 1950s, nearly 65 million acres (26.3 million hectares) have been lost, and logging continues at a rate of 568,330 acres (230,000 hectares) a year. Within the province, 15.3 million acres (6.2 million hectares) are permanently protected from logging.

Many communities in the Pacific Northwest are dependent on the cutting and processing of old-growth trees for jobs and for revenues paid to the states from gross receipts of federal timber sales. (In fiscal year 1990, Washington, Oregon, and California received a total of over $232 million.) Logging companies have already cut most of the ancient forests on privately owned lands. Publicly owned forests in the United States and Canada provide the only significant source of remaining old growth.

To the American public, however, these forests are valuable for more than timber. (See box, Cancer Drug from the

Forest.) They are remnants of unique temperate rainforest ecosystems that harbor a rich diversity of plant and animal species. They play important roles in stabilizing soils and maintaining water quality in rivers and streams. This, in turn, protects salmon nurseries and habitat for many other fish. Over 60,000 jobs are dependent on sport and commercial fisheries in Washington, Oregon, and northern California. Old-growth forests also provide habitat for the spotted owl, a species officially listed as threatened in 1990.

The continued logging of old-growth forests in the Pacific Northwest has triggered a national controversy that often is portrayed as pitting people's jobs against environmental protection. Others say, however, the real issue is how to convert the old-growth

Timber Harvests in the Lower 48 States
(1986 and projection to 2000)

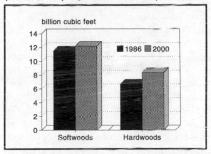

Source: U.S. Department of Agriculture, Forest Service, *An Analysis of the Timber Situation in the United States: 1989–2040*, Table 114, p. 147.

industry into a sustainable business and still preserve healthy stands of for-

Sustainable Forestry

Throughout the nation's forests, clearcutting is a standard logging practice. There are good reasons, however, for reconsidering the wisdom of this approach. Clearcutting requires the construction of roads into forests so that all trees over large areas (usually 80–100 acres) can be felled and removed. Road construction and clearcutting lead to erosion and irreplaceable losses of topsoil. The silt pollutes waterways, ruining salmon spawning grounds and killing fish. This logging process replaces mixed-age, diverse forests with even-aged, several-species stands. Clearcutting in the Pacific Northwest has fragmented the old-growth forests, turning the landscape into a checkerboard of towering woods and charred stumps.

Sustainable forestry, an alternative to clearcutting, is emerging as a more environmentally sound tactic. According to the Public Forestry Foundation, sustainable forestry focuses on what one leaves rather than on what one takes. Areas are never

clearcut. Instead, individual trees are identified and removed, with the intention of retaining the diversity and health of the forest ecosystem. The Forest Service is experimenting with sustainable forestry techniques in the Pacific Northwest.

Managers of private forests are also putting sustainable forestry theory into practice. The Collins-Almanor Forest in northern California, a 90,000-acre mixed conifer forest, has been managed sustainably since 1940. A commercial venture, the forest, provides 30 million board feet a year. This is accomplished without clearcutting, artificial replanting, herbicides, insecticides, or fertilizers.

Revival of another sustainable logging practice evokes visions of logging in bygone days. Horses and mules are being used to remove selectively cut logs. These animals cause much less damage to forests than the standard heavy machinery does, and they do not need roads to gain access to trees.

ests. Loggers will soon run out of more old growth to cut, regardless of whether more old-growth forests are protected. Inevitably, jobs will be lost and the industry will have to adapt. The question is, will industry change before or after it has cut down all of the remaining old growth?

From 1986 to 1988, record harvests of old growth occurred, with 100,000 acres cleared each year. If logging continued at this rate, the last of our unprotected old-growth forests would be gone in 15 to 20 years. In an effort to stave off such a future, conservation organizations have gone to court and have won injunctions against timber sales on forests under Forest Service and Bureau of Land Management jurisdiction. Judges have required the federal agencies to evaluate the environmental impacts that timber sales will have on spotted owl populations and develop management plans before sales can continue.

In response to its court injunction, the Forest Service prepared an environmental impact statement. Under this plan, 5.9 million acres of national forests will be "set aside" for spotted owls. Logging will be restricted on these areas for now, but they are not permanently protected from logging. (Much of this acreage was already off-limits to commercial cutting before the plan was devised.) According to U.S. Fish and Wildlife Service data, this level of protection in the Forest Service's plan will still result in at least a 50 percent decline in spotted owl populations. The Forest Service also estimated that 33,000 timber-related jobs could also be lost over the next 20 years, but spotted owl protection would not be the only cause. Other factors include overall reductions in the region's timber harvest and increased use of machinery rather than people for logging operations.

This region has already experienced significant job declines for reasons unrelated to conservation. Increased mechanization and modernization of logging and processing operations continue to claim many jobs. Mill positions have been sacrificed as a result of heavy export of whole logs cut on private lands. Over 3 billion board feet are exported each year, with most destined for Japan. If just half of these logs were processed in the region instead of being sent overseas unprocessed, the 30,000 jobs that would be lost from protection of old growth could be recovered. The export of logs cut from federal lands is prohibited.

The question in the Pacific Northwest is not *whether* the logging of old growth should stop, but *when*. The supply of ancient trees is limited. Advocates for old growth such as the Wilderness Society and the Native Forest Council want logging to halt while enough forests still stand to maintain healthy ecosystems and the plant and animals that depend on them. At the same time, they generally support legislation that would encourage diversification of timber-dependent economies and retraining of people for other occupations. The future of old-growth forests and the people connected to them will depend on whether the nation can address the real short-term needs without compromising the long-term health of both forest and human communities.

This chapter was written by Kathleen Rude, an environmental writer based in Deerfield, Illinois.

Industry

Tough regulations, consumer demand, and a growing trend toward corporate environmentalism spur industry's search for cleaner ways to produce goods and services.

As the toll of environmental abuse and degradation mounts, leaders of industry are facing what could be their greatest challenge: to maintain economic growth without compromising the environmental resources that sustain us. As companies try to regain the trust of a public made skeptical by toxic spills and decades of unchecked pollution, they are learning to provide services and produce goods in a less wasteful, more efficient manner. In the process, many businesses are finding that what is good for the environment is good for business.

Waste and pollution are still the rule, not the exception. But change is in the works from the boardroom to the loading dock. More companies are trying to prevent pollution at its source, finding new ways to make products and render services. Increasingly, consumers are demanding products that do not harm the environment. These currents are transforming business in ways that enhance both the environment and, some claim, the economy. The firms operating most effectively in this new climate focus ultimately on quality—goods and services that satisfy customers without diminishing their surroundings.

The developments described in this chapter focus on the United States and Canada, but change is in the works around the world. As *Changing Course*, a 1992 report prepared by the international 50-member Business Council for Sustainable Development, notes, businesses that recognize the advantages of corporate environmentalism "may expect to reap advantages over their competitors who lack vision. Companies that fail to change can expect to become obsolete."

Changing Attitudes

Many forces have caused the goals of environmentalists and corporate leaders to converge in ways undreamed of only a few years ago. For 25 years, environmental activists have hammered home the point that wasteful industrial practices (as well as individual habits) despoil the environment, jeopardize wildlife, and threaten human health and safety. Their efforts are paying off: Thanks to landmark federal laws that mandate that industry clean up, the air and waterways are significantly cleaner than they were only two decades ago.

Much of industry's new ecological bent can be traced straight to the bottom line. The cost of federally required pollution control and cleanup in the United States reached $100 billion in 1990 (nearly two thirds was paid by industry; taxpayers paid the rest). (See table, Manufacturers' Expenditures on Pollution Abatement.)

A 1990 survey by researchers at Stanford University found that 75 percent of the 80 firms questioned had incurred state or federal penalties averaging $300,000 each for failing to meet environmental guidelines, and that

these expenses were dwarfed by legal fees and cleanup costs. The researchers also reported that a large industrial firm can expect to pay as much as $450 million a year to comply with environmental regulations.

Consumer preferences are important motivators as well. Industry cannot afford to ignore the growing demand for goods and services that are environmentally benign, or "green," especially when consumers express willingness to pay premium prices.

Thus, it is not surprising that when more than 220 senior executives from more than 15 different industries responded to a survey conducted by Booz-Allen & Hamilton, a major environmental consulting firm, the proportion who believed environmental issues are "extremely important" to their company had increased threefold in the past two years.

Reducing Toxic Pollution

Conventional pollutants such as those produced by burning fuels have been regulated in the United States for more than 20 years. But toxic chemicals and materials—used in manufacturing and

Industry News

Houston, 1/31/92—*Texas industries discharged at least 941,000 pounds of toxics into Galveston Bay in 1988, according to a study released by the Galveston Bay Foundation. The actual amount is probably higher, the report said, because municipal and other dumping does not have to be disclosed under federal Toxic Release Inventory laws. The foundation's director said the sheer volume of toxics dumped was shocking.*

in a variety of service industries such as dry cleaning—represent a far more

Manufacturers' Expenditures on Pollution Abatement
(1986)

State	Million $	State	Million $
Alabama	36.7	Montana	2.0
Alaska	1.5	Nebraska	3.7
Arizona	30.2	Nevada	1.5
Arkansas	21.2	New Hampshire	4.0
California	292.2	New Jersey	87.3
Colorado	9.6	New Mexico	5.6
Connecticut	18.6	New York	109.3
Delaware	56.3	North Carolina	47.9
Florida	56.4	North Dakota	3.7
Georgia	177.7	Ohio	145.6
Hawaii	1.8	Oklahoma	9.9
Idaho	18.8	Oregon	23.6
Illinois	83.0	Pennsylvania	92.9
Indiana	115.4	Rhode Island	2.0
Iowa	19.0	South Carolina	52.3
Kansas	69.9	South Dakota	3.5
Kentucky	50.2	Tennessee	118.8
Louisiana	137.0	Texas	291.2
Maine	8.0	Utah	6.6
Maryland	24.4	Vermont	15.5
Massachusetts	146.9	Virginia	66.3
Michigan	162.3	Washington	45.8
Minnesota	18.7	West Virginia	25.9
Mississippi	14.0	Wisconsin	59.7
Missouri	50.4	Wyoming	2.2

Source: U.S. Bureau of the Census, *State and Metropolitan Area Data Book, 1991* (U.S. Government Printing Office, Washington, D.C., 1991), Table E: States, Item 627, p. 240.

subtle type of pollution. Literally tens of thousands of such chemicals and materials are used by industry. While toxic emissions and wastes may be very small compared to emissions of conventional pollutants, their effects can be extremely hazardous to human health as well as damaging to plants and animals.

Corporate attitudes toward toxic pollutants changed radically in the United States in 1986 when the Emergency Planning and Community Right to-Know Act went into effect. This law is more commonly known as Title III of the Superfund Amendments and Reauthorization Act (SARA Title III), or simply, "Superfund." It requires that companies with nine or more employees detail their releases of any of 313 listed toxic chemicals and chemical compounds to air, water, or underground wells. The report is used to compile a national Toxics Release Inventory (TRI). For the first time, the public was able to scrutinize industry's pollution performance. The TRI quickly became a valuable source of environmental data, useful to citizens, the press, regulators and lawmakers, and industry itself. (See box, For More Information about TRI.)

Companies had tracked the pollutants they released in order to comply

For More Information about TRI

A key provision of the Emergency Planning and Community Right to Know Act of 1986 is that the U.S. Environmental Protection Agency (EPA) must make the information reported available to the public. The Toxics Release Inventory (TRI) is the first publicly accessible on-line computer database mandated by federal law.

If you are interested in learning about the TRI, a good place to start is the Working Group on Community Right-to-Know, an affiliation of more than a dozen environmental and public interest organizations. This network provides information and publishes *Working Notes*, a newsletter covering right-to-know about toxic pollution ($15 per year). The Working Group is hosted by the U.S. Public Interest Research Group Education Fund at 215 Pennsylvania Avenue, S.E., Washington, DC 20003-1155. (202) 546-9707.

Other useful sources include:

EPA's Toxics Release Inventory User Support Service (TRI-US). This service helps citizens locate and access TRI data.
(202) 260-1531, 8:00-4:30 EST, M--F;
Fax: (202) 260-4659

Right-to-Know Computer Network (RTK NET). Provides access to TRI and other environmental data.
(202) 234-8494

On-Line Computer Database (TOXNET).
(301) 496-1131 (for account information).
Cost: $25-$35 per hour. Ask for a Quick Reference Guide and a TRI Demo Disk.

Useful documents:

To obtain these and other documents call EPA's Emergency Planning Community Right-to-Know (EPCRA) Hotline, (800) 535-0202 or (703) 920-9877, 8:30--4:30 EST, M--F

"Roadmaps Toxicity Matrix"
Helps citizens obtain quick reference toxicity information for TRI chemicals.

"Common Synonyms" (for chemicals listed under Section 313 of EPCRA) EPA 560/4-91-005, January 1991.

"Pocket Guide for Chemical Hazards," National Institute for Occupational Safety and Health, 1990.
Helps citizens identify TRI chemicals under various common names.
(800) 35NIOSH

"Making the Difference: Using the Right to Know in the Fight against Toxics"
Explains citizen use of TRI data.
The Center for Policy Alternatives
1875 Connecticut Avenue, N.W., Suite 710
Washington, DC 20009
(202) 387-6030

"A Citizen's Toxic Waste Audit Manual"
Greenpeace
1436 U Street, N.W.
Washington, DC 20009
(202) 462-1177

Source: Working Group on Community Right-to-Know, 1992.

with specific pollution control regulations. The 1987 TRI was the first time, however, that these data had been collected in a way that provided an overall picture of company emissions. Many top-level managers, and the communities that surround their plants, were shocked by the numbers. Now, nearly every major manufacturer is taking steps to cut emissions of substances in the inventory.

The U.S. Environmental Protection Agency (EPA) estimates that in 1990, the latest year for which figures are available, 4.83 billion pounds of the 313 listed toxic chemicals were released

Toxic Releases to Public Water Facilities
(top 15 industries, 1990)

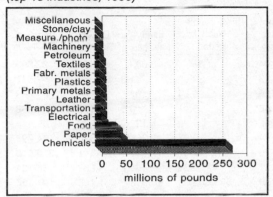

Source: U.S. Environmental Protection Agency (EPA), *1990 Toxics Release Inventory: Public Data Release* (EPA, Office of Pollution Prevention and Toxics, Washington, D.C., 1992), Table 17, p. 58.
Note: The category "Measure./photo." includes toxics created by medical and dental x-ray instruments and related measuring devices, and photographic equipment and supplies.

from manufacturing facilities or transferred off-site for treatment and disposal. Of this total, 2.2 billion pounds were emitted to the air, 197 million pounds were released into water, 441 million pounds were released to land, and 725 million pounds were injected underground. EPA also estimates that 448 million pounds of toxic chemicals were transferred (sent to municipal wastewater treatment plants for processing and disposal). Another 815 million pounds were removed from factories for treatment, storage, or disposal. (See table, Toxic Chemicals Released, by Industry.)

While the depth of commitment to environmental concerns varies among companies, there are clear signs that companies are moving to reduce the amount of toxic material they release to the environment and to improve community relations. For example:

- The Chemical Manufacturers Association (CMA) reports that between 1987 and 1990 its members decreased their releases of TRI-listed chemicals to the environment by about one third.

- By April 1992, 734 companies, which contribute a significant percentage of the nation's toxic releases, had joined EPA's voluntary "33/50" program. Participating firms committed to cut emissions of 17 toxic chemicals by one third by 1992, and halve them by 1995. Results will be published in 1993 along with 1992 TRI data.

- Nationwide, citizens have formed more than 160 community action panels. Initiated after the catastrophic chemical leak in Bhopal, India, in December 1984, these groups meet at least bimonthly with plant managers on topics that range from emergency response to corporate charitable contributions.

Rethinking the Inventory

Many observers, while conceding the usefulness of the TRI, express concern about gaps in the data. For example, the TRI does not reflect hazardous materials incorporated into products themselves, because the reporting requirement applies only to wastes released to the environment. Only two thirds of the factories and other facilities covered by the reporting requirement actually comply. And the list of toxic substances is itself incomplete. In

Toxic Chemicals Released, by Industry
(distribution, in thousand pounds, 1990)

Industry	Air Emissons	Surface Water Discharges	Underground Well Injection	Land Releases	Off-Site Transfers	Total Transfers and Releases
Food	26,886	5,404	36	8,689	9,116	92,393
Tobacco	2,475	23	0	1.5	39	2,547
Textiles	33,967	556	0.04	37	3,120	45,663
Apparel	1,600	48	0	0.8	170	1,968
Lumber	37,649	209	0.08	127	7,326	45,414
Furniture	60,051	4	0.07	7,368	4,328	64,796
Paper	243,936	37,676	0.07	7,368	18,441	359,510
Printing	52,035	1	0.35	4.7	4,383	56,734
Chemicals	695,358	133,479	658,662	98,518	251,193	2,107,156
Petroleum	71,299	4,987	37,851	3,114	9,249	134,214
Plastics	192,541	463	15	200	22,455	224,534
Leather	11,846	388	0	21	2,552	24,428
Stone/clay	21,869	175	7,555	2,283	12,001	45,651
Metals	351,509	12,501	20,052	315,591	364,125	1,081,447
Machinery	52,777	209	0.568	139	13,564	69,427
Electrical	81,867	416	19	2,736	35,119	132,656
Transportation	193,522	235	0.32	1,949	39,537	244,941
Measure./photo.	32,780	58	0.02	5.3	9,785	44,447
Miscellaneous	24,891	17	0.09	40	6,486	32,073

Source: U.S. Environmental Protection Agency (EPA), *1990 Toxics Release Inventory: Public Data Release* (EPA, Office of Pollution Prevention and Toxics, Washington, D.C., 1992), Table 17, p. 58.
Note: The category "Measure./photo." includes toxics created by medical and dental x-ray instruments and related measuring devices, and photographic equipment and supplies.

1991, the U.S. General Accounting Office reported that current law allows as much as 95 percent of all chemical emissions to go unreported.

The Pollution Prevention Act (1990) extended reporting requirements to include the amount of chemicals recycled on- or off-site, as well as the amount of waste *not* generated because of steps a manufacturer has taken to prevent pollution. But the law does not require that producers outline how toxic chemicals are used in the production process or how they are incorporated into the products themselves.

These concerns prompted introduction in the U.S. House of Representatives of the "Community Right to Know More Act of 1991." One of the goals of this bill is to generate information on how much chemical is used per unit of product. This would enhance efforts to reduce use of toxics and to make comparisons between specific industries and companies. A similar bill was introduced in the Senate.

Trends in Industrial Toxic Releases
(by distribution, 1987–90)

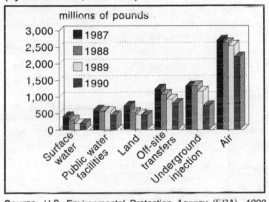

millions of pounds

- 1987
- 1988
- 1989
- 1990

Categories (x-axis): Surface water, Public water facilities, Land, Off-site transfers, Underground injection, Air

Source: U.S. Environmental Protection Agency (EPA), *1990 Toxics Release Inventory: Public Data Release* (EPA, Office of Pollution Prevention and Toxics, Washington, D.C., 1992), Table 19, p. 62.

It is difficult to make straightforward comparisons of TRI data from different years, for many reasons:

- For each chemical on the TRI in 1990, companies were required to report releases of 25,000 pounds or more. That number was lowered from 75,000 pounds in 1987. As a result, 1990 figures reflect reporting by more companies.

- The database changes continually as chemicals are added to or removed from the list.

- The numbers do not reflect fluctuations in production. Output by the U.S. chemical industry has grown by 10.1 percent since 1987. The TRI figures show that the amount of toxic material released has dropped, but not that production has also increased.

- Companies have modified and improved methods of calculating the quantities of toxic substances they release.

Nonetheless, overall emissions of toxic substances appear to be decreasing. (See graph, Trends in Industrial Toxic Releases.)

When interpreting TRI data, it is useful to remember that not all substances reported are equally toxic. The characteristics of a compound can be more important than the quantity released. Thus, a small release of a highly toxic chemical can be more significant than release of a large volume of a less toxic chemical. Of the 313 substances on the TRI list, 43 are known or suspected to cause cancer. (See table, Known or Suspected TRI Carcinogens.) The CMA, whose members produce 90 percent of the chemicals made in the United States, reports that in 1990 known or suspected carcinogens made up 3 percent of TRI releases by members and 4 percent of toxic materials transferred off-site.

Toward Zero Wastes

One way to avoid harm to human health and the environment by toxic substances is to stop releasing them, in the form of industrial byproducts and wastes, to the environment. This goal is known as pollution prevention or source reduction. An even better option, where possible, is not to use toxic substances in the first place.

Efforts to reduce use of toxics and to prevent pollution often require back-to-the-basics planning. Manufacturers can redesign processes, upgrade cleaning practices, and improve operating procedures, for example, to minimize spills. Managers and engineers can rethink their choice of raw materials and solvents to avoid or reduce the use of toxics and can modify product packaging, loading, and transportation.

The result is a radical but very sensible new approach. Pollution control has long relied on familiar "end-of-the-

pipe" technologies such as scrubbers, incinerators, and filters to control or reduce the toxicity of pollutants. Such methods do not affect the processes that produce the wastes, and all of them add to production costs. In contrast, pollution prevention relies on more efficient processes that reduce wastes while producing more product per unit of raw material.

A goal of zero wastes gives rise to a hierarchy of waste management options. Source reduction has the least effect on the environment, followed by recycling and reuse of wastes, especially when they can be recycled directly back into the process. Waste treatment to detoxify or neutralize wastes comes next, followed by the least desirable option—disposal of what cannot be treated.

Industry experience in the past few years supports an assertion by the congressional Office of Technology Assessment that existing technology could prevent half of industrial waste releases. In 1992, the nonprofit group INFORM looked again at 29 chemical manufacturing plants whose pollution prevention activities it had studied in 1985. The analysis of 181 individual activities or processes—44 from the 1985 study and 137 in the interim—reveals progress in waste reduction and rapid cost savings:

- Amounts of waste reduced were reported for 80 of the 181 activities for a total annual waste reduction of 128.7 million pounds. Six large plants—belonging to Aristech, Dow, DuPont, Exxon, Merck, and Monsanto—reported reductions of more than 10 million pounds of waste annually.

- Of the 99 source reduction activities for which percent reductions were reported, more than 25 percent totally eliminated the target waste stream, while more than half cut targeted wastes by 90 percent or more. Average reduction in individual waste streams was 71 percent.

- Of 62 source reduction activities for which cost information was reported, 15 percent saved $1 million or more a year. Twenty-five percent of the programs involved no capital investment.

- For two thirds of the 38 programs for which payback data were provided, companies recouped their initial investments in six months or less.

The following examples suggest the range of successful industry efforts to improve environmental performance.

Cleaner production. When American Cyanamid modified the manufacturing process of a yellow dye, it was able to eliminate the use of a toxic solvent. Equipment modification that allowed recycling of a substitute solvent cost $100,000 and saved the company $200,000 a year in reduced disposal and energy costs.

Equipment change. Rhône-Poulenc spent $10,000 to install in-line condensers for its salicylaldehyde process to avoid product loss during the drying stage. Product yield rose 0.5 percent. The plant saved $30,000 in the first year.

Chemical substitution. Intertox America, a paper processor, developed a way to bleach paper using hydrogen peroxide, thereby eliminating its use of toxic chlorine bleaching agents. Intertox now consults with other paper processing companies to help them switch to the new process.

Industry cooperatives. Northern Telecom (Canada) and AT&T joined forces in 1989 to found the Industry Cooperative for Ozone Layer Protection. Now, the co-op's members, 12 multinational electronics and aerospace manufacturers, provide information and technical support to companies trying to make the transition to substances free of ozone-depleting compounds.

Industrial partnerships. S.C. Johnson, a producer of household cleaning materials, invited its top suppliers to participate in a conference focused on the suppliers' environmental performance as well as on Johnson's. Johnson representatives report that the conference accelerated improvements in packag-

Known or Suspected TRI Carcinogens

1,2-Dibromoethane (ethylene dibromide)	Creosote
4-Aminobiphenyl	Diethyl sulfate
4-Nitrobiphenyl	Dimethyl sulfate
Acrylonitrile	Dimethylcarbaryl chloride
Arsenic	Epichlorohydrin
Arsenic compounds	Ethylene oxide
Asbestos (friable)	Formaldehyde
Benzene	Isopropyl alcohol[a]
Benzidine	Mustard gas
Beryllium	Nickel
Beryllium compounds	Nickel compounds
β-Naphthylamine	Nitrogen mustard
Bis(chloromethyl) ether	N-Nitrosodiethylamine
C.I. Direct Black 38	N-Nitrosodimethylamine
C.I. Direct Blue 6	Propylene oxide
C.I. Direct Brown 95	Styrene oxide
Cadmium	Thorium dioxide
Cadmium compounds	o-Toluidine hydrochloride
Chloromethyl methyl ether	Tris (2,3-dibromopropyl) phosphate
Chromium	Vinyl bromide
Chromium compounds	Vinyl chloride

Source: Chemical Manufacturers Association (CMA), *Preventing Pollution in the Chemical Industry: 1987–1000* (CMA, Washington, D.C., 1992), Table 12, p. 15.
Note: a. The carcinogenic classification applies to manufacturing by the strong acid process, not to isopropyl alcohol itself.

In Pursuit of Green Labeling

Q: Can a "biodegradable" plastic trash bag degrade if it is buried in an airtight landfill?

Q: Is a deodorant environmentally safer than others since, as its label claims, it contains no CFCs?

Q: Does the triangular "chasing arrows" symbol mean that a product can be recycled?*

Such questions are familiar to consumers trying to sort out the confusing and conflicting claims manufacturers make on behalf of their products. Opinion surveys in the past few years show two distinct trends in consumer attitudes toward "green" marketing.

On the one hand, the percentages of people who say they buy products on the basis of the manufacturer's or product's environmental reputation are rising. One poll by the Roper Organization showed that consumers in the United States would be willing to pay an average 6.6 percent more and as much as 19.6 percent more for products that they think will not harm the environment.

On the other hand, many consumers do not trust business to act responsibly when it comes to environmental issues. Some environmental claims for products are valid, but many are misleading or even deceptive. While many people prefer to select products that will not harm the environment, they do not want to fall for yet another marketing gimmick. How can an ecoconscious buyer tell which claims are legitimate?

Many countries are taking their lead from Germany, which launched the "Blue Angel," the first national ecolabel, in 1978. So far, Japan, Canada, Sweden, and Nor-

way have introduced their own environmental seals, and several other European nations have proposed them.

The programs have different criteria for judging a product's fitness for a seal. Germany has been criticized for judging a product on a few key attributes and awarding the seal even when other qualities are no better than those of similar products. This example has inspired some other countries to analyze each product's effect on the environment through its whole "life cycle"—from the raw materials used, through emissions released in manufacturing, through a consumer's use, to disposal. Canada's Eco-logo, bestowed by the Environmental Choice program established in 1988, attempts to follow this approach.

For a number of political and scientific reasons, the United States has no plans for a national ecolabel. An important one, as other countries have learned, is the extreme difficulty of devising a sound methodology for setting product standards. The goal of accurate life cycle assessments is elusive so far.

Federal reluctance to enter the labeling fray has given rise to a bewildering array of definitions, product seals, and logos as environmental groups and state legislators step in to fill the void. Two private

ing and elimination from its products of specific chemicals that may have adverse environmental effects.

Industry and environmental group collaboration. Several Canadian companies, such as Dow Chemical Canada,

Nova Corp., and Dofasco, are working with environmental groups, including Friends of the Earth and Pollution Probe, to gather data on toxic waste emissions in Canada and to eliminate the worst problems by 1994.

In Pursuit of Green Labeling *(continued)*

sector groups, Green Seal (started by Earth Day founder Denis Hayes), and Green Cross, a division of Scientific Certification Systems, a California-based organization, are trying independently to develop a widely recognized U.S. ecological product seal that earns respect from both consumers and industry. The programs are in early stages. They show promise, but to succeed they must resolve the same problems of methodology and standards faced by other labeling programs. The seals have yet to win widespread acceptance.

Alarmed by the emerging trend toward advertising products based on alleged environmental qualities, 10 state attorney generals formed a task force to study environmental product claims.

The ensuing report, "Green Report II," was published by the National Association of Attorney Generals in 1991. It summarized the problems and suggested some solutions. Doug Blanke, who represented Minnesota's attorney general on the task force, said that the overriding recommendation was for national leadership—federal definitions, guidelines, and standards that would help companies advertise products as environmentally superior. On July 28, 1992, the Federal Trade Commission responded by issuing guidelines to help clarify potentially deceptive "green" phrases in advertising. After the new standards have been in place for three years, a Commission spokesman said, they may be modified on the basis of suggestions from consumers and advertisers.

The task force suggests that businesses should avoid broad terminology, using phrases such as "earth friendly," "green," or "environmentally safe" only if they are defined. More specific guidelines from "Green Report II" include the following:

- Previously existing or previously unadvertised green attributes should not be promoted to create the appearance of recent modifications or improvements.

- Only post-consumer materials should be referred to as "recycled" material.

- Recaptured factory materials should be termed "reprocessed" or "recaptured."

- Product life cycle studies should not be used to advertise or promote specific products until methods for conducting them are standardized.

- A clear distinction should be made between the environmental attributes of a *product* and the environmental attributes of its *packaging*.

- A nationally sold product should not be described as compostable unless a significant amount of the product is currently being composted everywhere the product is sold. Likewise, if consumers have little or no opportunity to recycle a product, recyclability claims should not be made.

*Answers: 1) No. 2) No, none of them contains CFCs. 3) Only if there is a recycling facility that can accept it and a market for resale. Many plastic items bear a symbol with a number, but it only identifies which combination of resins was used, not that the plastic is recyclable.

Waste tracking and accounting. Polaroid's Environmental Accounting and Reporting System (EARS) monitors all substances that enter Polaroid facilities, not just those regulated by the government. These substances are divided into five categories depending on their potential environmental impact. EARS, an industry model, measures waste reduced per unit of production,

Steps for Company Managers

How should the sensible company chairman turn environmental ideas into action? Here are a few suggestions to begin with:

1. Put the most senior person possible in charge of environmental policy. A member of the board should have clear responsibility, and there should be a well-defined management structure. All the golden intentions in the world are pointless unless the chairman cares and is known to care.

2. Draft a policy, then make it public. Make it clear. Include targets, with numbers and dates; this will not be possible unless you also follow the remaining suggestions.

3. Measure. Nothing concentrates the mind like numbers. In particular, discover what wastes you are creating and what energy you are using.

4. Institute a regular environmental audit to check on what is happening. While an outside consultant may be a help with the first three steps, this one can be done in-house. Pay particular attention to the follow-up: there is no point in knowing what is wrong if nothing is done to fix it.

5. Consider ways to reduce the range of materials you use that could do environmental harm. Do you really need so many toxic chemicals?

6. Think about the materials in your product. If you had responsibility for disposing of it when your customer threw it out (and one day, legislators may well dump that burden on your firm), could you do so? In an environmentally benign way? If not, consider changing the design and materials you use.

7. Remember that you may be able to make a business opportunity out of disposing of your product when the customer has finished with it. If your customer brings back used paint drums or old refrigerators, it offers a chance to build a new link—and to make your customer dependent on you in a new way.

8. If you invest in a country where environmental standards are low, do not expect them to stay that way. If one country finds a way of forcing companies to clean up, others will follow. Better to assume that standards everywhere will rise than to risk an expensive and disagreeable surprise.

9. Accept that environmental regulations will tend to converge upward. What is compulsory in the most energetically environmental markets (California, Germany, Scandinavia) will probably reach your home market. If you accept the highest standards before they are made compulsory, you steal a market advantage.

10. Remember that greenery is often a proxy for quality—in the eyes of your customers, your workers, and your managers. A truly green company is unlikely to be badly managed. Conversely, a well-managed company finds it relatively easy to be green.

Source: Reprinted with permission from Frances Cairncross, *Costing the Earth: The Challenge for Governments, the Opportunities for Business* (Harvard Business School Press ed., Boston, 1992; Economist Books Ltd., 1991), pp. 317–318.

whereas TRI data only reflect absolute quantity. This allows Polaroid to compare progress from year to year regardless of company expansion or production cutbacks.

Companywide involvement. The 3M Company, which has pioneered corporate pollution prevention, introduced its Pollution Prevention Pays (3P) program in 1975. 3M reports that in more

Selected Reading

For Consumers

A Citizen's Guide to Promoting Toxic Waste Reduction, 1990, $15 plus $2.50 per order for shipping.
INFORM
381 Park Avenue South
New York, NY 10016-8806
Write to request a list of other INFORM publications.

Shopping for a Better World, 4th ed. 1992, $6.45 includes shipping; and *The Better World Investment Guide*, 1991, $22.95 includes shipping.
Council on Economic Priorities
30 Irving Place
New York, NY 10003
(202) 420-1133
For consumers and investors who want to learn about, support, and influence a company on the basis of its environmental and human rights performance.

"Green Consumer Letter"
Tilden Press
1526 Connecticut Avenue, N.W.
Washington, DC 20036
(800) 955-GREEN
$27 per year/U.S., $30 per year/Canada. Monthly newsletter with news and pointers for environmentally aware consumers.

For Managers

Business Recycling Manual
INFORM, Inc., and Recourse Systems, Inc., 1991, $85 plus $3 for shipping and handling.
INFORM
381 Park Avenue South
New York, NY 10016-8806

"The Green Business Letter"
Tilden Press
1526 Connecticut Avenue, N.W.
Washington, DC 20036
(800) 955-GREEN
$97 per year/U.S., $102 per year/Canada. Monthly news and tips for environmentally conscious companies.

Environmental Self-Assessment Program
A Corporate Self-Assessment of Environmental Performance.
GEMI/ESAP Document
c/o The Environmental Policy Center
2000 L Street, Suite 710
Washington, DC 20036
$25 payable to GEMI to cover shipping. For more information, contact Charles McGlashan, (415) 296-2289.

Costing the Earth: The Challenge for Governments, the Opportunities for Business, by Frances Cairncross
Harvard Business School Press ed., 1992, $24.95
How market incentives can correct environmental problems and why conventional regulatory systems do not work. By the environment editor of *The Economist.*

"Green Market Alert"
345 Wood Creek Road
Bethlehem, CT 06751
(203) 266-5049
$145/$175/$295 per year, depending on subscriber group type and revenues.
Monthly newsletter with forecasts, reports, news, and statistics on the business impacts of green consumerism.

Changing Course, by Stephan Schmidheiny with the Business Council for Sustainable Development, MIT Press, 1992.
$35.00 hardcover, $16.95 softcover
Can industry and a healthy environment coexist? The 50-some members of the Business Council for Sustainable Development answer a resounding "yes." But, as this lively analysis shows, it is not always easy to meld corporate concerns with the goals of sustainable development.

Environmental Dividends: Cutting More Chemical Wastes, Mark H. Dorfman, Warren R. Muir, Ph.D., Catherine G. Miller, Ph.D., 1992. $75, plus $3 postage.
INFORM
381 Park Avenue South
New York, NY 10016-8806

than 3,000 3P projects, it has cut wastewater by 1 billion gallons, air pollutants by 120,000 tons, and solid waste by more than 400,000 tons. Savings so far exceed $530 million.

Components of Change

One indication of the corporate turn toward more environmentally sound practices is the surge of corporate commitments to cut toxic emissions substantially and finally eliminate such releases altogether. Codes of environmental ethics also may raise corporate commitment to develop less polluting products and processes. Some, like the Responsible Care programs started by the Canadian Chemical Producers Association in 1985 and adopted by members of the CMA in 1988, promote responsible management of chemicals throughout industry operations. Association members also commit to improve their operations continually, through reevaluation, goal-setting, and input from employees and the public.

Codes of environmental ethics strike some observers as corporate PR-as-usual. Experience in the past few years has shown, however, that companies where top managers make a public commitment to reducing waste and increasing efficiency are the most successful in meeting their goals. (See box, Steps for Company Managers.) At ICI and Union Carbide, for instance, top managers review all major strategic plans for minimizing waste. The INFORM study found that while leadership is important, plants making the greatest environmental strides also emphasize cost accounting and employee involvement.

As the impetus for an industrial transformation grows, blueprints for action are proliferating. One of the most lofty, and influential, is the Business Charter for Sustainable Development, 16 principles for environmental management detailed by the International Chamber of Commerce. So far, more than 900 companies worldwide have signed the charter.

While the goals set out by the principles are admirable, the realities of transforming them into concrete steps can be daunting for a business of any size. Thus, the Global Environmental Management Initiative, an international business consortium, has collaborated with the management firm Deloitte & Touche to develop an environmental self-assessment program that helps a company measure its progress in living up to each of the principles. (See box, Selected Reading.) The results can be used by a company to set priorities for improving its environmental performance and to translate strategy into action.

Author Cheryl Simon Silver, based in Silver Spring, Maryland, is also senior editor of the 1993 Information Please Environmental Almanac.

Green Metro Areas

A new ranking covering the 75 largest metro areas reveals some surprises in who's clean and green. Also, 37 major cities provide environmental self-portraits.

What defines a city? Is it the political entity that administers environmental laws and provides environmental services such as waste collection? Or is it the mass of humanity whose homes and workplaces often sprawl across political boundaries within an extended metro area? The U.S. Census Bureau has struggled with this question, and so have the editors of this *Almanac*. The result is that this chapter ranks the 75 largest U.S. metro areas—those with a population of over 500,000—on measures of environmental quality and performance ap-

propriate to metro areas as a whole. It also compares 37 major cities on measures of environmental quality and performance appropriate to specific political entities.

The metro area rankings are summarized in a Green Metro Index, based on federal data and other national data sources. The comparisons of cities as political entities are based on environmental self-portraits provided by the cities themselves; some 37 cities returned a detailed questionnaire to the *Almanac* (see box, City Environmental Self Portraits).

The results of these two different but complementary looks at the environmental aspects of U.S. metro areas reveal some strong similarities. They also show, however, some fascinating and important differences that reinforce the need for a dual approach to capture the complexity of the environmental problems in our urban areas.

Perhaps the most critical factor forcing a dual approach is the growing divergence between the human geography of cities and their political geography. As an urban entity, the New York metropolitan area sprawls far beyond the boundaries of the political entity that is New York City. As measured by the U.S. Census Bureau, beginning with the 1990 census, the consolidated metropolitan area extends to parts of three states—New York, New Jersey, and Connecticut—some 23 counties in all. Likewise, the Chicago metro area stretches from Gary, Indiana, through Illinois and into southern Wisconsin; the Washington, D.C., metro area extends far into Maryland and Virginia; the Philadelphia metro area now includes both Wilmington, Delaware, and Trenton, New Jersey; and the San Francisco metro area includes Oakland and San Jose.

In effect, the Census Bureau has changed the definition of what constitutes a metropolitan area to include not just the central city but also the suburbs and contiguous urban areas, however far they stretch. This change in definition has significantly altered the sizes and even the entries in the list of the largest U.S. metro areas (see table, 75 Largest U.S. Metro Areas). New York is now a behemoth with a population approaching 18 million people. Los Angeles has 14.5 million, greater Chicago 8 million, and the consolidated San Francisco region, with 6.3 million,

City Environmental Self-Portraits

The *Environmental Almanac* invited 64 cities (those ranked in the *1992 Environmental Almanac*) to return a detailed questionnaire covering some 27 environmental practices and policies and to provide other information relevant to the city's environmental efforts.

We were not certain that the cities would respond to our challenge to provide environmental self-portraits, because the questionnaire required cities to pull together data from many different agencies and programs in order to assemble an in-depth picture. Somewhat to our surprise, a total of 37 cities did respond. One city manager told us, "These are tough questions, but they are just the kind of questions cities should be asking themselves."

We present descriptions and comparisons based on those self-portraits in a series of boxes throughout this chapter.

is the country's fourth largest. Some 38 metro areas now have populations over 1 million, and there are 75 U.S. metro areas with populations larger than 500,000, including Little Rock, Arkansas; Charleston, South Carolina; and New Bedford, Massachusetts. Cities such as Albuquerque, New Mexico (ranked the 38th largest U.S. city under the old definitions), or Wichita, Kansas (formerly the 50th largest), are not even on the list of the 75 largest. Other cities have been statistically swallowed by the surrounding metropolitan area, with Santa Ana, California, disappearing into the Los Angeles metro area and Newark, New Jersey, into the New York metro area.

From an environmental point of view, the new and expanded definition of a metro area reflects an important reality. Air pollution, water and energy

75 Largest U.S. Metro Areas

Metro Area	Population	Rank	Metro Area	Population	Rank
New York-Northern New Jersey-Long Island, NY-NJ-CT	17,953,372	1	Columbus, OH	1,377,419	29
			San Antonio, TX	1,302,099	30
			Indianapolis, IN	1,249,822	31
Los Angeles-Anaheim-Riverside, CA	14,531,529	2	New Orleans, LA	1,238,816	32
			Buffalo-Niagara Falls, NY	1,189,288	33
Chicago-Gary-Lake County, IL-IN-WI	8,065,633	3	Charlotte-Gastonia-Rock Hill, NC-SC	1,162,093	34
San Francisco-Oakland-San Jose, CA	6,253,311	4	Hartford-New Britain-Middletown, CT	1,123,678	35
Philadelphia-Wilmington-Trenton, PA-NJ-DE-MD	5,899,345	5	Orlando, FL	1,072,748	36
			Salt Lake City-Ogden, UT	1,072,227	37
Detroit-Ann Arbor, MI	4,665,236	6	Rochester, NY	1,002,410	38
Washington, DC-MD-VA	3,923,574	7	Nashville, TN	985,026	39
Dallas-Ft. Worth, TX	3,885,415	8	Memphis, TN-AR-MS	981,747	40
Boston-Lawrence-Salem, MA-NH	3,783,817	9	Oklahoma City, OK	958,839	41
			Louisville, KY-IN	952,662	42
Houston-Galveston-Brazoria, TX	3,711,043	10	Dayton-Springfield, OH	951,270	43
Miami-Ft. Lauderdale, FL	3,192,582	11	Greensboro, NC	942,091	44
Atlanta, GA	2,833,511	12	Providence-Pawtucket-Fall River, RI-MA	916,270	45
Cleveland-Akron-Lorain, OH	2,759,823	13			
Seattle-Tacoma, WA	2,559,164	14	Birmingham, AL	907,810	46
San Diego, CA	2,498,016	15	Jacksonville, FL	906,727	47
Minneapolis-St. Paul, MN-WI	2,464,124	16	Albany-Schenectady-Troy, NY	874,304	48
St. Louis, MO-IL	2,444,099	17	Richmond-Petersburg, VA	865,640	49
Baltimore, MD	2,382,172	18	West Palm Beach-Boca Raton-Delray Beach, FL	863,518	50
Pittsburgh-Beaver Valley, PA	2,242,798	19			
Phoenix, AZ	2,122,101	20	Honolulu, HI	836,231	51
Tampa-St. Petersburg-Clearwater, FL	2,067,959	21	New Haven-Waterbury-Meriden, CT	804,219	52
Denver-Boulder, CO	1,848,319	22	Austin, TX	781,572	53
Cincinnati-Hamilton, OH-KY-IN	1,744,124	23	Las Vegas, NV	741,459	54
Milwaukee-Racine, WI	1,607,183	24	Raleigh-Durham, NC	735,480	55
Kansas City, MO-KS	1,566,280	25	Scranton-Wilkes-Barre, PA	734,175	56
Sacramento, CA	1,481,102	26	Worcester-Fitchburg-Leominster, MA	709,705	57
Portland-Vancouver, OR-WA	1,477,895	27	Tulsa, OK	708,954	58
Norfolk-Virginia Beach-Newport News, VA	1,396,107	28	Grand Rapids, MI	688,399	59
			Allentown-Bethlehem, PA-NJ	686,688	60

Continued on next page

75 Largest U.S. Metro Areas (cont.)

Metro Area	Population	Rank	Metro Area	Population	Rank
Fresno, CA	667,490	61	Harrisburg-Lebanon-	587,986	70
Tucson, AZ	666,880	62	Carlisle, PA		
Syracuse, NY	659,864	63	Bakersfield, CA	543,477	71
Greenville-	640,861	64	Baton Rouge, LA	528,264	72
Spartanburg, SC			Little Rock-North	513,117	73
Omaha, NE-IA	618,262	65	Little Rock, AR		
Toledo, OH	614,128	66	Charleston, SC	506,875	74
Knoxville, TN	604,816	67	New Bedford-Fall	506,325	75
Springfield, MA	602,878	68	River-Attleboro, MA		
El Paso, TX	591,610	69			

Source: U.S. Bureau of the Census, *State and Metropolitan Data Book, 1991.*

consumption, transportation needs and options, opportunities for access to nature in the form of parks, and potential exposure to industrial pollutants all reflect conditions, political performance, and individual behaviors in the entire metro region, not just in the central city. The collection of federal data—and our Green Metro Index—increasingly reflects these new Census Bureau definitions.

Yet it is important to acknowledge that the mayor or the city manager of, say, Los Angeles, does not control environmental regulations in Santa Monica, Long Beach, or Riverside—all parts of the consolidated Los Angeles metro area. To judge the performance of city officials on environmental matters requires data specific to the political jurisdiction that they manage. That is the importance of the environmental self-portraits provided by 37 cities.

Environmental Indicators

Nine environmental indicators are included in the Green Metro Index, measuring air quality (two indicators), drinking water quality, transportation practices, past and present sources of toxic chemicals in the metro environment (two indicators), and energy use

and price (three indicators). Since conditions change and federal data sometimes lag behind, the Green Metro Index should be viewed as a snapshot of the level of environmental quality at a given moment in time.

In addition, we report comparisons based on 19 additional environmental indicators drawn from the completed questionnaires we received—data provided directly by the cities themselves. These data span such categories as water use, wastes, sources of energy used to generate electricity, transportation, parks and other environmental amenities, and the presence or absence of a variety of environmental policies, from recycling and tree planting programs to incentives for the use of mass transit. These data are not included in the Green Metro Index; instead, cities that returned our questionnaire are compared separately on those data, which in most instances relates to a specific political entity, not to the entire metro area.

Air Quality

Air quality is perhaps the most widely used environmental indicator, in part because data are widely available but also because air quality has such an immediate impact on our lives. For the Green Metro Index, the ambient quality of air in our cities is determined by daily readings of ambient levels of five pollutants, all regulated by the Clean Air Act: sulfur dioxide, nitrogen oxides, particulate matter, carbon monoxide, and ozone.

The U.S. Environmental Protection Agency (EPA) integrates daily monitoring information for these five pollutants into an overall Pollutant Standards Index (PSI), taking account of the differing standards and monitoring techniques for each pollutant. The single PSI number represents the worst daily air quality experienced in an extended metro area and is often used to report air quality by the news media. PSI levels above 100 are characterized as unhealthful, above 200 as very unhealthful, and above 300 as hazardous.

The EPA publishes PSI data for only a few cities. However, it calculates the index for most large cities and metro areas. The *Environmental Almanac* filed a Freedom of Information request to obtain those data for the 75 largest U.S. metro areas. In the Green Metro Index, we include both the annual average

Average Air Quality

Metro Area	Average PSI	Metro Area	Average PSI
Honolulu	15	Tulsa	42
San Francisco-Oakland	20	Detroit	43
Kansas City	28	Grand Rapids	43
Washington, DC	32	Dallas-Ft. Worth	43
Pittsburgh	32	Milwaukee	44
Scranton	33	Las Vegas	44
Chicago	33	St. Louis	45
Louisville	33	Toledo	45
Albany	33	New York	46
Rochester	34	Columbus	46
Allentown	34	Jacksonville	46
Cleveland	35	Tampa-St. Petersburg	46
Harrisburg	35	Atlanta	47
Providence	35	Baton Rouge	47
Salt Lake City	36	El Paso	48
New Haven	36	Phoenix	48
Nashville	37	Memphis	49
Omaha	37	Tucson	49
Austin	38	Indianapolis	49
New Orleans	38	Bakersfield	51
Denver	39	Sacramento	51
Baltimore	39	Knoxville	52
Philadelphia	39	Charlotte	54
Worcester	39	San Diego	54
San Antonio	39	Houston	56
Cincinnati	40	Raleigh-Durham	56
Oklahoma City	41	Fresno	56
Dayton	42	Los Angeles	73
Orlando	42		

Source: EPA Aeromatic Information Retrieval System, Pollutant Standard Index Summary, 1990.

ENVIRONMENTAL SELF-PORTRAITS

City Water Use

Data on residential water use come from questionnaires and show a very wide range. Western cities generally used more water than their eastern counterparts. At one extreme, daily use in Birmingham and Denver is about 165 gallons per person (see table, Residential Water Use Per Capita). New York and Honolulu were also comparatively wasteful (in Honolulu's case, surprisingly so, since virtually all of its supply comes from groundwater). At the other extreme, Pittsburgh residents each use less than one quarter as much— 41 gallons per day. Buffalo, Seattle, and St. Paul were also sparing in their use of water in the home. Such large variations in water use—a fourfold difference—suggest that many cities could significantly improve their water conservation practices. Even within a metro area, different cities reported very different practices: Dallas residents, for example, used nearly 50 percent more water per person than their neighbors in Ft. Worth and Arlington.

Total water use within a city depends not only on residential use but also on how much is used by industry and commercial establishments. Cities reported total daily use ranging from 280 (Chicago) to 88 gallons (Virginia Beach). Newark reported high total daily use, 274 gallons, yet has relatively low residential use. Denver and Dallas, with high total daily use of 247 and 232 gallons, respectively, are also high in residential use. Pittsburgh, Kansas City, and Omaha are all in the top half of cities reporting total use, but in the bottom half for residential use.

Water reduction programs can make a difference. Omaha, for example, tries to control use by charging higher prices in times of heavy use. New York City offers education in elementary schools and free water surveys for homes, including installment of low-flow shower heads and toilet displacement bags. Los Angeles makes available low-flow shower heads and toilet displacement bags.

The source of water supplies is critical to a city's long-term future. Arid cities such as Tucson, San Antonio, and El Paso, for example, rely almost exclusively on groundwater and are thus living on borrowed time.

Residential Water Use Per Capita

City	Gallons per Day
Pittsburgh	41
Buffalo	45
Seattle	55
St. Paul	56
Kansas City	61
Portland	61
Milwaukee	65
Oakland	65
Newark	67
Cincinnati	67
Virginia Beach	69
Arlington	77
Ft. Worth	78
Toledo	79
Oklahoma City	79
Omaha	84
Columbus	95
Tulsa	103
Tucson	106
El Paso	107
San Antonio	108
Los Angeles	110
Austin	110
Wichita	113
Dallas	116
Honolulu	127
New York	140
Denver	165
Birmingham	167

Unhealthy Air Pollution Days
(16 worst metro areas, 1990)

Metro Area	Number of Days
Los Angeles	70
Houston	36
San Diego	14
New York	13
Baton Rouge	10
Fresno	10
Phoenix	8
Sacramento	6
Dallas-Ft. Worth	5
El Paso	4
Philadelphia	4
Atlanta	3
Seattle-Tacoma	2
Grand Rapids	2
Tulsa	2
Baltimore	2

Source: EPA Aeromatic Information Retrieval System, Pollutant Standard Index Summary, 1990.

PSI—a measure of chronic levels of air pollution—and the number of days in a year in which the PSI rose above 100—a measure of the number of acute air pollution episodes that reached the unhealthful level. Both measures provide useful information about how clean the air is in a given metro area.

In 1990, chronic air pollution was worst in Los Angeles, with an average PSI of 73 (see table, Average Air Quality). Bakersfield, Charlotte, Fresno, Houston, Raleigh-Durham, and Sacramento all had average PSIs above 50. In contrast, of those metro areas for which federal data existed, Honolulu had the cleanest air, with an average PSI of 15. The San Francisco-Oakland area was close behind with a PSI of 20. Albany, Allentown, Chicago, Kansas City, Louisville, Pittsburgh, Rochester, Scranton, and Washington, D.C., all had ratings below 35.

Unhealthy air pollution episodes followed a somewhat similar pattern.

Los Angeles had by far the most unhealthful days (with a PSI over 100)—70 days in 1990. Baton Rouge, Fresno, Houston, and New York each had 10 or more such days (see table, Unhealthy Air Pollution Days). Some 31 of our 75 cities had not a single day in 1990 in which the PSI reached 100. Even for some of the worst performers, however, 1990 represented a significant improvement over levels common in the mid-1980s, when Los Angeles often recorded more than 200 unhealthful days annually and New York more than 50.

Water Quality

In much of the world, safe drinking water is relatively rare. In the United States, however, many people take drinking-water quality almost for granted. At least in the 75 largest metro areas, that assumption appears to be a good one.

Drinking-Water Quality Violations
(1990–91)

Metro Area	Number of Violations
Other ranked metro areas	0
Buffalo	1
Columbus	1
Denver	1
Houston	1
Indianapolis	1
Louisville	1
Miami	1
San Francisco-Oakland	1
Syracuse	1
Detroit	2
Orlando	2
Sacramento	2
Seattle-Tacoma	4

Source: Federal Data Reporting System, Public Water System Summary Violations for Systems Serving More Than 100,000, Fiscal Year 1991.

ENVIRONMENTAL SELF-PORTRAITS
Access to Nature

Urban Parkland

City	Parkland (percent of area)	City	Parkland (percent of area)
Honolulu	40.68	Columbus	5.80
Washington, DC	20.60	Los Angeles	5.30
Minneapolis	17.30	Toledo	5.30
Tulsa	14.00	Miami	5.10
St. Paul	12.00	Indianapolis	5.00
El Paso	11.70	Newark	5.00
Buffalo	11.50	Ft. Worth	4.70
Portland	11.00	Denver	4.00
Chicago	10.50	Oklahoma City	4.00
Seattle	10.00	New Orleans	3.60
Omaha	9.80	Arlington	3.00
Dallas	9.00	Birmingham	3.00
Cincinnati	9.00	Tucson	2.91
Pittsburgh	7.30	Fresno	1.56
Virginia Beach	7.10	Milwaukee	1.00
Oakland	7.00	Kansas City	0.05
Austin	6.80	Jacksonville	0.01
Wichita	5.99		

Access to urban parks affect city dwellers's quality of life. A city with little parkland can be intimidating and sterile. Even if large parks are just beyond the city, as they often are in the West, getting there requires a special trip. A city broken up with green spaces, on the other hand, can provide recreation and aesthetic experiences, make the climate milder, and provide habitat for wildlife.

Of the 35 cities providing data on parkland, Honolulu—which included the entire island of Oahu in its figures—counts 251 square miles of park (40 percent of land area)—more than double its nearest rivals (see table, Urban Parkland). Washington, D.C., Minneapolis, Tulsa, and St. Paul also rank high in percentage of land area devoted to parks or nature preserves.

Because of wide variation in land area, cities with many square miles of parkland do not always have the highest percentage of parkland. For example, Dallas's 73 square miles of parkland (the second highest) make up only 9 percent of the total area, while Buffalo's 2.2 square miles take up 11.5 percent of its area.

About half of the cities allow swimming, and all but a few permit fishing in urban lakes and rivers. All but three of the cities that returned the survey have tree-planting programs.

The EPA requires public water systems serving more than 100,000 persons to monitor their water for levels of nearly 75 different contaminants, from bacteria to hazardous chemicals to ra-diation. In 1990 and 1991, federal data show that most violations of water quality standards occurred in small communities. Of the 75 largest cities covered in this chapter, 62 reported no violations at all. Only 13 recorded violations, led by Seattle-Tacoma, Sacramento, Orlando, and Detroit (see table, Drinking-Water Quality Violations). Even in these cities, however, the water is clearly safe to drink. Violations as recorded in the federal data included failures to take a sample or to file a report in a particular month, as well as detection of levels of a single contaminant above standards. The majority of the violations reported here are of the failure to sample or report type—not necessarily reassuring, but not direct evidence of poor water quality. Many of the remaining violations are for high turbidity levels, meaning water that contains soil or other sediments. No violations for our 75 cities concerned chemicals or radiation, and only a few violations reported levels of bacteria higher than standards. The small number of violations and violators means that water quality ratings have almost no effect on a metro area's overall standing in our ratings. Nonetheless, we have included the number of water quality violations in the Green Metro Index, because opinion polls show that drinking-water quality is something people value highly and expect their cities to provide.

In many cities, however, this high-quality water is used wastefully (see box, City Water Use).

Toxic Chemicals

Beginning in 1987, the EPA began requiring nearly all industrial facilities in the United States that make or use some 300 toxic chemicals to report annually the amounts that are released to the environment or transferred to other sites for treatment or disposal. The total amounts are staggering—4.83 billion pounds in 1990 (see the "Industry" chapter).

Superfund Sites
(15 worst metro areas)

Metro Area	Number of Sites
New York	101
Philadelphia	77
San Francisco-Oakland	34
Los Angeles	24
Chicago	23
Minneapolis-St. Paul	21
Miami	19
Seattle-Tacoma	16
Boston	15
Houston	15
Detroit	13
Grand Rapids	12
Providence	11
Denver	10
Tampa-St. Petersburg	10

Source: EPA Superfund Program, CERCLIS, 1992.

Likewise, the EPA maintains a list of sites contaminated by past releases of toxic chemicals. More than 37,000 such sites have been identified in connection with the agency's Superfund efforts. Of these, 1,200 sites are included on the National Priorities List for remedial action. More than 60 percent of the priority Superfund sites are located in our 75 metro areas.

Releases and transfers of toxic chemicals in congested metro areas do not necessarily mean that humans will be exposed to them, and not all chemicals classified as toxic are equally hazardous to human health. Likewise, Superfund sites represent already-contaminated areas that cannot be used at present and that have the potential for human exposure or additional contamination through natural processes (such as runoff or leaching of chemicals from the site) or during cleanup. Regardless of the actual danger (which may be relatively low), it is clear that

ENVIRONMENTAL SELF-PORTRAITS

City Waste and Recycling

We all produce garbage—about 1,460 pounds each per year, according to U.S. Environmental Protection Agency (EPA) estimates. But according to our survey, most major cities produce more per capita than the EPA amount. With 34 cities reporting figures for solid waste per capita, the figures ranged from about 360 pounds a year in Indianapolis and 380 pounds in Buffalo to 3,480 pounds a year in Jacksonville (see table, Solid Waste Collected). Such wide differences suggest that cities at

burgh. Omaha, Cincinnati, and Miami offer curbside pickup to half or more of their residents. Other cities do not yet appear to be making much effort.

Solid Waste Collected
(per capita)

City	Pounds per Year
Indianapolis	360
Buffalo	380
Chicago	740
Omaha	800
Oklahoma City	800
Kansas City	860
Pittsburgh	920
El Paso	920
Minneapolis	930
Milwaukee	1,000
Birmingham	1,000
Denver	1,000
Ft. Worth	1,000
Toledo	1,000
Cincinnati	1,060
Fresno	1,340
Newark	1,460
Oakland	1,600
Tulsa	1,880
St. Paul	2,000
Los Angeles	2,000
Honolulu	2,200
Arlington	2,200
Austin	2,400
San Antonio	2,400
Tucson	2,460
Dallas	2,540
Miami	2,560
Washington, DC	2,680
Portland	2,680
Wichita	2,880
Seattle	2,900
Virginia Beach	3,000
Jacksonville	3,480

Top 10 Cities in Recycling

City	Percent Recycled
Honolulu	72
Newark	51
Seattle	40
St. Paul	39
Portland	38
Jacksonville	35
Minneapolis	27
Virginia Beach	22
Los Angeles	20
Washington, DC	20

the high end of the range could make significant improvements in reducing trash.

Preventing so much waste in the first place would be ideal. Recycling is the next best thing. Of those cities reporting, Honolulu recycles the highest proportion of its solid waste—72 percent. Newark, Seattle, St. Paul, Portland, and Jacksonville are also among the leading recyclers (see table, Top 10 Cities in Recycling).

Another measure of a city's efforts in recycling, however, is whether it offers curbside pickup to its residents. Most of the top 10 recyclers (except Honolulu, Los Angeles, and Virginia Beach) offer this service to all their residents, as do Austin, Buffalo, Fresno, New Orleans, and Pitts-

Toxic Chemical Releases and Transfers, 1990

Metro Area	Amount (pounds per year)	Metro Area	Amount (pounds per year)
West Palm Beach	943,459	Sacramento	11,849,792
Fresno	1,054,243	Dayton	12,278,554
Washington, DC	1,107,218	Atlanta	12,915,673
Honolulu	1,213,025	Syracuse	13,116,558
Tucson	1,235,512	Cincinnati	13,753,370
El Paso	1,517,720	Charleston	13,954,715
Harrisburg	1,988,790	Kansas City	14,031,849
Las Vegas	2,399,549	Baltimore	14,997,426
Bakersfield	2,498,033	Nashville	15,386,028
Little Rock	2,826,267	Dallas-Ft. Worth	16,669,699
Orlando	3,006,612	Seattle-Tacoma	17,185,029
Raleigh-Durham	4,034,662	Boston	17,491,237
San Antonio	4,036,402	Greensboro	17,570,847
Oklahoma City	4,269,395	Tulsa	17,594,760
Knoxville	4,506,671	Louisville	19,321,492
Miami	4,822,142	San Francisco-Oakland	19,521,589
Austin	4,931,825	Buffalo	19,818,835
New Bedford	5,627,807	Columbus	20,520,317
San Diego	6,089,986	Milwaukee	21,383,959
Denver	6,617,837	Indianapolis	21,522,919
Scranton	7,062,692	Grand Rapids	21,611,428
Tampa-St. Petersburg	7,171,038	Charlotte	21,833,254
Worcester	7,292,509	Minneapolis-St. Paul	24,813,330
Allentown	7,367,033	Memphis	26,891,707
Hartford	7,389,714	Pittsburgh	30,689,769
Phoenix	7,473,876	Richmond	34,410,782
Norfolk	7,634,591	Cleveland	44,832,133
Providence	8,237,427	Philadelphia	72,824,789
Rochester	8,485,852	St. Louis	83,949,520
Springfield	9,053,780	Baton Rouge	84,540,370
Toledo	9,401,840	Detroit	85,046,048
Omaha	9,564,863	Los Angeles	90,368,911
Jacksonville	9,690,225	Salt Lake City	110,789,489
Birmingham	10,450,063	New York	144,773,930
Greenville	10,510,580	Chicago	162,833,008
Portland	10,976,256	New Orleans	186,704,887
New Haven	11,575,334	Houston	264,880,496

Source: EPA, All Toxic Chemical Release Inventory Submissions in TRIS as of March 22, 1992.

most people do not want to live or work or have their children go to school near toxic waste dumps such as Superfund sites or industrial facilities that emit significant quantities of toxic chemicals.

To provide an index of the toxic burden on metro environments from present industrial activity, we added the total releases and transfers for each county included in our 75 metro areas. (The EPA database records toxic releases and transfers to air, water, land, and deep well injection; it also records transfers to municipal sewage systems or to other off-site disposal facilities.) Houston has by far the largest amount of toxic releases and transfers, followed by New Orleans, Chicago, New York, and Salt Lake City, all with more than 100 million pounds of toxics per year. (See table, Toxic Chemical Releases and Transfers, 1990.) West Palm Beach, Fresno, Washington, D.C., Honolulu, Tucson, El Paso, and Harrisburg put only a small toxic burden on the environment, according to the EPA data. However, the El Paso metro area extends across the U.S.-Mexico border into the town of Juarez, where manufacturing plants are less tightly regulated and toxic emissions are reputedly high. Thus, El Paso might be ranked significantly lower if data were available from the non-U.S. portion of the metro area.

To provide an index of the toxic burden on metro environments from the past, we added the total number of Superfund sites (from the National Priorities List) located in each county included in our 75 metro areas. The New York metro area has the most Superfund sites, 101 in all, followed by Philadelphia and San Francisco-Oakland (see table, Superfund Sites). Fifteen metro areas have 10 or more sites. Some 11 metro areas have no Superfund sites. Larger metro areas tend to have more Superfund sites, although not necessarily more toxic releases.

Transportation

Transportation systems play an important role in tying together the extended metro areas in which we increasingly live. But how we commute to work or travel on other daily tasks also affects the quality of the environment in which we live. Metro areas differ widely both in the transportation options they provide their residents and in the use residents make of them. Use of mass transit in our 75 metro areas, measured as passenger miles traveled per year per capita, provides an index of transportation behavior. We com-

---

ENVIRONMENTAL SELF-PORTRAITS

City Environmental Policies

Cities answered a series of yes-or-no questions about their environmental activities: Do you have energy or water conservation programs? Policies to buy recycled products? Parking taxes or other incentives to reduce traffic and encourage use of public transit?

The best news is that energy and water conservation programs are running in virtually every city. Only three cities among the respondents lack either water or energy conservation programs.

The hopeful news is that two thirds of the city governments buy recycled products. Newark, which had the first mandatory program in the United States, is no longer alone. Although most programs are limited to buying recycled paper—and then only if the price is competitive—it is a start. Omaha requires all letterhead and copy paper to have a minimum of 20 percent recycled content.

The bad news is that over half the cities have no policies to discourage auto travel or encourage mass transportation. Those that do include Chicago, Cincinnati, Columbus, Denver, Fresno, Ft. Worth, Honolulu, Los Angeles, Miami, New Orleans, Newark, Oakland, Omaha, Pittsburgh, Portland, Seattle, and Tucson. The policies vary. Ft. Worth and Honolulu, for example, subsidize bus passes for city employees. Honolulu also reduces parking prices for carpoolers, and Los Angeles levies a 10 percent tax on parking spaces.

Mass Transit Passenger Miles
(per capita, 1991)

Metro Area	Thousand Miles Per Year	Metro Area	Thousand Miles Per Year
New York	1.0141	Tucson	0.0984
Washington, DC	0.5934	Albany	0.0953
Honolulu	0.5640	St. Louis	0.0953
Chicago	0.5566	Rochester	0.0918
San Francisco-Oakland	0.4648	Detroit	0.0885
Atlanta	0.3919	Buffalo	0.0849
Boston	0.3502	Jacksonville	0.0788
Seattle-Tacoma	0.3477	Memphis	0.0780
Philadelphia	0.2992	Springfield	0.0771
Pittsburgh	0.2239	Providence	0.0762
Baltimore	0.2235	Phoenix	0.0758
Austin	0.2154	Las Vegas	0.0731
Los Angeles	0.2086	Nashville	0.0693
Houston	0.1986	Tampa-St. Petersburg	0.0676
San Diego	0.1956	Orlando	0.0664
Portland	0.1922	Kansas City	0.0652
New Orleans	0.1898	Bakersfield	0.0621
Milwaukee	0.1651	Toledo	0.0603
San Antonio	0.1631	Indianapolis	0.0593
Salt Lake City	0.1627	Norfolk	0.0588
Miami	0.1539	Worcester	0.0505
Denver	0.1520	Omaha	0.0485
Minneapolis-St. Paul	0.1498	Charleston	0.0478
Charlotte	0.1333	Grand Rapids	0.0435
El Paso	0.1287	Little Rock	0.0424
Louisville	0.1278	Allentown	0.0421
Cleveland	0.1226	Baton Rouge	0.0396
Hartford	0.1200	Scranton	0.0388
Richmond	0.1145	Harrisburg	0.0386
Cincinnati	0.1128	Tulsa	0.0359
Syracuse	0.1102	Birmingham	0.0349
Sacramento	0.1071	Knoxville	0.0338
Dayton	0.1006	West Palm Beach	0.0309
Columbus	0.1000	Raleigh-Durham	0.0297
Dallas-Ft. Worth	0.0994	Greenville	0.0226
New Bedford	0.0993	Oklahoma City	0.0199
New Haven	0.0989	Greensboro	0.0022
Fresno	0.0987		

Source: U.S. Department of Transportation, *National Urban Mass Transportation Statistics*, November 1990, Table 3.16, p. 3-315. Apparent ties are the result of rounding.

piled the total passenger miles traveled in 1989 from federal data for each of the many transit systems in our 75 metro areas and then divided by the appropriate (1989) population figure to get per capita mass transit miles.

Not surprisingly, the larger and more densely populated cities are also

ENVIRONMENTAL SELF-PORTRAITS

City Sources of Electric Power

Electricity is a clean source of energy at its point of use. But different methods of generating that power have very different environmental consequences. Burning coal, for example, releases far more carbon dioxide—a greenhouse gas—than does oil; natural gas releases still less. All three fu-

Electricity from Nuclear Power Plants
(top five cities)

City	Percent
Chicago	75
Toledo	55
Virginia Beach	45
Omaha	43
Newark	43

els contribute to smog and to acid precipitation when burned. Nuclear power and hydroelectricity release no greenhouse gases or other air pollutants, but contribute to other environmental problems.

For cities responding to the questionnaire, the most common source of electricity, by far, is coal. Five cities get virtually every kilowatt-hour from coal (Buffalo, Cincinnati, Denver, Indianapolis, and Tucson). Two thirds of the cities responding get more than 40 percent of their electrical power from coal (see table, Electricy from Coal).

Gas, the cleanest-burning fuel, is a major source of power for cities in Texas, Okla-

Electricity from Coal

City	Percent
Seattle	6
El Paso	12
Portland	15
Chicago	20
Newark	22
Virginia Beach	36
San Antonio	42
Dallas	42
Arlington	44
Ft. Worth	44
Toledo	45
Austin	49
Tulsa	50
Wichita	51
Minneapolis	54
Omaha	55
St. Paul	59
Oklahoma City	61
Los Angeles	65
Milwaukee	68
Kansas City	69
Birmingham	70
Jacksonville	71
Pittsburgh	76
Columbus	84
Honolulu	85
Denver	98
Tucson	99
Indianapolis	100
Cincinnati	100
Buffalo	100

Electricity from Gas
(top five cities)

City	Percent
New Orleans	76
Tulsa	50
Oklahoma City	39
Arlington	37
Ft. Worth	37

homa, and Louisiana (see table, Electricity from Gas). Nuclear power is more common in the Midwest and East (see table, Electricity from Nuclear Power.) Seattle and Portland in the Northwest get more than three quarters of their electricity from hydropower. Oil plays a very small role in electricity production for most cities, with Miami the only city in our survey that relies heavily on this fuel.

Residential Energy Use Index

15 best		15 worst	
Metro Area	Index Value	Metro Area	Index Value
San Diego	2,126	Minneapolis-St. Paul	8,669
Los Angeles	2,323	Milwaukee	7,796
San Francisco-Oakland	3,276	Albany	7,421
Jacksonville	3,922	Omaha	7,360
Sacramento	3,970	Buffalo	7,274
New Orleans	4,176	Chicago	7,195
Miami	4,294	Detroit	7,178
Houston	4,310	Hartford	6,840
Honolulu	4,389	Cleveland	6,790
Atlanta	4,691	Salt Lake City	6,783
El Paso	4,760	Denver	6,694
Charlotte	4,888	Indianapolis	6,638
Norfolk	4,904	Kansas City	6,616
Portland	5,023	Pittsburgh	6,595
Phoenix	5,188	Columbus	6,548

Source: U.S. National Oceanic and Atmospheric Administration, *Climatography of the United States*, No. 81, September 1982.

those with the highest use of mass transit. Residents of the New York metro area are the most extensive users of mass transit, annually averaging about 1,000 miles per person (see table, Mass Transit Passenger Miles). Washington, D.C., Honolulu, Chicago, and San Francisco-Oakland also made extensive use of mass transit. Smaller metro areas generally depend far more on the automobile and made only minimal use of mass transit. The median for all our 75 cities, in fact, is just 100 miles per person—one tenth that of New York City.

Cities also differ in whether and how they offer incentives to use mass transit or to discourage commuting by automobile (see box, City Environmental Policies).

Energy Use and Price

Energy use is one of the major sources of environmental pollution. Combustion of fossil fuels contributes to local air pollution, to regional problems such as acid precipitation, and to global warming. Because of the way in which energy use statistics are collected, however, relatively few national data exist on energy use in metro areas.

One important use of energy for which some measures exist is space heating and cooling, usually the most energy-intensive activity in the home. An index of heating and cooling needs is given by heating degree days and cooling degree days—defined as the number of days the temperature is above or below 65° F), the optimum temperature, with each day weighted by the number of degrees above or below 65° F. We combined these two indicators into a single measure, heating and cooling degree days, which provides an index of residential energy use. Those cities that are blessed with a moderate climate year-round have the lowest energy use for space heating and cooling. Not surprisingly, California metro areas top the list—San Diego and Los Angeles, with less than 2,400

Average Gasoline Price, May 1992
(unleaded regular self-serve)

Metro Area	Price (dollars per gallon)	Metro Area	Price (dollars per gallon)
Las Vegas	1.25	El Paso	1.10
Portland	1.25	Knoxville	1.10
San Francisco-Oakland	1.25	Philadelphia	1.10
San Diego	1.22	Pittsburgh	1.10
Chicago	1.21	Tampa-St. Petersburg	1.10
Denver	1.20	Charlotte	1.09
Buffalo	1.19	Jacksonville	1.09
Omaha	1.18	Memphis	1.09
Sacramento	1.17	Miami	1.09
Boston	1.14	Nashville	1.09
Seattle	1.14	Oklahoma City	1.09
Albany	1.13	Orlando	1.09
Cincinnati	1.13	San Antonio	1.09
Indianapolis	1.13	Dallas-Ft. Worth	1.08
Providence	1.13	Detroit	1.08
Baltimore	1.12	Washington, DC	1.08
Cleveland	1.12	Little Rock	1.07
Fresno	1.12	Toledo	1.07
Los Angeles	1.12	Birmingham	1.06
Minneapolis-St. Paul	1.12	Houston	1.06
New Orleans	1.12	Kansas City	1.06
Phoenix	1.12	Richmond	1.06
Salt Lake City	1.12	Columbus	1.05
Louisville	1.11	St. Louis	1.03
Milwaukee	1.11	Atlanta	0.96

Source: Computer Petroleum Corporation, Minneapolis, Minnesota, 1992.

in combined heating and cooling degree days, and San Francisco next, with 3,276 (see table, Residential Energy Use Index). Those cities with climatic extremes (both heat and cold) use more energy to keep residents comfortable. As might be predicted, the Minneapolis-St. Paul area is at the bottom of the list, with an energy need for heating and cooling that is four times that of San Diego. Milwaukee, Albany, Omaha, Buffalo, Chicago, and Detroit also have heating and cooling degree days over 7,000.

Energy prices play an important role in energy use. There is good evi-dence that we use more gasoline or electricity when it is cheap and less when it becomes more expensive. Higher energy prices are therefore a positive factor from an environmental point of view, delivering benefits such as lower pollution. Indices that compare energy prices among metro areas thus provide important indirect measures of energy use, as well as an indication of local energy policies such as gasoline or other energy taxes, state or regional regulatory decisions, and federal subsidies (for hydropower plants built with public funds in many parts of the country, for example, and for

Residential Electricity Price Index

15 best		15 Worst	
Metro Area	Index Price per 1,000 Kilowatt-hours	Metro Area	Index Price per 1,000 Kilowatt-hours
New York	$143.28	Seattle-Tacoma	$33.59
Philadelphia	$126.70	Portland	$46.23
Pittsburgh	$123.55	Las Vegas	$49.49
New Bedford	$117.56	Kansas City	$56.22
Toledo	$114.80	Knoxville	$56.80
New Haven	$114.42	Nashville	$57.87
Chicago	$107.79	Indianapolis	$57.95
Springfield	$105.89	Memphis	$58.04
Bakersfield	$104.14	Louisville	$60.79
Fresno	$104.14	Washington, DC	$61.01
San Francisco-Oakland	$104.14	Tulsa	$62.43
Cleveland	$103.89	Columbus	$64.63
Boston	$101.92	San Antonio	$65.17
Hartford	$101.00	Milwaukee	$65.69
San Diego	$100.73	Dallas-Ft. Worth	$65.99

Source: Energy Information Administration, *Electric Sales and Revenue*, 1990.

energy produced by the Tennessee Valley Authority in the Southeast).

We chose to look at two key energy prices—for gasoline and for electricity. For gasoline prices, we used national survey data gathered for most metro areas by the Computer Petroleum Corporation for May 1992. Gasoline prices tend to change rapidly, so current figures are important. The prices are average metro prices for unleaded self-serve regular, the most widely sold type of gasoline. For electricity prices, we used an index based on average revenue per kilowatt-hour for utility systems serving metro areas, the data were gathered by the U.S. Department of Energy for 1990.

The most expensive gasoline in our survey month was found in San Francisco-Oakland, Portland, and Las Vegas. Chicago, Denver, and Buffalo also had prices at the high end of the list (see table, Average Gasoline Price, May 1992). Atlanta, St. Louis, and Columbus had the least expensive gaso-

line. The most expensive electricity was found in New York City, followed by Philadelphia, Pittsburgh, New Bedford, Toledo, and New Haven (see table, Residential Electricity Price Index). Seattle-Tacoma, Portland, and Las Vegas had the lowest electricity prices.

The sources of the electricity generated for each metro area—and their environmental impact—vary greatly (see box, City Sources of Electric Power).

Green Metro Index

To get an overall environmental ranking of our 75 metro areas, we ranked them—from most environmentally favorable to least environmentally favorable—on each of our nine metrowide indicators separately. These ranks were then combined to yield an overall score, giving equal weight to each indicator. The procedure was to average the individual ranks to give a rank score, whose value determined the overall comparative rank of each metro

ENVIRONMENTAL SELF-PORTRAITS
Special City Initiatives

When asked on a questionnaire to describe their best environmental efforts, many cities told of awards: Seattle was recognized for providing money to neighborhood tree planting and cleanup efforts; Toledo for recycling waste sludge into a nutrient-rich topsoil supplement; Dallas for its water quality; Austin for encouraging the use of sustainable building materials.

Austin's award for excellence in local environmental initiatives from the United Nations Local Government Honours Programme was the only U.S. winner. The city also considers itself one of the most progressive in eliminating water pollution from runoff.

Besides Seattle's winning program, tree-planting is popular in most cities. Washington, Chicago, and Toledo called their programs exemplary. Los Angeles's Operation Clean Sweep not only plants trees but assists with cleanup projects and graffiti paint-outs.

Oklahoma City promotes a different kind of tree-planting with xeriscape, landscaping with plants that thrive in dry conditions. In addition to reducing outdoor watering by as much as 50 percent, xeriscape requires fewer lawn chemicals and fertilizers. In Oklahoma City, two demonstration gardens use a variety of native and adapted plants, turfs, and trees.

Other city garden projects take over vacant lots to beautify as well as to grow food. Honolulu provides water and land to more than 2,000 gardeners for fees of less than $12. Newark in 1991 delivered over 100 truckloads of compost to 266 community and 540 backyard gardens that produced 2,000 pounds of fruits and vegetables for senior citizens and shelters. Seattle found that its garden program not only produced food but also helped to create a better sense of community.

Oakland recently started a 15-year, multi-million-dollar project to buy parkland. Washington recycles 100 percent of its sewage sludge.

A few cities mentioned their efforts to deal with automobile traffic. Chicago is considering making permanent a temporary weekday ban on street parking downtown. Portland tore out a four-lane highway and replaced it with a park; over half the people who work there now take public transportation. Honolulu has banned commercial traffic from Hanauma Bay Park.

Incidental to auto traffic, Newark replaced 16,000 old street lights with high-pressure sodium units that save money and provide twice the illumination. Chicago buys recycled asphalt, and Dallas buries shredded tires to await resale.

Not every city is waiting to use its garbage. Jacksonville recycles freon into the air conditioners of public housing units and sells old appliances for scrap. Honolulu burns 60 percent of its waste to supply 6 percent of its electricity needs.

area—the Green Metro Index; the index is effectively a rank of ranks. Lower rankings indicate better environmental quality or performance.

The results contain some surprises (see table, Green Metro Index, p. 220). Honolulu is the top-ranked Green Metro Area in the United States by a significant margin. Despite only average rankings for electricity prices, it has consistently good rankings in air quality, transportation, control of toxics, and residential energy use. San Diego was ranked second overall, with San Francisco-Oakland and El Paso tied for third. Again, a caveat may be appropriate regarding El Paso; as discussed above, its high ranking might well decline if data were available for the portions of that metro area outside the

Special City Initiatives *(continued)*

Within four months of its formation last spring, Chicago's new Department of the Environment was tested by the flooding of a large part of downtown. The department responded with air and water quality testing and counseled businesses on asbestos removal and cleanup procedures.

To prevent a similar flood, Kansas City is replacing a 60-year-old tunnel with a new one capable of moving 210 million gallons of water a day. Cincinnati solved an environmental maintenance problem with an in-house program to remove 50 underground gasoline tanks on city property at one tenth the estimated cost; the city

also put together a booklet to help other cities with similar problems.

In the area of legislation, Newark has tightly regulated ozone-depleting chemicals since 1989 with landmark laws. New York requires that only low-water toilets, faucets, and showers be sold. Seattle and San Antonio coordinate departments to address environmental problems.

Toledo became one of the first cities to address air quality, health, and pollution back in 1906 with a Smoke Inspection Department. Today the city considers its Division of Pollution Control one of the country's most advanced.

United States. Washington, D.C., Austin, Fresno, New Bedford, Tucson, and New Haven round out the top 10.

What is noteworthy about the Index is that high-ranked metro areas include both large and small urban areas: San Francisco-Oakland is the fourth largest; New Bedford is the 75th. There is no geographical pattern, with high- and low-ranked metro areas found in every region of the country. Many older industrial metro areas are ranked in the lower half of the list, yet metro

Why Some Metro Areas Ranked Low

A few metro areas may have been unfairly penalized in our Green Metro Index ranking system because of a lack of data from federal sources. Thus, Greensboro and Greenville are both ranked at the bottom of our list, in part because of poor mass transit and toxics rankings. But had we been able to obtain air pollution data, residential energy use data, and gasoline price data, they both might have ranked considerably higher. Missing data may also have been a factor in the low rankings of Minneapolis-St. Paul and Charleston.

areas that have cleaned up—such as Pittsburgh, Toledo, and Baltimore—are ranked high.

The Green Metro Index and its component rankings are a kind of statistical mirror. The reflection it provides is not a perfect image of environmental quality or behavior, but it does lead to provocative questions. The most important comparisons are those among metro areas on a single indicator—within the accuracy of the data, those rankings have very specific meanings. New York City does have more Superfund sites than other metro areas; it also has higher electricity prices (a positive factor) and uses more mass transit. The method of combining the separate rankings into an overall one (we weighted each component equally) is necessarily arbitrary. But since we also provide the rankings for each measure included in the index, you can weight more heavily those measures most important to you or leave out measures that you think are not important (see table, Green Metro Rankings) to determine your own overall rankings. We believe that the Green Metro Index as presented here is a reasonably fair

Green Metro Rankings
(1 = best, 75 = worst)

Metro Area	Average Air Quality	Acute Air Quality	Water Quality Violations	Toxic Releases
Albany	5	1	1	NA
Allentown	6	1	1	24
Atlanta	19	4	1	40
Austin	10	1	1	17
Bakersfield	22	1	1	9
Baltimore	11	3	1	45
Baton Rouge	19	9	1	67
Birmingham	NA	NA	1	34
Boston	NA	2	1	49
Buffalo	NA	NA	2	54
Charleston	NA	NA	1	43
Charlotte	24	1	1	59
Chicago	5	1	1	72
Cincinnati	12	1	1	42
Cleveland	7	1	1	64
Columbus	18	2	2	55
Dallas-Ft. Worth	15	6	1	47
Dayton	14	1	1	39
Denver	11	1	2	20
Detroit	15	1	3	68
El Paso	20	5	1	6
Fresno	25	9	1	2
Grand Rapids	15	3	1	58
Greensboro	NA	NA	1	50
Greenville	NA	NA	1	35
Harrisburg	7	2	1	7
Hartford	NA	NA	1	25
Honolulu	NA	1	1	4
Houston	25	12	2	74
Indianapolis	21	2	2	57
Jacksonville	18	1	1	33
Kansas City	3	1	1	44
Knoxville	23	1	1	15
Las Vegas	16	2	1	8
Little Rock	NA	NA	1	10
Los Angeles	26	13	1	69
Louisville	5	1	2	52
Memphis	21	1	1	61
Miami	NA	NA	2	16
Milwaukee	16	2	1	56
Minneapolis-St. Paul	NA	NA	1	60
Nashville	9	1	1	46
New Bedford	NA	NA	1	18
New Haven	8	1	1	37
New Orleans	10	1	1	73
New York	18	10	1	71

Green Metro Rankings (cont.)
(1 = best, 75 = worst)

Superfund Sites	Mass Transit Use	Residential Energy Use	Gasoline Price	Electricity Price	Rank Score
1	40	44	9	21	15.25
10	64	NA	NA	29	19.29
1	6	10	19	36	15.11
1	12	NA	NA	43	12.14
3	55	NA	NA	9	14.29
7	11	24	10	33	16.11
6	65	NA	NA	35	28.86
2	69	NA	16	45	27.83
15	7	28	8	11	15.13
8	44	42	5	21	25.14
3	61	NA	NA	44	30.40
7	24	12	13	39	20.00
19	4	41	3	7	17.00
3	30	29	9	50	19.67
3	27	38	10	10	17.89
2	34	32	17	53	23.89
4	35	17	14	50	21.00
7	33	NA	NA	38	19.00
11	22	36	4	40	16.33
14	43	40	14	19	24.11
1	25	11	12	16	10.78
8	38	NA	10	9	12.75
13	62	NA	NA	48	28.57
1	75	NA	NA	39	33.20
7	73	NA	NA	41	31.40
3	67	NA	NA	29	16.57
5	28	39	NA	12	18.03
3	3	9	NA	17	4.75
15	14	8	16	25	21.22
6	57	35	9	58	27.44
8	45	4	13	42	18.33
5	54	34	NA	61	25.38
2	70	NA	12	60	23.00
1	50	NA	1	62	17.63
4	63	16	15	20	18.43
20	13	2	10	22	19.56
7	26	25	11	56	20.56
7	46	18	13	57	25.00
17	21	7	13	28	14.86
9	18	45	11	51	23.22
18	23	56	10	47	30.71
1	51	21	13	59	22.44
6	36	NA	NA	4	13.00
5	37	NA	NA	6	13.57
2	17	6	10	37	17.44
23	1	26	NA	1	18.88

Continued on next page

Green Metro Rankings (cont.)
(1 = best, 75 = worst)

Metro Area	Average Air Quality	Acute Air Quality	Water Quality Violations	Toxic Releases
Norfolk	NA	NA	1	27
Oklahoma City	13	1	1	14
Omaha	9	1	1	32
Orlando	14	1	3	11
Philadelphia	11	5	1	65
Phoenix	20	8	1	26
Pittsburgh	4	1	1	62
Portland	NA	NA	1	36
Providence	7	2	1	28
Raleigh-Durham	25	2	1	12
Richmond	NA	NA	1	63
Rochester	6	1	1	29
Sacramento	22	7	3	38
Salt Lake City	8	1	1	70
San Antonio	11	1	1	13
San Diego	24	11	1	19
San Francisco-Oakland	2	1	2	53
Scranton	5	1	1	21
Seattle-Tacoma	NA	3	4	48
Springfield	NA	NA	1	30
St. Louis	17	2	1	66
Syracuse	NA	NA	2	41
Tampa-St. Petersburg	18	2	1	22
Toledo	17	1	1	31
Tucson	21	1	1	5
Tulsa	14	3	1	51
Washington, DC	4	1	1	3
West Palm Beach	NA	NA	1	1
Worcester	11	2	1	23

method of providing an environmental rating for metrowide aspects of major metro areas. When combined with data for the performance of specific political entities within those metro areas (such as central or component cities), the statistical portrait becomes even more useful as a guide to citizens or city managers wanting to know where their city needs improvement.

The two sets of data allow some fascinating intercomparisons. For example, Dallas, Ft. Worth, and Arlington all returned completed questionaires. The Dallas-Ft. Worth metro area, which includes all three political entities, is the eighth-largest metro area by population in the nation. The three component cities pursue generally enlightened but not identical environmental policies; Arlington and Ft. Worth in particular rank relatively high in many of the comparisons on the basis of the environmental self-portraits provided by the cities themselves, while Dallas ranks somewhat lower. Yet overall, the Dallas-Ft. Worth area is ranked in the lower third of the Green Metro Index, based on national data sources. Clearly, Arlington and Ft.

se

s a measure of
and potential
. Contrary to in-
rgy use tends to
tates than urban
Alaska, one of the
on average use al-
energy used by resi-
rk, one of the most
gy use and its pollu-
vever, is widely dis-
al states but highly
such urban states as
New Jersey. On aver-
of energy-producing
s Texas, Louisiana, and
a also use large amounts

Top 10 States for Per Capita Use of Energy

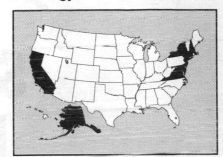

Per Capita Energy Use

	Million Btus	State	Million Btus
	991	Oregon	318
g	786	Utah	316
ia	783	Maine	309
	569	Illinois	308
Dakota	467	Virginia	306
na	446	Minnesota	305
sas	423	Pennsylvania	300
tana	415	North Carolina	300
st Virginia	415	Michigan	298
lahoma	396	New Jersey	296
abama	393	Missouri	294
shington	389	Wisconsin	288
ntucky	376	South Dakota	284
ssissippi	358	Colorado	273
ho	354	Maryland	268
nnessee	350	Arizona	258
aware	349	California	246
o	348	Hawaii	243
w Mexico	347	Florida	237
vada	337	Connecticut	234
braska	334	Vermont	232
a	333	Massachusetts	229
th Carolina	330	New Hampshire	224
nsas	330	Rhode Island	218
rgia	322	New York	200

Green Metro Rankings (cont.)
(1 = best, 75 = worst)

Superfund Sites	Mass Transit Use	Residential Energy Use	Gasoline Price	Electricity Price	Rank Score
7	58	13	NA	32	23.00
7	74	23	13	46	21.33
1	60	43	6	49	22.44
3	53	NA	13	34	16.50
22	9	27	12	2	17.11
8	49	15	10	18	17.22
4	10	33	12	3	14.44
8	16	14	1	63	19.86
12	48	31	9	15	17.00
3	72	NA	NA	26	20.14
5	29	19	16	32	23.57
3	42	NA	NA	14	13.71
5	32	5	7	27	16.22
10	20	37	10	NA	19.63
1	19	NA	13	52	13.88
2	15	1	2	13	9.78
21	5	3	1	9	10.78
10	66	NA	NA	NA	17.33
16	8	20	NA	64	23.29
2	47	NA	NA	8	17.60
10	41	30	18	30	23.89
6	31	NA	NA	21	20.20
11	52	NA	12	31	18.63
1	56	NA	15	5	15.88
2	39	NA	NA	24	13.29
3	68	NA	NA	54	27.71
1	2	22	14	55	11.44
2	71	NA	NA	28	20.60
2	59	NA	NA	23	17.29

Note: NA = not available.

Worth—and to a lesser extent, Dallas—are to be commended for their individual efforts. Yet it is also clear that the environmental quality and performance of the metro area as a whole leaves much to be desired. The Minneapolis-St. Paul metro area shows a similar pattern. The twin cities are ranked very highly on many of the environmental measures pertinent to the political entities themselves, yet the metro area as a whole is ranked near the bottom of the Green Metro Index, through the combination of high toxic emissions (past and present), high residential energy use, and relatively low energy prices.

The complementarity of these two sets of data, city and national, is important. It is not that one set of data is wrong and another is right. Rather, the two data sets measure largely different things, and both are important for providing a comprehensive picture of environmental conditions and practices in our metropolitan areas.

Green Metro Index
(1 = best, 75 = worst)

Metro Area	Rank	Rank Score	Metro Area	Rank	Rank Score
Honolulu	1	4.75	New York	39	18.88
San Diego	2	9.78	Dayton	40	19.00
San Francisco-Oakland	3	10.78	Allentown	41	19.29
El Paso	3	10.78	Los Angeles	42	19.56
Washington	5	11.44	Salt Lake City	43	19.63
Austin	6	12.14	Cincinnati	44	19.67
Fresno	7	12.75	Portland	45	19.86
New Bedford	8	13.00	Charlotte	46	20.00
Tucson	9	13.29	Raleigh-Durham	47	20.14
New Haven	10	13.57	Syracuse	48	20.20
Rochester	11	13.71	Louisville	49	20.56
San Antonio	12	13.88	West Palm Beach	50	20.60
Bakersfield	13	14.29	Dallas-Ft. Worth	51	21.00
Pittsburgh	14	14.44	Houston	52	21.22
Miami	15	14.86	Oklahoma City	53	21.33
Atlanta	16	15.11	Nashville	54	22.44
Boston	17	15.13	Omaha	54	22.44
Albany	18	15.25	Knoxville	56	23.00
Toledo	19	15.88	Norfolk	57	23.00
Baltimore	20	16.11	Milwaukee	58	23.22
Sacramento	21	16.22	Seattle-Tacoma	59	23.29
Denver	22	16.33	Richmond	60	23.57
Orlando	23	16.50	Columbus	61	23.89
Harrisburg	24	16.57	St. Louis	61	23.89
Chicago	25	17.00	Detroit	63	24.11
Providence	25	17.00	Memphis	64	25.00
Philadelphia	27	17.11	Buffalo	65	25.14
Phoenix	28	17.22	Kansas City	66	25.38
Worcester	29	17.29	Indianapolis	67	27.44
Scranton	30	17.33	Tulsa	68	27.71
New Orleans	31	17.44	Birmingham	69	27.83
Springfield	32	17.60	Grand Rapids	70	28.57
Las Vegas	33	17.63	Baton Rouge	71	28.86
Cleveland	34	17.89	Charleston	72	30.40
Hartford	35	18.33	Minneapolis-St. Paul	73	30.71
Jacksonville	36	18.33	Greenville	74	31.40
Little Rock	37	18.43	Greensboro	75	33.20
Tampa-St. Petersburg	38	18.63			

Note: Except where indicated by equal rank, apparent ties are the result of rounding.

This chapter was written by Allen Hammond, editor-in-chief of the 1993 Information Please Environmental Almanac. Additional research, reporting, and writing was contributed by Dale Hopper, editorial assistant and now a Washington, D.C.-based freelancer. Susan L. Cutter, professor of geography at Rutgers University, consulted and advised on the creation of the Green Metro Index.

STATE AND PROVINC...

Per Capita Energy U...

Per capita energy use i...
both energy efficiency...
environmental impact...
tuition, per capita en...
be higher in rural s...
states. Residents of...
most rural states,...
most five times the...
dents of New Yo...
urban states. Ene...
tion impact, ho...
bursed in rur...
concentrated i...
New York an...
age, citizens...
states such...
West Virgin...
of energy.

Annual ...

State	
Alaska	
Wyomin...	
Louisia...	
Texas	
North...	
India...	
Kan...	
Mo...	
W...	

Comp...

*Canada and the United S...
of nearly 7.5 million square...
treatment of environmenta...
worst?*

Alaska is the largest state and Rhode Island the smallest. That much most schoolchildren know. But most of us know far less about the environmental geography of the United States and Canada.

Which states, for example, use the most energy on a per capita basis? Which region uses the most water? Where are current releases of toxic chemicals highest? Which states emit the most climate-altering greenhouse gases? Which Canadian p... highest on greenhouse ga... and per capita energy use?

This chapter provides an... such questions. If the answers f... state or province trouble you, o... want more information regarding vironmental issues in your area, t... chapter also provides names, dresses, and phone numbers of o... cials with responsibilities in ... environment.

Toxic Releases

The federal Toxic Release Inventory allows citizens access to information on where and how much of more than 300 chemicals known to be toxic (such as creosote, ammonia, toluene, phosphoric acid, zinc compounds, or hydrochloric acid, among others) are released to the environment (whether to the land, air, underground wells, or water). This information is useful to hold to account specific industrial plants and is a useful measure of how well each state performs relative to all the others. Toxic releases in Louisiana (213,700 tons) and Texas (209,400 tons), both energy-producing states, have twice as many releases as the next leading state, Tennessee (103,700). Many states release only small amounts of

Top 10 States for Releases of Toxic Chemicals

these toxins. New Jersey (the state with the most priority Superfund sites) currently releases only 13,000 tons of these toxic materials. Fourteen states release less than 10,000 tons.

Toxic Releases

State	Thousand tons	State	Thousand tons
Louisiana	213.7	Kentucky	21.2
Texas	209.4	Washington	20.7
Tennessee	103.7	Iowa	20.3
Indiana	84.4	West Virginia	19.1
Ohio	84.2	Oklahoma	16.6
Utah	62.7	New Mexico	16.3
North Carolina	62.0	New Jersey	13.0
Michigan	59.9	Oregon	11.3
Illinois	59.5	Connecticut	10.7
Alabama	56.3	Massachusetts	10.4
Florida	53.3	Alaska	10.3
Mississippi	51.8	Nebraska	8.7
California	48.5	Maryland	8.0
Kansas	44.9	Maine	7.4
Pennsylvania	44.7	Wyoming	5.8
Virginia	39.8	Idaho	5.8
Georgia	38.9	New Hampshire	4.1
Arizona	36.0	Colorado	3.7
Missouri	34.3	Delaware	3.3
South Carolina	33.6	Rhode Island	2.6
New York	30.2	Nevada	1.6
Arkansas	28.9	South Dakota	1.5
Minnesota	26.0	North Dakota	1.1
Wisconsin	22.5	Vermont	0.5
Montana	21.3	Hawaii	0.4

Per Capita Water Use

Per capita water use in the United States is highest in the heavily irrigated states of the arid and semi-arid west. Idaho's Snake River, for example, is dammed and diverted to the otherwise arid but now highly productive agricultural lands in the southern part of the state. What flows in the remains of the Snake is warmed and eutrophied by drainage of excess irrigation water. The problem of water supply is most acute in the West, where issues of inter-basin water transfers are grist for the political mill. But, the limitations of water supply and the constant need to deal with potential human, agricultural, and industrial pollution require balancing the need for a safe water with maintenance of a healthy aquatic environments.

Top 10 States for Per Capita Use of Water

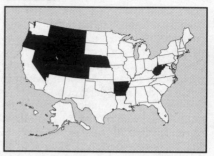

Per Capita Water Use

State	Gallons per day	State	Gallons per day
Idaho	22,200	Texas	1,230
Wyoming	12,200	Missouri	1,210
Montana	10,500	Pennsylvania	1,210
Nebraska	6,250	Ohio	1,180
Colorado	4,190	Kentucky	1,130
Nevada	3,860	Hawaii	1,100
West Virginia	2,810	Massachusetts	1,070
Utah	2,540	Iowa	960
Arkansas	2,500	South Dakota	956
Oregon	2,450	Georgia	899
New Mexico	2,320	Mississippi	885
Kansas	2,310	Virginai	853
Louisiana	2,210	Maine	733
Alabama	2,140	Alaska	727
South Carolina	2,040	New Hampshire	688
Arizona	1,960	Minnesota	676
Tennessee	1,770	Florida	554
North Dakota	1,690	New York	508
Washington	1,600	Oklahoma	386
Indiana	1,470	Connecticut	375
California	1,420	Maryland	321
Wisconsin	1,400	New Jersey	307
Michigan	1,270	Vermont	235
North Carolina	1,260	Delaware	222
Illinois	1,250	Rhode Island	152

Greenhouse Gas Emissions

Concentrations in the atmosphere of trace gases that trap heat continue to increase from human activity. Carbon dioxide, methane, and chlorofluorocarbons are the three most important of these "greenhouse gases." Their emissions are highly correlated with energy production and use, industrial activity, and agriculture (especially rice and cattle production). The two largest producers of greenhouse gases are Texas and California——both states with large energy production and industrial activities, as well as significant rice and cattle production. Both of those states produce 50 percent more emissions than Illinois, the next largest emitter.

Top 10 States for Greenhouse Gas Emissions

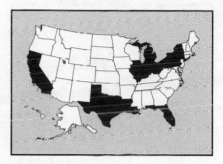

Illinois. Other northern industrial and coal producing states are also large emitters of these warming gases.

Greenhouse Gas Emissions Per Capita

State	Million tons of CO₂ per year	State	Million tons of CO₂ per year
Texas	459.0	Colorado	72.3
California	443.2	Kansas	70.8
Illinois	298.9	Iowa	68.5
Ohio	255.2	Arizona	64.1
Pennsylvania	254.6	Arkansas	62.4
New York	219.0	South Carolina	60.5
Indiana	217.1	Wyoming	54.8
Michigan	181.5	New Mexico	54.2
Louisiana	172.9	Mississippi	51.0
Florida	167.4	Connecticut	47.3
Georgia	145.4	North Dakota	43.5
North Carolina	126.5	Utah	42.8
Alabama	120.0	Nebraska	39.6
Missouri	112.8	Oregon	38.4
Virginia	112.6	Montana	26.4
Tennessee	110.2	Nevada	21.0
Kentucky	109.6	Maine	20.6
New Jersey	107.2	Idaho	17.1
Wisconsin	99.9	South Dakota	16.1
West Virginia	95.9	New Hampshire	15.0
Oklahoma	90.7	Delaware	14.2
Massachusetts	89.9	Rhode Island	11.7
Minnesota	83.1	Vermont	8.4
Maryland	77.9	Hawaii	NA
Washington	76.7	Alaska	NA

The Three Provinces with the Highest Per Capita Income

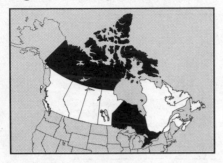

Per Capita Income

Province	$(Can.)
Yukon Territory	$25,846
N.W. Territories	$25,556
Ontario	$25,151
British Columbia	$22,433
Alberta	$21,971
Quebec	$20,568
Manitoba	$19,251
Nova Scotia	$18,154
Saskatchewan	$17,774
New Brunswick	$17,062
Prince Edward Island	$16,292
Newfoundland	$15,860

The Three Provinces with the Greatest Per Capita Energy Use

Per Capita Energy Use

Province	Gigajoules
Alberta	675.3
Saskatchewan	364.0
British Columbia	259.6
Ontario	255.3
New Brunswick	243.1
Newfoundland	235.7
Manitoba	231.7
Quebec	213.0
Nova Scotia	196.7
Prince Edward Island	161.8
N.W. Territories	NA
Yukon Territory	NA

The Three Provinces with the Greatest Greenhouse Gas Emissions

Greenhouse Gas Emissions

Province	Metric tons of CO_2 equivalent
Ontario	42,045,128
Alberta	28,690,136
Quebec	17,357,792
British Columbia	16,653,906
Saskatchewan	8,355,606
Nova Scotia	4,741,408
New Brunswick	3,908,083
Manitoba	3,414,615
Newfoundland	2,294,304
N.W. Territories	545,282
Yukon Territory	545,282
Prince Edward Island	427,949

Environmental Officers

What follows is a list of state environmental officers available to take citizens' questions regarding environmental issues in their state. This U.S. information, based on a list provided by the National Governor's Association, was confirmed in July 1992. Phone numbers for Public information Offices are labeled (P.I.O.). EPA stands for Environmental Protection Agency. Information for provincial and territorial environmental officers is on page 223.

United States

AL Mr. Leigh Pegues, Director
AL Dept. of Envmtl. Mgmt.
1751 Congressman
   W.L. Dickinson Dr.
Montgomery, AL 36130
(205) 271-7706
(205) 271-7950 Fax

AK Mr. John Sandor
Commissioner
Dept. of Envmtl. Conservation
410 Willoughby Ave., Suite 105
Juneau, AK 99801-1795
(907) 465-5050
(907) 465-5070 Fax

AZ Mr. Edward Z. Fox, Director
Dept. of Envmtl. Quality
3033 North Central Ave.
Phoenix, AZ 85012
(602) 207-2300
(602) 207-2218 Fax

AR Mr. Randall Mathis, Director
Dept. of Pollution Ctrl. and
   Ecology
8001 National Dr.
Little Rock, AR 72209
(501) 562-7444
(501) 562-4632 Fax

CA Mr. James M. Stock
Secretary for Envmtl.
   Protection
California EPA
555 Capitol Mall, Suite 235
Sacramento, CA 95814
(916) 445-3846
(916) 445-6401 Fax

CT Mr. Timothy R.E. Keeney
Commissioner
Dept. of Envmtl. Protection
165 Capitol Ave.
Hartford, CT 06106
(203) 566-5599
(203) 566-7932 Fax

CO Mr. Thomas P. Looby
Director
Office of Environment Colorado
   Dept. of Health
4210 East 11th Ave.
Denver, CO 80220
(303) 331-4510

Mr. Kenneth L. Salazar
   Executive Director
Dept. of Natural Resources
1313 Sherman St., Room 718
Denver, CO 80203
(303) 866-3311
(303) 866-2115 Fax

DE Mr. David S. Small, Chief
Information and Education
Dept. of Natural Resources and
   Environmental Control
89 Kings Hwy., P.O. Box 1401
Dover, DE 19903
(302) 739-4506
(302) 739-6242 Fax

FL Mr. Jim Lewis
Communications Director
Dept. of Envmtl. Regulation
2600 Blair Rd.
Tallahassee, FL 32399-2400
(904) 488-9334
(904) 487-4938 Fax

GA Mr. Joe D. Tanner
Commissioner
GA Dept. of Natural Resources
205 Butler St., Suite 1252
Atlanta, GA 30334
(404) 656-3500
(404) 656-2285 Fax

Mr. Harold F. Reheis, Director
Environmental Protection Division
GA Dept. of Natural Resources
205 Butler Street, Suite 1152
Atlanta, GA 30334
(404) 656-4713
(404) 651-5778 Fax

HI Mr. Bruce Anderson
Deputy Director
Environmental Health
HI State Dept. of Health
P.O. Box 3378
Honolulu, HI 96801
(808) 586-4424
(808) 586-4444 Fax

IA Mr. Larry Wilson, Director
Dept. of Natural Resources
Wallace State Office Building
900 East Grand
Des Moines, IA 50319
(515) 281-5385
(515) 281-8895 or 6794 Fax

ID Mr. Joe Nagal
Administrator
Division of Envmtl. Quality
ID Dept. of Health and Welfare
State House Mail
Boise, ID 83720
(208) 334-5840
(208) 334-0417 Fax

IL Ms. Mary Gade, Director
Illinois EPA
2200 Churchill Rd.
Springfield, IL 62706
(217) 782-3397
(217) 782-9039 Fax

Mr. John S. Moore, Director
IL Dept. of Energy and
   Natural Resources
325 W. Adams St
Springfield, IL 62704
(217) 785-2800
(217) 785-2618 Fax

IN Ms. Kathy Prosser
Commissioner
Dept. of Envmtl. Mgmt.
105 South Meridian, 5th Fl.
Indianapolis, IN 46225
(317) 232-8162
(317) 232-8564 Fax

IN Mr. Patrick Ralston
Executive Director
Natural Resources Dept.
402 W. Washington St.
Rm. W256
Indianapolis, IN 46204
(317) 232-4020
(317) 232-8036 Fax

KS Mr. Charles Jones, Director
Division of Environment
KS Dept. of Health and Envmt.
Forbes Field, Bldg. 740
Topeka, KS 66620
(913) 296-1535
(913) 296-6247 Fax

KY Senator Greg Hidgon
Acting Commissioner
Dept. for Envmtl. Protection
Fort Boone Plaza
14 Reilly Rd.
Frankfort, KY 40601
(502) 564-2150
(502) 564-4245 Fax

LA Mr. Kai Midboe, Secretary
Dept. of Envmtl. Quality
P.O. Box 82263
Baton Rouge, LA 70884-2263
(504) 765-0741
(504) 765-0746 Fax

ME Mr. Dean C. Marriott
Commissioner
ME Dept. of Envmtl. Protection
State House Station #17
Augusta, ME 04333
(207) 289-2812
(207) 289-7826 Fax

MD Mr. Robert Perciasepe
Secretary
Dept. of the Environment
2500 Broening Hwy.
Baltimore, MD 21224
(410) 631-3084
(410) 631-3888 Fax

MA Mr. Daniel S. Greenbaum
Commissioner
Dept. of Envmtl. Protection
One Winter St., 3rd Fl.
Boston, MA 02108
(617) 292-5500
(617) 556-1049 Fax

Mr. Peter Webber
Commissioner
Dept. of Envmtl. Mgmt.
100 Cambridge St., 19th Fl.
Boston, MA 02202
(617) 727-3180
(617) 727-9402 Fax

MI Mr. Roland Harmes, Director
MI Dept. of Natural Resources
Executive Division
P.O. Box 30028
Lansing, MI 48909
(517) 373-2329
(517) 335-4242 Fax

MN Mr. Charles Williams
Commissioner
MN Pollution Control Agency
520 Lafayette Rd.
St. Paul, MN 55155-3898
(612) 296-6300
(612) 296-7923 Fax

Mr. Rodney Sando
Commissioner
Dept. of Natural Resources
500 Layfayette Rd.
St. Paul, MN 55155-4037
(612) 296-6157
(800) 766-6000 (In-state calls)
(612) 296-3500 Fax

MS Mr. J.I. Palmer, Jr.
Executive Director
Dept. of Envmtl. Quality
P.O. Box 20305
Jackson, MS 32909
(601) 961-5000
(601) 961-5015 (P.I.O.)
(601) 354-6965 Fax

MO Mr. G. Tracy Mehan
Director
MO Dept. of Natural Resources
P.O. Box 176
Jefferson City, MO 65102
(314) 751-4422
(800) 334-6946 (In-state calls)
(314) 751-3443 (P.I.O.)
(314) 751-7627 Fax

MT Mr. Dennis Iverson, Director
Dept. of Health and Envmtl.
Sciences
Cogswell Bldg.
Helena, MT 59620
(406) 444-2544
(406) 444-2606 Fax

Ms. Karen L. Barclay Fagg
Director
Dept. of Natural Resources
and Conservation
1520 E. 6th Ave.
Helena, MT 59620
(406) 444-6699
(406) 444-6721 Fax

NE Mr. Randolph Wood
Director
Dept. of Envmtl. Quality
P.O. Box 98922
State House Station
Lincoln, NE 68509-8922
(402) 471-2186
(402) 471-2909 Fax

NV Mr. Lewis Dodgion
Administrator
Envmtl. Protection Division
Dept. of Conservation and Natural Resources
333 West Nye Lane
Carson City, NV 89710
(702) 687-4670
(702) 885-0868 Fax

Mr. Pete Morros, Director
Dept. of Conservation and
Natural Resources
123 West Nye Lane, Rm. 230
Carson City, NV 89710
(7020 687-4360
(702) 687-6972 Fax

NH Mr. John Dabuliewicz
Assistant Commissioner
New Hampshire Dept. of Envmtl.
Services
6 Hazen Drive
Concord, NH 03301
(603) 271-3503
(603) 271-2867 Fax

Mr. Timothy Drew
Administrator
Public Info. and Permitting Unit
Dept. of Envmtl. Services
6 Hazen Dr.
P.O. Box 95
Concord, NH 03302-0095
(603) 271-2975
(603) 271-2867 Fax

NJ Mr. Scott A. Weiner
Commissioner
NJ Dept. of Envmtl. Protection
and Energy
CN 402
Trenton, NJ 08625
(609) 777-3373
(609) 984-3962 Fax

NM Ms. Judith M. Espinosa
Secretary
New Mexico Envmt. Dept.
1190 St. Francis Dr.
Santa Fe, NM 87502
(505) 827-2850
(505) 827-2836 Fax

NY Mr. Thomas Jorling
Commissioner
NY State Dept. of Envmtl.
Conservation
50 Wolf Rd., 6th Fl.
Albany, NY 12233
(518) 457-3446
(518) 457-6996 Fax

NC Mr. A Preston Howard, Jr.
Director
Division of Envmtl. Mgmt.
Dept. of Envmt., Health, and Nat.
Resources
512 N. Salisbury St.
Raleigh, NC 27604
(919) 733-7015
(919) 733-2496 Fax

ND Mr. Francis Schwindt, Chief
Envmtl. Health Section
ND Dept. of Health and Consolidated Laboratories
1200 Missouri Ave.
Bismarck, ND 58502
(701) 221-5150
(701) 221-5200 Fax

OH Mr. Donald Schregardus
Director
Ohio EPA
P.O. Box 1049
1800 Watermark Dr.
Columbus, OH 43215
(614) 644-2782
(614) 644-3184 Fax

OK Mr. Mark Coleman
Deputy Commissioner
Environmental Health Services
Envmtl. Health Admin. 0200
OK State Dept. of Health
1000 N.E. Tenth St.
Oklahoma City, OK 73117-1299
(405) 271-8056
(405) 271-7339 Fax

OR Mr. Fred Hansen, Director
Dept. of Envmtl. Quality
811 S.W. Sixth Ave.
Portland, OR 97204 1004
(503) 229-5301
(503) 229-6271 (P.I.O.)
(503) 229-6124 Fax

PA Mr. Arthur Davis, Secretary
Dept. of Envmtl. Resources
P.O. Box 2063
Harrisburg, PA 17105-2063
(717) 787-2814
(717) 783-8926 Fax

PR Mr. Santos Rohena Betancourt, Secretary
Dept. of Nat. Resources
P.O. Box 5887
Correo de Puerta de Tierra
San Juan, PR 00906
(809) 723-2055
(809) 722-2785 Fax

Mr. Pedro A. Naldonado Ojeda
President
PR Envmtl. Quality Board
P.O. Box 11488
San Turce, PR 00910
(809) 767-8058 or 8056
Call for new fax number

RI Ms. Louise Durfee, Director
Dept. of Envmtl. Mgmt.
9 Hayes St.
Providence, RI 02908
(401) 277-2771
(401) 277-6802 Fax

SC Mr. Lewis Shaw
Deputy Commissioner
Envmtl. Quality Control
Dept. of Health and Envmtl. Ctrl.
2600 Bull St.
Columbia, SC 29201
(803) 734-5360
(803) 734-5407 Fax

SD Mr. Robert F. Roberts
Secretary
Dept. of Envmt. and
Natural Resources
523 E. Capitol Ave.
Pierre, SD 57501-3181
(605) 773-3151
(605) 773-6035 Fax

TN Mr. J.W. Luna
Commissioner
TN Dept. of Health and Envmt.
401 Church St., Suite 2100
Nashville, TN 37243-0435
(615) 741-3111
(615) 741-2491
(These numbers will change in
fall 1992; please call directory
assistance.)

Mr. Wayne Scharber
Assistant Commissioner
Bureau of Environment
150 Ninth Ave., North
Nashville, TN 37243
(615) 741-3657
(615) 741-4608 Fax

TX Dr. David R. Smith
Commissioner
Texas Dept. of Health
1100 West 49th St.
Austin, TX 78756
(512) 458-7375
(512) 458-7477 Fax

Mr. Josus Garza
Executive Director
Texas Water Commission
P.O. Box 13087, Capitol Station
Austin, TX 78711-3087
(512) 463-7860
(512) 475-2332 Fax

UT Mr. Ken Alkema
Executive Director
Dept. of Envmtl. Quality
288 North 1460 West
Salt Lake City, UT 84116
(801) 538-6421
(801) 538-6016 Fax

VI Mr. Roy E. Adams
Commissioner
Dept. of Planning and
Natural Resources
Nisky Center, Suite 231
Charlotte Amalie, VI 00802
(809) 774-3320
(809) 775-5706 Fax

VT Ms. Jan S. Eastman, Secretary
Agency of Natural Resources
103 South Main St.
Waterbury, VT 05671-0301
(802) 244-7347
(802) 244-1102 Fax

VA Mr. Keith J. Buttleman
Administrator
VA Council on the Envmt.
202 N. Ninth St., Suite 900
Richmond, VA 23219
(804) 786-4500
(804) 225-3933 Fax

Ms. Elizabeth Haskell
Secretary
Natural Resources Office
202 Ninth St., North, 7th Fl.
Richmond, VA 23219
(804) 786-0044
(804) 371-8333 Fax

DC Ms. Barbara E. Brown
Acting Director
Dept. of Consumer and Regulatory Affairs
614 "H" St., N.W.
Washington, D.C. 20001
(202) 727-7170
(202) 727-7842 Fax

WV Mr. David Callaghan, Director
WV Div. of Envmtl. Protection
10 McJunkin Rd.
Nitro, WV 25143
(304) 759-0515
(304) 759-0526 Fax

Mr. J. Edward Hamrick III
Director
WV Div. of Nat. Resources
1900 Kanawha Blvd.
Charlestown, WV 25305
(304) 558-2754
(304) 384-2768 Fax

WA Mr. Chuck Clarke, Director
Dept. of Ecology
P.O. Box 47600
Olympia, WA 98504-7600
(206) 459-6168
(206) 493-9495 Fax

WI Mr. Lyman Wible
Adminstrator
Div. for Envmtl. Quality
Dept. of Natural Resources
P.O. Box 7921
Madison, WI 53707
(608) 266-2121
(608) 267-3579 Fax

WY Mr. Dennis Hemmer
Director
Dept. of Envmtl. Quality
Herschler Bldg., 4th Fl. West
122 W. 25th St.
Cheyenne, WY 82002
(307) 777-7938
(307) 777-7682 Fax

CANADA

AB Jim Dau
Communications Director
Communications Division
Alberta Environment
9820 106 St., Main Fl.
Edmonton, AB T5K 2J6
(403) 427-6267
(403) 422-3571 Fax

BC General Inquiries
Ministry of Environment
Public Affairs & Communications
  Branch
810 Blanshard St., 4th Fl.
Victoria, BC V8V 1X4
(604) 387-1161
(604) 387-5669 Fax

MB Manitoba Environment
Management Division
Bldg. 2
139 Tuxedo Ave.
Winnipeg, MB R3N 0H6
(204) 945-7100
(204) 945-5229 Fax

NB Gerry Hill
Director, Communications
& Envmtl. Education
Dept. of the Environment
P.O. Box 6000
Fredericton, NB E3B 5H1
(506) 453-3700
(506) 453-3843 Fax

NF Cheryl Ford
Public Relations Specialist
Dept. of Environment & Lands
Confederation Bldg., West Block
P.O, Box 8700
St. John's, NF A1B 4J6
(709) 729-3394
(709) 729-1930 Fax

NS Margaret Murphy
Media Relations
Dept. of the Environment
P.O. Box 2107
Halifax, NS B3J 3B7
(902) 424-2575
(902) 424-0503 Fax

NT Stewart Lewis
Director, Policy and Planning
Dept. of Renewable Resources
Government of Northwest Terri-
tories
P.O. Box 1320
Yellowknife, NT X1A 2L9
(403) 920-8046
(403) 873-0114 Fax

ON Public Affairs & Communications Branch
Ministry of the Environment
135 St. Clair Ave. W.
Toronto, ON M4V 1P5
(416) 323-4321
(416) 323-4264 Fax

PE Lee Bartley
Communications Officer
Dept. of the Environment
P.O. Box 2000
Charlottetown, PE C1A 7N8
(902) 368-5000
(902) 368-5830 Fax

PQ Cecile Gaudreault
Direction des communica-
tions
Ministere de l'Environnement
3900, rue Marle
Sainte-Foy, PQ G1X 4E4
(418) 644-3284
(418) 528-0406 Fax

SK Deanne Cairns
Public Affairs Branch
Dept. of Environment & Public
  Safety
3085 Albert St., Room 218
Regina, SK S4S 0B1
(306) 787-6127
(306) 787-0930 Fax

YT Joe Ballantyne
Manager, Envmtl.
  Protection
Government of Yukon Territories
P.O. Box 2703
Whitehorse, YT Y1A 2C6
(403) 667-5683
(403) 667-3641 Fax

State Profiles

How does your state measure up in environmental quality?

How much does your state government spend on managing environmental resources? How many hazardous waste sites are found within your borders? What is the average per capita number of miles that a typical state resident travels in a year—is your state closer to the low end, at 5,900 (New York) or the high end, at 12,800 (Wyoming)? How much gas do you and your fellow citizens consume? These numbers and many others are in the 50 pages that follow.

From these profiles of state data, you can investigate trends—current population and estimates for the year 2010, whether your state has increased or decreased its overall energy use in the past 15 years—and statistics—your state's ranking for output of air emissions that negatively effect the world's greenhouse gases. The data provide fascinating glimpses of lifestyle (for example, energy and water use per capita) and practices within your state, as well as hints at how your state fits into the bigger national picture. When you want to know more about a particular topic, refer to the Profile Data Notes that begin on page 282.

ALABAMA

Important Facts

Population 1990: 4,041,000 **(22)**
Estimated pop. 2010: 4,469,000 **(22)**
Number of households 1990: 1,507,000
Per capita average income: $9,615 **(40)**
Metropolitan area population: 67.4%
Total area: 52,423 sq. mi. **(30)**
Land area: 50,750 sq. mi.
Water area: 1,673 sq. mi.
National Parks: 6,534 acres
State Park/rec. areas: 49,000 acres
Environmental Voting Record (1991):
    U.S. House 30%   U.S. Senate 10%

Energy Use and Production

Total consumed/year: 1,614 tr. Btu
    per capita: 393 m. Btu **(11)**
Change in use 1973–88: 9.42%
Chief sources:
    petroleum: 36%
    gas: 15%
    coal: 40%
Renewables as source of total energy
    used: 17.25%
Average price per kWh of electricity
    for residents: 6.6¢
Consumption by end use:
    residential: 18%
    commercial: 12%
    industrial: 47%
    transportation: 23%

Wastes

Total solid waste: 4,500 t. tons
    per capita: 1.11 tons **(16)**
Municipal landfills: 108
Curbside recycling programs: 8
Hazardous Waste Sites: 12 **(22)**
Municipal incinerators: 2

Transportation

Miles driven per year: 42,347 m. mi.
    per capita: 10,500 mi. **(5)**
Motor fuel consumed: 2,688 m. gal.
Registered motor vehicles: 4,075,000

Highway expenditures: $865.8 m.
How workers commute:
    drive alone: 69.7%
    carpool: 23.4%
    public transportation: 1.4% **(40)**

Water

Total used per day: 8,600 m. gal.
    per capita: 2,140 gal. **(14)**
Withdrawals by sector:
    public supply: 7.6%
    thermoelectric: 80.5%
    industrial and mining: 9.9%
    irrigation: 0.8%

Pollutant Releases

Toxics released: 56.3 t. tons **(10)**
    per capita: 27.86 pounds **(9)**
Toxics transferred: 9.4 t. tons **(19)**
Smog precursors: 2.5 m. tons
Acid precip. precursors: 954.2 t. tons
Greenhouse gas emissions (CO_2
    equiv.): 120.0 m. tons **(13)**
    per capita: 29.25 tons **(9)**

Environmental Expenditures

Budget spent on environmental and
    natural resources: 1.02% **(41)**
    per capita: $15.82 **(42)**
Per capita budget by category:
    air quality: $0.49 **(45)**
    drinking water: in water quality
    forestry: $5.30 **(11)**
    fish & wildlife: $3.28 **(42)**
    geological survey: $0.63 **(17)**
    hazardous waste: in solid waste
    land management: $0.17 **(28)**
    marine & coastal progs.: $0.49 **(18)**
    mining reclamation: $1.03 **(16)**
    nuclear waste: $0.17 **(13)**
    pesticides control: $0.15 **(34)**
    soil conservation: $0.31 **(22)**
    solid waste: $0.53 **(27)**
    water quality: $2.13 **(34)**
    water resources: $1.13 **(30)**

Btu = British thermal unit; **m.** = million; **sq. mi.** = square mile; **t.** = thousand; **tr.** = trillion

ALASKA

Important Facts
Population 1990: 550,000 **(49)**
Estimated pop. 2010: 669,000 **(47)**
Number of households 1990: 189,000
Per capita average income: $13,263 **(7)**
Metropolitan area population: 41.1%
Total area: 656,424 sq. mi. **(1)**
Land area: 570,374 sq. mi.
Water area: 86,051 sq. mi.
National Parks: 52,918,010 acres
State Park/rec. areas: 3,237,000 acres
Environmental Voting Record (1991):
 U.S. House 0%   U.S. Senate 20%

Energy Use and Production
Total consumed/year: 520 tr. Btu
 per capita: 991 m. Btu **(1)**
Change in use 1973–88: 168.04%
Chief sources:
 petroleum: 42%
 gas: 56%
 hydropower: 2%
Renewables as source of total energy
 used: 3.07%
Average price per kWh of electricity
 for residents: 10.1¢
Consumption by end use:
 residential: 8%
 commercial: 10%
 industrial: 53%
 transportation: 29%

Wastes
Total solid waste: 500 t. tons
 per capita: 0.91 tons **(30)**
Municipal landfills: 740
Curbside recycling programs: 0
Hazardous Waste Sites: 6 **(27)**
Municipal incinerators: 3

Transportation
Miles driven per year: 3,979 m. mi.
 per capita: 7,200 mi. **(48)**
Motor fuel consumed: 355 m. gal.
Registered motor vehicles: 367,000

Highway expenditures: $335.6 m.
How workers commute:
 drive alone: 52.3%
 carpool: 21.5%
 public transportation: 3.2% **(23)**

Water
Total used per day: 406 m. gal.
 per capita: 727 gal. **(39)**
Withdrawals by sector:
 public supply: 21.2%
 thermoelectric: 7.4%
 industrial and mining: 32.8%
 irrigation: 0.0%

Pollutant Releases
Toxics released: 10.3 t. tons **(36)**
 per capita: 37.41 pounds **(6)**
Toxics transferred: 0.0 t. tons **(50)**
Smog precursors: NA
Acid precip. precursors: 21.2 t. tons
Greenhouse gas emissions (CO_2
 equiv.): NA
 per capita: NA

Environmental Expenditures
Budget spent on environmental and
 natural resources: 4% **(4)**
 per capita: $251.31 **(2)**
Per capita budget by category:
 air quality: $2.97 **(3)**
 drinking water: $2.61 **(2)**
 forestry: $44.26 **(1)**
 fish & wildlife: $147.30 **(1)**
 geological survey: $5.93 **(1)**
 hazardous waste: $3.95 **(6)**
 land management: $23.49 **(1)**
 marine & coastal progs.: $6.17 **(2)**
 mining reclamation: $1.18 **(15)**
 nuclear waste: $0.00
 pesticides control: $0.26 **(19)**
 soil conservation: $0.60 **(15)**
 solid waste: $1.17 **(17)**
 water quality: $9.90 **(11)**
 water resources: $1.52 **(28)**

Btu = British thermal unit; **m.** = million; **sq. mi.** = square mile; **t.** = thousand; **tr.** = trillion

ARIZONA

Important Facts
Population 1990: 3,665,000 **(24)**
Estimated pop. 2010: 5,537,000 **(18)**
Number of households 1990: 1,369,000
Per capita average income: $11,521 **(21)**
Metropolitan area population: 79.0%
Total area: 114,006 sq. mi. **(6)**
Land area: 113,642 sq. mi.
Water area: 364 sq. mi.
National Parks: 2,671,486 acres
State Park/rec. areas: 39,000 acres
Environmental Voting Record (1991):
  U.S. House 13%   U.S. Senate 33%

Energy Use and Production
Total consumed/year: 898 tr. Btu
  per capita: 258 m. Btu **(41)**
Change in use 1973–88: 35.44%
Chief sources:
  petroleum: 39%
  coal: 34%
  nuclear: 27%
Renewables as source of total energy
  used: 8.87%
Average price per kWh of electricity
  for residents: 9.0¢
Consumption by end use:
  residential: 22%
  commercial: 22%
  industrial: 19%
  transportation: 37%

Wastes
Total solid waste: 2,900 t. tons
  per capita: 0.79 tons **(40)**
Municipal landfills: 85
Curbside recycling programs: 13
Hazardous Waste Sites: 10 **(24)**
Municipal incinerators: 0

Transportation
Miles driven per year: 35,456 m. mi.
  per capita: 9,700 mi. **(16)**
Motor fuel consumed: 2,025 m. gal.
Registered motor vehicles: 2,785,000
Highway expenditures: $1,525.4 m.
How workers commute:
  drive alone: 67.7%
  carpool: 19.8%
  public transportation: 2.0% **(31)**

Water
Total used per day: 6,430 m. gal.
  per capita: 1,960 gal. **(16)**
Withdrawals by sector:
  public supply: 10.0%
  thermoelectric: 0.9%
  industrial and mining: 2.1%
  irrigation: 85.8%

Pollutant Releases
Toxics released: 36.0 t. tons **(18)**
  per capita: 19.65 pounds **(15)**
Toxics transferred: 1.3 t. tons **(39)**
Smog precursors: 1.3 m. tons
Acid precip. precursors: 753.3 t. tons
Greenhouse gas emissions (CO_2
  equiv.): 64.1 m. tons **(29)**
  per capita: 18.37 tons **(33)**

Environmental Expenditures
Budget spent on environmental and
  natural resources: 0.96% **(43)**
  per capita: $13.36 **(45)**
Per capita budget by category:
  air quality: $0.81 **(32)**
  drinking water: $0.32 **(30)**
  forestry: $0.23 **(48)**
  fish & wildlife: $3.87 **(39)**
  geological survey: $0.11 **(42)**
  hazardous waste: $1.34 **(17)**
  land management: $1.96 **(13)**
  marine & coastal progs.: $0.00
  mining reclamation: $0.01 **(37)**
  nuclear waste: NA
  pesticides control: $0.04 **(47)**
  soil conservation: $0.05 **(35)**
  solid waste: In Hazardous Waste
  water quality: $1.51 **(37)**
  water resources: $3.11 **(19)**

Btu = British thermal unit; **m.** = million; **sq. mi.** = square mile; **t.** = thousand; **tr.** = trillion

ARKANSAS

Important Facts
Population 1990: 2,351,000 **(33)**
Estimated pop. 2010: 2,559,000 **(31)**
Number of households 1990: 891,000
Per capita average income: $9,061 **(46)**
Metropolitan area population: 40.1%
Total area: 53,182 sq. mi. **(29)**
Land area: 52,075 sq. mi.
Water area: 1,107 sq. mi.
National Parks: 101,350 acres
State Park/rec. areas: 48,000 acres
Environmental Voting Record (1991):
  U.S. House 25%   U.S. Senate 37%

Energy Use and Production
Total consumed/year: 790 tr. Btu
  per capita: 330 m. Btu **(24)**
Change in use 1973–88: .38%
Chief sources:
  petroleum: 39%
  gas: 28%
  coal: 28%
Renewables as source of total energy
  used: 16.25%
Average price per kWh of electricity
  for residents: 8.1¢
Consumption by end use:
  residential: 21%
  commercial: 13%
  industrial: 38%
  transportation: 29%

Wastes
Total solid waste: 2,000 t. tons
  per capita: 0.85 tons **(33)**
Municipal landfills: 64
Curbside recycling programs: 2
Hazardous Waste Sites: 12 **(22)**
Municipal incinerators: 5

Transportation
Miles driven per year: 21,011 m. mi.
  per capita: 8,900 mi. **(48)**
Motor fuel consumed: 1,647 m. gal.
Registered motor vehicles: 1,436,000

Highway expenditures: $455.8 m.
How workers commute:
  drive alone: 68.7%
  carpool: 22.6%
  public transportation: 0.8% **(48)**

Water
Total used per day: 5,910 m. gal.
  per capita: 2,500 gal. **(9)**
Withdrawals by sector:
  public supply: 5.4%
  thermoelectric: 18.4%
  industrial and mining: 3.0%
  irrigation: 65.5%

Pollutant Releases
Toxics released: 28.9 t. tons **(22)**
  per capita: 24.60 pounds **(12)**
Toxics transferred: 5.0 t. tons **(30)**
Smog precursors: 1.2 m. tons
Acid precip. precursors: 217.5 t. tons
Greenhouse gas emissions (CO_2
  equiv.): 62.4 m. tons **(30)**
  per capita: 26.04 tons **(13)**

Environmental Expenditures
Budget spent on environmental and
  natural resources: 1.15% **(39)**
  per capita: $18.45 **(39)**
Per capita budget by category:
  air quality: $0.39 **(47)**
  drinking water: $0.27 **(32)**
  forestry: $4.60 **(14)**
  fish & wildlife: $7.84 **(18)**
  geological survey: $0.36 **(26)**
  hazardous waste: $0.61 **(27)**
  land management: in water resources
  marine & coastal progs.: $0.00
  mining reclamation: $0.46 **(24)**
  nuclear waste: $0.18 **(12)**
  pesticides control: $0.05 **(43)**
  soil conservation: in water resources
  solid waste: $0.14 **(33)**
  water quality: $0.77 **(45)**
  water resources: $2.78 **(20)**

Btu = British thermal unit; **m.** = million; **sq. mi.** = square mile; **t.** = thousand; **tr.** = trillion

CALIFORNIA

Important Facts

Population 1990: 29,760,000 **(1)**
Estimated pop. 2010: 38,096,000 **(1)**
Number of households 1990: 10,381,000
Per capita average income: $13,197 **(8)**
Metropolitan area population: 95.7%
Total area: 163,707 sq. mi. **(3)**
Land area: 155,973 sq. mi.
Water area: 7,734 sq. mi.
National Parks: 4,574,693 acres
State Park/rec. areas: 1,287,000 acres
Environmental Voting Record (1991):
  U.S. House 50%   U.S. Senate 47%

Energy Use and Production

Total consumed/year: 6,970 tr. Btu
  per capita: 246 m. Btu **(42)**
Change in use 1973–88: 17.40%
Chief sources:
  petroleum: 50%
  gas: 27%
  nuclear: 5%
Renewables as source of total energy
  used: 13.44%
Average price per kWh of electricity
  for residents: 10.0¢
Consumption by end use:
  residential: 18%
  commercial: 17%
  industrial: 26%
  transportation: 39%

Wastes

Total solid waste: 45,000 t. tons
  per capita: 1.51 tons **(1)**
Municipal landfills: 353
Curbside recycling programs: 369
Hazardous Waste Sites: 95 **(3)**
Municipal incinerators: 3

Transportation

Miles driven per year: 258,926 m. mi.
  per capita: 8,700 mi. **(33)**
Motor fuel consumed: 15,152 m. gal.
Registered motor vehicles: 21,657,000

Highway expenditures: $4,294.4 m.
How workers commute:
  drive alone: 67.8%
  carpool: 16.9%
  public transportation: 5.8% **(8)**

Water

Total used per day: 49,700 m. gal.
  per capita: 1,420 gal. **(21)**
Withdrawals by sector:
  public supply: 11.0%
  thermoelectric: 24.5%
  industrial and mining: 2.3%
  irrigation: 61.6%

Pollutant Releases

Toxics released: 48.5 t. tons **(13)**
  per capita: 3.26 pounds **(46)**
Toxics transferred: 29.0 t. tons **(8)**
Smog precursors: 9.8 m. tons
Acid precip. precursors: 296.4 t. tons
Greenhouse gas emissions (CO_2
  equiv.): 443.2 m. tons **(2)**
  per capita: 15.65 tons **(39)**

Environmental Expenditures

Budget spent on environmental and
  natural resources: 2.60% **(9)**
  per capita: $52.49 **(8)**
Per capita budget by category:
  air quality: $2.25 **(6)**
  drinking water: $0.35 **(26)**
  forestry: $11.60 **(4)**
  fish & wildlife: $4.16 **(37)**
  geological survey: $0.37 **(25)**
  hazardous waste: $3.09 **(9)**
  land management: $0.71 **(20)**
  marine & coastal progs.: $0.53 **(17)**
  mining reclamation: $0.09 **(32)**
  nuclear waste: NA
  pesticides control: $1.15 **(2)**
  soil conservation: $0.03 **(37)**
  solid waste: $3.13 **(4)**
  water quality: $3.76 **(23)**
  water resources: $21.24 **(3)**

Btu = British thermal unit; **m.** = million; **sq. mi.** = square mile; **t.** = thousand; **tr.** = trillion

Important Facts

Population 1990: 3,294,000 **(26)**
Estimated pop. 2010: 3,385,000 **(27)**
Number of households 1990: 1,282,000
Per capita average income: $12,271 **(17)**
Metropolitan area population: 81.5%
Total area: 104,100 sq. mi. **(8)**
Land area: 103,730 sq. mi.
Water area: 371 sq. mi.
National Parks: 596,653 acres
State Park/rec. areas: 230,000 acres
Environmental Voting Record (1991):
  U.S. House 36%   U.S. Senate 58%

Energy Use and Production

Total consumed/year: 902 tr. Btu
  per capita: 273 m. Btu **(39)**
Change in use 1973–88: 13.60%
Chief sources:
  petroleum: 38%
  gas: 25%
  coal: 34%
Renewables as source of total energy
  used: 5.33%
Average price per kWh of electricity
  for residents: 7.0¢
Consumption by end use:
  residential: 23%
  commercial: 25%
  industrial: 22%
  transportation: 30%

Wastes

Total solid waste: 2,400 t. tons
  per capita: 0.73 tons **(43)**
Municipal landfills: 140
Curbside recycling programs: 20
Hazardous Waste Sites: 17 **(19)**
Municipal incinerators: 0

Transportation

Miles driven per year: 27,178 m. mi.
  per capita: 8,300 mi. **(40)**
Motor fuel consumed: 1,753 m. gal.
Registered motor vehicles: 2,932,000

Highway expenditures: $713.9 m.
How workers commute:
  drive alone: 64.2%
  carpool: 20.2%
  public transportation: 4.2% **(16)**

Water

Total used per day: 13,600 m. gal.
  per capita: 4,,190 gal. **(5)**
Withdrawals by sector:
  public supply: 5.5%
  thermoelectric: 0.8%
  industrial and mining: 1.6%
  irrigation: 91.2%

Pollutant Releases

Toxics released: 3.7 t. tons **(43)**
  per capita: 2.25 pounds **(48)**
Toxics transferred: 2.0 t. tons **(36)**
Smog precursors: 1.9 m. tons
Acid precip. precursors: 94.9 t. tons
Greenhouse gas emissions (CO_2
  equiv.): 72.3 m. tons **(26)**
  per capita: 21.89 tons **(23)**

Environmental Expenditures

Budget spent on environmental and
  natural resources: 1.65% **(23)**
  per capita: $23.07 **(33)**
Per capita budget by category:
  air quality: $1.95 **(8)**
  drinking water: $0.07 **(37)**
  forestry: $1.33 **(37)**
  fish & wildlife: $11.71 **(13)**
  geological survey: $0.29 **(31)**
  hazardous waste: $1.17 **(21)**
  land management: $0.42 **(23)**
  marine & coastal progs.: $0.00
  mining reclamation: $0.84 **(17)**
  nuclear waste: in geological survey
  pesticides control: $0.16 **(32)**
  soil conservation: $0.20 **(26)**
  solid waste: in hazardous waste
  water quality: $1.36 **(39)**
  water resources: $3.57 **(17)**

Btu = British thermal unit; **m.** = million; **sq. mi.** = square mile; **t.** = thousand; **tr.** = trillion

CONNECTICUT

Important Facts

Population 1990: 3,287,000 **(27)**
Estimated pop. 2010: 3,514,000 **(26)**
Number of households 1990: 1,230,000
Per capita average income: $16,094 **(1)**
Metropolitan area population: 92.4%
Total area: 5,544 sq. mi. **(48)**
Land area: 4,845 sq. mi.
Water area: 698 sq. mi.
National Parks: 5,701 acres
State Park/rec. areas: 170,000 acres
Environmental Voting Record (1991):
  U.S. House 64%   U.S. Senate 87%

Energy Use and Production

Total consumed/year: 757 tr. Btu
  per capita: 234 m. Btu **(45)**
Change in use 1973–88: 3.70%
Chief sources:
  petroleum: 64%
  gas: 12%
  nuclear: 32%
Renewables as source of total energy
  used: 9.04%
Average price per kWh of electricity
  for residents: 10.0¢
Consumption by end use:
  residential: 31%
  commercial: 22%
  industrial: 18%
  transportation: 29%

Wastes

Total solid waste: 2,900 t. tons
  per capita: 0.88 tons **(32)**
Municipal landfills: 60
Curbside recycling programs: 150
Hazardous Waste Sites: 15 **(20)**
Municipal incinerators: 5

Transportation

Miles driven per year: 26,303 m. mi.
  per capita: 8,000 mi. **(41)**
Motor fuel consumed: 1,531 m. gal.
Registered motor vehicles: 2,695,000

Highway expenditures: $1,203.7 m.
How workers commute:
  drive alone: 67.6%
  carpool: 19.6%
  public transportation: 5.1% **(11)**

Water

Total used per day: 3,780 m. gal.
  per capita: 375 gal. **(45)**
Withdrawals by sector:
  public supply: 10.6%
  thermoelectric: 84.9%
  industrial and mining: 3.9%
  irrigation: 0.1%

Pollutant Releases

Toxics released: 10.7 t. tons **(34)**
  per capita: 6.49 pounds **(38)**
Toxics transferred: 6.6 t. tons **(25)**
Smog precursors: 1.0 m. tons
Acid precip. precursors: 113.9 t. tons
Greenhouse gas emissions (CO_2
  equiv.): 47.3 m. tons **(35)**
  per capita: 14.63 tons **(42)**

Environmental Expenditures

Budget spent on environmental and
  natural resources: 0.77% **(46)**
  per capita: $19.18 **(37)**
Per capita budget by category:
  air quality: $2.65 **(4)**
  drinking water: $1.23 **(5)**
  forestry: $1.34 **(36)**
  fish & wildlife: $5.73 **(27)**
  geological survey: in water resources
  hazardous waste: $4.43 **(4)**
  land management: $0.00
  marine & coastal progs.: in water quality
  mining reclamation: $0.00
  nuclear waste: in air quality
  pesticides control: in hazardous waste
  soil conservation: in water quality
  solid waste: in hazardous waste
  water quality: $3.81 **(22)**
  water resources: in water quality

Btu = British thermal unit; **m.** = million; **sq. mi.** = square mile; **t.** = thousand; **tr.** = trillion

Important Facts

Population 1990: 666,000 **(46)**
Estimated pop. 2010: 933,000 **(44)**
Number of households 1990: 247,000
Per capita average income: $12,785 **(10)**
Metropolitan area population: 66.3%
Total area: 2,489 sq. mi. **(49)**
Land area: 1,955 sq. mi.
Water area: 535 sq. mi.
National Parks: NA
State Park/rec. areas: 12,000 acres
Environmental Voting Record (1991):
  U.S. House 69%   U.S. Senate 83%

Energy Use and Production

Total consumed/year: 230 tr. Btu
  per capita: 349 m. Btu **(17)**
Change in use 1973–88: -2.13%
Chief sources:
  petroleum: 62%
  gas: 13%
  coal: 30%
Renewables as source of total energy
  used: 4.16%
Average price per kWh of electricity
  for residents: 8.4¢
Consumption by end use:
  residential: 20%
  commercial: 14%
  industrial: 38%
  transportation: 27%

Wastes

Total solid waste: 750 t. tons
  per capita: 1.13 tons **(15)**
Municipal landfills: 3
Curbside recycling programs: 0
Hazardous Waste Sites: 20 **(17)**
Municipal Incinerators: 1

Transportation

Miles driven per year: 6,548 m. mi.
  per capita: 9,800 mi. **(12)**
Motor fuel consumed: 400 m. gal.
Registered motor vehicles: 529,000

Highway expenditures: $315.4 m.
How workers commute:
  drive alone: 66.4%
  carpool: 21.3%
  public transportation: 4.1% **(17)**

Water

Total used per day: 1,650 m. gal.
  per capita: 222 gal. **(49)**
Withdrawals by sector:
  public supply: 5.3%
  thermoelectric: 67.9%
  industrial and mining: 24.8%
  irrigation: 1.6%

Pollutant Releases

Toxics released: 3.3 t. tons **(44)**
  per capita: 9.88 pounds **(31)**
Toxics transferred: 2.9 t. tons **(33)**
Smog precursors: 0.4 m. tons
Acid precip. precursors: 158.6 t. tons
Greenhouse gas emissions (CO_2
  equiv.): 14.2 m. tons **(46)**
  per capita: 21.53 tons **(24)**

Environmental Expenditures

Budget spent on environmental and
  natural resources: 1.80% **(19)**
  per capita: $50.26 **(9)**
Per capita budget by category:
  air quality: $2.10 **(7)**
  drinking water: in water resources
  forestry: $2.01 **(30)**
  fish & wildlife: $15.26 **(6)**
  geological survey: $1.13 **(10)**
  hazardous waste: $7.58 **(1)**
  land management: in forestry
  marine & coastal progs.: $7.32 **(1)**
  mining reclamation: $0.00
  nuclear waste: in water resources
  pesticides control: $0.41 **(10)**
  soil conservation: in marine/coastal
  solid waste: in hazardous waste
  water quality: in water resources
  water resources: $14.45 **(7)**

Btu = British thermal unit; **m.** = million; **sq. mi.** = square mile; **t.** = thousand; **tr.** = trillion

FLORIDA

Important Facts

Population 1990: 12,938,000 **(4)**
Estimated pop. 2010: 19,702,000 **(2)**
Number of households 1990: 5,135,000
Per capita average income: $12,456 **(12)**
Metropolitan area population: 90.8%
Total area: 65,758 sq. mi. **(22)**
Land area: 53,997 sq. mi.
Water area: 11,761 sq. mi.
National Parks: 2,298,000 acres
State Park/rec. areas: 419,000 acres
Environmental Voting Record (1991):
  U.S. House 45%   U.S. Senate 47%

Energy Use and Production

Total consumed/year: 2,929 tr. Btu
  per capita: 237 m. Btu **(44)**
Change in use 1973–88: 50.51%
Chief sources:
  petroleum: 53%
  gas: 10%
  coal: 21%
Renewables as source of total energy
  used: 5.78%
Average price per kWh of electricity
  for residents: 7.8¢
Consumption by end use:
  residential: 26%
  commercial: 22%
  industrial: 15%
  transportation: 38%

Wastes

Total solid waste: 18,700 t. tons
  per capita: 1.45 tons **(5)**
Municipal landfills: 170
Curbside recycling programs: 200
Hazardous Waste Sites: 55 **(6)**
Municipal incinerators: 13

Transportation

Miles driven per year: 109,997 m. mi.
  per capita: 8,500 mi. **(36)**
Motor fuel consumed: 7,043 m. gal.
Registered motor vehicles: 11,378,000

Highway expenditures: $1,677.3 m.
How workers commute:
  drive alone: 69.2%
  carpool: 20.3%
  public transportation: 2.7% **(24)**

Water

Total used per day: 17,000 m. gal.
  per capita: 554 gal. **(42)**
Withdrawals by sector:
  public supply: 11.4%
  thermoelectric: 66.8%
  industrial and mining: 4.0%
  irrigation: 17.1%

Pollutant Releases

Toxics released: 53.3 t. tons **(11)**
  per capita: 8.24 pounds **(34)**
Toxics transferred: 12.2 t. tons **(16)**
Smog precursors: 4.5 m. tons
Acid precip. precursors: 1135.8 t. tons
Greenhouse gas emissions (CO_2
  equiv.): 167.4 m. tons **(10)**
  per capita: 13.57 tons **(46)**

Environmental Expenditures

Budget spent on environmental and
  natural resources: 2.51% **(11)**
  per capita: $37.75 **(13)**
Per capita budget by category:
  air quality: $0.58 **(38)**
  drinking water: $0.88 **(7)**
  forestry: $3.81 **(18)**
  fish & wildlife: $6.05 **(25)**
  geological survey: $0.12 **(39)**
  hazardous waste: $2.35 **(13)**
  land management: $0.38 **(25)**
  marine & coastal progs.: $1.61 **(11)**
  mining reclamation: $0.15 **(28)**
  nuclear waste: $0.01 **(26)**
  pesticides control: $0.23 **(24)**
  soil conservation: $0.11 **(31)**
  solid waste: $1.98 **(10)**
  water quality: $4.49 **(17)**
  water resources: $14.98 **(5)**

Btu = British thermal unit; **m.** = million; **sq. mi.** = square mile; **t.** = thousand; **tr.** = trillion

Important Facts

Population 1990: 6,478,000 **(11)**
Estimated pop. 2010: 9,378,000 **(8)**
Number of households 1990: 2,367,000
Per capita average income: $11,406 **(24)**
Metropolitan area population: 65.0%
Total area: 59,441 sq. mi. **(24)**
Land area: 57,919 sq. mi.
Water area: 1,522 sq. mi.
National Parks: 40,492 acres
State Park/rec. areas: 62,000 acres
Environmental Voting Record (1991):
  U.S. House 55%   U.S. Senate 50%

Energy Use and Production

Total consumed/year: 2,038 tr. Btu
  per capita: 322 m. Btu **(25)**
Change in use 1973–88: 38.26%
Chief sources:
  petroleum: 41%
  gas: 16%
  coal: 34%
Renewables as source of total energy
  used: 15.94%
Average price per kWh of electricity
  for residents: 7.5¢
Consumption by end use:
  residential: 21%
  commercial: 15%
  industrial: 30%
  transportation: 34%

Wastes

Total solid waste: 4,400 t. tons
  per capita: 0.68 tons **(48)**
Municipal landfills: 180
Curbside recycling programs: 20
Hazardous Waste Sites: 13 **(21)**
Municipal incinerators: 1

Transportation

Miles driven per year: 72,746 m. mi.
  per capita: 11,200 mi. **(2)**
Motor fuel consumed: 4,439 m. gal.
Registered motor vehicles: 5,385,000

Highway expenditures: $1,277.8 m.
How workers commute:
  drive alone: 67.5%
  carpool: 22.1%
  public transportation: 3.9% **(20)**

Water

Total used per day: 5,450 m. gal.
  per capita: 899 gal. **(35)**
Withdrawals by sector:
  public supply: 17.2%
  thermoelectric: 61.0%
  industrial and mining: 12.0%
  irrigation: 8.3%

Pollutant Releases

Toxics released: 38.9 t. tons **(17)**
  per capita: 12.02 pounds **(24)**
Toxics transferred: 11.4 t. tons **(17)**
Smog precursors: 3.3 m. tons
Acid precip. precursors: 1397.6 t. tons
Greenhouse gas emissions (CO_2
  equiv.): 145.4 m. tons **(11)**
  per capita: 22.93 tons **(19)**

Environmental Expenditures

Budget spent on environmental and
  natural resources: 1.07% **(40)**
  per capita: $14.72 **(44)**
Per capita budget by category:
  air quality: $0.55 **(40)**
  drinking water: $0.39 **(24)**
  forestry: $6.39 **(9)**
  fish & wildlife: $4.20 **(36)**
  geological survey: $0.41 **(22)**
  hazardous waste: $0.37 **(37)**
  land management: $0.07 **(34)**
  marine & coastal progs.: $0.34 **(21)**
  mining reclamation: $0.00
  nuclear waste: $0.30 **(27)**
  pesticides control: $0.30 **(15)**
  soil conservation: $0.27 **(24)**
  solid waste: $0.19 **(30)**
  water quality: $1.15 **(41)**
  water resources: $0.08 **(46)**

Btu = British thermal unit; **m.** = million; **sq. mi.** = square mile; **t.** = thousand; **tr.** = trillion

HAWAII

Important Facts

Population 1990: 1,108,000 **(41)**
Estimated pop. 2010: 1,590,000 **(38)**
Number of households 1990: 356,000
Per capita avg. income: $12,290 **(15)**
Metropolitan area population: 75.5%
Total area: 10,932 sq. mi. **(43)**
Land area: 6,423 sq. mi.
Water area: 4,508 sq. mi.
National Parks: 245,640 acres
State Park/rec. areas: 25,000 acres
Environmental Voting Record (1991):
  U.S. House 85%   U.S. Senate 50%

Energy Use and Production

Total consumed/year: 266 tr. Btu
  per capita: 243 m. Btu **(43)**
Change in use 1973–88: 17.18%
Chief sources:
  petroleum: 98%
  gas: 1%
Renewables as source of total energy
  used: 8.05%
Average price per kWh of electricity
  for residents: 10.3¢
Consumption by end use:
  residential: 9%
  commercial: 14%
  industrial: 23%
  transportation: 54%

Wastes

Total solid waste: 1,300 t. tons
  per capita: 1.17 tons **(10)**
Municipal landfills: 13
Curbside recycling programs: 2
Hazardous Waste Sites: 2 **(31)**
Municipal incinerators: 1

Transportation

Miles driven per year: 8,066 m. mi.
  per capita: 7,300 mi. **(46)**
Motor fuel consumed: 412 m. gal.
Registered motor vehicles: 719,000
Highway expenditures: $297.4 m.

How workers commute:
  drive alone: 55.3%
  carpool: 23.2%
  public transportation: 8.3% **(6)**

Water

Total used per day: 2,150 m. gal.
  per capita: 1,100 gal. **(31)**
Withdrawals by sector:
  public supply: 10.0%
  thermoelectric: 45.1%
  industrial and mining: 0.9%
  irrigation: 42.1%

Pollutant Releases

Toxics released: 0.4 t. tons **(50)**
  per capita: 0.77 pounds **(50)**
Toxics transferred: 0.2 t. tons **(43)**
Smog precursors: NA
Acid precip. precursors: 82.1 t. tons
Greenhouse gas emissions (CO_2
  equiv.): NA
  per capita: NA

Environmental Expenditures

Budget spent on environmental and
  natural resources: 0.85% **(44)**
  per capita: $25.35 **(29)**
Per capita budget by category:
  air quality: $6.13 **(1)**
  drinking water: $0.65 **(13)**
  forestry: $3.61 **(19)**
  fish & wildlife: $0.63 **(50)**
  geological survey: $0.08 **(46)**
  hazardous waste: in air quality
  land management: $5.03 **(6)**
  marine & coastal progs.: $0.13 **(25)**
  mining reclamation: $0.00
  nuclear waste: $0.00
  pesticides control: $0.45 **(9)**
  soil conservation: in land mgmt.
  solid waste: $1.27 **(15)**
  water quality: in air quality
  water resources: $7.36 **(10)**

Btu = British thermal unit; **m.** = million; **sq. mi.** = square mile; **t.** = thousand; **tr.** = trillion

Important Facts

Population 1990: 1,007,000 **(42)**
Estimated pop. 2010: 985,000 **(43)**
Number of households 1990: 361,000
Per capita average income: $9,159 **(45)**
Metropolitan area population: 20.4%
Total area: 83,574 sq. mi. **(14)**
Land area: 82,751 sq. mi.
Water area: 823 sq. mi.
National Parks: 97,656 acres
State Park/rec. areas: 47,000 acres
Environmental Voting Record (1991):
  U.S. House 43%   U.S. Senate 14%

Energy Use and Production

Total consumed/year: 355 tr. Btu
  per capita: 354 m. Btu **(15)**
Change in use 1973–88: 8.56%
Chief sources:
  petroleum: 32%
  gas: 12%
  hydropower: 20%
Renewables as source of total energy
  used: 46.47%
Average price per kWh of electricity
  for residents: 4.9¢
Consumption by end use:
  residential: 21%
  commercial: 19%
  industrial: 36%
  transportation: 24%

Wastes

Total solid waste: 850 t. tons
  per capita: 0.84 tons **(34)**
Municipal landfills: 83
Curbside recycling programs: 2
Hazardous Waste Sites: 9 **(25)**
Municipal incinerators: 1

Transportation

Miles driven per year: 9,849 m. mi.
  per capita: 9,800 mi. **(11)**
Motor fuel consumed: 626 m. gal.
Registered motor vehicles: 953,000

Highway expenditures: $300.4 m.
How workers commute:
  drive alone: 64.5%
  carpool: 17.4%
  public transportation: 2.5% **(26)**

Water

Total used per day: 22,300 m. gal.
  per capita: 22,300 gal. **(1)**
Withdrawals by sector:
  public supply: 1.3%
  thermoelectric: 0.0%
  industrial and mining: 1.5%
  irrigation: 92.4%

Pollutant Releases

Toxics released: 5.8 t. tons **(40)**
  per capita: 11.51 pounds **(26)**
Toxics transferred: 1.5 t. tons **(37)**
Smog precursors: 1.5 m. tons
Acid precip. precursors: 38.6 t. tons
Greenhouse gas emissions (CO_2
  equiv.): 17.1 m. tons **(43)**
  per capita: 17.02 tons **(36)**

Environmental Expenditures

Budget spent on environmental and
  natural resources: 4.22% **(3)**
  per capita: $61.26 **(6)**
Per capita budget by category:
  air quality: $0.77 **(35)**
  drinking water: $0.57 **(17)**
  forestry: $9.91 **(5)**
  fish & wildlife: $23.73 **(4)**
  geological survey: $0.33 **(27)**
  hazardous waste: $1.72 **(16)**
  land management: $1.28 **(17)**
  marine & coastal progs.: $0.00
  mining reclamation: $0.37 **(26)**
  nuclear waste: $0.00
  pesticides control: $0.38 **(12)**
  soil conservation: $0.64 **(14)**
  solid waste: $0.10 **(38)**
  water quality: $10.05 **(10)**
  water resources: $11.39 **(8)**

Btu = British thermal unit; **m.** = million; **sq. mi.** = square mile; **t.** = thousand; **tr.** = trillion

ILLINOIS

Important Facts

Population 1990: 11,431,000 **(6)**
Estimated pop. 201010: 11,571,000 **(6)**
Number of households 1990: 4,202,000
Per capita average income: $12,437 **(13)**
Metropolitan area population: 82.7%
Total area: 57,918 sq. mi. **(25)**
Land area: 55,593 sq. mi.
Water area: 2,325 sq. mi.
National Parks: 12 acres
State Park/rec. areas: 401,000 acres
Environmental Voting Record (1991):
U.S. House 52%   U.S. Senate 70%

Energy Use and Production

Total consumed/year: 3,577 tr. Btu
per capita: 308 m. Btu **(29)**
Change in use 1973–88: -10.35%
Chief sources:
petroleum: 35%
gas: 27%
nuclear: 21%
Renewables as source of total energy
used: 2.20%
Average price per kWh of electricity
for residents: 9.9¢
Consumption by end use:
residential: 25%
commercial: 19%
industrial: 35%
transportation: 22%

Wastes

Total solid waste: 14,600 t. tons
per capita: 1.28 tons **(6)**
Municipal landfills: 110
Curbside recycling programs: 200
Hazardous Waste Sites: 37 **(10)**
Municipal incinerators: 1

Transportation

Miles driven per year: 83,334 m. mi.
per capita: 7,300 mi. **(45)**
Motor fuel consumed: 6,348 m. gal.
Registered motor vehicles: 8,091,000

Highway expenditures: $2,644.9 m.
How workers commute:
drive alone: 61.0%
carpool: 17.9%
public transportation: 12.0% **(2)**

Water

Total used per day: 14,500 m. gal.
per capita: 1,250 gal. **(25)**
Withdrawals by sector:
public supply: 13.2%
thermoelectric: 80.7%
industrial and mining: 4.4%
irrigation: 0.5%

Pollutant Releases

Toxics released: 59.5 t. tons **(9)**
per capita: 10.41 pounds **(30)**
Toxics transferred: 56.6 t. tons **(2)**
Smog precursors: 4.8 m. tons
Acid precip. precursors: 1697.2 t. tons
Greenhouse gas emissions (CO_2
equiv.): 298.9 m. tons **(3)**
per capita: 25.74 tons **(14)**

Environmental Expenditures

Budget spent on environmental and
natural resources: 2.26% **(14)**
per capita: $33.83 **(18)**
Per capita budget by category:
air quality: $2.36 **(5)**
drinking water: $0.53 **(19)**
forestry: $0.32 **(47)**
fish & wildlife: $1.14 **(48)**
geological survey: $0.52 **(20)**
hazardous waste: $3.17 **(8)**
land management: $0.00
marine & coastal progs.: $0.03 **(28)**
mining reclamation: $2.24 **(8)**
nuclear waste: $1.10 **(1)**
pesticides control: $0.16 **(31)**
soil conservation: $0.45 **(17)**
solid waste: $1.38 **(13)**
water quality: $15.54 **(5)**
water resources: $4.88 **(12)**

Btu = British thermal unit; **m.** = million; **sq. mi.** = square mile; **t.** = thousand; **tr.** = trillion

Important Facts

Population 1990: 5,544,000 **(14)**
Estimated pop. 2010: 5,655,000 **(1716)**
Number of households 1990: 2,065,000
Per capita average income: $11,078 **(30)**
Metropolitan area population: 68.5%
Total area: 36,420 sq. mi. **(38)**
Land area: 35,870 sq. mi.
Water area: 550 sq. mi.
National Parks: 9,917 acres
State Park/rec. areas: 57,000 acres
Environmental Voting Record (1991):
　U.S. House 55%　　U.S. Senate 24%

Energy Use and Production

Total consumed/year: 2,478 tr. Btu
　per capita: 446 m. Btu **(6)**
Change in use 1973–88: .57%
Chief sources:
　petroleum: 32%
　gas: 19%
　coal: 52%
Renewables as source of total energy
　used: 2.04%
Average price per kWh of electricity
　for residents: 6.9¢
Consumption by end use:
　residential: 18%
　commercial: 11%
　industrial: 48%
　transportation: 23%

Wastes

Total solid waste: 5,700 t. tons
　per capita: 1.03 tons **(20)**
Municipal landfills: 76
Curbside recycling programs: 40
Hazardous Waste Sites: 33 **(11)**
Municipal incinerators: 2

Transportation

Miles driven per year: 53,697 m. mi.
　per capita: 9,700 mi. **(14)**
Motor fuel consumed: 3,422 m. gal.
Registered motor vehicles: 4,265,000

Highway expenditures: $1,217.7 m.
How workers commute:
　drive alone: 69.9%
　carpool: 20.0%
　public transportation: 1.7% **(37)**

Water

Total used per day: 8,030 m. gal.
　per capita: 1,470 gal. **(20)**
Withdrawals by sector:
　public supply: 8.9%
　thermoelectric: 55.8%
　industrial and mining: 34.3%
　irrigation: 0.6%

Pollutant Releases

Toxics released: 84.4 t. tons **(4)**
　per capita: 30.45 pounds **(8)**
Toxics transferred: 21.4 t. tons **(9)**
Smog precursors: 3.8 m. tons
Acid precip. precursors: 2526.2 t. tons
Greenhouse gas emissions (CO_2
　equiv.): 217.1 m. tons **(7)**
　per capita: 39.07 tons **(5)**

Environmental Expenditures

Budget spent on environmental and
　natural resources: 0.68% **(47)**
　per capita: $9.50 **(49)**
Per capita budget by category:
　air quality: $0.85 **(28)**
　drinking water: $0.07 **(38)**
　forestry: $1.14 **(40)**
　fish & wildlife: $1.52 **(46)**
　geological survey: $0.37 **(24)**
　hazardous waste: $1.15 **(22)**
　land management: NA
　marine & coastal progs.: $0.00
　mining reclamation: $0.56 **(21)**
　nuclear waste: NA
　pesticides control: $0.21 **(26)**
　soil conservation: $0.34 **(20)**
　solid waste: $0.02 **(40)**
　water quality: $0.59 **(47)**
　water resources: $2.67 **(21)**

Btu = British thermal unit; **m.** = million; **sq. mi.** = square mile; **t.** = thousand; **tr.** = trillion

IOWA

Important Facts

Population 1990: 2,777,000 **(30)**
Estimated pop. 2010: 2,251,000 **(33)**
Number of households 1990: 1,064,000
Per capita average income: $11,198 **(28)**
Metropolitan area population: 44.0%
Total area: 56,276 sq. mi. **(26)**
Land area: 55,875 sq. mi.
Water area: 401 sq. mi.
National Parks: 1,663 acres
State Park/rec. areas: 83,000 acres
Environmental Voting Record (1991):
  U.S. House 30%   U.S. Senate 53%

Energy Use and Production

Total consumed/year: 942 tr. Btu
  per capita: 333 m. Btu **(22)**
Change in use 1973–88: -1.77%
Chief sources:
  petroleum: 36%
  gas: 26%
  coal: 32%
Renewables as source of total energy
  used: 8.35%
Average price per kWh of electricity
  for residents: 7.8¢
Consumption by end use:
  residential: 24%
  commercial: 15%
  industrial: 37%
  transportation: 25%

Wastes

Total solid waste: 2,300 t. tons
  per capita: 0.83 tons **(37)**
Municipal landfills: 82
Curbside recycling programs: 35
Hazardous Waste Sites: 20 **(17)**
Municipal incinerators: 1

Transportation

Miles driven per year: 22,993 m. mi.
  per capita: 8,300 mi. **(39)**
Motor fuel consumed: 1,752 m. gal.
Registered motor vehicles: 2,613,000

Highway expenditures: $868.5 m.
How workers commute:
  drive alone: 62.1%
  carpool: 18.4%
  public transportation: 1.9% **(34)**

Water

Total used per day: 2,770 m. gal.
  per capita: 960 gal. **(33)**
Withdrawals by sector:
  public supply: 15.0%
  thermoelectric: 65.3%
  industrial and mining: 9.4%
  irrigation: 2.4%

Pollutant Releases

Toxics released: 20.3 t. tons **(28)**
  per capita: 14.65 pounds **(19)**
Toxics transferred: 5.7 t. tons **(27)**
Smog precursors: 1.3 m. tons
Acid precip. precursors: 388.6 t. tons
Greenhouse gas emissions (CO_2
  equiv.): 68.5 m. tons **(28)**
  per capita: 24.16 tons **(17)**

Environmental Expenditures

Budget spent on environmental and
  natural resources: 1.44% **(32)**
  per capita: $31.07 **(22)**
Per capita budget by category:
  air quality: $0.38 **(48)**
  drinking water: $0.32 **(29)**
  forestry: $0.77 **(42)**
  fish & wildlife: $6.46 **(22)**
  geological survey: $0.80 **(13)**
  hazardous waste: $0.19 **(42)**
  land management: $0.00
  marine & coastal progs.: $0.00
  mining reclamation: $0.64 **(19)**
  nuclear waste: $0.00
  pesticides control: $0.24 **(21)**
  soil conservation: $5.08 **(1)**
  solid waste: $0.14 **(34)**
  water quality: $15.50 **(6)**
  water resources: $0.56 **(37)**

Btu = British thermal unit; **m.** = million; **sq. mi.** = square mile; **t.** = thousand; **tr.** = trillion

Important Facts

Population 1990: 2,478,000 **(32)**
Estimated pop. 2010: 2,488,000 **(32)**
Number of households 1990: 945,000
Per capita average income: $11,520 **(22)**
Metropolitan area population: 53.8%
Total area: 82,282 sq. mi. **(15)**
Land area: 81,823 sq. mi.
Water area: 459 sq. mi.
National Parks: 696 acres
State Park/rec. areas: 30,000 acres
Environmental Voting Record (1991):
 U.S. House 34%   U.S. Senate 27%

Energy Use and Production

Total consumed/year: 1,057 tr. Btu
 per capita: 423 m. Btu **(7)**
Change in use 1973–88: 9.88%
Chief sources:
 petroleum: 41%
 gas: 33%
 coal: 25%
Renewables as source of total energy
 used: 0.28%
Average price per kWh of electricity
 for residents: 7.8¢
Consumption by end use:
 residential: 18%
 commercial: 16%
 industrial: 39%
 transportation: 28%

Wastes

Total solid waste: 2,400 t. tons
 per capita: 0.97 tons **(25)**
Municipal landfills: 115
Curbside recycling programs: 10
Hazardous Waste Sites: 11 **(23)**
Municipal incinerators: 0

Transportation

Miles driven per year: 22,849 m. mi.
 per capita: 9,200 mi. **(24)**
Motor fuel consumed: 1,560 m. gal.
Registered motor vehicles: 2,237,000

Highway expenditures: $697.0 m.
How workers commute:
 drive alone: 67.6%
 carpool: 19.2%
 public transportation: 1.0% **(46)**

Water

Total used per day: 5,670 m. gal.
 per capita: 2,310 gal. **(12)**
Withdrawals by sector:
 public supply: 6.3%
 thermoelectric: 7.3%
 industrial and mining: 1.7%
 irrigation: 83.4%

Pollutant Releases

Toxics released: 44.9 t. tons **(14)**
 per capita: 36.28 pounds **(7)**
Toxics transferred: 5.5 t. tons **(28)**
Smog precursors: 1.5 m. tons
Acid precip. precursors: 330.8 t. tons
Greenhouse gas emissions (CO_2
 equiv.): 70.8 m. tons **(27)**
 per capita: 28.38 tons **(10)**

Environmental Expenditures

Budget spent on environmental and
 natural resources: 1.23% **(37)**
 per capita: $19.17 **(38)**
Per capita budget by category:
 air quality: $1.00 **(20)**
 drinking water: $1.05 **(6)**
 forestry: $0.00
 fish & wildlife: $3.74 **(40)**
 geological survey: $1.51 **(7)**
 hazardous waste: $0.56 **(31)**
 land management: $0.00
 marine & coastal progs.: $0.00
 mining reclamation: $1.63 **(13)**
 nuclear waste: in air quality
 pesticides control: $0.64 **(6)**
 soil conservation: $0.14 **(30)**
 solid waste: $0.54 **(26)**
 water quality: $4.17 **(18)**
 water resources: $4.19 **(14)**

Btu = British thermal unit; **m.** = million; **sq. mi.** = square mile; **t.** = thousand; **tr.** = trillion

KENTUCKY

Important Facts

Population 1990: 3,685,000 **(23)**
Estimated pop. 2010: 3,562,000 **(25)**
Number of households 1990: 1,380,000
Per capita average income: $9,380 **(42)**
Metropolitan area population: 46.5%
Total area: 40,411 sq. mi. **(37)**
Land area: 39,732 sq. mi.
Water area: 679 sq. mi.
National Parks: 108,722 acres
State Park/rec. areas: 42,000 acres
Environmental Voting Record (1991):
  U.S. House 24%   U.S. Senate 10%

Energy Use and Production

Total consumed/year: 1,401 tr. Btu
  per capita: 376 m. Btu **(13)**
Change in use 1973–88: 14.09%
Chief sources:
  petroleum: 37%
  gas: 14%
  coal: 59%
Renewables as source of total energy
  used: 6.49%
Average price per kWh of electricity
  for residents: 5.7¢
Consumption by end use:
  residential: 20%
  commercial: 12%
  industrial: 41%
  transportation: 27%

Wastes

Total solid waste: 3,500 t. tons
  per capita: 0.95 tons **(27)**
Municipal landfills: 34
Curbside recycling programs: 10
Hazardous Waste Sites: 19 **(18)**
Municipal incinerators: 0

Transportation

Miles driven per year: 33,639 m. mi.
  per capita: 9,100 mi. **(25)**
Motor fuel consumed: 2,337 m. gal.
Registered motor vehicles: 2,841,000

Highway expenditures: $1,007.9 m.
How workers commute:
  drive alone: 65.3%
  carpool: 22.8%
  public transportation: 2.5% **(27)**

Water

Total used per day: 4,200 m. gal.
  per capita: 1,130 gal. **(30)**
Withdrawals by sector:
  public supply: 10.7%
  thermoelectric: 81.2%
  industrial and mining: 6.3%
  irrigation: 0.2%

Pollutant Releases

Toxics released: 21.2 t. tons **(26)**
  per capita: 11.51 pounds **(27)**
Toxics transferred: 12.9 t. tons **(15)**
Smog precursors: 2.1 m. tons
Acid precip. precursors: 1174.7 t. tons
Greenhouse gas emissions (CO_2
  equiv.): 109.6 m. tons **(17)**
  per capita: 29.41 tons **(8)**

Environmental Expenditures

Budget spent on environmental and
  natural resources: 1.64% **(24)**
  per capita: $32.28 **(21)**
Per capita budget by category:
  air quality: $1.16 **(17)**
  drinking water: in water quality
  forestry: $2.44 **(24)**
  fish & wildlife: $3.87 **(38)**
  geological survey: $0.45 **(21)**
  hazardous waste: in solid waste
  land management: $0.08 **(32)**
  marine & coastal progs.: $0.00
  mining reclamation: $14.82 **(2)**
  nuclear waste: $0.22 **(10)**
  pesticides control: $0.31 **(14)**
  soil conservation: $1.13 **(8)**
  solid waste: $1.08 **(18)**
  water quality: $6.72 **(14)**
  water resources: in water quality

Btu = British thermal unit; **m.** = million; **sq. mi.** = square mile; **t.** = thousand; **tr.** = trillion

LOUISIANA

Important Facts
Population 1990: 4,220,000 **(21)**
Estimated pop. 2010: 3,876,000 **(24)**
Number of households 1990: 1,499,000
Per capita average income: $8,961 **(48)**
Metropolitan area population: 69.5%
Total area: 51,843 sq. mi. **(31)**
Land area: 43,566 sq. mi.
Water area: 8,277 sq. mi.
National Parks: 9,722 acres
State Park/rec. areas: 38,000 acres
Environmental Voting Record (1991):
  U.S. House 18%   U.S. Senate 17%

Energy Use and Production
Total consumed/year: 3,450 tr. Btu
  per capita: 783 m. Btu **(3)**
Change in use 1973–88: 8.52%
Chief sources:
  petroleum: 44%
  gas: 44%
  coal: 6%
Renewables as source of total energy
  used: 5.37%
Average price per kWh of electricity
  for residents: 7.4¢
Consumption by end use:
  residential: 8%
  commercial: 7%
  industrial: 64%
  transportation: 20%

Wastes
Total solid waste: 3,500 t. tons
  per capita: 0.83 tons **(36)**
Municipal landfills: 31
Curbside recycling programs: 17
Hazardous Waste Sites: 12 **(22)**
Municipal incinerators: 0

Transportation
Miles driven per year: 37,667 m. mi.
  per capita: 8,900 mi. **(28)**
Motor fuel consumed: 2,265 m. gal.
Registered motor vehicles: 2,984,000

Highway expenditures: $922.5 m.
How workers commute:
  drive alone: 67.3%
  carpool: 21.4%
  public transportation: 4.3% **(15)**

Water
Total used per day: 10,400 m. gal.
  per capita: 2,210 gal. **(13)**
Withdrawals by sector:
  public supply: 6.5%
  thermoelectric: 57.3%
  industrial and mining: 20.2%
  irrigation: 14.2%

Pollutant Releases
Toxics released: 213.7 t. tons **(1)**
  per capita: 101.28 pounds **(1)**
Toxics transferred: 7.8 t. tons **(20)**
Smog precursors: 3.4 m. tons
Acid precip. precursors: 1008.9 t. tons
Greenhouse gas emissions (CO_2
  equiv.): 172.9 m. tons **(9)**
  per capita: 39.23 tons **(4)**

Environmental Expenditures
Budget spent on environmental and
  natural resources: 2.64% **(7)**
  per capita: $43.97 **(11)**
Per capita budget by category:
  air quality: $1.16 **(16)**
  drinking water: $0.59 **(16)**
  forestry: $2.24 **(25)**
  fish & wildlife: $6.31 **(24)**
  geological survey: in marine/coastal
  hazardous waste: $1.18 **(20)**
  land management: $0.20 **(27)**
  marine & coastal progs.: $4.51 **(4)**
  mining reclamation: $1.63 **(12)**
  nuclear waste: in air quality
  pesticides control: $0.45 **(8)**
  soil conservation: $4.33 **(2)**
  solid waste: in hazardous waste
  water quality: $1.37 **(38)**
  water resources: $19.99 **(4)**

Btu = British thermal unit; **m.** = million; **sq. mi.** = square mile; **t.** = thousand; **tr.** = trillion

MAINE

Important Facts

Population 1990: 1,228,000 **(38)**
Estimated pop. 2010: 1,430,000 **(41)**
Number of households 1990: 465,000
Per capita average income: $10,478 **(34)**
Metropolitan area population: 35.9%
Total area: 35,387 sq. mi. **(39)**
Land area: 30,865 sq. mi.
Water area: 4,523 sq. mi.
National Parks: 69,190 acres
State Park/rec. areas: 70,000 acres
Environmental Voting Record (1991):
  U.S. House 81%   U.S. Senate 87%

Energy Use and Production

Total consumed/year: 372 tr. Btu
  per capita: 309 m. Btu **(28)**
Change in use 1973–88: 9.09%
Chief sources:
  petroleum: 69%
  hydropower: 16%
  nuclear: 15%
Renewables as source of total energy
  used: 27.00%
Average price per kWh of electricity
  for residents: 9.3¢
Consumption by end use:
  residential: 23%
  commercial: 14%
  industrial: 30%
  transportation: 33%

Wastes

Total solid waste: 950 t. tons
  per capita: 0.77 tons **(41)**
Municipal landfills: 190
Curbside recycling programs: 16
Hazardous Waste Sites: 9 **(25)**
Municipal incinerators: 3

Transportation

Miles driven per year: 11,871 m. mi.
  per capita: 9,700 mi. **(15)**
Motor fuel consumed: 722 m. gal.
Registered motor vehicles: 988,000

Highway expenditures: $332.1 m.
How workers commute:
  drive alone: 59.3%
  carpool: 24.6%
  public transportation: 1.5% **(39)**

Water

Total used per day: 1,520 m. gal.
  per capita: 733 gal. **(38)**
Withdrawals by sector:
  public supply: 8.4%
  thermoelectric: 70.4%
  industrial and mining: 16.4%
  irrigation: 0.1%

Pollutant Releases

Toxics released: 7.4 t. tons **(39)**
  per capita: 12.07 pounds **(23)**
Toxics transferred: 1.1 t. tons **(40)**
Smog precursors: 0.6 m. tons
Acid precip. precursors: 112.2 t. tons
Greenhouse gas emissions (CO_2
  equiv.): 20.6 m. tons **(42)**
  per capita: 17.11 tons **(35)**

Environmental Expenditures

Budget spent on environmental and
  natural resources: 1.88% **(16)**
  per capita: $32.64 **(19)**
Per capita budget by category:
  air quality: $0.55 **(41)**
  drinking water: in water quality
  forestry: $0.49 **(45)**
  fish & wildlife: $14.70 **(7)**
  geological survey: $0.09 **(45)**
  hazardous waste: $1.29 **(19)**
  land management: $2.64 **(10)**
  marine & coastal progs.: $1.89 **(9)**
  mining reclamation: $0.00
  nuclear waste: $0.25 **(9)**
  pesticides control: $0.25 **(20)**
  soil conservation: $0.07 **(33)**
  solid waste: $6.64 **(1)**
  water quality: $3.62 **(25)**
  water resources: $0.16 **(44)**

Btu = British thermal unit; **m.** = million; **sq. mi.** = square mile; **t.** = thousand; **tr.** = trillion

MARYLAND

Important Facts

Population 1990: 4,781,000 **(19)**
Estimated pop. 2010: 6,446,000 **(13)**
Number of households 1990: 1,749,000
Per capita average income: $14,697 **(3)**
Metropolitan area population: 92.8%
Total area: 12,407 sq. mi. **(42)**
Land area: 9,775 sq. mi.
Water area: 2,633 sq. mi.
National Parks: 41,279 acres
State Park/rec. areas: 222,000 acres
Environmental Voting Record (1991):
U.S. House 61%   U.S. Senate 90%

Energy Use and Production

Total consumed/year: 1,240 tr. Btu
per capita: 268 m. Btu **(40)**
Change in use 1973–88: 5.35%
Chief sources:
petroleum: 41%
gas: 14%
coal: 24%
Renewables as source of total energy
used: 4.55%
Average price per kWh of electricity
for residents: 7.2¢
Consumption by end use:
residential: 26%
commercial: 14%
industrial: 32%
transportation: 28%

Wastes

Total solid waste: 5,100 t. tons
per capita: 1.07 tons **(17)**
Municipal landfills: 30
Curbside recycling programs: NA
Hazardous Waste Sites: 10 **(24)**
Municipal incinerators: 4

Transportation

Miles driven per year: 40,536 m. mi.
per capita: 8,500 mi. **(35)**
Motor fuel consumed: 2,446 m. gal.
Registered motor vehicles: 3,539,000

Highway expenditures: $1,464.4 m.
How workers commute:
drive alone: 60.7%
carpool: 23.1%
public transportation: 8.8% **(5)**

Water

Total used per day: 6,710 m. gal.
per capita: 321 gal. **(46)**
Withdrawals by sector:
public supply: 12.4%
thermoelectric: 80.9%
industrial and mining: 5.5%
irrigation: 0.5%

Pollutant Releases

Toxics released: 8.0 t. tons **(38)**
per capita: 3.36 pounds **(42)**
Toxics transferred: 3.7 t. tons **(32)**
Smog precursors: 1.5 m. tons
Acid precip. precursors: 491.1 t. tons
Greenhouse gas emissions (CO_2
equiv.): 77.9 m. tons **(24)**
per capita: 16.85 tons **(37)**

Environmental Expenditures

Budget spent on environmental and
natural resources: 1.60% **(25)**
per capita: $32.47 **(20)**
Per capita budget by category:
air quality: $0.99 **(22)**
drinking water: in water quality
forestry: $1.95 **(31)**
fish & wildlife: $4.71 **(34)**
geological survey: $1.12 **(11)**
hazardous waste: $0.56 **(30)**
land management: $7.71 **(1)**
marine & coastal progs.: $2.94 **(6)**
mining reclamation: $0.58 **(20)**
nuclear waste: $0.18 **(11)**
pesticides control: $0.13 **(38)**
soil conservation: $1.16 **(7)**
solid waste: $1.83 **(11)**
water quality: $4.54 **(16)**
water resources: $4.07 **(15)**

Btu = British thermal unit; **m.** = million; **sq. mi.** = square mile; **t.** = thousand; **tr.** = trillion

MASSACHUSETTS

Important Facts

Population 1990: 6,016,000 **(13)**
Estimated pop. 2010: 6,431,000 **(14)**
Number of households 1990: 2,247,000
Per capita average income: $14,389 **(4)**
Metropolitan area population: 90.4%
Total area: 10,555 sq. mi. **(44)**
Land area: 7,838 sq. mi.
Water area: 2,717 sq. mi.
National Parks: 32,636 acres
State Park/rec. areas: 269,000 acres
Environmental Voting Record (1991):
  U.S. House 78%   U.S. Senate 97%

Energy Use and Production

Total consumed/year: 1,346 tr. Btu
  per capita: 229 m. Btu **(47)**
Change in use 1973–88: -12.37%
Chief sources:
  petroleum: 63%
  gas: 16%
  coal: 9%
Renewables as source of total energy
  used: 5.20%
Average price per kWh of electricity
  for residents: 9.7¢
Consumption by end use:
  residential: 30%
  commercial: 23%
  industrial: 16%
  transportation: 31%

Wastes

Total solid waste: 6,800 t. tons
  per capita: 1.13 tons **(14)**
Municipal landfills: 139
Curbside recycling programs: 82
Hazardous Waste Sites: 26 **(13)**
Municipal incinerators: 8

Transportation

Miles driven per year: 46,130 m. mi.
  per capita: 7,700 mi. **(43)**
Motor fuel consumed: 2,693 m. gal.
Registered motor vehicles: 3,791,000

Highway expenditures: $1,054.9 m.
How workers commute:
  drive alone: 61.0%
  carpool: 19.1%
  public transportation: 9.3% **(3)**

Water

Total used per day: 9,660 m. gal.
  per capita: 1,070 gal. **(32)**
Withdrawals by sector:
  public supply: 8.3%
  thermoelectric: 87.5%
  industrial and mining: 1.6%
  irrigation: 0.2%

Pollutant Releases

Toxics released: 10.4 t. tons **(35)**
  per capita: 3.46 pounds **(41)**
Toxics transferred: 10.2 t. tons **(18)**
Smog precursors: 1.8 m. tons
Acid precip. precursors: 362.1 t. tons
Greenhouse gas emissions (CO_2
  equiv.): 89.9 m. tons **(22)**
  per capita: 15.27 tons **(40)**

Environmental Expenditures

Budget spent on environmental and
  natural resources: 1.56% **(26)**
  per capita: $40.40 **(12)**
Per capita budget by category:
  air quality: $0.83 **(31)**
  drinking water: $9.57 **(1)**
  forestry: $1.36 **(34)**
  fish & wildlife: $1.57 **(45)**
  geological survey: $0.03 **(48)**
  hazardous waste: $4.32 **(5)**
  land management: $0.00
  marine & coastal progs.: $2.64 **(7)**
  mining reclamation: $0.00
  nuclear waste: $0.01 **(24)**
  pesticides control: $0.19 **(28)**
  soil conservation: $0.02 **(40)**
  solid waste: $0.82 **(23)**
  water quality: $16.89 **(3)**
  water resources: $2.14 **(23)**

Btu = British thermal unit; **m.** = million; **sq. mi.** = square mile; **t.** = thousand; **tr.** = trillion

Important Facts

Population 1990: 9,295,000 **(8)**
Estimated pop. 2010: 9,301,000 **(9)**
Number of households 1990: 3,419,000
Per capita average income: $11,973 **(19)**
Metropolitan area population: 80.1%
Total area: 96,810 sq. mi. **(11)**
Land area: 56,809 sq. mi.
Water area: 40,001 sq. mi.
National Parks: 632,053 acres
State Park/rec. areas: 262,000 acres
Environmental Voting Record (1991):
 U.S. House 54%   U.S. Senate 70%

Energy Use and Production

Total consumed/year: 2,753 tr. Btu
 per capita: 298 m. Btu **(34)**
Change in use 1973–88: -9.77%
Chief sources:
 petroleum: 35%
 gas: 28%
 coal: 30%
Renewables as source of total energy
 used: 4.26%
Average price per kWh of electricity
 for residents: 7.8¢
Consumption by end use:
 residential: 26%
 commercial: 16%
 industrial: 33%
 transportation: 25%

Wastes

Total solid waste: 11,700 t. tons
 per capita: 1.26 tons **(7)**
Municipal landfills: 55
Curbside recycling programs: 100
Hazardous Waste Sites: 77 **(5)**
Municipal incinerators: 5

Transportation

Miles driven per year: 81,091 m. mi.
 per capita: 8,700 mi. **(32)**
Motor fuel consumed: 4,902 m. gal.
Registered motor vehicles: 7,293,000

Highway expenditures: $1,526.2 m.
How workers commute:
 drive alone: 72.5%
 carpool: 17.8%
 public transportation: 2.5% **(28)**

Water

Total used per day: 11,400 m. gal.
 per capita: 1,270 gal. **(23)**
Withdrawals by sector:
 public supply: 12.0%
 thermoelectric: 73.6%
 industrial and mining: 12.1%
 irrigation: 1.8%

Pollutant Releases

Toxics released: 59.9 t. tons **(8)**
 per capita: 12.89 pounds **(21)**
Toxics transferred: 37.8 t. tons **(7)**
Smog precursors: 4.1 m. tons
Acid precip. precursors: 833.7 t. tons
Greenhouse gas emissions (CO_2
 equiv.): 181.5 m. tons **(8)**
 per capita: 19.65 tons **(28)**

Environmental Expenditures

Budget spent on environmental and
 natural resources: 1.42% **(33)**
 per capita: $23.96 **(32)**
Per capita budget by category:
 air quality: $0.85 **(30)**
 drinking water: $0.02 **(39)**
 forestry: $2.46 **(23)**
 fish & wildlife: $4.88 **(33)**
 geological survey: $0.10 **(43)**
 hazardous waste: $0.42 **(36)**
 land management: $1.33 **(16)**
 marine & coastal progs.: $1.27 **(13)**
 mining reclamation: $0.11 **(30)**
 nuclear waste: $0.09 **(16)**
 pesticides control: $0.15 **(35)**
 soil conservation: $0.28 **(23)**
 solid waste: $0.94 **(21)**
 water quality: $10.73 **(9)**
 water resources: $0.33 **(40)**

Btu = British thermal unit; **m.** = million; **sq. mi.** = square mile; **t.** = thousand; **tr.** = trillion

MINNESOTA

Important Facts

Population 1990: 4,375,000 **(20)**
Estimated pop. 2010: 4,632,000 **(21)**
Number of households 1990: 1,648,000
Per capita average income: $12,281 **(16)**
Metropolitan area population: 67.7%
Total area: 86,943 sq. mi. **(12)**
Land area: 79,617 sq. mi.
Water area: 7,326 sq. mi.
National Parks: 141,298 acres
State Park/rec. areas: 200,000 acres
Environmental Voting Record (1991):
  U.S. House 61%   U.S. Senate 77%

Energy Use and Production

Total consumed/year: 1,315 tr. Btu
  per capita: 305 m. Btu **(31)**
Change in use 1973–88: 6.31%
Chief sources:
  petroleum: 39%
  gas: 22%
  coal: 23%
Renewables as source of total energy
  used: 9.04%
Average price per kWh of electricity
  for residents: 6.8¢
Consumption by end use:
  residential: 24%
  commercial: 15%
  industrial: 35%
  transportation: 26%

Wastes

Total solid waste: 4,400 t. tons
  per capita: 1.01 tons **(22)**
Municipal landfills: 53
Curbside recycling programs: 488
Hazardous Waste Sites: 41 **(8)**
Municipal incinerators: 16

Transportation

Miles driven per year: 38,946 m. mi.
  per capita: 8,900 mi. **(30)**
Motor fuel consumed: 2,412 m. gal.
Registered motor vehicles: 3,267,000

Highway expenditures: $1,228.2 m.
How workers commute:
  drive alone: 60.6%
  carpool: 19.0%
  public transportation: 5.5% **(9)**

Water

Total used per day: 2,830 m. gal.
  per capita: 676 gal. **(41)**
Withdrawals by sector:
  public supply: 21.3%
  thermoelectric: 51.9%
  industrial and mining: 16.1%
  irrigation: 7.4%

Pollutant Releases

Toxics released: 26.0 t. tons **(23)**
  per capita: 11.90 pounds **(25)**
Toxics transferred: 5.7 t. tons **(26)**
Smog precursors: 2.3 m. tons
Acid precip. precursors: 316.2 t. tons
Greenhouse gas emissions (CO_2
  equiv.): 83.1 m. tons **(23)**
  per capita: 19.30 tons **(31)**

Environmental Expenditures

Budget spent on environmental and
  natural resources: 1.46% **(31)**
  per capita: $29.31 **(28)**
Per capita budget by category:
  air quality: $0.78 **(34)**
  drinking water: $0.35 **(27)**
  forestry: $9.90 **(6)**
  fish & wildlife: $8.21 **(17)**
  geological survey: $0.22 **(33)**
  hazardous waste: $2.41 **(12)**
  land management: in forestry
  marine & coastal progs.: $0.24 **(23)**
  mining reclamation: $0.39 **(25)**
  nuclear waste: $0.00
  pesticides control: $0.26 **(17)**
  soil conservation: in water resources
  solid waste: $2.35 **(8)**
  water quality: $2.24 **(32)**
  water resources: $1.97 **(24)**

Btu = British thermal unit; **m.** = million; **sq. mi.** = square mile; **t.** = thousand; **tr.** = trillion

Important Facts

Population 1990: 2,573,000 **(31)**
Estimated pop. 2010: 2,858,000 **(29)**
Number of households 1990: 911,000
Per capita average income: $8,088 **(50)**
Metropolitan area population: 30.1%
Total area: 48,434 sq. mi. **(32)**
Land area: 46,914 sq. mi.
Water area: 1,520 sq. mi.
National Parks: 107,612 acres
State Park/rec. areas: 23,000 acres
Environmental Voting Record (1991):
U.S. House 32%   U.S. Senate 14%

Energy Use and Production

Total consumed/year: 938 tr. Btu
per capita: 358 m. Btu **(14)**
Change in use 1973–88: 14.53%
Chief sources:
petroleum: 47%
gas: 23%
coal: 14%
Renewables as source of total energy
used: 16.02%
Average price per kWh of electricity
for residents: 6.9¢
Consumption by end use:
residential: 18%
commercial: 11%
industrial: 38%
transportation: 34%

Wastes

Total solid waste: 1,400 t. tons
per capita: 0.54 tons **(50)**
Municipal landfills: 75
Curbside recycling programs: 25
Hazardous Waste Sites: 2 **(31)**
Municipal incinerators: 1

Transportation

Miles driven per year: 24,398 m. mi.
per capita: 9,500 mi. **(19)**
Motor fuel consumed: 1,593 m. gal.
Registered motor vehicles: 1,811,000

Highway expenditures: $528.7 m.
How workers commute:
drive alone: 66.2%
carpool: 25.3%
public transportation: 1.2% **(44)**

Water

Total used per day: 2,510 m. gal.
per capita: 885 gal. **(36)**
Withdrawals by sector:
public supply: 13.1%
thermoelectric: 26.7%
industrial and mining: 9.4%
irrigation: 35.3%

Pollutant Releases

Toxics released: 51.8 t. tons **(12)**
per capita: 40.28 pounds **(5)**
Toxics transferred: 2.6 t. tons **(34)**
Smog precursors: 1.4 m. tons
Acid precip. precursors: 238.2 t. tons
Greenhouse gas emissions (CO_2
equiv.): 51.0 m. tons **(34)**
per capita: 19.48 tons **(30)**

Environmental Expenditures

Budget spent on environmental and
natural resources: 1.40% **(34)**
per capita: $20.67 **(35)**
Per capita budget by category:
air quality: $0.50 **(43)**
drinking water: $0.47 **(22)**
forestry: $8.10 **(8)**
fish & wildlife: $5.52 **(30)**
geological survey: $0.31 **(28)**
hazardous waste: $0.29 **(40)**
land management: $0.08 **(33)**
marine & coastal progs.: $3.19 **(5)**
mining reclamation: $0.10 **(31)**
nuclear waste: $0.11 **(15)**
pesticides control: $0.17 **(29)**
soil conservation: $0.20 **(28)**
solid waste: $0.13 **(37)**
water quality: $1.10 **(42)**
water resources: $0.39 **(39)**

Btu = British thermal unit; **m.** = million; **sq. mi.** = square mile; **t.** = thousand; **tr.** = trillion

MISSOURI

Important Facts

Population 1990: 5,117,000 **(15)**
Estimated pop. 2010: 5,665,000 **(16)**
Number of households 1990: 1,961,000
Per capita average income: $11,203 **(27)**
Metropolitan area population: 66.2%
Total area: 69,709 sq. mi. **(21)**
Land area: 68,898 sq. mi.
Water area: 811 sq. mi.
National Parks: 63,430 acres
State Park/rec. areas: 109,000 acres
Environmental Voting Record (1991):
  U.S. House 39%   U.S. Senate 20%

Energy Use and Production

Total consumed/year: 1,511 tr. Btu
  per capita: 294 m. Btu **(36)**
Change in use 1973–88: 8.01%
Chief sources:
  petroleum: 42%
  gas: 17%
  coal: 36%
Renewables as source of total energy
  used: 4.81%
Average price per kWh of electricity
  for residents: 7.4¢
Consumption by end use:
  residential: 26%
  commercial: 19%
  industrial: 23%
  transportation: 31%

Wastes

Total solid waste: 7,500 t. tons
  per capita: 1.47 tons **(2)**
Municipal landfills: 78
Curbside recycling programs: 30
Hazardous Waste Sites: 23 **(15)**
Municipal incinerators: 0

Transportation

Miles driven per year: 50,883 m. mi.
  per capita: 9,900 mi. **(9)**
Motor fuel consumed: 3,346 m. gal.
Registered motor vehicles: 3,873,000

Highway expenditures: $937.4 m.
How workers commute:
  drive alone: 65.3%
  carpool: 21.8%
  public transportation: 3.8% **(21)**

Water

Total used per day: 6,110 m. gal.
  per capita: 1,210 gal. **(28)**
Withdrawals by sector:
  public supply: 11.4%
  thermoelectric: 80.7%
  industrial and mining: 1.9%
  irrigation: 5.0%

Pollutant Releases

Toxics released: 34.3 t. tons **(19)**
  per capita: 13.43 pounds **(20)**
Toxics transferred: 20.1 t. tons **(10)**
Smog precursors: 2.6 m. tons
Acid precip. precursors: 1412.1 t. tons
Greenhouse gas emissions (CO_2
  equiv.): 112.8 m. tons **(14)**
  per capita: 21.93 tons **(22)**

Environmental Expenditures

Budget spent on environmental and
  natural resources: 1.73% **(27)**
  per capita: $23.32 **(34)**
Per capita budget by category:
  air quality: $0.47 **(46)**
  drinking water: $0.15 **(35)**
  forestry: $3.48 **(20)**
  fish & wildlife: $5.73 **(26)**
  geological survey: $0.41 **(23)**
  hazardous waste: $0.58 **(29)**
  land management: $0.14 **(30)**
  marine & coastal progs.: $0.00
  mining reclamation: $2.35 **(7)**
  nuclear waste: $0.00
  pesticides control: $0.38 **(13)**
  soil conservation: $1.44 **(5)**
  solid waste: In hazardous waste
  water quality: $8.01 **(13)**
  water resources: $0.18 **(43)**

Btu = British thermal unit; **m.** = million; **sq. mi.** = square mile; **t.** = thousand; **tr.** = trillion

MONTANA

Important Facts

Population 1990: 799,000 **(44)**
Estimated pop. 2010: 692,000 **(46)**
Number of households 1990: 306,000
Per capita average income: $9,322 **(43)**
Metropolitan area population: 23.9%
Total area: 147,046 sq. mi. **(4)**
Land area: 145,556 sq. mi.
Water area: 1,490 sq. mi.
National Parks: 1,221,177 acres
State Park/rec. areas: 51,000 acres
Environmental Voting Record (1991):
  U.S. House 27%   U.S. Senate 47%

Energy Use and Production

Total consumed/year: 334 tr. Btu
  per capita: 415 m. Btu **(9)**
Change in use 1973–88: -2.05%
Chief sources:
  petroleum: 43%
  coal: 54%
  hydropower: 25%
Renewables as source of total energy
  used: 28.42%
Average price per kWh of electricity
  for residents: 5.4¢
Consumption by end use:
  residential: 17%
  commercial: 15%
  industrial: 43%
  transportation: 25%

Wastes

Total solid waste: 600 t. tons
  per capita: 0.75 tons **(42)**
Municipal landfills: 90
Curbside recycling programs: 3
Hazardous Waste Sites: 0 **(26)**
Municipal incinerators: 1

Transportation

Miles driven per year: 8,332 m. mi.
  per capita: 10,400 mi. **(7)**
Motor fuel consumed: 573 m. gal.
Registered motor vehicles: 733,000

Highway expenditures: $302.5 m.
How workers commute:
  drive alone: 59.6%
  carpool: 17.3%
  public transportation: 1.1% **(45)**

Water

Total used per day: 8,650 m. gal.
  per capita: 10,500 gal. **(3)**
Withdrawals by sector:
  public supply: 2.0%
  thermoelectric: 0.8%
  industrial and mining: 0.7%
  irrigation: 96.0%

Pollutant Releases

Toxics released: 21.3 t. tons **(25)**
  per capita: 53.41 pounds **(3)**
Toxics transferred: 0.2 t. tons **(44)**
Smog precursors: 1.3 m. tons
Acid precip. precursors: 145.3 t. tons
Greenhouse gas emissions (CO_2
  equiv.): 26.4 m. tons **(40)**
  per capita: 32.83 tons **(7)**

Environmental Expenditures

Budget spent on environmental and
  natural resources: 4.29% **(2)**
  per capita: $86.41 **(3)**
Per capita budget by category:
  air quality: $1.48 **(13)**
  drinking water: $0.65 **(14)**
  forestry: $12.60 **(3)**
  fish & wildlife: $24.97 **(3)**
  geological survey: $1.59 **(5)**
  hazardous waste: $6.18 **(2)**
  land management: $1.06 **(18)**
  marine & coastal progs.: $0.00
  mining reclamation: $8.27 **(4)**
  nuclear waste: $0.00
  pesticides control: $1.30 **(1)**
  soil conservation: $0.88 **(12)**
  solid waste: $1.38 **(14)**
  water quality: $2.19 **(33)**
  water resources: $23.85 **(2)**

Btu = British thermal unit; **m.** = million; **sq. mi.** = square mile; **t.** = thousand; **tr.** = trillion

NEBRASKA

Important Facts

Population 1990: 1,578,000 **(36)**
Estimated pop. 2010: 1,443,000 **(40)**
Number of households 1990: 602,000
Per capita average income: $11,139 **(29)**
Metropolitan area population: 48.5%
Total area: 77,358 sq. mi. **(16)**
Land area: 76,878 sq. mi.
Water area: 481 sq. mi.
National Parks: 5,854 acres
State Park/rec. areas: 149,000 acres
Environmental Voting Record (1991):
U.S. House 44%   U.S. Senate 67%

Energy Use and Production

Total consumed/year: 536 tr. Btu
per capita: 334 m. Btu **(21)**
Change in use 1973–88: 3.28%
Chief sources:
petroleum: 41%
gas: 22%
coal: 26%
Renewables as source of total energy
used: 3.08%
Average price per kWh of electricity
for residents: 6.2¢
Consumption by end use:
residential: 24%
commercial: 21%
industrial: 25%
transportation: 30%

Wastes

Total solid waste: 1,300 t. tons
per capita: 0.82 tons **(38)**
Municipal landfills: 36
Curbside recycling programs: 4
Hazardous Waste Sites: 8 **(26)**
Municipal incinerators: 0

Transportation

Miles driven per year: 13,958 m. mi.
per capita: 8,800 mi. **(31)**
Motor fuel consumed: 1,016 m. gal.
Registered motor vehicles: 1,340,000

Highway expenditures: $448.9 m.
How workers commute:
drive alone: 62.8%
carpool: 17.8%
public transportation: 2.5% **(25)**

Water

Total used per day: 10,000 m. gal.
per capita: 6,250 gal. **(4)**
Withdrawals by sector:
public supply: 2.7%
thermoelectric: 22.1%
industrial and mining: 1.7%
irrigation: 72.7%

Pollutant Releases

Toxics released: 8.7 t. tons **(37)**
per capita: 11.02 pounds **(28)**
Toxics transferred: 4.2 t. tons **(31)**
Smog precursors: 0.8 m. tons
Acid precip. precursors: 164.1 t. tons
Greenhouse gas emissions (CO_2
equiv.): 39.6 m. tons **(38)**
per capita: 24.75 tons **(16)**

Environmental Expenditures

Budget spent on environmental and
natural resources: 1.29% **(36)**
per capita: $17.47 **(40)**
Per capita budget by category:
air quality: $0.34 **(49)**
drinking water: $0.22 **(33)**
forestry: $0.42 **(46)**
fish & wildlife: $7.30 **(19)**
geological survey: $1.64 **(4)**
hazardous waste: $0.25 **(41)**
land management: $1.48 **(15)**
marine & coastal progs.: $0.00
mining reclamation: $0.00
nuclear waste: $0.07 **(17)**
pesticides control: $0.05 **(46)**
soil conservation: $1.26 **(6)**
solid waste: $0.38 **(29)**
water quality: $3.11 **(27)**
water resources: $0.96 **(32)**

Btu = British thermal unit; **m.** = million; **sq. mi.** = square mile; **t.** = thousand; **tr.** = trillion

Important Facts

Population 1990: 1,202,000 **(39)**
Estimated pop. 2010: 1,618,000 **(37)**
Number of households 1990: 466,000
Per capita average income: $12,603 **(11)**
Metropolitan area population: 82.9%
Total area: 110,567 sq. mi. **(7)**
Land area: 109,806 sq. mi.
Water area: 761 sq. mi.
National Parks: 776,937 acres
State Park/rec. areas: 142,000 acres
Environmental Voting Record (1991):
  U.S. House 27%   U.S. Senate 60%

Energy Use and Production

Total consumed/year: 355 tr. Btu
  per capita: 337 m. Btu **(20)**
Change in use 1973–88: 54.35%
Chief sources:
  petroleum: 48%
  gas: 14%
  coal: 52%
Renewables as source of total energy
  used: 9.93%
Average price per kWh of electricity
  for residents: 5.7¢
Consumption by end use:
  residential: 21%
  commercial: 18%
  industrial: 24%
  transportation: 37%

Wastes

Total solid waste: 1,000 t. tons
  per capita: 0.83 tons **(35)**
Municipal landfills: 110
Curbside recycling programs: 2
Hazardous Waste Sites: 1 **(32)**
Municipal incinerators: 0

Transportation

Miles driven per year: 10,215 m. mi.
  per capita: 8,500 mi. **(38)**
Motor fuel consumed: 784 m. gal.
Registered motor vehicles: 835,000

Highway expenditures: $308.6 m.
How workers commute:
  drive alone: 69.1%
  carpool: 19.5%
  public transportation: 1.9% **(32)**

Water

Total used per day: 3,740 m. gal.
  per capita: 3,860 gal. **(6)**
Withdrawals by sector:
  public supply: 8.0%
  thermoelectric: 0.6%
  industrial and mining: 0.9%
  irrigation: 89.6%

Pollutant Releases

Toxics released: 1.6 t. tons **(46)**
  per capita: 2.72 pounds **(47)**
Toxics transferred: 0.1 t. tons **(48)**
Smog precursors: 0.5 m. tons
Acid precip. precursors: 94.9 t. tons
Greenhouse gas emissions (CO_2
  equiv.): 21.0 m. tons **(41)**
  per capita: 19.89 tons **(27)**

Environmental Expenditures

Budget spent on environmental and
  natural resources: 2.57% **(10)**
  per capita: $34.62 **(16)**
Per capita budget by category:
  air quality: $0.52 **(42)**
  drinking water: $0.53 **(20)**
  forestry: $4.43 **(17)**
  fish & wildlife: $9.80 **(14)**
  geological survey: $0.09 **(44)**
  hazardous waste: $0.47 **(33)**
  land management: $0.40 **(34)**
  marine & coastal progs.: $0.00
  mining reclamation: NA
  nuclear waste: $0.00
  pesticides control: $0.08 **(40)**
  soil conservation: $0.02 **(38)**
  solid waste: $0.00
  water quality: $16.05 **(4)**
  water resources: $2.21 **(22)**

Btu = British thermal unit; **m.** = million; **sq. mi.** = square mile; **t.** = thousand; **tr.** = trillion

NEW HAMPSHIRE

Important Facts

Population 1990: 1,109,000 **(40)**
Estimated pop. 2010: 1,650,000 **(36)**
Number of households 1990: 411,000
Per capita average income: $13,529 **(6)**
Metropolitan area population: 56.1%
Total area: 9,351 sq. mi. **(46)**
Land area: 8,969 sq. mi.
Water area: 382 sq. mi.
National Parks: 8,745 acres
State Park/rec. areas: 33,000 acres
Environmental Voting Record (1991):
U.S. House 50%   U.S. Senate 52%

Energy Use and Production

Total consumed/year: 243 tr. Btu
per capita: 224 m. Btu **(48)**
Change in use 1973–88: 19.70%
Chief sources:
petroleum: 66%
coal: 14%
hydropower: 8%
Renewables as source of total energy
used: 18.39%
Average price per kWh of electricity
for residents: 10.3¢
Consumption by end use:
residential: 30%
commercial: 16%
industrial: 22%
transportation: 32%

Wastes

Total solid waste: 1,100 t. tons
per capita: 0.99 tons **(23)**
Municipal landfills: 50
Curbside recycling programs: 26
Hazardous Waste Sites: 17 **(19)**
Municipal incinerators: 16

Transportation

Miles driven per year: 9,844 m. mi.
per capita: 8,900 mi. **(29)**
Motor fuel consumed: 561 m. gal.
Registered motor vehicles: 976,000

Highway expenditures: $298.6 m.
How workers commute:
drive alone: 62.9%
carpool: 23.7%
public transportation: 1.3% **(43)**

Water

Total used per day: 894 m. gal.
per capita: 688 gal. **(40)**
Withdrawals by sector:
public supply: 12.4%
thermoelectric: 60.7%
industrial and mining: 26.7%
irrigation: 0.1%

Pollutant Releases

Toxics released: 4.1 t. tons **(42)**
per capita: 7.48 pounds **(37)**
Toxics transferred: 0.9 t. tons **(41)**
Smog precursors: 0.4 m. tons
Acid precip. precursors: 109.2 t. tons
Greenhouse gas emissions (CO_2
equiv.): 15.9 m. tons **(45)**
per capita: 14.62 tons **(43)**

Environmental Expenditures

Budget spent on environmental and
natural resources: 2.41% **(12)**
per capita: $30.96 **(23)**
Per capita budget by category:
air quality: $0.89 **(27)**
drinking water: $0.48 **(21)**
forestry: $1.45 **(33)**
fish & wildlife: $6.64 **(21)**
geological survey: $0.07 **(47)**
hazardous waste: $5.05 **(3)**
land management: in forestry
marine & coastal progs.: $0.10 **(26)**
mining reclamation: $0.00
nuclear waste: $0.02 **(23)**
pesticides control: $0.14 **(37)**
soil conservation: NA
solid waste: $0.58 **(25)**
water quality: $13.75 **(7)**
water resources: $1.80 **(25)**

Btu = British thermal unit; **m.** = million; **sq. mi.** = square mile; **t.** = thousand; **tr.** = trillion

NEW JERSEY

Important Facts
Population 1990: 7,730,000 **(9)**
Estimated pop. 2010: 8,846,000 **(10)**
Number of households 1990: 2,795,000
Per capita average income: $15,028 **(2)**
Metropolitan area population: 100.0%
Total area: 8,722 sq. mi. **(47)**
Land area: 7,419 sq. mi.
Water area: 1,303 sq. mi.
National Parks: 34,962 acres
State Park/rec. areas: 301,000 acres
Environmental Voting Record (1991):
  U.S. House 69%   U.S. Senate 94%

Energy Use and Production
Total consumed/year: 2,286 tr. Btu
  per capita: 296 m. Btu **(35)**
Change in use 1973–88: 6.18%
Chief sources:
  petroleum: 56%
  gas: 19%
  nuclear: 11%
Renewables as source of total energy
  used: 1.29%
Average price per kWh of electricity
  for residents: 10.4¢
Consumption by end use:
  residential: 23%
  commercial: 20%
  industrial: 23%
  transportation: 34%

Wastes
Total solid waste: 7,100 t. tons
  per capita: 0.92 tons **(29)**
Municipal landfills: 25
Curbside recycling programs: 525
Hazardous Waste Sites: 108 **(1)**
Municipal incinerators: 4

Transportation
Miles driven per year: 58,923 m. mi.
  per capita: 7,600 mi. **(44)**
Motor fuel consumed: 3,787 m. gal.
Registered motor vehicles: 5,894,000

Highway expenditures: $1,830.6 m.
How workers commute:
  drive alone: 64.4%
  carpool: 18.3%
  public transportation: 9.2% **(4)**

Water
Total used per day: 6,940 m. gal.
  per capita: 307 gal. **(47)**
Withdrawals by sector:
  public supply: 16.1%
  thermoelectric: 65.5%
  industrial and mining: 16.4%
  irrigation: 1.9%

Pollutant Releases
Toxics released: 13.0 t. tons **(32)**
  per capita: 3.36 pounds **(43)**
Toxics transferred: 44.4 t. tons **(6)**
Smog precursors: 2.3 m. tons
Acid precip. precursors: 513.7 t. tons
Greenhouse gas emissions (CO_2
  equiv.): 107.2 m. tons **(18)**
  per capita: 13.88 tons **(45)**

Environmental Expenditures
Budget spent on environmental and
  natural resources: 3.61% **(5)**
  per capita: $67.85 **(4)**
Per capita budget by category:
  air quality: $1.68 **(10)**
  drinking water: in water resources
  forestry: $0.68 **(43)**
  fish & wildlife: $1.51 **(47)**
  geological survey: $0.18 **(36)**
  hazardous waste: $2.86 **(11)**
  land management: NA
  marine & coastal progs.: $0.72 **(16)**
  mining reclamation: $0.00
  nuclear waste: $0.64 **(5)**
  pesticides control: $0.17 **(30)**
  soil conservation: $0.20 **(27)**
  solid waste: $0.93 **(22)**
  water quality: $57.96 **(1)**
  water resources: $0.33 **(41)**

Btu = British thermal unit; **m.** = million; **sq. mi.** = square mile; **t.** = thousand; **tr.** = trillion

NEW MEXICO

Important Facts

Population 1990: 1,515,000 **(37)**
Estimated pop. 2010: 1,922,000 **(34)**
Number of households 1990: 543,000
Per capita average income: $9,434 **(41)**
Metropolitan area population: 48.4%
Total area: 121,598 sq. mi. **(5)**
Land area: 121,365 sq. mi.
Water area: 234 sq. mi.
National Parks: 349,085 acres
State Park/rec. areas: 119,000 acres
Environmental Voting Record (1991):
  U.S. House 31%   U.S. Senate 27%

Energy Use and Production

Total consumed/year: 524 tr. Btu
  per capita: 347 m. Btu **(19)**
Change in use 1973–88: 11.02%
Chief sources:
  petroleum: 42%
  gas: 35%
  coal: 51%
Renewables as source of total energy
  used: 2.96%
Average price per kWh of electricity
  for residents: 8.9¢
Consumption by end use:
  residential: 14%
  commercial: 19%
  industrial: 30%
  transportation: 37%

Wastes

Total solid waste: 1,500 t. tons
  per capita: 0.99 tons **(24)**
Municipal landfills: 153
Curbside recycling programs: 3
Hazardous Waste Sites: 10 **(24)**
Municipal incinerators: 0

Transportation

Miles driven per year: 16,148 m. mi.
  per capita: 10,700 mi. **(3)**
Motor fuel consumed: 1,034 m. gal.
Registered motor vehicles: 1,247,000

Highway expenditures: $408.6 m.
How workers commute:
  drive alone: 67.1%
  carpool: 20.2%
  public transportation: 1.8% **(36)**

Water

Total used per day: 3,280 m. gal.
  per capita: 2,320 gal. **(11)**
Withdrawals by sector:
  public supply: 8.0%
  thermoelectric: 1.8%
  industrial and mining: 2.5%
  irrigation: 86.0%

Pollutant Releases

Toxics released: 16.3 t. tons **(31)**
  per capita: 21.55 pounds **(13)**
Toxics transferred: 0.2 t. tons **(45)**
Smog precursors: 1.3 m. tons
Acid precip. precursors: 466.4 t. tons
Greenhouse gas emissions (CO_2
  equiv.): 54.2 m. tons **(33)**
  per capita: 35.96 tons **(6)**

Environmental Expenditures

Budget spent on environmental and
  natural resources: 1.48% **(29)**
  per capita: $29.72 **(27)**
Per capita budget by category:
  air quality: $0.99 **(21)**
  drinking water: $1.37 **(4)**
  forestry: $1.29 **(38)**
  fish & wildlife: $8.78 **(16)**
  geological survey: $1.71 **(3)**
  hazardous waste: $3.61 **(7)**
  land management: $3.31 **(9)**
  marine & coastal progs.: $0.00
  mining reclamation: $2.01 **(10)**
  nuclear waste: $0.74 **(4)**
  pesticides control: $0.00
  soil conservation: $0.22 **(25)**
  solid waste: $0.13 **(36)**
  water quality: $0.99 **(43)**
  water resources: $4.58 **(13)**

Btu = British thermal unit; **m.** = million; **sq. mi.** = square mile; **t.** = thousand; **tr.** = trillion

Important Facts

Population 1990: 17,990,000 **(2)**
Estimated pop. 2010: 18,129,000 **(3)**
Number of households 1990: 6,639,000
Per capita average income: $13,167 **(9)**
Metropolitan area population: 91.1%
Total area: 54,475 sq. mi. **(27)**
Land area: 47,224 sq. mi.
Water area: 7,251 sq. mi.
National Parks: 35,914 acres
State Park/rec. areas: 258,000 acres
Environmental Voting Record (1991):
  U.S. House 60%   U.S. Senate 67%

Energy Use and Production

Total consumed/year: 3,586 tr. Btu
  per capita: 200 m. Btu **(50)**
Change in use 1973–88: -18.28%
Chief sources:
  petroleum: 51%
  gas: 23%
  hydropower: 10%
Renewables as source of total energy
  used: 10.62%
Average price per kWh of electricity
  for residents: 11.4¢
Consumption by end use:
  residential: 29%
  commercial: 28%
  industrial: 19%
  transportation: 24%

Wastes

Total solid waste: 22,000 t. tons
  per capita: 1.22 tons **(8)**
Municipal landfills: 193
Curbside recycling programs: 200
Hazardous Waste Sites: 84 **(4)**
Municipal incinerators: 17

Transportation

Miles driven per year: 106,902 m. mi.
  per capita: 5,900 mi. **(50)**
Motor fuel consumed: 6,857 m. gal.
Registered motor vehicles: 10,184,000

Highway expenditures: $2,874.5 m.
How workers commute:
  drive alone: 46.1%
  carpool: 15.9%
  public transportation: 26.5% **(1)**

Water

Total used per day: 15,200 m. gal.
  per capita: 508 gal. **(43)**
Withdrawals by sector:
  public supply: 20.1%
  thermoelectric: 71.5%
  industrial and mining: 7.1%
  irrigation: 0.3%

Pollutant Releases

Toxics released: 30.2 t. tons **(21)**
  per capita: 3.36 pounds **(44)**
Toxics transferred: 18.3 t. tons **(11)**
Smog precursors: 4.4 m. tons
Acid precip. precursors: 748.9 t. tons
Greenhouse gas emissions (CO_2
  equiv.): 219.0 m. tons **(6)**
  per capita: 12.23 tons **(47)**

Environmental Expenditures

Budget spent on environmental and
  natural resources: 0.59% **(50)**
  per capita: $13.20 **(46)**
Per capita budget by category:
  air quality: $0.90 **(26)**
  drinking water: $0.56 **(18)**
  forestry: $2.09 **(29)**
  fish & wildlife: $1.66 **(44)**
  geological survey: $0.11 **(41)**
  hazardous waste: in solid waste
  land management: in forestry
  marine & coastal progs.: $0.19 **(24)**
  mining reclamation: $0.03 **(36)**
  nuclear waste: $0.07 **(18)**
  pesticides control: in solid waste
  soil conservation: NA
  solid waste: $3.06 **(5)**
  water quality: $4.54 **(15)**
  water resources: in water quality

Btu = British thermal unit; **m.** = million; **sq. mi.** = square mile; **t.** = thousand; **tr.** = trillion

NORTH CAROLINA

Important Facts

Population 1990: 6,629,000 **(10)**
Estimated pop. 2010: 8,735,000 **(11)**
Number of households 1990: 2,517,000
Per capita average income: $10,856 **(32)**
Metropolitan area population: 56.7%
Total area: 53,821 sq. mi. **(28)**
Land area: 48,718 sq. mi.
Water area: 5,103 sq. mi.
National Parks: 380,078 acres
State Park/rec. areas: 129,000 acres
Environmental Voting Record (1991):
  U.S. House 45%   U.S. Senate 37%

Energy Use and Production

Total consumed/year: 1,947 tr. Btu
  per capita: 300 m. Btu **(33)**
Change in use 1973–88: 30.85%
Chief sources:
  petroleum: 40%
  coal: 26%
  nuclear: 16%
Renewables as source of total energy
  used: 12.57%
Average price per kWh of electricity
  for residents: 7.8¢
Consumption by end use:
  residential: 23%
  commercial: 16%
  industrial: 31%
  transportation: 30%

Wastes

Total solid waste: 6,000 t. tons
  per capita: 0.91 tons **(31)**
Municipal landfills: 140
Curbside recycling programs: 58
Hazardous Waste Sites: 23 **(15)**
Municipal incinerators: 3

Transportation

Miles driven per year: 62,707 m. mi.
  per capita: 9,500 mi. **(20)**
Motor fuel consumed: 3,964 m. gal.
Registered motor vehicles: 5,201,000
Highway expenditures: $1,428.5 m.
How workers commute:
  drive alone: 66.2%
  carpool: 24.7%
  public transportation: 1.5% **(38)**

Water

Total used per day: 8,760 m. gal.
  per capita: 1,260 gal. **(24)**
Withdrawals by sector:
  public supply: 8.7%
  thermoelectric: 82.9%
  industrial and mining: 6.2%
  irrigation: 1.5%

Pollutant Releases

Toxics released: 62.0 t. tons **(7)**
  per capita: 18.70 pounds **(17)**
Toxics transferred: 7.3 t. tons **(22)**
Smog precursors: 3.3 m. tons
Acid precip. precursors: 709.9 t. tons
Greenhouse gas emissions (CO_2
  equiv.): 126.5 m. tons **(12)**
  per capita: 19.49 tons **(29)**

Environmental Expenditures

Budget spent on environmental and
  natural resources: 1.00% **(42)**
  per capita: $14.94 **(43)**
Per capita budget by category:
  air quality: $0.50 **(44)**
  drinking water: $0.38 **(25)**
  forestry: $4.57 **(15)**
  fish & wildlife: $3.31 **(41)**
  geological survey: $0.12 **(40)**
  hazardous waste: $0.53 **(32)**
  land management: $0.73 **(19)**
  marine & coastal progs.: $1.12 **(15)**
  mining reclamation: $0.00
  nuclear waste: $0.01 **(25)**
  pesticides control: $0.24 **(22)**
  soil conservation: $1.75 **(3)**
  solid waste: $0.15 **(32)**
  water quality: $1.28 **(40)**
  water resources: $0.26 **(42)**

Btu = British thermal unit; **m.** = million; **sq. mi.** = square mile; **t.** = thousand; **tr.** = trillion

NORTH DAKOTA

Important Facts

Population 1990: 639,000 **(47)**
Estimated pop. 2010: 531,000 **(49)**
Number of households 1990: 241,000
Per capita average income: $9,641 **(39)**
Metropolitan area population: 40.3%
Total area: 70,704 sq. mi. **(19)**
Land area: 68,994 sq. mi.
Water area: 1,710 sq. mi.
National Parks: 71,340 acres
State Park/rec. areas: 17,000 acres
Environmental Voting Record (1991):
  U.S. House 15%   U.S. Senate 54%

Energy Use and Production

Total consumed/year: 311 tr. Btu
  per capita: 467 m. Btu **(5)**
Change in use 1973–88: 59.49%
Chief sources:
  petroleum: 38%
  gas: 10%
  coal: 119%
Renewables as source of total energy
  used: 5.13%
Average price per kWh of electricity
  for residents: 6.3¢
Consumption by end use:
  residential: 17%
  commercial: 12%
  industrial: 49%
  transportation: 22%

Wastes

Total solid waste: 400 t. tons
  per capita: 0.63 tons **(49)**
Municipal landfills: 47
Curbside recycling programs: 5
Hazardous Waste Sites: 2 **(01)**
Municipal incinerators: 0

Transportation

Miles driven per year: 5,910 m. mi.
  per capita: 9,200 mi. **(23)**
Motor fuel consumed: 444 m. gal.
Registered motor vehicles: 662,000

Highway expenditures: $189.4 m.
How workers commute:
  drive alone: 56.6%
  carpool: 16.4%
  public transportation: 0.7% **(49)**

Water

Total used per day: 1,160 m. gal.
  per capita: 1,690 gal. **(18)**
Withdrawals by sector:
  public supply: 7.2%
  thermoelectric: 76.9%
  industrial and mining: 1.1%
  irrigation: 13.3%

Pollutant Releases

Toxics released: 1.1 t. tons **(48)**
  per capita: 3.30 pounds **(45)**
Toxics transferred: 0.1 t. tons **(46)**
Smog precursors: 0.5 m. tons
Acid precip. precursors: 326.4 t. tons
Greenhouse gas emissions (CO_2
  equiv.): 43.5 m. tons **(36)**
  per capita: 65.22 tons **(2)**

Environmental Expenditures

Budget spent on environmental and
  natural resources: 2.32% **(13)**
  per capita: $48.76 **(10)**
Per capita budget by category:
  air quality: $1.65 **(11)**
  drinking water: $0.75 **(10)**
  forestry: $1.26 **(39)**
  fish & wildlife: $12.37 **(11)**
  geological survey: $1.27 **(9)**
  hazardous waste: $0.60 **(28)**
  land management: $7.94 **(3)**
  marine & coastal progs.: $0.00
  mining reclamation: $4.10 **(6)**
  nuclear waste: $0.00
  pesticides control: $0.80 **(5)**
  soil conservation: $0.83 **(13)**
  solid waste: $0.15 **(31)**
  water quality: $2.25 **(31)**
  water resources: $14.80 **(6)**

Btu = British thermal unit; **m.** = million; **sq. mi.** = square mile; **t.** = thousand; **tr.** = trillion

OHIO

Important Facts
Population 1990: 10,847,000 **(7)**
Estimated pop. 2010: 10,803,000 **(7)**
Number of households 1990: 4,088,000
Per capita average income: $11,323 **(25)**
Metropolitan area population: 79.0%
Total area: 44,828 sq. mi. **(34)**
Land area: 40,953 sq. mi.
Water area: 3,875 sq. mi.
National Parks: 17,564 acres
State Park/rec. areas: 208,000 acres
Environmental Voting Record (1991):
    U.S. House 38%   U.S. Senate 83%

Energy Use and Production
Total consumed/year: 3,785 tr. Btu
    per capita: 348 m. Btu **(18)**
Change in use 1973–88: -9.88%
Chief sources:
    petroleum: 30%
    gas: 22%
    coal: 39%
Renewables as source of total energy
    used: 2.37%
Average price per kWh of electricity
    for residents: 8.0¢
Consumption by end use:
    residential: 23%
    commercial: 15%
    industrial: 41%
    transportation: 21%

Wastes
Total solid waste: 15,700 t. tons
    per capita: 1.45 tons **(4)**
Municipal landfills: 87
Curbside recycling programs: 130
Hazardous Waste Sites: 33 **(11)**
Municipal incinerators: 10

Transportation
Miles driven per year: 86,972 m. mi.
    per capita: 8,000 mi. **(42)**
Motor fuel consumed: 5,761 m. gal.
Registered motor vehicles: 8,820,000

Highway expenditures: $2,270.8 m.
How workers commute:
    drive alone: 71.7%
    carpool: 17.3%
    public transportation: 4.0% **(18)**

Water
Total used per day: 12,700 m. gal.
    per capita: 1,180 gal. **(29)**
Withdrawals by sector:
    public supply: 12.3%
    thermoelectric: 82.7%
    industrial and mining: 4.3%
    irrigation: 0.1%

Pollutant Releases
Toxics released: 84.2 t. tons **(5)**
    per capita: 15.52 pounds **(18)**
Toxics transferred: 51.6 t. tons **(3)**
Smog precursors: 5.4 m. tons
Acid precip. precursors: 3320.3 t. tons
Greenhouse gas emissions (CO_2
    equiv.): 255.2 m. tons **(4)**
    per capita: 23.51 tons **(18)**

Environmental Expenditures
Budget spent on environmental and
    natural resources: 0.65% **(48)**
    per capita: $11.58 **(48)**
Per capita budget by category:
    air quality: $1.02 **(19)**
    drinking water: $0.30 **(31)**
    forestry: $0.83 **(41)**
    fish & wildlife: $2.07 **(43)**
    geological survey: $0.13 **(37)**
    hazardous waste: $1.10 **(23)**
    land management: $0.12 **(31)**
    marine & coastal progs.: $0.07 **(27)**
    mining reclamation: $1.69 **(11)**
    nuclear waste: NA
    pesticides control: $0.06 **(42)**
    soil conservation: $0.98 **(10)**
    solid waste: $1.01 **(19)**
    water quality: $1.58 **(36)**
    water resources: $0.62 **(36)**

Btu = British thermal unit; **m.** = million; **sq. mi.** = square mile; **t.** = thousand; **tr.** = trillion

OKLAHOMA

Important Facts

Population 1990: 3,146,000 **(28)**
Estimated pop. 2010: 2,660,000 **(30)**
Number of households 1990: 1,206,000
Per capita average income: $9,927 **(37)**
Metropolitan area population: 59.4%
Total area: 69,903 sq. mi. **(20)**
Land area: 68,679 sq. mi.
Water area: 1,224 sq. mi.
National Parks: 9,517 acres
State Park/rec. areas: 96,000 acres
Environmental Voting Record (1991):
   U.S. House 31%   U.S. Senate 20%

Energy Use and Production

Total consumed/year: 1,280 tr. Btu
   per capita: 396 m. Btu **(10)**
Change in use 1973–88: 25.98%
Chief sources:
   petroleum: 33%
   gas: 48%
   coal: 21%
Renewables as source of total energy
   used: 3.16%
Average price per kWh of electricity
   for residents: 6.6¢
Consumption by end use:
   residential: 19%
   commercial: 15%
   industrial: 40%
   transportation: 26%

Wastes

Total solid waste: 3,000 t. tons
   per capita: 0.95 tons **(26)**
Municipal landfills: 130
Curbside recycling programs: 11
Hazardous Waste Sites: 10 **(24)**
Municipal incinerators: 3

Transportation

Miles driven per year: 33,081 m. mi.
   per capita: 10,500 mi. **(4)**
Motor fuel consumed: 2,107 m. gal.
Registered motor vehicles: 2,581,000

Highway expenditures: $826.7 m.
How workers commute:
   drive alone: 70.5%
   carpool: 20.3%
   public transportation: 1.0% **(47)**

Water

Total used per day: 1,270 m. gal.
   per capita: 386 gal. **(44)**
Withdrawals by sector:
   public supply: 43.1%
   thermoelectric: 10.6%
   industrial and mining: 8.9%
   irrigation: 35.0%

Pollutant Releases

Toxics released: 16.6 t. tons **(30)**
   per capita: 10.53 pounds **(29)**
Toxics transferred: 7.1 t. tons **(23)**
Smog precursors: 1.9 m. tons
Acid precip. precursors: 332.3 t. tons
Greenhouse gas emissions (CO_2
   equiv.): 90.7 m. tons **(21)**
   per capita: 27.99 tons **(11)**

Environmental Expenditures

Budget spent on environmental and
   natural resources: 0.79% **(45)**
   per capita: $12.61 **(47)**
Per capita budget by category:
   air quality: $0.61 **(37)**
   drinking water: $0.10 **(36)**
   forestry: $1.95 **(32)**
   fish & wildlife: $5.09 **(32)**
   geological survey: $0.64 **(16)**
   hazardous waste: $0.31 **(39)**
   land management: $0.25 **(26)**
   marine & coastal progs.: $0.00
   mining reclamation: $0.52 **(22)**
   nuclear waste: $0.02 **(22)**
   pesticides control: $0.54 **(7)**
   soil conservation: $0.94 **(11)**
   solid waste: $0.14 **(35)**
   water quality: $0.75 **(46)**
   water resources: $0.74 **(34)**

Btu = British thermal unit; **m.** = million; **sq. mi.** = square mile; **t.** = thousand; **tr.** = trillion

STATE PROFILES

OREGON

Important Facts

Population 1990: 2,842,000 **(29)**
Estimated pop. 2010: 2,922,000 **(28)**
Number of households 1990: 1,103,000
Per capita average income: $11,045 **(31)**
Metropolitan area population: 68.5%
Total area: 98,386 sq. mi. **(9)**
Land area: 96,003 sq. mi.
Water area: 2,383 sq. mi.
National Parks: 194,716 acres
State Park/rec. areas: 90,000 acres
Environmental Voting Record (1991):
  U.S. House 57%   U.S. Senate 20%

Energy Use and Production

Total consumed/year: 880 tr. Btu
  per capita: 318 m. Btu **(26)**
Change in use 1973–88: 9.86%
Chief sources:
  petroleum: 40%
  gas: 10%
  hydropower: 42%
Renewables as source of total energy
  used: 47.46%
Average price per kWh of electricity
  for residents: 4.7¢
Consumption by end use:
  residential: 22%
  commercial: 18%
  industrial: 28%
  transportation: 32%

Wastes

Total solid waste: 3,300 t. tons
  per capita: 1.16 tons **(11)**
Municipal landfills: 93
Curbside recycling programs: 115
Hazardous Waste Sites: 9 **(25)**
Municipal incinerators: 1

Transportation

Miles driven per year: 26,738 m. mi.
  per capita: 9,400 mi. **(21)**
Motor fuel consumed: 1,704 m. gal.
Registered motor vehicles: 2,367,000

Highway expenditures: $765.1 m.
How workers commute:
  drive alone: 65.6%
  carpool: 17.6%
  public transportation: 5.0% **(13)**

Water

Total used per day: 6,540 m. gal.
  per capita: 2,450 gal. **(10)**
Withdrawals by sector:
  public supply: 7.6%
  thermoelectric: 0.2%
  industrial and mining: 4.6%
  irrigation: 87.3%

Pollutant Releases

Toxics released: 11.3 t. tons **(33)**
  per capita: 7.99 pounds **(35)**
Toxics transferred: 5.0 t. tons **(29)**
Smog precursors: 1.7 m. tons
Acid precip. precursors: 30.5 t. tons
Greenhouse gas emissions (CO_2
  equiv.): 38.4 m. tons **(39)**
  per capita: 13.89 tons **(44)**

Environmental Expenditures

Budget spent on environmental and
  natural resources: 3.03% **(6)**
  per capita: $67.38 **(5)**
Per capita budget by category:
  air quality: $3.84 **(2)**
  drinking water: in water quality
  forestry: $21.99 **(2)**
  fish & wildlife: $17.91 **(5)**
  geological survey: $0.73 **(14)**
  hazardous waste: in solid waste
  land management: $9.79 **(2)**
  marine & coastal progs.: $1.67 **(10)**
  mining reclamation: $0.17 **(27)**
  nuclear waste: $0.02 **(20)**
  pesticides control: $0.23 **(23)**
  soil conservation: $0.16 **(29)**
  solid waste: $4.61 **(2)**
  water quality: $2.26 **(30)**
  water resources: $3.98 **(16)**

Btu = British thermal unit; **m.** = million; **sq. mi.** = square mile; **t.** = thousand; **tr.** = trillion

PENNSYLVANIA

Important Facts

Population 1990: 11,882,000 **(5)**
Estimated pop. 2010: 12,038,000 **(5)**
Number of households 1990: 4,496,000
Per capita average income: $11,544 **(20)**
Metropolitan area population: 84.8%
Total area: 46,058 sq. mi. **(33)**
Land area: 44,820 sq. mi.
Water area: 1,239 sq. mi.
National Parks: 47,614 acres
State Park/rec. areas: 276,000 acres
Environmental Voting Record (1991):
U.S. House 34%   U.S. Senate 63%

Energy Use and Production

Total consumed/year: 3,601 tr. Btu
per capita: 300 m. Btu **(32)**
Change in use 1973–88: -15.25%
Chief sources:
petroleum: 37%
gas: 19%
coal: 41%
Renewables as source of total energy
used: 2.68%
Average price per kWh of electricity
for residents: 9.2¢
Consumption by end use:
residential: 24%
commercial: 14%
industrial: 38%
transportation: 24%

Wastes

Total solid waste: 9,500 t. tons
per capita: 0.80 tons **(39)**
Municipal landfills: 44
Curbside recycling programs: 603
Hazardous Waste Sites: 100 **(?)**
Municipal Incinerators: 6

Transportation

Miles driven per year: 85,708 m. mi.
per capita: 7,200 mi. **(47)**
Motor fuel consumed: 5,593 m. gal.
Registered motor vehicles: 7,922,000

Highway expenditures: $2,884.8 m.
How workers commute:
drive alone: 61.1%
carpool: 20.2%
public transportation: 8.2% **(7)**

Water

Total used per day: 14,300 m. gal.
per capita: 1,210 gal. **(27)**
Withdrawals by sector:
public supply: 12.5%
thermoelectric: 71.3%
industrial and mining: 15.4%
irrigation: 0.1%

Pollutant Releases

Toxics released: 44.7 t. tons **(15)**
per capita: 7.52 pounds **(36)**
Toxics transferred: 45.0 t. tons **(4)**
Smog precursors: 4.8 m. tons
Acid precip. precursors: 1815.7 t. tons
Greenhouse gas emissions (CO_2
equiv.): 254.6 m. tons **(5)**
per capita: 21.22 tons **(25)**

Environmental Expenditures

Budget spent on environmental and
natural resources: 1.49% **(28)**
per capita: $24.06
Per capita budget by category:
air quality: $0.95 **(24)**
drinking water: $0.84 **(9)**
forestry: $2.13 **(27)**
fish & wildlife: $5.59 **(29)**
geological survey: $0.20 **(34)**
hazardous waste: $1.94 **(15)**
land management: NA
marine & coastal progs.: $0.46 **(19)**
mining reclamation: $5.23 **(5)**
nuclear waste: $0.87 **(3)**
pesticides control: $0.11 **(39)**
soil conservation: $0.08 **(32)**
solid waste: $0.95 **(20)**
water quality: $3.69 **(24)**
water resources: $1.02 **(31)**

Btu = British thermal unit; **m.** = million; **sq. mi.** = square mile; **t.** = thousand; **tr.** = trillion

RHODE ISLAND

Important Facts
Population 1990: 1,003,000 **(43)**
Estimated pop. 2010: 1,105,000 **(42)**
Number of households 1990: 378,000
Per capita average income: $12,351 **(14)**
Metropolitan area population: 92.5%
Total area: 1,545 sq. mi. **(50)**
Land area: 1,045 sq. mi.
Water area: 500 sq. mi.
National Parks: 5 acres
State Park/rec. areas: 9,000 acres
Environmental Voting Record (1991):
  U.S. House 85%   U.S. Senate 90%

Energy Use and Production
Total consumed/year: 216 tr. Btu
  per capita: 218 m. Btu **(49)**
Change in use 1973–88: -4.85%
Chief sources:
  petroleum: 56%
  gas: 15%
  hydropower: 3%
Renewables as source of total energy
  used: 4.10%
Average price per kWh of electricity
  for residents: 9.8¢
Consumption by end use:
  residential: 30%
  commercial: 21%
  industrial: 20%
  transportation: 29%

Wastes
Total solid waste: 1,200 t. tons
  per capita: 1.20 tons **(9)**
Municipal landfills: 4
Curbside recycling programs: 19
Hazardous Waste Sites: 12 **(22)**
Municipal incinerators: 0

Transportation
Miles driven per year: 7,024 m. mi.
  per capita: 7,000 mi. **(49)**
Motor fuel consumed: 420 m. gal.
Registered motor vehicles: 687,000

Highway expenditures: $213.8 m.
How workers commute:
  drive alone: 65.3%
  carpool: 21.4%
  public transportation: 4.3% **(14)**

Water
Total used per day: 409 m. gal.
  per capita: 152 gal. **(50)**
Withdrawals by sector:
  public supply: 29.8%
  thermoelectric: 63.8%
  industrial and mining: 4.9%
  irrigation: 0.7%

Pollutant Releases
Toxics released: 2.6 t. tons **(45)**
  per capita: 5.25 pounds **(39)**
Toxics transferred: 1.5 t. tons **(38)**
Smog precursors: 0.2 m. tons
Acid precip. precursors: 14.9 t. tons
Greenhouse gas emissions (CO_2
  equiv.): 11.7 m. tons **(47)**
  per capita: 11.76 tons **(48)**

Environmental Expenditures
Budget spent on environmental and
  natural resources: 1.86% **(17)**
  per capita: $36.13 **(15)**
Per capita budget by category:
  air quality: $0.78 **(33)**
  drinking water: $0.62 **(15)**
  forestry: $1.34 **(35)**
  fish & wildlife: $5.70 **(28)**
  geological survey: $0.13 **(38)**
  hazardous waste: $2.89 **(10)**
  land management: in forestry
  marine & coastal progs.: $4.55 **(3)**
  mining reclamation: $0.00
  nuclear waste: $0.00
  pesticides control: $0.26 **(18)**
  soil conservation: $0.02 **(39)**
  solid waste: $2.38 **(7)**
  water quality: $9.70 **(12)**
  water resources: $7.76 **(9)**

Btu = British thermal unit; **m.** = million; **sq. mi.** = square mile; **t.** = thousand; **tr.** = trillion

SOUTH CAROLINA

Important Facts

Population 1990: 3,487,000 **(25)**
Estimated pop. 2010: 4,304,000 **(23)**
Number of households 1990: 1,258,000
Per capita average income: $9,967 **(36)**
Metropolitan area population: 60.6%
Total area: 32,007 sq. mi. **(40)**
Land area: 30,111 sq. mi.
Water area: 1,896 sq. mi.
National Parks: 25,935 acres
State Park/rec. areas: 79,000 acres
Environmental Voting Record (1991):
  U.S. House 60%   U.S. Senate 37%

Energy Use and Production

Total consumed/year: 1,143 tr. Btu
  per capita: 330 m. Btu **(23)**
Change in use 1973–88: 34.31%
Chief sources:
  petroleum: 33%
  coal: 26%
  nuclear: 38%
Renewables as source of total energy
  used: 11.67%
Average price per kWh of electricity
  for residents: 7.1¢
Consumption by end use:
  residential: 20%
  commercial: 14%
  industrial: 43%
  transportation: 24%

Wastes

Total solid waste: 4,000 t. tons
  per capita: 1.15 tons **(13)**
Municipal landfills: 59
Curbside recycling programs: 6
Hazardous Waste Sites: 24 **(14)**
Municipal incinerators: 2

Transportation

Miles driven per year: 34,376 m. mi.
  per capita: 9,900 mi. **(10)**
Motor fuel consumed: 2,288 m. gal.
Registered motor vehicles: 2,474,000

Highway expenditures: $585.3 m.
How workers commute:
  drive alone: 65.3%
  carpool: 25.6%
  public transportation: 1.3% **(42)**

Water

Total used per day: 6,820 m. gal.
  per capita: 2,040 gal. **(15)**
Withdrawals by sector:
  public supply: 6.2%
  thermoelectric: 76.0%
  industrial and mining: 16.6%
  irrigation: 0.5%

Pollutant Releases

Toxics released: 33.6 t. tons **(20)**
  per capita: 19.28 pounds **(16)**
Toxics transferred: 6.8 t. tons **(24)**
Smog precursors: 1.7 m. tons
Acid precip. precursors: 423.6 t. tons
Greenhouse gas emissions (CO_2
  equiv.): 60.5 m. tons **(31)**
  per capita: 17.44 tons **(34)**

Environmental Expenditures

Budget spent on environmental and
  natural resources: 1.21% **(38)**
  per capita: $20.50 **(36)**
Per capita budget by category:
  air quality: $0.26 **(50)**
  drinking water: $0.45 **(23)**
  forestry: $4.91 **(12)**
  fish & wildlife: $9.18 **(15)**
  geological survey: $0.19 **(35)**
  hazardous waste: $0.76 **(24)**
  land management: $0.68 **(21)**
  marine & coastal progs.: $1.18 **(14)**
  mining reclamation: $0.09 **(33)**
  nuclear waste: $0.47 **(6)**
  pesticides control: $0.23 **(25)**
  soil conservation: in land management
  solid waste: in hazardous waste
  water quality: $0.82 **(44)**
  water resources: $1.27 **(29)**

Btu = British thermal unit; **m.** = million; **sq. mi.** = square mile; **t.** = thousand; **tr.** = trillion

SOUTH DAKOTA

Important Facts
Population 1990: 696,000 **(45)**
Estimated pop. 2010: 704,000 **(45)**
Number of households 1990: 259,000
Per capita average income: $8,910 **(49)**
Metropolitan area population: 29.5%
Total area: 77,121 sq. mi. **(17)**
Land area: 75,898 sq. mi.
Water area: 1,224 sq. mi.
National Parks: 263,549 acres
State Park/rec. areas: 92,000 acres
Environmental Voting Record (1991):
  U.S. House 69%   U.S. Senate 37%

Energy Use and Production
Total consumed/year: 203 tr. Btu
  per capita: 284 m. Btu **(38)**
Change in use 1973–88: 15.34%
Chief sources:
  petroleum: 52%
  coal: 17%
  hydropower: 27%
Renewables as source of total energy
  used: 29.20%
Average price per kWh of electricity
  for residents: 6.9¢
Consumption by end use:
  residential: 27%
  commercial: 16%
  industrial: 26%
  transportation: 32%

Wastes
Total solid waste: 800 t. tons
  per capita: 1.15 tons **(12)**
Municipal landfills: 100
Curbside recycling programs: 1
Hazardous Waste Sites: 4 **(29)**
Municipal incinerators: 0

Transportation
Miles driven per year: 6,989 m. mi.
  per capita: 10,000 mi. **(8)**
Motor fuel consumed: 494 m. gal.
Registered motor vehicles: 707,000

Highway expenditures: $232.3 m.
How workers commute:
  drive alone: 58.1%
  carpool: 14.3%
  public transportation: 0.4% **(50)**

Water
Total used per day: 675 m. gal.
  per capita: 956 gal. **(34)**
Withdrawals by sector:
  public supply: 14.2%
  thermoelectric: 0.6%
  industrial and mining: 6.8%
  irrigation: 68.1%

Pollutant Releases
Toxics released: 1.5 t. tons **(47)**
  per capita: 4.22 pounds **(40)**
Toxics transferred: 0.3 t. tons **(42)**
Smog precursors: 0.6 m. tons
Acid precip. precursors: 67.3 t. tons
Greenhouse gas emissions (CO_2
  equiv.): 16.1 m. tons **(44)**
  per capita: 22.55 tons **(20)**

Environmental Expenditures
Budget spent on environmental and
  natural resources: 1.85% **(18)**
  per capita: $29.82 **(26)**
Per capita budget by category:
  air quality: $1.07 **(18)**
  drinking water: in water quality
  forestry: $4.44 **(16)**
  fish & wildlife: $13.81 **(9)**
  geological survey: $2.05 **(2)**
  hazardous waste: in air quality
  land management: $0.44 **(22)**
  marine & coastal progs.: $0.00
  mining reclamation: $0.68 **(18)**
  nuclear waste: in air quality
  pesticides control: $0.39 **(11)**
  soil conservation: $0.57 **(16)**
  solid waste: in air quality
  water quality: $2.85 **(28)**
  water resources: $3.52 **(18)**

Btu = British thermal unit; **m.** = million; **sq. mi.** = square mile; **t.** = thousand; **tr.** = trillion

Important Facts

Population 1990: 4,877,000 **(17)**
Estimated pop. 2010: 5,727,000 **(15)**
Number of households 1990: 1,854,000
Per capita average income: $10,448 **(35)**
Metropolitan area population: 67.7%
Total area: 42,146 sq. mi. **(36)**
Land area: 41,220 sq. mi.
Water area: 926 sq. mi.
National Parks: 425,381 acres
State Park/rec. areas: 133,000 acres
Environmental Voting Record (1991):
  U.S. House 39%   U.S. Senate 63%

Energy Use and Production

Total consumed/year: 1,714 tr. Btu
  per capita: 350 m. Btu **(16)**
Change in use 1973–88: 8.96%
Chief sources:
  petroleum: 34%
  gas: 13%
  coal: 36%
Renewables as source of total energy
  used: 12.55%
Average price per kWh of electricity
  for residents: 5.7¢
Consumption by end use:
  residential: 22%
  commercial: 11%
  industrial: 41%
  transportation: 27%

Wastes

Total solid waste: 5,000 t. tons
  per capita: 1.03 tons **(21)**
Municipal landfills: 99
Curbside recycling programs: 3
Hazardous Waste Sites: 15 **(20)**
Municipal incinerators: 5

Transportation

Miles driven per year: 46,710 m. mi.
  per capita: 9,600 mi. **(18)**
Motor fuel consumed: 3,102 m. gal.
Registered motor vehicles: 4,382,000

Highway expenditures: $1,173.7 m.
How workers commute:
  drive alone: 68.2%
  carpool: 23.2%
  public transportation: 2.5% **(29)**

Water

Total used per day: 8,450 m. gal.
  per capita: 1,770 gal. **(17)**
Withdrawals by sector:
  public supply: 8.2%
  thermoelectric: 71.7%
  industrial and mining: 19.1%
  irrigation: 0.1%

Pollutant Releases

Toxics released: 103.7 t. tons **(3)**
  per capita: 42.54 pounds **(4)**
Toxics transferred: 16.1 t. tons **(13)**
Smog precursors: 2.6 m. tons
Acid precip. precursors: 1307.7 t. tons
Greenhouse gas emissions (CO_2
  equiv.): 110.2 m. tons **(16)**
  per capita: 22.52 tons **(21)**

Environmental Expenditures

Budget spent on environmental and
  natural resources: 1.34% **(35)**
  per capita: $16.58 **(41)**
Per capita budget by category:
  air quality: $0.58 **(39)**
  drinking water: in water quality
  forestry: $3.03 **(22)**
  land management: in mining recl.
  fish & wildlife: $4.41 **(35)**
  geological survey: $0.25 **(32)**
  hazardous waste: $0.74 **(25)**
  marine & coastal progs.: $0.00
  mining reclamation: $0.47 **(23)**
  nuclear waste: $0.28 **(8)**
  pesticides control: $0.20 **(27)**
  soil conservation: $0.31 **(21)**
  solid waste: $0.68 **(24)**
  water quality: $3.92 **(21)**
  water resources: $1.72 **(26)**

Btu = British thermal unit; **m.** = million; **sq. mi.** = square mile; **t.** = thousand; **tr.** = trillion

TEXAS

Important Facts
Population 1990: 16,987,000 **(3)**
Estimated pop. 2010: 17,990,000 **(4)**
Number of households 1990: 6,071,000
Per capita average income: $10,645 **(33)**
Metropolitan area population: 81.6%
Total area: 268,601 sq. mi. **(2)**
Land area: 261,914 sq. mi.
Water area: 6,687 sq. mi.
National Parks: 1,161,390 acres
State Park/rec. areas: 433,000 acres
Environmental Voting Record (1991):
 U.S. House 30%   U.S. Senate 30%

Energy Use and Production
Total consumed/year: 9,583 tr. Btu
 per capita: 569 m. Btu **(4)**
Change in use 1973–88: 19.64%
Chief sources:
 petroleum: 47%
 gas: 38%
 coal: 13%
Renewables as source of total energy
 used: 0.34%
Average price per kWh of electricity
 for residents: 7.2¢
Consumption by end use:
 residential: 12%
 commercial: 10%
 industrial: 56%
 transportation: 23%

Wastes
Total solid waste: 18,000 t. tons
 per capita: 1.06 tons **(18)**
Municipal landfills: 750
Curbside recycling programs: 10
Hazardous Waste Sites: 29 **(12)**
Municipal incinerators: 7

Transportation
Miles driven per year: 162,232 m. mi.
 per capita: 9,600 mi. **(17)**
Motor fuel consumed: 10,269 m. gal.
Registered motor vehicles: 12,565,000

Highway expenditures: $3,001.0 m.
How workers commute:
 drive alone: 69.8%
 carpool: 21.1%
 public transportation: 2.3% **(30)**

Water
Total used per day: 25,300 m. gal.
 per capita: 1,230 gal. **(26)**
Withdrawals by sector:
 public supply: 12.2%
 thermoelectric: 43.5%
 industrial and mining: 10.9%
 irrigation: 32.1%

Pollutant Releases
Toxics released: 209.4 t. tons **(2)**
 per capita: 24.65 pounds **(11)**
Toxics transferred: 58.4 t. tons **(1)**
Smog precursors: 10.4 m. tons
Acid precip. precursors: 2407.5 t. tons
Greenhouse gas emissions (CO_2
 equiv.): 459.0 m. tons **(1)**
 per capita: 27.26 tons **(12)**

Environmental Expenditures
Budget spent on environmental and
 natural resources: 0.60% **(49)**
 per capita: $6.76 **(50)**
Per capita budget by category:
 air quality: $0.68 **(36)**
 drinking water: $0.15 **(34)**
 forestry: $0.52 **(44)**
 fish & wildlife: $0.93 **(49)**
 geological survey: $0.66 **(15)**
 hazardous waste: $0.47 **(34)**
 land management: $1.55 **(14)**
 marine & coastal progs.: $0.26 **(22)**
 mining reclamation: $0.13 **(29)**
 nuclear waste: $0.06 **(19)**
 pesticides control: $0.29 **(16)**
 soil conservation: $0.07 **(34)**
 solid waste: $0.08 **(39)**
 water quality: $0.22 **(48)**
 water resources: $0.67 **(35)**

Btu = British thermal unit; **m.** = million; **sq. mi.** = square mile; **t.** = thousand; **tr.** = trillion

Important Facts

Population 1990: 1,723,000 **(35)**
Estimated pop. 2010: 1,879,000 **(35)**
Number of households 1990: 537,000
Per capita average income: $9,288 **(44)**
Metropolitan area population: 77.5%
Total area: 84,904 sq. mi. **(13)**
Land area: 82,168 sq. mi.
Water area: 2,736 sq. mi.
National Parks: 2,022,481 acres
State Park/rec. areas: 116,000 acres
Environmental Voting Record (1991):
U.S. House 31%   U.S. Senate 13%

Energy Use and Production

Total consumed/year: 534 tr. Btu
per capita: 316 m. Btu **(27)**
Change in use 1973–88: 17.88%
Chief sources:
petroleum: 39%
gas: 22%
coal: 63%
Renewables as source of total energy
used: 3.25%
Average price per kWh of electricity
for residents: 7.1¢
Consumption by end use:
residential: 18%
commercial: 16%
industrial: 38%
transportation: 28%

Wastes

Total solid waste: 1,200 t. tons
per capita: 0.70 tons **(45)**
Municipal landfills: 30
Curbside recycling programs: 3
Hazardous Waste Sites: 13 **(21)**
Municipal incinerators: 1

Transportation

Miles driven per year: 14,646 m. mi.
per capita: 8,500 mi. **(37)**
Motor fuel consumed: 910 m. gal.
Registered motor vehicles: 1,188,000

Highway expenditures: $354.7 m.
How workers commute:
drive alone: 64.1%
carpool: 22.8%
public transportation: 3.5% **(22)**

Water

Total used per day: 4,320 m. gal.
per capita: 2,540 gal. **(8)**
Withdrawals by sector:
public supply: 10.5%
thermoelectric: 0.6%
industrial and mining: 4.9%
irrigation: 83.1%

Pollutant Releases

Toxics released: 62.7 t. tons **(6)**
per capita: 72.80 pounds **(2)**
Toxics transferred: 44.5 t. tons **(5)**
Smog precursors: 1.2 m. tons
Acid precip. precursors: 135.6 t. tons
Greenhouse gas emissions (CO_2
equiv.): 42.8 m. tons **(37)**
per capita: 25.33 tons **(15)**

Environmental Expenditures

Budget spent on environmental and
natural resources: 1.80% **(20)**
per capita: $30.43 **(24)**
Per capita budget by category:
air quality: $1.24 **(14)**
drinking water: $0.84 **(8)**
forestry: in land management
fish & wildlife: $13.66 **(10)**
geological survey: $1.36 **(8)**
hazardous waste: $1.30 **(18)**
land management: $2.05 **(12)**
marine & coastal progs.: $0.00
mining reclamation: $1.57 **(14)**
nuclear waste: $0.13 **(14)**
pesticides control: $0.07 **(41)**
soil conservation: $0.04 **(36)**
solid waste: $0.00
water quality: $1.66 **(35)**
water resources: $6.51 **(11)**

Btu = British thermal unit; **m.** = million; **sq. mi.** = square mile; **t.** = thousand; **tr.** = trillion

VERMONT

Important Facts

Population 1990: 563,000 **(48)**
Estimated pop. 2010: 658,000 **(48)**
Number of households 1990: 211,000
Per capita average income: $11,234 **(26)**
Metropolitan area population: 23.4%
Total area: 9,615 sq. mi. **(45)**
Land area: 9,249 sq. mi.
Water area: 366 sq. mi.
National Parks: 6,578 acres
State Park/rec. areas: 170,000 acres
Environmental Voting Record (1991):
   U.S. House 85%   U.S. Senate 94%

Energy Use and Production

Total consumed/year: 129 tr. Btu
   per capita: 232 m. Btu **(46)**
Change in use 1973–88: 7.50%
Chief sources:
   petroleum: 57%
   hydropower: 29%
   nuclear: 34%
Renewables as source of total energy
   used: 22.64%
Average price per kWh of electricity
   for residents: 9.3¢
Consumption by end use:
   residential: 27%
   commercial: 19%
   industrial: 20%
   transportation: 34%

Wastes

Total solid waste: 390 t. tons
   per capita: 0.69 tons **(47)**
Municipal landfills: 60
Curbside recycling programs: 12
Hazardous Waste Sites: 8 **(26)**
Municipal incinerators: 0

Transportation

Miles driven per year: 5,838 m. mi.
   per capita: 10,400 mi. **(6)**
Motor fuel consumed: 332 m. gal.
Registered motor vehicles: 473,000

Highway expenditures: $165.0 m.
How workers commute:
   drive alone: 55.9%
   carpool: 24.9%
   public transportation: 1.4% **(41)**

Water

Total used per day: 126 m. gal.
   per capita: 235 gal. **(48)**
Withdrawals by sector:
   public supply: 51.6%
   thermoelectric: 0.8%
   industrial and mining: 43.7%
   irrigation: 0.8%

Pollutant Releases

Toxics released: 0.5 t. tons **(49)**
   per capita: 1.81 pounds **(49)**
Toxics transferred: 0.1 t. tons **(47)**
Smog precursors: 0.3 m. tons
Acid precip. precursors: 1.7 t. tons
Greenhouse gas emissions (CO_2
   equiv.): 8.4 m. tons **(48)**
   per capita: 15.17 tons **(41)**

Environmental Expenditures

Budget spent on environmental and
   natural resources: 1.94% **(15)**
   per capita: $36.31 **(14)**
Per capita budget by category:
   air quality: $1.60 **(12)**
   drinking water: in water quality
   forestry: $5.50 **(10)**
   fish & wildlife: $11.92 **(12)**
   geological survey: $0.54 **(19)**
   hazardous waste: in solid waste
   land management: $7.30 **(5)**
   marine & coastal progs.: $0.00
   mining reclamation: $0.00
   nuclear waste: $0.43 **(7)**
   pesticides control: $0.99 **(4)**
   soil conservation: $1.72 **(4)**
   solid waste: $2.60 **(6)**
   water quality: $3.57 **(26)**
   water resources: $0.15 **(45)**

Btu = British thermal unit; **m.** = million; **sq. mi.** = square mile; **t.** = thousand; **tr.** = trillion

Important Facts

Population 1990: 6,187,000 **(12)**
Estimated pop. 2010: 8,222,000 **(12)**
Number of households 1990: 2,292,000
Per capita average income: $13,658 **(5)**
Metropolitan area population: 72.5%
Total area: 42,769 sq. mi. **(35)**
Land area: 39,598 sq. mi.
Water area: 3,171 sq. mi.
National Parks: 315,438 acres
State Park/rec. areas: 52,000 acres
Environmental Voting Record (1991):
  U.S. House 33%   U.S. Senate 54%

Energy Use and Production

Total consumed/year: 1,840 tr. Btu
  per capita: 306 m. Btu **(30)**
Change in use 1973–88: 33.04%
Chief sources:
  petroleum: 43%
  coal: 19%
  nuclear: 12%
Renewables as source of total energy
  used: 11.10%
Average price per kWh of electricity
  for residents: 7.2¢
Consumption by end use:
  residential: 23%
  commercial: 20%
  industrial: 25%
  transportation: 32%

Wastes

Total solid waste: 9,000 t. tons
  per capita: 1.45 tons **(3)**
Municipal landfills: 131
Curbside recycling programs: 61
Hazardous Waste Sites: 22 **(16)**
Municipal incinerators: 9

Transportation

Miles driven per year: 60,178 m. mi.
  per capita: 9,700 mi. **(13)**
Motor fuel consumed: 3,564 m. gal.
Registered motor vehicles: 4,729,000

Highway expenditures: $1,873.9 m.
How workers commute:
  drive alone: 61.1%
  carpool: 25.2%
  public transportation: 5.1% **(12)**

Water

Total used per day: 7,250 m. gal.
  per capita: 853 gal. **(37)**
Withdrawals by sector:
  public supply: 9.5%
  thermoelectric: 79.4%
  industrial and mining: 9.3%
  irrigation: 0.7%

Pollutant Releases

Toxics released: 39.8 t. tons **(16)**
  per capita: 12.87 pounds **(22)**
Toxics transferred: 13.1 t. tons **(14)**
Smog precursors: 2.6 m. tons
Acid precip. precursors: 430.1 t. tons
Greenhouse gas emissions (CO_2
  equiv.): 112.6 m. tons **(15)**
  per capita: 18.72 tons **(32)**

Environmental Expenditures

Budget spent on environmental and
  natural resources: 1.47% **(30)**
  per capita: $25.29 **(30)**
Per capita budget by category:
  air quality: $0.93 **(25)**
  drinking water: $0.34 **(28)**
  forestry: $3.28 **(21)**
  fish & wildlife: $5.28 **(31)**
  geological survey: $0.56 **(18)**
  hazardous waste: $0.46 **(35)**
  land management: $2.51 **(11)**
  marine & coastal progs.: $2.51 **(8)**
  mining reclamation: $2.11 **(9)**
  nuclear waste: $0.02 **(21)**
  pesticides control: $0.05 **(45)**
  soil conservation: $1.11 **(9)**
  solid waste: $1.19 **(16)**
  water quality: $4.07 **(19)**
  water resources: $0.88 **(33)**

Btu = British thermal unit; **m.** = million; **sq. mi.** = square mile; **t.** – thousand; **tr.** = trillion

WASHINGTON

Important Facts

Population 1990: 4,867,000 **(18)**
Estimated pop. 2010: 5,369,000 **(19)**
Number of households 1990: 1,872,000
Per capita average income: $12,184 **(18)**
Metropolitan area population: 81.7%
Total area: 71,303 sq. mi. **(18)**
Land area: 66,582 sq. mi.
Water area: 4,721 sq. mi.
National Parks: 1,930,785 acres
State Park/rec. areas: 231,000 acres
Environmental Voting Record (1991):
  U.S. House 52%   U.S. Senate 64%

Energy Use and Production

Total consumed/year: 1,807 tr. Btu
  per capita: 389 m. Btu **(12)**
Change in use 1973–88: 26.45%
Chief sources:
  petroleum: 39%
  gas: 8%
  hydropower: 39%
Renewables as source of total energy
  used: 53.54%
Average price per kWh of electricity
  for residents: 4.4¢
Consumption by end use:
  residential: 20%
  commercial: 16%
  industrial: 35%
  transportation: 28%

Wastes

Total solid waste: 5,100 t. tons
  per capita: 1.05 tons **(19)**
Municipal landfills: 65
Curbside recycling programs: 81
Hazardous Waste Sites: 49 **(7)**
Municipal incinerators: 5

Transportation

Miles driven per year: 44,695 m. mi.
  per capita: 9,200 mi. **(22)**
Motor fuel consumed: 2,674 m. gal.
Registered motor vehicles: 4,075,000

Highway expenditures: $1.250.8 m.
How workers commute:
  drive alone: 64.9%
  carpool: 18.9%
  public transportation: 5.3% **(10)**

Water

Total used per day: 7,030 m. gal.
  per capita: 1,600 gal. **(19)**
Withdrawals by sector:
  public supply: 15.0%
  thermoelectric: 6.1%
  industrial and mining: 8.0%
  irrigation: 70.3%

Pollutant Releases

Toxics released: 20.7 t. tons **(27)**
  per capita: 8.51 pounds **(33)**
Toxics transferred: 2.5 t. tons **(35)**
Smog precursors: 3.0 m. tons
Acid precip. precursors: 198.1 t. tons
Greenhouse gas emissions (CO_2
  equiv.): 76.7 m. tons **(25)**
  per capita: 16.51 tons **(38)**

Environmental Expenditures

Budget spent on environmental and
  natural resources: 2.63% **(8)**
  per capita: $53.11 **(7)**
Per capita budget by category:
  air quality: $1.21 **(15)**
  drinking water: $2.24 **(3)**
  forestry: $8.84 **(7)**
  fish & wildlife: $14.56 **(8)**
  geological survey: $0.31 **(29)**
  hazardous waste: $2.24 **(14)**
  land management: $4.02 **(8)**
  marine & coastal progs.: $1.57 **(12)**
  mining reclamation: $0.08 **(34)**
  nuclear waste: $0.89 **(2)**
  pesticides control: $1.07 **(3)**
  soil conservation: NA
  solid waste: $3.69 **(3)**
  water quality: $10.81 **(8)**
  water resources: $1.59 **(27)**

Btu = British thermal unit; **m.** = million; **sq. mi.** = square mile; **t.** = thousand; **tr.** = trillion

WEST VIRGINIA

Important Facts
Population 1990: 1,793,000 **(34)**
Estimated pop. 2010: 1,482,000 **(39)**
Number of households 1990: 689,000
Per capita average income: $8,980 **(47)**
Metropolitan area population: 36.4%
Total area: 24,231 sq. mi. **(41)**
Land area: 24,087 sq. mi.
Water area: 145 sq. mi.
National Parks: 41,020 acres
State Park/rec. areas: 207,000 acres
Environmental Voting Record (1991):
U.S. House 48%   U.S. Senate 57%

Energy Use and Production
Total consumed/year: 778 tr. Btu
per capita: 415 m. Btu **(8)**
Change in use 1973–88: -14.32%
Chief sources:
petroleum: 34%
gas: 17%
coal: 118%
Renewables as source of total energy
used: 2.97%
Average price per kWh of electricity
for residents: 5.9¢
Consumption by end use:
residential: 17%
commercial: 11%
industrial: 53%
transportation: 19%

Wastes
Total solid waste: 1,700 t. tons
per capita: 0.95 tons **(28)**
Municipal landfills: 39
Curbside recycling programs: 50
Hazardous Waste Sites: 5 **(28)**
Municipal incinerators: 0

Transportation
Miles driven per year: 15,418 m. mi.
per capita: 8,600 mi. **(34)**
Motor fuel consumed: 1,038 m. gal.
Registered motor vehicles: 1,321,000

Highway expenditures: $605.5 m.
How workers commute:
drive alone: 64.5%
carpool: 24.7%
public transportation: 1.9% **(35)**

Water
Total used per day: 5,440 m. gal.
per capita: 2,810 gal. **(7)**
Withdrawals by sector:
public supply: 3.2%
thermoelectric: 77.4%
industrial and mining: 18.9%
irrigation: 0.1%

Pollutant Releases
Toxics released: 19.1 t. tons **(29)**
per capita: 21.30 pounds **(14)**
Toxics transferred: 7.7 t. tons **(21)**
Smog precursors: 1.5 m. tons
Acid precip. precursors: 1341.8 t. tons
Greenhouse gas emissions (CO_2
equiv.): 95.9 m. tons **(20)**
per capita: 51.14 tons **(3)**

Environmental Expenditures
Budget spent on environmental and
natural resources: 1.68% **(22)**
per capita: $29.95 **(25)**
Per capita budget by category:
air quality: $0.85 **(29)**
drinking water: $0.72 **(11)**
forestry: $2.13 **(28)**
fish & wildlife: $6.40 **(23)**
geological survey: $1.01 **(12)**
hazardous waste: $0.69 **(26)**
land management: $0.15 **(29)**
marine & coastal progs.: $0.00
mining reclamation: $12.67 **(3)**
nuclear waste: NA
pesticides control: $0.16 **(33)**
soil conservation: $0.43 **(18)**
solid waste: $2.35 **(9)**
water quality: $2.40 **(29)**
water resources: in water quality

Btu = British thermal unit; **m.** = million; **sq. mi.** = square mile; **t.** = thousand; **tr.** = trillion

WISCONSIN

Important Facts

Population 1990: 4,892,000 **(16)**
Estimated pop. 2010: 4,652,000 **(20)**
Number of households 1990: 1,822,000
Per capita average income: $11,417 **(23)**
Metropolitan area population: 67.4%
Total area: 65,503 sq. mi. **(23)**
Land area: 54,314 sq. mi.
Water area: 11,190 sq. mi.
National Parks: 71,816 acres
State Park/rec. areas: 120,000 acres
Environmental Voting Record (1991):
  U.S. House 47%   U.S. Senate 57%

Energy Use and Production

Total consumed/year: 1,392 tr. Btu
  per capita: 288 m. Btu **(37)**
Change in use 1973–88: 5.69%
Chief sources:
  petroleum: 35%
  gas: 23%
  coal: 28%
Renewables as source of total energy
  used: 7.90%
Average price per kWh of electricity
  for residents: 6.6¢
Consumption by end use:
  residential: 26%
  commercial: 17%
  industrial: 33%
  transportation: 24%

Wastes

Total solid waste: 3,400 t. tons
  per capita: 0.70 tons **(46)**
Municipal landfills: 150
Curbside recycling programs: 190
Hazardous Waste Sites: 40 **(9)**
Municipal incinerators: 5

Transportation

Miles driven per year: 44,277 m. mi.
  per capita: 9,100 mi. **(26)**
Motor fuel consumed: 2,541 m. gal.
Registered motor vehicles: 4,043,000

Highway expenditures: $978.6 m.
How workers commute:
  drive alone: 61.7%
  carpool: 19.2%
  public transportation: 3.9% **(19)**

Water

Total used per day: 6,740 m. gal.
  per capita: 1,400 gal. **(22)**
Withdrawals by sector:
  public supply: 9.8%
  thermoelectric: 80.7%
  industrial and mining: 6.8%
  irrigation: 1.2%

Pollutant Releases

Toxics released: 22.5 t. tons **(24)**
  per capita: 9.20 pounds **(32)**
Toxics transferred: 17.2 t. tons **(12)**
Smog precursors: 2.2 m. tons
Acid precip. precursors: 545.2 t. tons
Greenhouse gas emissions (CO_2
  equiv.): 99.9 m. tons **(19)**
  per capita: 20.58 tons **(26)**

Environmental Expenditures

Budget spent on environmental and
  natural resources: 1.70% **(21)**
  per capita: $34.56 **(17)**
Per capita budget by category:
  air quality: $0.96 **(23)**
  drinking water: $0.66 **(12)**
  forestry: $4.81 **(13)**
  fish & wildlife: $6.67 **(20)**
  geological survey: $0.30 **(30)**
  hazardous waste: in solid waste
  land management: NA
  marine & coastal progs.: $0.39 **(20)**
  mining reclamation: $0.03 **(35)**
  nuclear waste: $0.00
  pesticides control: $0.15 **(36)**
  soil conservation: NA
  solid waste: $1.46 **(12)**
  water quality: $18.63 **(2)**
  water resources: $0.50 **(38)**

Btu = British thermal unit; **m.** = million; **sq. mi.** = square mile; **t.** = thousand; **tr.** = trillion

Important Facts

Population 1990: 454,000 **(50)**
Estimated pop. 2010: 366,000 **(50)**
Number of households 1990: 169,000
Per capita average income: $9,826 **(38)**
Metropolitan area population: 29.6%
Total area: 97,818 sq. mi. **(10)**
Land area: 97,105 sq. mi.
Water area: 714 sq. mi.
National Parks: 2,393,200 acres
State Park/rec. areas: 119,000 acres
Environmental Voting Record (1991):
  U.S. House 0%   U.S. Senate 10%

Energy Use and Production

Total consumed/year: 377 tr. Btu
  per capita: 786 m. Btu **(2)**
Change in use 1973–88: 34.64%
Chief sources:
  petroleum: 36%
  gas: 23%
  coal: 118%
Renewables as source of total energy
  used: 2.52%
Average price per kWh of electricity
  for residents: 6.0¢
Consumption by end use:
  residential: 10%
  commercial: 11%
  industrial: 57%
  transportation: 22%

Wastes

Total solid waste: 320 t. tons
  per capita: 0.70 tons **(44)**
Municipal landfills: 80
Curbside recycling programs: 0
Hazardous Waste Sites: 3 **(30)**
Municipal incinerators: 0

Transportation

Miles driven per year: 5,833 m. mi.
  per capita: 12,800 mi. **(1)**
Motor fuel consumed: 483 m. gal.
Registered motor vehicles: 491,000

Highway expenditures: $296.6 m.
How workers commute:
  drive alone: 60.9%
  carpool: 22.8%
  public transportation: 1.9% **(33)**

Water

Total used per day: 6,220k m. gal.
  per capita: 12,200 gal. **(2)**
Withdrawals by sector:
  public supply: 1.8%
  thermoelectric: 3.8%
  industrial and mining: 3.0%
  irrigation: 91.0%

Pollutant Releases

Toxics released: 5.8 t. tons **(41)**
  per capita: 25.51 pounds **(10)**
Toxics transferred: 0.0 t. tons **(49)**
Smog precursors: 0.8 m. tons
Acid precip. precursors: 164.5 t. tons
Greenhouse gas emissions (CO_2
  equiv.): 54.8 m. tons **(32)**
  per capita: 114.40 tons **(1)**

Environmental Expenditures

Budget spent on environmental and
  natural resources: 7.73% **(1)**
  per capita: $267.33 **(1)**
Per capita budget by category:
  air quality: $1.86 **(9)**
  drinking water: in water quality
  forestry: $2.22 **(26)**
  fish & wildlife: $43.79 **(2)**
  geological survey: $1.56 **(6)**
  hazardous waste: $0.37 **(38)**
  land management: $4.44 **(7)**
  marine & coastal progs.: $0.00
  mining reclamation: $69.57 **(1)**
  nuclear waste: $0.00
  pesticides control: $0.05 **(44)**
  soil conservation: $0.40 **(19)**
  solid waste: $0.39 **(28)**
  water quality: $3.94 **(20)**
  water resources: $138.75 **(1)**

Btu = British thermal unit; **m.** = million; **sq. mi.** = square mile; **t.** = thousand; **tr.** = trillion

State Profiles

All entries are annual figures unless otherwise indicated. Following some data entries, a rank is indicated by a number in parentheses. This indicates the relative ranking of the state compared with the other 49 states. The largest numerical value is given the rank of (1) and the smallest numerical value is given the rank of (50). NA means not available.

Important Facts

General references in this section to the U.S. Bureau of the Census indicate that data are from *Statistical Abstract of the United States: 1991* (111th ed.), Washington, DC, 1991, unless otherwise indicated. **Population 1990:** U.S. Bureau of the Census. **Estimated population 2010:** U.S. Bureau of the Census, "Projections of the Population of States, by Age, Sex, and Race: 1989 to 2010," *Current Population Reports, Series P-25, No. 1053.* **Number of households 1990, Metropolitan area population,** and **Per-capita average income:** U.S. Bureau of the Census. **Total area** includes land and water. U.S. Bureau of the Census. **National Parks:** National Park Service, Land Resources Division, "Master Deed Listing: Listing of Acreages by State" (December 31, 1991). **State Park/recreation areas:** U.S. Bureau of the Census. **Environmental Voting Record (1991):** Percentage of votes cast by a state's U.S. representatives and senators (from Jan.—Nov. 1991, 102nd Congress) in favor of environmental issues. League of Conservation Voters, *1991 National Environmental Scorecard* (Jan. 1992), "Voting Summary: State Averages."

Energy Use and Production

Total consumption per year, and per capita consumption: U.S. Bureau of the Census. **Change in energy use 1973–88:** Reflects an increase or decrease in the total amount of energy used within the state. U.S. Bureau of the Census, *State and Metropolitan Area Data Book, 1991.* **Chief sources:** The top three sources of energy used, by state. U.S. Bureau of the Census. Percentages were calculated. Totals that add to over 100 reflect energy exported, as in the cases of Vermont, North Dakota, and West Virginia. **Renewables as**

source of total energy used: Includes a state's use of solar, wind, geothermal, running water, and biomass energy. Public Citizen's Critical Mass Energy Project, *The Power of the States: A Fifty-State Survey of Renewable Energy,* June 1990. **Average price per Kwh of electricity for residents:** 1990 data. U.S. Department of Energy, *Electric Power Annual 1990,* Jan. 1992. **Consumption by end use:** U.S. Bureau of the Census. Reflects the percentages of total energy used by various sectors.

Wastes

Total solid wastes: Reflects the state's estimate of total municipal solid waste generated in 1991. Jim Glenn, "The State of Garbage in America," *BioCycle,* April 1992. For types of waste included in each state's total assessment, see the "Wastes" chapter, table, U.S. Solid Waste Output and Management, by State. Per capita waste output was calculated using 1990 population data. **Municipal landfills, Municipal incinerators, and Curbside recycling programs:** Jim Glenn, "The State of Garbage in America," *BioCycle,* April 1992. **Hazardous Waste Sites:** Number of sites that, according to the Resource Conservation and Recovery Act (Superfund), warrant classification on the National Priorities List (NPL). Includes existing and proposed NPL sites (general and federal). U.S. Environmental Protection Agency (EPA), "Background Information: National Priorities List, Proposed Rule" (Intermittent Bulletin, Vol. 2, No. 1, U.S. EPA, Office of Emergency and Remedial Response, Hazardous Site Evaluation Division), February 1992.

Transportation

Miles driven per year and per capita: The total number of rural and urban miles traveled within a state in 1990. U.S. Department of Transportation (DOT), Federal Highway Administration, *Highway Statistics 1990.* Per capita and rank were calculated based on 1990 population. **Motor fuel consumed:** Millions of gallons of gasoline and gasohol used in 1990. U.S. DOT. **Registered motor vehicles:** For 1989, including cars, buses, and trucks. U.S. Bureau of the Census. **Highway expenditures:** Total disbursements in

1990, including interstate and other highways, maintenance, administration, and highway police. U.S. DOT. **How workers commute:** U.S. Bureau of the Census, *State and Metropolitan Area Data Book 1986.* Rank for persons using public transport was calculated. Data are for 1980, the most recent year available.

Water

Total used per day, per capita, and withdrawals by sector: U.S. Bureau of the Census, based on U.S. Geological Survey, *Circular 1004,* "Estimated Use of Water in the United States in 1985" (1988). Numbers include fresh and saline water.

Pollutant Releases

Toxics released and per capita: 1990 data include industrial releases of EPA-classified toxic chemicals to air, land, water, underground well, land surface, and transfers to public-owned water treatment facilities as reported for 1990. Per capita data is based on 1990 population. **Toxics transferred** represent toxic chemicals moved from the producing industry to other sites for disposal or treatment. U.S. EPA, *1990 Toxics Release Inventory: Public Data Release* (May 1992). **Smog precursors** and **Greenhouse gas emissions (CO_2 equiv.):** U.S. EPA, *National- and State-Level Emissions Estimates of Radiatively Important Trace Gases (RITGs) from Anthropogenic Sources* (October 1990). Smog precursors include emissions of volatile organic carbons, nitrogen oxides, and carbon monoxide. Greenhouse gas emissions include methane, carbon dioxide, and cloroflourocarbons 11 and 12, converted to the heating value of an equivalent weight of carbon dioxide. Per capita based on 1988 population. **Acid precipitation precursors:** Annual state emissions of sulfur dioxide and nitrogen oxides as of April 1992. U.S. EPA, National Air Data Branch, printout, "AFS Emissions by SIC Report" (AFS633).

Environmental Expenditures

Budget spent on environment and natural resources: Reflects fiscal year 1988 expenditures, except in the case of Pennsylvania, which is 1987. Council of State Governments, *Resource Guide to State Environmental*

Management, 2nd ed., 1990. **Per capita budget by category** expenditures (1988 populations) grouped under another category are noted as such (e.g., drinking water: in water quality). $0.00 typically means that expenses in that category are not applicable, however, data for Utah's and Nevada's solid waste expenditures were zero. **Air quality** expenses are for administration of state clean air laws and the Clean Air Act; **drinking water** funds are for administering the Clean Water Act and public laws (testing, monitoring, systems construction and maintenance); **forestry** monies are used to manage the state's forest resources; **fish & wildlife** funds go toward protecting, managing, and enhancing fish and wildlife resources and enforcing the state's fish and game laws; **geological survey** funds go to research terrain, mineral resources, and potential geological hazards; **hazardous waste** expenses help maintain a management program (which might include cleanup of Superfund sites and leaking underground storage tanks in some states); **land management** expenditures are directed toward state owned or administered lands, including rangelands and wetlands, different from state parks or recreation areas; **marine & coastal program** funds are used for putting into place research and development plans for coastal zones; **mining reclamation** monies enforce mining reclamation standards and cleanup of abandoned mines; **nuclear waste** expenses go toward a comprehensive low-level and high-level nuclear waste management program; **pesticides control** covers regulating the sale, use, content, and disposal of agricultural and/or commercial pesticides; **soil conservation** funds are used to run programs for protecting the state's soil resources from erosion and other sediment loss; **solid waste** expenses support solid waste management programs (litter control, recycling programs); **water quality** expenses help develop and maintain quality protection and pollution abatement programs that fall under state or Clean Water Act requirements; **water resources** monies cover water conservation, development, use and planning programs.

PROFILE DATA NOTES

Province Profiles

All entries are annual figures unless otherwise indicated. Following some data entries, a rank is indicated by a number in parentheses. This indicates the relative ranking of the province or territory compared with the other 11 provinces or territories. The largest numerical value is given the rank of (1) and the smallest numerical value is given the rank of (12). NA means not available. Unless otherwise specified, data are from Statistics Canada.

Important Facts

Population and **Number of dwellings** data are from *1991 Census of Population* and *Population Projections for Canada, Provinces and Territories, 1989–2011.* **Area** and **National** and **Provincial parks** information is from the *1992 Canada Year Book* and the *National Conservation Areas Data Base, 1990.*

Economic Profile

Budget figures are from Statistics Canada's Public Institutions Division, 1990.

Energy Use and Production

Total energy consumed per year is 1991 data, given in petajoules (one petajoule = 10^{15} joules = 0.00095 quadrillion Btus) or in gigajoules (one gigajoule = 10^9 joules = 950,000 Btus). **Change in energy use 1990–91** reflects an increase or decrease in the total amount of energy used over the period. **Renewables as source of primary electricity**, primary electricity is hydro and nuclear power. Primary energy is coal, crude oil, natural gas, gas plant, steam, hydro, and nuclear power. Gas plant includes propane, butane, and ethane. **Use** and **Average price per kilowatt-hour** figures are from *Quarterly Report on Energy Supply-Demand in Canada*, 1990.

Wastes

Percent of national hazardous waste generated shows the share of national hazardous waste output, based on 1988 data from Fenco Newfoundland Lavalin, as cited in *The State of Canada's Environment*, 1991. **Total**
solid wastes and **per capita** output reflect residential, all commercial, industrial, and institutional solid waste produced in 1988. Data for New Brunswick also include construction/demolition debris. Data for Newfoundland also include construction/demolition debris and sewage sludge. Both sets of data are from Environment Canada. **Disposal sites in use** are the number of active and inactive landfills. **Hazardous waste sites** are those presenting a high risk potential to health and the environment. Environment Canada, *State of the Environment Report for Canada*, May 1986. The number of **Municipal incinerators** is from Environment Canada's Office of Waste Management, August 1992. Of 18 total incinerators, nine are heat recovery plants.

Transportation

Kilometers driven reflect the total number of kilometers driven in the province or territory in 1988. **Registered motor vehicles** (1988) reflects the total number for the province or territory. **Personal autos** includes cars for personal use. The *1992 Canada Year Book.* **Average fuel used per car** (1988) data are from Statistics Canada's *Fuel Consumption Survey.*

Water

Total water used per day, per capita data, and **Withdrawals by sector** are from Environment Canada, *Municipal Water Use in Canada, 1989.*

Pollutant Releases

Smog precursors data include air emissions of volatile organic compounds, nitrogen dioxide, and carbon monoxide. **Acid rain precursors** reflect sulfur dioxide and nitrogen oxide emissions. Both categories are calculated from Environment Canada, *Canadian Emissions Inventory of Common Air Contaminants (1985)*, March 1990. **Greenhouse gas emissions in CO_2 equivalents** are taken from Environment Canada, *National Inventory of Sources and Emissions of Carbon Dioxide (1987)*, May 1990. **Chemicals applied to agricultural land** (1990) information is from the *1991 Census of Agriculture.*

Province Profiles

How does Canada approach environmental issues? Here is an overview of some of our northern neighbor's concerns and strategies.

As the second largest country in the world, Canada is responsible for a significant portion of the global environment. Bounded by the longest coastline of any nation (150,000 miles), the country holds nearly one quarter of Earth's wetlands and freshwater resources and one tenth of its global forest resources.

Despite the vastness of its land and a very low overall population density, Canada is an urban country. More than three-quarters of its 27 million inhabitants live in urban places. All but a handful of these metropolitan areas are in a relatively narrow band just north of the United States; almost three quarters of Canada's people are within a two-hour drive of the U.S. border.

Even though Canadians enjoy an environment with a high carrying capacity in relation to the size of the population, the natural world is showing signs of strain. Because of the great diversity of climate, landforms, vegetation, resources, and economic activities across the nation, environmental stresses are varied. A broad diagnosis of environmental quality is presented in the government report, *The State of*

Canada's Environment, 1991. The report analyzes how the environment is changing and describes the progress that has been made as well as the problems that remain.

The report indicates that despite the remoteness of the Arctic, lead, PCBs, pesticides, and other contaminants are found there. Waste is another perplexing problem. Canadians, already among the highest producers of waste in the world, continued to increase the volume of both municipal and hazardous wastes in the 1980s. Many communities are now faced with major waste disposal problems. Finally, greenhouse gas emissions have grown significantly in the last 50 years, mainly as a byproduct of increased energy use.

With regard to wildlife populations, as of 1991, 193 species, subspecies or populations of Canadian wildlife—plants, birds, and animals—were considered at risk of eventual disappearance, mostly as a result of the loss or degradation of critical habitats.

Land-based species are not the only ones that have suffered from the demands of modern society. Fish populations—on the Atlantic and Pacific coasts and in the Great Lakes—have been severely overfished and their habitats have been polluted. Current restrictions on commercial fishing may allow fish populations to regenerate, but the reduced catches have hurt local economies, especially on the Atlantic.

Preserving land that has so far been unprotected from human activity is among Canada's foremost environmental concerns. Specifically, the conversion of natural forest and grassland to farmland and urban areas has contributed over the years to the country's worst land use problems. As urban areas grow, they also consume natural and formerly agricultural lands. This causes more stress to the remaining farmland as farmers add chemicals and water to maintain levels of food production. As a result, some sections of soil on the prairies have lost over one half their original organic material. Erosion is an even greater problem and occurs in some areas at rates more than 25 times faster than the natural rate of soil replacement.

Human activities and demands have also taken their toll on wetlands. About 70 percent of prairie and Ontario wetlands have been converted to other uses since European settlement.

But Canada has had a number of environmental successes. Air quality in Canadian cities has improved notably, with ambient air levels of lead dropping by 93 percent between 1974 and 1989. Levels of carbon monoxide have also showed a large decrease. With sulfur dioxide levels dropping by more than 50 percent in the same period, good progress has also been made with respect to acid rain.

In addition, the amount of pollution flowing into Canadian waters from both industrial and municipal sources has decreased. Significant initiatives for preserving wildlife habitat, expanding protected areas, managing toxic chemicals, and phasing out the production of ozone-depleting chemicals are also under way.

A number of new regulatory mechanisms have been put into effect in the last few years, and these should noticeably affect the output of pollutants. In particular, the Canadian Environmental Protection Act (CEPA) of 1988 established a strong legislative base for controlling priority toxic substances.

New partnerships involving nongovernment organizations, communities, and businesses are emerging to address environmental issues. Among these is the 1.5 billion, 15-year North American Waterfowl Management Plan, which involves both Canadian and U.S. governments, hunters, farmers, and conservation groups in helping landowners and managers build habitat management into their activities. Remedial action plans now exist for the Atlantic provinces, the Great Lakes, and the St. Lawrence and Fraser rivers.

Canadians continue to map out long-term environmental goals and relate these to social and economic priorities by involving representatives from government, business, and non government organizations, as well as academics and private citizens in round table discussions. The round tables have been set up by the federal government, the provinces and territories, and some regional jurisdictions. Such deliberations have helped to identify specific roles that business, governments, and individuals can play in solving environmental problems and have provided guidance to government in the development of action strategies.

Canadians have recognized their responsibilities to the global environment as well. The government joined other country leaders in 1987 to sign the International Protocol on Substances that Deplete the Ozone Layer, better known as the Montreal Protocol, which commits signees to making a 50 percent reduction in their use of ozone-depleting chlorofluourocarbons (CFCs) and halons by the year 2000. More recently Canada has pushed its own deadline for phasing out the production and export of CFCs to the end of 1995.

The Canadian government introduced a comprehensive $3 billion, six-year Green Plan in 1990. Building on a broad public consultation process, the Green Plan advocates sustainable development and outlines new federal policies, programs, and standards for cleaning up and protecting the environment. The Plan contains initiatives for reducing energy use and waste. It promotes global environmental security, environmentally responsible decision making, and deals with the country's preparedness for environmental emergencies.

In some respects the Canadian environment is healthier than it was a generation ago. New means of environmental management have been developed, some of the most polluting technologies have been replaced or regulated. Many of the more visible problems are being addressed, particularly those involving pollution hot spots or toxic substances. Overall, the Green Plan has committed Canada to a path toward sustainable development, but there remains considerable distance to travel to reach this goal.

Metric Conversions

Use these calculations to convert the metric data given in the following provincial or territorial profile to English measurement.

Metric	Calculation	To obtain
kilometers (km.)	x 0.6214	miles
square kilometers (sq. km.)	x 0.3861	square miles
hectares (ha.)	÷ 259	square miles
liters (l.)	x .2642	gallons (U.S.)
metric ton (mt. ton)	x 1.102	tons (short)

ALBERTA

Important Facts
Population 1991: 2,545,553 **(4)**
Estimated pop. 2011: 3,298,700 **(4)**
Number of dwellings: 914,720
Urban area population 1991: 79.8%
Total area: 661,190 sq. km. **(5)**
Land area: 644,390 sq. km.
Water area: 16,800 sq. km.
National parks: 49,583 sq. km.
Prov. parks/forests: 12,514 sq. km.

Economic Profile
Per capita average income: $21,971 **(5)**
Budget spent on environmental and
   natural resources: 3.8% **(1)**
   per capita: $277 **(3)**

Energy Use and Production
Total consumed/year: 1,719 PJ
   per capita: 675.3 GJ **(1)**
Change in use 1990–91: –5.2%
Chief sources:
   natural gas: 49%
   petroleum: 33%
   primary electricity: 16%
Renewables as source of primary
   energy produced:
   hydroelectric: 0.1%
Money spent on residential electricity
   (thousands): $412,008
Average price per kWh of electricity
   for residents: 7¢

Consumption by end use:
   industrial: 36.5%
   transportation: 25.1%
   residential and farms: 21.2%
   government and commercial: 17.2%

Wastes
Percent of national hazardous waste
   generated: 1.6% **(4)**
Total solid wastes: 1.8 m. mt. tons
   per capita: 0.7 mt. tons
Disposal sites: 1,190
Hazardous waste sites: 65
Municipal incinerators: 0

Transportation
Kilometers driven per year:
   14,543 m. km.
   per capita: 6,276 km. **(4)**
Registered motor vehicles: 1,820,141
Number of personal autos: 768,200
Average fuel per car: 2,330 t. liters

Water
Total used per day: 1141 cu. meters
   per capita: 0.342 cu. meters **(9)**
Withdrawals by sector:
   domestic: 52.9%
   commercial/institutional: 23.2%
   industrial: 14.1%
   other/unaccounted loss: 9.8%

Pollutant Releases
Smog precursors: 1,952 t. mt. tons **(4)**
Acid rain precurs.: 986 t. mt. tons **(3)**
Greenhouse gas emissions (CO_2
   equiv.): 28,690 t. mt. tons
   per capita: 11.51 mt. tons **(1)**
Chemicals applied to agricultural
   land (no. of hectares):
   fertilizer: 6,349,884
   herbicides: 5,670,592
   pesticides: 553,280

GJ = gigajoules; **PJ** = petajoules; **m.** = million; **mt.** = metric; **t.** = thousand

BRITISH COLUMBIA

Important Facts
Population 1991: 3,282,061 **(3)**
Estimated pop. 2011: 3,997,800 **(3)**
Number of dwellings: 1,251,414
Urban area population 1991: 80.4%
Total area: 947,800 sq. km. **(4)**
Land area: 929,730 sq. km.
Water area: 18,070 sq. km.
National parks: 6,299 sq. km.
Prov. parks/forests: 53,359 sq. km.

Economic Profile
Per capita average income: $22,433 **(4)**
Budget spent on environmental and
   natural resources: 3.3% **(6)**
   per capita: $194 **(8)**

Energy Use and Production
Total consumed/year: 852 PJ
   per capita: 259.6 GJ **(3)**
Change in use 1990–91: 2.2%
Chief sources:
   petroleum: 42%
   natural gas: 31%
   primary electricity: 25%
Renewables as source of primary
   energy produced:
   hydroelectric: 14.0%
Money spent on residential electricity
   (thousands): $685,884
Average price per kWh of electricity
   for residents: 5¢
Consumption by end use:
   industrial: 33.1%
   transportation: 33.7%
   residential and farms: 17.1%
   government and commercial: 16.0%

Wastes
Percent of national hazardous waste
   generated: 1.4% **(5)**
Total solid wastes: 2.63 m. mt. tons
   per capita: 0.8 mt. tons

Disposal sites: 141
Hazardous waste sites: 7
Municipal incinerators: 6

Transportation
Kilometers driven per year:
   14,499 m. km.
   per capita: 5,144 km. **(7)**
Registered motor vehicles: 2,350,437
Number of personal autos: 984,600
Average fuel per car: 1,810 t. liters

Water
Total used per day: 1790.2 cu. meters
   per capita: 0.447 cu. meters **(4)**
Withdrawals by sector:
   domestic: 52.2%
   commercial/institutional: 21.5%
   industrial: 10.6%
   other/unaccounted loss: 15.7%

Pollutant Releases
Smog precursors: 2,983 t. mt. tons **(2)**
Acid rain precurs.: 368 t. mt. tons **(7)**
Greenhouse gas emissions (CO_2
   equiv.): 16,654 t. mt. tons
   per capita: 5.24 mt. tons **(6)**
Chemicals applied to agricultural
   land (no. of hectares):
   fertilizer: 330,937
   herbicides: 126,472
   pesticides: 38,102

GJ = gigajoules; **PJ** = petajoules; **m.** = million; **mt.** = metric; **t.** = thousand

MANITOBA

Important Facts

Population 1991: 1,091,942 **(5)**
Estimated pop. 2011: 1,223,700 **(5)**
Number of dwellings: 407,089
Urban area population 1991: 72.1%
Total area: 649,950 sq. km. **(7)**
Land area: 548,360 sq. km.
Water area: 101,590 sq. km.
National parks: 2,976 sq. km.
Prov. parks/forests: 15,000 sq. km.

Economic Profile

Per capita average income: $19,251 **(7)**
Budget spent on environmental and
  natural resources: 3.1% **(8)**
  per capita: $194 **(8)**

Energy Use and Production

Total consumed/year: 253 PJ
  per capita: 231.7 GJ **(7)**
Change in use 1990–91: –2.1%
Chief sources:
  petroleum: 38%
  natural gas: 37%
  primary electricity: 23%
Renewables as source of primary
  energy produced:
  hydroelectric: 71.3%
Money spent on residential electricity
  (thousands): $255,273
Average price per kWh of electricity
  for residents: 5¢

Consumption by end use:
  industrial: 17.4%
  transportation: 34.3%
  residential and farms: 27.8%
  government and commercial: 20.5%

Wastes

Percent of national hazardous waste
  generated: 0.8% **(8)**
Total solid wastes: 1.02 m. mt. tons
  per capita: 0.9 mt. tons
Disposal sites: 760
Hazardous waste sites: 194
Municipal incinerators: 0

Transportation

Kilometers driven per year:
  6,255 m. km.
  per capita: 5,986 km. **(5)**
Registered motor vehicles: 769,976
Number of personal autos: 340,700
Average fuel per car: 2,450 t. liters

Water

Total used per day: 358.2 cu. meters
  per capita: 0.429 cu. meters **(5)**
Withdrawals by sector:
  domestic: 74.3%
  commercial/institutional: 5.0%
  industrial: 5.8%
  other/unaccounted loss: 14.9%

Pollutant Releases

Smog precursors: 583 t. mt. tons **(6)**
Acid rain precurs.: 554 t. mt. tons **(4)**
Greenhouse gas emissions (CO_2
  equiv.): 3,415 t. mt. tons
  per capita: 3.19 mt. tons **(10)**
Chemicals applied to agricultural
  land (no. of hectares):
  fertilizer: 3,688,335
  herbicides: 3,263,182
  pesticides: 583,346

GJ = gigajoules; **PJ** = petajoules; **m.** = million; **mt.** = metric; **t.** = thousand

NEW BRUNSWICK

Important Facts
Population 1991: 723,900 **(8)**
Estimated pop. 2011: 740,600 **(8)**
Number of dwellings: 255,042
Urban area population 1991: 47.7%
Total area: 73,440 sq. km. **(10)**
Land area: 72,090 sq. km.
Water area: 1,350 sq. km.
National parks: 444 sq. km.
Prov. parks/forests: 249 sq. km.

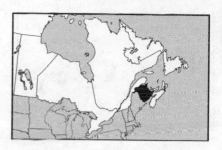

Economic Profile
Per capita avg. income: $17,062 **(10)**
Budget spent on environmental and
  natural resources: 2.1% **(11)**
  per capita: $1?? **(11)**

Energy Use and Production
Total consumed/year: 176 PJ
  per capita: 243.1 GJ **(5)**
Change in use 1990–91: –0.8%
Chief sources:
  petroleum: 66%
  primary electricity: 31%
  gas plant: 2%
Renewables as source of primary
  energy produced:
  hydroelectric: 27.2%
Money spent on residential electricity
  (thousands): $258,154
Average price per kWh of electricity
  for residents: 6¢
Consumption by end use:
  industrial: 29.2%
  transportation: 33.0%
  residential and farms: 21.6%
  government and commercial: 16.2%

Wastes
Percent of national hazardous waste
  generated: 1.1% **(6)**
Total solid wastes: 0.45 m. mt. tons
  per capita: 0.6 mt. tons

Disposal sites: 436
Hazardous waste sites: 9
Municipal incinerators: 0

Transportation
Kilometers driven per year:
  4,280 m. km.
  per capita: 8,179 km. **(1)**
Registered motor vehicles: 451,562
Number of personal autos: 232,000
Average fuel per car: 2,150 t. liters

Water
Total used per day: 400.5 cu. meters
  per capita: 0.516 cu. meters **(2)**
Withdrawals by sector:
  domestic: 44.8%
  commercial/institutional: 18.1%
  industrial: 34.3%
  other/unaccounted loss: 2.9%

Pollutant Releases
Smog precursors: 380 t. mt. tons **(8)**
Acid rain precurs.: 184 t. mt. tons **(6)**
Greenhouse gas emissions (CO_2
  equiv.): 3,908 t. mt. tons
  per capita: 5.38 mt. tons **(4)**
Chemicals applied to agricultural
  land (no. of hectares):
  fertilizer: 78,136
  herbicides: 39,860
  pesticides: 24,089

GJ = gigajoules; **PJ** = petajoules; **m.** = million; **mt.** = metric; **t.** = thousand

NEWFOUNDLAND

Important Facts
Population 1991: 568,474 **(9)**
Estimated pop. 2011: 566,100 **(9)**
Number of dwellings: 175,665
Urban area population 1991: 53.6%
Total area: 405,720 sq. km. **(9)**
Land area: 371,690 sq. km.
Water area: 34,030 sq. km.
National parks: 2,342 sq. km.
Prov. parks/forests: 4,394 sq. km.

Economic Profile
Per capita avg. income: $15,860 **(12)**
Budget spent on environmental and
 natural resources: 2.8% **(10)**
 per capita: $176 **(10)**

Energy Use and Production
Total consumed/year: 134 PJ
 per capita: 235.7 GJ **(6)**
Change in use 1990–91: –2.7%
Chief sources:
 petroleum: 68%
 primary electricity: 30%
 coke: 1%
Renewables as source of primary
 energy produced:
 hydroelectric: 100.0%
Money spent on residential electricity
 (thousands): $193,050
Average price per kWh of electricity
 for residents: 7¢

Consumption by end use:
 industrial: 31.0%
 transportation: 34.4%
 residential and farms: 17.3%
 government and commercial: 17.4%

Wastes
Percent of national hazardous waste
 generated: 0.4% **(9)**
Total solid wastes: 0.73 m. mt. tons
 per capita: 1.3 mt. tons
Disposal sites: 239
Hazardous waste sites: 1
Municipal incinerators: 2

Transportation
Kilometers driven per year:
 2,303 m. km.
 per capita: 4,156 km. **(10)**
Registered motor vehicles: 307,049
Number of personal autos: 139,700
Average fuel per car: 2,000 t. liters

Water
Total used per day: 250.2 cu. meters
 per capita: 0.507 cu. meters **(3)**
Withdrawals by sector:
 domestic: 50.2%
 commercial/institutional: 9.6%
 industrial: 9.8%
 other/unaccounted loss: 30.4%

Pollutant Releases
Smog precursors: 269 t. mt. tons **(9)**
Acid rain precurs.: 79 t. mt. tons **(9)**
Greenhouse gas emissions (CO_2
 equiv.): 2,294 t. mt. tons
 per capita: 3.99 mt. tons **(8)**
Chemicals applied to agricultural
 land (no. of hectares):
 fertilizer: 5,434
 herbicides: 572
 pesticides: 556

GJ = gigajoules; **PJ** = petajoules; **m.** = million; **mt.** = metric; **t.** = thousand

NORTHWEST TERRITORIES

Important Facts

Population 1991: 57,649 **(11)**
Estimated pop. 2011: 71,800 **(11)**
Number of dwellings: 16,349
Urban area population 1991: 36.7%
Total area: 3,426,320 sq. km. **(1)**
Land area: 3,239,020 sq. km.
Water area: 133,300 sq. km.
National parks: 77,454 sq. km.
Prov. parks/forests: NA

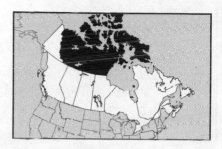

Economic Profile

Per capita average income: $25,556 **(2)**
Budget spent on environmental and
  natural resources: 3.5% **(4)**
  per capita: $693 **(1)**

Energy Use and Production

Total consumed/year: NA
  per capita: NA
Change in use 1990–91: NA
Chief sources:
  NA
  NA
  NA
Renewables as source of primary
  energy produced:
  NA
Money spent on residential electricity
  (thousands): $34,997
Average price per kWh of electricity
  for residents: 23¢
Consumption by end use:
  industrial: NA
  transportation: NA
  residential and farms: NA
  government and commercial: NA

Wastes

Percent of national hazardous waste
  generated: NA
Total solid wastes: 0.03 m. mt. tons
  per capita: 0.5 mt. tons
Disposal sites: 432

Hazardous waste sites: 20
Municipal incinerators: 0

Transportation

Kilometers driven per year: NA
  per capita: NA
Registered motor vehicles: 23,931
Number of personal autos: NA
Average fuel per car: NA

Water

Total used per day: 32.6 cu. meters*
  per capita: 0.369 cu. meters **(7)***
Withdrawals by sector:
  domestic: 46.3%*
  commercial/institutional: 24.9%*
  industrial: 3.6%*
other/unaccounted loss: 25.2%*

Pollutant Releases

Smog precursors: 52 t. mt. tons **(12)**
Acid rain precurs.: 16 t. mt. tons **(12)**
Greenhouse gas emissions (CO_2
  equiv.): 545 t. mt. tons*
  per capita: 6.72 mt. tons **(3)***
Chemicals applied to agricultural
  land (no. of hectares):
  fertilizer: NA
  herbicides: NA
  pesticides: NA

  * Northwest Territories and
    Yukon combined.

GJ = gigajoules; **PJ** = petajoules; **m.** = million; **mt.** = metric; **t.** = thousand

NOVA SCOTIA

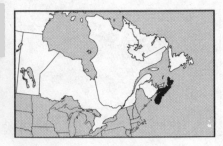

Important Facts

Population 1991: 899,942 **(7)**
Estimated pop. 2011: 963,800 **(7)**
Number of dwellings: 326,484
Urban area population 1991: 53.5%
Total area: 55,490 sq. km. **(11)**
Land area: 52,840 sq. km.
Water area: 2,650 sq. km.
National parks: 1,354 sq. km.
Prov. parks/forests: 218 sq. km.

Economic Profile

Per capita average income: $18,154 **(8)**
Budget spent on environmental and
  natural resources: 3.5% **(4)**
  per capita: $208 **(7)**

Energy Use and Production

Total consumed/year: 177 PJ
  per capita: 196.7 GJ **(9)**
Change in use 1990–91: –4.5%
Chief sources:
  petroleum: 76%
  primary electricity: 21%
  gas plant: 2%
Renewables as source of primary
  energy produced:
  hydroelectric, wind & tidal: 4.2%
Money spent on residential electricity
  (thousands): $275,584
Average price per kWh of electricity
  for residents: 8¢

Consumption by end use:
  industrial: 13.5%
  transportation: 40.1%
  residential and farms: 25.8%
  government and commercial: 20.6%

Wastes

Percent of national hazardous waste
  generated: 2.6% **(3)**
Total solid wastes: 0.6 m. mt. tons
  per capita: 0.7 mt. tons
Disposal sites: 242
Hazardous waste sites: 15
Municipal incinerators: 1

Transportation

Kilometers driven per year:
  4,161 m. km.
  per capita: 4,885 km. **(8)**
Registered motor vehicles: 512,067
Number of personal autos: 236,900
Average fuel per car: 1,960 t. liters

Water

Total used per day: 273.7 cu. meters
  per capita: 0.381 cu. meters **(6)**
Withdrawals by sector:
  domestic: 40.7%
  commercial/institutional: 11.5%
  industrial: 13.1%
  other/unaccounted loss: 34.7%

Pollutant Releases

Smog precursors: 430 t. mt. tons **(7)**
Acid rain precurs.: 248 t. mt. tons **(5)**
Greenhouse gas emissions (CO_2
  equiv.): 4,741 t. mt. tons
  per capita: 5.3 mt. tons **(5)**
Chemicals applied to agricultural
  land (no. of hectares):
  fertilizer: 82,267
  herbicides: 22,383
  pesticides: 13,466

GJ = gigajoules; **PJ** = petajoules; **m.** = million; **mt.** = metric; **t.** = thousand

ONTARIO

Important Facts

Population 1991: 10,084,885 **(1)**
Estimated pop. 2011: 11,843,200 **(1)**
Number of dwellings: 3,661,671
Urban area population 1991: 81.8%
Total area: 1,068,580 sq. km. **(3)**
Land area: 891,190 sq. km.
Water area: 177,390 sq. km.
National parks: 2,191 sq. km.
Prov. parks/forests: 63,284 sq. km.

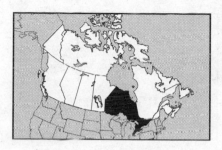

Economic Profile

Per capita average income: $25,151 **(3)**
Budget spent on environmental and
  natural resources: 3.8% **(1)**
  per capita: $237 **(5)**

Energy Use and Production

Total consumed/year: 2,575 PJ
  per capita: 255.3 GJ **(4)**
Change in use 1990–91: –0.7%
Chief sources:
  natural gas: 36%
  petroleum: 33%
  primary electricity: 21%
Renewables as source of primary
  energy produced:
  hydroelectric: 36.3%
Money spent on residential electricity
  (thousands): $3,111,421
Average price per kWh of electricity
  for residents: 7¢
Consumption by end use:
  industrial: 32.8%
  transportation: 27.7%
  residential and farms: 22.6%
  government and commercial: 17.0%

Wastes

Percent of national hazardous waste
  generated: 68.1% **(1)**
Total solid wastes: 7.42 m. mt. tons
  per capita: 0.7 mt. tons

Disposal sites: 220
Hazardous waste sites: 7
Municipal incinerators: 5

Transportation

Kilometers driven per year:
  58,579 m. km.
  per capita: 6,383 km. **(3)**
Registered motor vehicles: 5,804,105
Number of personal autos: 3,280,500
Average fuel per car: 2,090 t. liters

Water

Total used per day: 4722.4 cu. meters
  per capita: 0.300 cu. meters **(11)**
Withdrawals by sector:
  domestic: 42.0%
  commercial/institutional: 20.1%
  industrial: 21.6%
  other/unaccounted loss: 16.3%

Pollutant Releases

Smog precursors: 4,449 t. mt. tons **(1)**
Acid rain precurs.: 2.025 t. mt. tons **(1)**
Greenhouse gas emissions (CO_2
  equiv.): 42,045 t. mt. tons
  per capita 1.20 mt. tons **(7)**
Chemicals applied to agricultural
  land (no. of hectares):
  fertilizer: 2,273,448
  herbicides: 1,791,483
  pesticides: 456,171

GJ = gigajoules; **PJ** = petajoules; **m.** = million; **mt.** = metric; **t.** = thousand

PRINCE EDWARD ISLAND

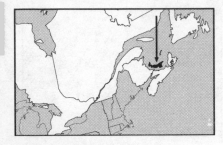

Important Facts

Population 1991: 129,765 **(10)**
Estimated pop. 2011: 139,000 **(10)**
Number of dwellings: 44,751
Urban area population 1991: 39.9%
Total area: 5,660 sq. km. **(12)**
Land area: 5,660 sq. km.
Water area: 0 sq. km.
National parks: 26 sq. km.
Prov. parks/forests: 15 sq. km.

Economic Profile

Per capita avg. income: $16,292 **(11)**
Budget spent on environmental and
  natural resources: 1.3% **(12)**
  per capita: $78 **(12)**

Energy Use and Production

Total consumed/year: 21 PJ
  per capita: 161.8 GJ **(10)**
Change in use 1990–91: −1.8%
Chief sources:
  petroleum: 83%
  primary electricity: 12%
  gas plant: 3%
Renewables as source of primary
  energy produced:
  0.0%
Money spent on residential electricity
  (thousands): $27,156
Average price per kWh of electricity
  for residents: 11¢

Consumption by end use:

  industrial: 5.5%
  transportation: 38.5%
  residential and farms: 33.5%
  government and commercial: 22.5%

Wastes

Percent of national hazardous waste
  generated: 0.01% **(10)**
Total solid wastes: 0.06 m. mt. tons
  per capita: 0.5 mt. tons
Disposal sites: 461
Hazardous waste sites: 11
Municipal incinerators: 1

Transportation

Kilometers driven per year:
  856 m. km.
  per capita: 6,909 km. **(2)**
Registered motor vehicles: 82,531
Number of personal autos: 43,000
Average fuel per car: 2,480 t. liters

Water

Total used per day: 19.7 cu. meters
  per capita: 0.227 cu. meters **(12)**
Withdrawals by sector:
  domestic: 39.6%
  commercial/institutional: 24.2%
  industrial: 20.9%
  other/unaccounted loss: 15.3%

Pollutant Releases

Smog precursors: 81 t. mt. tons **(10)**
Acid rain precurs.: 8 t. mt. tons **(11)**
Greenhouse gas emissions (CO_2
  equiv.): 428 t. mt. tons
  per capita: 3.24 mt. tons **(9)**
Chemicals applied to agricultural
  land (no. of hectares):
  fertilizer: 102,117
  herbicides: 73,783
  pesticides: 36,161

GJ = gigajoules; **PJ** = petajoules; **m.** = million; **mt.** = metric; **t.** = thousand

QUEBEC

Important Facts
Population 1991: 6,895,963 **(2)**
Estimated pop. 2011: 7,684,300 **(2)**
Number of dwellings: 2,650,111
Urban area population 1991: 77.6%
Total area: 1,540,680 sq. km. **(2)**
Land area: 1,356,790 sq. km.
Water area: 183,890 sq. km.
National parks: 935 sq. km.
Prov. parks/forests: 71,000 sq. km.

Economic Profile
Per capita average income: $20,568 **(6)**
Budget spent on environmental and
  natural resources: 3.7% **(3)**
  per capita: $244 **(4)**

Energy Use and Production
Total consumed/year: 1,469 PJ
  per capita: 213.0 GJ **(8)**
Change in use 1990–91: –3.8%
Chief sources:
  primary electricity: 41%
  petroleum: 41%
  natural gas: 16%
Renewables as source of primary
  energy produced:
  hydroelectric: 96.7%
Money spent on residential electricity
  (thousands): $2,344,670
Average price per kWh of electricity
  for residents: 5¢
Consumption by end use:
  industrial: 36.5%
  transportation: 26.3%
  residential and farms: 20.8%
  government and commercial: 16.4%

Wastes
Percent of national hazardous waste
  generated: 22.2% **(2)**
Total solid wastes: 5.6 m. mt. tons
  per capita: 0.8 mt. tons

Disposal sites: 48
Hazardous waste sites: 11
Municipal incinerators: 3

Transportation
Kilometers driven per year:
  33,566 m. km.
  per capita: 5,261 km. **(6)**
Registered motor vehicles: 3,432,035
Number of personal autos: 1,826,000
Average fuel per car: 2,060 t. liters

Water
Total used per day: 4503.4 cu. meters
  per capita: 0.519 cu. meters **(1)**
Withdrawals by sector:
  domestic: 46.3%
  commercial/institutional: 11.4%
  industrial: 16.6%
  other/unaccounted loss: 25.7%

Pollutant Releases
Smog precursors: 2,513 t. mt. tons **(3)**
Acid rain precurs.: 933 t. mt. tons **(2)**
Greenhouse gas emissions (CO_2
  equiv.): 17,357 t. mt. tons
  per capita: 2.56 mt. tons **(11)**
Chemicals applied to agricultural
  land (no. of hectares):
  fertilizer: 996,722
  herbicides: 564,330
  pesticides: 96,285

GJ = gigajoules; **PJ** = petajoules; **m.** = million; **mt.** = metric; **t.** = thousand

SASKATCHEWAN

Important Facts
Population 1991: 988,928 **(6)**
Estimated pop. 2011: 1,124,600 **(6)**
Number of dwellings: 366,075
Urban area population 1991: 63.0%
Total area: 652,330 sq. km. **(6)**
Land area: 570,700 sq. km.
Water area: 81,630 sq. km.
National parks: 4,781 sq. km.
Prov. parks/forests: 9,080 sq. km.

Economic Profile
Per capita average income: $17,774 **(9)**
Budget spent on environmental and
  natural resources: 3.1% **(8)**
  per capita: $211 **(6)**

Energy Use and Production
Total consumed/year: 360 PJ
  per capita: 364.0 GJ **(2)**
Change in use 1990–91: +5.3%
Chief sources:
  natural gas: 48%
  petroleum: 36%
  primary electricity: 14%
Renewables as source of primary
  energy produced:
  hydroelectric: 1.7%
Money spent on residential electricity
  (thousands): $178,419
Average price per kWh of electricity
  for residents: 7¢

Consumption by end use:
  industrial: 26.0%
  transportation: 30.1%
  residential and farms: 30.5%
  government and commercial: 13.4%

Wastes
Percent of national hazardous waste
  generated: 0.9% **(7)**
Total solid wastes: 0.77 m. mt. tons
  per capita: 0.8 mt. tons
Disposal sites: 1,324
Hazardous waste sites: 97
Municipal incinerators: 0

Transportation
Kilometers driven per year:
  4,748 m. km.
  per capita: 4,819 km. **(9)**
Registered motor vehicles: 755,350
Number of personal autos: 305,200
Average fuel per car: 2,130 t. liters

Water
Total used per day: 363.1 cu. meters
  per capita: 0.330 cu. meters **(10)**
Withdrawals by sector:
  domestic: 50.9%
  commercial/institutional: 23.3%
  industrial: 14.4%
  other/unaccounted loss: 11.4%

Pollutant Releases
Smog precurs.: 796 t. mt. tons **(5)**
Acid rain precurs.: 244 t. mt. tons **(8)**
Greenhouse gas emissions (CO_2
  equiv.): 8,356 t. mt. tons
  per capita: 8.27 mt. tons **(2)**
Chemicals applied to agricultural
  land (no. of hectares):
  fertilizer: 7,654,551
  herbicides: 10,045,850
  pesticides: 973,365

GJ = gigajoules; **PJ** = petajoules; **m.** = million; **mt.** = metric; **t.** = thousand

YUKON TERRITORIES

Important Facts
Population 1991: 27,797 **(12)**
Estimated pop. 2011: 36,600 **(12)**
Number of dwellings: 10,071
Urban area population 1991: 58.8%
Total area: 483,450 sq. km. **(8)**
Land area: 478,970 sq. km.
Water area: 4,480 sq. km.
National parks: 32,183 sq. km.
Prov. parks/forests: NA sq. km.

Economic Profile
Per capita average income: $25,846 **(1)**
Budget spent on environmental and
  natural resources: 3.2% **(7)**
  per capita: $415 **(2)**

Energy Use and Production
Total consumed/year: NA
  per capita: NA
Change in use 1990–91: NA
Chief sources:
  NA
  NA
  NA
Renewables as source of primary
  energy produced:
  NA
Money spent on residential electricity
  (thousands): $9,233
Average price per kWh of electricity
  for residents: 8¢
Consumption by end use:
  industrial: NA
  transportation: NA
  residential and farms: NA
  government and commercial: NA

Wastes
Percent of national hazardous waste
  generated: NA
Total solid wastes: 0.04 m. mt. tons
  per capita: 1.4 mt. tons
Disposal sites: 16

Hazardous waste sites: NA
Municipal incinerators: 0

Transportation
Kilometers driven per year: NA
  per capita: NA
Registered motor vehicles: 27,077
Number of personal autos: NA
Average fuel per car: NA t. liters

Water
Total used per day: 32.6 cu. meters*
  per capita: .369 cu. meters **(7)***
Withdrawals by sector:
  domestic: 46.3%*
  commercial/institutional: 24.9%*
  industrial: 3.6%*
  other/unaccounted loss: 25.2%*

Pollutant Releases
Smog precursors: 17 t. mt. tons **(11)**
Acid rain precurs.: 2 t. mt. tons **(10)**
Greenhouse gas emissions (CO_2
  equiv.): 545 t. mt. tons*
  per capita: 6.72 mt. tons **(3)***
Chemicals applied to agricultural
  land (no. of hectares):
  fertilizer: NA
  herbicides: NA
  pesticides: NA

* Yukon and Northwest
  Territories combined.

GJ = gigajoules; PJ = petajoules; **m.** = million; **mt.** = metric; **t.** = thousand

A Global View

Environmental problems differ greatly among the countries of the world, but they add up to global trouble.

What global pollutant is currently six times natural levels and expected to continue rising at least until the year 2000? What has partially destroyed 11 percent of the Earth's fertile soils over the last 45 years? Why does the government of Australia now require schoolchildren to wear hats when playing outside? Is U.S. use of pesticides and fertilizers, the highest of any country in the world, increasing or decreasing? What type of tree grows in semiarid regions, thrives on poor soil, and is a source of substances that repel pests, fight tooth decay, have antiviral and

antibacterial properties, and may even yield a male birth control pill?

Which continent has the largest area of degraded land? Do you risk damage to your eyes from the sun's ultraviolet radiation if you only wear cheap sun glasses at the beach? After the United States, which country is the worst climate polluter as measured by industrial emissions of carbon dioxide—Japan, China, or Germany? How might cleaning emissions of acidic particles from industrial facilities worsen global warming? Which country has the largest known number of mammal species (more than 500)? Of bird species? Of flowering plants?

This section takes an international look at environmental problems. In it you will find the answers to the questions above, and many more. In additional to chapters on ozone depletion, greenhouse warming, and land degradation (including a discussion about the world's diminishing biodiversity), there are explicit comparisons among countries on a number of environmentally-important topics. You will also find environmental profiles for 143 countries (and some former countries, such as Yugoslavia), organized by continent. We also include mini-profiles of the 15 new republics emerging from the former Soviet Union. The country profiles provide a brief snapshot of each country's natural resource and environmental conditions.

Ozone Depletion

The global decline in the stratospheric ozone layer intensifies—and the worst is still to come.

In the last decade, ozone depletion has overtaken smog and acid rain and has gone to the top of the list of human insults to Earth's atmosphere. Assaulted by a potent brew of chlorine-containing chemicals released over the last 60 years, Earth's ozone shield—a thin veil of molecules in the stratosphere that absorbs the worst of the sun's ultraviolet (UV) rays before they reach the ground—has begun to erode at an alarming pace.

Depending on its severity, ozone depletion could have profound effects on human health, natural ecosystems, the durability of outdoor materials, weather, and even the rate of global warming. Increased incidence of skin cancers and cataracts, reduced crop yields, and disruption of delicate food chains are just some of the known effects of the increase in biologically damaging UV radiation expected to come with a thinner ozone shield.

Chlorofluorocarbons (CFCs), the ubiquitous family of chemicals used as refrigerants and in the manufacture of a host of consumer products from foam insulation to computer chips, are the primary culprits in the ozone's unnatural demise. Over the years, some 20 million tons of CFCs have been released to the atmosphere, where, after a decade or so of random drift, they eventually reach the stratosphere. There, intense sunlight tears them apart, releasing their destructive chlorine. CFCs are tremendously efficient ozone killers; one CFC-spawned chlorine atom can catalyze the destruction of as many as 100,000 ozone molecules.

Ozone destruction proceeds most rapidly at the Earth's poles, where it was first observed in 1985. Over Antarctica, an unfortunate synergy of weather conditions and chlorine chemistry conspires to deplete the strato-

> **Ozone News**
> London, 2/7/92—*Scientists are anticipating a potential three-year gap in satellite collection of data on the ozone layer. NASA's Upper Atmosphere Research Satellite is slated to go out of commission in the mid-1990s. Unless backers of a German satellite, Atmos, find unlikely funding, data will not be gathered until the next planned launch—of the U.S. Earth Observing System—in 1998.*

sphere of more than half of its ozone when the sun returns each spring, creating the infamous Antarctic ozone hole. Beneath the hole, UV intensities two or more times the normal level are common. In the Arctic, a similar but weaker springtime scenario consumes some 10 percent of the north polar ozone.

But the threat to the ozone layer is no longer confined to the poles. Recent findings show that substantial wintertime ozone losses have also occurred over temperate latitudes, where much of the world's population resides. For example, the winter ozone concentra-

tion above northern midlatitudes, a region spanning most of the United States and Canada and much of Europe, fell by 8 percent over the last decade.

Perhaps more importantly, these losses have been found to persist into spring and summer, when solar radiation is greater and UV levels peak. Summertime ozone levels dropped about 3 percent over northern midlatitudes during the 1980s.

And the worst is still to come. For the next decade or so, stratospheric chlorine levels will continue to rise as the ozone-destroying chemicals that remain in the lower atmosphere drift slowly upward. The natural background level of chlorine in the atmosphere, attributed to volcanoes and other natural sources, is 0.6 parts per billion (ppb). Today's chlorine concentrations are nearly six times that level, 3.5 ppb, and still rising at a rate of about 5 percent per year. Assuming worldwide CFC production is curtailed by the year 2000, as required by international treaty (the Montreal Protocol), chlorine levels are expected to peak at approximately 4.1 ppb around the turn of the century.

That much chlorine will push the ozone destruction cycle faster, resulting in double-digit depletion over midlatitudes. The U.S. Environmental Protection Agency (EPA) believes that peak ozone losses over northern midlatitudes will probably reach well over 10 percent. Others have placed loss figures as high as 20–30 percent, a range that the EPA deems unlikely but not impossible.

Healing the ozone layer will take time. When the chemistry of the stratosphere is in balance, oxygen molecules energized by radiation from the sun form ozone at the same rate that ozone

Rising Amounts of CFCs in the Atmosphere, 1976–90

CFC-11

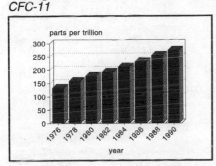

CFC-12

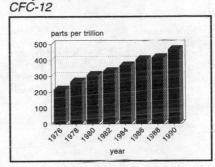

Source: *World Resources 1992–93* (Oxford University Press, New York, 1992), Table 24.3, p. 350.

is removed by naturally occurring chemical reactions. The ozone layer is unlikely to regain equilibrium any time soon. Returning to chlorine levels of 2.0 ppb, the level at which the Antarctic ozone hole first appeared, will probably take 70–80 years if we curtail CFC use on schedule. A more thorough purging to natural background levels will undoubtedly require much longer. Indeed, some 6 percent of CFCs now in the atmosphere are expected to persist intact beyond the year 2300.

In the meantime, learning to live with our legacy of atmospheric insult will mean redefining our relationship with the outdoors. This will entail spending less time outside and donning protective gear when we do venture out. Parents will need to be careful that their children are protected from sunburn. For all of us, the hat, shades, and sunscreen that earlier seemed optional are fast becoming mandatory.

The Aerosol Factor

As if the projections of faster, more extensive ozone loss were not sobering enough, additional findings over the last year have increased international anxiety.

First, atmospheric researchers have demonstrated that tiny particles called stratospheric aerosols have come to play an important role in ozone depletion. Because they have a large surface area relative to their size, these particles remain aloft—and provide the surfaces upon which the reactions that destroy ozone can take place. This greatly speeds an otherwise piecemeal process.

Several years ago, chemists discovered that stratospheric clouds played a similar but much enhanced role at the poles. The ice particles that make up these clouds act as platforms for reactions that both release chlorine from CFCs and remove ozone-friendly nitrogen compounds that occur naturally in the stratosphere. These nitrogen compounds protect the ozone layer by binding with chlorine atoms and preventing the chain reactions that result in severe ozone depletion.

Stratospheric clouds require extreme cold to form, however, and generally occur only over the north and south poles. This explains why ozone loss at the poles is many times greater than at lower latitudes. Stratospheric aerosols, on the other hand, are ubiqui-

Fighting Ozone Loss: What You Can Do

Like it or not, ozone depleters surround us, from the coolant in your refrigerator to the solvent in your spot remover. In addition to CFCs, hydrochlorofluorocarbons (HCFCs), carbon tetrachloride, methyl chloroform, halons, and bromine contribute to destruction of ozone. No one wants to be an unwitting agent in the ozone layer's destruction, but being an ozone-friendly consumer takes effort and attention. Here are some tips:

1. *Repair and maintain your auto air conditioner.* Auto air conditioners are notoriously leaky, accounting for perhaps 20 percent of CFC emissions in the United States, where some 130 million units are on the road. Have your system checked regularly for leaks. At accredited service stations, recycling of the coolant is now common practice. Before you leave your car for servicing, make sure your station routinely captures and recycles the used CFCs.

2. *Service and dispose of your refrigerator or home air conditioner responsibly.* Virtually every home refrigerator currently on the market uses CFCs as the coolant, and most home air conditioners use HCFCs. If yours needs repair, make sure the service company captures and recycles the coolant. If it is beyond repair, contact the manufacturer about proper disposal or find a local service shop that can help you drain the coolant.

3. *Avoid halon fire extinguishers.* Some 30 percent of home fire extinguishers currently in use in the United States are made with halons, which are as much as 10 times more destructive to ozone than CFCs. Halon extinguishers offer no advantage; in fact, dry-chemical extinguishers work better. If you already have a halon extinguisher, store it until a reclamation program becomes available.

4. *Choose fiberglass or cellulose insulation.* CFCs are used to manufacture most rigid polyurethane foam insulation, though manufacturers are rapidly switching to alternatives. Until rigid insulation is certifiably CFC-free, use fiberglass or cellulose.

5. *Avoid products containing methyl chloroform, also known as 1,1,1-trichloroethane.* Unfortunately, a wide variety of consumer products, including bug sprays, fabric protectors, and spot removers, contain this lesser-known ozone depleter. Look for it on the label.

In time, ozone-friendly consuming will become easier. Manufacturers are rapidly switching to CFC alternatives, and frequently advertise that fact. Government labeling laws will also help. By May 1993, U.S. law will require manufacturers to label products containing CFCs, halons, carbon tetrachloride, or methyl chloroform. Unfortunately, HCFCs, to which many manufacturers are switching, will not require labeling until the year 2015.

tous and are especially common over the temperate latitudes, where, for example, sulfate aerosols from the burning of fossil fuels are present at high levels. By taking into account the way these aerosols behave chemically, atmospheric scientists can partially explain how ozone loss may occur over temperate and perhaps even tropical latitudes where stratospheric clouds do not form.

These findings took on even greater importance in June 1991 when Mt. Pinatubo in the Philippines erupted, spewing an estimated 20 million tons of sulfate aerosols into the stratosphere. Some scientists believe this massive pulse of aerosols could trigger substantial ozone loss over midlatitudes in the next few years. Ozone levels apparently dipped some 10 percent over the Northern Hemisphere the year after the eruption of Mexico's El Chichon volcano in 1982, which injected only about one third as many sulfate aerosols into the stratosphere as Pinatubo.

Another troubling discovery recently prompted scientists to worry once more about Pinatubo's ozone effects. Observations over the tropics, an area of the stratosphere previously unaffected by ozone loss, showed a distinct ozone decline associated with the additional aerosols. Scientists do not know if the loss is caused by chlorine added to the atmosphere through human activity or results from other disruptions in natural ozone cycles. Nonetheless, the decline is real, and worrisome in that it may indicate another blind spot in our understanding of how the atmosphere behaves.

A Northern Ozone Hole?

Six months after the Pinatubo eruption, the year's most disturbing ozone news seemed to confirm scientists' fears that the other shoe was about to drop. Researchers detected chlorine monoxide, the chemical directly responsible for ozone destruction, in extremely high concentrations over populated northern latitudes far to the south of the pole. In addition, scientists found reduced levels of protective nitrogen compounds in the same regions. Volcanic aerosols from Pinatubo were thought to have contributed to these effects, but not to be wholly to blame.

The high chlorine levels observed raised the possibility that rapid ozone depletion could take place in the next few years over northern regions of North America, Europe, and Asia—in

Global Ozone Loss
(amount of peak depletion)

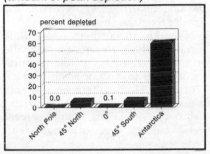

percent depleted

Source: Adapted from World Meteorological Organization (WMO) and United Nations Environment Programme (UNEP), "Scientific Assessment of Stratospheric Ozone, 1991," executive summary (WMO, October 22, 1991), pp. 2 and 4.

effect, creating a northern "ozone hole," with ozone losses of 30–40 percent possible within the hole. At the time of the measurements, the area beneath the potential hole included populous regions of Canada, New England, Scandinavia, Russia, Germany, and even parts of Britain and France.

Fortunately, the combination of factors that allows rapid ozone loss—extreme cold, the presence of ozone-eating chemicals, and sunlight—did not persist long enough to form a full-blown ozone hole. A warm spell in January 1992 kept Arctic ozone losses to about 10 percent.

The unseasonably warm temperatures cut short the cycle of ozone loss by disrupting the Arctic vortex—an air mass over the north pole so cold that stratospheric ice clouds can form. The ice clouds chemically "prime" the surrounding stratosphere for rapid ozone loss. For the severe ozone depletion typical of an ozone hole to occur, this vortex must remain relatively stable and cold in springtime, when sunlight returns to drive the chain reactions that ultimately consume ozone. In general, the longer the frigid vortex persists, the greater the ozone loss will be.

Though no northern ozone hole formed in 1992, researchers find little reason for optimism. Satellite measurements show that ozone levels over the Northern Hemisphere as a whole dipped to a new low in January and February 1992, falling 10 to 15 percent below average over northern midlatitude regions.

Moreover, scientists warn that sometime within the next decade the Arctic vortex will probably persist long enough for a northern ozone hole to form. This year's vortex reached the critical cold temperatures for only 39 days, but the average Arctic vortex maintains its cold for almost 70 days. Some years, the cold vortex has lasted 100 days or more. To make matters worse, stratospheric chlorine levels are still rising, which will allow ozone loss to progress more rapidly when the right atmospheric conditions do occur. Even if no ozone hole forms this spring, researchers warn, the chances are good that sometime within the next decade, the arctic vortex will persist long enough for a northern ozone hole to form.

Human and Environmental Effects

As the ozone shield thins, greater amounts of biologically damaging UV radiation—known as UV-B—are expected to reach Earth's surface, leading to a variety of ill effects. Among humans, for example, the DNA damage that excessive UV-B causes is expected to increase the risk of skin cancer and cataracts.

The United Nations Environment Programme estimates that sustained

Under the Hole Down Under

What will life be like under an ozone-depleted sky? Australia, which is already subject to infusions of ozone-poor air when the Antarctic vortex breaks up each spring, may be a good example of what lies in store for many Northern Hemisphere residents.

Both public policy and personal habits have begun to change down under in response to the threat of increasing UV exposure. The incidence of skin cancer among fair-skinned Australians is already very high, so the Australian government now issues alerts when UV levels are expected to be dangerous. The government has begun public awareness campaigns about the dangers of exposure to the sun and the need to use protective measures.

Sun-conscious policy has even reached the schoolyard, where the government has mandated hats as required equipment for schoolchildren playing outside. Efforts are also under way to plant more shade trees on school grounds and to adjust student schedules to avoid outdoor activities during the sunniest times of the day.

exposure to the extra UV associated with a 10 percent ozone loss—a very real possibility within just a few years—could eventually result in a 26 percent increase in the incidence of nonmelanoma skin cancers, or about 300,000 new cases per year worldwide. At the same time, about 1.6 million new cataract cases would be expected per year. Excessive UV exposure has also been linked to suppression of the human immune system, possibly increasing the risk of contracting infectious diseases.

While the impact of higher UV levels on human health will be great, the effects on other organisms and ecosystems will be even more widespread.

OZONE DEPLETION

These effects are not yet well understood, but the evidence points to substantial possible damage.

Studies have shown that UV radiation can impair photosynthesis and plant metabolism in a number of species, including many important food crops, such as soybeans, potatoes, beans, and sugar beets. In Australia, where UV levels have already climbed as a result of the country's proximity to the Antarctic ozone hole, plant scientists have reported damage to wheat, sorghum, and pea crops as well. Many tree species, such as the loblolly pine common in the southeastern United States, also show UV sensitivity, sparking concern that forest productivity may decline as UV levels rise.

Marine ecosystems, which account for much of the productivity from photosynthesis at the base of the world's food webs, may be particularly vulnerable to damage by increased UV-B, which can penetrate beneath the ocean surface. All other wildlife in Antarctica depends on the health of various plankton species. But a recent study found that the high UV levels under the ozone hole suppressed the productivity of the plankton at the base of the Antarctic food chain by 6–12 percent. Moreover, some species were more resistant to UV damage, raising the likelihood that these more UV-resistant plankton populations will become dominant as less resistant species die out, further upsetting the region's delicately balanced food chain.

Pollution Protection

In an ironic twist, some atmospheric pollutants may actually decrease the amount of UV-B reaching the surface, partially offsetting the effects of ozone depletion. For instance, sulfate aerosols from power plants and other in-

Sources of CFCs
(percent)

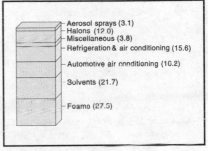

Aerosol sprays (3.1)
Halons (12.0)
Miscellaneous (3.8)
Refrigeration & air conditioning (15.6)
Automotive air conditioning (16.2)
Solvents (21.7)
Foams (27.5)

Source: U.S. Environmental Protection Agency, 1991.
Note: Totals do not add to 100 percent due to rounding.

dustries form a haze that scatters sunlight, cutting surface UV levels as much as 18 percent in some heavily industrialized areas. Volcanic aerosols from Mt. Pinatubo will presumably increase this UV scattering, even as they help to destroy the ozone shield.

The increasing concentration of ozone lower in the atmosphere also offsets the effects of stratospheric ozone loss. Though ozone is the prime ingredient of photochemical smog and thus a serious pollutant in the lower atmosphere, it still performs its UV-absorbing role and may block as much as 10 percent of the UV that would otherwise strike the surface.

These pollution effects are thought to be the reason that the expected increases in UV due to ozone thinning have not as yet been detected in urban areas of the United States and elsewhere. As emission controls for a variety of air pollutants become more effective in the future and pollution levels fall, scientists expect surface UV levels to climb, perhaps more quickly than previously anticipated.

Protecting Yourself

Ozone depletion will be with us for the next century or so, so start protecting yourself now from the dangers posed by rising UV levels. Besides sunburn and premature aging, skin can become cancerous from solar radiation. One in six Americans (600,000 a year) will develop skin cancer, 90 percent as a result of overexposure to the sun.

The damaging rays are not necessarily hot, nor do shade and clouds necessarily protect you. UV light can reflect off sand, snow, water, or patio floors. Three quarters of the burning power can penetrate clouds and under water. The sun can burn through gauzy clothes and wet t-shirts.

For the most part, these strategies for avoiding the sun's ill effects are the same ones dermatologists have been recommending for years:

- Reduce exposure during midday, when UV levels are highest—between 10 AM and 3 PM.

- When work or recreation takes you outdoors, wear protective clothing, such as broad-brimmed hats, long-sleeved shirts, and tightly woven fabrics.

- When you go outside, use sunscreen with a protection factor of 15 or higher on any exposed skin.

- Don't tan with sunlamps.

- Wear sunglasses treated to absorb UV. The combination of hat and sunglasses dramatically cuts the amount of UV damage to the eyes, reducing the risk of cataract formation.

Danger: Melanoma

Because of a 20- to 30-year lag between UV exposure and cancer development, most basal cell or squamous cell skin cancers (which make up 95 percent of all skin cancer types) are not discovered until later in life. However, a child or adolescent with only one severe sunburn has double the normal chance of developing these cancers. Melanomas, which make up 5 percent of diagnosed U.S. skin cancers but account for 75 percent of related deaths, are growing at the rate of 4 percent per year. In the 30 years after 1950, malignant melanomas increased by 500 percent. In 1992 alone, the American Academy of Dermatology estimated 32,000 new cases of malignant melanoma would be discovered—one quarter of which in persons aged 39 or younger.

The fair-skinned, especially blond or red-headed, are most at risk and should always take such precautions as using sunscreen and wearing hats and loose clothing that covers the skin when out in the sun. People who take antibiotics or birth control pills may discover they are more susceptible to sunburn. Even people with dark skin should be aware of their risk for damage from the sun.

Tanning is a natural defense system against sunburn. The ability to produce melanin, the brown-black granules in the skin that appear as a tan, is different for everyone. The darker the skin, the more melanin present. The most melanin protection high-risk people can produce amounts to scattered freckles on pale skin. Blacks, with the greatest amount, are at low risk for skin cancer.

Interestingly, some of ozone depletion's most profound effects may stem not from higher UV levels but from a change in the heat balance in the upper atmosphere that occurs as ozone levels drop. When ozone molecules intercept UV radiation, they generate heat, making the stratosphere warmer than the atmosphere beneath. This juxtaposition of warm and cool helps to create the stratospheric winds that drive global weather patterns. As ozone depletion has progressed, scientists have found that the lower stratosphere,

Protecting Yourself *(continued)*

How Sunscreen Works

Sunscreen absorbs, reflects, or scatters the sun's ultraviolet rays similar to the way melanin does. Most suncreens protect against both UV-A and UV-B, although the latter is responsible for most skin damage. The number on a sunscreen bottle (the sun protection factor or SPF) represents a multiple of the time (beyond the normal amount when no sunscreen has been applied) that a person may stay in the sun before getting burned. For example, a person who would normally get a burn in just 30 minutes' exposure would be protected for 2 hours with an SPF4. The higher the SPF, the more protection is provided. (See table, SPF Protection.)

All SPF ratings are based on using 1 ounce of sunscreen product, which comes as a surprise to many. The common practice of using less than the recommended amount simply means that the user gets significantly less effective protection.

The Benefits of Sunglasses

Skin is not the only organ damaged by too much sun. Eyes are vulnerable, too. UV-B, the shortest wavelength of light, has been linked to cataracts, an opaquing of the eye's lens. These rays also damage the cornea, but it repairs itself quickly. Prolonged exposure may also contribute to a retinal disease that causes blindness in people over 60.

Contrary to rumors that sunglasses may dilate the pupil without filtering UV rays, even dark sunglasses dilate only slightly and even cheap sunglasses filter effectively, according to tests by *Consumer Reports* magazine. People whose cataracts have been removed, or those taking drugs that increase their eyes' sensitivity to sunlight, need to be sure their sunglasses prevent damage. For the most protection from both UV-A and UV-B, however, *Consumer Reports* recommends buying glasses that "absorb UV up to 400 nm."

For More Information

If you want to find out more about how to prevent skin cancer from overexposure to the sun, call the American Cancer Society toll free at (800) 227-2345 or send a SASE to the American Academy of Dermatology, 930 Meacham Road, P.O. Box 681069, Shaumburg, Illinois 60168-1069.

To review *Consumer Reports'* study of sunscreen effectiveness, see the June 1988 issue; for UV protection from sunglasses, see the August 1988 issue.

Sun Protection Factors in Sunscreens

SPF Level	Protection from Sunburn	Tanning Level Allowed
2 – less than 4	Minimal	Permits tanning
4 – less than 6	Moderate	Some
6 – less than 8	Extra	Limited
8 – less than 15	Maximal	Little or none
15 or greater	Most	None

Source: Food and Drug Administration advisory panel.

where ozone depletion is centered, has become cooler, raising concerns that the world climate system may be thrown off kilter.

But the stratospheric cooling may also have an unanticipated benefit by helping to offset the global warming expected from the increase in greenhouse gases that has occurred over the last 200 years. Ozone losses may have already masked a portion of the current greenhouse warming, and climate modelers predict they may have to lower their estimates of eventual global warming by as much as 20 percent. (See "Greenhouse Warming" chapter.)

The International Response

One bright spot in this year's ozone story is the alarm and, in some cases, quick action these findings have evoked among many international policymakers. Over the last several years, the international community has responded relatively quickly to the steadily worsening ozone prognosis.

In 1990, the Montreal Protocol, the landmark treaty regulating emissions of ozone-depleting chemicals, was tightened to provide a complete phaseout of most ozone-eating compounds by the year 2000. Further treaty negotiations are set for November 1992, and it is widely expected that phaseout schedules will be moved up, perhaps to 1996 or 1997. It is also possible that new requirements for the eventual phaseout of HCFCs—less harmful but still destructive substitutes for CFCs—will be added to the treaty.

In the meantime, several nations have acted unilaterally to further restrict their use of CFCs and other ozone-depleting substances and shorten the timetable for ending their production. Germany, for instance, will ban CFC production after 1994. Both the United States and Canada have promised to phase out CFCs by 1996. Such actions, if widely adopted and faithfully applied, could help hold down future ozone losses and hasten the day when chlorine concentrations return to safe levels.

Aiding the rapid phaseout of CFCs is the surprising ease with which some industries, such as computer chip makers and polystyrene manufacturers, have been able to find CFC alternatives. The wider marketing of chemical substitutes, such as HCFCs and hydrofluorocarbons (HFCs), has also begun to drive down worldwide CFC use, which is reported to have declined some 40 percent in the last five years. These CFC mimics are finding increasing use in the refrigeration industry, which has had a rougher time than most in weaning itself from CFCs.

The downside is that many of these substitutes are not completely benign themselves. HCFCs do still release chlorine—though only at a fraction of the rate of CFCs—and HFCs, while they do not contain chlorine, are potent greenhouse gases. (See graph, Sources of CFCs.) The regulation and eventual phaseout of CFC substitutes are thus increasingly controversial, even though all parties agree they must eventually be retired.

While experts in atmospheric science hone their predictions concerning the trends in loss of Earth's ozone, the global community will continue to make its own response. In some regions, this will likely mean a change in lifestyle where vacations, work, and recreation are typically experienced outdoors—in direct exposure to harmful UV radiation. Current changes in the atmosphere are indeed affecting the way we perceive the outdoors, altering a centuries-old pattern.

This chapter was compiled by Gregory Mock, a science writer in Ben Lomond, California.

Greenhouse Warming

New findings illuminate our complex atmosphere as it responds to natural and human forces.

At the Earth Summit in 1992, 153 countries signed the United Nations Framework Convention on Climate Change requiring them to use their best efforts to halt the growth in emissions of the greenhouse gases that are warming Earth's atmosphere. Additional countries are expected to sign later. The treaty does not set binding targets or require specific actions—largely at the insistence of the United States. But it nonetheless marks the first time that nations have formally recognized that human activities are threatening to alter the climate and have committed themselves in principle to take steps to deal with the problem. Thus, the treaty may prove an important precedent, establishing a legal framework—and possibly a stronger moral obligation—for protection of the atmosphere, one of Earth's great global commons.

The immediate impact of the treaty is likely to be modest. It calls for—but does not require—stabilizing emissions of greenhouse gases at 1990 levels in the industrial countries by the end of the century. An international body of scientists—the United Nations' Intergovernmental Panel on Climate

What Is the Greenhouse Effect?

Although much remains unknown about Earth's atmosphere, some properties are known with certainty. One of these is that trace gases trap heat near Earth's surface, much as the glass panels of a greenhouse allow sunlight to enter and trap heat inside. This property is called the greenhouse effect. Without the naturally occurring gases, especially water vapor and carbon dioxide, Earth's average temperature would be much lower, and conditions here would be much less suitable for human life. Other important greenhouse gases are methane, chlorofluorocarbons and hydrogenated chlorofluorocarbons, ozone, and nitrous oxide.

Today's concern about the greenhouse effect arises because concentrations of these gases are building up in the atmosphere at unprecedented rates. Human activities, particularly deforestation and burning of coal, oil, and natural gas, inject billions of tons of carbon into the atmosphere each year. Since the Industrial Revolution began, atmospheric levels of carbon dioxide have increased 25 percent. The concentration of carbon dioxide is increasing by about 0.4 percent each year (see graph, Carbon Dioxide Concentrations in the Atmosphere.) Other trace gases absorb infrared radiation more effectively than carbon dioxide does, but their concentrations are lower. Their combined effect, however, may nearly equal that of carbon dioxide. As global warming occurs, water vapor will increase in the atmosphere, further enhancing the warming process.

The projected increase is likely to occur many times faster than previous natural warmings, and temperatures will be much warmer than most organisms alive today have ever experienced. The actual rate of warming will depend on how quickly concentrations of greenhouse gases increase, natural fluctuations in the climate system, and responses of oceans and glacial ice, which may be considerably delayed.

Researchers trying to predict global warming rely on sophisticated computer models of Earth's climate system. Modelers are working continually to refine their ability to simulate how climate variables like temperature, humidity, wind direction and speed, sea ice, and soil moisture change over time. To gauge a model's credibility, scientists use three tests: Can the model simulate today's climate, including the large swings in temperature that occur with the seasons? Can it simulate individual aspects of the climate system, such as cloudiness? And can it duplicate long-term changes, such as those that produced the varied climates of ancient Earth?

The current models are far from perfect, but they are getting better. They are only tools, however. The real experiment is occurring in the Earth system itself.

Greenhouse Gases and Their Sources

Greenhouse Gas	Sources	Life Span in Atmosphere
Carbon dioxide (CO_2)	Fossil fuels, deforestation, soil destruction	500 years
Methane (CH_4)	Cattle, biomass, rice paddies, gas leaks, mining, termites	7–10 years
Nitrous oxide (N_2O)	Fossil fuels, soil cultivation, deforestation	140–190 years
Chlorofluorocarbons (CFCs 11 and 12)	Refrigeration, air conditioning, aerosols, foam blowing, solvents	65–110 years
Ozone and other trace gases	Photochemical processes, cars, power plants, solvents	Hours to days in upper troposphere

Source: Adapted from Francesca Lyman et al., *The Greenhouse Trap*, World Resources Institute (Beacon Press, Boston, 1990), p. 10.

Change (IPCC)—has estimated that a 60 percent reduction in emissions of gases such as carbon dioxide would be required to keep atmospheric concentrations at present levels. Because such a reduction is not immediately forthcoming, amounts of greenhouse gases in the atmosphere will continue to rise, at least for the foreseeable future.

Just what impact these gases—and their heating effects on the atmosphere—will have on the global climate is still uncertain. Although computer models of climate suggest that continued accumulation of greenhouse gases could warm the climate an average of 2° to 9° F by the middle of the next century, scientists cannot be sure how much warming will occur or how quickly. New research, however, drives home the fact that what occurs in one part of the Earth's system can affect another part in unexpected ways. The findings also highlight how much we have to learn, even as human activities such as combustion of fossil fuels (coal, oil, and natural gas), deforestation, and agriculture continue to change the composition of the atmosphere.

The findings pertain to two other areas of concern about the atmosphere: depletion of Earth's protective ozone

How the Greenhouse Effect Works

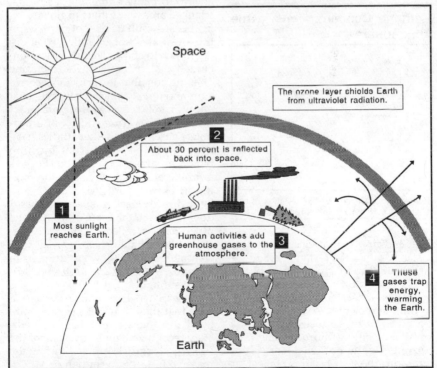

Source: Adapted from Mack/Remillard, *The Christian Science Monitor,* 1988.

Carbon Dioxide Concentrations in the Atmosphere

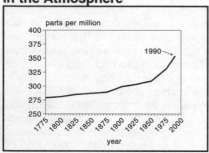

Source: *World Resources 1992–93* (Oxford University Press, New York, 1992), Table 24.3, p. 350.

Methane Concentrations in the Atmosphere

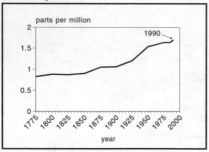

Source: *World Resources 1992–93* (Oxford University Press, New York, 1992), Table 24.3, p. 350.

layer and air pollution closer to Earth's surface. In the first instance, scientists have concluded that depletion of stratospheric ozone—itself a greenhouse gas—cools the atmosphere by an amount sufficient to offset the warming effect of the industrial chemicals known as chlorofluorocarbons (see "Ozone Depletion" chapter). Chlorofluorocarbons (CFCs), proficient at trapping heat, are expected to contrib-

ute about 20 percent of projected global warming. (See table, Greenhouse Gases and Their Sources.)

A Challenge to Scientists

These findings have spurred scientists to rethink how different greenhouse gases may contribute to global warming. (See box, What Is the Greenhouse Effect?) Until recently, it was assumed that international efforts to reduce CFC emissions would reduce greenhouse warming. Now, efforts to control emissions of other major greenhouse gases such as carbon dioxide have acquired greater urgency.

In another pivotal finding, scientists have realized that the pollutants that enshroud many of the world's industrialized areas contribute to global *cooling* because sulfate or soot particles in the lower atmosphere reflect solar energy back to space. The IPCC has concluded that acidic particles (the same ones responsible for acid rain, corrosion, and forest damage) have reflected enough solar energy to counteract much of the warming effect of greenhouse gases so far. Other studies have suggested that soot from burning biomass—grasslands and forests—has a similar effect. About half of the cooling arises from particles reflecting sunlight directly back to space, so that it does not reach the Earth's surface. The other half is reflected indirectly because the sulfate or soot particles increase the number of water droplets in a cloud. The cloud then reflects additional sunlight.

Researchers have known for a long time that these tiny haze particles are good at scattering light. They immediately recognized, for example, that the sulfur-rich particles ejected during the massive June 1991 eruption of Mt. Pinatubo in the Philippines could reflect enough light to cause substantial, though temporary, cooling. The mean surface temperature is expected to drop about 1° F in the next two to four years as a fine mist of sulfuric acid from Pinatubo reduces the amount of sunlight reaching the Earth's surface. (Whether the actual cooling will match expectations will provide researchers with an important test of their climate simulation models.)

The recently discovered additional cooling from the haze of conventional pollutants such as soot and acid particles is an ongoing effect. The cooling may be masking global warming and may continue to offset some of the warming as greenhouse gases accumulate, meaning that temperatures would rise at a slower rate than scientists expected. Paradoxically, the new findings may also mean that as air pollution is

What to Expect from a Warmer Climate

Heat waves, hurricanes, and droughts in recent years offer modern reminders that human society is deeply vulnerable to extreme weather conditions. Such events are likely to be more frequent as the climate warms, but no one can accurately predict the effects of a large and rapid warming in detail. It is likely that Earth's surface temperature will increase unevenly, with regions experiencing change at different times and by different magnitudes. Some regions may benefit, but many are likely to suffer as climate changes transform the world's natural, agricultural, and social systems. A U.S. National Academy of Sciences panel noted recently that the amount of warming projected by the end of the next century "could cause extremely unpleasant surprises." Possible changes include the following:

● *Ecosystems* unable to adapt quickly to warmer conditions may be torn apart.

● *Global precipitation* may increase because of increased evaporation, though some individual regions may experience decreased precipitation.

● *Sea level* is virtually certain to rise as the oceans absorb heat from the atmosphere and expand as a result, and as some land ice melts. The United Nations Intergovernmental Panel on Climate Change predicts an 8-inch rise in global sea level in the next 40 years, with higher levels later if global warm-

ing continues. Even modest increases in sea level would flood coastal areas inhabited by half of the world's people. Rising waters would also jeopardize or inundate some low-lying and island nations, including the Maldives, the Seychelles, and parts of Egypt, Bangladesh, and Indonesia.

● *Soil moisture* in the midlatitude continental areas such as the U.S. corn belt may decrease in summer because warmer temperatures may cause periods of snowmelt and rain to end earlier and evaporation to increase.

● *Tropical storms* may be more frequent and more intense.

● *Northern polar regions* will experience much warmer winter surface temperatures. This could result in thinner sea ice. Higher Arctic temperatures could cause permafrost to thaw gradually, releasing large amounts of methane and amplifying greenhouse warming.

● *Agriculture* will adapt, though markets and food supplies may be disrupted. Some regions and crops will become more competitive, but no one can predict which ones with any certainty. Researchers are trying to assess how plant water use and photosynthesis may change in response to higher carbon dioxide levels.

reduced through the Clean Air Act and other cleanup efforts, global warming will accelerate.

A Warmer 21st Century

Scientists expect that the warming predicted by computer models should be clear within a few decades—well within the life spans of most people living today. The IPCC predicts that the gases already in the atmosphere will boost the average global temperature by about 1.8° F by 2025. By the end of the next century, the temperature could be 10° F warmer than today's temperature. These numbers sound relatively small, but in fact they represent a large increase and a huge change in climate. The last time Earth's temperature was as much as 7° F warmer than today was 40 million years ago; during the last ice age, however, when ice blanketed much of North America, Earth's average temperature was only 9° F cooler than it is today.

In the pattern familiar to scientists trying to understand the atmospheric system, the new research findings answer some questions but raise others. One answer addresses a problem that has troubled scientists for years. The computer models used by researchers to simulate Earth's climate indicate that warming in the Northern Hemisphere due to the added greenhouse gases should be twice as great as actually recorded. Now it appears that the curtain of sulfate particles over industrialized regions may have prevented enough light from reaching Earth's surface to counteract about half of the warming.

This finding increases modelers' confidence that they can, in fact, simulate the climate, at least in general terms. The specific effects of the pollutant screen are unclear, however. Because the haze particles are spread unevenly over the globe, warming may also be uneven, affecting regional precipitation patterns.

The presence of pollutant haze may also help explain why much of the warmer temperatures seem to be occurring at night. Researchers from the United States, the former Soviet Union, and China (which together total 25 percent of Earth's land area) have studied 40 years of climate records from those countries. They have found that average yearly high temperatures changed little or not at all over this period, but that minimum (night) temperatures were considerably higher. One explanation is that the particles reflect solar energy to space only in the daytime, while greenhouse gases absorb heat around the clock. Another possible explanation is that, over North America at least, the lack of warmer daytime temperatures is the result of increased cloudiness that may be due to natural causes or to the warming climate itself.

The recent findings show that ozone depletion, air pollution, and greenhouse warming are not separate phenomena but are closely interconnected. Policy decisions will need to take the whole picture into account.

Greenhouse News

San Diego, 7/16/92—*A new study reveals that temperatures in the top layer of the ocean off southern California have increased by about 1° F over the last 42 years. Dean Roemmich, professor at the Scripps Institution of Oceanography and author of the report, is not certain whether the warming is a result of natural climate changes or human activity, such as the greenhouse effect. But, he said, accelerated warming and sea level rise cause concerns for coastal flooding.*

Slowing the Trend

The projected warming poses an unprecedented challenge to world leaders who must make decisions that will affect conditions in unknowable ways for generations to come. The dramatic and unexpected depletion of stratospheric ozone over Earth's poles provides a useful parallel. Twenty years ago, scientists warned that CFCs were destroying the ozone layer that shields the planet from damaging ultraviolet radiation. Only minor steps were taken to control CFC emissions, until it became clear in 1985 that ozone depletion was well under way; now it will take more than 50 years for the ozone layer to fully recover. In the case of greenhouse gases, policymakers again must decide whether to wait for evidence or act now, buying time for Earth's social and natural systems to adapt. Because greenhouse gases such as carbon dioxide and nitrous oxide remain in the atmosphere for many decades, scientists believe we are already committed to some warming.

Sources of Greenhouse Gases

The most important greenhouse gas, carbon dioxide, is emitted when fossil fuels are burned and when land, including tropical forest, is cleared for agriculture. Rates at which carbon dioxide has built up in the atmosphere closely parallel our use of energy, which has risen continuously since the beginnings of industrialization. Over the past 20 years, efforts to increase energy efficiency have slowed the growth of energy use in some industrial countries, but the spread of industrialization around the globe has insured continued increases in carbon dioxide emissions.

Fossil fuel combustion and other industrial operations such as the manufacture of cement make up the largest single source of global CO_2 buildup. The United States releases the most at more than 5 billion tons every year. It is also the largest "climate polluter" of carbon dioxide from industrial sources on a per capita basis, nearly 22 tons annually for each U.S. inhabitant, compared with less than 3 tons per capita for Chinese citizens. After the United States, the largest emitters are the former Soviet Union, China, Japan, Germany, and India. The western industrial countries account for about 47 percent of the global total, while the former Soviet Union plus Central Europe account for 23 percent. (See table, Top 15 Countries for Carbon Dioxide Releases.) In the United States, electric utilities are the greatest source of CO_2, followed closely by transporta-

Top 15 Countries for Carbon Dioxide Releases
(1989 industrial emissions)

Country	Total CO_2 Emissions (million tons)
United States	5,365,644
Soviet Union, former	4,192,009
China	2,632,252
Japan	1,146,691
Germany [a]	1,062,359
India	718,433
United Kingdom	626,433
Canada	501,994
Poland	485,904
Italy	429,501
France	393,594
Mexico	352,312
South Africa	306,872
Australia	283,743
Czechoslovakia	249,434

Source: *World Resources 1992–93* (Oxford University Press, New York, 1992), Table 13.6, p. 211.
Note: a. Data for Germany include the former Federal Republic of Germany and the German Democratic Republic.

U.S. CO$_2$ Emissions, by Sector
(percent, 1987)

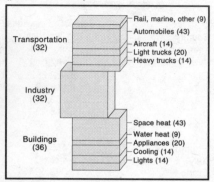

Transportation (32)
- Rail, marine, other (9)
- Automobiles (43)
- Aircraft (14)
- Light trucks (20)
- Heavy trucks (14)

Industry (32)

Buildings (36)
- Space heat (43)
- Water heat (9)
- Appliances (20)
- Cooling (14)
- Lights (14)

Source: U.S. Congress, Office of Technology Assessment, *Changing by Degrees: Steps to Reduce Greenhouse Gases* (OTA-0-482, Washington, DC: U.S. Government Printing Office, 1991), Figure 1-4, p. 8.

tion (such as cars and trucks); each produces one third of CO$_2$ emissions in the United States. (See graph, U.S. CO$_2$ Emissions, by Sector.)

Land use practices such as burning forests for agriculture in developing countries also contribute substantially to the potential for global warming. Efforts of developing countries to raise their standards of living are likely to increase industrial emissions of carbon dioxide from those regions in coming decades, even though per capita emissions are still far below those in industrial countries.

To stabilize atmospheric levels of carbon dioxide any time soon and thus avoid the risks of global warming, therefore, would require drastic cuts in the use of fossil fuels in industrial countries such as the United States—actions that go far beyond those contemplated in the Convention on Climate Change. More likely, even with conservation efforts to keep emis-

sions from industrial countries from rising, we are likely to incur the risk of a significant amount of global warming. Eventually, switching to new, nonfossil sources of energy may be required to keep global warming within tolerable limits.

Costs of Action and Inaction

Many scientists believe that despite uncertainties about the timing and magnitude of the projected warming, there is enough evidence and risk to warrant broad efforts to slow the atmospheric buildup of greenhouse gases, thereby slowing the expected warming. Such efforts could buy time for people and other natural systems to adapt. The costs of these efforts are difficult to estimate, however, and are a topic of heated debate.

In a recent study, Institute of International Economics economist William R. Cline argues that estimates of the potential damage from climate change, already high by most standards, are far too low. The problem, Cline points out, is that most estimates, based on climate models, focus on warming caused by a "benchmark doubling" of carbon dioxide. This expression refers to the accumulation of carbon dioxide and other greenhouse gases at levels that together trap heat equivalent to a doubling of carbon dioxide alone. The carbon dioxide concentration will not reach twice its preindustrial level for some time, but the benchmark doubling could occur by 2025, and the corresponding warming by 2050, because of the ocean's delayed response.

The benchmark doubling is an arbitrary level, however, and atmospheric accumulations of greenhouse gases—and the prospective warming—will continue if nothing is done to limit the growth of emissions. "The IPCC itself

Per Capita Carbon Dioxide Emissions
(top 15 countries, 1989)

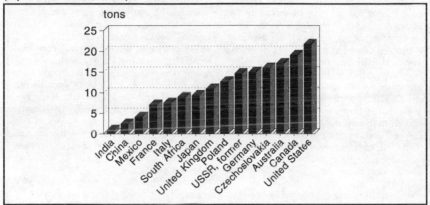

Source: Carbon Dioxide Information Analysis Center (CDIAC), Oak Ridge National Laboratory, unpublished data (CDIAC, Oak Ridge, Tennessee, August 1989).

calculates that, under business as usual, the commitment to warming would reach 5.7° C [10.3° F] by the year 2100," Cline writes. He adds that further warming would be likely to continue through at least the year 2300, when deep ocean mixing could begin to partially reverse the greenhouse gas buildup. At this level, an increase of 18° F is possible.

With this grim reminder, Cline presents new estimates of the costs of global warming. Overall U.S. impacts including agricultural losses from heat stress and drought, sea-level rise, forest losses, and increased human mortality caused by heat stress would cost nearly $60 billion if the average global temperature increased 4.5° F. Damages would be higher if warming continued over the very long term. Cline estimates that an 18° F warming could cost six times as much.

While the Bush administration has argued that efforts to limit carbon dioxide emissions would be too expensive,

Cline and others, including government analysts, environmentalists, scientists, and economists, say that the efforts could save or even make money in the long run. A recent study by four major environmental groups examined the role that energy efficiency and renewable energy technologies could play in reducing environmental damages caused by global warming. Aggressive actions over the next 40 years could cost about $2.7 trillion—but could *save* consumers and industry $5 trillion in fuel and electricity costs. Low-tech solutions can have a significant impact as well. The U.S. National Academy of Sciences suggests that the United States could reduce or offset its greenhouse gas emissions by 10 to 40 percent of 1990 levels at little or no cost, or at some net savings.

Reductions in the near future can be achieved by exploiting the best technologies available, improving energy efficiency, and enhancing efforts to conserve energy at all levels of society.

Can Forests Migrate?

Climate changes have occurred repeatedly throughout Earth's history, but the amount of warming possible in the next century may occur 10 times faster than any warming trend in the past 10,000 years. The biosphere has adjusted to warming and cooling before, but at a gradual pace. Scientists do not know how quickly ecosystems and species can adapt, and they are worried that many species of plants and animals will not be able to migrate to cooler climates fast enough to survive. Some members of ecosystems may successfully relocate, but others may perish. Thus, ecosystems may re-form in other locations in new combinations.

Researchers who studied forest responses to previous warmings estimate that the ranges of the eastern hemlock, yellow birch, beech, and sugar maple, for example, would gradually shift 300 to 600 miles north if carbon dioxide concentrations double their pre-industrial levels in the next century as predicted. Most adult trees could grow at their present locations for several decades, but growth rates would slow, and seedlings at the southern ends of the ranges would not survive. In the north part of the ranges, the species would mostly die out, and so would the other plants and animals that live within the forest habitats.

Rapid warming would jeopardize species in a variety of ways. Some species require a narrow range of temperature and moisture. Monarch butterflies, which winter in Mexico's mountains, and edelweiss, which grows in a narrow zone on the Alps, are two species whose habitats could be erased by warming. Coastal wetlands and mangrove swamps could be flooded by rising seas. Northern species such as the polar bear and walrus would have nowhere to migrate and would disappear. What's more, wildlife reserves around the world, designed to protect a diversity of species, would become useless because many resident species would be forced to migrate. Some species might succeed in this effort, but others, thwarted not only by inhospitable temperature and moisture but by human barriers, would perish.

Perhaps the greatest reason for concern is that ecosystems are important themselves in maintaining a stable atmosphere because they transfer energy and absorb and emit gases. Member plants, trees, animals, and microbes are often interdependent, and the absence or removal of a key member may cause the collapse of the ecosystem, which could weaken the whole global web of life.

World Wildlife Fund International notes the types of ecosystems at greatest risk include coral reefs, mangroves, Arctic seas, coastal wetlands, Arctic tundra, mountain ecosystems, savannas, and tropical forests.

This trend is already under way, as industry and utilities attempt to streamline operations and increase profits. The track record for changes in energy use through conservation is already well established. Between 1973 and 1986, U.S. energy consumption remained level while CO_2 emissions dropped, all in a time of rapid economic expansion.

The threat of greenhouse warming is a new kind of environmental concern. It is global, potentially affecting temperatures, rainfall patterns, and sea levels in virtually all countries. It is also long term, with the consequences of today's actions or inactions felt most strongly by generations still to come.

Author Cheryl Simon Silver, a Maryland-based writer, is senior editor of the 1993 *Information Please Environmental Almanac.*

Land Degradation

Human activity has so altered the Earth's landscape that in many places soils are degraded, forests and species are disappearing, and the productive capacity of the planet is at risk.

Despite the refusal of the Bush administration to sign the Convention on Biological Diversity at the 1992 Earth Summit in Rio de Janeiro, the treaty did attract significant support. (See "State of the Planet" chapter.) Widespread adoption of the Convention endorses the recognition that humankind is increasingly responsible for the biological future of the planet—a future that may be threatened. The Convention also marks a first step toward the preservation of the millions of different species inhabiting the Earth—the rich genetic heritage produced by 3 billion years of evolution—and of the thou-sands of ecosystems functioning in intricate networks that support the Earth's biological productivity.

Humanity thrives within the biosphere, a thin veneer of interacting animal, plant, fungal, and bacterial life that clings to the Earth's surface. For most of the time our human ancestors walked the Earth, their activities produced only local and short-lived consequences. In the last 40 years, however, human activities have changed the face of the Earth to such a degree and at such a rate that the planet's capacity to support many forms of life is being drastically altered.

Many researchers have become convinced in recent years that the components of the Earth work together as a system. In this view, trees and plants, as well as microbes in bodies of water and on land, interact with the oceans and atmosphere to maintain a stable climate, cleanse the air and waterways, and help form the soils and hold them in place. No one knows if, or at what point, the gradual disruption and loss of ecosystems will affect the general health of the biosphere.

Among the most recognizable changes to the Earth are the increasing areas of degraded and deforested land and the loss of species diversity. While local crises might be well documented, the global rate of these losses could only be guessed at until data were collected from around the world. Recent assessments offer valuable insights into the degree to which human activities have altered the biosphere.

Land Degradation News
Bhopal, India, 8/4/92—The Madhya Pradesh government in central India has proposed a new plan to help stop desertification. The state plans to spend about $800,000 on afforestation projects and the development of fodder farms, green belts, and lakes. The project will begin in the western part of the state.

Soil Degradation

At the bottom of the land-based food chains that connect regal, solitary predators to the simplest bacteria lies the soil. Humans became aware of soil's importance with the development of agriculture. Early on, the first farmers learned the dangers of losing soil and the benefits of practicing soil conservation.

Throughout history, societies have suffered from incidents of local or regional land degradation. One of the world's first civilizations flourished, for instance, through irrigation of the Euphrates River plain beginning as early as 4100 B.C. By 1700 B.C., the once-fertile lowlands were abandoned because the over-irrigated soils had become too salty for growing crops.

The pace of land degradation has accelerated since World War II, as rapidly increasing numbers of people try to meet their needs for food and fuel. A recent study sponsored by the United Nations Environment Programme found that over the last 45 years, 11 percent of the Earth's plant-supporting soils had been degraded to the point that their original biotic function—their ability to process nutrients into a form that plants can use—had been partially destroyed. (See table, Degraded Lands around the World, 1945–90.) This area, nearly 3 billion acres, is as large as the combined areas of China and India. Reclamation, where possible, is expensive and often beyond the means of individual farmers.

Degraded Lands around the World, 1945–90
(million acres)

Region	Total Degraded Area
World	4,854.0
Europe	540.9
Africa	1,221.2
Asia	1,845.8
Oceania	254.3
North America	236.0
Central America and Mexico	155.2
South America	601.4

Source: *World Resources 1992–93* (Oxford University Press, New York, 1992), Table 8.1, p. 112.

Another 1.8 billion acres of soil have been lightly degraded. This means that biotic activity is still intact and the soil can be restored through farm conservation methods that can be applied by individual efforts. In all, 17 percent of all vegetated land on Earth has suffered some degree of degradation.

Poor agricultural practices, overgrazing, and deforestation all contribute to land degradation. (See graph, Causes of World Soil Degradation.) An estimated 28 percent of land degradation has been caused by incorrect cultivation of hillsides, which causes water erosion. When fields are allowed to lie fallow without protective ground cover, wind erosion increases. The modern machinery designed to lighten the farmer's burden is too heavy for fragile soils. When soil is compacted by heavy weight, the structure of the soil itself may change. As the soil is compressed, it becomes less porous, which discourages root growth and encourages water runoff and erosion.

In North America, most land degradation is related to agriculture, especially the misuse of modern farming technologies. Irrigation systems, for instance, require that certain amounts of water be applied at certain times and drained away at other times. If too little water is supplied, salts build up in the soil; if there is too much water, crops may drown. Insufficient drainage may draw salts up into the root zone, while drainage that is too rapid may erode the topsoil.

Improper use—including overuse—of chemical fertilizers, pesticides, and herbicides also degrade the soil. These agricultural chemicals were developed to encourage growth, eliminate pests, and kill weeds. (See graphs, Cropland Chemicals in the United States and Canada.) But too much fertilizer can make the soil overly acidic, and pesticides can kill soil bacteria essential for nutrient recycling.

Causes of World Soil Degradation
(percent)

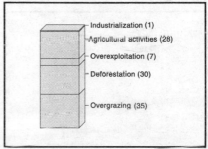

- Industrialization (1)
- Agricultural activities (28)
- Overexploitation (7)
- Deforestation (30)
- Overgrazing (35)

Source: *World Resources 1992–93* (Oxford University Press, New York, 1992), Figure 8.2, p. 114.

Overgrazing is responsible for 35 percent of global soil degradation. When animals crop their pastures too low, new growth is inhibited, grasses and legumes do not reseed, and the nutrient-rich topsoil is exposed to wind erosion. Compaction by animals that trample the ground reduces the number of small pores between particles where water and air accumulate. Thus, when rain falls, less water enters the soil, running instead along the surface and eroding the topsoil. Overgrazing is the dominant cause of soil degradation in Africa, and it is also an important cause of degradation elsewhere. (See box, Australia's Soils.)

In developing countries, the numbers of cattle, sheep, and goats have been increasing since the 1950s. Improved veterinary practices mean more animals survive disease and injury; expanding human populations mean more herds. Unfortunately, the amount of good pasture has not increased proportionally. Instead, herds graze marginally productive lands or

Cropland Chemicals in the United States and Canada

Fertilizers

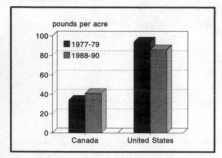

Pesticides

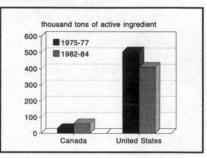

Source: *World Resources 1992–93* (Oxford University Press, New York, 1992), Table 8.2, p. 274.

are restricted to smaller areas. Overgrazing is also a problem in Canada and the United States, where it causes 30 percent of the soil degradation.

Deforestation

Deforestation degrades the soil more intensively than any other activity. An estimated 40 percent of soil degradation in Asia and 41 percent in South America is the result of deforestation, including both careless logging practices and land clearing for agriculture. Deforestation in some parts of North America has geologists debating some odd, long-term effects to soil surfaces. (See box, "Good Fences" or Rock Dumps?)

The worst damage to soil results from current methods used to remove the forest cover. First, heavy logging machinery or bulldozers destroy soil structure. After trees are cleared, the tract is often burned. Some of the nutrients from the burning plant cover quickly reenter the soil as ash. But these mobile nutrients also leach out rapidly, so that initial bumper crops drop off after a few harvests. What nutrients remain after wind or water erosion can

hardly permeate the compacted and sometimes chemically-altered crust.

The United Nations Food and Agriculture Organization has released preliminary results from a global forest study that considered tropical deforestation from land clearing between 1981 and 1990. It found that the world is losing its tropical forests at the alarming rate of almost 42 million acres per year, an increase of 50 percent from an estimate made a decade earlier. This means that nearly 1.3 acres of tropical forest disappear every second. The largest areas of forest loss occurred in Latin America, followed by Africa. However, when deforestation is measured as a percentage of the remaining forest, the most losses occurred in Asia, where 1.2 percent of the forest was destroyed per year during the 1980s. (See table, Deforestation around the World.) At the current rate, tropical forests will be gone within 115 years.

Tropical forests can be economically valuable, but they are also biologically valuable as habitat for the most diverse forms of life on the planet. Rainforests in particular—among the various types of tropical forests—sup-

Deforestation around the World

Region	Number of Countries	Area Deforested Annually, 1981–90 (thousand acres)	Annual Rate of Change, 1981–90 (percent)
Latin America	32	20,509.3	−0.9
Asia	15	8,905.6	−1.2
Africa	40	12,355	−0.8

Source: *World Resources 1992–93* (Oxford University Press, New York, 1992), Table 8.2, p. 119.

Australia's Soils

Soil degradation in Australia is caused mainly by overgrazing. Seventy-five percent of the continent is arid, and only half of that area is suitable as pasture. Although most of the arid and semiarid pastureland has been grazed for less than 150 years, animals introduced by the European colonists have substantially reduced soil productivity.

Australian soils were always deficient in essential nutrients. Many of the soils developed from ancient, deeply weathered material. Because it has escaped glaciation for 250 million years, the continent missed out on the rejuvenating influence of glacial erosion and redistribution of minerals that enriched the soils of Europe and North America.

Native plant species were well adapted to the low nutrient levels and dry conditions, and the soil productivity remained in balance until hooved animals were imported in the 1800s. The animals initiated a process of soil compaction that worsened with growing numbers of stock. During that same period, introduced rabbits became major pests since they had no natural predators to keep their numbers in check. While cattle and sheep could be removed to allow pastures to recover, the rabbits continued to graze on tender new shoots and prevent establishment of new growth. The rabbit problem abated during the 1950s as the rabbits succumbed to an introduced disease, myxomatosis. Recent reports indicate, however, that the numbers of rabbits resistant to the disease are on the rise. In 1988 they were again causing severe damage to perennial range plants and to young trees.

Further complications involve the low levels of organic matter in Australian soils, despite adequate animal droppings. It turns out that Australia lacks native insects of the type that breaks down animal droppings, which would recycle the organic matter that feeds the flocks and herds and replenish soil nutrients. In an attempt to remedy this problem, scientists have introduced dung beetles. They have yet to see whether their strategy will help to rejuvenate Australia's struggling soils.

port countless species of animals, plants, fungi, and bacteria. A single volcanic mountain in the rainforests of Indonesia is capable of supporting more species of plants than exist in the entire United States. All these species are involved in locally complex, interdependent networks that are vulnerable at every level to assault by human activities.

The rainforest offers an example of how natural systems maintain a complex and delicate balance involving soil, forest, and biotic diversity. Except in volcanic regions, rainforests grow on poor soils, and the greatest proportion of organic matter and minerals remains above the Earth's surface. Tropical rainforests are characterized by a tall, thick canopy that encloses a very hu-

"Good Fences" or Rock Dumps?

The thousands of miles of low stone walls that crisscross New England are beloved by poets, artists, tourists, and residents alike. Conventional wisdom has always held that the walls embody the ingenuity of the thrifty Yankee farmer. The walls were thought to be stone fences that accomplished two purposes: they kept livestock in, and they gave the farmers a place to put the stones dug from the rocky fields. Now some researchers, including geologist Robert M. Thorson of the University of Connecticut, suggest that the walls are evidence of the environmental disruption caused by the massive deforestation of that part of North America.

When European settlers came to this continent, they cleared away 75 percent of the New England forest cover to establish farms. This deforestation may have removed the land's natural insulation, initiating freeze-thaw cycles that continue to produce yearly "rock crops" at the soil surface. In fact, New England's rock crops were not mentioned in historical literature until the late 1700s and early 1800s, a generation or two after the area was cleared for agriculture. Local historians acknowledge the link between the walls and deforestation but defend the ingenious-farmer view, claiming that the fences were built with stones because wood was scarce.

Thorson claims that the walls are in fact mere refuse heaps: when the fields started yielding rocks, the farmers had to put them somewhere, so they stacked the rocks at the perimeters of the fields. Thorson points out that, even accounting for natural decay, most of the walls are too low or have too many gaps to be useful for fencing livestock, and they waver for miles at varying heights like extended dump heaps of rock.

There is no question that regional soil conditions result in frost heave, which brings new rocks to the surface every spring. The area is covered by a melange of clay, sand, gravel, cobbles, and boulders left behind by glaciers after the last ice sheet melted 10,000 years ago. Moisture accumulates around the stones in these surface layers. When the water freezes, it expands, lifting the stones and allowing sand and clay to sift into the spaces left underneath. Eventually, the stones rise to the surface. The rate of a stone's journey is affected by soil temperature, which in turn is controlled by insulating forest cover, snow, and decomposing leaves and wood.

The "rock crop" may not be unique to New England. In other formerly glaciated areas of North America, farmlands have been completely turned over to pasture because the soils have become too rocky to cultivate. It has been suggested that England's Dartmoor area was deforested, farmed, and subsequently abandoned because of degenerating conditions more than 2,000 years ago. Local legends recount fantastic origins for the thick crops of boulders scattered over the hills of southern England; in fact, they may simply be evidence of ancient deforestation and land use practices.

mid, nearly windless microclimate. Here, mammals, birds, and insects spread the pollen and seeds that replenish plant life. When the forest is cut down and burned, not only do the plants and animals disappear—some species, perhaps, forever—but the thin soils also disappear, washing away or undergoing chemical changes that render them unusable.

Widely diverse perspectives flavor the disputes over tropical deforestation. About 25 percent of the carbon dioxide released to the atmosphere comes from carbon released when forests are cleared. Thus, environmentalists worry that further deforestation will contribute to global warming, which in turn may lead to further extinction of many species as temperatures, habitats, and conditions change. (See "Greenhouse Warming" chapter.) But governments in many tropical countries hope to resettle burgeoning populations in forest areas they consider useless space. They say the use of forest resources will help meet their economic needs. Finally, those who have lived off the forest for generations without felling the trees demand a voice in the future of their homes and their way of life.

As the threat that unchecked deforestation poses to the global environment becomes clear, governments, environmental groups, and indigenous peoples are struggling to slow the destruction and still meet everyone's needs. With advice from scientists and economists, they are defining policies that could preserve the forests and slow the destruction. Achieving these goals will require actions that include reforming national policies; creating new international agreements on trade, aid, and debt relief; and recognizing the rights of indigenous peoples.

Biodiversity Loss

As deforestation proceeds, biodiversity shrinks. Destruction of an entire forest, of course, destroys the ecosystems sheltered under its canopy. But some researchers fear too that destruction of an individual species may remove a vital link in a whole system and begin a spiral of environmental deterioration. In tropical rainforests, where many habitats coexist within a small area, elimination of even a patch may cause many species to die.

While the vivid image of slashed and smoldering rainforests is widely known, other ecosystems are also threatened by the pressures that growing numbers of humans are placing on the biosphere. Coral reefs and aquatic

The Incredible Neem

Environmentalists who claim that deforestation and loss of biodiversity will destroy potential sources of miracle drugs could use the neem tree as an example of what bounty might await researchers looking for pharmaceutical materials.

The neem tree, a member of the mahogany family native to the Indian subcontinent, may be one of the most useful plants known. Extracts from neem seeds and leaves repel pests and have antiviral, antibacterial, and antifungal properties. There is even evidence that the neem produces substances that fight inflammation, reduce high blood pressure, and protect against ulcers. But that is not all: Neem protects against tooth decay and gum disease, can act as a spermicide, and might be used in producing a male birth control pill.

The neem grows in semiarid regions, thrives on poor soil, and produces a canopy that offers dense shade. It is considered a viable species for reforesting degraded lands that are poor in organic matter.

Many of the neem's capabilities have not been rigorously tested in scientific laboratories, but experiments are under way. The results look promising even if they do not turn out to produce miraculous improvements and cures. The effects of neem tree extracts appear to be slow acting and may be best used as preventive measures. The U.S. National Academy of Sciences is urging continued research into the best ways to use the neem. The potential of the neem has reinvigorated scientists searching for other natural sources of medicines and pest repellents in the vast pharmacopeia that remains within Earth's system.

communities of algae, plankton, and fish larvae, for instance, may be endangered by pollution and climate change and by the increased ultraviolet radiation levels allowed by depletion of

Top 30 Countries for Mammals, Birds, Reptiles and Amphibians
(number of known species)

Country	Total	Mammals	Birds	Reptiles & Amphibians
Brazil	2,937	394	1,573	970
Colombia	2,870	359	1,721	790
Indonesia	2,815	515	1,519	781
Peru	2,588	344	1,705	539
Mexico	2,401	439	961	1,001
Ecuador	2,386	271	1,435	680
China	1,966	394	1,100	472
Bolivia	1,897	280	1,257	360
India	1,881	317	969	595
Australia	1,733	282	571	880
Venezuela	1,727	288	1,308	131[a]
Tanzania	1,688	306	1,016	366
Kenya	1,651	309	1,067	275
Zaire	1,587	415	1,086	86[b]
Panama	1,530	218[b]	922	390[b]
Uganda	1,467	315	989	163
Myanmar	1,445	300	867	278
Costa Rica	1,429	205	848	376
South Africa	1,415	247	774	394
Thailand	1,272	251	616	405
Nigeria	>1,265	274	831	>160
Papua New Guinea	1,252	242	578	432
Cameroon	1,229	297	848	84[a]
Sudan	1,213	267	938	8[a]
Malaysia	1,191	264	501	426
Angola	1,189	276	872	41[a]
Viet Nam	1,171	273	638	260
Ethiopia	1,127	255	836	36[a]
United States	1,118	346	650	122[c]
Zimbabwe	1,104	196	635	273

Source: World Conservation Monitoring Centre, *Global Biodiversity: Status of the Earth's Living Resources,* Brian Groombridge, ed. (Chapman & Hall, London, 1992), adapted from Table 13.1, pp. 139–141.

Notes:

a. Represents only species unique or native to that country.
b. May include marine species.
c. Represents native species of amphibians only.

stratospheric ozone. Wetlands, drained and filled in lockstep with expanding agriculture and urbanization, disappear. With them are lost countless plant and animal species, as well as critical nesting grounds for migratory waterfowl. (See "Forests and Wetlands" chapter.) As overgrazing strips grassland vegetation and damages the soil, these ecosystems also vanish.

Temperate coastlines also support interdependent biological systems. Sea otters, for example, which thrive from Alaska to California, feed on sea urchins. The sea urchins, in turn, feed on kelp. In these North Pacific kelp beds, where scientists say the highest measured productivity on Earth exists, the kelp supports a rich diversity of plants and animals along the shallow coastal waters. When otter populations are eliminated by hunting, water pollution, or other causes, sea urchins devour the expansive kelp beds and cover the ocean floor. Once the kelp is gone, the species it supports are lost.

Rainforest destruction receives so much attention because, although these ecosystems cover only 7 percent of the Earth's surface, they contain more than 50 percent of its species. So far throughout the world, 1.4 million species have been named, but projections for the total number range from 5 million to 30 million. At present rates of habitat destruction, many of the planet's diverse species will disappear before we even know what they are.

Recovery will not be easy. The following long-term examples provide a glimpse. Well over 500 years after the Khmer capital of Angkor in Cambodia was abandoned in 1431, researchers can observe differences in structure between a fully mature rainforest and one that has regenerated. On the Indonesian island of Krakatoa, nearly all life was destroyed by a massive volcanic eruption in 1883. Today, while some trees in regenerated areas are 4 meters in circumference and 40 meters tall, the number of species found there is only 10 percent of that found in comparable areas that have not been disturbed.

Adding species to an ecosystem can be just as dangerous as removing species. Along the Great Rift Valley of East Africa, lakes support a rich variety of fish. But in Lake Victoria, Africa's largest lake, at least half of the original 400 fish species have been lost since the

Top 15 Countries for Flowering Plants

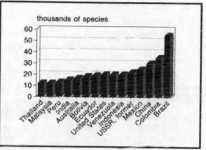

thousands of species

Source: World Conservation Monitoring Centre, *Global Biodiversity: Status of the Earth's Living Resources,* Brian Groombridge, ed. (Chapman & Hall, London, 1992), adapted from Table 8.3, pp. 81–82.

Nile perch, a predatory fish, was introduced for commercial harvest.

Conservation Strategies

In early 1992, the World Conservation Union, the United Nations Environment Programme, and the World Resources Institute suggested a global strategy for curtailing biodiversity loss. The strategy focuses on opportunities that will yield the greatest benefits and outlines five key actions. The first concerns the establishment of international standards through the adoption of the Convention on Biological Diversity presented in June 1992 at the Earth Summit in Rio de Janeiro. Other objectives include a United Nations declaration of an International Biodiversity Decade from 1994 to 2003 to heighten global awareness and the establishment of an International Panel on Biodiversity Conservation to ensure broad participation in decisionmaking. Information such as an early warning network would be provided to monitor threats to biodiversity and to mobilize defenses. Finally, a system would be established to coordinate global efforts to preserve species diversity with national policies worldwide.

At current rates, natural systems are being destroyed before they can even begin to adjust to altered conditions. But humanity can recognize the dangers of accelerated change and act to prevent irrevocable loss.

Biodiversity News

London, 7/25/92—*A record seizure of illegally exported coral has raised new fears about the impact of the aquarium and marine curio trade on the world's coral reefs. British customs officials confiscated more than 80 tons of Philippine coral valued at more than $750,000. Marine conservationists, already worried about the declining health of the world's coral reefs, are "trying to focus public attention on the trade in the same way that ivory was scutinized three years ago," according to the London* Times.

During the "Age of Exploration" that marked the expansion of Western European culture, exotic species were preserved in zoos, conservatories, and private collections. But the time for collecting samples of exotica is past. Today, serious attempts to preserve the expanse and variety of existing natural conditions are addressing a number of critical fronts that vary in scale from the regional to the microscopic.

Both developed and developing countries acknowledge the need for parks and reserves that ban most human activities within their boundaries. Usually these reserves are established around impressive examples of large animals, geologic phenomena, or historic sites. This approach has recently been suggested for the protection of biologically diverse areas as well. Zoos and conservatories have reoriented their missions to serve as sponsors of captive breeding, scientific research, and public education. Other approaches to conservation of biological diversity include seed banks and gene banks. All of these efforts are part of science's attempt to preserve biological diversity for future generations.

Some of the most ambitious programs aimed at identifying and benefiting from species diversity are being carried out in tropical countries. In Costa Rica, an effort is under way to collect information and catalog existing species. Local people are trained to make initial assessments of the country's rich flora and fauna. The private, nonprofit organization that supports the program, the Instituto Nacional de Biodiversidad (INBIO), has contracted with the world's largest pharmaceutical company to search for potential product material. Merck & Company, Inc., hopes that future insect repellents, growth inhibitors, or antibiotics may be synthesized from the natural materials found in the Costa Rican forests; in return, Merck helps to support Costa Rica's nature reserves.

In Indonesia's Arfak Mountains Nature Reserve, local citizens are organized to protect and manage the reserve lying within their traditional territory. The project may serve as a model for future efforts as it strives to maintain a naturally regenerating rainforest while benefiting local people, allowing them to continue traditional uses, and encouraging environmental awareness.

The author, Catherine McMullen, is based in Ottawa, Ontario.

Country Comparisons

Highlights of how countries differ in population density, quality of life, and use of natural resources.

The most crowded country on Earth? No, it's not China, although it counts many Chinese among its inhabitants.

In how many countries is life so difficult and dangerous that the average person cannot expect to reach the age of 50? (Hint: more than 25 countries.) Is the average life expectancy higher in Sri Lanka or in Saudi Arabia? In Cuba or in a wealthy state like Germany?

Does it shock you that the average resident of India has less than one tenth the water for cooking, washing, bathing, and drinking that a Canadian has? Or that the Dutch, surrounded by the sea, nonetheless use only one fifth as much water in their homes as do Americans? And which country has more cars per 1,000 residents, Iceland or Italy?

This chapter answers these questions and many more. It provides a quick means of comparison among countries, showing how each ranks on a number of environmentally important scales, from per capita energy use to the percentage of land area in nature preserves or under other forms of protection. These comparisons are not meant to imply that one country is better or worse than another, but rather to interest and intrigue the reader, in hopes of provoking further inquiry. More detailed information on each country is given in the country profiles that follow this chapter.

Population Density

Country	Density (people per square mile)	Rank	Country	Density (people per square mile)	Rank
Singapore	11,562	1	Romania	262	46
Malta	2,857	2	Cuba	250	47
Bangladesh	2,300	3	Uganda	244	48
Bahrain	1,965	4	Yugoslavia	241	49
Barbados	1,536	5	(former)		
Mauritius	1,515	6	Malawi	241	50
Netherlands	1,142	7	Cape Verde	238	51
Korea, South	1,123	8	Austria	237	52
Japan	849	9	Gambia, The	223	53
Belgium	843	10	Guatemala	220	54
Rwanda	760	11	Bulgaria	211	55
India	743	12	Spain	203	56
Sri Lanka	690	13	Greece	199	57
Lebanon	684	14	Cyprus	196	58
El Salvador	657	15	Turkey	188	59
Trinidad and Tobago	647	17	Syrian Arab Rep	176	60
Comoros	639	18	Ghana	169	61
United Kingdom	614	19	Togo	168	62
Haiti	612	20	Myanmar	164	63
Jamaica	587	21	Costa Rica	153	64
Israel	586	22	Lesotho	151	65
Germany	575	23	Sierra Leone	150	66
Burundi	553	24	Morocco	145	67
Philippines	542	25	Malaysia	141	68
Viet Nam	531	26	Ireland	140	69
Italy	503	27	Egypt	136	70
Korea, North	468	28	Tunisia	136	71
Switzerland	430	29	Cambodia	121	72
Pakistan	412	30	Mexico	120	73
Dominican Rep	384	31	Honduras	119	74
Luxembourg	373	32	Swaziland	119	75
Nepal	362	33	Jordan	117	76
Poland	327	34	Ethiopia	116	77
Czechoslovakia	324	35	Iraq	112	78
China	316	36	Kenya	109	79
Denmark	314	37	Benin	108	80
Nigeria	309	38	Fiji	108	81
Albania	307	39	Ecuador	99	82
Kuwait	296	40	Senegal	99	83
Hungary	296	41	Cote d'Ivoire	98	84
Portugal	290	42	Guinea-Bissau	89	85
Thailand	282	43	Qatar	87	86
France	264	44	Iran	86	87
Indonesia	263	45	Burkina Faso	85	88

Life Expectancy	Rank	Country	Life Expectancy	Rank
58	58	Malta	73	31
69	57	Kuwait	73	30
69	56	Singapore	74	29
69	55	Portugal	74	28
69	54	Ireland	74	27
69	53	Austria	74	26
69	52	Luxembourg	74	25
70	51	Barbados	75	24
70	50	Costa Rica	75	23
70	49	Germany	75	22
70	48	Belgium	75	21
		New Zealand	75	20
70	47	Finland	75	19
		Cuba	75	18
70	46	United Kingdom	75	17
70	45	Israel	75	16
70	44	Denmark	75	15
70	43	United States	76	14
71	42	Cyprus	76	13
71	41	Italy	76	12
		Greece	76	11
71	40	France	76	10
72	39	Australia	76	9
72	38	Canada	77	8
72	37	Spain	77	7
72	36	Norway	77	6
72	35	Netherlands	77	5
72	34	Sweden	77	4
72	33	Switzerland	77	3
		Iceland	78	2
73	32	Japan	78	1

Population Density (cont.)

Country	Density (people per square mile)	Rank	Country	Density (people per square mile)	Rank
Nicaragua	84	89	Somalia	31	119
Bhutan	84	90	Argentina	31	120
Panama	82	91	Solomon Islands	30	121
Colombia	82	92			
Tanzania	80	93	Zambia	29	122
South Africa	75	94	Paraguay	28	123
United States	70	95	Sudan	27	124
Liberia	69	96	Algeria	27	125
Cameroon	66	97	Papua New Guinea	22	126
Afghanistan	66	98			
Zimbabwe	65	99	Belize	21	127
Guinea	61	100	Angola	21	128
Venezuela	58	101	Mali	20	129
Yemen	57	102	Oman	18	130
Madagascar	53	103	Bolivia	17	131
Sweden	53	104	Congo	17	132
Mozambique	52	105	Saudi Arabia	17	133
United Arab Emirates	49	106	Niger	16	134
Laos	46	107	Central African Rep	13	135
Brazil	46	108	Gabon	12	136
Uruguay	46	109	Chad	12	137
Djibouti	46	110	Guyana	10	138
Chile	46	111	Canada	7	139
Peru	44	112	Suriname	7	140
Finland	42	113	Libya	7	141
Zaire	41	114	Iceland	7	142
Norway	36	115	Botswana	6	143
Soviet Union (former)	34	116	Australia	6	144
New Zealand	33	117	Namibia	6	145
Equatorial Guinea	33	118	Mauritania	5	146
			Mongolia	4	147

Life Expectancy

n, people live so long that the ment is becoming concerned the "graying" of their popula Afghanistan, inhabitants are re- ng from (and in some cases still g) a brutal civil war that has dev- d the land; life expectancy is only y more than half that of Japan. e expectancy depends on many , including diet and access to health care. Overall, however, it reflects the conditions under which life is lived. In 26 countries, conditions are so grim and difficult that the average person cannot hope to live out five decades. All but four of those countries lie in Africa—testimony to the chronic poverty, famine, environmental degradation, and civil strife that inflict much of that continent.

Population Density

The Earth's peoples live under many different conditions, some crowded together, others spread far apart. The city-state of Singapore is easily the most crowded nation. Malta and Bahrain are also very small countries, not much more than city-states. But Bangladesh and the island states of Barbados and Mauritius are simply very crowded.

At the other extreme, Australia is still a nearly empty continent. Also sparsely settled because of their large deserts are countries such as Libya,

Population Density (cont.)

Mauritania, and Mongolia. Other uncrowded countries include Canada—where the majority of the population lives within 100 miles of the U.S. border.

The more crowded a country, the fewer natural resources—such as fertile land and water—there are to go around. High population densities can also intensify environmental degradation, leading to deforestation, overgrazing, soil erosion, and depletion of wildlife.

Automobile Ownership

The automobile has been part of the American dream for several generations. Not surprisingly, the United States leads the world in the number of cars per 1,000 people. That is nearly 500 times as many cars per capita as China. European countries and those industrial countries with large distances to cross (Australia, Canada) are also high on the list. In contrast, Africa and Asia, with three quarters of the world's population, have only 12 percent of the world's cars. The world automobile fleet is growing rapidly, however, with serious environmental consequences.

Automobile Ownership (top 50)

Country	Cars per 1,000 People	Rank	Country	Cars per 1,000 People	Rank
United States	573	1	Saudi Arabia	173	26
Australia	500	2	Hungary	169	27
Iceland	489	3	Portugal	155	28
New Zealand	485	4	Bulgaria	137	29
Luxembourg	470	5	Yugoslavia (former)	131	30
Canada	457	6	Venezuela	129	31
Switzerland	439	7	Poland	128	32
Italy	424	8	Argentina	127	33
Sweden	421	9	Greece	127	34
France	410	10	Israel	116	35
Finland	382	11	Brazil	104	36
Norway	382	12	South Africa	96	37
Austria	381	13	Uruguay	96	38
Belgium	366	14	Malaysia	88	39
Netherlands	362	15	Singapore	88	40
United Kingdom	337	16	Suriname	86	41
Denmark	323	17	Mexico	71	42
Spain	295	18	Chile	53	43
Japan	265	19	Romania	53	44
Ireland	263	20	Costa Rica	53	45
Kuwait	244	21	Soviet Union (former)	51	46
Cyprus	238	22	Jordan	45	47
Trinidad and Tobago	205	23	Mauritius	41	48
Czechoslovakia	200	24	Tunisia	40	49
Lebanon	174	25	Fiji	39	50

Life Expectancy
(years)

Country	Life Expectancy	
Sierra Leone	41	
Guinea-Bissau	42	
Afghanistan	42	
Guinea	43	
Gambia, The	43	
Mali	44	
Ethiopia	44	
Angola	45	
Niger	45	
Somalia	45	
Chad	46	13
Mauritania	46	13
Benin	46	132
Equatorial Guinea	46	131
Mozambique	47	130
Djibouti	47	129
Malawi	47	128
Burkina Faso	47	127
Senegal	47	126
Burundi	48	125
Bhutan	48	124
Lao People's Dem Rep	49	123
Cambodia	49	122
Central African Rep	49	121
Rwanda	49	120
Sudan	50	119
Yemen	50	118
Nigeria	51	117
Bangladesh	51	116
Nepal	51	115
Uganda	51	114
Gabon	52	113
Zaire	52	112
Cote d'Ivoire	52	111
Cameroon	53	110
Congo	53	109
Tanzania	53	108
Liberia	53	107
Togo	53	106
Bolivia	53	105
Zambia	53	104
Madagascar	54	103

Life Expectancy (cont.)
(years)

Country	Life Expectancy
Colombia	
Qatar	
Suriname	
Mexico	
Mauritius	
China	
Korea, South	
Malaysia	
Venezuela	
Korea, North	
United Arab Emirates	
Soviet Union (former)	
Hungary	
Romania	
Sri Lanka	
Bahrain	
Argentina	
Pe...	
Vie...	
Gua...	Trinidad and Tobago
El Sa...	Czechoslovakia
Guya...	Poland
Saudi A...	Chile
Nicarag...	Albania
Philippin...	Uruguay
Fiji	Bulgaria
Oman	Panama
Iraq	Yugoslavia (former)
Honduras	Jamaica
Algeria	
Turkey	
Brazil	
Thailand	
Syrian Arab Rep	
Lebanon	
Iran	
Ecuador	
Tunisia	
Dominican Rep	
Jordan	
Cape Verde	
Paraguay	6.

Life Ex...

In Japa... govern... about... tion... cove... figh... as... s...

Continue...

Life Expectancy (cont.)

The figures also reveal some success stories. Both Sri Lanka and China are poor countries, yet their peoples have life expectancies comparable to those of the former Soviet Union and signifi-cantly higher than those of the oil-rich inhabitants of Saudi Arabia. Cubans live as long as most Europeans and, on average, 20 years longer than the residents of Haiti.

Municipal Solid Waste

Trash is increasingly a problem in the United States. We make a lot of it, and we are running out of places to put it. Even so, Australia, New Zealand, France, and Canada generate more municipal solid waste per capita than the United States does. Also high on the list of the top 50 producers are the oil-rich nations of the Middle East and most European nations. In the United States, recycling of metals, paper, and even plastic is beginning to make a significant difference in the amount of waste that must be disposed of.

Municipal Solid Waste (top 50)

Country	Waste (lbs. per capita per day)	Rank	Country	Waste (lbs. per capita per day)	Rank
Australia	4.2	1	Spain	1.9	26
New Zealand	4.0	2	Germany	1.8	27
France	4.0	3	Iceland	1.8	28
Canada	3.7	4	Hungary	1.6	29
United States	3.3	5	Greece	1.5	30
Norway	2.9	6	Italy	1.5	31
Netherlands	2.6	7	Portugal	1.5	32
Denmark	2.6	8	Soviet Union (former)	1.3	33
Finland	2.4	9			
Bahrain	2.4	10	Czechoslovakia	1.3	34
United Arab Emirates	2.4	11	Albania	1.3	35
			Bulgaria	1.3	36
Saudi Arabia	2.4	12	Austria	1.3	37
Kuwait	2.4	13	Poland	1.3	38
Oman	2.4	14	Romania	1.3	39
Israel	2.4	15	Indonesia	1.3	40
Qatar	2.4	16	Colombia	1.2	41
Iraq	2.4	17	Guatemala	1.1	42
Luxembourg	2.2	18	Liberia	1.1	43
Switzerland	2.2	19	Cote d'Ivoire	1.1	44
United Kingdom	2.2	20	Malta	1.1	45
Belgium	2.0	21	Gabon	1.1	46
Sweden	2.0	22	Kenya	1.1	47
Japan	2.0	23	Trinidad and Tobago	1.1	48
Ireland	2.0	24			
Singapore	1.9	25	Cape Verde	1.1	49
			Mozambique	1.1	50

COUNTRY COMPARISONS

Domestic Water Use

Country	Water Use (gallons per capita day per)	Rank	Country	Water Use (gallons per capita per day)	Rank
Bahrain	264	1	Germany	50	45
United States	188	2	Mauritius	48	46
Australia	151	3	South Africa	47	47
Canada	142	4	Yugoslavia	46	48
Korea, North	131	5	(former)		
Malaysia	127	6	United Arab	45	49
New Zealand	126	7	Emirates		
Sweden	125	8	Barbados	44	50
Venezuela	120	9	Greece	42	51
Portugal	115	10	Mauritania	41	52
Japan	114	11	Cyprus	41	53
Kuwait	110	12	Peru	40	54
Qatar	108	13	Iran	39	55
Spain	102	14	Zambia	39	56
Italy	100	15	Mexico	39	57
Iraq	99	16	Malta	37	58
Philippines	90	17	Netherlands	37	59
France	84	18	Jordan	36	60
Switzerland	84	19	Luxembourg	36	61
Saudi Arabia	83	20	Hungary	33	62
Bulgaria	81	21	Ireland	31	63
Iceland	78	22	Tunisia	31	64
United Kingdom	73	23	Trinidad and	29	65
Belgium	73	24	Tobago		
Norway	71	25	Ecuador	28	66
Chile	71	26	Singapore	27	67
Argentina	69	27	Gabon	27	68
Libya	68	28	Algeria	26	69
Finland	67	29	Korea, South	24	70
Nicaragua	67	30	Syrian Arab Rep	23	71
Romania	66	31	Costa Rica	23	72
Brazil	66	32	Morocco	22	73
Panama	65	33	Mongolia	22	74
Czechoslovakia	63	34	Lebanon	22	75
Denmark	63	35	China	20	76
Egypt	61	36	Togo	18	77
Soviet Union	58	37	Thailand	17	78
(former)			Dominican Rep	16	79
Austria	57	38	Swaziland	15	80
Cuba	57	39	Pakistan	15	81
Turkey	55	40	Honduras	15	82
Poland	55	41	Bolivia	13	83
Colombia	53	42	India	13	84
Israel	52	43	Laos	13	85
Suriname	51	44	Zimbabwe	13	86

Domestic Water Use (cont.)

Country	Water Use (gallons per capita per day)	Rank	Country	Water Use (gallons per capita per day)	Rank
El Salvador	12	87	Malawi	5	116
Madagascar	12	88	Tanzania	5	117
Paraguay	12	89	Fiji	5	118
Cote d'Ivoire	11	90	Benin	5	119
Liberia	11	91	Papua New	5	120
Uruguay	10	92	Guinea		
Afghanistan	10	93	Myanmar	5	121
Cameroon	10	94	Comoros	5	122
Nigeria	10	95	Solomon Islands	5	123
Cape Verde	10	96	Burundi	5	124
Kenya	9	97	Sierra Leone	5	125
Zaire	9	98	Uganda	5	126
Mozambique	9	99	Bangladesh	5	127
Guatemala	9	100	Nepal	4	128
Indonesia	9	101	Angola	4	129
Congo	9	102	Central African	4	130
Ghana	9	103	Rep		
Guinea	8	104	Albania	4	131
Haiti	8	105	Burkina Faso	4	132
Jamaica	8	106	Chad	4	133
Sudan	8	107	Guinea-Bissau	4	134
Viet Nam	8	108	Rwanda	4	135
Sri Lanka	7	109	Bhutan	4	136
Senegal	7	110	Ethiopia	4	137
Oman	7	111	Somalia	4	138
Niger	7	112	Botswana	4	139
Equatorial	6	113	Namibia	3	140
Guinea			Cambodia	2	141
Djibouti	6	114	Mali	2	142
Lesotho	5	115	Gambia, The	2	143

Domestic Water Use

With the exception of the oil-rich country of Bahrain, the United States is the most profligate country in the world in its use of water in the home 100 gallons a day per person. Canada and Australia also use large quantities.

In many parts of the world, however, the concern is not wasting water: it is finding enough for daily use. More than half the world's people must make do with less than 25 gallons a day each, and with no guarantee that the water is safe to drink.

Among the most water-short are a number of African countries, where periodic drought and rising populations have combined to make obtaining enough water to meet minimal personal and household needs a burdensome daily chore.

Agricultural Water Use (top 50)

Country	Water Use (gallons per capita per day)	Rank	Country	Water Use (gallons per capita per day)	Rank
Iraq	3,046	1	Ecuador	365	27
Pakistan	1,456	2	Sri Lanka	350	28
Madagascar	1,200	3	Libya	338	29
Chile	1,047	4	Honduras	334	30
Afghanistan	1,029	5	Japan	331	31
Korea, North	871	6	Morocco	330	32
Iran	857	7	Greece	329	33
Sudan	781	8	United Arab	327	34
Egypt	766	9	Emirates		
Suriname	761	10	Philippines	306	35
Australia	728	11	Dominican	292	36
United States	657	12	Rep		
Bulgaria	637	13	China	291	37
Soviet Union,	626	14	Mauritania	288	38
former			Swaziland	279	39
Mexico	561	15	Syrian Arab	270	40
Argentina	560	16	Rep		
Cuba	559	17	Malaysia	260	41
Cyprus	532	18	Israel	256	42
Spain	527	19	Netherlands	252	43
Costa Rica	502	20	Mauritius	231	44
Romania	489	21	Oman	221	45
Italy	420	22	South Africa	196	46
Panama	415	23	Tunisia	188	47
India	412	24	Lebanon	167	48
Thailand	390	25	Korea, South	162	49
Portugal	369	26	Uruguay	159	50

Agricultural Water Use

The amounts of water used in homes are small compared with the amounts used in farming. Worldwide, irrigation is the largest use of water. When improperly done, irrigation can lead to the buildup of salts in the soil and loss of fertility. But irrigation also makes possible the growing of food in many areas that would otherwise be too arid to support present populations.

The extent of dependence on irrigation varies widely. Iraq, with a history of irrigation extending over thousands of years, uses by far the most agricultural water on a per capita basis.

Also in the top 50 countries worldwide are the United States, Mexico, India, Japan, and several European countries. Many of the heavily irrigated countries lie partly or wholly in arid zones. In some cases, such as California, shortages of water for urban areas are attributable to the extensive use of limited supplies by agriculture.

Commercial Energy Consumption

Country	Energy Use (million Btus per capita)	Rank	Country	Energy Use (million Btus per capita)	Rank
Qatar	671.8	1	Korea, South	70.8	42
United Arab Emirates	553.0	2	Cyprus	70.8	43
			Argentina	61.5	44
Bahrain	434.9	3	Gabon	59.4	45
Luxembourg	432.6	4	Cuba	58.7	46
Canada	399.7	5	Mongolia	58.4	47
Norway	369.7	6	Malta	56.9	48
United States	308.9	7	Guadeloupe	56.0	49
Iceland	281.7	8	Portugal	55.3	50
Sweden	265.8	9	Hong Kong	53.9	51
Kuwait	230.7	10	Mexico	51.6	52
Finland	222.4	11	Suriname	51.1	53
Australia	214.7	12	Barbados	51.1	54
Soviet Union (former)	194.0	13	Brazil	47.4	55
			Albania	46.5	56
Belgium	189.0	14	Malaysia	45.3	57
Netherlands	188.7	15	Iran	44.1	58
New Zealand	187.7	16	Chile	43.7	59
Czechoslovakia	180.3	17	Lebanon	43.1	60
Germany	178.8	18	Reunion	36.9	61
Saudi Arabia	176.9	19	Uruguay	36.5	62
Trinidad and Tobago	159.2	20	Colombia	35.1	63
			Costa Rica	32.8	64
Switzerland	155.4	21	Fiji	31.7	65
United Kingdom	150.1	22	Swaziland	31.5	66
France	149.3	23	Turkey	30.6	67
Bulgaria	145.4	24	Panama	30.5	68
Austria	144.2	25	Iraq	29.7	69
Singapore	138.4	26	Zimbabwe	29.7	70
Denmark	137.9	27	Syrian Arab Rep	29.3	71
Romania	132.1	28	Ecuador	28.3	72
Japan	127.8	29	Thailand	28.2	73
Poland	127.4	30	Jordan	28.1	74
Hungary	120.5	31	Algeria	26.8	75
Italy	115.3	32	Mauritius	26.7	76
Libya	112.7	33	Jamaica	26.1	77
Ireland	102.8	34	China	24.3	78
Oman	95.4	35	Zambia	23.4	79
Venezuela	91.7	36	Tunisia	23.4	80
Greece	90.7	37	Liberia	23.0	81
Korea, North	89.7	38	Papua New Guinea	22.7	82
Israel	83.7	39			
Spain	82.5	40	Egypt	22.4	83
Yugoslavia (former)	81.4	41	Peru	21.7	84

Continued on next page

Commercial Energy Consumption (cont.)

Country	Energy Use (million Btus per capita)	Rank	Country	Energy Use (million Btus per capita)	Rank
Paraguay	21.2	85	Senegal	11.0	114
Botswana	20.4	86	Djibouti	10.7	115
Mauritania	20.0	87	Pakistan	10.6	116
Bhutan	19.4	88	Somalia	10.6	117
Congo	19.2	89	Mozambique	10.3	118
Nicaragua	17.9	90	Laos	10.2	119
Kenya	17.8	91	Haiti	9.9	120
Honduras	16.9	92	Sudan	9.8	121
Cameroon	16.9	93	Yemen	9.7	122
Guatemala	16.5	94	Burkina Faso	9.4	123
Malawi	16.4	95	Guinea	9.4	124
Guyana	16.3	96	Afghanistan	9.2	125
Equatorial Guinea	16.2	97	Sierra Leone	8.7	126
			Sri Lanka	8.6	127
El Salvador	16.0	98	Rwanda	8.4	128
Dominican Rep	15.5	99	Ethiopia	8.2	129
Ghana	15.4	100	Burundi	7.7	130
Philippines	15.3	101	Angola	7.6	131
Indonesia	15.0	102	Uganda	7.5	132
Nigeria	14.3	103	Madagascar	7.1	133
Bolivia	14.0	104	Niger	7.0	134
Cote d'Ivoire	13.8	105	Cambodia	6.8	135
Gambia, The	12.9	106	Viet Nam	6.8	136
Central African Rep	12.2	107	Chad	6.2	137
			Mali	6.2	138
Tanzania	12.2	108	Myanmar	6.2	139
India	12.1	109	Guinea-Bissau	6.2	140
Zaire	11.6	110	Togo	4.3	141
Nepal	11.5	111	Bangladesh	4.2	142
Benin	11.4	112	Cape Verde	2.9	143
Morocco	11.1	113	Comoros	1.3	144

Energy Use

It takes energy to pump oil from the ground and refine it. Thus, oil-producing nations that have small populations—like Qatar, the United Arab Emirates, and Bahrain—have high per capita energy use.

Canada, the United States, and many European countries also use a lot of energy per person to heat homes, fuel cars, and power factories. Japan uses far less energy than most other industrial nations—less than half as much per capita as the United States.

Commercial energy consumption includes only those types of energy that are bought and sold on world markets. It does not include fuelwood or dung, which in many developing countries is the major source of energy for domestic use. Thus, this index un-

Commercial Energy Use (cont.)

derstates the energy consumption for such countries; figures for both types of energy are given in the country profiles that follow this chapter.

Commercial energy use especially of fossil fuels such as coal, oil, and natural gas—is a major source of local, regional, and global pollution. Burning of these fuels contributes to smog, acid rain, and the buildup in the atmosphere of greenhouse gases that can cause global warming.

Protected Areas

Preservation of forests, mountains, lakes, and other spectacular natural sites was the rationale for the U.S. National Park system, one of the best-known and best-maintained in the world. Now another reason for nature preserves has emerged—to conserve the biodiversity resources that represent the Earth's genetic treasures.

Many countries have now set aside significant protected areas. Ecuador and Venezuela, for example, have set aside large areas covered with the Amazon tropical forest.

Protected Areas (top 50)

Country	National Land Area (% protected)	Rank	Country	National Land Area (% protected)	Rank
Ecuador	38	1	Malawi	9	26
Venezuela	22	2	Iceland	0	27
Bhutan	20	3	France	9	28
Austria	19	4	Zambia	8	29
United Kingdom	19	5	Colombia	8	30
Chile	18	6	Benin	7	31
Botswana	17	7	Uganda	7	32
Panama	17	8	Zimbabwe	7	33
Czechoslovakia	15	9	Poland	7	34
Norway	15	10	Spain	7	35
Germany	14	11	Nepal	7	36
Tanzania	13	12	Gabon	7	37
Namibia	13	13	Cuba	6	38
Rwanda	12	14	Japan	6	39
Sri Lanka	12	15	Honduras	6	40
Costa Rica	12	16	Central African Rep	6	41
Togo	11	17			
Senegal	11	18	Cote d'Ivoire	6	42
Israel	11	19	Bolivia	6	43
United States	10	20	Australia	6	44
New Zealand	10	21	Korea, South	6	45
Thailand	10	22	Kenya	6	46
Denmark	10	23	Hungary	5	47
Netherlands	10	24	South Africa	5	48
Indonesia	9	25	Ethiopia	5	49
			Algeria	5	50

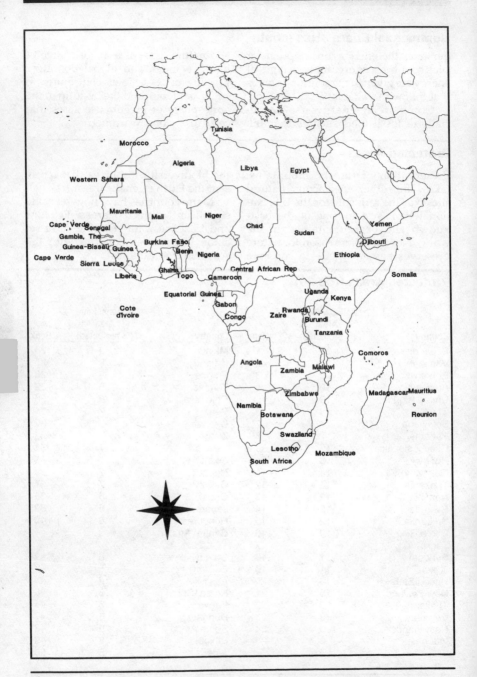

Africa

This chapter contains environmental profiles for the African countries listed. Technical notes and data sources are given beginning on page 641.

ALGERIA

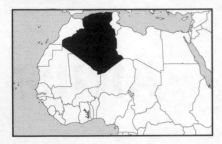

Total Area: 919,575 sq. miles
Global Rank: 10   Per Capita: 23.6 acres
Population: 24,960,000
Global Rank: 35   Growth Rate: 2.72%
Gross National Product: $47,304 m.
Global Rank: 36   Per Capita: $1,947
Greenhouse Gas Emissions
Global Share: 0.21%   Per Capita Rank: 110

Almost one third the size of the continental United States, this oil-rich Islamic nation on the southern shore of the Mediterranean is divided into a fertile coastal plain, a high and largely barren plateau surrounded by the rugged Atlas and Sahara Atlas mountains, and, in the southern portion of the country, part of the Sahara Desert. Nearly 80 percent of this arid and semiarid country is desert, wasteland, and mountains.

Algeria's 25 million people live mostly in the narrow coastal plain, 45 percent of them in urban areas. The population is growing very rapidly at an annual rate of 2.7 percent, and is of Arab and Berber origins.

Algeria has the world's fourth largest reserves of natural gas and significant amounts of petroleum, phosphates, uranium, and some metal ores. Despite efforts to improve agriculture in recent years, the country imports a third of its food. Algeria has large industrial and government sectors, but the economy is still largely dependent on oil and natural gas exports. The per capita national income of $2,450 is ranked in the upper middle of all countries.

Major Environmental Problems

Land degradation. Algeria has extensive soil erosion from farming in marginal areas, overgrazing, and destruction of vegetation from the gathering of firewood or use as animal fodder. The depletion of vegetation also destroys soils, grasslands, and watersheds, lowering the capacity of the land to support life and increasing the rate of desertification.

Water. Water is scarce in Algeria, and drought is common. The cost of new water supplies is very high, limiting further economic development. Poorly maintained water supply systems make matters worse, leading to wasting of scarce water resources and an urgent need for water conservation efforts. Poorly managed irrigation systems have led to siltation of reservoirs and occasional flooding. Sewage treatment is rare; tap water is usually not potable, and bottled water is recommended for travelers. Because of water pollution, waterborne diseases are a frequent problem.

Pollution. Untreated urban sewage is a major cause of water pollution; wastes from petroleum refining and industrial effluents are also often dumped untreated into sewage systems or rivers. These pollutants, together with silt from land erosion and oil pollution in coastal waters, contribute to the increasing pollution and overfertilization of the Mediterranean Sea.

Quality of Life

Life Expectancy (years)	64.0
Infant Mortality (per 1000)	74.0
Population Under 15 Years	41.6%
Population Over 65 Years	3.4%
Literacy Rate	57.4%
Malnourished Children	14.0%

Land Use and Habitats

Cropland (sq. miles):	29,363
per capita (acres)	0.8
global rank	59
Permanent Pasture (sq. miles):	120,367
total livestock (millions)	19.2
Forest and Woodlands (sq. miles):	18,143
1985 deforestation (sq. miles)	154
Wilderness Area (sq. miles)	542,179
Maritime Areas (EEZ, sq. miles)	530
Protected Areas (sq. miles):	45,937
percent of total	5.0%
No. of Threatened Species:	
mammals	12
birds	15
plants	144

Energy and Industry

Energy Production:	
solids (trillion BTUs)	0
liquids (trillion BTUs)	2,254
gas (trillion BTUs)	1,412
nuclear (gigawatt-hours)	0
hydroelectric (gigawatt-hours)	228
Energy Requirements:	
traditional fuels (trillion BTUs)	17
total (trillion BTUs)	650
per capita (million BTUs)	27
per capita (global rank)	8
Industrial Share of GDP	43.2%
Industrial Energy Index	6
Metal Reserve Index (world=100%)	0.0%
No. of Motor Vehicles/1000 Persons	30

Water

Renewable Supply (cubic miles)	4.5
Total Use (cubic miles):	0.7
in agriculture	74.0%
in industry	4.0%
in homes and cities	22.0%
Access to Safe Water:	
urban population	NA
rural population	NA

Urban Centers and Waste

No. of Cities Over 1 Million:	1
percent of population	12.2%
Solid Wastes (million tons)	2.6
Urban Sanitation Access	NA

Population and Gross National Product

Population	GNP
(millions)	(billion $US)

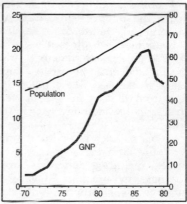

Commercial Energy Use

Total Energy Use	Per Capita Energy Use
(trillion BTUs)	(million BTUs)

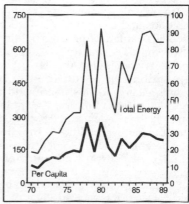

ANGOLA

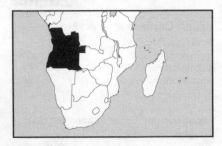

Total Area: 481,343 sq. miles
  Global Rank: 21   Per Capita: 30.7 acres
Population: 10,020,000
  Global Rank: 65   Growth Rate: 2.70%
Gross National Product: $6,031 m.
  Global Rank: 79   Per Capita: $618
Greenhouse Gas Emissions
  Global Share: 0.12%   Per Capita Rank: 88

The People's Republic of Angola is located on the southwestern shore of Africa and is adjacent to Zaire, Zambia, and Namibia. Two times the size of Texas, Angola has a terrain that varies from flatland on the coast to a high plateau in the east. The climate also varies from semiarid in the south to a two-season dry and rainy cycle in the north.

Angola has rich agricultural land, petroleum, and prized mineral resources, including diamonds, iron, phosphate, and uranium. However, a 15-year civil war has until recently disrupted the economy and the nation's ability to manage its resources wisely. Nonetheless, petroleum production is increasing, and this source of income has kept the economy from collapsing.

Angola still produces and exports diamonds and coffee, but production of food has suffered from both fighting and drought. The country now imports most of its food. Half of Angola's urban population can obtain food only through emergency assistance, and a large percentage of the rural population, still uncounted in 1988, is also subject to famine conditions. The situation became acute in recent years, especially in central and southern Angola.

With hunger and displacement because of war, the very survival of at least one fourth of the population is challenged. Environmental concerns are fundamental and desperate, but they are receiving little attention.

Major Environmental Problems

Unsafe drinking water. Drought and unusually high population growth rates combine to make safe drinking water scarce. The shortage is of particular concern in the cities on the coast. Luanda, Angola's capital city, saw a widespread outbreak of cholera in 1987. Other waterborne diseases are a continuing threat as well.

Land degradation. Under pressure to produce food for Angola's quickly increasing population, land is often mismanaged. Deforestation, soil erosion, and overuse of pastures are the result. Severe soil erosion has led to siltation of rivers and dams, contributing to water pollution.

Deforestation. The tropical rainforest in extreme northeast Angola supports tree species that are harvested for high profits on the international market: rosewood, sandalwood, ebony, and others. Throughout Angola, other tree species are cut from forests and are used domestically for timber and for fuel in rural areas. But indiscriminate logging has led to deteriorating land quality and loss of animal and plant species.

Quality of Life

Life Expectancy (years)	44.5
Infant Mortality (per 1000)	137.0
Population Under 15 Years	45.1%
Population Over 65 Years	2.6%
Literacy Rate	41.7%
Malnourished Children	NA

Land Use and Habitats

Cropland (sq. miles):	13,900
per capita (acres)	0.9
global rank	46
Permanent Pasture (sq. miles):	111,969
total livestock (millions)	4.9
Forest and Woodlands (sq. miles):	204,440
1985 deforestation (sq. miles)	363
Wilderness Area (sq. miles)	104,436
Maritime Areas (EEZ, sq. miles)	2,339
Protected Areas (sq. miles):	10,394
percent of total	2.2%
No. of Threatened Species:	
mammals	14
birds	12
plants	19

Energy and Industry

Energy Production:	
solids (trillion BTUs)	0
liquids (trillion BTUs)	898
gas (trillion BTUs)	6
nuclear (gigawatt-hours)	0
hydroelectric (gigawatt-hours)	1,351
Energy Requirements:	
traditional fuels (trillion BTUs)	41
total (trillion BTUs)	74
per capita (million BTUs)	8
per capita (global rank)	131
Industrial Share of GDP	NA
Industrial Energy Index	NA
Metal Reserve Index (world=100%)	0.0%
No. of Motor Vehicles/1000 Persons	7

Water

Renewable Supply (cubic miles)	37.9
Total Use (cubic miles):	0.1
in agriculture	76.0%
in industry	10.0%
in homes and cities	14.0%
Access to Safe Water:	
urban population	75.0%
rural population	19.0%

Urban Centers and Waste

No. of Cities Over 1 Million:	1
percent of population	17.1%
Solid Wastes (million tons)	0.6
Urban Sanitation Access	25.0%

Population and Gross National Product

Population (millions) GNP (billion $US)

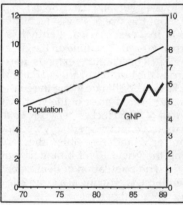

Commercial Energy Use

Total Energy Use (trillion BTUs) Per Capita Energy Use (million BTUs)

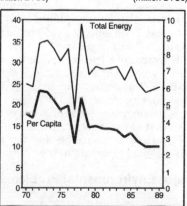

BENIN

Total Area: 43,482 sq. miles
Global Rank: 93   Per Capita: 6.0 acres
Population: 4,630,000
Global Rank: 93   Growth Rate: 3.00%
Gross National Product: $1,637 m.
Global Rank: 118   Per Capita: $364
Greenhouse Gas Emissions
Global Share: 0.03%   Per Capita Rank: 120

Benin is a generally flat, tropical country about the size of Pennsylvania. Located in West Africa, Benin has a narrow 60-mile coastline on the Gulf of Guinea. The country extends northward to the borders of Niger and Burkina Faso. The climate along the coast is hot and humid most of the year, with rainfall of 30-50 inches per year. To the north, the country gradually becomes more arid and resembles the Sahel along the Niger River boundary with Niger. The population of Benin, about 4.7 million, is growing at a rapid rate of over 3 percent per year.

In addition to extensive forests, Benin has internal waterways that provide both lagoon fisheries and the potential for energy production. It also possesses deposits of oil, gold, iron, and limestone that remain largely unexploited for lack of capital. The Seme oil field produces about 5,500 barrels per day.

Upwards of 80 percent of the population is engaged in subsistence agriculture but must contend with drought, few roads, and low prices for crops; fertilizer use per acre is only one-third that of the average African country. Agriculture accounts for almost half of Benin's gross domestic product.

Major Environmental Problems

Threat of Desertification. In recent years, a significant shortage of rainfall has led to widespread drought. This condition, along with population pressure, poor land management techniques, and wildfires, have seriously degraded extensive areas of the country's north.

Deforestation. During the 1980s, Benin lost its forests at an average annual rate of about 1.7 percent, or roughly three times the rate of loss for Africa as a whole. About 59 percent of Benin's original forest cover has been lost. Most of the losses, which have been primarily caused by shifting agriculture and fire, have been in the southern section of the country.

Wildlife protection. The "W" and Pendjari national parks and several hunting zones form a chain of protected areas that overlaps the borders with Burkina Faso and Niger. However, some important species remain unprotected in nearby habitats, and illegal hunting remains a problem. Cattle grazing, agricultural encroachment, and uncontrolled brush fires also threaten the parks and protected areas.

Unsafe drinking water. About 65 percent of the population lacks access to safe drinking water. Sanitation services are almost nonexistent, especially in rural areas. Unsafe drinking water is a major causes of disease.

Quality of Life

Life Expectancy (years)	46.0
Infant Mortality (per 1000)	90.0
Population Under 15 Years	47.0%
Population Over 65 Years	2.5%
Literacy Rate	23.4%
Malnourished Children	NA

Land Use and Habitats

Cropland (sq. miles):	7,181
per capita (acres)	1.0
global rank	35
Permanent Pasture (sq. miles):	1,707
total livestock (millions)	3.5
Forest and Woodlands (sq. miles):	13,591
1985 deforestation (sq. miles)	259
Wilderness Area (sq. miles)	4,669
Maritime Areas (EEZ, sq. miles)	105
Protected Areas (sq. miles):	3,257
percent of total	7.5%
No. of Threatened Species:	
mammals	11
birds	1
plants	3

Energy and Industry

Energy Production:	
solids (trillion BTUs)	NA
liquids (trillion BTUs)	12
gas (trillion BTUs)	NA
nuclear (gigawatt-hours)	NA
hydroelectric (gigawatt-hours)	NA
Energy Requirements:	
traditional fuels (trillion BTUs)	44
total (trillion BTUs)	51
per capita (million BTUs)	11
per capita (global rank)	112
Industrial Share of GDP	12.1%
Industrial Energy Index	3
Metal Reserve Index (world=100%)	NA
No. of Motor Vehicles/1000 Persons	NA

Water

Renewable Supply (cubic miles)	6.2
Total Use (cubic miles):	0.0
in agriculture	58.0%
in industry	14.0%
in homes and cities	28.0%
Access to Safe Water:	
urban population	66.0%
rural population	46.0%

Urban Centers and Waste

No. of Cities Over 1 Million:	0
percent of population	0.0%
Solid Wastes (million tons)	0.4
Urban Sanitation Access	42.0%

Population and Gross National Product

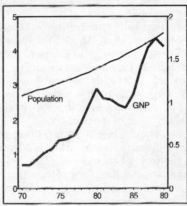

Population — (millions)
GNP — (billion $US)

Commercial Energy Use

Total Energy Use (trillion BTUs)
Per Capita Energy Use (million BTUs)

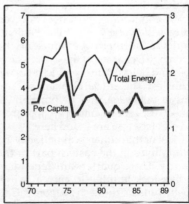

BOTSWANA

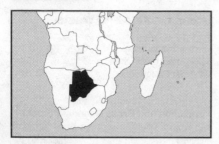

Total Area: 224,602 sq. miles
  Global Rank: 43   Per Capita: 110.2 acres
Population: 1,304,000
  Global Rank: 124   Growth Rate: 3.71%
Gross National Product: $2,212 m.
  Global Rank: 109   Per Capita: $1,760
Greenhouse Gas Emissions
  Global Share: 0.02%   Per Capita Rank: 82

The Republic of Botswana is a landlocked country in southern Africa, bounded by South Africa to the south and east, Zimbabwe to the northeast, and Namibia to the west and north. The climate is subtropical semiarid to arid, with large areas of desert and savanna and some wetlands and forest in the northern part of the country.

Botswana is one of the few flourishing multiparty democracies in Africa. At the time of its independence from Britain in 1966, it was one of the world's poorest countries. Recently, economic growth has been strong but somewhat unbalanced, led primarily by rapid expansion in diamond production. Botswana produces over 15 million carats annually, making it one of the world's top three diamond exporters.

The country also is richly endowed with a wide variety of wildlife habitats, from the northern wetlands of the Okavango Delta (one of the world's largest inland deltas) to the semidesert of the southwest. The African elephant is abundant in Botswana, and hippopotamus, rhinoceros, zebras, antelopes, leopards, and cheetahs also are found here.

Most of the human population of 1.3 million lives in the eastern part of the country. Three quarters are dependent on livestock farming to earn a living, mostly outside the cash economy. Cattle raising has long been a dominant part of Botswana's economy and social structure. The national herd has more than doubled in size since independence, and cattle continue to outnumber Botswana's human inhabitants by almost two to one.

Major Environmental Problems

Overgrazing. Overgrazing is not a new phenomenon in Botswana, but it is more intense and widespread than ever before. Landsat imagery reveals devegetated areas throughout the country. If recent trends continue, over half of Botswana's land area could be degraded early in the next century.

Wildlife protection. Rapid expansion of livestock farming also has meant that as grazing areas in eastern Botswana are filled, new grazing areas are being opened up in the west and the north, reducing the area available for wildlife. Especially serious has been the expanding network of cordon fences established by ranchers. Intended to control outbreaks of disease among cattle, the fences also block wildlife migration paths. Up to 50,000 wildebeest died along cordon fences in one year alone.

Water resources. Water is Botswana's scarcest resource. The country faces shortages caused by population growth and density.

Quality of Life

Life Expectancy (years)	58.6
Infant Mortality (per 1000)	67.0
Population Under 15 Years	48.7%
Population Over 65 Years	3.1%
Literacy Rate	73.6%
Malnourished Children	51.0%

Land Use and Habitats

Cropland (sq. miles):	5,328
per capita (acres)	2.7
global rank	5
Permanent Pasture (sq. miles):	127,413
total livestock (millions)	4.9
Forest and Woodlands (sq. miles):	42,162
1985 deforestation (sq. miles)	77
Wilderness Area (sq. miles)	120,675
Maritime Areas (EEZ, sq. miles)	0
Protected Areas (sq. miles):	38,707
percent of total	17.2%
No. of Threatened Species:	
mammals	9
birds	6
plants	4

Energy and Industry

Energy Production:	
solids (trillion BTUs)	18
liquids (trillion BTUs)	0
gas (trillion BTUs)	0
nuclear (gigawatt-hours)	0
hydroelectric (gigawatt-hours)	0
Energy Requirements:	
traditional fuels (trillion BTUs)	NA
total (trillion BTUs)	26
per capita (million BTUs)	20
per capita (global rank)	86
Industrial Share of GDP	54.8%
Industrial Energy Index	NA
Metal Reserve Index (world=100%)	0.1%
No. of Motor Vehicles/1000 Persons	15

Water

Renewable Supply (cubic miles)	0.2
Total Use (cubic miles):	0.0
in agriculture	85.0%
in industry	10.0%
in homes and cities	5.0%
Access to Safe Water:	
urban population	70.0%
rural population	NA

Urban Centers and Waste

No. of Cities Over 1 Million:	0
percent of population	0.0%
Solid Wastes (million tons)	0.1
Urban Sanitation Access	98.0%

Population and Gross National Product

Population	GNP
(millions)	(billion $US)

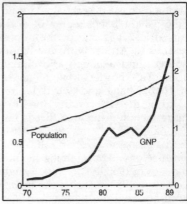

BURKINA FASO

Total Area: 105,867 sq. miles
Global Rank: 68   Per Capita: 7.5 acres
Population: 8,996,000
Global Rank: 71   Growth Rate: 2.66%
Gross National Product: $2,579 m.
Global Rank: 105   Per Capita: $294
Greenhouse Gas Emissions
Global Share: 0.06%   Per Capita Rank: 121

Burkina Faso is a desert nation located in the Sahara/Sahel region of northwest Africa. It is one of the poorest countries in Africa, with few natural resources and a harsh, arid climate. Burkina Faso borders Mali, Niger, Benin, Togo, Ghana, and Cote d' Ivoire.

During the 11th century, the Mossi empire included the area that is now Burkina Faso. In the 19th century, Burkina Faso, then Upper Volta, was a French colony. After gaining its independence in 1960, it was initially a democracy. In 1983, a coup d'état made it a military regime, which it has remained. Soon thereafter, the country officially changed its name from Upper Volta, the name given by the French, to Burkina Faso.

Burkina Faso has several ethnic groups, and indigenous languages are spoken by 90 percent of the population. French is the official language. A fast-growing populace puts significant pressures on the environment, as well as on the government's attempts to meet its citizens' needs.

About 82 percent of the work force works in the agricultural sector, despite the poor Sahelian agricultural conditions. Peanuts, shea nuts, sesame, cotton, millet, corn, and rice are among the country's primary crops. About 20 percent of the men migrate seasonally to other countries for work.

Fuels other than wood must be imported, and wood is increasingly scarce in some areas.

Major Environmental Problems

Desertification. Drought is endemic to the Sahel region, in which Burkina Faso is situated. Desertification is largely caused by this lack of rainfall, but population pressure and overgrazing also contribute. On the Mossi Plateau in Burkina Faso, for example, the population density is an estimated 33 percent higher than that which can be sustained by indigenous agricultural resources. Herding on the plain leads to a loss of vegetation, which in turn contributes to the destruction of soils and protective brush and ultimately to desertification.

Soil degradation. The limited area of arable land is a significant factor in the soil degradation within Burkina Faso. In many villages within the Yatenga region, well over half the area of the immediate surroundings is used to grow crops. Population pressures, drought, overuse, and overgrazing have resulted in the degradation of the soils. Although many farmers abandon their fields and migrate from regions with degraded soils, more and more are applying soil conservation techniques in an attempt to preserve their livelihood.

Quality of Life

Life Expectancy (years)	47.2
Infant Mortality (per 1000)	138.0
Population Under 15 Years	44.6%
Population Over 65 Years	2.5%
Literacy Rate	18.2%
Malnourished Children	NA

Land Use and Habitats

Cropland (sq. miles):	13,761
per capita (acres)	1.0
global rank	37
Permanent Pasture (sq. miles):	38,610
total livestock (millions)	12.3
Forest and Woodlands (sq. miles):	25,714
1985 deforestation (sq. miles)	309
Wilderness Area (sq. miles)	2,894
Maritime Areas (EEZ, sq. miles)	0
Protected Areas (sq. miles):	2,853
percent of total	2.7%
No. of Threatened Species:	
mammals	10
birds	1
plants	0

Energy and Industry

Energy Production:	
solids (trillion BTUs)	0
liquids (trillion BTUs)	0
gas (trillion BTUs)	0
nuclear (gigawatt-hours)	0
hydroelectric (gigawatt-hours)	0
Energy Requirements:	
traditional fuels (trillion BTUs)	76
total (trillion BTUs)	83
per capita (million BTUs)	9
per capita (global rank)	123
Industrial Share of GDP	24.3%
Industrial Energy Index	NA
Metal Reserve Index (world=100%)	0.0%
No. of Motor Vehicles/1000 Persons	3

Water

Renewable Supply (cubic miles)	0.7
Total Use (cubic miles):	0.0
in agriculture	67.0%
in industry	5.0%
in homes and cities	28.0%
Access to Safe Water:	
urban population	44.0%
rural population	72.0%

Urban Centers and Waste

No. of Cities Over 1 Million:	0
percent of population	0.0%
Solid Wastes (million tons)	0.2
Urban Sanitation Access	35.0%

Population and Gross National Product

Population (millions)   GNP (billion \$US)

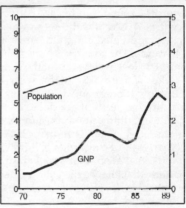

Commercial Energy Use

Total Energy Use (trillion BTUs)   Per Capita Energy Use (million BTUs)

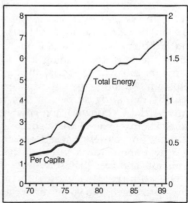

BURUNDI

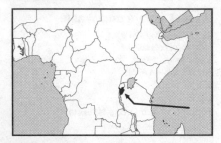

Total Area: 10,745 sq. miles
Global Rank: 123   Per Capita: 1.3 acres
Population: 5,472,000
Global Rank: 88   Growth Rate: 2.91%
Gross National Product: $1,078 m.
Global Rank: 124   Per Capita: $203
Greenhouse Gas Emissions
Global Share: 0.00%   Per Capita Rank: 161

Burundi is a small, landlocked country in central Africa; it is the second most densely populated nation in Africa after Rwanda. The country is hilly, rising from 2,600 feet in elevation at the shore of Lake Tanganyika in the west to mountains more than 9,000 feet high. Burundi has untapped deposits of nickel, vanadium, uranium, and other minerals and generally fertile soils.

Nearly all of Burundi's 5.5 million inhabitants live on small family farms, a pattern that shapes the country's society but also has put great pressure on its land and resources because the population is growing at nearly 3 percent a year. This growth, combined with the traditional inheritance system, has led to an increasingly atomized pattern of very small landholdings and ever greater pressure on the already densely settled land. Problems stem from the intense use of the land for farming and for raising far too many cattle for the land to sustain. Although the importance of cattle is declining somewhat, as in many African countries, the cow remains a status symbol and a social institution, and closely packed citizens need ever more room to graze their ruminants and feed themselves.

The country also grows coffee, which provides 80 to 90 percent of export earnings, and is increasing its tea production.

Major Environmental Problems

Deforestation. Forests, an important climate regulator, could be exhausted in the near future. Only a few percent of the nation's landscape remains forested. The need for new farmland and for fuel wood has already placed an intolerable burden on Burundi's tiny forest lands and no practical alternative to fuel wood now exists. Reforestation projects are under way, but alternate fuels must be found.

Soil degradation. The problem is made worse by the nearly total use of farmable land, so that lands are not permitted to lie fallow. Pasture land is severely overgrazed by large cattle herds; in many places, quality grasses have been replaced with less nutritious varieties.

Erosion. In hilly country, forests are essential for rain catchment and retention. As deforestation has proceeded in Burundi, erosion has worsened. Failure to employ adequate control measures has caused serious loss of topsoil. Improper terracing—critical in this hilly country—encourages soil erosion.

Wildlife depletion. Because of the high density of humans and cattle and the resulting competition for habitat, wildlife populations are suffering.

Quality of Life

Life Expectancy (years)	47.5
Infant Mortality (per 1000)	119.0
Population Under 15 Years	46.2%
Population Over 65 Years	2.8%
Literacy Rate	50.0%
Malnourished Children	60.0%

Land Use and Habitats

Cropland (sq. miles):	5,158
per capita (acres)	0.6
global rank	71
Permanent Pasture (sq. miles):	3,529
total livestock (millions)	1.7
Forest and Woodlands (sq. miles):	255
1985 deforestation (sq. miles)	4
Wilderness Area (sq. miles)	0
Maritime Areas (EEZ, sq. miles)	0
Protected Areas (sq. miles):	146
percent of total	1.4%
No. of Threatened Species:	
mammals	4
birds	5
plants	0

Energy and Industry

Energy Production:	
solids (trillion BTUs)	0
liquids (trillion BTUs)	0
gas (trillion BTUs)	0
nuclear (gigawatt-hours)	0
hydroelectric (gigawatt-hours)	106
Energy Requirements:	
traditional fuels (trillion BTUs)	38
total (trillion BTUs)	41
per capita (million BTUs)	8
per capita (global rank)	130
Industrial Share of GDP	15.0%
Industrial Energy Index	NA
Metal Reserve Index (world=100%)	NA
No. of Motor Vehicles/1000 Persons	NA

Water

Renewable Supply (cubic miles)	0.9
Total Use (cubic miles):	0.0
in agriculture	64.0%
in industry	0.0%
in homes and cities	36.0%
Access to Safe Water:	
urban population	100.0%
rural population	34.0%

Urban Centers and Waste

No. of Cities Over 1 Million:	0
percent of population	0.0%
Solid Wastes (million tons)	0.1
Urban Sanitation Access	80.0%

Population and Gross National Product

Population (millions) GNP (billion $US)

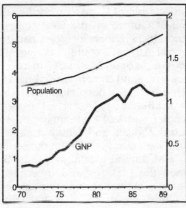

Commercial Energy Use

Total Energy Use (trillion BTUs) Per Capita Energy Use (million BTUs)

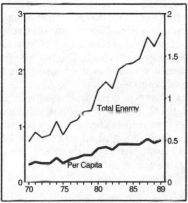

CAMEROON

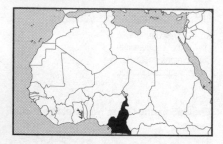

Total Area: 183,564 sq. miles
Global Rank: 49   Per Capita: 9.9 acres
Population: 11,833,000
Global Rank: 58   Growth Rate: 3.27%
Gross National Product: $10,760 m.
Global Rank: 64   Per Capita: $940
Greenhouse Gas Emissions
Global Share: 0.31%   Per Capita Rank: 52

The Republic of Cameroon borders the Gulf of Guinea on the west coast of Africa. Its neighbors include Chad, the Central African Republic, Congo, Gabon, Guinea, and Nigeria. Cameroon's geography and climate are diverse and include semiarid hot plains that stretch toward the Sahara Desert on the north, a cooler and less arid climate on the central plateau, and a humid climate with year-round rainfall on the southern plateau and coastal lowlands. Between the plateaus and the coastal plain rise highlands and mountains.

There are more than 200 tribal groups included in Cameroon's population of 11.8 million; 60 percent live in rural areas. The population is increasing at 3.3 percent annually. About 40 percent of the population is Christian, 21 percent is Muslim, and the remaining 39 percent follows traditional religious beliefs. French is the official language, although English is frequently spoken, as are more than 80 tribal languages.

Cameroon's natural resources include oil, natural gas, bauxite, and iron ore. It also has extensive forests and a rich and varied plant and animal life, with examples of nearly every habitat that exists in Africa. National parks and reserves cover nearly 5 percent of the country.

Nearly 70 percent of the population is employed in agriculture. Chief crops include coffee, cocoa, timber, and rubber, all of which are grown primarily for export as cash crops.

Major Environmental Problems

Deforestation. Cameroon is destroying both its forests and wildlife habitats at a rapid rate. Although forest reserves exist, logging activities and poaching within their boundaries are threatening their integrity, especially in the country's coastal forests.

Range degradation. Drought and overgrazing by cattle have severely damaged the semiarid rangelands of northern Cameroon, and in some areas the vegetation has virtually disappeared. At the same time, however, much of the rangeland is underutilized because of tsetse fly infestation, which is responsible for trypanosomiasis (sleeping sickness). More careful management of rangeland will be necessary to prevent further destruction.

Water-related diseases. Malaria—Cameroon's most critical health care issue—affects more than 90 percent of the population and contributes to poor health and low resistance to other diseases. In the absence of other environmentally safe methods of controlling malaria-carrying mosquitoes, drainage of stagnant water can help.

Quality of Life

Life Expectancy (years)	52.5
Infant Mortality (per 1000)	94.0
Population Under 15 Years	47.4%
Population Over 65 Years	2.9%
Literacy Rate	54.1%
Malnourished Children	43.0%

Land Use and Habitats

Cropland (sq. miles):	27,058
per capita (acres)	1.5
global rank	14
Permanent Pasture (sq. miles):	32,046
total livestock (millions)	12.4
Forest and Woodlands (sq. miles):	95,174
1985 deforestation (sq. miles)	425
Wilderness Area (sq. miles)	5,096
Maritime Areas (EEZ, sq. miles)	59
Protected Areas (sq. miles):	8,107
percent of total	4.4%
No. of Threatened Species:	
mammals	27
birds	17
plants	74

Energy and Industry

Energy Production:	
solids (trillion BTUs)	0
liquids (trillion BTUs)	318
gas (trillion BTUs)	0
nuclear (gigawatt-hours)	0
hydroelectric (gigawatt-hours)	2,630
Energy Requirements:	
traditional fuels (trillion BTUs)	95
total (trillion BTUs)	193
per capita (million BTUs)	17
per capita (global rank)	93
Industrial Share of GDP	27.9%
Industrial Energy Index	3
Metal Reserve Index (world=100%)	0.2%
No. of Motor Vehicles/1000 Persons	8

Water

Renewable Supply (cubic miles)	49.9
Total Use (cubic miles):	0.1
in agriculture	35.0%
in industry	19.0%
in homes and cities	46.0%
Access to Safe Water:	
urban population	100.0%
rural population	96.0%

Urban Centers and Waste

No. of Cities Over 1 Million:	0
percent of population	0.0%
Solid Wastes (million tons)	1.0
Urban Sanitation Access	NA

Population and Gross National Product

Population (millions)   GNP (billion $US)

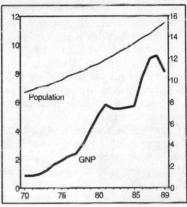

Commercial Energy Use

Total Energy Use (trillion BTUs)   Per Capita Energy Use (million BTUs)

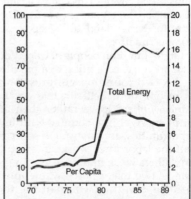

CAPE VERDE

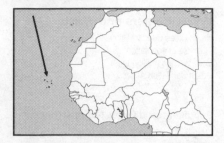

Total Area: 1,556 sq. miles
Global Rank: 139   Per Capita: 2.7 acres
Population: 370,000
Global Rank: 139   Growth Rate: 2.65%
Gross National Product: $282 m.
Global Rank: 136   Per Capita: $783
Greenhouse Gas Emissions
Global Share: 0.00%   Per Capita Rank: NA

Cape Verde is an archipelago consisting of 10 rocky islands and five islets, divided into the windward Banlavento and leeward Sotavento groups. The islands are mostly level, though mountains are found on several of them. Mineral resources are salt, limestone, and posslana, a volcanic rock used in cement production.

Cape Verde was uninhabited until the Portuguese discovered it in 1456 and brought African slaves there to work. At that time, the islands were green and well-watered. Some were even forested. However, centuries of intense exploitation for fuel, construction material, grazing, and agriculture have destroyed the natural vegetation. The country now lacks natural water supplies and suffers from chronic drought and periodic famines. Surface water supplies are lost because the barren land and steep slopes promote runoff.

Of the 1 million people of Cape Verdean ancestry, consisting of a mixture of the two founding cultures, only about one third actually live on the islands. Others leave rather than attempt survival in a country with few opportunities and natural resources. Half the labor force works in agriculture; others work in service jobs in the islands' two major ports, where international shipping companies stop regularly, and in other parts of the archipelago.

Islanders have built over 600 miles of stone walls to help trap surface water and have planted more than 3 million trees to help improve their habitat. The Center for Agrarian Studies, established in 1980, is attempting to control soil erosion and promote effective water use, but it lacks adequate staff, money, and authority to fully accomplish its goals. The government is committed to trying to reverse the causes of the drought but lacks the resources for an effective program. Outside aid will be necesary.

Major Environmental Problems

Drought. Cape Verde has always experienced periodic drought. The problem has become more severe as vegetation is destroyed and soil eroded, and it is now perhaps the country's major problem. Reforestation and revegetation are essential to any permanent restoration of Cape Verde's environment.

Erosion and desertification. Sand carried by high winds has caused erosion on all the islands, especially the windward ones. The lack of natural vegetation in the uplands and coast contributes to erosion, which in turn makes reforestation harder. Desertification problems differ among the 10 islands, but degradation of vegetation and erosion are common to all of them.

Quality of Life

Life Expectancy (years)	66.1
Infant Mortality (per 1000)	44.0
Population Under 15 Years	45.3%
Population Over 65 Years	4.6%
Literacy Rate	NA
Malnourished Children	25.8%

Land Use and Habitats

Cropland (sq. miles):	151
per capita (acres)	0.3
global rank	115
Permanent Pasture (sq. miles):	97
total livestock (millions)	0.2
Forest and Woodlands (sq. miles):	4
1985 deforestation (sq. miles)	0
Wilderness Area (sq. miles)	0
Maritime Areas (EEZ, sq. miles)	3,048
Protected Areas (sq. miles):	0
percent of total	0.0%
No. of Threatened Species:	
mammals	0
birds	3
plants	1

Energy and Industry

Energy Production:	
solids (trillion BTUs)	0
liquids (trillion BTUs)	0
gas (trillion BTUs)	0
nuclear (gigawatt-hours)	0
hydroelectric (gigawatt-hours)	0
Energy Requirements:	
traditional fuels (trillion BTUs)	0
total (trillion BTUs)	1
per capita (million BTUs)	3
per capita (global rank)	143
Industrial Share of GDP	17.1%
Industrial Energy Index	NA
Metal Reserve Index (world=100%)	NA
No. of Motor Vehicles/1000 Persons	NA

Water

Renewable Supply (cubic miles)	0.0
Total Use (cubic miles):	0.0
in agriculture	89.0%
in industry	2.0%
in homes and cities	9.0%
Access to Safe Water:	
urban population	87.0%
rural population	65.0%

Urban Centers and Waste

No. of Cities Over 1 Million:	0
percent of population	0.0%
Solid Wastes (million tons)	NA
Urban Sanitation Access	35.0%

Population and Gross National Product

Population (millions)   GNP (billion $US)

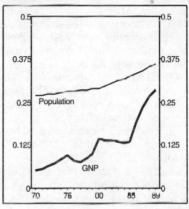

Commercial Energy Use

Total Energy Use (trillion BTUs)   Per Capita Energy Use (million BTUs)

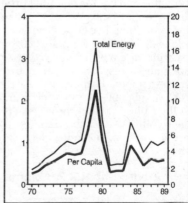

CENTRAL AFRICAN REPUBLIC

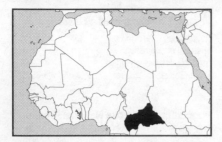

Total Area: 240,529 sq. miles
  Global Rank: 41   Per Capita: 50.7 acres
Population: 3,039,000
  Global Rank: 108   Growth Rate: 2.77%
Gross National Product: $1,056 m.
  Global Rank: 126   Per Capita: $357
Greenhouse Gas Emissions
  Global Share: 0.04%   Per Capita Rank: 87

The Central African Republic is a landlocked country nearly the size of Texas. It consists mainly of a vast, well-watered plateau drained by two major river systems, the northern one flowing into Lake Chad and the southern one draining into the Oubangui. The rivers provide the country with a significant source of hydroelectric energy. Other resources include diamonds, uranium, gold, oil, and extensive forests and wildlife.

Most of the country is wooded, and wildlife populations are strongest in the nearly uninhabited northeast and eastern sections. Seventy-five percent of the population is engaged in subsistence farming. Nevertheless, the country is nearly self-sufficient in food production and has the potential to become a regional exporter. If recent trends continue, livestock production could well double by the year 2000, but at significant environmental cost. An inadequate transportation infrastructure has hampered exports of meat.

Diamonds now account for nearly half the nation's export earnings, with coffee, cotton, and timber making up the other portion. The industrial sector is limited.

Major Environmental Problems

Desertification. Nomads who come into the Central African Republic from Chad and the Sudan bring cattle with them, giving rise to the local observation that the country has more cattle than people. The cattle are crowded onto the limited grasslands, depleting their productivity, while the herdsmen cut brush and trees in the savannas for fuel. The result is devegetation, soil degradation, and eventually, desertification.

Wildlife poaching. Nomads leave their cattle with herd boys and range through forests hunting elephants, rhinos, and other animals; they take hides and tusks back across the borders for later sale.

The Central African Republic is considered one of the last great refuges of the African elephant, but poaching has taken a severe toll. The elephant population is estimated to have dropped from 150,000 to 15,000 during the last 30 years, and has decreased 85 percent since 1982 alone.

The government banned elephant hunting in 1985 and hopes to increase its enforcement staff, but nomadic populations who enter the country and poach in game preserves are numerous and hard to monitor. Observers say the government is intensely interested in conservation and the situation is not unrecoverable. Several major projects are under way to preserve or create game parks and reserves.

CENTRAL AFRICAN REPUBLIC

Quality of Life

Life Expectancy (years)	48.5
Infant Mortality (per 1000)	104.0
Population Under 15 Years	45.3%
Population Over 65 Years	3.4%
Literacy Rate	37.7%
Malnourished Children	NA

Land Use and Habitats

Cropland (sq. miles):	7,745
per capita (acres)	1.7
global rank	9
Permanent Pasture (sq. miles).	11,583
total livestock (millions)	4.2
Forest and Woodlands (sq. miles):	138,263
1985 deforestation (sq. miles)	212
Wilderness Area (sq. miles)	80,760
Maritime Areas (EEZ, sq. miles)	0
Protected Areas (sq. miles):	15,073
percent of total	6.3%
No. of Threatened Species:	
mammals	12
birds	2
plants	0

Energy and Industry

Energy Production:	
solids (trillion BTUs)	0
liquids (trillion BTUs)	0
gas (trillion BTUs)	0
nuclear (gigawatt-hours)	0
hydroelectric (gigawatt-hours)	73
Energy Requirements:	
traditional fuels (trillion BTUs)	32
total (trillion BTUs)	36
per capita (million BTUs)	12
per capita (global rank)	107
Industrial Share of GDP	15.3%
Industrial Energy Index	NA
Metal Reserve Index (world=100%)	NA
No. of Motor Vehicles/1000 Persons	0.4

Water

Renewable Supply (cubic miles)	33.8
Total Use (cubic miles):	0.0
in agriculture	74.0%
in industry	5.0%
in homes and cities	21.0%
Access to Safe Water:	
urban population	13.0%
rural population	11.0%

Urban Centers and Waste

No. of Cities Over 1 Million:	0
percent of population	0.0%
Solid Wastes (million tons)	0.3
Urban Sanitation Access	NA

Population and Gross National Product

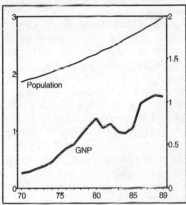

Population (millions) — GNP (billion $US)

Commercial Energy Use

Total Energy Use (trillion BTUs) — Per Capita Energy Use (million BTUs)

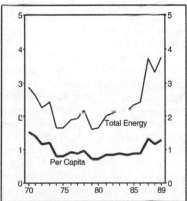

CHAD

Total Area: 495,744 sq. miles
Global Rank: 19   Per Capita: 55.9 acres
Population: 5,678,000
Global Rank: 87   Growth Rate: 2.47%
Gross National Product: $1,002 m.
Global Rank: 128   Per Capita: $181
Greenhouse Gas Emissions
Global Share: 0.06%   Per Capita Rank: 102

Chad is an arid, landlocked country in the Sahel region of Africa. It has known human habitation since time immemorial. The oldest skull found in Chad is more than 1 million years old. Artifacts from tombs in the Tibesti region have been carbon dated back to 4,900 B.C. Around that time, the North Central Basin, now in the Sahara, was filled with water, and people lived and farmed around its shores.

Chad is shaped like a shallow basin, rising gradually from 750 feet above sea level at Lake Chad to the Tibesti Mountains in the north. The northern half of the country is within the Sahara Desert, and arable land is very limited.

The country is home to more than 200 ethnic groups. Muslims constitute the largest religious group. French and Arabic are the official languages, although many indigenous languages are spoken as well.

The country has relatively few natural resources and one of the lowest per capita incomes in the world. All fuels other than wood must be imported. Cotton drives the economy, and the government has continued to subsidize it, though production costs far exceed sales. It is difficult to grow cotton in Chad now; drought and continuing hostilities in the civil war between the southern-led government and the Muslim north and east have ravaged agricultural lands and industrial production as well. Most of the population make their living from subsistence agriculture, fishing, and raising livestock. Livestock and cotton are the major exports. Chad was self-sufficient in grain production until the drought that began in 1967.

Major Environmental Problems

Desertification. Erosion of precious topsoil by wind is a major problem. This is compounded by devegetation, caused by overgrazing of livestock and cutting of trees and shrubs for firewood, and drought. Wind-driven sand also covers roads and croplands as the desert moves southward, as it did until recently.

Civil war. Nearly 25 years of endemic civil war between the Moslem regions of the country to the north and east and the southern region controlled by the government have devastated the country economically and environmentally and prevented any sustained developmental efforts. The result is a country that can barely sustain its growing population at a subsistence level.

Drought. Drought is endemic in Chad, and water scarcity affects virtually every aspect of life, from agriculture to the distribution of population. Loss of vegetation contributes to the problem.

Quality of Life

Life Expectancy (years)	45.5
Infant Mortality (per 1000)	132.0
Population Under 15 Years	43.3%
Population Over 65 Years	3.2%
Literacy Rate	29.8%
Malnourished Children	NA

Land Use and Habitats

Cropland (sq. miles):	12,375
per capita (acres)	1.4
global rank	16
Permanent Pasture (sq. miles):	173,745
total livestock (millions)	9.7
Forest and Woodlands (sq. miles):	49,459
1985 deforestation (sq. miles)	309
Wilderness Area (sq. miles)	236,503
Maritime Areas (EEZ, sq. miles)	NA
Protected Areas (sq. miles):	440
percent of total	0.1%
No. of Threatened Species:	
mammals	18
birds	4
plants	14

Energy and Industry

Energy Production:	
solids (trillion BTUs)	0
liquids (trillion BTUs)	0
gas (trillion BTUs)	0
nuclear (gigawatt-hours)	0
hydroelectric (gigawatt-hours)	0
Energy Requirements:	
traditional fuels (trillion BTUs)	32
total (trillion BTUs)	35
per capita (million BTUs)	6
per capita (global rank)	137
Industrial Share of GDP	20.0%
Industrial Energy Index	NA
Metal Reserve Index (world=100%)	NA
No. of Motor Vehicles/1000 Persons	NA

Water

Renewable Supply (cubic miles)	9.2
Total Use (cubic miles):	0.0
in agriculture	82.0%
in industry	2.0%
in homes and cities	16.0%
Access to Safe Water:	
urban population	NA
rural population	NA

Urban Centers and Waste

No. of Cities Over 1 Million:	0
percent of population	0.0%
Solid Wastes (million tons)	0.3
Urban Sanitation Access	NA

Population and Gross National Product

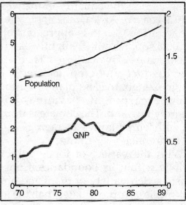

Population (millions)   GNP (billion $US)

Commercial Energy Use

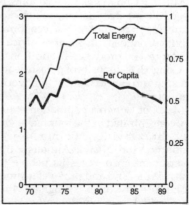

Total Energy Use (trillion BTUs)   Per Capita Energy Use (million BTUs)

CONGO

Total Area: 132,044 sq. miles
  Global Rank: 58   Per Capita: 37.2 acres
Population: 2,271,000
  Global Rank: 115   Growth Rate: 3.16%
Gross National Product: $2,008 m.
  Global Rank: 112   Per Capita: $913
Greenhouse Gas Emissions
  Global Share: 0.04%   Per Capita Rank: 77

Lying astride the equator on the west central coast of Africa, the People's Republic of the Congo is approximately 132,000 square miles, slightly larger than the state of New Mexico. There are four distinct topographical regions within Congo: treeless plain, well-forested escarpment, savanna, and swampy lowland. The climate is tropical, with temperatures averaging 70° to 80° Fahrenheit year-round.

With the variety of topographical regions within its boundaries, Congo boasts a rich variety of plant and animal species. Approximately half the total land area is covered by rainforest, in which elephants, wild boars, giraffes, and monkeys live. The savanna supports jackals, hyenas, and cheetahs.

Much of Congo's export economy is based on oil production, which accounts for 15 percent of total economic activity. Congo is sub-Saharan Africa's fifth largest oil producer. In addition to oil, Congo has deposits of potash, lead, and zinc and exports timber and wood products.

Much of Congo's population is urban, concentrated in the four major cities: Brazzaville, Pointe-Noire, Loubomo, and Nkayi. Although the government encourages its people to return to the land and pursue farming, agriculture in Congo is stagnant; this has resulted in heavy dependence on imports to feed the growing urban population. Despite the ideal climatic and topographic conditions for farming, less than 1 percent of the total land area is devoted to agriculture, and the potential for future development is great. The high forest region is home to small groups of pygmies.

Major Environmental Problems

Deforestation. Congo has abundant forest resources, but it has gone through periods when overexploitation was prevalent. From 1981 to 1985, deforestation proceeded at a rate of 85 square miles per year. In addition, itinerant farming practices typically involve clearing land by burning, which has devastated forests and made reforesting difficult.

Urban growth. Rapid urban growth has brought congestion and air pollution caused by cars. Other problems include inadequate waste disposal and water pollution caused by dumping of untreated sewage.

Protecting biodiversity. Congo's current system of protected area reserves is inadequate. The reserves that do exist lack proper equipment and personnel, so that enforcement is sporadic and ineffective. In addition, illegal hunting and deforestation threaten the native wildlife and floral biodiversity.

Quality of Life

Life Expectancy (years)	52.7
Infant Mortality (per 1000)	73.0
Population Under 15 Years	46.6%
Population Over 65 Years	2.9%
Literacy Rate	56.6%
Malnourished Children	23.0%

Land Use and Habitats

Cropland (sq. miles):	649
per capita (acres)	0.2
global rank	132
Permanent Pasture (sq. miles):	38,610
total livestock (millions)	0.5
Forest and Woodlands (sq. miles):	81,776
1985 deforestation (sq. miles)	85
Wilderness Area (sq. miles)	45,703
Maritime Areas (EEZ, sq. miles)	95
Protected Areas (sq. miles):	5,147
percent of total	3.9%
No. of Threatened Species:	
mammals	12
birds	3
plants	4

Energy and Industry

Energy Production:	
solids (trillion BTUs)	0
liquids (trillion BTUs)	292
gas (trillion BTUs)	0
nuclear (gigawatt-hours)	0
hydroelectric (gigawatt-hours)	399
Energy Requirements:	
traditional fuels (trillion BTUs)	17
total (trillion BTUs)	42
per capita (million BTUs)	19
per capita (global rank)	89
Industrial Share of GDP	35.5%
Industrial Energy Index	1
Metal Reserve Index (world=100%)	0.0%
No. of Motor Vehicles/1000 Persons	NA

Water

Renewable Supply (cubic miles)	13.4
Total Use (cubic miles):	0.0
in agriculture	11.0%
in industry	27.0%
in homes and cities	62.0%
Access to Safe Water:	
urban population	92.0%
rural population	2.0%

Urban Centers and Waste

No. of Cities Over 1 Million:	0
percent of population	0.0%
Solid Wastes (million tons)	0.2
Urban Sanitation Access	NA

Population and Gross National Product

Population (millions)	GNP (billion $US)

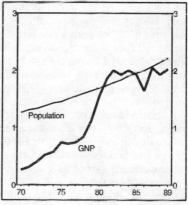

Commercial Energy Use

Total Energy Use (trillion BTUs)	Per Capita Energy Use (million BTUs)

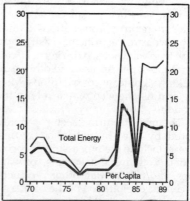

COTE D'IVOIRE

Total Area: 124,500 sq. miles
  Global Rank: 63   Per Capita: 6.6 acres
Population: 11,997,000
  Global Rank: 57   Growth Rate: 3.78%
Gross National Product: $8,337 m.
  Global Rank: 70   Per Capita: $722
Greenhouse Gas Emissions
  Global Share: 0.94%   Per Capita Rank: 4

The Republic of the Cote d'Ivoire (Ivory Coast) is located on the west coast of Africa between Ghana to the east and Liberia to the west, with Guinea, Mali, and Burkina Faso to the north and the Gulf of Guinea to the south. Covering an area of 124,500 square miles, it is divided into a coastal plain and an interior plateau. The land is predominantly flat, with tropical forests situated in the southern third of the country and an inland savanna covering the northern part of the country.

The climate of the Cote d'Ivoire varies from hot and humid in the coastal zone to dry, hot, savanna-like in the northern areas.

Although its economy is relatively diversified, agriculture has been the keystone to the Cote d'Ivoire's development into one of sub-Saharan Africa's more prosperous nations. Coffee and cocoa are the principal cash crops, with tropical woods, palm kernels, cotton, rubber, pineapples, and other fruit making significant contributions. Mining and fishing also play a role in the economy.

The manufacturing sector is dominated by agro-industrial activities. These include the processing of cocoa, coffee, cotton, palm kernels, pineapples, and fish, among other products. Excessive exploitation of the country's forest resources has led to a decline in the importance of this sector.

Major Environmental Problems

Deforestation. Studies of tropical forest endowments have concluded that the Cote d'Ivoire has experienced the most rapid deforestation rates in the world. The principal causes of deforestation have been shifting cultivation, logging, and conversion to agricultural uses. With higher than average fertility rates and immigration from its very low income neighbors such as Burkina Faso and Mali, it is possible that population pressure has been one cause of the shift of cultivation into areas opened up by logging. Government tax, land-clearing, and plantation policies also have had the effect of accelerating deforestation. Efforts to reforest have met with limited success because of inadequate implementation, poor maintenance, and forest fires.

Pollution. Sprawling urbanization and the parallel development of lands for industrial and agricultural use have combined to create a water pollution problem in the coastal lagoons. Mining wastes and sewage disposal contribute to pollution in the rural areas.

Endangered species. Overfishing and removal of lagoon sediments for construction have reduced the fish and shrimp population on which many birds depend for food.

COTE D'IVOIRE

Quality of Life

Life Expectancy (years)	52.4
Infant Mortality (per 1000)	96.0
Population Under 15 Years	48.9%
Population Over 65 Years	2.1%
Literacy Rate	53.8%
Malnourished Children	20.0%

Land Use and Habitats

Cropland (sq. miles):	14,131
per capita (acres)	0.8
global rank	58
Permanent Pasture (sq. miles):	50,193
total livestock (millions)	3.4
Forest and Woodlands (sq. miles):	29,459
1985 deforestation (sq. miles)	1,969
Wilderness Area (sq. miles)	16,479
Maritime Areas (EEZ, sq. miles)	404
Protected Areas (sq. miles):	7,799
percent of total	6.3%
No. of Threatened Species:	
mammals	18
birds	9
plants	70

Energy and Industry

Energy Production:	
solids (trillion BTUs)	0
liquids (trillion BTUs)	8
gas (trillion BTUs)	0
nuclear (gigawatt-hours)	0
hydroelectric (gigawatt-hours)	1,254
Energy Requirements:	
traditional fuels (trillion BTUs)	95
total (trillion BTUs)	160
per capita (million BTUs)	14
per capita (global rank)	105
Industrial Share of GDP	24.0%
Industrial Energy Index	6
Metal Reserve Index (world=100%)	NA
No. of Motor Vehicles/1000 Persons	19

Water

Renewable Supply (cubic miles)	17.8
Total Use (cubic miles):	0.2
in agriculture	67.0%
in industry	11.0%
in homes and cities	22.0%
Access to Safe Water:	
urban population	100.0%
rural population	75.0%

Urban Centers and Waste

No. of Cities Over 1 Million:	1
percent of population	18.1%
Solid Wastes (million tons)	1.0
Urban Sanitation Access	69.0%

Population and Gross National Product

Population (millions)   GNP (billion $US)

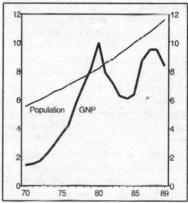

Commercial Energy Use

Total Energy Use (trillion BTUs)   Per Capita Energy Use (million BTUs)

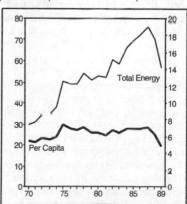

EGYPT

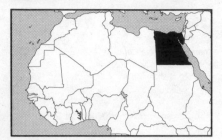

Total Area: 386,654 sq. miles
Global Rank: 28   Per Capita: 4.7 acres
Population: 52,426,000
Global Rank: 21   Growth Rate: 2.39%
Gross National Product: $30,684 m.
Global Rank: 48   Per Capita: $599
Greenhouse Gas Emissions
Global Share: 0.30% Per Capita Rank: 129

Egypt is the most populous country in the Arab world and the second most populous country on the African continent. Egypt also has a strategic location, sitting atop the Suez Canal and with coasts on the Mediterranean and Red seas and the Gulf of Aqaba. It is bounded by Libya, Sudan, and Israel. The country is part of the wide band of desert that stretches from the Atlantic coast of Africa into the Middle East. The exception to the desert is the abundance of water and soil carried by the mighty Nile River, which supports virtually all of Egypt's population.

Egypt's rapidly growing population is extremely dense, averaging 2,500 persons per square mile. More than one third of the labor force is engaged directly in farming, and many others work in the processing or trading of agricultural products. The climate and ready availability of water for irrigation permit multiple cropping. This almost doubles the actual crop area per year. Cotton, rice, onions and beans are the principal ones.

Egypt also has deposits of petroleum, natural gas, phosphates, and iron ore. Egypt's biological resources are of utmost importance. Its deserts and oases contain rare and endangered plants and animals. Egypt recognizes this threat and has passed laws to protect its unique plants, animals, and ecosystems.

Major Environmental Problems

Loss of agricultural land. For the past 20 years, urban growth has annually consumed between 45 and 80 square miles of the best agricultural land.

Soil damage and loss. Soil damage and loss is the result of salinization caused by irrigation. At least 28 percent of Egypt's irrigated soils suffer from some degree of salinization. Continued pressure for increased food production prevents soils from recovering their ancient fertility, especially in the lands near the coast. Windblown sands and urban sprawl entirely remove arable soil from use.

Oil pollution. Oil pollution presents a significant threat to Egypt's coral reefs, commercial fisheries, birds, mangroves, and coastal and marine resources. The Egyptian coast, including the beaches and offshore reefs, is coated with tar and petroleum residues from ships, offshore oil facilities, and oil pipelines. Oil pollution plagues beaches and harms fisheries and birds.

Water pollution. In Egypt, water pollution results from many causes, including runoff of salinized drainage water from irrigated areas, use of agricultural pesticides, lack of adequate sewage disposal, and industrial effluents.

Quality of Life

Life Expectancy (years)	59.1
Infant Mortality (per 1000)	65.0
Population Under 15 Years	37.7%
Population Over 65 Years	3.4%
Literacy Rate	48.4%
Malnourished Children	32.0%

Land Use and Habitats

Cropland (sq. miles):	9,927
per capita (acres)	0.1
global rank	136
Permanent Pasture (sq. miles):	0
total livestock (millions)	16.2
Forest and Woodlands (sq. miles):	120
1985 deforestation (sq. miles)	0
Wilderness Area (sq. miles)	164,249
Maritime Areas (EEZ, sq. miles)	670
Protected Areas (sq. miles):	2,646
percent of total	0.7%
No. of Threatened Species:	
mammals	9
birds	16
plants	93

Energy and Industry

Energy Production:	
solids (trillion BTUs)	0
liquids (trillion BTUs)	1,770
gas (trillion BTUs)	238
nuclear (gigawatt-hours)	0
hydroelectric (gigawatt-hours)	6,399
Energy Requirements:	
traditional fuels (trillion BTUs)	41
total (trillion BTUs)	1,148
per capita (million BTUs)	22
per capita (global rank)	83
Industrial Share of GDP	25.0%
Industrial Energy Index	38
Metal Reserve Index (world=100%)	0.0%
No. of Motor Vehicles/1000 Persons	16

Water

Renewable Supply (cubic miles)	0.40
Total Use (cubic miles):	13.53
in agriculture	88.0%
in industry	5.0%
in homes and cities	7.0%
Access to Safe Water:	
urban population	96.0%
rural population	82.0%

Urban Centers and Waste

No. of Cities Over 1 Million:	2
percent of population	24.3%
Solid Wastes (million tons)	3.0
Urban Sanitation Access	100.0%

Population and Gross National Product

Population
(millions)

GNP
(billion $US)

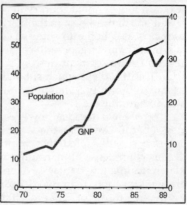

Commercial Energy Use

Total Energy Use
(trillion BTUs)

Per Capita Energy Use
(million BTUs)

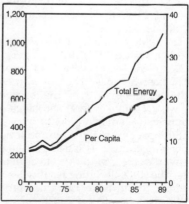

ETHIOPIA

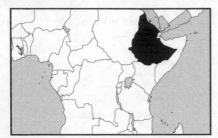

Total Area: 471,768 sq. miles
Global Rank: 23   Per Capita: 6.1 acres
Population: 49,240,000
Global Rank: 22   Growth Rate: 2.67%
Gross National Product: $5,959 m.
Global Rank: 80   Per Capita: $124
Greenhouse Gas Emissions
Global Share: 0.17%   Per Capita Rank: 146

The oldest independent country in Africa and one of the oldest in the world, Ethiopia is also home to some of Africa's most famous geographical features. Its central plateau descends to the Great Rift Valley, which splits the plateau diagonally. The Blue Nile River rises from Lake Tana.

In the past two decades, however, a series of natural and man-made catastrophes has bankrupted the country and caused immense human suffering and environmental damage. A civil war raged for more than two decades after the overthrow of Emperor Haile Selassie in the mid 1970s. This caused environmental problems and prevented economic development that might have provided jobs and food for the country's rapidly growing population and thus helped stem its environmental deterioration.

Drought and famine have recurred five times since 1972, striking every 2 to 3 years instead of every 7 to 10 years as in past decades. The government estimates that in 1991, 8.7 million people were victims of food shortages or famine-caused displacement.

Ethiopia has small textile and food-processing industries, but 85 percent of the work force is employed in agriculture. The soil's declining fertility leads farmers to cultivate marginal land, putting it at risk of erosion. The country lacks major mineral resources, though it has good but as yet unexploited hydroelectric potential.

At present, however, the population depends overwhelmingly on traditional fuels, which puts further pressure on the overtaxed and depleted land.

Major Environmental Problems

Drought. Dry periods recur in cycles and have been particularly severe and frequent over the last decade. They are caused by changed rainfall patterns resulting in part from destruction of vegetation and forest lands.

Desertification and erosion. Overgrazing and cultivation of slopes cause 600,000 acres of topsoil to wash away each year. Many areas, once rich with vegetation, are now bare and rocky. Cattle grazing has severely degraded Awash National Park, one of only two protected wildlife reserves in Ethiopia.

Deforestation. Droughts, war, and the cutting and burning of trees for fuelwood and to clear land for cultivation destroy nearly 340 square miles of forest every year. Fifty years ago, more than 30 percent of the Ethiopian plateau was forested; now, 3 percent is. The destruction will take generations to overcome. In some areas, villagers have to walk 10 miles for firewood.

Quality of Life

Life Expectancy (years)	44.0
Infant Mortality (per 1000)	137.0
Population Under 15 Years	46.2%
Population Over 65 Years	2.6%
Literacy Rate	NA
Malnourished Children	43.0%

Land Use and Habitats

Cropland (sq. miles):	53,784
per capita (acres)	0.7
global rank	63
Permanent Pasture (sq. miles):	173,552
total livestock (millions)	79.2
Forest and Woodlands (sq. miles):	105,019
1985 deforestation (sq. miles)	340
Wilderness Area (sq. miles)	76,123
Maritime Areas (EEZ, sq. miles)	293
Protected Areas (sq. miles):	24,025
percent of total	5.1%
No. of Threatened Species:	
mammals	25
birds	14
plants	44

Energy and Industry

Energy Production:	
solids (trillion BTUs)	0
liquids (trillion BTUs)	0
gas (trillion BTUs)	0
nuclear (gigawatt-hours)	0
hydroelectric (gigawatt-hours)	659
Energy Requirements:	
traditional fuels (trillion BTUs)	355
total (trillion BTUs)	392
per capita (million BTUs)	8
per capita (global rank)	129
Industrial Share of GDP	16.8%
Industrial Energy Index	6
Metal Reserve Index (world=100%)	0.0%
No. of Motor Vehicles/1000 Persons	1

Water

Renewable Supply (cubic miles)	26.4
Total Use (cubic miles).	0.5
in agriculture	86.0%
in industry	3.0%
in homes and cities	11.0%
Access to Safe Water:	
urban population	70.0%
rural population	11.0%

Urban Centers and Waste

No. of Cities Over 1 Million:	1
percent of population	3.8%
Solid Wastes (million tons)	1.3
Urban Sanitation Access	97.0%

Population and Gross National Product

Population (millions)   GNP (billion $US)

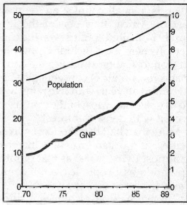

Commercial Energy Use

Total Energy Use (trillion BTUs)   Per Capita Energy Use (million BTUs)

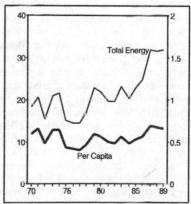

GABON

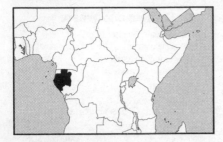

Total Area: 103,346 sq. miles
  Global Rank: 70   Per Capita: 56.4 acres
Population: 1,172,000
  Global Rank: 126   Growth Rate: 3.47%
Gross National Product: $3,208 m.
  Global Rank: 100   Per Capita: $2,834
Greenhouse Gas Emissions
  Global Share: 0.05%   Per Capita Rank: 20

Gabon is a small country on the west coast of Africa. It is one of the less densely inhabited countries on the continent. Its neighbors include Cameroon and Congo. Gabon straddles the equator and its climate is consequently hot and humid all year, with two rainy and two dry seasons. Most of the country is covered with dense rainforest.

More than half the population lives in cities, and urban growth is increasing almost twice as fast as that of total population as people leave the countryside in search of employment.

Gabon's natural resources include petroleum, uranium, manganese, gold, and iron, in addition to its vast forests. Mining contributes almost 30 percent of gross domestic product and 60 percent of exports, and the country is the third largest producer of oil in Africa.

Mineral production has provided one of the highest standards of living in Africa and, until now, has kept pressure off the forests. In consequence, Gabon has large areas of undisturbed forests that are among the most biologically diverse in Africa. The floral riches of Gabon surpass those of all of West Africa. Wildlife is abundant. Elephants live throughout the forest, and Gabon holds the largest and probably the most stable population of this species. It is also home to at least 20 species of primates—one of which, the sun-tailed guenon, was discovered only in

1984—and to large populations of lowland gorillas and chimpanzees. Little attention has been paid to conservation, but lack of roads and low populations in forest regions has achieved the same result.

Gabon has the second highest per capita gross domestic product in sub-Saharan Africa. It is one of the few sub-Saharan countries to have a trade surplus in recent years. Gabon accounts for 90 percent of the world's market in okoume, a timber tree preferred for veneer and plywood.

Major Environmental Problems

Risk of deforestation. Recent drops in prices for Gabon's exports have shifted emphasis to the forestry sector, increasing pressure to boost timber production. However, there is no management plan for forests and consequent danger of wasteful exploitation and damage. Protected areas covering 6.7 percent of the country have been set aside. Hunting in these is prohibited, but enforcement is weak.

Wildlife destruction. Professional hunters who provide meat for whole towns can wipe out the animal life of a small area very quickly. Hunters bring about four tons of animal meat to Libreville every month, and this form of hunting is beginning to spread. Ivory poaching is on the increase.

Quality of Life

Life Expectancy (years)	51.5
Infant Mortality (per 1000)	103.0
Population Under 15 Years	36.1%
Population Over 65 Years	4.9%
Literacy Rate	60.7%
Malnourished Children	NA

Land Use and Habitats

Cropland (sq. miles):	1,745
per capita (acres)	1.0
global rank	39
Permanent Pasture (sq. miles):	625
total livestock (millions)	0.4
Forest and Woodlands (sq. miles):	77,220
1985 deforestation (sq. miles)	58
Wilderness Area (sq. miles)	28,313
Maritime Areas (EEZ, sq. miles)	825
Protected Areas (sq. miles):	6,911
percent of total	6.7%
No. of Threatened Species:	
mammals	14
birds	4
plants	80

Energy and Industry

Energy Production:	
solids (trillion BTUs)	0
liquids (trillion BTUs)	425
gas (trillion BTUs)	10
nuclear (gigawatt-hours)	0
hydroelectric (gigawatt-hours)	676
Energy Requirements:	
traditional fuels (trillion BTUs)	23
total (trillion BTUs)	67
per capita (million BTUs)	59
per capita (global rank)	45
Industrial Share of GDP	46.5%
Industrial Energy Index	3
Metal Reserve Index (world=100%)	0.4%
No. of Motor Vehicles/1000 Persons	18

Water

Renewable Supply (cubic miles)	39.1
Total Use (cubic miles):	0.0
in agriculture	6.0%
in industry	22.0%
in homes and cities	72.0%
Access to Safe Water:	
urban population	90.0%
rural population	50.0%

Urban Centers and Waste

No. of Cities Over 1 Million:	0
percent of population	0.0%
Solid Wastes (million tons)	0.1
Urban Sanitation Access	NA

Population and Gross National Product

Population (millions)   GNP (billion $US)

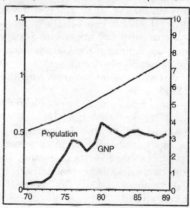

Commercial Energy Use

Total Energy Use (trillion BTUs)   Per Capita Energy Use (million BTUs)

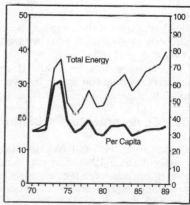

GAMBIA, THE

Total Area: 4,363 sq. miles
  Global Rank: 133   Per Capita: 3.2 acres
Population: 861,000
  Global Rank: 129   Growth Rate: 2.89%
Gross National Product: $196 m.
  Global Rank: 140   Per Capita: $234
Greenhouse Gas Emissions
  Global Share: 0.01%   Per Capita Rank: 114

The Gambia is a small, flat country on the West African coast that extends as a narrow strip 200 miles into Senegal along the course of the Gambia River. The vegetation is dominated by mangrove swamps and savanna forests in upland areas.

Over 75 percent of the people in this densely populated country are engaged in agriculture, primarily producing peanuts, The Gambia's major export. Raising livestock, fishing, and tourism are also important activities.

Agricultural production is limited by rainfall and the availability of arable land. Although rainfall averages from 35 to 55 inches per year, it occurs during a single seven-month rainy season; annual precipitation has declined since the 1960s. At present, irrigated agriculture is only possible along the nonsaline tributaries of the Gambia, as the main body of the river is tidal throughout the country.

The Gambia has few natural resources other than the fish in its rivers and off its shores.

Major Environmental Problems

Desertification. Rainfall has dropped 30 percent since 1960, allowing saltwater to intrude ever farther upriver. Increasingly large stretches of agricultural land have become saline; acid-sulfate soils, which turn into barren wastes incapable of supporting vegetation, continue to expand. The water table has also dropped. Human and livestock populations continue to grow, however, putting increasing pressure on already fragile soils.

Deforestation. Ninety-one percent of the original forest habitat of this country has been lost through cutting for fuelwood and clearing for new agricultural land. Nonmangrove swamp areas are under heavy pressure from farmers and other rural inhabitants. Almost all of The Gambia's big game animals have disappeared, as a result of loss of habitat. The Gambia's first national park was recently established.

Waterborne diseases. Because The Gambia is dominated by riverine habitat, its population is particularly vulnerable to malaria, schistosomiasis, onchocerciasis, and other diseases. Intestinal diseases are also rampant because of poor sanitation facilities in Banjul and other towns along the river.

Damage to Fisheries. Overfishing threatens to curtail production of fish, shrimp, and oysters, a major industry. Government incentives have encouraged the number of fishing companies to grow from 2 in 1980 to 20 in 1989. Foreign poachers add to the overfishing problem.

Quality of Life

Life Expectancy (years)	43.0
Infant Mortality (per 1000)	143.0
Population Under 15 Years	44.2%
Population Over 65 Years	2.4%
Literacy Rate	27.2%
Malnourished Children	35.0%

Land Use and Habitats

Cropland (sq. miles):	687
per capita (acres)	0.5
global rank	82
Permanent Pasture (sq. miles):	347
total livestock (millions)	0.8
Forest and Woodlands (sq. miles):	625
1985 deforestation (sq. miles)	19
Wilderness Area (sq. miles)	0
Maritime Areas (EEZ, sq. miles)	75
Protected Areas (sq. miles):	46
percent of total	1.1%
No. of Threatened Species:	
mammals	7
birds	1
plants	0

Energy and Industry

Energy Production:	
solids (trillion BTUs)	0
liquids (trillion BTUs)	0
gas (trillion BTUs)	0
nuclear (gigawatt-hours)	0
hydroelectric (gigawatt-hours)	0
Energy Requirements:	
traditional fuels (trillion BTUs)	8
total (trillion BTUs)	11
per capita (million BTUs)	13
per capita (global rank)	106
Industrial Share of GDP	10.3%
Industrial Energy Index	NA
Metal Reserve Index (world=100%)	NA
No. of Motor Vehicles/1000 Persons	7

Water

Renewable Supply (cubic miles)	0.7
Total Use (cubic miles):	0.0
in agriculture	91.0%
in industry	2.0%
in homes and cities	7.0%
Access to Safe Water:	
urban population	92.0%
rural population	73.0%

Urban Centers and Waste

No. of Cities Over 1 Million:	0
percent of population	0.0%
Solid Wastes (million tons)	NA
Urban Sanitation Access	NA

Population and Gross National Product

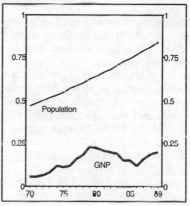

Population (millions)	GNP (billion $US)

Commercial Energy Use

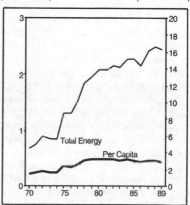

Total Energy Use (trillion BTUs)	Per Capita Energy Use (million BTUs)

GHANA

Total Area: 92,099 sq. miles
Global Rank: 74   Per Capita: 3.9 acres
Population: 15,028,000
Global Rank: 51   Growth Rate: 3.15%
Gross National Product: $5,145 m.
Global Rank: 83   Per Capita: $353
Greenhouse Gas Emissions
Global Share: 0.11%   Per Capita Rank: 118

Ghana, located on the west coast of Africa, covers an area slightly smaller than Oregon. It is a lowlying country, half of it less than 500 feet above sea level. The coastline is mostly a low, sandy shore backed by plains and scrub. A tropical rainforest belt, broken by heavily forested hills and many streams and rivers, extends north from the shore. North of this belt, known as the Ashanti, the country is covered with low bush, savanna, and grassy plains.

Once the world's leading producer of cocoa, Ghana now produces only 15 percent of the world's cocoa output. Its natural resources include bauxite, gold, timber, and industrial diamonds. Mining is the major industry.

Half the population works in agriculture, but the urban and industrial sector is growing. Forty percent of the population lived in cities in 1985. However, years of government instability have damaged the country's industry and infrastructure, leaving a heavy debt. Only in the past several years has Ghana's fragile economy begun to recover.

Meanwhile, the population is growing by 3.2 percent annually, leaving agriculture hard-pressed to keep up with increasing demand for food and export products. Farmers have had to expand their acreage, at the expense of woodlands. The timber industry is also expanding.

Major Environmental Problems

Desertification. The northwestern third of the country faces a moderate to serious threat of desertification because increased population pressure has led to overgrazing, overcultivation, and reduced fallow periods. Rangelands, forests, and agricultural lands are all endangered.

Deforestation. Forests covered much of the country at the turn of century. Now they cover only about 34 percent. Forest loss is estimated at 278 square miles a year.

Water pollution. Ghana has inadequate and hazardous supplies of drinking water. Pollution by industrial, commercial, domestic, and community wastes is common. Existing dams and water conservation practices have spread onchocerciasis, schistosomiasis, and mosquito-borne diseases.

Wildlife depletion. Ghana has legislation to protect native wild species, but enforcement is poor. Even within reserves, fauna and flora are only partially protected from hunting and logging, activities that are widespread. Ghanian forests contain 2,100 plant species and many rare animals, including the forest elephant, the bongo, and the giant forest hog.

Quality of Life

Life Expectancy (years)	54.0
Infant Mortality (per 1000)	90.0
Population Under 15 Years	45.8%
Population Over 65 Years	2.4%
Literacy Rate	60.3%
Malnourished Children	39.0%

Land Use and Habitats

Cropland (sq. miles):	10,502
per capita (acres)	0.5
global rank	91
Permanent Pasture (sq. miles):	19,305
total livestock (millions)	6.3
Forest and Woodlands (sq. miles):	31,429
1985 deforestation (sq. miles)	278
Wilderness Area (sq. miles)	0
Maritime Areas (EEZ, sq. miles)	842
Protected Areas (sq. miles):	4,149
percent of total	4.5%
No. of Threatened Species:	
mammals	13
birds	8
plants	34

Energy and Industry

Energy Production:	
solids (trillion BTUs)	0
liquids (trillion BTUs)	0
gas (trillion BTUs)	0
nuclear (gigawatt-hours)	0
hydroelectric (gigawatt-hours)	4,819
Energy Requirements:	
traditional fuels (trillion BTUs)	149
total (trillion BTUs)	224
per capita (million BTUs)	15
per capita (global rank)	100
Industrial Share of GDP	17.9%
Industrial Energy Index	19
Metal Reserve Index (world=100%)	0.1%
No. of Motor Vehicles/1000 Persons	NA

Water

Renewable Supply (cubic miles)	12.7
Total Use (cubic miles):	0.1
in agriculture	52.0%
in industry	13.0%
in homes and cities	35.0%
Access to Safe Water:	
urban population	93.0%
rural population	39.0%

Urban Centers and Waste

No. of Cities Over 1 Million:	1
percent of population	7.3%
Solid Wastes (million tons)	0.5
Urban Sanitation Access	64.0%

Population and Gross National Product

Population (millions)	GNP (billion $US)

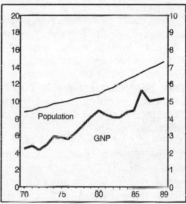

Commercial Energy Use

Total Energy Use (trillion BTUs)	Per Capita Energy Use (million BTUs)

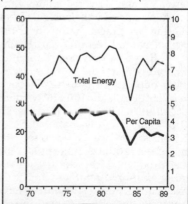

GUINEA

Total Area: 94,925 sq. miles
Global Rank: 72   Per Capita: 10.6 acres
Population: 5,755,000
Global Rank: 86   Growth Rate: 2.86%
Gross National Product: $2,551 m.
Global Rank: 106   Per Capita: $456
Greenhouse Gas Emissions
Global Share: 0.12%   Per Capita Rank: 66

The Republic of Guinea is situated on the west coast of Africa, roughly 10 degrees north of the equator. It is surrounded by Senegal to the north, Mali and Cote d'Ivoire to the east, Sierra Leone and Liberia to the south, and Guinea-Bissau to the west. Its climate is tropical, remaining hot and humid year-round, with a rainy season from April to November.

Guinea's flat coastal areas contain estuaries, stretches of swampland, and coastal plains. The northern region is covered with moist savanna and upland evergreen forests, and contains the Fouta Djallon Mountains. To the east is a combination of plateaus and river basins dominated by tall grasses and brush. To the south lie highlands, interior savanna-covered plains, and mountains topped with tropical forest.

Guinea is graced with an abundance of natural resources, including forests, fisheries, iron ore, diamonds, gold, and perhaps the world's largest known deposits of bauxite. Twenty-two rivers originate within its borders. Agriculture, which accounts for nearly half of Guinea's gross national product, consists of rice, corn, coffee, bananas, palm products, pineapples, and forest products. Other industries are mining, minor manufacturing, and construction. Guinea's resources have not been adequately developed and the country remains very poor.

Major Environmental Problems

Public health. The lack of safe drinking water and environmental sanitation services is a major concern in Guinea, where most diseases are environment-related. Among those spread by insect or animal vectors are sleeping sickness and river blindness. Parasitic infections, including amoebiasis and hookworm, are widespread. Nutritional deficiencies are also common. The average life expectancy is only about 42, and infant mortality is very high.

Land degradation. A variety of land use practices, such as farming, livestock herding, hydroelectric development, and especially mining, threaten Guinea's scarce and fragile soils. The lack of land use management has resulted in the widespread contamination, depletion, and erosion of soils, the loss of vegetative cover, desertification, and groundwater pollution.

Deforestation. Guinea has recently begun efforts to commercially exploit its forest resources, leading to the wasteful and destructive harvest of trees. While there is little enforced protection of forests, the government has recently declared Guinea's first national park, and other sites have been designated as biosphere reserves.

Quality of Life

Life Expectancy (years)	42.5
Infant Mortality (per 1000)	145.0
Population Under 15 Years	47.1%
Population Over 65 Years	2.3%
Literacy Rate	24.0%
Malnourished Children	NA

Land Use and Habitats

Cropland (sq. miles):	2,811
per capita (acres)	0.3
global rank	109
Permanent Pasture (sq. miles):	23,745
total livestock (millions)	2.8
Forest and Woodlands (sq. miles):	56,525
1985 deforestation (sq. miles)	332
Wilderness Area (sq. miles)	0
Maritime Areas (EEZ, sq. miles)	274
Protected Areas (sq. miles):	499
percent of total	0.5%
No. of Threatened Species:	
mammals	17
birds	6
plants	36

Energy and Industry

Energy Production:	
solids (trillion BTUs)	0
liquids (trillion BTUs)	0
gas (trillion BTUs)	0
nuclear (gigawatt-hours)	0
hydroelectric (gigawatt-hours)	171
Energy Requirements:	
traditional fuels (trillion BTUs)	38
total (trillion BTUs)	53
per capita (million BTUs)	9
per capita (global rank)	124
Industrial Share of GDP	NA
Industrial Energy Index	NA
Metal Reserve Index (world=100%)	1.7%
No. of Motor Vehicles/1000 Persons	NA

Water

Renewable Supply (cubic miles)	54.2
Total Use (cubic miles):	0.2
in agriculture	87.0%
in industry	3.0%
in homes and cities	10.0%
Access to Safe Water:	
urban population	55.0%
rural population	24.0%

Urban Centers and Waste

No. of Cities Over 1 Million:	1
percent of population	22.5%
Solid Wastes (million tons)	0.3
Urban Sanitation Access	65.0%

Population and Gross National Product

Population (millions)   GNP (billion $US)

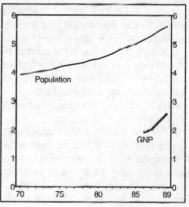

Commercial Energy Use

Total Energy Use (trillion BTUs)   Per Capita Energy Use (million BTUs)

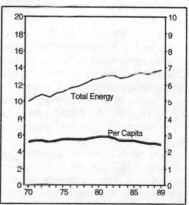

GUINEA-BISSAU

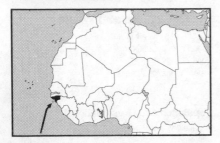

Total Area: 13,946 sq. miles
Global Rank: 117   Per Capita: 9.3 acres
Population: 964,000
Global Rank: 128   Growth Rate: 1.99%
Gross National Product: $167 m.
Global Rank: 142   Per Capita: $177
Greenhouse Gas Emissions
Global Share: 0.05%   Per Capita Rank: 11

The rivers of Guinea-Bissau, a country located on the northwest coast of Africa, were one of the first areas in Africa explored by the Portuguese during the 15th century. Yet under the Portuguese colonial rule, little was built; much of what existed was destroyed during the country's 12-year struggle for independence.

Guinea-Bissau is today among the world's least developed nations. Much of the country is a low coastal plain, gradually rising to a savanna in the east. Inlets pierce the coast, and offshore there are more than a dozen small islands. Palm trees and mangrove thickets cover most of the lowland along the rivers and the coast. A transitional zone of hardwood gives way to the tree-covered grasslands of the interior.

About 80 percent of the population is employed in agriculture. The principal cash crops are cashew nuts, which account for half of export earnings, plus palm kernels, peanuts, and cotton. The mining sector is undeveloped, though the nation possesses large reserves of bauxite and phosphate and also undeveloped deposits of petroleum.

Unlike other Sahelian countries, desertification has not yet reached serious levels. The government is implementing a program to control degradation of its land. Guinea-Bissau believes that it has an advantage over other African nations in that it can institute environmental protection measures before it embarks on extensive economic development.

Major Environmental Problems

Fire. In the dry season, brush fires are a serious hazard and can be widespread, leading the United Nations to call brush fires "a real catastrophe for Guinea-Bissau." Brush fires destroy significant areas of the country's forest and brush cover each year.

Deforestation. Deforestation is the result largely of itinerant, slash-and-burn agricultural practices, in addition to losses from brush fires. Estimates made in 1981 suggested that deforestation was claiming about 220 square miles (about 2.7 percent of the remaining forest) per year, but the damage may have become more serious in the intervening decade. In coastal areas, mangrove forests are cleared as rice growing areas are expanded.

Soil degradation. Drought, reduction in vegetation cover through overgrazing of livestock, erosion, failure to allow agricultural lands to lie fallow long enough, and overgrazing have all contributed to a loss of fertile topsoil. Soil loss reduces the small area of fertile land suitable for growing crops.

GUINEA-BISSAU

Quality of Life

Life Expectancy (years)	41.5
Infant Mortality (per 1000)	151.0
Population Under 15 Years	41.7%
Population Over 65 Years	3.7%
Literacy Rate	36.5%
Malnourished Children	NA

Land Use and Habitats

Cropland (sq. miles):	1,293
per capita (acres)	0.9
global rank	49
Permanent Pasture (sq. miles):	4,170
total livestock (millions)	1.0
Forest and Woodlands (sq. miles):	4,131
1985 deforestation (sq. miles)	220
Wilderness Area (sq. miles)	0
Maritime Areas (EEZ, sq. miles)	581
Protected Areas (sq. miles):	0
percent of total	0.0%
No. of Threatened Species:	
mammals	5
birds	2
plants	0

Energy and Industry

Energy Production:	
solids (trillion BTUs)	0
liquids (trillion BTUs)	0
gas (trillion BTUs)	0
nuclear (gigawatt-hours)	0
hydroelectric (gigawatt-hours)	0
Energy Requirements:	
traditional fuels (trillion BTUs)	4
total (trillion BTUs)	6
per capita (million BTUs)	6
per capita (global rank)	140
Industrial Share of GDP	15.8%
Industrial Energy Index	NA
Metal Reserve Index (world=100%)	NA
No. of Motor Vehicles/1000 Persons	NA

Water

Renewable Supply (cubic miles)	7.4
Total Use (cubic miles):	0.0
in agriculture	63.0%
in industry	6.0%
in homes and cities	31.0%
Access to Safe Water:	
urban population	18.0%
rural population	27.0%

Urban Centers and Waste

No. of Cities Over 1 Million:	0
percent of population	0.0%
Solid Wastes (million tons)	NA
Urban Sanitation Access	30.0%

Population and Gross National Product

Population (millions)	GNP (billion $US)

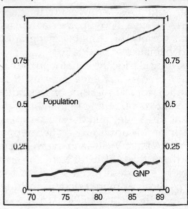

Commercial Energy Use

Total Energy Use (trillion BTUs)	Per Capita Energy Use (million BTUs)

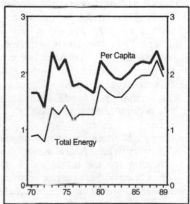

KENYA

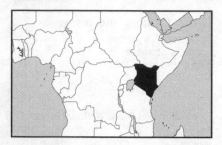

Total Area: 224,077 sq. miles
Global Rank: 44   Per Capita: 6.0 acres
Population: 24,031,000
Global Rank: 36   Growth Rate: 3.58%
Gross National Product: $7,931 m.
Global Rank: 72   Per Capita: $342
Greenhouse Gas Emissions
Global Share: 0.09%   Per Capita Rank: 144

Although best known for its game parks, Kenya encompasses a remarkable variety of climates, geography, and habitats.

Lying astride the equator on the east coast of Africa, Kenya rises up from humid, tropical coastline on the Indian Ocean to cool, rolling highlands of the great Rift Valley and the snow-capped peak of Mount Kenya, then slopes down to Lake Victoria in the west. The northern three fifths of Kenya is arid, mostly semidesert; the southern two fifths receives more rain and includes some of the richest soil in Africa.

Most of the economic activity and 85 percent of the growing population are located in the south. Nomads inhabit the arid north, along with increasing numbers of subsistence farmers forced onto marginal lands by an annual population growth rate estimated at 3.6 percent. The fertile lands in the central and western regions have become seriously overcrowded, leading to overcultivation and the farming of increasingly marginal lands. Overgrazing has become a serious problem in some areas.

Although Kenya is the most industrialized country in East Africa, agriculture and ranching are the mainstay of the Kenyan economy. Subsistence farming accounts for one-half of all agriculture. Coffee and tea, along with tourism, are the main earners of foreign exchange.

Nearly 6 percent of the land area in Kenya is protected, much of it in game reserves. Tourism makes the protection of wildlife a major economic, as well as ecological, concern. An aggressive antipoaching program has reduced, but not eliminated, the threat to elephant and rhino populations.

Major Environmental Problems

Land degradation. Soil erosion is a serious problem in both fertile and semiarid areas. Fertilizer use has risen, often to compensate for lost topsoil. In arid and semiarid areas, up to 2 million people may be threatened by desertification. Some parks have also suffered from a high rate of tourism and overgrazing by wild herbivores.

Deforestation. Natural forests, now scattered and covering only 3 percent of the surface area, are being rapidly lost. Much of the clearing is for new agricultural lands or fuelwood. Forest dwellers are also suffering because of deforestation.

Pollution. Water pollution due to urban and industrial wastes, some of them untreated, has become an increasing problem around Nairobi and the coastal city of Mombasa. Increased use of pesticides and fertilizers in agriculture is affecting water quality in many areas.

Quality of Life

Life Expectancy (years)	58.4
Infant Mortality (per 1000)	72.0
Population Under 15 Years	48.9%
Population Over 65 Years	2.6%
Literacy Rate	69.0%
Malnourished Children	42.0%

Land Use and Habitats

Cropland (sq. miles):	9,375
per capita (acres)	0.3
global rank	116
Permanent Pasture (sq. miles):	147,104
total livestock (millions)	28.2
Forest and Woodlands (sq. miles):	9,112
1985 deforestation (sq. miles)	151
Wilderness Area (sq. miles)	43,325
Maritime Areas (EEZ, sq. miles)	456
Protected Areas (sq. miles):	12,925
percent of total	5.8%
No. of Threatened Species:	
mammals	15
birds	18
plants	144

Energy and Industry

Energy Production:	
solids (trillion BTUs)	0
liquids (trillion BTUs)	0
gas (trillion BTUs)	0
nuclear (gigawatt-hours)	0
hydroelectric (gigawatt-hours)	2,467
Energy Requirements:	
traditional fuels (trillion BTUs)	324
total (trillion BTUs)	412
per capita (million BTUs)	18
per capita (global rank)	91
Industrial Share of GDP	19.5%
Industrial Energy Index	15
Metal Reserve Index (world=100%)	0.0%
No. of Motor Vehicles/1000 Persons	6

Water

Renewable Supply (cubic miles)	3.6
Total Use (cubic miles):	0.3
in agriculture	62.0%
in industry	11.0%
in homes and cities	27.0%
Access to Safe Water:	
urban population	NA
rural population	NA

Urban Centers and Waste

No. of Cities Over 1 Million:	1
percent of population	6.3%
Solid Wastes (million tons)	1.1
Urban Sanitation Access	NA

Population and Gross National Product

Population (millions) — GNP (billion $US)

Commercial Energy Use

Total Energy Use (trillion BTUs) — Per Capita Energy Use (million BTUs)

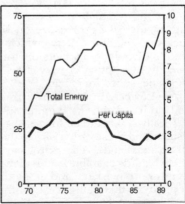

LESOTHO

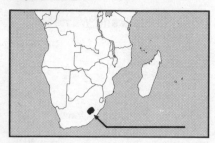

Total Area: 11,718 sq. miles
Global Rank: 119   Per Capita: 4.2 acres
Population: 1,774,000
Global Rank: 120   Growth Rate: 2.85%
Gross National Product: $754 m.
Global Rank: 131   Per Capita: $437
Greenhouse Gas Emissions
Global Share: NA   Per Capita Rank: NA

One of the few nations entirely surrounded by another, little Lesotho is an island about the size of Maryland floating in a sea of South African territory. Its high veld, plateau, and wooded mountains are home to people who farm, raise livestock, and work as migrant laborers in a variety of jobs in South Africa. The country's Alpine scenery is virtually unique in Africa and has contributed to an increasingly flourishing tourism industry. The Lesotho National Development Corporation has stimulated foreign investment in a number of ventures, including a $12 million hotel.

Only about one quarter of the country, situated in the lowlands, is fully suitable for agriculture. The highlands experience frost up to 200 days a year. A growing population, however, is putting increasing pressure on the stock of agricultural land, which is steadily dwindling. Farmers often respond by attempting to grow crops in land better suited for grazing.

As elsewhere in Africa, overuse of the land has changed the topography drastically. There are no forests left in Lesotho, and livestock have taken their toll on grasslands. A key problem is that two thirds of arable land is owned by migrant workers and is sharecropped in their absence by other workers, who have no incentive to practice conservation measures.

Economically, the country is largely dependent on South Africa, with up to one fourth of the population employed there. Highland water, which Lesotho sells to its neighbor, is the most important natural resource and has the potential for hydroelectric development. Other resources include some diamond and other mineral deposits.

Major Environmental Problems

Erosion. The country's most serious environmental problem, erosion, arises mainly from unrestricted grazing, along with overcultivation and other poor farming practices. The government estimates that 58 percent of croplands in the lowlands and 28 percent in the mountains face severe erosion threats, as do half the rangelands. Much of the soil lacks fertility because of low organic content. Both agricultural and livestock yields are falling. Deforestation has also left denuded areas vulnerable to erosion.

Deforestation. Fuelwood provides about three fourths of residential energy use. Trees cleared for firewood have left barren areas or grasslands in their place. Some reforestation has occurred, but not enough to keep pace with the growing demand. Without trees, firewood is scarce, rainfall is not retained, and erosion is increased.

Quality of Life

Life Expectancy (years)	56.0
Infant Mortality (per 1000)	100.0
Population Under 15 Years	43.5%
Population Over 65 Years	3.2%
Literacy Rate	NA
Malnourished Children	23.0%

Land Use and Habitats

Cropland (sq. miles):	1,236
per capita (acres)	0.5
global rank	92
Permanent Pasture (sq. miles):	7,722
total livestock (millions)	3.4
Forest and Woodlands (sq. miles):	0
1985 deforestation (sq. miles)	NA
Wilderness Area (sq. miles)	8,236
Maritime Areas (EEZ, sq. miles)	NA
Protected Areas (sq. miles):	26
percent of total	0.2%
No. of Threatened Species:	
mammals	2
birds	7
plants	7

Energy and Industry

Energy Production:	
solids (trillion BTUs)	NA
liquids (trillion BTUs)	0
gas (trillion BTUs)	0
nuclear (gigawatt-hours)	0
hydroelectric (gigawatt-hours)	0
Energy Requirements:	
traditional fuels (trillion BTUs)	NA
total (trillion BTUs)	NA
per capita (million BTUs)	NA
per capita (global rank)	NA
Industrial Share of GDP	29.8%
Industrial Energy Index	NA
Metal Reserve Index (world=100%)	NA
No. of Motor Vehicles/1000 Persons	4

Water

Renewable Supply (cubic miles)	1.0
Total Use (cubic miles).	0.0
in agriculture	56.0%
in industry	22.0%
in homes and cities	22.0%
Access to Safe Water:	
urban population	59.0%
rural population	45.0%

Urban Centers and Waste

No. of Cities Over 1 Million:	NA
percent of population	NA
Solid Wastes (million tons)	0.1
Urban Sanitation Access	14.0%

Population and Gross National Product

Population (millions)	GNP (billion $US)

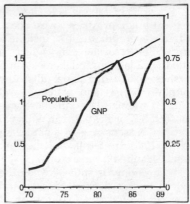

LIBERIA

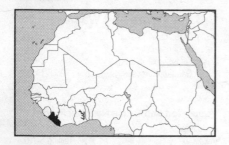

Total Area: 42,999 sq. miles
Global Rank: 95   Per Capita: 10.7 acres
Population: 2,575,000
Global Rank: 112   Growth Rate: 3.16%
Gross National Product: $1,063 m.
Global Rank: 125   Per Capita: $454
Greenhouse Gas Emissions
Global Share: 0.11%   Per Capita Rank: 22

The Republic of Liberia is located on the great bulge of Africa's west coast. Its four geographic regions include a narrow, level coastal plain which is dotted with lagoons, tidal creeks, and marshes; a belt of rolling hills; low mountain ranges and plateaus; and northern highlands. Rainfall ranges from 79 to 177 inches per year, with two short dry seasons. Water is abundant and the soils are fertile, but they are often best suited for tree crops.

The economy is split between the modern, foreign-dominated sector and the traditional sector. Exploitation of iron ore, diamonds, and rubber employs 40 percent of the workers. Farmers grow rice, cassava, bananas, and vegetables under a system of shifting cultivation.

In 1816 the American Colonization Society of the United States, a private organization, sent freed slaves to the west coast of Africa. Settlers landed at the site of the present Liberian capital, Monrovia, and later united to form the first independent republic in Africa. Liberia has recently gone through a painful and bloody internal conflict, with troops from neighboring West African countries having to establish peace.

Major Environmental Problems

Basic human needs. Development is at a standstill. The first priority for envi-

ronmental protection is to reestablish governmental authority, protect human rights, and meet basic needs for food and shelter.

Deforestation and loss of biodiversity. Many areas of remaining tropical rainforests are being cleared by smallholder agriculturalists, but the trend depends principally on the location of major logging roads, which depends on the companies holding concessions. National Forest Reserves are extensive and in the past were well managed. Communal forests were established and protected by tribal authorities. The status of both systems depends on constant monitoring and training, programs that have been cut back.

With political instability, illegal hunting and poaching are not being controlled. As of 1987 only 1 of 13 areas proposed for inclusion into a national system of parks and nature reserves had been established. Legislation has been proposed to protect biodiversity, but it has not been passed and there is little enforcement capacity available.

Soil erosion. Over 40 percent of the country is devoted to cultivation of traditional crops. Traditionally, only a portion of the land is planted to crops at any one time. With population growth, fallow periods have been reduced and erosion has increased.

Quality of Life

Life Expectancy (years)	53.0
Infant Mortality (per 1000)	142.0
Population Under 15 Years	45.9%
Population Over 65 Years	3.1%
Literacy Rate	39.5%
Malnourished Children	24.4%

Land Use and Habitats

Cropland (sq. miles):	1,440
per capita (acres)	0.4
global rank	101
Permanent Pasture (sq. miles):	22,008
total livestock (millions)	0.7
Forest and Woodlands (sq. miles):	6,795
1985 deforestation (sq. miles)	178
Wilderness Area (sq. miles)	5,483
Maritime Areas (EEZ, sq. miles)	887
Protected Areas (sq. miles):	505
percent of total	1.2%
No. of Threatened Species:	
mammals	18
birds	10
plants	1

Energy and Industry

Energy Production:	
solids (trillion BTUs)	0
liquids (trillion BTUs)	0
gas (trillion BTUs)	0
nuclear (gigawatt-hours)	0
hydroelectric (gigawatt-hours)	317
Energy Requirements:	
traditional fuels (trillion BTUs)	44
total (trillion BTUs)	57
per capita (million BTUs)	23
per capita (global rank)	81
Industrial Share of GDP	NA
Industrial Energy Index	NA
Metal Reserve Index (world=100%)	0.1%
No. of Motor Vehicles/1000 Persons	3

Water

Renewable Supply (cubic miles)	55.7
Total Use (cubic miles):	0.0
in agriculture	60.0%
in industry	13.0%
in homes and cities	27.0%
Access to Safe Water:	
urban population	93.0%
rural population	22.0%

Urban Centers and Waste

No. of Cities Over 1 Million:	0
percent of population	0.0%
Solid Wastes (million tons)	0.2
Urban Sanitation Access	4.0%

Population and Gross National Product

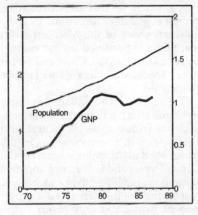

Commercial Energy Use

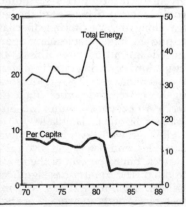

LIBYA

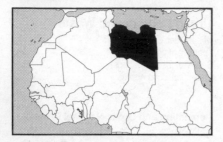

Total Area: 679,347 sq. miles
  Global Rank: 15   Per Capita: 95.7 acres
Population: 4,545,000
  Global Rank: 95   Growth Rate: 3.65%
Gross National Product: $22,214 m.
  Global Rank: 56   Per Capita: $5,069
Greenhouse Gas Emissions
  Global Share: 0.12%   Per Capita Rank: 48

This oil-rich Islamic nation has the longest coastline of any country on the southern shore of the Mediterranean Sea. Libya is bordered on the east by Egypt and the Sudan, Chad and Niger on the south, and Algeria and Tunisia on the west.

The country itself is largely desert and semidesert: hills south of the capital city of Tripoli, rocky plains and sand in the interior, and mountains in the south. Most of the country is part of the Sahara Desert and is very hot and dry. Rainfall averages less than 8 inches per year in the interior. There are no permanent rivers, and only about 1 percent of the country is available as cropland and 7.5 percent as pasture.

Libya is sparsely populated, with 90 percent of the country's 4.5 million people living in 10 percent of the land area along the Mediterranean coast. Despite an inhospitable climate and limited agricultural resources, the population is growing rapidly at about 3.7 percent per year. The population is largely of Arab and Berber ethnic origins. Most people are Sunni Muslims. Arabic is the official language.

Libya grows wheat, barley, olives, vegetables, and dates, and also raises livestock, but 65 percent of the food is imported. The country has significant reserves of oil, natural gas, and iron ore. Libya exports an average of about 1 million barrels of oil per day and the economy is heavily dependent on oil revenues.

Major Environmental Problems

Water. Because of the arid climate and absence of rivers, water is very scarce in Libya. Much of the water supply is pumped from underground resources at rates that far exceed rates of natural replenishment. Excessive pumping is likely to cause saltwater intrusion into underground aquifers. An ambitious but expensive effort pumps water from aquifers in the south for agricultural and urban use in the north.

Land degradation. Soil erosion from farming in marginal areas, overgrazing of livestock, and destruction of vegetation are significant problems. The depletion of vegetation also erodes soils and grasslands, lowering the capacity of the land to support life and increasing desertification.

Pollution. Untreated urban sewage and wastes from petroleum refining and industrial effluents are a significant problem. Waste disposal has contaminated coastal areas that are badly needed for food production. Effluents from untreated sewage, mining, industrial operations, and oil contribute to the increasing pollution and overfertilization of the Mediterranean Sea.

Quality of Life

Life Expectancy (years)	60.5
Infant Mortality (per 1000)	82.0
Population Under 15 Years	45.7%
Population Over 65 Years	1.9%
Literacy Rate	63.8%
Malnourished Children	NA

Land Use and Habitats

Cropland (sq. miles):	8,301
per capita (acres)	1.2
global rank	27
Permanent Pasture (sq. miles):	51,351
total livestock (millions)	7.3
Forest and Woodlands (sq. miles):	2,645
1985 deforestation (sq. miles)	0
Wilderness Area (sq. miles)	252,883
Maritime Areas (EEZ, sq. miles)	1,305
Protected Areas (sq. miles):	598
percent of total	0.1%
No. of Threatened Species:	
mammals	12
birds	9
plants	58

Energy and Industry

Energy Production:	
solids (trillion BTUs)	0
liquids (trillion BTUs)	2,201
gas (trillion BTUs)	261
nuclear (gigawatt-hours)	0
hydroelectric (gigawatt-hours)	0
Energy Requirements:	
traditional fuels (trillion BTUs)	5
total (trillion BTUs)	494
per capita (million BTUs)	113
per capita (global rank)	33
Industrial Share of GDP	NA
Industrial Energy Index	22
Metal Reserve Index (world=100%)	0.0%
No. of Motor Vehicles/1000 Persons	NA

Water

Renewable Supply (cubic miles)	0.2
Total Use (cubic miles):	0.7
in agriculture	75.0%
in industry	10.0%
in homes and cities	15.0%
Access to Safe Water:	
urban population	100.0%
rural population	80.0%

Urban Centers and Waste

No. of Cities Over 1 Million:	1
percent of population	45.4%
Solid Wastes (million tons)	0.6
Urban Sanitation Access	100.0%

Population and Gross National Product

Population (millions)	GNP (billion $US)

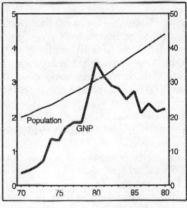

Commercial Energy Use

Total Energy Use (trillion BTUs)	Per Capita Energy Use (million BTUs)

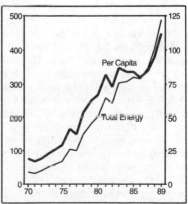

MADAGASCAR

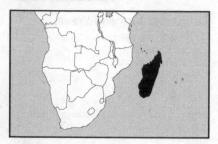

Total Area: 226,652 sq. miles
  Global Rank: 42   Per Capita: 12.1 acres
Population: 12,004,000
  Global Rank: 56   Growth Rate: 3.18%
Gross National Product: $2,283 m.
  Global Rank: 108   Per Capita: $196
Greenhouse Gas Emissions
  Global Share: 0.38%   Per Capita Rank: 36

Madagascar, a large island, lies in the Indian Ocean 250 miles off the coast of Mozambique. Separated by geological forces from the African continent about 100 million years ago, Madagascar developed its own unique variety of more than 200,000 plant and animal species, three fourths of which exist nowhere else in the world. The island is host to more than one half of the world's chameleon species and 1,000 species of orchids. It also is home to 5 percent of the world's total species.

Despite the country's biological wealth, the population lives in relative poverty. Inequitable land distribution, an export-based economy, and rapid population growth all contribute to the poverty. Agriculture, which includes slash-and-burn techniques, employs 83 percent of the labor force. In the lowlands and valleys, rice is the major crop.

More electricity comes from hydropower than from fossil fuels. Those too poor to purchase kerosene or oil burn charcoal for heat and cooking, augmenting deforestation and air pollution, a minor but growing problem. A recently discovered titanium deposit could help alleviate Madagascar's $3.4 billion external debt; however, the deposit lies beneath a protected forest area.

Madagascar established a system of nature reserves as early as 1927. Today, two national parks and 34 nature reserves protect the deciduous forest in the west and rainforests in the east. The first African debt-for-nature swap, between Madagascar and the World Wildlife Fund, relieved the country of $3 million in debt. As part of this exchange, ecology is now standard curriculum in all schools.

Major Environmental Problems

Deforestation. Seventy-five percent of forested lands are already destroyed, and at current rates, total denudation is expected in all but the steepest inclines in 35 years. Despite numerous reforestation projects, second-growth stands have little chance of reaching maturity. Clearcut areas are set afire each year to promote grass for cattle grazing.

Local customs also work against forest preservation efforts. Plowing is taboo because it "turns the earth's back on god." Without plowing, a field's productive lifetime is dramatically reduced, forcing farmers to seek out and deforest new land. The forest floor is mainly laterite, an iron-red clay that bakes to concrete hardness in the tropical sun.

Water quality. Only 10 percent of the people in rural areas have access to safe drinking water. Surface water is heavily contaminated with untreated sewage and other organic wastes.

Quality of Life

Life Expectancy (years)	53.5
Infant Mortality (per 1000)	120.0
Population Under 15 Years	45.6%
Population Over 65 Years	2.5%
Literacy Rate	80.2%
Malnourished Children	56.0%

Land Use and Habitats

Cropland (sq. miles):	11,938
per capita (acres)	0.7
global rank	68
Permanent Pasture (sq. miles):	131,274
total livestock (millions)	13.6
Forest and Woodlands (sq. miles):	60,541
1985 deforestation (sq. miles)	602
Wilderness Area (sq. miles)	2,669
Maritime Areas (EEZ, sq. miles)	4,988
Protected Areas (sq. miles):	4,161
percent of total	1.8%
No. of Threatened Species:	
mammals	53
birds	28
plants	193

Energy and Industry

Energy Production:	
solids (trillion BTUs)	0
liquids (trillion BTUs)	0
gas (trillion BTUs)	0
nuclear (gigawatt-hours)	0
hydroelectric (gigawatt-hours)	317
Energy Requirements:	
traditional fuels (trillion BTUs)	68
total (trillion BTUs)	83
per capita (million BTUs)	7
per capita (global rank)	133
Industrial Share of GDP	14.4%
Industrial Energy Index	NA
Metal Reserve Index (world=100%)	0.0%
No. of Motor Vehicles/1000 Persons	3

Water

Renewable Supply (cubic miles)	9.6
Total Use (cubic miles):	3.9
in agriculture	99.0%
in industry	0.0%
in homes and cities	1.0%
Access to Safe Water:	
urban population	62.0%
rural population	10.0%

Urban Centers and Waste

No. of Cities Over 1 Million:	0
percent of population	0.0%
Solid Wastes (million tons)	0.6
Urban Sanitation Access	NA

Population and Gross National Product

Population — GNP
(millions) — (billion $US)

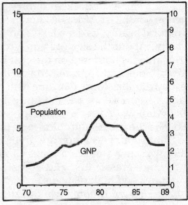

Commercial Energy Use

Total Energy Use — Per Capita Energy Use
(trillion BTUs) — (million BTUs)

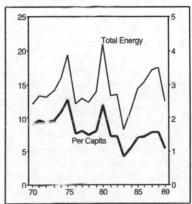

MALAWI

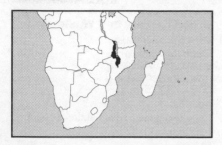

Total Area: 45,744 sq. miles
  Global Rank: 92   Per Capita: 3.3 acres
Population: 8,754,000
  Global Rank: 72   Growth Rate: 3.52%
Gross National Product: $1,540 m.
  Global Rank: 119   Per Capita: $182
Greenhouse Gas Emissions
  Global Share: 0.17%   Per Capita Rank: 69

Malawi, a small landlocked country located in southeast Africa, is known for its natural beauty, its deep lake, and its poverty. About the size of Pennsylvania, Malawi is bordered on the east by Mozambique and Tanzania and on the west by Zambia. More than one fifth of Malawi's surface area is made up by Lake Malawi, Africa's third largest lake. The climate is subtropical, and the geography and vegetation are diverse, encompassing flat savanna, woodlands and grasslands, and forested mountains and high plateaus.

Lake Malawi is home to a dazzling variety of fish, containing more endemic species than any other in the world. Fish from Lake Malawi provide 70 percent of the animal protein consumed in the country. Malawi possesses few mineral resources, and its per capita income is among the lowest in the world. Agriculture supports 85 percent of the population and provides over 90 percent of the nation's export earnings. Nine percent of the country has been set aside as wilderness area, including the southern tip of Lake Malawi.

Population density is one of the highest in Africa, as is population growth, contributing to environmental problems. These conditions have been worsened by a huge influx of 800,000 refugees fleeing the civil war in neighboring Mozambique.

Major Environmental Problems

Deforestation. Population growth coupled with the influx of refugees has given Malawi the second highest rate of deforestation in Africa, next to Cote d'Ivoire. The problem is most severe in the central and southern regions, where trees are cleared both for fuel and for cropland. Strong measures are needed to conserve the remaining forest areas.

Land degradation. Land pressure has forced many farmers onto smaller and increasingly marginal plots. As the land is not allowed to recover, the soil is increasingly depleted of nutrients and the result—decreasing yields— has contributed to one of the highest rates of child malnutrition in Africa. Much of the best land is reserved for estates growing export crops.

Threats to fish. Siltation of spawning grounds, caused by agricultural runoff and deforestation, threatens some fish species with local extinction. Pollution by sewage, agricultural chemicals, and industrial wastes also threaten fish.

Wildlife preservation. Poaching has severely threatened elephant and rhino populations in the parks. Forestry and wildlife officials often come in conflict with local people in search of food, fuelwood, or agricultural land.

Quality of Life

Life Expectancy (years)	47.0
Infant Mortality (per 1000)	150.0
Population Under 15 Years	49.1%
Population Over 65 Years	2.1%
Literacy Rate	NA
Malnourished Children	61.0%

Land Use and Habitats

Cropland (sq. miles):	9,301
per capita (acres)	0.7
global rank	65
Permanent Pasture (sq. miles):	7,104
total livestock (millions)	2.4
Forest and Woodlands (sq. miles):	14,440
1985 deforestation (sq. miles)	579
Wilderness Area (sq. miles)	3,014
Maritime Areas (EEZ, sq. miles)	0
Protected Areas (sq. miles):	4,119
percent of total	9.0%
No. of Threatened Species:	
mammals	10
birds	7
plants	61

Energy and Industry

Energy Production:	
solids (trillion BTUs)	0
liquids (trillion BTUs)	0
gas (trillion BTUs)	0
nuclear (gigawatt-hours)	0
hydroelectric (gigawatt-hours)	570
Energy Requirements:	
traditional fuels (trillion BTUs)	125
total (trillion BTUs)	138
per capita (million BTUs)	16
per capita (global rank)	95
Industrial Share of GDP	20.1%
Industrial Energy Index	NA
Metal Reserve Index (world=100%)	NA
No. of Motor Vehicles/1000 Persons	2

Water

Renewable Supply (cubic miles)	??
Total Use (cubic miles):	0.0
in agriculture	49.0%
in industry	17.0%
in homes and cities	34.0%
Access to Safe Water:	
urban population	66.0%
rural population	49.0%

Urban Centers and Waste

No. of Cities Over 1 Million:	0
percent of population	0.0%
Solid Wastes (million tons)	0.2
Urban Sanitation Access	0.0%

Population and Gross National Product

Population	GNP
(millions)	(billion $US)

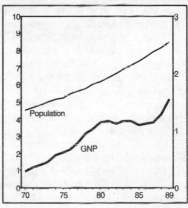

Commercial Energy Use

Total Energy Use	Per Capita Energy Use
(trillion BTUs)	(million BTUs)

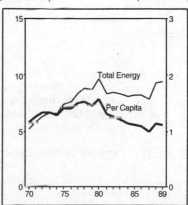

MALI

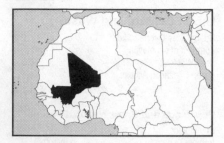

Total Area: 478,830 sq. miles
Global Rank: 22   Per Capita: 33.3 acres
Population: 9,214,000
Global Rank: 68   Growth Rate: 3.04%
Gross National Product: $1,978 m.
Global Rank: 115   Per Capita: $221
Greenhouse Gas Emissions
Global Share: 0.04% Per Capita Rank: 135

Mali, a landlocked country located in northwestern Africa, is larger than Texas and California combined. The agriculturally productive part of the nation is located in the transitional savanna region, just north of the border with Burkina Faso and Cote d'Ivoire. The Niger and Senegal rivers support both biodiversity and a large share of Mali's rural income.

Gold, salt, phosphate, marble, and limestone resources are currently utilized. Deposits of bauxite, iron ore, manganese, uranium, and other minerals are thus far undeveloped. One half of Mali's gross domestic product consists of agricultural products, including millet, sorghum, corn, rice, livestock, sugar, cotton, and peanuts. Mali is extremely poor and has high rates of infant mortality and low rates of literacy.

Mali's population of diverse ethnic groups coexist peacefully; most share similar historic, cultural, and religious (Muslim) traditions. Each ethnic group traditionally is tied to a specific occupation such as farming, fishing, or herding. French is the official language.

Major Environmental Problems

Water scarcity. Recurring drought has had severe consequences in Mali. Where vegetation once flourished, there are withered crops, impover-

ished soil, bone-dry wells, and abandoned villages. Destruction of trees for firewood, overcultivation, and overgrazing in wet years all lead to land degradation, which together with a lack of soil and water conservation contribute to the cycle of aridity.

The country's water supply comes from river sources or open wells, which are often contaminated by organisms that cause such diseases as onchocerciasis and schistosomiasis. Only 9 percent of Malians have access to adequate and sanitary water supplies for drinking and household use.

The not-yet-fully-operational Manantali Dam was built to control flooding of the Senegal River for increased irrigation, shipping, and electrical power. However, it will eliminate the floodpulse upon which many Malians depend, discourage traditional methods of cultivation, and greatly reduce the pasture area in the dry season. Wetland species and fisheries will also be adversely affected by the dam.

Wildlife resources. Drought, poaching, and loss of habitat have decimated much of the wildlife. A once rich variety of animals has declined to the point where there are likely to be no significant large mammal populations left in 10 years. Oryx, elephants, lions, cheetahs, elands, giraffes, and ostriches are declining rapidly or are locally extinct.

Quality of Life

Life Expectancy (years)	44.0
Infant Mortality (per 1000)	169.0
Population Under 15 Years	47.4%
Population Over 65 Years	2.2%
Literacy Rate	32.0%
Malnourished Children	34.0%

Land Use and Habitats

Cropland (sq. miles):	8,081
per capita (acres)	0.6
global rank	74
Permanent Pasture (sq. miles):	115,830
total livestock (millions)	17.1
Forest and Woodlands (sq. miles):	26,950
1985 deforestation (sq. miles)	139
Wilderness Area (sq. miles)	227,080
Maritime Areas (EEZ, sq. miles)	0
Protected Areas (sq. miles):	3,433
percent of total	0.7%
No. of Threatened Species:	
mammals	16
birds	4
plants	15

Energy and Industry

Energy Production:	
solids (trillion BTUs)	0
liquids (trillion BTUs)	0
gas (trillion BTUs)	0
nuclear (gigawatt-hours)	0
hydroelectric (gigawatt-hours)	171
Energy Requirements:	
traditional fuels (trillion BTUs)	48
total (trillion BTUs)	56
per capita (million BTUs)	6
per capita (global rank)	138
Industrial Share of GDP	12.2%
Industrial Energy Index	NA
Metal Reserve Index (world=100%)	NA
No. of Motor Vehicles/1000 Persons	NA

Water

Renewable Supply (cubic miles)	14.9
Total Use (cubic miles):	0.3
in agriculture	97.0%
in industry	1.0%
in homes and cities	2.0%
Access to Safe Water:	
urban population	100.0%
rural population	36.0%

Urban Centers and Waste

No. of Cities Over 1 Million:	0
percent of population	0.0%
Solid Wastes (million tons)	0.4
Urban Sanitation Access	94.0%

Population and Gross National Product

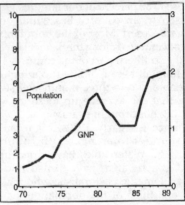

Population (millions)   GNP (billion $US)

Commercial Energy Use

Total Energy Use (trillion BTUs)   Per Capita Energy Use (million BTUs)

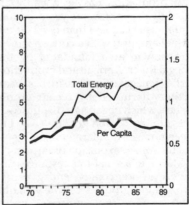

MAURITANIA

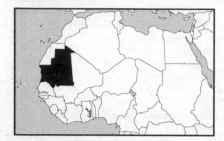

Total Area: 395,947 sq. miles
  Global Rank: 27   Per Capita: 125.2 acres
Population: 2,024,000
  Global Rank: 118   Growth Rate: 2.73%
Gross National Product: $943 m.
  Global Rank: 129   Per Capita: $479
Greenhouse Gas Emissions
  Global Share: 0.02%   Per Capita Rank: 109

Close to 80 percent of this large, coastal west African country lies within the Sahara Desert. Most of the population is concentrated along the Senegal River in the southern part of the country.

Rainfall here is limited to a highly variable two-to-three-month wet season that can average up to 26 inches during nondrought years.

Since the early 1970s, Mauritania has undergone near continuous drought. Water holes have dried up, and grazing areas have turned to desert. Nomadic pastoralists, who make up one third of the population, have lost most of their livestock and have been forced to settle around urban areas where food aid was available.

Dryland and floodplain agricultural production has been badly affected by drought. Some years, annual rainfall has been less than one half the normal amount, with a corresponding reduction in area inundated by the Senegal River. Agricultural production in the Senegal River basin has been further disrupted by recent ethnic clashes, which began as a dispute over access to dry season grazing areas between nomads and farmers. The result was the forced expulsion of farmers.

Mauritania's natural resources include iron ore, copper, and gypsum. Rich fishing grounds off the Atlantic coast provide the country's largest revenue source. Most of the annual catch is taken by foreign trawlers, which have leased fishing rights from the government.

Major Environmental Problems

Desertification. Overgrazing and the destruction of trees by pastoralists to provide new grazing areas for their livestock has contributed to the rapid desertification of much of Sahelian Mauritania over the past two decades. Denuded of vegetative cover, soils have been subjected to heavy wind erosion. Drought has also contributed to the gradual encroachment of the desert.

Water development. A project to dam and develop the Senegal River basin seeks to maintain a sufficient level of water in the river year-round so that more land can be brought under irrigated cultivation. When fully operational, the dams will end annual flooding of the river valley and may increase food production. This will disrupt the ecology of the area, however, drying the spawning habitats of local fish populations and altering the wetland areas used as wintering grounds by migratory birds. Forests whose resident plant species depend on annual inundation will also be affected. The dams will limit traditional agricultural practices and the availability of seasonal floodplain pasture for livestock.

MAURITANIA

Quality of Life

Life Expectancy (years)	46.0
Infant Mortality (per 1000)	127.0
Population Under 15 Years	45.0%
Population Over 65 Years	2.7%
Literacy Rate	34.0%
Malnourished Children	37.0%

Land Use and Habitats

Cropland (sq. miles):	768
per capita (acres)	0.2
global rank	119
Permanent Pasture (sq. miles):	151,544
total livestock (millions)	9.7
Forest and Woodlands (sq. miles).	19,073
1985 deforestation (sq. miles)	50
Wilderness Area (sq. miles)	275,559
Maritime Areas (EEZ, sq. miles)	596
Protected Areas (sq. miles):	6,691
percent of total	1.7%
No. of Threatened Species:	
mammals	14
birds	5
plants	3

Energy and Industry

Energy Production:	
solids (trillion BTUs)	0
liquids (trillion BTUs)	0
gas (trillion BTUs)	0
nuclear (gigawatt-hours)	0
hydroelectric (gigawatt-hours)	24
Energy Requirements:	
traditional fuels (trillion BTUs)	0
total (trillion BTUs)	39
per capita (million BTUs)	20
per capita (global rank)	87
Industrial Share of GDP	24.1%
Industrial Energy Index	NA
Metal Reserve Index (world=100%)	0.0%
No. of Motor Vehicles/1000 Persons	9

Water

Renewable Supply (cubic miles)	0.1
Total Use (cubic miles):	0.2
in agriculture	84.0%
in industry	4.0%
in homes and cities	12.0%
Access to Safe Water:	
urban population	67.0%
rural population	65.0%

Urban Centers and Waste

No. of Cities Over 1 Million:	0
percent of population	0.0%
Solid Wastes (million tons)	0.2
Urban Sanitation Access	34.0%

Population and Gross National Product

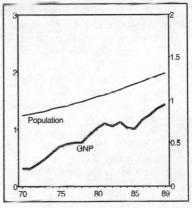

Population (millions)

GNP (billion $US)

Commercial Energy Use

Total Energy Use (trillion BTUs)

Per Capita Energy Use (million BTUs)

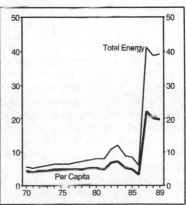

MAURITIUS

Total Area: 718 sq. miles
Global Rank: 142   Per Capita: 0.4 acres
Population: 1,082,000
Global Rank: 127   Growth Rate: 1.17%
Gross National Product: $2,055 m.
Global Rank: 111   Per Capita: $1,922
Greenhouse Gas Emissions
Global Share: 0.00%   Per Capita Rank: 149

The island of Mauritius lies 500 miles east of Madagascar in the Indian Ocean. Also including Rodrigues and St. Brandon islands and a number of outlying smaller islands, the land mass of the state of Mauritius covers an area about the size of Rhode Island.

The main island is of volcanic origin and is entirely surrounded by coral reefs. It has a small natural resource base. Originally inhabited only by the now extinct dodo, Mauritius owes its settlement and development to sugar cane, its staple crop, which now grows on 98 percent of the main island's cultivated land, or 45 percent of its total land area.

Because of the absence of mineral resources and its distance from major markets, Mauritius must rely on imports for most of its basic needs. However, Mauritius is self-sufficient for one fourth of its electrical needs, which it derives from hydroelectric sources and from the recycling of sugar by-products, particularly dried sugar cane pulp. Standards of nutrition, health care, and general education greatly exceed those of neighboring countries.

In an effort to increase its income base, Mauritius has widely promoted tourism as a major industry. Since the mid 1980s, there has been a steady increase in the number of visitors. Increased tourism, however, has added to environmental pressures.

Major Environmental Problems

Land degradation. Intensive monoculture in a tropical climate customarily involves large quantities of pesticides and fertilizers. Overuse of these chemicals threatens soil fertility, as well as ground and surface waters. Such overuse can also destroy nontarget organisms, including natural enemies of pest species, which can lead to the development of pesticide resistance and appearance of new pest species.

Water pollution. Rapid economic development, including tourism, has resulted in a proliferation of industries that use a range of potentially hazardous materials. The existing infrastructure for sewage and solid waste collection has proved inadequate. As a result, sewage threatens drinking water supplies and coastal ecology.

Species conservation. Mauritius has many unique endemic plants and animals that have come under stress from increased tourism and the resulting lack of consideration for native ecosystems. In addition, native flora and fauna are also threatened by coastal pollution and overfishing, illegal logging, deforestation for the purposes of deer ranching, and the introduction of exotic plants or animals that overtake indigenous species.

Quality of Life

Life Expectancy (years)	69.0
Infant Mortality (per 1000)	23.0
Population Under 15 Years	25.8%
Population Over 65 Years	4.3%
Literacy Rate	NA
Malnourished Children	22.0%

Land Use and Habitats

Cropland (sq. miles):	409
per capita (acres)	0.2
global rank	120
Permanent Pasture (sq. miles):	27
total livestock (millions)	0.1
Forest and Woodlands (sq. miles):	220
1985 deforestation (sq. miles)	0
Wilderness Area (sq. miles)	0
Maritime Areas (EEZ, sq. miles)	4,568
Protected Areas (sq. miles):	16
percent of total	2.2%
No. of Threatened Species:	
mammals	3
birds	10
plants	240

Energy and Industry

Energy Production:	
solids (trillion BTUs)	0
liquids (trillion BTUs)	0
gas (trillion BTUs)	0
nuclear (gigawatt-hours)	0
hydroelectric (gigawatt-hours)	106
Energy Requirements:	
traditional fuels (trillion BTUs)	15
total (trillion BTUs)	29
per capita (million BTUs)	27
per capita (global rank)	76
Industrial Share of GDP	32.0%
Industrial Energy Index	NA
Metal Reserve Index (world=100%)	NA
No. of Motor Vehicles/1000 Persons	41

Water

Renewable Supply (cubic miles)	0.5
Total Use (cubic miles):	0.1
in agriculture	77.0%
in industry	7.0%
in homes and cities	16.0%
Access to Safe Water:	
urban population	100.0%
rural population	92.0%

Urban Centers and Waste

No. of Cities Over 1 Million:	0
percent of population	0.0%
Solid Wastes (million tons)	0.1
Urban Sanitation Access	92.0%

Population and Gross National Product

Population
(millions)

GNP
(billion $US)

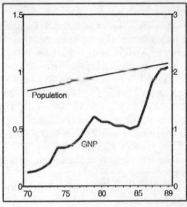

Commercial Energy Use

Total Energy Use
(trillion BTUs)

Per Capita Energy Use
(million BTUs)

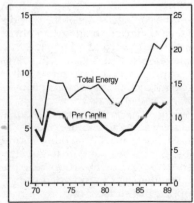

MOROCCO

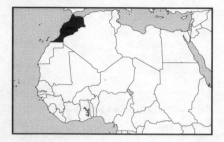

Total Area: 172,410 sq. miles
 Global Rank: 52   Per Capita: 4.4 acres
Population: 25,061,000
 Global Rank: 34   Growth Rate: 2.58%
Gross National Product: $21,186 m.
 Global Rank: 57   Per Capita: $867
Greenhouse Gas Emissions
 Global Share: 0.10%   Per Capita Rank: 142

Perhaps best known for the cities of Casablanca, Marrakesh, and Tangier, Morocco sits at the extreme northwest corner of Africa. The country faces both the Mediterranean Sea and the Atlantic Ocean and is bordered on the east by Algeria and on the south by the western Sahara. Morocco has a fertile coastal plain and the rugged Atlas Mountains, as well as a desert.

The country's 25 million inhabitants, most of whom live in the coastal plain, are of Arab-Berber ethnic origins. Morocco's capital is Rabat, and the dominant religion is Sunni Muslim. The population is growing at the rate of about 2.6 percent annually. Arabic is Morocco's official language, but French and Berber dialects are also spoken.

Morocco's long Atlantic Ocean coastline contains some of the world's richest fisheries. It also has three fourths of the world's known phosphate reserves and is the world's largest exporter of phosphate. Other economic sectors include food processing and leather goods.

About 40 percent of the work force is employed in agriculture, mostly as subsistence farmers. The country is not self-sufficient in food. With few energy resources except hydropower, the country depends on imported energy supplies. But surface water resources, with several major river systems, arc the most plentiful in arid Africa.

Major Environmental Problems

Land degradation. Soil erosion is a major problem in Morocco. Erosion results from several factors, including the expansion of farming into marginal areas, overgrazing of livestock, destruction of vegetation for firewood, and conversion of forested land to farmland.

The depletion of vegetation, especially grasslands, from overgrazing also destroys the soil and contributes to additional deterioration through wind erosion. Some efforts to reverse this process, largely through reforestation programs, have been undertaken.

Water and wildlife mismanagement. Massive irrigation projects associated with the expansion of agriculture have resulted in the silting of reservoirs and an increased incidence of diseases. The major watersheds need immediate attention and careful management.

Uncontrolled hunting and habitat destruction are rapidly depleting wildlife stocks; several species are close to extinction.

Pollution. Untreated urban sewage is the primary cause of severe contamination of water supplies. Morocco faces some oil contamination of its coastal waters. Rapid industrial development has increased effluents and created waste disposal problems.

Quality of Life

Life Expectancy (years)	60.7
Infant Mortality (per 1000)	82.0
Population Under 15 Years	38.8%
Population Over 65 Years	3.4%
Literacy Rate	49.5%
Malnourished Children	34.0%

Land Use and Habitats

Cropland (sq. miles):	35,680
per capita (acres)	0.9
global rank	44
Permanent Pasture (sq. miles):	80,695
total livestock (millions)	28.3
Forest and Woodlands (sq. miles):	30,618
1985 deforestation (sq. miles)	50
Wilderness Area (sq. miles)	0
Maritime Areas (EEZ, sq. miles)	1,074
Protected Areas (sq. miles):	1,422
percent of total	0.8%
No. of Threatened Species:	
mammals	9
birds	14
plants	194

Energy and Industry

Energy Production:	
solids (trillion BTUs)	15
liquids (trillion BTUs)	1
gas (trillion BTUs)	2
nuclear (gigawatt-hours)	0
hydroelectric (gigawatt-hours)	1,156
Energy Requirements:	
traditional fuels (trillion BTUs)	13
total (trillion BTUs)	270
per capita (million BTUs)	11
per capita (global rank)	113
Industrial Share of GDP	35.7%
Industrial Energy Index	6
Metal Reserve Index (world=100%)	0.1%
No. of Motor Vehicles/1000 Persons	24

Water

Renewable Supply (cubic miles)	7.8
Total Use (cubic miles):	2.6
in agriculture	91.0%
in industry	3.0%
in homes and cities	6.0%
Access to Safe Water:	
urban population	100.0%
rural population	25.0%

Urban Centers and Waste

No. of Cities Over 1 Million:	2
percent of population	17.1%
Solid Wastes (million tons)	2.4
Urban Sanitation Access	100.0%

Population and Gross National Product

Population	GNP
(millions)	(billion $US)

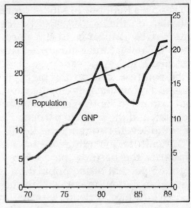

Commercial Energy Use

Total Energy Use	Per Capita Energy Use
(trillion BTUs)	(million BTUs)

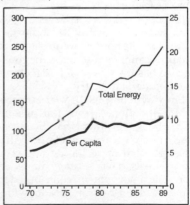

MOZAMBIQUE

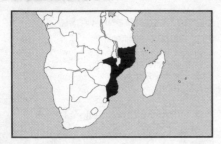

Total Area: 309,489 sq. miles
  Global Rank: 33   Per Capita: 12.7 acres
Population: 15,656,000
  Global Rank: 50   Growth Rate: 2.65%
Gross National Product: $1,081 m.
  Global Rank: 123   Per Capita: $71
Greenhouse Gas Emissions
  Global Share: NA   Per Capita Rank: NA

The People's Republic of Mozambique is located on the east coast of Africa, bordered by Tanzania to the north, Malawi, Zambia, and Zimbabwe to the west, and South Africa and Swaziland to the south. Except in the high plateaus and mountains, its climate varies from tropical to subtropical. Rainfall is irregular, and the south in particular is subject to severe droughts and floods.

Agriculture (including forestry and fishing) is the base of the economy. About 85 percent of the population is engaged in agriculture, mostly in subsistence farming. Agriculture provides much of the country's exports; the principal cash crops are tea, cashews, sugar, and cotton. Shrimp accounts for up to 40 percent of the national economy. Transport services are economically important, too, as several busy ports are linked by rail to landlocked states along its borders. With extensive untapped mineral resources, the country also has the potential to develop a strong mineral industry.

Since winning its 10-year struggle for independence from Portugal in 1975, the government has been engaged in civil war with a South African-supported opposition group. The war's effects have severely impeded economic development, contributed to plunging export earnings and widespread malnutrition and starvation, and devastated the environment. Severe drought and lack of government agricultural incentives are also factors in agricultural productivity decline. Population pressures in areas affected by refugees from the war have made the environment more vulnerable.

Major Environmental Problems

Health. Mozambique has a very high infant mortality rate, and disease and malnutrition are the principal causes of death for the population as a whole. Droughts, floods, and civil strife interplay to make the country extremely susceptible to food shortages and famine, as illustrated during the 1980s. Disease and epidemics are widespread in camps housing those displaced by famine and war, contributing to the high morbidity and mortality rates. Further, the civil war has disabled the government's efforts to provide infrastructure and health and social services.

Deforestation. Mozambique's mangrove forests, which comprised 48 percent of the coastline, have been reduced by 70 percent over the last 20 years. Mangrove wood is exploited locally for firewood and fuel, especially for the sugar industry. Loss of these forests makes coastlines more vulnerable to erosion, adversely affecting marine populations and the country's shrimp industry.

MOZAMBIQUE

Quality of Life

Life Expectancy (years)	46.5
Infant Mortality (per 1000)	141.0
Population Under 15 Years	44.2%
Population Over 65 Years	2.8%
Literacy Rate	32.9%
Malnourished Children	NA

Land Use and Habitats

Cropland (sq. miles):	11,969
per capita (acres)	0.5
global rank	87
Permanent Pasture (sq. miles):	888
total livestock (millions)	2.1
Forest and Woodlands (sq. miles):	55,521
1985 deforestation (sq. miles)	463
Wilderness Area (sq. miles)	23,669
Maritime Areas (EEZ, sq. miles)	2,170
Protected Areas (sq. miles):	8
percent of total	0.0%
No. of Threatened Species:	
mammals	10
birds	11
plants	84

Energy and Industry

Energy Production:	
solids (trillion BTUs)	1
liquids (trillion BTUs)	0
gas (trillion BTUs)	0
nuclear (gigawatt-hours)	0
hydroelectric (gigawatt-hours)	49
Energy Requirements:	
traditional fuels (trillion BTUs)	140
total (trillion BTUs)	156
per capita (million BTUs)	10
per capita (global rank)	118
Industrial Share of GDP	22.0%
Industrial Energy Index	8
Metal Reserve Index (world=100%)	0.1%
No. of Motor Vehicles/1000 Persons	NA

Water

Renewable Supply (cubic miles)	10.9
Total Use (cubic miles):	0.2
in agriculture	66.0%
in industry	10.0%
in homes and cities	24.0%
Access to Safe Water:	
urban population	44.0%
rural population	17.0%

Urban Centers and Waste

No. of Cities Over 1 Million:	1
percent of population	10.1%
Solid Wastes (million tons)	0.8
Urban Sanitation Access	61.0%

Population and Gross National Product

Population (millions)	GNP (billion $US)

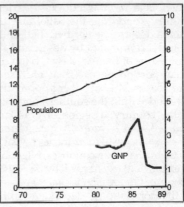

Commercial Energy Use

Total Energy Use (trillion BTUs)	Per Capita Energy Use (million BTUs)

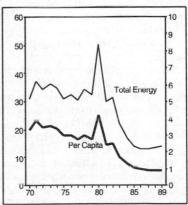

NIGER

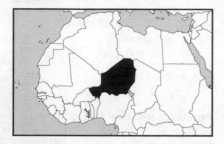

Total Area: 489,181 sq. miles
  Global Rank: 20   Per Capita: 40.5 acres
Population: 7,731,000
  Global Rank: 77   Growth Rate: 3.14%
Gross National Product: $1,987 m.
  Global Rank: 113   Per Capita: $265
Greenhouse Gas Emissions
  Global Share: 0.04%   Per Capita Rank: 134

Niger is a landlocked West African country straddling the Sahel and the Sahara desert. The northern half of the country, dominated by desert and the mountains of the Aïr Massif, is too dry to support people except at a few scattered oases. Most of Niger's population is found within the southern one third of the country, a region of grassland and wooded savanna, where rainfall averages from 10 to 32 inches a year.

Of the Sahelian countries, Niger has been particularly hard hit by periods of drought. One reason is that 90 percent of the population is dependent on the drought-vulnerable livestock and agricultural sectors of the economy for a living. The drought of 1967 to 1973 wiped out close to half the country's cattle herd. Niger went from self-sufficiency in grain production during the early 1960s to dependency on outside aid and emergency food imports in 1985.

Niger is one of the poorest countries in the world. Although it holds 15 percent of the world's proven uranium reserves, income from uranium, the country's primary export, fell during the 1980s as a result of a depressed world market. Drought and poverty have led to high emigration levels, both from the countryside to urban areas and from Niger to other countries. Niger has one of the highest urbanization rates in the Sahel. The population of Niamey, the capital, grows by an average of 10 percent annually.

Major Environmental Problems

Deforestation. Drought has killed or weakened many of the country's trees. Overbrowsing of new growth is preventing the regeneration of woody vegetation. Woodland areas are also threatened by slash-and-burn agricultural practices.

Soil erosion. Because of climatic conditions, Niger is naturally prone to topsoil loss. Drought and devegetation of the landscape have hastened this process through wind and water erosion.

Declining wildlife populations. Despite a ban on hunting, poaching is widespread. Illegal hunting by the military is a particular problem. Populations of elephant, hippo, lion, and other game can still be found in Park W, one of West Africa's largest national parks. Much of the wildlife in this trinational park— which also overlaps the borders of Burkina Faso and Benin—is found in the Niger sector. Plans to mine phosphates and dam rivers in the park, if carried out, could destroy remaining large game populations. These projects would also attract more settlers within Park W, exposing wildlife to higher levels of poaching and habitat destruction.

Quality of Life

Life Expectancy (years)	44.5
Infant Mortality (per 1000)	135.0
Population Under 15 Years	48.1%
Population Over 65 Years	2.1%
Literacy Rate	28.4%
Malnourished Children	38.0%

Land Use and Habitats

Cropland (sq. miles):	13,919
per capita (acres)	1.2
global rank	28
Permanent Pasture (sq. miles):	35,792
total livestock (millions)	15.9
Forest and Woodlands (sq. miles):	7,954
1985 deforestation (sq. miles)	259
Wilderness Area (sq. miles)	253,409
Maritime Areas (EEZ, sq. miles)	0
Protected Areas (sq. miles):	6,387
percent of total	1.3%
No. of Threatened Species:	
mammals	15
birds	1
plants	1

Energy and Industry

Energy Production:	
solids (trillion BTUs)	4
liquids (trillion BTUs)	0
gas (trillion BTUs)	0
nuclear (gigawatt-hours)	0
hydroelectric (gigawatt-hours)	0
Energy Requirements:	
traditional fuels (trillion BTUs)	38
total (trillion BTUs)	52
per capita (million BTUs)	7
per capita (global rank)	134
Industrial Share of GDP	12.6%
Industrial Energy Index	NA
Metal Reserve Index (world=100%)	0.0%
No. of Motor Vehicles/1000 Persons	1

Water

Renewable Supply (cubic miles)	3.1
Total Use (cubic miles):	0.1
in agriculture	74.0%
in industry	5.0%
in homes and cities	21.0%
Access to Safe Water:	
urban population	100.0%
rural population	52.0%

Urban Centers and Waste

No. of Cities Over 1 Million:	0
percent of population	0.0%
Solid Wastes (million tons)	0.3
Urban Sanitation Access	39.0%

Population and Gross National Product

Population (millions) — GNP (billion $US)

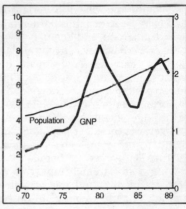

Commercial Energy Use

Total Energy Use (trillion BTUs) — Per Capita Energy Use (million BTUs)

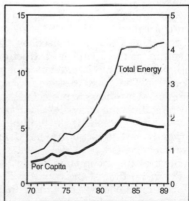

NIGERIA

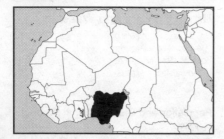

Total Area: 356,662 sq. miles
Global Rank: 30   Per Capita: 2.1 acres
Population: 108,542,000
Global Rank: 10   Growth Rate: 3.30%
Gross National Product: $27,515 m.
Global Rank: 54   Per Capita: $262
Greenhouse Gas Emissions
Global Share: 1.14%   Per Capita Rank: 103

The Federal Republic of Nigeria is located in West Africa. It is bordered by Niger, Cameroon, and Benin.

Nigeria is made up of a coastal plain, which is characterized by mangrove swamps; a central plateau, the Jos Plateau; an eastern mountain range; and in the north, a semidesert. Its chief rivers are the Niger, Benue, and Kaduna.

Nigeria is the most populous, and potentially one of the richest, countries in Africa. However, its population is growing at an extremely rapid rate, 3.3 percent annually, and this growth is straining Nigeria's natural resources. These resources include oil, tin, iron ore, and coal, as well as productive agricultural lands and forests. Major exports include oil, cocoa, cotton, and rubber.

Substantial increases in the production and sale of oil in the 1970s generated revenues that were used by the government to expand infrastructure and implement other development programs. These activities were not accompanied by efforts to protect the environment. In the early 1980s, oil and cocoa prices crashed, development stopped, and the country faced an acute debt crisis.

Most of the inhabitants live in the southern portion of the country. The population is composed of more than 250 tribal groups. English is the official language.

Major Environmental Problems

Soil degradation. Nigeria faces soil loss from an expanding population that creates pressures for land, which in turn alters the tradition of allowing land to stay fallow. The resulting overuse hastens erosion. In addition, unsuitable farming techniques and the lack of watershed protection contribute to erosion.

Water contamination. Household and industrial sources, especially in urban areas with burgeoning populations, pose significant health and treatment problems. Poor sanitation and wastewater treatment, inadequate solid waste disposal, and weak regulatory institutions are the key causes of these difficulties.

Deforestation. During the 1980s, an average of 5 percent of the country's closed forests were lost to deforestation every year. Nigeria has lost between 70 and 80 percent of all its original forest, savanna, and wetland areas.

As of late 1988, only 1.7 percent of Nigeria's land area was protected, with another 1.1 percent proposed for protection. "Protected" areas, many of which are inadequately staffed, continue to suffer from the effects of poaching, illegal logging, farming, and grazing.

Quality of Life

Life Expectancy (years)	50.5
Infant Mortality (per 1000)	105.0
Population Under 15 Years	47.3%
Population Over 65 Years	2.1%
Literacy Rate	50.7%
Malnourished Children	NA

Land Use and Habitats

Cropland (sq. miles):	120,985
per capita (acres)	0.7
global rank	61
Permanent Pasture (sq. miles):	154,440
total livestock (millions)	45.0
Forest and Woodlands (sq. miles):	47,104
1985 deforestation (sq. miles)	1,544
Wilderness Area (sq. miles)	5,891
Maritime Areas (EEZ, sq. miles)	814
Protected Areas (sq. miles):	5,971
percent of total	1.7%
No. of Threatened Species:	
mammals	25
birds	10
plants	9

Energy and Industry

Energy Production:	
solids (trillion BTUs)	4
liquids (trillion BTUs)	3,380
gas (trillion BTUs)	160
nuclear (gigawatt-hours)	0
hydroelectric (gigawatt-hours)	2,214
Energy Requirements:	
traditional fuels (trillion BTUs)	931
total (trillion BTUs)	1,506
per capita (million BTUs)	14
per capita (global rank)	103
Industrial Share of GDP	44.1%
Industrial Energy Index	5
Metal Reserve Index (world=100%)	0.0%
No. of Motor Vehicles/1000 Persons	NA

Water

Renewable Supply (cubic miles)	62.6
Total Use (cubic miles):	0.9
in agriculture	54.0%
in industry	15.0%
in homes and cities	31.0%
Access to Safe Water:	
urban population	100.0%
rural population	20.0%

Urban Centers and Waste

No. of Cities Over 1 Million:	2
percent of population	8.3%
Solid Wastes (million tons)	7.7
Urban Sanitation Access	NA

Population and Gross National Product

Population (millions)   GNP (billion $US)

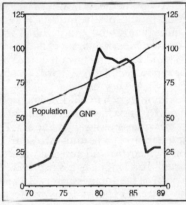

Commercial Energy Use

Total Energy Use (trillion BTUs)   Per Capita Energy Use (million BTUs)

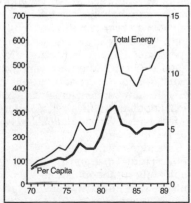

411

RWANDA

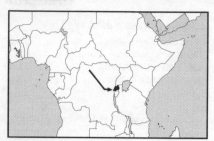

Total Area: 10,170 sq. miles
Global Rank: 25   Per Capita: 0.9 acres
Population: 7,237,000
Global Rank: 82   Growth Rate: 3.41%
Gross National Product: $2,168 m.
Global Rank:110   Per Capita: $310
Greenhouse Gas Emissions
Global Share:0.01%   Per Capita Rank: 157

Located in the heart of central Africa, the Republic of Rwanda is a small country whose topography is characterized by mountains and valleys in the west and by rolling terrain in the east. The renowned National Park of Volcanoes is in the northwest.

Although rich in wildlife and vegetation, Rwanda has meager mineral resources of cassiterite and wolfram. The exploitation of these mineral resources, from which tin and tungsten are extracted, has languished since 1986. In its profuse mountain streams, Rwanda also possesses enormous hydroelectric potential, which is beginning to be tapped through joint projects with Burundi and Zaire.

Rwanda is among the most densely populated countries in Africa, and it has an alarmingly high fertility rate—each woman bears 8.6 children, on average. A rapidly growing population dependent on relatively few resources results in what may be, for Rwanda, an unsustainably large population. In 1981, the government created a National Population Office, whose efforts to deal with overpopulation appear, thus far, ineffectual.

Rwandans comprise three ethnic groups: Hutu, Tutsi, and Twa. The predominantly rural population—90 percent—is unevenly distributed, largely because of significant variations in soil quality.

Major Environmental Problems

Deforestation. As the source of fuelwood and charcoal, the forests provide Rwanda with over 90 percent of total energy consumption. Meeting the country's energy needs is having a significant impact on the forest. In addition, land clearing on fertile hills and highlands is widespread.

Land degradation. In order to provide food for its massive population, Rwanda needs to double agricultural production by the year 2000. The vast majority of farming is done on a subsistence level: bananas, beans, peas, and sweet potatoes. Rwanda's cash crops are coffee, tea, pyrethrum, and cotton. Environmental problems arise because all available arable land has been used and reused until its agricultural capacity is exhausted and, in many cases, the soil is eroded.

Preserving biological diversity. In the middle 1980s, mountain gorilla populations were plummeting because of uncontrolled hunting by poachers and encroachment into their natural habitat by farmers. The gorillas' plight was made known to the world, largely through the efforts of George Schaller and Dian Fossey, and the resulting attention and support proved invaluable in reversing this trend.

Quality of Life

Life Expectancy (years)	48.5
Infant Mortality (per 1000)	122.0
Population Under 15 Years	48.9%
Population Over 65 Years	2.0%
Literacy Rate	50.2%
Malnourished Children	36.6%

Land Use and Habitats

Cropland (sq. miles):	4,452
per capita (acres)	0.4
global rank	99
Permanent Pasture (sq. miles):	1,819
total livestock (millions)	2.2
Forest and Woodlands (sq. miles):	2,151
1985 deforestation (sq. miles)	19
Wilderness Area (sq. miles)	0
Maritime Areas (EEZ, sq. miles)	0
Protected Areas (sq. miles):	1,263
percent of total	12.4%
No. of Threatened Species:	
mammals	11
birds	7
plants	0

Energy and Industry

Energy Production:	
solids (trillion BTUs)	0
liquids (trillion BTUs)	0
gas (trillion BTUs)	0
nuclear (gigawatt-hours)	0
hydroelectric (gigawatt-hours)	171
Energy Requirements:	
traditional fuels (trillion BTUs)	52
total (trillion BTUs)	59
per capita (million BTUs)	8
per capita (global rank)	128
Industrial Share of GDP	22.8%
Industrial Energy Index	NA
Metal Reserve Index (world=100%)	NA
No. of Motor Vehicles/1000 Persons	1

Water

Renewable Supply (cubic miles)	1.5
Total Use (cubic miles):	0.0
in agriculture	68.0%
in industry	8.0%
in homes and cities	24.0%
Access to Safe Water:	
urban population	46.0%
rural population	64.0%

Urban Centers and Waste

No. of Cities Over 1 Million:	0
percent of population	0.0%
Solid Wastes (million tons)	0.1
Urban Sanitation Access	45.0%

Population and Gross National Product

Population (millions) — GNP (billion $US)

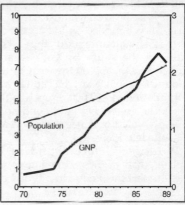

Commercial Energy Use

Total Energy Use (trillion BTUs) — Per Capita Energy Use (million BTUs)

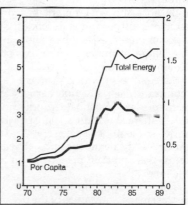

SENEGAL

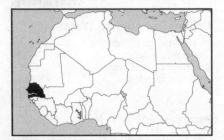

Total Area: 75,952 sq. miles
  Global Rank: 80   Per Capita: 6.6 acres
Population: 7,327,000
  Global Rank: 80   Growth Rate: 2.78%
Gross National Product: $4,429 m.
  Global Rank: 89   Per Capita: $622
Greenhouse Gas Emissions
  Global Share: 0.05%   Per Capita Rank: 119

The Republic of Senegal, a Sahelian country, is the westernmost nation in Africa. It is bounded on the north and northeast by Mauritania, on the east by Mali, on the south by Guinea and Guinea-Bissau, and on the west by the Atlantic Ocean. Dakar, the capital, has a population of 850,000. French is the official language. Drought conditions have prevailed in Senegal most years since the late 1960s.

Wildlife is more abundant in Senegal than in most Sahelian countries. In part this is due to a broad diversity of vegetation and an accompanying variety of animal species. Vegetation ranges from dry steppe in the north to tropical dry forest in the south, with savanna woodland in the middle.

Because the government has protected over 10 percent of the country as parks and reserves, elephant, lion, and other large mammal populations still remain in some areas.

Senegal's economy is primarily agricultural. Major revenue earners are peanuts, fish, phosphate production, and tourism. Peanuts are grown primarily in the midcoastal section of the country—"the peanut basin"—that encompasses about 40 percent of all arable land.

The rural population density is greatest in the rainy areas of the peanut basin. A shortage of land here has forced peasants to cultivate marginal dry lands in the interior of the country. Others have left the countryside seeking work in Dakar, the capital, and other cities. About 35 percent of Senegal's population is now located in urban areas.

Major Environmental Problems

Land degradation. Senegal has serious problems both with deforestation and desertification. Fuelwood harvesting, charcoal production, and overgrazing by livestock have denuded much of the landscape. Illegal cutting is rampant in the woodland.

Wildlife poaching. Poaching and overharvesting of birds and game are serious problems. Senegal is the world's largest exporter of exotic birds. Exports are approximately eight times higher than official quotas, which are set at levels considered sustainable for continued production. Elephant, crocodile, and sea turtle populations also suffer from heavy poaching.

Water development. A project to dam and develop the Senegal River basin, located on the country's northern border, threatens to disrupt the ecology of the area. When fully operational, the dam will disrupt breeding cycles of anadromous and riverine fish.

Quality of Life

Life Expectancy (years)	47.3
Infant Mortality (per 1000)	87.0
Population Under 15 Years	44.8%
Population Over 65 Years	2.5%
Literacy Rate	38.3%
Malnourished Children	28.0%

Land Use and Habitats

Cropland (sq. miles):	20,178
per capita (acres)	1.8
global rank	8
Permanent Pasture (sq. miles):	22,008
total livestock (millions)	8.9
Forest and Woodlands (sq. miles):	22,942
1985 deforestation (sq. miles)	193
Wilderness Area (sq. miles)	6,125
Maritime Areas (EEZ, sq. miles)	794
Protected Areas (sq. miles):	8,420
percent of total	11.1%
No. of Threatened Species:	
mammals	11
birds	5
plants	32

Energy and Industry

Energy Production:	
solids (trillion BTUs)	0
liquids (trillion BTUs)	0
gas (trillion BTUs)	0
nuclear (gigawatt-hours)	0
hydroelectric (gigawatt-hours)	0
Energy Requirements:	
traditional fuels (trillion BTUs)	40
total (trillion BTUs)	79
per capita (million BTUs)	11
per capita (global rank)	114
Industrial Share of GDP	31.1%
Industrial Energy Index	5
Metal Reserve Index (world=100%)	NA
No. of Motor Vehicles/1000 Persons	14

Water

Renewable Supply (cubic miles)	5.6
Total Use (cubic miles):	0.3
in agriculture	92.0%
in industry	3.0%
in homes and cities	5.0%
Access to Safe Water:	
urban population	79.0%
rural population	38.0%

Urban Centers and Waste

No. of Cities Over 1 Million:	1
percent of population	20.4%
Solid Wastes (million tons)	0.6
Urban Sanitation Access	87.0%

Population and Gross National Product

Population (millions)	GNP (billion $US)

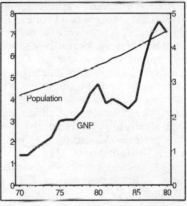

Commercial Energy Use

Total Energy Use (trillion BTUs)	Per Capita Energy Use (million BTUs)

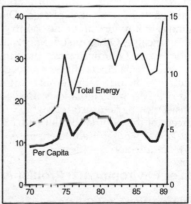

SIERRA LEONE

Total Area: 27,698 sq. miles
  Global Rank: 107   Per Capita: 4.3 acres
Population: 4,151,000
  Global Rank: 98   Growth Rate: 2.49%
Gross National Product: $904 m.
  Global Rank: 130   Per Capita: $223
Greenhouse Gas Emissions
  Global Share: 0.02%   Per Capita Rank: 133

The first Portuguese explorers, who visited what is now Sierra Leone in the 15th century, named the area "lion mountains" for the peaks they saw as they approached from the sea. One of Africa's smaller countries, Sierra Leone is dominated by the mountains of its western peninsula, a narrow belt of coastal swamplands, and plains that rise gradually to a broad eastern region of low plateaus. Mountain masses include 6,390-foot Loma Mansa, West Africa's highest point. The capital, Freetown, has a population of about 500,000.

Rich in minerals, Sierra Leone has relied upon mining, and especially diamonds, for its economic base. Other mineral resources include titanium, bauxite, iron, chromium, and gold, some of them not yet exploited. Diamonds account for half of the country's export income. Other major exports include bauxite (aluminum ore), titanium ore, and cocoa. In addition to cocoa, chief crops include palm kernels, coffee, and rice. Much of the land is used for subsistence agriculture, on which 75 percent of the population depends. Sierra Leone is not self-sufficient in food, and malnutrition is widespread.

Major Environmental Problems

Deforestation. Intrinsic to Sierra Leonean culture and life is the "bush fallow" agricultural system. Under this system, trees are cut to grow crops for a few seasons, and then the forest is allowed to regrow. As a consequence, most of the original forest of the country has been replaced with regrowth forest.

However, the bush fallow system is breaking down. With rapid population growth—a nearly 80 percent increase between 1963 and 1990—the demand for food and for land on which to grow it have outstripped the supply of land. There is no time for forest regrowth to replenish soil nutrients. As a result, forest area is declining and more and more of the soils are exhausted.

Additional pressure on forests comes from the timber industry. Overharvesting of timber is causing significant loss of forestlands. Little of Sierra Leone's forestland is protected.

Habitat loss. Sierra Leone has lost approximately 85 percent of its wildlife habitats. The country has only about 389 square miles of protected land. The loss of habitat means greatly reduced wildlife populations and, perhaps, local extinction of some species.

Soil compaction. Machinery is increasingly used to harvest rice, corn, millet, cassava, and some other annual crops. On some soils, use of this equipment has compacted the soil.

SIERRA LEONE

Quality of Life

Life Expectancy (years)	41.0
Infant Mortality (per 1000)	154.0
Population Under 15 Years	45.0%
Population Over 65 Years	2.8%
Literacy Rate	20.7%
Malnourished Children	42.8%

Land Use and Habitats

Cropland (sq. miles):	6,954
per capita (acres)	1.1
global rank	32
Permanent Pasture (sq. miles):	8,510
total livestock (millions)	0.9
Forest and Woodlands (sq. miles):	7,992
1985 deforestation (sq. miles)	23
Wilderness Area (sq. miles)	0
Maritime Areas (EEZ, sq. miles)	601
Protected Areas (sq. miles):	389
percent of total	1.4%
No. of Threatened Species:	
mammals	13
birds	7
plants	12

Energy and Industry

Energy Production:	
solids (trillion BTUs)	0
liquids (trillion BTUs)	0
gas (trillion BTUs)	0
nuclear (gigawatt-hours)	0
hydroelectric (gigawatt-hours)	0
Energy Requirements:	
traditional fuels (trillion BTUs)	27
total (trillion BTUs)	35
per capita (million BTUs)	9
per capita (global rank)	126
Industrial Share of GDP	12.4%
Industrial Energy Index	NA
Metal Reserve Index (world=100%)	0.1%
No. of Motor Vehicles/1000 Persons	NA

Water

Renewable Supply (cubic miles)	38.4
Total Use (cubic miles):	0.1
in agriculture	89.0%
in industry	4.0%
in homes and cities	7.0%
Access to Safe Water:	
urban population	83.0%
rural population	22.0%

Urban Centers and Waste

No. of Cities Over 1 Million:	0
percent of population	0.0%
Solid Wastes (million tons)	0.3
Urban Sanitation Access	59.0%

Population and Gross National Product

Population (millions)	GNP (billion $US)

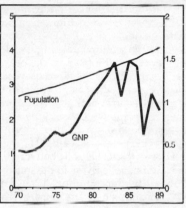

Commercial Energy Use

Total Energy Use (trillion BTUs)	Per Capita Energy Use (million BTUs)

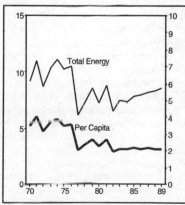

SOMALIA

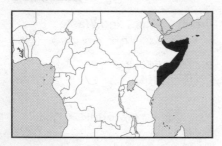

Total Area: 246,197 sq. miles
Global Rank: 40   Per Capita: 21.0 acres
Population: 7,497,000
Global Rank: 79   Growth Rate: 3.26%
Gross National Product: $1,053 m.
Global Rank: 127   Per Capita: $145
Greenhouse Gas Emissions
Global Share: 0.06%   Per Capita Rank: 104

A thousand years ago, Arab traders established ports and founded a sultanate on the coast of this dry, half-hilly, half-flat continental bulge, which together with Ethiopia and Djibouti is often referred to as the Horn of Africa.

Today, as in the past, 60 percent of all Somalis are nomadic or semi-nomadic people who raise cattle, camels, sheep, and goats for a living. Twenty-five percent are settled farmers who live in the fertile zone between the Juba and Shebelle rivers in the south.

Somali herders traditionally enjoyed free passage across the border with Ethiopia, providing pasture for their animals on the flat grasslands known as the Ogaden. Fighting that erupted between Somalia and Ethiopia over the Ogaden resulted in Ethiopia's closure of the border, and Somali livestock now trample increasingly crowded and less productive plots of earth.

The cattle must also share space with refugees, who began to stream across the border from Ethiopia in 1977. The large number of refugees overwhelm the nation's land and already inadequate infrastructure. The recent civil war has compounded these problems.

The country has no range management system, and residents are plagued by fuel shortages and health problems from the use of contaminated water.

Major Environmental Problems

Drought. Coping with drought is a way of life for Somalia, where two out of every five years are expected to be drought periods. Recent droughts have been aggravated by overstocking, which forces herders onto marginal grazing lands and leaves their animals more vulnerable. Livestock previously grazed only during the rainy season; sinking of wells has allowed year-round grazing, leaving no time for grasses to regenerate.

Desertification. Somalis have always raised and sold livestock on a small scale, but in the 1960s, livestock replaced bananas as the country's major source of export earnings. Livestock production provides a living for two-thirds of the population and constitutes 80 percent of export revenues. This population explosion among livestock, however, triggered a desertification process that worsened dramatically during the Ogaden crisis in 1977–1978. Now only thorn bushes remain in areas once rich with grass and shrubs.

Marine resource degradation. Overfishing and blast fishing have damaged coral reefs and sea grasses. The destruction eliminates habitat for many species of fish and could limit future catches.

Quality of Life

Life Expectancy (years)	45.1
Infant Mortality (per 1000)	132.0
Population Under 15 Years	47.7%
Population Over 65 Years	2.4%
Literacy Rate	24.1%
Malnourished Children	NA

Land Use and Habitats

Cropland (sq. miles):	4,012
per capita (acres)	0.4
global rank	104
Permanent Pasture (sq. miles):	166,023
total livestock (millions)	46.5
Forest and Woodlands (sq. miles):	35,019
1985 deforestation (sq. miles)	52
Wilderness Area (sq. miles)	40,387
Maritime Areas (EEZ, sq. miles)	3,022
Protected Areas (sq. miles):	0
percent of total	0.0%
No. of Threatened Species:	
mammals	16
birds	7
plants	51

Energy and Industry

Energy Production:	
solids (trillion BTUs)	0
liquids (trillion BTUs)	0
gas (trillion BTUs)	0
nuclear (gigawatt-hours)	0
hydroelectric (gigawatt-hours)	0
Energy Requirements:	
traditional fuels (trillion BTUs)	65
total (trillion BTUs)	77
per capita (million BTUs)	11
per capita (global rank)	117
Industrial Share of GDP	9.6%
Industrial Energy Index	NA
Metal Reserve Index (world=100%)	NA
No. of Motor Vehicles/1000 Persons	NA

Water

Renewable Supply (cubic miles)	2.8
Total Use (cubic miles):	0.2
in agriculture	97.0%
in industry	0.0%
in homes and cities	3.0%
Access to Safe Water:	
urban population	50.0%
rural population	29.0%

Urban Centers and Waste

No. of Cities Over 1 Million:	0
percent of population	0.0%
Solid Wastes (million tons)	0.5
Urban Sanitation Access	41.0%

Population and Gross National Product

Population (millions) GNP (billion $US)

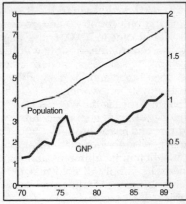

Commercial Energy Use

Total Energy Use (trillion BTUs) Per Capita Energy Use (million BTUs)

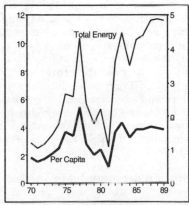

SOUTH AFRICA

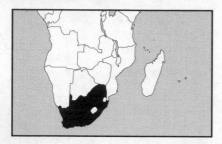

Total Area: 471,436 sq. miles
Global Rank: 24   Per Capita: 8.6 acres
Population: 35,282,000
Global Rank: 28   Growth Rate: 2.22%
Gross National Product: $86,748 m.
Global Rank: 26   Per Capita: $2,514
Greenhouse Gas Emissions
Global Share: 1.08%   Per Capita Rank: 38

South Africa describes itself as a "world in one country," and ecologically, it is. Home to 25,000 native plant species, mountains, desert, wildlife, breathtaking seacoasts, modern cities, and open rangeland, its geography is filled with striking variety.

South Africa is the world's leading producer of gold, gem diamonds, vanadium, and ferro-chromium, and it is a major producer of platinum-group metals, titanium, antimony, and manganese. Its supply of gold makes up almost half of the world's total known reserves.

Yet South Africa's environment and natural resources are endangered by land use and economic development policies. Coincident with the country's emergence from apartheid, it is also emerging from an era of rapid development and is beginning to assess environmental damage.

One region of special concern is an area east of Pretoria known as the Highveld; 80 percent of the country's electricity is generated there by coal-fired power stations. Stagnant air masses allow pollution to build up to extremely high levels, causing severe acid rain.

Major Environmental Problems

Water quality and supply. If current growth in water use continues, demand will outpace supply in some areas before the end of this decade. Salinization, a natural process in the drier regions, poses a major threat. In addition, urban discharge and agricultural runoff has led to eutrophication of most major rivers.

Soil erosion. Particularly in the homelands where the country's apartheid policies have forced many black people to live, cultivation of hilly areas on fragile soil combined with too many people and livestock are causing millions of tons of soil to be washed into the sea every year. Annual soil losses nationally amount to an estimated 300 million to 400 million tons.

Air pollution. The air pollution problem is especially severe in the Eastern Transvaal Highveld region. Deposition of acid precipitation and sulfur in this area is three to four times greater than in Germany and in Great Britain.

Desertification. The dry ranges of the Karoo have been moving eastward for at least 100 years, but no one knows why. Within the area, the grasslands on which sheep are stocked are deteriorating. Overgrazing is thought to be one cause, because it is estimated that the Karoo can safely support only 7.5 million sheep; the actual population is 10 million.

Quality of Life

Life Expectancy (years)	60.4
Infant Mortality (per 1000)	72.0
Population Under 15 Years	36.5%
Population Over 65 Years	3.7%
Literacy Rate	NA
Malnourished Children	NA

Land Use and Habitats

Cropland (sq. miles):	50,865
per capita (acres)	0.9
global rank	41
Permanent Pasture (sq. miles):	314,201
total livestock (millions)	50.7
Forest and Woodlands (sq. miles):	17,432
1985 deforestation (sq. miles)	0
Wilderness Area (sq. miles)	0
Maritime Areas (EEZ, sq. miles)	5,998
Protected Areas (sq. miles):	24,362
percent of total	5.2%
No. of Threatened Species:	
mammals	26
birds	13
plants	1,145

Energy and Industry

Energy Production:	
solids (trillion BTUs)	3,658
liquids (trillion BTUs)	0
gas (trillion BTUs)	0
nuclear (gigawatt-hours)	3,932
hydroelectric (gigawatt-hours)	602
Energy Requirements:	
traditional fuels (trillion BTUs)	NA
total (trillion BTUs)	NA
per capita (million BTUs)	NA
per capita (global rank)	NA
Industrial Share of GDP	43.9%
Industrial Energy Index	32
Metal Reserve Index (world=100%)	11.1%
No. of Motor Vehicles/1000 Persons	96

Water

Renewable Supply (cubic miles)	12.0
Total Use (cubic miles):	2.2
in agriculture	67.0%
in industry	17.0%
in homes and cities	16.0%
Access to Safe Water:	
urban population	NA
rural population	NA

Urban Centers and Waste

No. of Cities Over 1 Million:	4
percent of population	17.6%
Solid Wastes (million tons)	4.2
Urban Sanitation Access	NA

Population and Gross National Product

Population	GNP
(millions)	(billion $US)

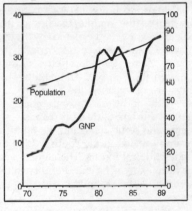

SUDAN

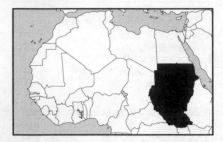

Total Area: 967,478 sq. miles
Global Rank: 9   Per Capita: 24.6 acres
Population: 25,203,000
Global Rank: 33   Growth Rate: 2.88%
Gross National Product: $11,175 m.
Global Rank: 62   Per Capita: $456
Greenhouse Gas Emissions
Global Share: 0.35%   Per Capita Rank: 83

The largest country in Africa, Sudan lies across the middle reaches of the Nile River and is bordered by Egypt, Libya, Chad, the Central African Republic, Zaire, Uganda, Kenya, Ethiopia, and the Red Sea. The country has three major regions: the northern desert with sandy, arid hills; the plains of central Sudan with semitropical savanna and scrublands; and the Sudd or swampy region in the south, which includes tropical forests. The climate varies from extreme heat and aridity in the northern deserts to milder southern climates.

Sudan's principal resources are agricultural. Cotton and cottonseed account for over one half of the country's export earnings; Sudan also produces four fifths of the world's supply of gum arabic. The limited industrial development consists mainly of agricultural processing.

A continuing civil war has had a major detrimental effect on Sudan's environment, as well as on its ability to feed its population. Famines have been frequent.

Major Environmental Problems

Desertification. The process leads to a substantial loss of agricultural land. Causes include over-intensive cultivation, overgrazing, wood cutting and brush removal for fuelwood, and burning of grasslands, scrub, and forests.

These practices lead to erosion of the soil by wind and water. The desert is shifting southward at a rate of two to six miles per year.

Continued desertification has led populations to abandon certain regions entirely because the soil and lack of rainfall no longer support vegetation. Shifting sand dunes may also smother once-productive farmland.

Environmental health problems. Cases of malaria and bilharzia continue to rise because of the improper development of irrigation networks and surface-water resources. Contaminated water supplies and a lack of adequate sanitation facilities, especially in urban areas where population density is high, have led to widespread disease control problems.

Loss of wildlife. Although some game reserves and sanctuaries have been established, wildlife protection is minimal. Excessive hunting has caused a major decline in several species.

Susceptibility to plant and animal pests. Water hyacinth, which causes a sharp decline in the normal yield of the Nile's water, has infested the entire stretch of the Nile from Juba to the Jebel Aulia Dam. The plant clogs irrigation pumps and canals and improves the environment for disease-bearing snails.

Quality of Life

Life Expectancy (years)	49.8
Infant Mortality (per 1000)	108.0
Population Under 15 Years	44.8%
Population Over 65 Years	2.4%
Literacy Rate	27.1%
Malnourished Children	NA

Land Use and Habitats

Cropland (sq. miles):	48,301
per capita (acres)	1.3
global rank	23
Permanent Pasture (sq. miles):	378,378
total livestock (millions)	58.6
Forest and Woodlands (sq. miles):	174,286
1985 deforestation (sq. miles)	1,946
Wilderness Area (sq. miles)	306,475
Maritime Areas (EEZ, sq. miles)	354
Protected Areas (sq. miles):	29,851
percent of total	3.1%
No. of Threatened Species:	
mammals	17
birds	8
plants	9

Energy and Industry

Energy Production:	
solids (trillion BTUs)	0
liquids (trillion BTUs)	0
gas (trillion BTUs)	0
nuclear (gigawatt-hours)	0
hydroelectric (gigawatt-hours)	521
Energy Requirements:	
traditional fuels (trillion BTUs)	195
total (trillion BTUs)	241
per capita (million BTUs)	10
per capita (global rank)	121
Industrial Share of GDP	14.6%
Industrial Energy Index	NA
Metal Reserve Index (world=100%)	0.0%
No. of Motor Vehicles/1000 Persons	7

Water

Renewable Supply (cubic miles)	7.2
Total Use (cubic miles):	4.5
in agriculture	99.0%
in industry	0.0%
in homes and cities	1.0%
Access to Safe Water:	
urban population	90.0%
rural population	20.0%

Urban Centers and Waste

No. of Cities Over 1 Million:	1
percent of population	7.7%
Solid Wastes (million tons)	1.1
Urban Sanitation Access	40.0%

Population and Gross National Product

Population (millions) GNP (billion $US)

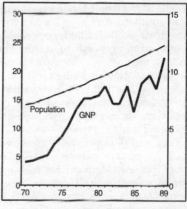

Commercial Energy Use

Total Energy Use (trillion BTUs) Per Capita Energy Use (million BTUs)

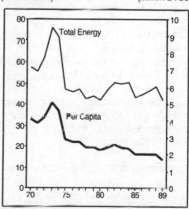

SWAZILAND

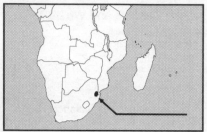

Total Area: 6,703 sq. miles
Global Rank: 132   Per Capita: 5.4 acres
Population: 788,000
Global Rank: 131   Growth Rate: 3.44%
Gross National Product: $645 m.
Global Rank: 132   Per Capita: $847
Greenhouse Gas Emissions
Global Share: 0.00%   Per Capita Rank: NA

Swaziland is a small, landlocked country in southern Africa. Its terrain contains four well-defined geographic regions running north to south. The land is mountainous in the west, changing to plateau in the center and in the east. Natural resources include asbestos, coal, clay, diamonds, and hydropower. Mining and agriculture are major economic activities.

Very rapid population growth—about 3.4 percent per year—has produced increased demand for fuel and building materials that threaten forests. About 17,000 Swazis are employed in neighboring South Africa. Small farmers, whose holdings dot the landscape, are expanding their operations with more cattle and more dairy output. The industrial sector is growing, as is exploitation of coal and diamonds.

Throughout the country, a number of exotic species of trees and shrubs have escaped from cultivation and threaten to suppress indigenous vegetation. The most serious case is that of the wattle tree, which has taken over the Highveld in areas cleared by grass fires, often set intentionally as part of slash-and-burn agriculture.

Major Environmental Problems

Land degradation. Overgrazing and overstocking have caused denudation of pasture and widespread soil erosion, bush encroachment, drying up of springs, dam siltation and low animal productivity. Erosion is high, causing extensive loss of soil every year and reducing the carrying capacity of the land. A system of communal grazing land eliminates individual responsibility for maintenance. Also, Swazis retain or increase cattle numbers under adverse environmental conditions.

Threats to forests. Overstocking, grass fires, expansion of agriculture, and the growing demand for fuelwood threaten Swaziland's forests. Fires beginning in high grass wiped out the forest of the Highveld and have probably changed the pattern of natural grasses and herbs almost everywhere in the country.

Poor sanitation. Especially in the Lowveld, waterborne diseases cause a high death rate. About 30 percent of school-age children have bilharzia, a waterborne parasitic disease, and only 7 percent of the rural population has access to safe water.

Threats to wildlife. Records from the late 1800s describe the vast herds of wild animals that ranged over the entire country. The wildlife were largely wiped out in the first half of the century, largely by foreign hunters. Today, wildlife is scarce outside Swaziland's two game reserves.

SWAZILAND

Quality of Life

Life Expectancy (years)	55.5
Infant Mortality (per 1000)	118.0
Population Under 15 Years	47.8%
Population Over 65 Years	2.5%
Literacy Rate	NA
Malnourished Children	NA

Land Use and Habitats

Cropland (sq. miles):	633
per capita (acres)	0.5
global rank	81
Permanent Pasture (sq. miles):	4,556
total livestock (millions)	1.0
Forest and Woodlands (sq. miles):	417
1985 deforestation (sq. miles)	0
Wilderness Area (sq. miles)	0
Maritime Areas (EEZ, sq. miles)	NA
Protected Areas (sq. miles):	153
percent of total	2.3%
No. of Threatened Species:	
mammals	0
birds	5
plants	25

Energy and Industry

Energy Production:	
solids (trillion BTUs)	5
liquids (trillion BTUs)	0
gas (trillion BTUs)	0
nuclear (gigawatt-hours)	0
hydroelectric (gigawatt-hours)	212
Energy Requirements:	
traditional fuels (trillion BTUs)	17
total (trillion BTUs)	24
per capita (million BTUs)	31
per capita (global rank)	66
Industrial Share of GDP	40.3%
Industrial Energy Index	NA
Metal Reserve Index (world=100%)	NA
No. of Motor Vehicles/1000 Persons	NA

Water

Renewable Supply (cubic miles)	1.7
Total Use (cubic miles):	0.1
in agriculture	93.0%
in industry	2.0%
in homes and cities	5.0%
Access to Safe Water:	
urban population	100.0%
rural population	7.0%

Urban Centers and Waste

No. of Cities Over 1 Million:	0
percent of population	0.0%
Solid Wastes (million tons)	0.1
Urban Sanitation Access	100.0%

Population and Gross National Product

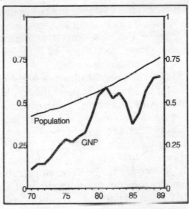

Population
(millions)

GNP
(billion $US)

Commercial Energy Use

Total Energy Use
(trillion BTUs)

Per Capita Energy Use
(million BTUs)

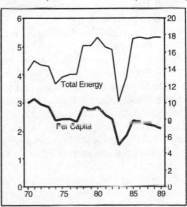

TANZANIA

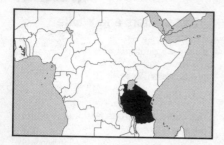

Total Area: 364,893 sq. miles
Global Rank: 29   Per Capita: 8.5 acres
Population: 27,318,000
Global Rank: 31   Growth Rate: 3.66%
Gross National Product: $2,642 m.
Global Rank: 104   Per Capita: $100
Greenhouse Gas Emissions
Global Share: 0.10%   Per Capita Rank: 138

Located on the eastern coast of southern Africa, Tanzania consists of a large mainland portion and the small, densely populated island of Zanzibar and its dependent islands.

Mainland population density is low, about 25 persons per square kilometer, and potentially productive spare land still exists. On Zanzibar, however, density is 10 times greater, making land relatively scarce. About 35 percent of Tanzania's mainland is arid or semiarid, but the remainder generally receives rainfall sufficient for cultivation. Tropical, savanna, and temperate conditions exist in various parts of the country, but much of the soil has low fertility. In the most fertile highland areas, population pressure on the land has begun to cause a loss of productive potential.

Forested areas, including woodlands, grasslands, and real forests, cover half the country. Tanzania possesses highly diverse and still plentiful wildlife, around which it has built a tourist industry that is a major earner of foreign exchange. The country is also home to many unique species of fish, plants, and butterflies. Illegal exploitation of forest resources continues to be a problem.

The economy depends mainly on cultivation of staple crops such as corn, rice, and wheat and export crops such as coffee, cotton, and cashews. Most food production is for subsistence. Though the country has a good potential for increasing livestock production, the tsetse fly limits herds in much of mainland Tanzania. Sizable coal deposits await exploitation.

Major Environmental Problems

Deforestation. Recent government estimates are that the country is losing mainland forest at about 1,350 square miles a year, a rate that will wipe out all the country's forests in roughly 100 years. Burning—whether for land clearance, tick control, or to smoke bees from hives—accounts for much of the destruction, in addition to fuelwood gathering.

Land degradation. Expansion of agriculture into arid and semiarid regions is the main cause of the desertification that threatens at least a third of the country. Even in the wettest parts of the country, soil fertility is dropping because of increasing population pressure and ever more intensive cultivation.

Destructive fishing methods. In order to increase their catch, small-scale fishermen sometimes use dynamite, which destroys the coral reefs that form feeding grounds for fish, help protect the coast from erosion, and attract tourists.

Quality of Life

Life Expectancy (years)	53.0
Infant Mortality (per 1000)	106.0
Population Under 15 Years	49.5%
Population Over 65 Years	1.9%
Literacy Rate	NA
Malnourished Children	NA

Land Use and Habitats

Cropland (sq. miles):	20,270
per capita (acres)	0.5
global rank	89
Permanent Pasture (sq. miles):	135,135
total livestock (millions)	26.6
Forest and Woodlands (sq. miles):	158,533
1985 deforestation (sq. miles)	502
Wilderness Area (sq. miles)	27,233
Maritime Areas (EEZ, sq. miles)	862
Protected Areas (sq. miles):	45,996
percent of total	12.6%
No. of Threatened Species:	
mammals	30
birds	26
plants	158

Energy and Industry

Energy Production:	
solids (trillion BTUs)	0
liquids (trillion BTUs)	0
gas (trillion BTUs)	0
nuclear (gigawatt-hours)	0
hydroelectric (gigawatt-hours)	619
Energy Requirements:	
traditional fuels (trillion BTUs)	290
total (trillion BTUs)	321
per capita (million BTUs)	12
per capita (global rank)	108
Industrial Share of GDP	7.5%
Industrial Energy Index	46
Metal Reserve Index (world=100%)	0.0%
No. of Motor Vehicles/1000 Persons	3

Water

Renewable Supply (cubic miles)	18.2
Total Use (cubic miles):	0.1
in agriculture	74.0%
in industry	5.0%
in homes and cities	21.0%
Access to Safe Water:	
urban population	75.0%
rural population	46.0%

Urban Centers and Waste

No. of Cities Over 1 Million.	1
percent of population	6.1%
Solid Wastes (million tons)	1.0
Urban Sanitation Access	76.0%

Population and Gross National Product

Population (millions)	GNP (billion $US)

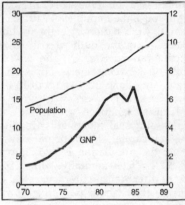

Commercial Energy Use

Total Energy Use (trillion BTUs)	Per Capita Energy Use (million BTUs)

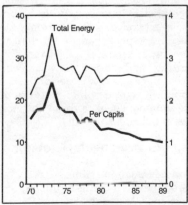

TUNISIA

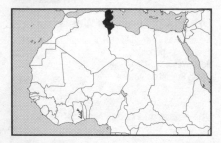

Total Area: 63,169 sq. miles
Global Rank: 84   Per Capita: 4.9 acres
Population: 8,180,000
Global Rank: 76   Growth Rate: 2.38%
Gross National Product: $9,599 m.
Global Rank: 66   Per Capita: $1,202
Greenhouse Gas Emissions
Global Share: 0.05%   Per Capita Rank: 124

With an area about the size of the state of Missouri, the Republic of Tunisia is a small Arab nation of eight million inhabitants on the southern coast of the Mediterranean Sea. On the east is Libya; on the west, Algeria. Tunisia has fertile land along the coast, but in the south the land is desert.

Tunisia's languages are Arabic and French; almost all inhabitants are Muslim. The capital and principal city is Tunis; the population is growing at about 2.4 percent annually. Tunisia has one of the highest literacy rates in North Africa, about 62 percent, and relatively good public health care.

The country's natural resources include oil, phosphates, iron, and other metal ores. Its chief crops include cereals and olives, but the country is not self-sufficient in food. Exports include textiles and olive oil, in addition to petroleum and phosphates. Important archeological ruins are found at Carthage, and tourism plays a sizable role in the economy. Other important economic activities include agriculture, mining, energy production, textiles, and manufacturing.

Major Environmental Problems

Land degradation. Tunisia has extensive soil erosion from its farmlands and rangelands. It is estimated that 76 percent of the land area in Tunisia is po-

tentially threatened by erosion, which completely strips the topsoil from more than 45,000 acres of land annually. The principal causes are the expansion of farming to marginal areas, population growth, overgrazing, and destruction of vegetation. The depletion of vegetation also destroys grasslands and watersheds, thus lowering the capacity of the land to support life and increasing desertification.

Water. Water is scarce in Tunisia, and drought is common. The cost of new water supplies is very high, limiting further economic development. Poorly maintained water supply systems make the situation worse, leading to the waste of scarce resources and an urgent need for water conservation efforts. Extensive construction of dams for large-scale irrigation is under way, and could lead to additional problems, including additional erosion.

Pollution and wastes. In Tunisia, as in many other countries in the region, all wastes are disposed together, including toxic and hazardous wastes, a dangerous practice that can lead to public health problems. In addition, disposal sites are often poorly designed and leak toxic materials. Untreated urban sewage is a problem; it contaminates water supplies and contributes to overfertilization of the Mediterranean Sea.

Quality of Life

Life Expectancy (years)	65.6
Infant Mortality (per 1000)	52.0
Population Under 15 Years	35.8%
Population Over 65 Years	3.4%
Literacy Rate	65.3%
Malnourished Children	23.0%

Land Use and Habitats

Cropland (sq. miles):	18,147
per capita (acres)	1.5
global rank	15
Permanent Pasture (sq. miles):	11,340
total livestock (millions)	7.5
Forest and Woodlands (sq. miles):	2,432
1985 deforestation (sq. miles)	19
Wilderness Area (sq. miles)	7,341
Maritime Areas (EEZ, sq. miles)	331
Protected Areas (sq. miles):	175
percent of total	0.3%
No. of Threatened Species:	
mammals	6
birds	14
plants	26

Energy and Industry

Energy Production:	
solids (trillion BTUs)	0
liquids (trillion BTUs)	200
gas (trillion BTUs)	13
nuclear (gigawatt-hours)	0
hydroelectric (gigawatt-hours)	33
Energy Requirements:	
traditional fuels (trillion BTUs)	28
total (trillion BTUs)	187
per capita (million BTUs)	23
per capita (global rank)	80
Industrial Share of GDP	32.8%
Industrial Energy Index	14
Metal Reserve Index (world=100%)	0.1%
No. of Motor Vehicles/1000 Persons	40

Water

Renewable Supply (cubic miles)	0.9
Total Use (cubic miles):	0.6
in agriculture	80.0%
in industry	7.0%
in homes and cities	13.0%
Access to Safe Water:	
urban population	100.0%
rural population	31.0%

Urban Centers and Waste

No. of Cities Over 1 Million:	1
percent of population	20.0%
Solid Wastes (million tons)	0.9
Urban Sanitation Access	71.0%

Population and Gross National Product

Population	GNP
(millions)	(billion $US)

Commercial Energy Use

Total Energy Use	Per Capita Energy Use
(trillion BTUs)	(million BTUs)

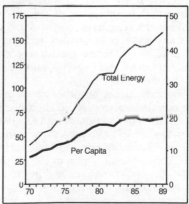

UGANDA

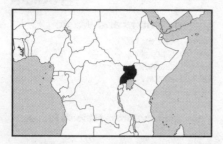

Total Area: 91,072 sq. miles
Global Rank: 77   Per Capita: 3.1 acres
Population: 18,794,000
Global Rank: 44   Growth Rate: 3.67%
Gross National Product: $4,642 m.
Global Rank: 86   Per Capita: $256
Greenhouse Gas Emissions
Global Share: 0.04%   Per Capita Rank: 152

A densely populated, landlocked nation in the heart of equatorial Africa, Uganda is rich in water resources—18 percent of the total area is lakes, rivers, and wetlands. Because of its high altitude, Uganda enjoys a moderate climate with little seasonal variation. The entire country is situated atop the east central African plateau and contains the source of the Nile River system, dominated by Lake Victoria.

The country lacks minerals and fossil fuels but has fertile soil, enormous hydroelectric potential, and many forms of wildlife: elephant, lion, giraffe, zebra, antelope, rhino, crocodile, ostrich, crane, and gorilla.

By 1987, much of the country's infrastructure was damaged or destroyed by war, and Uganda had to rebuild its economy with coffee (90 percent of its export earnings), tea, cotton, and tobacco. Most inhabitants rely on agriculture, forest products, commercial freshwater fisheries, and wildlife for their livelihoods.

Uganda, a net absorber of carbon dioxide, is biologically rich because it lies at the conjunction of four vegetation regions: Lake Victoria in the south, the dry Sudanian region in the north, the Somali-Masai region in the northeast, and the Afro-alpine and montane areas in the east. About three fourths of the country is now covered by cultivated land and savanna.

Major Environmental Problems

Wetland protection. Because wetlands are a source of malarial mosquitoes and bilharzia-carrying snails, they are called "wastelands" and considered useless. Wetlands are now being drained indiscriminately for agriculture, particularly rice.

Forest and wildlife management. More than 90 percent of residential energy requirements are met with fuelwoods, according to government figures, putting increasing pressure on forests. What little forested land remains is mostly in reserves and is being cleared for agriculture and other development projects. Conflicts are growing between the farmers and the authorities who are responsible for protecting the forests. Local and regional management plans that can make the best use of remaining resources are lacking.

Tsetse fly control. Sleeping sickness has been increasing since the mid-1970s. Cutting of the lantana bushes, which kept the tsetse fly populations down, was slowed down because of military conflicts and political instability. Controlling the tsetse fly with only limited use of pesticide spraying would increase areas for cattle grazing, improve health conditions, and protect wildlife.

UGANDA

Quality of Life

Life Expectancy (years)	51.0
Infant Mortality (per 1000)	103.0
Population Under 15 Years	50.3%
Population Over 65 Years	2.1%
Literacy Rate	48.3%
Malnourished Children	25.0%

Land Use and Habitats

Cropland (sq. miles):	25,888
per capita (acres)	0.9
global rank	47
Permanent Pasture (sq. miles):	6,950
total livestock (millions)	8.7
Forest and Woodlands (sq. miles):	21,660
1985 deforestation (sq. miles)	193
Wilderness Area (sq. miles)	2,047
Maritime Areas (EEZ, sq. miles)	0
Protected Areas (sq. miles):	6,778
percent of total	7.4%
No. of Threatened Species:	
mammals	16
birds	12
plants	11

Energy and Industry

Energy Production:	
solids (trillion BTUs)	0
liquids (trillion BTUs)	0
gas (trillion BTUs)	0
nuclear (gigawatt-hours)	0
hydroelectric (gigawatt-hours)	692
Energy Requirements:	
traditional fuels (trillion BTUs)	119
total (trillion BTUs)	136
per capita (million BTUs)	8
per capita (global rank)	132
Industrial Share of GDP	7.4%
Industrial Energy Index	NA
Metal Reserve Index (world=100%)	0.0%
No. of Motor Vehicles/1000 Persons	2

Water

Renewable Supply (cubic miles)	15.8
Total Use (cubic miles):	0.0
in agriculture	60.0%
in industry	8.0%
in homes and cities	32.0%
Access to Safe Water:	
urban population	45.0%
rural population	12.0%

Urban Centers and Waste

No. of Cities Over 1 Million:	0
percent of population	0.0%
Solid Wastes (million tons)	0.4
Urban Sanitation Access	40.0%

Population and Gross National Product

Population (millions)	GNP (billion $US)

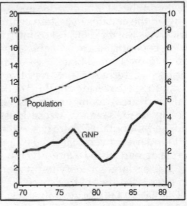

Commercial Energy Use

Total Energy Use (trillion BTUs)	Per Capita Energy Use (million BTUs)

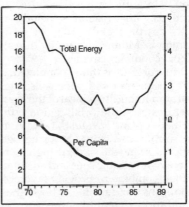

ZAIRE

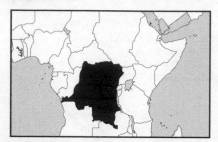

Total Area: 905,548 sq. miles
Global Rank: 11   Per Capita: 16.3 acres
Population: 35,568,000
Global Rank: 27   Growth Rate: 3.14%
Gross National Product: $8,546 m.
Global Rank: 69   Per Capita: $248
Greenhouse Gas Emissions
Global Share: 0.37%   Per Capita Rank: 96

The Republic of Zaire is located directly on the equator in eastern central Africa. It is the third largest country in Africa, covering an area roughly equal in size to the United States east of the Mississippi. Terrain varies from tropical rainforest (covering one third of the total land area) to mountainous terraces, plateau, savanna, dense grassland, and mountains. Zaire has within its boundaries several large lakes and the major part of the Zaire River system. Zaire's large primary forests contain over 100 different tree species.

The native fauna is widely considered to be one of Zaire's richest natural resources. Large grazing and browsing mammals, carnivores such as lions and leopards, and primates such as the mountain gorilla are major tourist attractions. Other resources include cobalt, copper, cadmium, oil, and diamonds. Mining and agriculture are major economic activities.

Most of Zaire is thinly populated, in part because of the poor soils, high heat, and humidity typical of the heavily forested equatorial regions, the northern upland savanna, and parts of the southern savanna. More densely populated are the eastern highlands, where rich volcanic soils and adequate rainfall combine to provide favorable conditions for farming. The highest population densities, however, are found in the cities, where population growth greatly exceeds that of the country as a whole.

Major Environmental Problems

Water pollution. Mainly a problem in the urban areas, water contamination is a major source of disease in Zaire. Although industrial pollution from oil and mining contribute to the problem, the most pervasive source of pollution is human waste, which is discharged untreated into rivers from open surface drains. The same water is used by downstream residents for washing, bathing, and even drinking.

Deforestation. Zaire has abundant and varied forest resources, including the second largest remaining area of tropical forest in the world (after Brazil). Poor management, limited knowledge of species vulnerability, and poor land use practices contribute to the permanent loss of trees.

Loss of wildlife. Some of Zaire's wildlife species are endangered, including the elephant and the square-lipped rhinoceros, whose horn is sold for use as an aphrodisiac. Poaching is clearly the most dangerous threat to Zaire's wildlife resources. Recent estimates are that within a few decades, the larger mammals will survive only within the national parks.

Quality of Life

Life Expectancy (years)	52.0
Infant Mortality (per 1000)	83.0
Population Under 15 Years	46.0%
Population Over 65 Years	2.2%
Literacy Rate	71.8%
Malnourished Children	43.3%

Land Use and Habitats

Cropland (sq. miles):	30,309
per capita (acres)	0.6
global rank	76
Permanent Pasture (sq. miles):	57,915
total livestock (millions)	6.3
Forest and Woodlands (sq. miles):	674,286
1985 deforestation (sq. miles)	1,429
Wilderness Area (sq. miles)	45,415
Maritime Areas (EEZ, sq. miles)	4
Protected Areas (sq. miles):	34,081
percent of total	3.8%
No. of Threatened Species:	
mammals	22
birds	27
plants	3

Energy and Industry

Energy Production:	
solids (trillion BTUs)	3
liquids (trillion BTUs)	51
gas (trillion BTUs)	0
nuclear (gigawatt-hours)	0
hydroelectric (gigawatt-hours)	5,251
Energy Requirements:	
traditional fuels (trillion BTUs)	304
total (trillion BTUs)	400
per capita (million BTUs)	12
per capita (global rank)	110
Industrial Share of GDP	32.1%
Industrial Energy Index	NA
Metal Reserve Index (world=100%)	3.5%
No. of Motor Vehicles/1000 Persons	NA

Water

Renewable Supply (cubic miles)	244.5
Total Use (cubic miles):	0.2
in agriculture	17.0%
in industry	25.0%
in homes and cities	58.0%
Access to Safe Water:	
urban population	59.0%
rural population	17.0%

Urban Centers and Waste

No. of Cities Over 1 Million:	1
percent of population	9.9%
Solid Wastes (million tons)	2.8
Urban Sanitation Access	14.0%

Population and Gross National Product

Population	GNP
(millions)	(billion $US)

Commercial Energy Use

Total Energy Use	Per Capita Energy Use
(trillion BTUs)	(million BTUs)

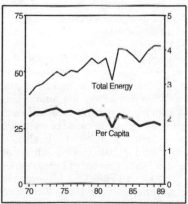

ZAMBIA

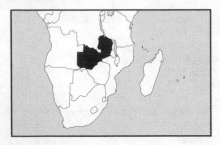

Total Area: 290,578 sq. miles
Global Rank: 37   Per Capita: 22.0 acres
Population: 8,452,000
Global Rank: 73   Growth Rate: 3.75%
Gross National Product: $4,328 m.
Global Rank: 90   Per Capita: $532
Greenhouse Gas Emissions
Global Share: 0.09%   Per Capita Rank: 94

Zambia is a large, landlocked country with comparatively few people, one half of whom live in towns and cities. It is named for the Zambezi River, which flows north to south, and is broken by Victoria Falls, one of the world's greatest waterfalls.

Most of Zambia lies on a high savanna-covered plateau and is between 3,280 and 5,249 feet above sea level. About 70 percent of the land is *miombo* woodland, which consists of an open mixture of shrubs, a variety of trees of moderate heights, and tall grasses. Zambia's wildlife is among the richest in Africa and includes herds of elephants, impalas, greater kudus, and other safari game, as well as 4,600 species of plants. Nineteen national parks have been established since Zambia gained independence from the Federation of Rhodesia and Nyasaland in 1964.

Zambia is more industrialized than most of sub-Saharan Africa—46 percent of its gross domestic product comes from mining, manufacturing, and construction—and it is self-sufficient in electricity because of its hydropower facilities. With the decline in copper and cobalt prices, which accounted for 16 percent of gross domestic product and more than 85 percent of export earnings in 1988, Zambians have begun to diversify their economy by increasing agriculture, expanding

tourism, and making more productive use of its wildlife and national parks.

Major Environmental Problems

Wildlife conservation. Poaching of ivory and rhino horn is a serious problem. In 1970 there were 65,000 black rhinos; in 1988 there were fewer than 4,500. In the Luangwa Valley, the elephant herd has been reduced from 86,000 to 30,000 in 10 years. The international ban on ivory imports to the developed world has helped to control demand.

Woodland destruction. Rapid destruction of the *miombo* woodland around towns and cities is a growing problem. Zambia loses about 0.5 percent of its woodlands each year to firewood and charcoal, shifting cultivation, clearing of land for large-scale agriculture, forest fires, which in some cases are set deliberately to drive animals into traps, and overcutting for logs and pulp.

Land degradation. Ninety percent of the cattle are owned by traditional herders. Cattle are important as status symbols and sources of dairy products, manure, and transportation. Herding is usually on a free-range system, and during the dry season cows are poorly fed and overcrowded, leading to land degradation and reduced production.

Quality of Life

Life Expectancy (years)	53.4
Infant Mortality (per 1000)	80.0
Population Under 15 Years	49.8%
Population Over 65 Years	2.0%
Literacy Rate	72.8%
Malnourished Children	NA

Land Use and Habitats

Cropland (sq. miles):	20,340
per capita (acres)	1.6
global rank	12
Permanent Pasture (sq. miles).	115,830
total livestock (millions)	3.6
Forest and Woodlands (sq. miles):	111,660
1985 deforestation (sq. miles)	270
Wilderness Area (sq. miles)	58,203
Maritime Areas (EEZ, sq. miles)	0
Protected Areas (sq. miles):	24,559
percent of total	8.5%
No. of Threatened Species:	
mammals	10
birds	10
plants	1

Energy and Industry

Energy Production:	
solids (trillion BTUs)	9
liquids (trillion BTUs)	0
gas (trillion BTUs)	0
nuclear (gigawatt-hours)	0
hydroelectric (gigawatt-hours)	6,700
Energy Requirements:	
traditional fuels (trillion BTUs)	110
total (trillion BTUs)	191
per capita (million BTUs)	23
per capita (global rank)	79
Industrial Share of GDP	43.0%
Industrial Energy Index	16
Metal Reserve Index (world=100%)	1.0%
No. of Motor Vehicles/1000 Persons	NA

Water

Renewable Supply (cubic miles)	23.0
Total Use (cubic miles):	0.1
in agriculture	26.0%
in industry	11.0%
in homes and cities	63.0%
Access to Safe Water:	
urban population	76.0%
rural population	43.0%

Urban Centers and Waste

No. of Cities Over 1 Million:	0
percent of population	0.0%
Solid Wastes (million tons)	0.8
Urban Sanitation Access	77.0%

Population and Gross National Product

Population   GNP
(millions)   (billion $US)

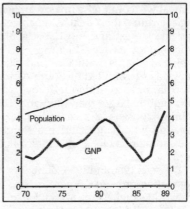

Commercial Energy Use

Total Energy Use   Per Capita Energy Use
(trillion BTUs)   (million BTUs)

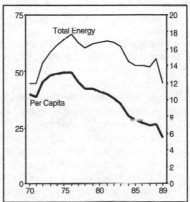

ZIMBABWE

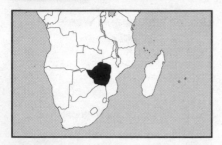

Total Area: 150,800 sq. miles
Global Rank: 55   Per Capita: 9.9 acres
Population: 9,709,000
Global Rank: 67   Growth Rate: 3.16%
Gross National Product: $5,731 m.
Global Rank: 81   Per Capita: $609
Greenhouse Gas Emissions
Global Share: 0.11%   Per Capita Rank:: 93

Zimbabwe contains a major archeological ruin—the Great Zimbabwe—and the largest and most spectacular waterfall in Africa—Victoria Falls—which it shares with Zambia. Zimbabwe is surrounded by South Africa, Zambia, and Mozambique; it covers an area slightly larger than Montana. The country consists of a central plateau, savanna woodlands and grasslands, and mountains along the eastern border.

Between 1980 and 1986, Zimbabwe's population grew at 3.8 percent, one of the world's highest rates, then fell to its present, still high, level. This growing number of humans, along with growing herds of cattle, puts increasing pressure on the land, on which 75 percent of the people depend for their livelihoods. Communal ownership of land by villages, which accounts for 42 percent of the country's territory, tends to encourage both ever larger herds and ever smaller plots. The result is pressure to use marginal lands.

Agriculture forms the backbone of the economy. Chief crops include tobacco, corn, tea, sugar, and cotton. The country's manufacturing sector and infrastructure are also strong. Zimbabwe possesses rich mineral deposits, including coal, chromium, asbestos, and gold, and has rapidly developed its hydroelectric potential, but wood is still the primary energy source for most people.

Zimbabwe has established an effective conservation program, with 7 percent of its total land area protected, including game reserves that support over 50,000 elephants and Africa's largest black rhinoceros population. The growing elephant populations have forced park officials to introduce population control measures to reduce habitat destruction.

Major Environmental Problems

Land degradation. Soil erosion in both the commercial and subsistence agricultural sectors is considered one of the country's most critical problems. The problem is most severe, however, in communal areas, where marginal land has been forced into overuse.

Deforestation. Although Zimbabwe has extensive natural forests, they are being depleted for firewood and through slash-and-burn agriculture, particularly in communal areas, at a rate that is cause for increasing concern. The government has made some efforts toward reforestation.

Pollution. Zimbabwe's industrialization has created pollution problems in both urban and rural areas. Several lakes have experienced eutrophication because of discharges of untreated sewage and industrial waste.

ZIMBABWE

Quality of Life

Life Expectancy (years)	58.3
Infant Mortality (per 1000)	66.0
Population Under 15 Years	44.1%
Population Over 65 Years	2.3%
Literacy Rate	66.9%
Malnourished Children	31.0%

Land Use and Habitats

Cropland (sq. miles):	10,849
per capita (acres)	0.7
global rank	60
Permanent Pasture (sq. miles):	18,749
total livestock (millions)	9.8
Forest and Woodlands (sq. miles):	74,170
1985 deforestation (sq. miles)	309
Wilderness Area (sq. miles)	0
Maritime Areas (EEZ, sq. miles)	0
Protected Areas (sq. miles):	10,929
percent of total	7.2%
No. of Threatened Species:	
mammals	9
birds	6
plants	96

Energy and Industry

Energy Production:	
solids (trillion BTUs)	142
liquids (trillion BTUs)	0
gas (trillion BTUs)	0
nuclear (gigawatt-hours)	0
hydroelectric (gigawatt-hours)	2,662
Energy Requirements:	
traditional fuels (trillion BTUs)	70
total (trillion BTUs)	279
per capita (million BTUs)	30
per capita (global rank)	70
Industrial Share of GDP	38.8%
Industrial Energy Index	35
Metal Reserve Index (world=100%)	0.8%
No. of Motor Vehicles/1000 Persons	30

Water

Renewable Supply (cubic miles)	5.5
Total Use (cubic miles):	0.3
in agriculture	79.0%
in industry	7.0%
in homes and cities	14.0%
Access to Safe Water:	
urban population	95.0%
rural population	80.0%

Urban Centers and Waste

No. of Cities Over 1 Million:	0
percent of population	0.0%
Solid Wastes (million tons)	0.5
Urban Sanitation Access	95.0%

Population and Gross National Product

Population	GNP
(millions)	(billion $US)

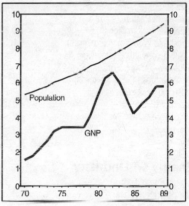

Commercial Energy Use

Total Energy Use	Per Capita Energy Use
(trillion BTUs)	(million BTUs)

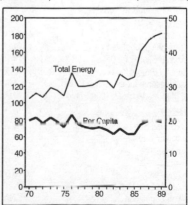

COMOROS

Quality of Life

Life Expectancy (years)	54.0
Infant Mortality (per 1000)	99.0
Population Under 15 Years	47.9%
Population Over 65 Years	2.2%
Literacy Rate	NA
Malnourished Children	NA

Land Use and Habitats

Cropland (sq. miles):	386
per capita (acres)	0.5
global rank	90
Permanent Pasture (sq. miles):	58
total livestock (millions)	0.2
Forest and Woodlands (sq. miles):	135
1985 deforestation (sq. miles)	4
Wilderness Area (sq. miles)	0
Maritime Areas (EEZ, sq. miles)	961
Protected Areas (sq. miles):	0
percent of total	0.0%
No. of Threatened Species:	
mammals	3
birds	5
plants	3

Energy and Industry

Energy Production:	
solids (trillion BTUs)	0
liquids (trillion BTUs)	0
gas (trillion BTUs)	0
nuclear (gigawatt-hours)	0
hydroelectric (gigawatt-hours)	0
Energy Requirements:	
traditional fuels (trillion BTUs)	0
total (trillion BTUs)	1
per capita (million BTUs)	1
per capita (global rank)	144
Industrial Share of GDP	14.1%
Industrial Energy Index	NA
Metal Reserve Index (world=100%)	NA
No. of Motor Vehicles/1000 Persons	NA

Water

Renewable Supply (cubic miles)	0.2
Total Use (cubic miles):	0.0
in agriculture	47.0%
in industry	5.0%
in homes and cities	48.0%
Access to Safe Water:	
urban population	NA
rural population	NA

Urban Centers and Waste

No. of Cities Over 1 Million:	0
percent of population	0.0%
Solid Wastes (million tons)	NA
Urban Sanitation Access	NA

Population and Gross National Product

Population (millions) GNP (billion $US)

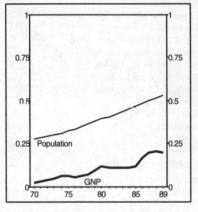

Commercial Energy Use

Total Energy Use (trillion BTUs) Per Capita Energy Use (million BTUs)

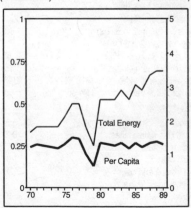

DJIBOUTI

Quality of Life

Life Expectancy (years)	47.0
Infant Mortality (per 1000)	122.0
Population Under 15 Years	45.4%
Population Over 65 Years	2.2%
Literacy Rate	NA
Malnourished Children	NA

Land Use and Habitats

Cropland (sq. miles):	9,981
per capita (acres)	16.1
global rank	1
Permanent Pasture (sq. miles):	772
total livestock (millions)	1.1
Forest and Woodlands (sq. miles):	23
1985 deforestation (sq. miles)	0
Wilderness Area (sq. miles)	0
Maritime Areas (EEZ, sq. miles)	24
Protected Areas (sq. miles):	39
percent of total	0.4%
No. of Threatened Species:	
mammals	6
birds	3
plants	3

Energy and Industry

Energy Production:	
solids (trillion BTUs)	0
liquids (trillion BTUs)	0
gas (trillion BTUs)	0
nuclear (gigawatt-hours)	0
hydroelectric (gigawatt-hours)	0
Energy Requirements:	
traditional fuels (trillion BTUs)	0
total (trillion BTUs)	4
per capita (million BTUs)	11
per capita (global rank)	115
Industrial Share of GDP	NA
Industrial Energy Index	NA
Metal Reserve Index (world=100%)	NA
No. of Motor Vehicles/1000 Persons	28

Water

Renewable Supply (cubic miles)	0.1
Total Use (cubic miles):	0.0
in agriculture	51.0%
in industry	21.0%
in homes and cities	28.0%
Access to Safe Water:	
urban population	50.0%
rural population	21.0%

Urban Centers and Waste

No. of Cities Over 1 Million:	0
percent of population	0.0%
Solid Wastes (million tons)	0.1
Urban Sanitation Access	94.0%

Population and Gross National Product

Population (millions) — GNP (billion $US)

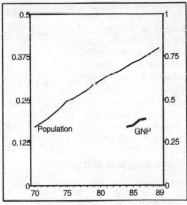

Commercial Energy Use

Total Energy Use (trillion BTUs) — Per Capita Energy Use (million BTUs)

EQUATORIAL GUINEA

Quality of Life

Life Expectancy (years)	46.0
Infant Mortality (per 1000)	127.0
Population Under 15 Years	43.2%
Population Over 65 Years	3.7%
Literacy Rate	50.2%
Malnourished Children	NA

Land Use and Habitats

Cropland (sq. miles):	888
per capita (acres)	1.7
global rank	10
Permanent Pasture (sq. miles):	402
total livestock (millions)	0.1
Forest and Woodlands (sq. miles):	5,000
1985 deforestation (sq. miles)	12
Wilderness Area (sq. miles)	0
Maritime Areas (EEZ, sq. miles)	1,093
Protected Areas (sq. miles):	0
percent of total	0.0%
No. of Threatened Species:	
mammals	15
birds	3
plants	NA

Energy and Industry

Energy Production:	
solids (trillion BTUs)	0
liquids (trillion BTUs)	0
gas (trillion BTUs)	0
nuclear (gigawatt-hours)	0
hydroelectric (gigawatt-hours)	0
Energy Requirements:	
traditional fuels (trillion BTUs)	4
total (trillion BTUs)	6
per capita (million BTUs)	16
per capita (global rank)	97
Industrial Share of GDP	10.3%
Industrial Energy Index	NA
Metal Reserve Index (world=100%)	NA
No. of Motor Vehicles/1000 Persons	NA

Water

Renewable Supply (cubic miles)	7.2
Total Use (cubic miles):	0.0
in agriculture	6.0%
in industry	13.0%
in homes and cities	81.0%
Access to Safe Water:	
urban population	NA
rural population	NA

Urban Centers and Waste

No. of Cities Over 1 Million:	0
percent of population	0.0%
Solid Wastes (million tons)	NA
Urban Sanitation Access	NA

Population and Gross National Product

Population (millions)   GNP (billion $US)

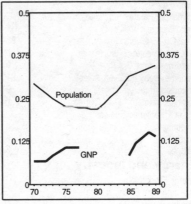

Commercial Energy Use

Total Energy Use (trillion BTUs)   Per Capita Energy Use (million BTUs)

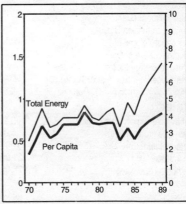

Quality of Life

Life Expectancy (years)	56.3
Infant Mortality (per 1000)	106.0
Population Under 15 Years	45.4%
Population Over 65 Years	2.8%
Literacy Rate	NA
Malnourished Children	NA

Land Use and Habitats

Cropland (sq. miles):	2,556
per capita (acres)	0.9
global rank	42
Permanent Pasture (sq. miles):	8
total livestock (millions)	11.3
Forest and Woodlands (sq. miles):	70,077
1985 deforestation (sq. miles)	116
Wilderness Area (sq. miles)	85,863
Maritime Areas (EEZ, sq. miles)	NA
Protected Areas (sq. miles):	39,947
percent of total	12.6%
No. of Threatened Species:	
mammals	11
birds	7
plants	18

Energy and Industry

Energy Production:	
solids (trillion BTUs)	NA
liquids (trillion BTUs)	0
gas (trillion BTUs)	0
nuclear (gigawatt-hours)	0
hydroelectric (gigawatt-hours)	0
Energy Requirements:	
traditional fuels (trillion BTUs)	NA
total (trillion BTUs)	NA
per capita (million BTUs)	NA
per capita (global rank)	NA
Industrial Share of GDP	NA
Industrial Energy Index	NA
Metal Reserve Index (world=100%)	0.1%
No. of Motor Vehicles/1000 Persons	NA

Water

Renewable Supply (cubic miles)	2.2
Total Use (cubic miles):	0.0
in agriculture	82.0%
in industry	12.0%
in homes and cities	6.0%
Access to Safe Water:	
urban population	NA
rural population	NA

Urban Centers and Waste

No. of Cities Over 1 Million:	0
percent of population	0.0%
Solid Wastes (million tons)	0.1
Urban Sanitation Access	NA

Population and Gross National Product

Population (millions)	GNP (billion $US)

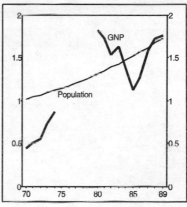

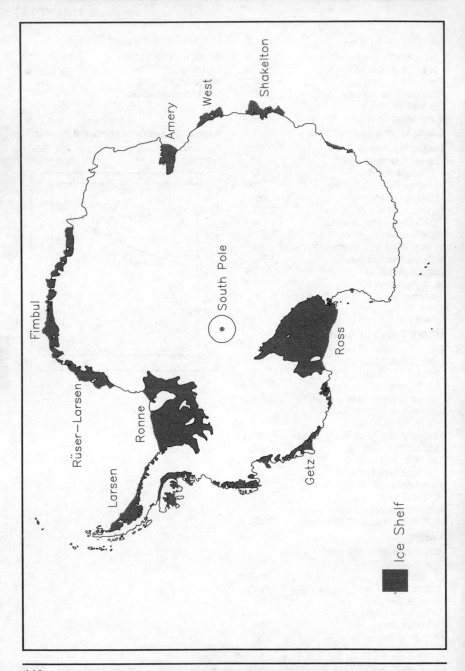

Antarctica

Most people associate the words *ozone hole* with Antarctica. The seasonal loss of the atmospheric shield that screens ultraviolet (UV) light was first observed by a British research group there in 1985. Since then, fear of the sun's damaging radiation has inspired treaties to reduce and eliminate the use of chlorofluorocarbons worldwide.

If global warming, a different problem, melted Antarctica's ice, ocean levels would rise by 200 feet. But do not expect a new coastline soon. The 5.4-million-square-mile continent holds 90 percent of the Earth's ice (equal to 70 percent of all fresh water), and it would take centuries to melt completely. Temperatures in Antarctica are still very low: the world record, −129° F, was recorded there in 1983.

For all its frigidity, Antarctica and the surrounding ocean support many plants, insects, and animals. Some have incredible adaptations, such as fish with a natural antifreeze and algae that grow on snow. The most familiar Antarctic animals are penguins, but the most important may be krill, 2-inch crustaceans that play a pivotal role in the Antarctic food chain. As UV light increases, scientists are concerned it may affect the phytoplankton that krill feed on, thus disrupting the chain.

Although the South Pole was first reached by humans in 1911, modern cooperation in Antarctic science and politics began during the International Geophysical Year of 1957–58, when twelve countries set up 60 research stations. In 1961, those countries agreed to make no territorial claims in Antarctica and to occupy it only for peaceful, scientific projects. A new treaty was approved in 1991 by 39 countries to continue the unique status of Antarctica for another 50 years.

No passport is required to visit Antarctica, and as many as 3,000 tourists a year make the trip. Many return home more concerned than ever about the environment, including Antarctica's. Although tours have been ecologically sensitive so far, increasing numbers of ships, planes, and feet now threaten the fragile and pristine environment of this icy continent.

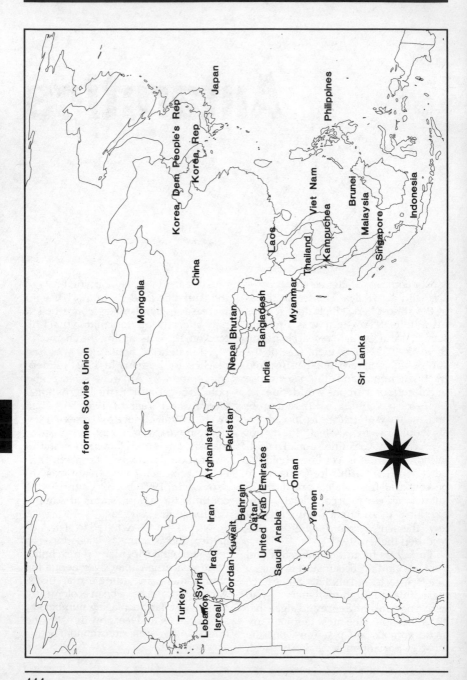

Asia

This chapter contains environmental profiles for the Asian countries listed. Technical notes and data sources are given beginning on page 641.

AFGHANISTAN

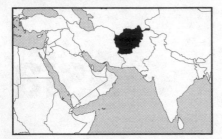

Total Area: 251,768 sq. miles
Global Rank: 39   Per Capita: 9.7 acres
Population: 16,557,000
Global Rank: 48   Growth Rate: 2.63%
Gross National Product: NA
Global Rank: NA   Per Capita: NA
Greenhouse Gas Emissions
Global Share: 0.05%   Per Capita Rank: 155

Afghanistan is a landlocked country bordering the Commonwealth of Independent States (C.I.S.), China, Pakistan, and Iran. Its terrain consists mostly of mountains and desert interspersed with small valleys and high plains or steppes. Afghanistan has an arid climate with dry, hot summers, cold winters, and a fairly well defined rainy season from November to February. Rangeland accounts for 45 percent of the country, on which oxen, sheep, goats, and other farm animals graze.

Afghanistan's natural resources include natural gas, oil, coal, and copper. The main energy resource, natural gas, is exported primarily to the republics of the C.I.S. via a pipeline that was temporarily capped between 1989 and 1990 but has been reopened. In addition, coal, salt, and chrome are exploited on a commercial scale. Other exports include cotton, wool, and the pelts of karakul lambs. Wheat, rice, fruit, and vegetables are among the major crops.

The people of Afghanistan have among the lowest life expectancy and literacy rates in the world, a situation tremendously exacerbated by the 13 years of warfare that followed the occupation by Soviet forces in 1979. The war destroyed much of the country's already meager land, maimed thousands of persons, and turned millions into refugees. In 1991, two major natural disasters, an earthquake measuring 6.8 on the Richter scale and flash flooding, also did extensive damage.

Major Environmental Problems

War devastation. More than a decade of civil war and Soviet occupation have left Afghanistan nearly destroyed. Roads, bridges, and whole villages were damaged by bombing. War-induced urbanization and mass exodus to other countries have turned many areas, particularly rural areas, into wastelands. The "scorched earth" policy practiced by occupying forces damaged many tracts of land to such an extent that they no longer sustain life. Unexploded bombs scattered by aircraft make many areas hazardous for farmers or herdsmen.

The war also depleted livestock herds, increasing rural poverty. A lack of draft animals makes traditional agricultural practices difficult, leading to increased dependence on mechanized methods of raising food.

Deforestation. A growing population in need of fuel and building materials threatens to destroy the country's few remaining forests, which cover less than 3 percent of the land area. Valuable oak and pistachio trees and old-growth stands have been cut for fuel.

AFGHANISTAN

Quality of Life

Life Expectancy (years)	41.5
Infant Mortality (per 1000)	172.0
Population Under 15 Years	39.8%
Population Over 65 Years	2.3%
Literacy Rate	29.4%
Malnourished Children	NA

Land Use and Habitats

Cropland (sq. miles):	31,097
per capita (acres)	1.2
global rank	25
Permanent Pasture (sq. miles):	115,830
total livestock (millions)	18.2
Forest and Woodlands (sq. miles):	7,336
1985 deforestation (sq. miles)	0
Wilderness Area (sq. miles)	33,747
Maritime Areas (EEZ, sq. miles)	0
Protected Areas (sq. miles):	550
percent of total	0.2%
No. of Threatened Species:	
mammals	13
birds	13
plants	2

Energy and Industry

Energy Production:	
solids (trillion BTUs)	4
liquids (trillion BTUs)	0
gas (trillion BTUs)	109
nuclear (gigawatt-hours)	0
hydroelectric (gigawatt-hours)	757
Energy Requirements:	
traditional fuels (trillion BTUs)	43
total (trillion BTUs)	149
per capita (million BTUs)	9
per capita (global rank)	125
Industrial Share of GDP	NA
Industrial Energy Index	NA
Metal Reserve Index (world=100%)	NA
No. of Motor Vehicles/1000 Persons	NA

Water

Renewable Supply (cubic miles)	12.0
Total Use (cubic miles).	6.3
in agriculture	99.0%
in industry	0.0%
in homes and cities	1.0%
Access to Safe Water:	
urban population	39.0%
rural population	17.0%

Urban Centers and Waste

No. of Cities Over 1 Million:	1
percent of population	9.5%
Solid Wastes (million tons)	0.6
Urban Sanitation Access	20.0%

Population and Gross National Product

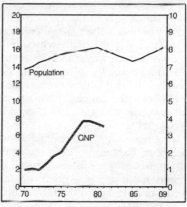

Population (millions) / GNP (billion $US)

Commercial Energy Use

Total Energy Use (trillion BTUs) / Per Capita Energy Use (million BTUs)

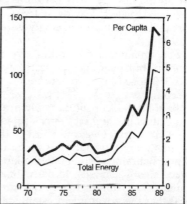

BAHRAIN

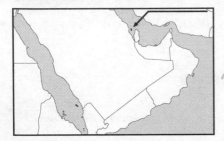

Total Area: 263 sq. miles
  Global Rank: 143   Per Capita: 0.3 acres
Population: 516,000
  Global Rank: 135   Growth Rate: 3.67%
Gross National Product: $3,019 m.
  Global Rank: 103   Per Capita: $6,070
Greenhouse Gas Emissions
  Global Share: 0.04%   Per Capita Rank: 3

Bahrain encompasses a group of 33 low-lying islands in the Persian Gulf, located between the Qatar Peninsula and Saudi Arabia (with which it is linked by a causeway). An interior plateau is located on the island of Bahrain, as is the hill Jabal Dukhan, which rises to 445 feet, the highest point in the country. The remaining land, most of the country, is desert.

Like many of its Middle Eastern neighbors, Bahrain is richly endowed with petroleum resources, especially oil and natural gas. Agriculture accounts for only 1 percent of the annual gross national product, and most foodstuffs are imported. About two thirds of the arable land is used for growing date palms. Most observers believe that in the next 20 years Bahrain's oil will be depleted, leaving it the first post-petroleum-based economy in the area.

Few mammals or reptiles live in Bahrain, but over 500 species of fish and 350 species of birds are found in the country.

Bahrain is a constitutional emirate and claims the highest literacy rate in the Arab world. Over one third of the population of the country is made up of non-Bahraini additions to the labor force, mostly Omanis, Indians, Pakistanis, and Iranians. It was not until 1980 that the government established an Environmental Protection Commit-

tee and began to address the country's problems in this area.

Major Environmental Problems

Coastal degradation. Oil spills and other discharges from large tankers, oil refineries, and distribution stations in Bahrain and neighboring countries cause damage to the coastlines, coral reefs, and sea vegetation. Experts believe that the nearby ruptures of Iran's Nowruz and Feridoon fields—in addition to the oil spills during the Persian Gulf War—pose a serious danger to marine life in the Persian Gulf.

Desertification. The government's economic emphasis on petroleum production has led to a neglect of agricultural development and degradation of the limited arable land. The area's sparse rainfall, combined with increasing desertification, gives rise to the potential for serious food shortages after the oil resources have been depleted.

Water scarcity. Bahrain has no surface water resources. Groundwater is the only source of water apart from the sea and a scanty amount of rainfall. The present rate of extraction of groundwater from wells, coupled with saltwater intrusions into underground aquifers, are depleting aquifers and pose a threat to Bahrain's future water supplies.

BAHRAIN

Quality of Life

Life Expectancy (years)	70.4
Infant Mortality (per 1000)	16.0
Population Under 15 Years	31.9%
Population Over 65 Years	1.6%
Literacy Rate	77.4%
Malnourished Children	NA

Land Use and Habitats

Cropland (sq. miles):	8
per capita (acres)	0.0
global rank	143
Permanent Pasture (sq. miles):	15
total livestock (millions)	0.0
Forest and Woodlands (sq. miles):	0
1985 deforestation (sq. miles)	NA
Wilderness Area (sq. miles)	0
Maritime Areas (EEZ, sq. miles)	20
Protected Areas (sq. miles):	0
percent of total	0.0%
No. of Threatened Species:	
mammals	1
birds	4
plants	NA

Energy and Industry

Energy Production:	
solids (trillion BTUs)	0
liquids (trillion BTUs)	92
gas (trillion BTUs)	185
nuclear (gigawatt-hours)	0
hydroelectric (gigawatt-hours)	0
Energy Requirements:	
traditional fuels (trillion BTUs)	0
total (trillion BTUs)	216
per capita (million BTUs)	435
per capita (global rank)	3
Industrial Share of GDP	43.1%
Industrial Energy Index	NA
Metal Reserve Index (world=100%)	NA
No. of Motor Vehicles/1000 Persons	NA

Water

Renewable Supply (cubic miles)	0.0
Total Use (cubic miles):	0.1
in agriculture	4.0%
in industry	36.0%
in homes and cities	60.0%
Access to Safe Water:	
urban population	100.0%
rural population	57.0%

Urban Centers and Waste

No. of Cities Over 1 Million:	0
percent of population	0.0%
Solid Wastes (million tons)	0.2
Urban Sanitation Access	100.0%

Population and Gross National Product

Population (millions)	GNP (billion $US)

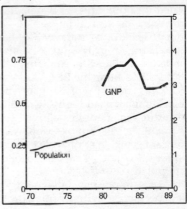

Commercial Energy Use

Total Energy Use (trillion BTUs)	Per Capita Energy Use (million BTUs)

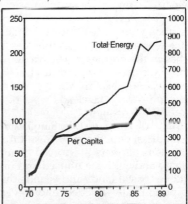

BANGLADESH

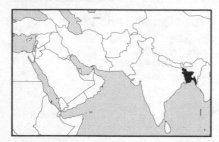

Total Area: 55,598 sq. miles
  Global Rank: 86   Per Capita: 0.3 acres
Population: 115,593,000
  Global Rank: 9   Growth Rate: 2.67%
Gross National Product: $20,387 m.
  Global Rank: 60   Per Capita: $181
Greenhouse Gas Emissions
  Global Share: 0.46%   Per Capita Rank: 141

Located in southern Asia, Bangladesh is one of the poorest and most densely populated countries in the world. It is a low-lying country largely surrounded by India, with a marshy, 370-mile coastline along the Bay of Bengal.

The vast majority of Bangladeshis live in rural areas and are engaged in agriculture. Bangladesh's alluvial soil is extremely fertile, but the people face a constant struggle to provide enough food for the country's rapidly increasing population.

The most important of the country's many pressing environmental problems involve water, which may be, variously, too plentiful, too scarce, and too polluted. The country forms the downriver and delta portions of one of the world's great river systems, which lies mostly beyond its borders. It also has among the highest annual rainfalls in the world, averaging as much as 85 inches in the northeast. The predominantly subsistence agricultural economy depends heavily on the erratic monsoon cycle, which leads to periodic flooding and drought.

Many of the people in Bangladesh are landless, with the tragic result that millions of farmers are forced to migrate to and cultivate unused and unsuitable coastal lands and islands that are periodically flooded and devastated by cyclones. For example, the 1991 cyclone, the worst on record,

killed 140,000 people. The potential of rising sea levels is also a threat to Bangladesh's heavily populated lowlands.

Major Environmental Problems

Water regulation. Deforestation of the Himalayas has reduced the capacity of the slopes to retain monsoon rains, causing increasingly savage floods downstream in the wet season and inadequate flow in the dry season. At the same time, the water table is dropping in the northern and central portions of Bangladesh, causing intermittent water shortages and allowing ever more intrusion of saltwater into cultivated areas.

Pollution and contamination. Industrial degradation of water and soil resources is widespread, and flood conditions result in the spread of polluted water across areas that are used for fishing and rice cultivation. Heavy use of commercial pesticides is also a concern.

Access to clean water. Many Bangladeshis have no access to potable water. The effect of waterborne diseases, together with chronic malnutrition and inadequate health services, is a high rate of infant mortality; 17 percent of children die before the age of 5 years.

BANGLADESH

Quality of Life

Life Expectancy (years)	50.7
Infant Mortality (per 1000)	119.0
Population Under 15 Years	42.1%
Population Over 65 Years	2.7%
Literacy Rate	35.3%
Malnourished Children	70.0%

Land Use and Habitats

Cropland (sq. miles):	35,876
per capita (acres)	0.2
global rank	131
Permanent Pasture (sq. miles):	2,317
total livestock (millions)	37.0
Forest and Woodlands (sq. miles):	7,529
1985 deforestation (sq. miles)	31
Wilderness Area (sq. miles)	0
Maritime Areas (EEZ, sq. miles)	297
Protected Areas (sq. miles):	374
percent of total	0.7%
No. of Threatened Species:	
mammals	15
birds	27
plants	6

Energy and Industry

Energy Production:	
solids (trillion BTUs)	0
liquids (trillion BTUs)	5
gas (trillion BTUs)	143
nuclear (gigawatt-hours)	0
hydroelectric (gigawatt-hours)	733
Energy Requirements:	
traditional fuels (trillion BTUs)	256
total (trillion BTUs)	475
per capita (million BTUs)	4
per capita (global rank)	142
Industrial Share of GDP	14.4%
Industrial Energy Index	32
Metal Reserve Index (world=100%)	NA
No. of Motor Vehicles/1000 Persons	NA

Water

Renewable Supply (cubic miles)	325.6
Total Use (cubic miles)	0.4
in agriculture	96.0%
in industry	1.0%
in homes and cities	3.0%
Access to Safe Water:	
urban population	37.0%
rural population	89.0%

Urban Centers and Waste

No. of Cities Over 1 Million:	2
percent of population	7.7%
Solid Wastes (million tons)	3.8
Urban Sanitation Access	37.0%

Population and Gross National Product

Population (millions)	GNP (billion $US)

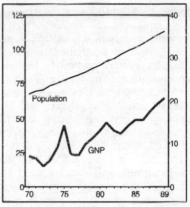

Commercial Energy Use

Total Energy Use (trillion BTUs)	Per Capita Energy Use (million BTUs)

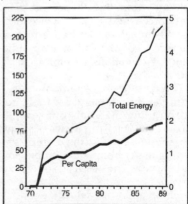

BHUTAN

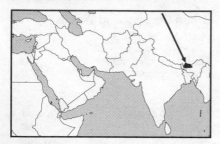

Total Area: 18,146 sq. miles
Global Rank: 113   Per Capita: 7.7 acres
Population: 1,516,000
Global Rank: 122   Growth Rate: 2.15%
Gross National Product: $258 m.
Global Rank: 138   Per Capita: $178
Greenhouse Gas Emissions
Global Share: 0.00%   Per Capita Rank: 154

Bhutan is a landlocked kingdom of 18,146 square miles—about the size of Vermont and New Hampshire combined—situated north of Bangladesh and at the eastern end of the Himalayan Mountains. The terrain is mostly mountainous, with elevations as high as 24,000 feet, and heavily forested. The Himalayas are a very young and still unstable range, giving rise to severe erosion.

Only about 8 percent of Bhutan's mountainous land can be used for farming or as pasture. When measured in terms of cropland per person, Bhutan ranks alongside such crowded countries as Bangladesh and China. All arable land is now in use, but a growing population puts growing pressure on that land. More than 90 percent of the work force works in subsistence farming and animal husbandry. Terrace agriculture is common, with rice paddies found at elevations as high as 8,000 feet.

The country has abundant forest resources, but demand for fuelwood and building materials outpaces reforestation. Diverse species of plants and animals inhabit the country, including many unique to Bhutan. Several rivers have hydroelectric potential.

The small industrial sector consists mostly of home-based handicrafts and privately owned small-to-medium-sized factories producing mostly consumer goods. Cement, plastic pipe, and calcium carbide factories have been built recently. Mineral resources include dolomite, limestone, coal, graphite, gypsum, slate, marble, lead, zinc, and copper; only dolomite, limestone, slate, and coal have been mined.

Both the country's Buddhist tradition and the government's formal policy emphasize preserving the environment. A late start at economic development has given the country the chance to plan carefully, learning from the mistakes of others.

Major Environmental Problems

Erosion. Roughly half the land is on steep slopes that are susceptible to erosion; about 15 percent of the land has shallow soils, which, in combination with steep slopes, are particularly susceptible. The road system, cut through the mountains, adds to the problem, which will grow as the road system expands.

Access to safe drinking water. Only about one fourth of the rural population has access to safe drinking water, and only about 7 percent has access to sanitation services. Health services are meager; there are roughly 50 doctors in the entire country.

BHUTAN

Quality of Life

Life Expectancy (years)	47.9
Infant Mortality (per 1000)	128.0
Population Under 15 Years	39.7%
Population Over 65 Years	3.0%
Literacy Rate	38.4%
Malnourished Children	56.0%

Land Use and Habitats

Cropland (sq. miles):	506
per capita (acres)	0.2
global rank	126
Permanent Pasture (sq. miles):	1,042
total livestock (millions)	0.6
Forest and Woodlands (sq. miles):	10,058
1985 deforestation (sq. miles)	4
Wilderness Area (sq. miles)	4,551
Maritime Areas (EEZ, sq. miles)	0
Protected Areas (sq. miles):	3,569
percent of total	19.7%
No. of Threatened Species:	
mammals	15
birds	10
plants	6

Energy and Industry

Energy Production:	
solids (trillion BTUs)	0
liquids (trillion BTUs)	0
gas (trillion BTUs)	0
nuclear (gigawatt-hours)	0
hydroelectric (gigawatt-hours)	651
Energy Requirements:	
traditional fuels (trillion BTUs)	27
total (trillion BTUs)	29
per capita (million BTUs)	19
per capita (global rank)	88
Industrial Share of GDP	29.3%
Industrial Energy Index	NA
Metal Reserve Index (world=100%)	NA
No. of Motor Vehicles/1000 Persons	NA

Water

Renewable Supply (cubic miles)	22.8
Total Use (cubic miles):	0.0
in agriculture	54.0%
in industry	10.0%
in homes and cities	36.0%
Access to Safe Water:	
urban population	100.0%
rural population	24.0%

Urban Centers and Waste

No. of Cities Over 1 Million:	0
percent of population	0.0%
Solid Wastes (million tons)	NA
Urban Sanitation Access	100.0%

Population and Gross National Product

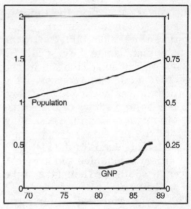

Population (millions) / GNP (billion $US)

Commercial Energy Use

Total Energy Use (trillion BTUs) / Per Capita Energy Use (million BTUs)

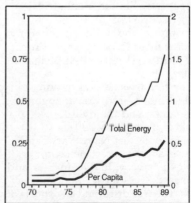

CAMBODIA

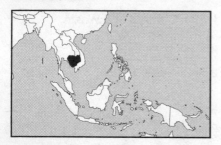

Total Area: 69,898 sq. miles
Global Rank: 82   Per Capita: 5.4 acres
Population: 8,246,000
Global Rank: 75   Growth Rate: 2.48%
Gross National Product: NA
Global Rank: NA   Per Capita: NA
Greenhouse Gas Emissions
Global Share: NA   Per Capita Rank: NA

Cambodia is located on the Indochinese peninsula in southeastern Asia. It is bordered by Thailand and Laos to the north, by Viet Nam to the east, and by the Gulf of Thailand to the south. The larger part of Cambodia consists of the plain of the lower Mekong River valley, with the western slopes of the Annamite Mountain chain in the east lying along the frontier with Viet Nam, and the isolated highlands of the Elephant and Cardamon mountains in the west, adjacent to southeast Thailand and the Gulf of Thailand.

The large Mekong River runs southward through the country's plains. The climate is tropical and humid, with monsoon rains from June to November. Nearly 700,000 live in the capital, Phnom Penh. Agriculture, fisheries, and rubber are the mainstays of the country's economy. Exports include rubber and timber. The country is not self-sufficient in food.

The country's natural resources include timber, iron ore, manganese, phosphates, and the hydropower potential of the Mekong River.

Before the Viet Nam War, Cambodia was a quiet, forest-rich country. It had extensive valuable forests and southeast Asia's most important wetlands. The war disrupted all aspects of the country's life for 20 years, and the ensuing civil war continued the disruption, with environmental consequences that will be felt for years to come.

Major Environmental Problems

Deforestation. Forests on the Annamite mountain range have largely been cleared and severely damaged by shifting cultivation. Prior to clearing they also suffered from defoliation and bombing during the Viet Nam War. The forests of the Elephant and Cardamon mountains, however, have not been affected as much because of the much smaller numbers of people living in the area.

Habitat loss. Cambodia has lost approximately three fourths of its wildlife habitat and has put at risk more than half of its wetlands. The main cause is deforestation. This has led to a decline in wildlife populations and the loss of some plant and animal species, thus reducing the country's biodiversity.

Mangrove destruction. Cambodia has a short coastline, only about 300 miles in length, but the mangrove swamps and estuaries found there are important to the country's fisheries and other wildlife. Much of these have been destroyed, and only discontinuous bands of mangrove now remain.

Quality of Life

Life Expectancy (years)	48.5
Infant Mortality (per 1000)	130.0
Population Under 15 Years	41.8%
Population Over 65 Years	2.3%
Literacy Rate	35.2%
Malnourished Children	NA

Land Use and Habitats

Cropland (sq. miles):	11,799
per capita (acres)	0.9
global rank	43
Permanent Pasture (sq. miles):	2,239
total livestock (millions)	4.3
Forest and Woodlands (sq. miles):	51,029
1985 deforestation (sq. miles)	116
Wilderness Area (sq. miles)	0
Maritime Areas (EEZ, sq. miles)	215
Protected Areas (sq. miles):	0
percent of total	0.0%
No. of Threatened Species:	
mammals	21
birds	13
plants	11

Energy and Industry

Energy Production:	
solids (trillion BTUs)	0
liquids (trillion BTUs)	0
gas (trillion BTUs)	0
nuclear (gigawatt-hours)	0
hydroelectric (gigawatt-hours)	33
Energy Requirements:	
traditional fuels (trillion BTUs)	48
total (trillion BTUs)	55
per capita (million BTUs)	7
per capita (global rank)	135
Industrial Share of GDP	NA
Industrial Energy Index	NA
Metal Reserve Index (world=100%)	NA
No. of Motor Vehicles/1000 Persons	NA

Water

Renewable Supply (cubic miles)	21.1
Total Use (cubic miles)	0.1
in agriculture	94.0%
in industry	1.0%
in homes and cities	5.0%
Access to Safe Water:	
urban population	NA
rural population	NA

Urban Centers and Waste

No. of Cities Over 1 Million:	0
percent of population	0.0%
Solid Wastes (million tons)	0.2
Urban Sanitation Access	NA

Population and Gross National Product

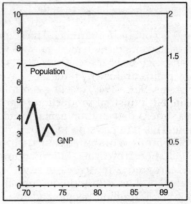

Population (millions) — GNP (billion $US)

Commercial Energy Use

Total Energy Use (trillion BTUs) — Per Capita Energy Use (million BTUs)

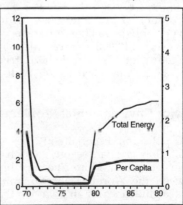

CHINA

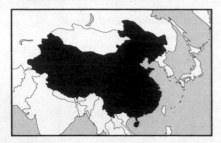

Total Area: 3,705,326 sq. miles
Global Rank: 3   Per Capita: 2.1 acres
Population: 1,139,060
Global Rank: 1   Growth Rate: 1.45%
Gross National Product: $419,466 m.
Global Rank: 10   Per Capita: $374
Greenhouse Gas Emissions
Global Share: 9.12%   Per Capita Rank: 111

China is slightly larger than the United States, but only about 10 percent of the land is suitable for farming. The country also contains high mountainous regions, rich coastal areas, deserts, and low plains drained by three large river systems. Since 1949, meeting centrally planned industrial production targets has superseded environmental protection. This emphasis on industrial development, combined with rapid population growth and little planning, has created some severe environmental problems. In addition, annually gaining 17 million people and losing about 1,150 square miles of cultivated land puts increasingly severe pressure on the remaining farmland.

In 1989, the national People's Congress revised the country's environmental protection law. China has established 600 nature reserves covering 150,000 square miles and is planting a shelterbelt of trees known as the Great Green Wall of China.

Major Environmental Problems

Air pollution. Especially in cities, air pollution is often severe enough to threaten health. More cities in China exceed the World Health Organization's guidelines for air pollution than in any other country. Coal, often burned in inefficient stoves and furnaces, provides 85 percent of the energy for urban residences, 75 percent for industry, and 73 percent for commercial uses. The resulting acid rain has damaged soils and trees over large parts of the country.

Water supply and pollution. A severe water shortage exists in China's north, which has 64 percent of the country's cultivated land but only 19 percent of its water. Nationwide, more than a third of the inhabitants lack access to water meeting sanitation standards. Industry accounts for most pollution, dumping 60 percent of its waste water without treatment. A 1989 survey found 436 out of 532 rivers polluted.

Deforestation. China has less than 490,000 square miles of forest—about 13 percent of the total land. In addition to threatening the habitats of many species, some unique to China, loss of forest cover contributes to severe soil erosion, especially in China's highland areas, and frequent flooding throughout the country. The Yellow River is among the world's most silt laden, carrying an estimated 1 billion tons of sediment annually.

Destruction of grasslands. At least 330,000 square miles show evidence of degradation.

Quality of Life

Life Expectancy (years)	69.4
Infant Mortality (per 1000)	32.0
Population Under 15 Years	26.3%
Population Over 65 Years	4.9%
Literacy Rate	73.3%
Malnourished Children	41.0%

Land Use and Habitats

Cropland (sq. miles):	371,100
per capita (acres)	0.2
global rank	128
Permanent Pasture (sq. miles):	1,231,969
total livestock (millions)	669.9
Forest and Woodlands (sq. miles):	488,282
1985 deforestation (sq. miles)	0
Wilderness Area (sq. miles)	813,807
Maritime Areas (EEZ, sq. miles)	5,235
Protected Areas (sq. miles):	84,738
percent of total	2.3%
No. of Threatened Species:	
mammals	30
birds	83
plants	841

Energy and Industry

Energy Production:	
solids (trillion BTUs)	20,614
liquids (trillion BTUs)	5,454
gas (trillion BTUs)	555
nuclear (gigawatt-hours)	0
hydroelectric (gigawatt-hours)	109,496
Energy Requirements:	
traditional fuels (trillion BTUs)	1,753
total (trillion BTUs)	27,302
per capita (million BTUs)	24
per capita (global rank)	78
Industrial Share of GDP	46.1%
Industrial Energy Index	66
Metal Reserve Index (world=100%)	8.4%
No. of Motor Vehicles/1000 Persons	NA

Water

Renewable Supply (cubic miles)	671.8
Total Use (cubic miles):	110.4
in agriculture	87.0%
in industry	7.0%
in homes and cities	6.0%
Access to Safe Water:	
urban population	87.0%
rural population	66.0%

Urban Centers and Waste

No. of Cities Over 1 Million:	38
percent of population	9.1%
Solid Wastes (million tons)	76.6
Urban Sanitation Access	100.0%

Population and Gross National Product

Population (millions)

GNP (billion $US)

Commercial Energy Use

Total Energy Use (trillion BTUs)

Per Capita Energy Use (million BTUs)

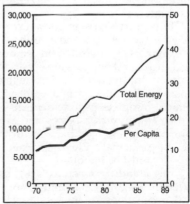

CYPRUS

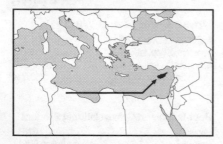

Total Area: 3,571 sq. miles
Global Rank: 137   Per Capita: 3.3 acres
Population: 701,000
Global Rank: 133   Growth Rate: 1.04%
Gross National Product: $4,552 m.
Global Rank: 88   Per Capita: $6,562
Greenhouse Gas Emissions
Global Share: 0.02%   Per Capita Rank: 63

The Republic of Cyprus is an island nation, about the size of Connecticut, located in the northeastern corner of the Mediterranean Sea. It comprises a fertile, central plain, a mostly barren mountain range running along the northern coastline, and a forest-covered range in the southwest. Over the past three decades, Cyprus has rapidly changed from an agrarian and rural society to a predominantly urban one with a thriving tourist trade. Tourists annually number twice the island's population, placing strains on the island's fragile ecosystem.

Cyprus depends largely on precipitation for its water supply, which is proving insufficient to the demand. About 90 percent of the island's rain falls between November and March.

The country's most important crops are wheat, barley, potatoes, carobs, olives, oranges, grapefruit, and lemons; citrus fruits and potatoes are exported. A significant amount of forest remains, mostly well protected and managed. Mineral resources include deposits of copper, iron pyrites, asbestos, and gypsum. Mining and light manufacturing are the principal industries. Energy supplies must be imported.

Long-standing tensions exist between the majority Greek and minority Turk populations. An invasion by Turkey in 1974 severely disrupted the country, leading to the defacto partition of the country into two separate economies.

The government has established departments for environmental protection and natural resource management, but rapid modernization and development and limited resources threaten their effectiveness.

Major Environmental Problems

Water management. Growing demands have begun to damage the island's scarce water supply. Over-pumping from coastal aquifers has allowed some intrusion of sea water. Sewage and industrial wastes have polluted some inland water sources. A risk of pollution by agricultural chemicals also exists.

Coastal degradation. Erosion and pollution threaten the coastline, primarily because of the expanding tourist trade, urban sprawl, and runoff from excessive pesticide use on farms.

Land use and wildlife management. Other strains on the environment include large irrigation schemes that consume scarce water resources and unplanned urban and industrial sprawl. Loss of habitat from commercial development is threatening wildlife.

Quality of Life

Life Expectancy (years)	75.7
Infant Mortality (per 1000)	12.0
Population Under 15 Years	25.4%
Population Over 65 Years	10.1%
Literacy Rate	NA
Malnourished Children	NA

Land Use and Habitats

Cropland (sq. miles):	602
per capita (acres)	0.6
global rank	75
Permanent Pasture (sq. miles):	19
total livestock (millions)	0.9
Forest and Woodlands (sq. miles):	475
1985 deforestation (sq. miles)	0
Wilderness Area (sq. miles)	0
Maritime Areas (EEZ, sq. miles)	384
Protected Areas (sq. miles):	0
percent of total	0.0%
No. of Threatened Species:	
mammals	NA
birds	NA
plants	44

Energy and Industry

Energy Production:	
solids (trillion BTUs)	0
liquids (trillion BTUs)	0
gas (trillion BTUs)	0
nuclear (gigawatt-hours)	0
hydroelectric (gigawatt-hours)	0
Energy Requirements:	
traditional fuels (trillion BTUs)	0
total (trillion BTUs)	49
per capita (million BTUs)	71
per capita (global rank)	43
Industrial Share of GDP	26.9%
Industrial Energy Index	NA
Metal Reserve Index (world=100%)	0.0%
No. of Motor Vehicles/1000 Persons	238

Water

Renewable Supply (cubic miles)	0.2
Total Use (cubic miles):	0.1
in agriculture	91.0%
in industry	2.0%
in homes and cities	7.0%
Access to Safe Water:	
urban population	100.0%
rural population	100.0%

Urban Centers and Waste

No. of Cities Over 1 Million:	0
percent of population	0.0%
Solid Wastes (million tons)	0.1
Urban Sanitation Access	100.0%

Population and Gross National Product

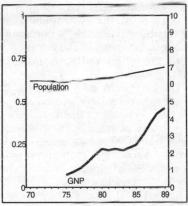

Population (millions) — GNP (billion $US)

Commercial Energy Use

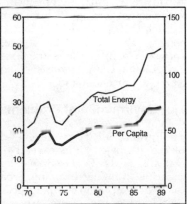

Total Energy Use (trillion BTUs) — Per Capita Energy Use (million BTUs)

INDIA

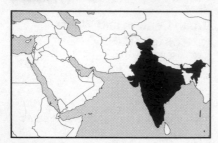

Total Area: 1,269,191 sq. miles
Global Rank: 7   Per Capita: 1.0 acres
Population: 853,094,000
Global Rank: 2   Growth Rate: 2.07%
Gross National Product: $262,414 m.
Global Rank: 13   Per Capita: $314
Greenhouse Gas Emissions
Global Share: 4.18%   Per Capita Rank: 132

India has only slightly more than twice the area of Alaska but counts nearly one sixth of the world's population among its inhabitants. The population is still growing rapidly, straining India's resources.

The geography and climate of the country vary widely, ranging from tropical lowlands in the south to the lofty peaks of the Himalayas in the north, from Thar, a nearly rainless desert, to Cherrapunji, the rainiest place on earth. Such varying habitats contribute to a wealth of biodiversity that includes 15,000 species of plants and 77,000 species of animals, many endemic to India.

The country has abundant resources of coal, iron ore, manganese, and bauxite. The major crops include rice and cotton, and agricultural products such as tea, coffee, and fish are among the chief exports. India is self-sufficient in food, but a large fraction of the population is undernourished and too poor to buy enough food.

Major Environmental Problems

Air pollution. Sulfur dioxide levels in 9 of the 10 major cities exceed national standards. Levels of particulates are also higher in many urban areas than they are in comparable areas of Europe and North America. Contributors to air pollution include power stations, industrial factories and automobiles.

Water pollution. India's rivers and streams suffer from very high levels of pollution. Untreated sewage and other nonindustrial wastes are the major cause, accounting for four times as much pollution as industrial effluents. Of 3,119 Indian towns and cities, only 209 have partial sewage treatment; only 8 have complete treatment. Waterborne diseases account for two thirds of all illnesses.

Soil degradation. India's soil resources are endangered. Soils covering at least 20 percent of the country are significantly degraded, the result of overgrazing, deforestation, and improper irrigation practices. Overcultivation has depleted some soils of nutrients. Use of marginal lands is widespread because of dire need.

Water shortages. India as a whole has abundant water resources, but some regions, particularly in the northeast, are arid and lack adequate water to grow crops. Occasional absences of the monsoon rains also can lead to water shortages and crop failures. A study by the Indian Institute of Technology predicts a state of nationwide water inadequacy before the turn of the century.

Quality of Life

Life Expectancy (years)	57.9
Infant Mortality (per 1000)	99.0
Population Under 15 Years	36.0%
Population Over 65 Years	3.8%
Literacy Rate	48.2%
Malnourished Children	NA

Land Use and Habitats

Cropland (sq. miles):	652,471
per capita (acres)	0.5
global rank	86
Permanent Pasture (sq. miles):	46,479
total livestock (millions)	443.7
Forest and Woodlands (sq. miles):	257,668
1985 deforestation (sq. miles)	568
Wilderness Area (sq. miles)	4,482
Maritime Areas (EEZ, sq. miles)	7,780
Protected Areas (sq. miles):	52,051
percent of total	4.1%
No. of Threatened Species:	
mammals	38
birds	72
plants	1,349

Energy and Industry

Energy Production:	
solids (trillion BTUs)	4,663
liquids (trillion BTUs)	1,353
gas (trillion BTUs)	299
nuclear (gigawatt-hours)	7,351
hydroelectric (gigawatt-hours)	63,760
Energy Requirements:	
traditional fuels (trillion BTUs)	2,506
total (trillion BTUs)	10,135
per capita (million BTUs)	12
per capita (global rank)	109
Industrial Share of GDP	28.5%
Industrial Energy Index	33
Metal Reserve Index (world=100%)	2.2%
No. of Motor Vehicles/1000 Persons	2

Water

Renewable Supply (cubic miles)	443.9
Total Use (cubic miles).	91.2
in agriculture	93.0%
in industry	4.0%
in homes and cities	3.0%
Access to Safe Water:	
urban population	79.0%
rural population	73.0%

Urban Centers and Waste

No. of Cities Over 1 Million:	24
percent of population	8.6%
Solid Wastes (million tons)	35.2
Urban Sanitation Access	38.0%

Population and Gross National Product

Population (millions) — GNP (billion $US)

Commercial Energy Use

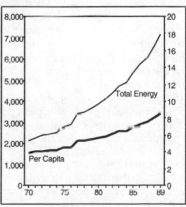

Total Energy Use (trillion BTUs) — Per Capita Energy Use (million BTUs)

INDONESIA

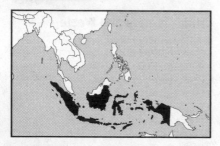

Total Area: 735,343 sq. miles
 Global Rank: 14   Per Capita: 2.6 acres
Population: 184,283,000
 Global Rank: 5   Growth Rate: 1.93%
Gross National Product: $89,373 m.
 Global Rank: 25   Per Capita: $494
Greenhouse Gas Emissions
 Global Share: 1.69%   Per Capita Rank: 105

The Republic of Indonesia is an archipelago of 17,508 islands, extending 2,900 miles along the equator between mainland southeastern Asia and Australia. Although nearly 6,000 islands are inhabited, 62 percent of the population of 187 million is found on the Inner Islands, which make up just 8 percent of the total land area.

Indonesia's abundant mineral resources include petroleum, coal, tin, nickel, bauxite, and copper. Indonesia exports oil and liquefied natural gas. Rich volcanic soils in Java and Bali sustain very high population densities and allow the republic to be self-sufficient in rice production. Principal crops, in addition to rice, are cassava, sugar cane, rubber, and coffee. Productive coastal and freshwater fisheries support both village and commercial industries. More than half of the country is covered by tropical rainforest. The archipelago is characterized by diverse and highly endemic flora and fauna.

Indonesia has made rapid strides towards alleviating absolute poverty, and its per capita gross national product has grown rapidly over the past 20 years. Although industrial activity has grown to more than one third of the gross national product, the economy remains dependent upon agriculture and natural resource extraction. Since the 1984 fall in world oil prices, the government has actively promoted forestry and mining, most recently in the eastern islands.

Major Environmental Problems

Rainforest degradation. The developing wood processing and pulp and paper industries call for the selective logging of nearly 3,000 square miles of virgin forest annually and the conversion of as much as 16,000 square miles to plantations by 1994. Shrimp ponds and logging concessions are destroying Indonesia's remaining mangrove forests. Overpopulation on the Inner Islands has driven both organized and spontaneous migration to the Outer Islands, opening large areas of undisturbed forest. Because of growing indigenous and immigrant populations, in many areas previously sustainable subsistence agriculture now results in irreversible deforestation.

Watershed degradation. Large areas of watershed lands are critically threatened. Industrial waste and sewage pollute rivers in port cities, presenting a serious health risk to urban dwellers dependent upon the rivers for water and fish and killing nearby coral reefs. Erosion, often caused by logging, threatens water transport, irrigation systems, and fisheries downstream.

INDONESIA

Quality of Life

Life Expectancy (years)	60.2
Infant Mortality (per 1000)	75.0
Population Under 15 Years	33.4%
Population Over 65 Years	3.3%
Literacy Rate	77.0%
Malnourished Children	46.0%

Land Use and Habitats

Cropland (sq. miles):	82,085
per capita (acres)	0.3
global rank	111
Permanent Pasture (sq. miles):	45,560
total livestock (millions)	37.3
Forest and Woodlands (sq. miles):	437,965
1985 deforestation (sq. miles)	2,394
Wilderness Area (sq. miles)	45,407
Maritime Areas (EEZ, sq. miles)	20,883
Protected Areas (sq. miles):	68,725
percent of total	9.3%
No. of Threatened Species:	
mammals	50
birds	135
plants	NA

Energy and Industry

Energy Production:	
solids (trillion BTUs)	126
liquids (trillion BTUs)	2,545
gas (trillion BTUs)	1,151
nuclear (gigawatt-hours)	0
hydroelectric (gigawatt-hours)	8,597
Energy Requirements:	
traditional fuels (trillion BTUs)	1,266
total (trillion BTUs)	2,703
per capita (million BTUs)	15
per capita (global rank)	102
Industrial Share of GDP	35.7%
Industrial Energy Index	11
Metal Reserve Index (world=100%)	1.5%
No. of Motor Vehicles/1000 Persons	6

Water

Renewable Supply (cubic miles)	607.1
Total Use (cubic miles):	4.0
in agriculture	76.0%
in industry	11.0%
in homes and cities	13.0%
Access to Safe Water:	
urban population	60.0%
rural population	40.0%

Urban Centers and Waste

No. of Cities Over 1 Million:	6
percent of population	10.0%
Solid Wastes (million tons)	12.9
Urban Sanitation Access	40.0%

Population and Gross National Product

Population	GNP
(millions)	(billion $US)

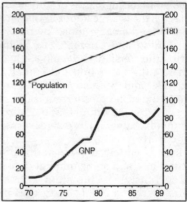

Commercial Energy Use

Total Energy Use	Per Capita Energy Use
(trillion BTUs)	(million BTUs)

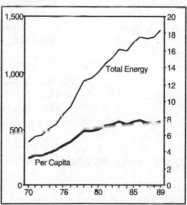

IRAN

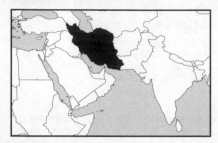

Total Area: 636,283 sq. miles
  Global Rank: 16   Per Capita: 7.5 acres
Population: 54,607,000
  Global Rank: 20   Growth Rate: 2.74%
Gross National Product: $154,584 m.
  Global Rank: 20   Per Capita: $2,909
Greenhouse Gas Emissions
  Global Share: 0.59%   Per Capita Rank: 95

Located in the highlands of southwestern Asia, the Islamic Republic of Iran is an arid land area bounded by the Soviet Union and Caspian Sea to the north, the Persian Gulf and Gulf of Oman to the south, Iraq and Turkey to the west, and Afghanistan and Pakistan to the east. Iran's terrain is distinguished by the Elburz and Zagros mountain chains and by extensive interior deserts.

Iran is endowed with petroleum, natural gas, and some mineral deposits, such as zinc, chromium, copper, sulfur, and iron ore. Its industries include petroleum production, oil refining, textiles, production of cement and other building materials, food processing, and metal fabricating.

Iran's population growth rate is high, adding to environmental strains. Tehran, the capital, is the second most populous city in the Middle East.

Iran's arid climate and fragile soil, combined with the destruction caused by the eight-year war with Iraq and the lack of management of many natural resources, has created an environmental crisis.

Major Environmental Problems

Deforestation. Only about 7,000 square miles of forest remain in the Caspian region, and the forests of the western mountains have been reduced to scattered woods. Other forests are threatened as well.

Water pollution. The almost completely landlocked Persian Gulf, with its shallow, highly saline water and narrow bottleneck at the Strait of Hormuz, has been plagued by pollution from heavy oil tanker traffic and a massive oil spill from the recent Persian Gulf War. Debris from oil tanker accidents and downed airplanes as well as black rain and toxic fumes from burning oil wells in Kuwait have made this body of water one of the most polluted in the world, threatening the marine food chain and the fishery on which many Iranians depend for protein. Hawksbill turtle, green turtle, dugong, whale, dolphin, shellfish, and bird populations are among those endangered by the continued pollution.

Water shortages. Many regions of the country are experiencing drought, with rainfall in recent years well below average. The drought, together with inefficient use of water resources, has created shortages of drinking water.

Air pollution. Iran's air is polluted, especially in urban areas, by emissions from cars, refinery operations, and industry.

Quality of Life

Life Expectancy (years)	65.2
Infant Mortality (per 1000)	52.0
Population Under 15 Years	41.9%
Population Over 65 Years	2.6%
Literacy Rate	54.0%
Malnourished Children	55.0%

Land Use and Habitats

Cropland (sq. miles):	57,259
per capita (acres)	0.7
global rank	67
Permanent Pasture (sq. miles):	169,884
total livestock (millions)	58.2
Forest and Woodlands (sq. miles):	69,575
1985 deforestation (sq. miles)	77
Wilderness Area (sq. miles)	60,561
Maritime Areas (EEZ, sq. miles)	601
Protected Areas (sq. miles):	29,069
percent of total	4.6%
No. of Threatened Species:	
mammals	15
birds	20
plants	1

Energy and Industry

Energy Production:	
solids (trillion BTUs)	33
liquids (trillion BTUs)	5,659
gas (trillion BTUs)	821
nuclear (gigawatt-hours)	0
hydroelectric (gigawatt-hours)	6,700
Energy Requirements:	
traditional fuels (trillion BTUs)	26
total (trillion BTUs)	2,345
per capita (million BTUs)	44
per capita (global rank)	58
Industrial Share of GDP	NA
Industrial Energy Index	40
Metal Reserve Index (world=100%)	0.2%
No. of Motor Vehicles/1000 Persons	39

Water

Renewable Supply (cubic miles)	28.2
Total Use (cubic miles):	10.9
in agriculture	87.0%
in industry	9.0%
in homes and cities	4.0%
Access to Safe Water:	
urban population	100.0%
rural population	75.0%

Urban Centers and Waste

No. of Cities Over 1 Million:	5
percent of population	23.3%
Solid Wastes (million tons)	6.2
Urban Sanitation Access	100.0%

Population and Gross National Product

Population	GNP
(millions)	(billion $US)

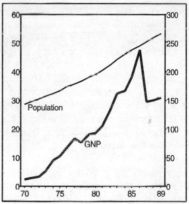

Commercial Energy Use

Total Energy Use	Per Capita Energy Use
(trillion BTUs)	(million BTUs)

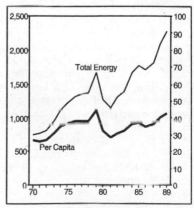

IRAQ

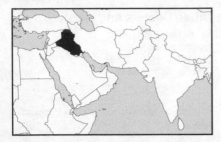

Total Area: 169,233 sq. miles
Global Rank: 53   Per Capita: 5.7 acres
Population: 18,920,000
Global Rank: 43   Growth Rate: 3.48%
Gross National Product: $35,000 m.
Global Rank: 45   Per Capita: $1,915
Greenhouse Gas Emissions
Global Share: 0.26%   Per Capita Rank: 84

Near the edge of western Asia, Iraq is an almost landlocked nation about the size of California. Along its northernmost border the country slopes downwards from mountains 10,000 feet above sea level toward a flat, alluvial plain that drains into reedy marshes in the southeast. In southwestern Iraq, much of the land is desert.

Once known as Mesopotamia, Iraq was the site of a flourishing ancient civilization. The population is overwhelmingly Muslim, split between the Shiite and Sunni sects, and is rapidly growing. Nearly 75 percent of the population lives on the fertile plain between Baghdad and Basra.

Iraq's natural resources include deposits of oil, natural gas, sulfur, and phosphates. The country claimed proven oil reserves of 79.5 billion barrels in 1986. The economy depends largely on oil production and agriculture. Oil makes up 95 percent of Iraq's exports. Iraq has abundant land and water resources but is dependent on imports for such foods as grains, meat, and dairy products.

Over the past decade, much of the country's resources have been focused on military activities, with little development in other sectors.

Iraq's invasion of Kuwait and the subsequent Persian Gulf War devastated much of Iraq's infrastructure, damaging or destroying roads, bridges, water treatment plants, factories, and military installations of all kinds. The country remains isolated and under United Nations sanctions that limit its ability to export oil and import the goods and services needed for rebuilding. Extensive loss of life in the war and the social disruption and civil war following Iraq's defeat have created very difficult conditions for the country's people. Interrupted agricultural activities and lack of imports have led to food shortages. Malnutrition is reported to be widespread.

Major Environmental Problems

War devastation. Extensive bombardment of Iraq during the Gulf War left the country's physical plant in ruins. Movements of tanks and troops caused extensive soil damage, particularly in the fragile desert soils near the border with Saudi Arabia.

Water contamination. Damage to water and sewage treatment facilities during the Gulf War has contaminated Iraq's water supply, particularly in Baghdad. Use of contaminated water has led to outbreaks of cholera and other waterborne diseases. The lack of adequate supplies of potable water is the country's most serious health problem.

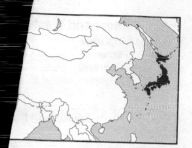

Total Area: 145,866 sq. miles
Global Rank: 56   Per Capita: 0.8 acres
Population: 123,460,000
Global Rank: 7   Growth Rate: 0.43%
Gross National Product: $2,836,300 m.
Global Rank: 2   Per Capita: $23,072
Greenhouse Gas Emissions
Global Share: 4.66%   Per Capita Rank: 29

consists of four large islands and
small ones in the western Pacific
n, near the coast of the Asian con-
nt. The country covers an area
tly smaller than California. Geo-
phic and geologic factors combine
give the country a limited natural
ource base. Although its climate is
orable for agriculture and more
an half the country is forested, most
the country is mountainous and
erefore not well suited for intensive
griculture or commercial forestry.
he country has no significant mineral
or energy deposits and imports virtually all its energy supplies. Japan is also
the world's leading importer of timber.

Less than 12 percent of the land is
arable, and much of it is intensely cultivated. Rice is the major crop. Japan
also has major fisheries along its coasts.
The country imports some foodstuffs,
particularly grains.

Japan's population is extremely homogeneous. Tokyo, the capital, has a
population of about 8 million.

The country has become one of the
world's leading industrial and financial powers, with an advanced technological and manufacturing capability
in the automotive and electronics sectors. Japan is one of the most efficient
users of energy among advanced industrial countries but is still a major
source of greenhouse gas emissions.
At the Rio Earth Summit, Japan

pledged to increase funding for environmental protection in developing
countries.

Major Environmental Problems

Air pollution. Concentrations of air
pollutants in such major urban areas as
Tokyo, Osaka, and Yokohama have increased steadily over the past decade.
Overall, however, Japan has tightened
its air quality regulations and has substantially reduced emissions of sulfur
dioxide and nitrogen oxides from its
power plants.

Nonetheless, acid rain is a serious
problem in many parts of the country
and has led to the significant degradation of water quality in many lakes and
reservoirs. Nearly one half of such
water bodies have experienced some
degree of acidification, threatening
aquatic life.

Marine degradation. Japan's fishing
industry is the largest in the world.
However, overfishing of many commercial species and increasing levels
of pollution in Japanese coastal waters have begun to reduce the catch.
Japan also leads the world in whaling
and in the use of drift net fishing—a
technique that indiscriminately kills
a large number of fish and sea mammals other than those sought by the
fishing fleet.

470

Quality of Life

Life Expectancy (years)	63.9
Infant Mortality (per 1000)	69.0
Population Under 15 Years	45.3%
Population Over 65 Years	2.2%
Literacy Rate	59.7%
Malnourished Children	NA

Land Use and Habitats

Cropland (sq. miles):	21,042
per capita (acres)	0.7
global rank	62
Permanent Pasture (sq. miles):	15,444
total livestock (millions)	13.3
Forest and Woodlands (sq. miles):	7,297
1985 deforestation (sq. miles)	0
Wilderness Area (sq. miles)	25,006
Maritime Areas (EEZ, sq. miles)	3
Protected Areas (sq. miles):	0
percent of total	0.0%
No. of Threatened Species:	
mammals	9
birds	17
plants	3

Energy and Industry

Energy Production:	
solids (trillion BTUs)	0
liquids (trillion BTUs)	5,497
gas (trillion BTUs)	181
nuclear (gigawatt-hours)	0
hydroelectric (gigawatt-hours)	594
Energy Requirements:	
traditional fuels (trillion BTUs)	1
total (trillion BTUs)	543
per capita (million BTUs)	30
per capita (global rank)	69
Industrial Share of GDP	NA
Industrial Energy Index	NA
Metal Reserve Index (world=100%)	0.0%
No. of Motor Vehicles/1000 Persons	37

Water

Renewable Supply (cubic miles)	8.2
Total Use (cubic miles):	10.3
in agriculture	92.0%
in industry	5.0%
in homes and cities	3.0%
Access to Safe Water:	
urban population	NA
rural population	NA

Urban Centers and Waste

No. of Cities Over 1 Million:	1
percent of population	21.4%
Solid Wastes (million tons)	6.0
Urban Sanitation Access	NA

Population and Gross National Product

Population (millions)   GNP (billion $US)

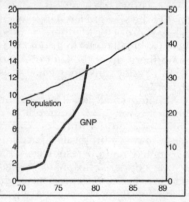

Commercial Energy Use

Total Energy Use (trillion BTUs)   Per Capita Energy Use (million BTUs)

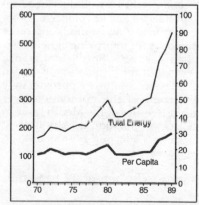

ISRAEL

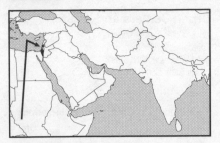

Total Area: 8,019 sq. miles
  Global Rank: 129   Per Capita: 1.1 acres
Population: 4,600,000
  Global Rank: 94   Growth Rate: 1.66%
Gross National Product: $44,887 m.
  Global Rank: 37   Per Capita: $9,922
Greenhouse Gas Emissions
  Global Share: 0.14%   Per Capita Rank: 37

Israel occupies a narrow strip of land roughly the size of New Jersey on the eastern shore of the Mediterranean Sea. There is a small outlet to the Red Sea at the northern tip of the Gulf of Aqaba. The Rift Valley runs along Israel's eastern border.

Although small, Israel has a remarkably wide range of geographical regions and environments: desert, alpine, and semitropical. The country has limited natural resources, which include copper, phosphates, potash, and clay. Israel is dependent on imported fossil fuels for most energy; some—particularly domestic—needs are met by locally developed solar-powered heaters.

Israel exports citrus and other fruits. The country has a well-developed industrial sector and has pioneered more efficient irrigation methods and other techniques for improving agriculture.

Israel is a nation of immigrants; over half of the population was born outside the country. Approximately 70 percent of the population lives within 10 miles of the Mediterranean seacoast. Population density is high, reaching 2,500 per square mile in some areas.

Major Environmental Problems

Water scarcity and pollution. Israel's available water supply is severely lim-

ited. Groundwater pollution caused by industrial and domestic waste, chemical fertilizers, pesticides, and seawater intrusion threatens this already limited resource. Surface water is also affected, as effluents and fertilizer runoffs find their way to the Jordan River and hence to the Sea of Galilee—the source of 40 percent of Israel's drinking water.

Coastal resources. Expansion and industrialization in urban coastal centers such as Tel Aviv and Haifa have created land-based marine pollution and have hampered efforts to protect coastal resources. Marine pollution from oil spills threatened Israel's coast at one time, but environmental legislation, combined with strict enforcement, have corrected the problem. Environmental pressures are increased by intensive recreational use of the coastal areas.

Air pollution. Power plants, quarries, cement factories, and oil refineries are major sources of air pollution in Israel. Emissions from cars and trucks exacerbate the problem. As of 1991, catalytic converters are required on some automobiles; by autumn 1993, all cars will have to have them. Unleaded gasoline is now available. These measures will contribute to the reduction of emissions.

Quality of Life

Life Expectancy (years)	75.4
Infant Mortality (per 1000)	12.0
Population Under 15 Years	29.6%
Population Over 65 Years	8.1%
Literacy Rate	NA
Malnourished Children	NA

Land Use and Habitats

Cropland (sq. miles):	1,672
per capita (acres)	0.2
global rank	121
Permanent Pasture (sq. miles):	568
total livestock (millions)	1.0
Forest and Woodlands (sq. miles):	425
1985 deforestation (sq. miles)	0
Wilderness Area (sq. miles)	0
Maritime Areas (EEZ, sq. miles)	90
Protected Areas (sq. miles):	872
percent of total	10.9%
No. of Threatened Species:	
mammals	8
birds	15
plants	39

Energy and Industry

Energy Production:	
solids (trillion BTUs)	0
liquids (trillion BTUs)	1
gas (trillion BTUs)	2
nuclear (gigawatt-hours)	0
hydroelectric (gigawatt-hours)	0
Energy Requirements:	
traditional fuels (trillion BTUs)	0
total (trillion BTUs)	379
per capita (million BTUs)	84
per capita (global rank)	39
Industrial Share of GDP	NA
Industrial Energy Index	NA
Metal Reserve Index (world=100%)	NA
No. of Motor Vehicles/1000 Persons	116

Water

Renewable Supply (cubic miles)	0.4
Total Use (cubic miles):	0.5
in agriculture	79.0%
in industry	5.0%
in homes and cities	16.0%
Access to Safe Water:	
urban population	100.0%
rural population	97.0%

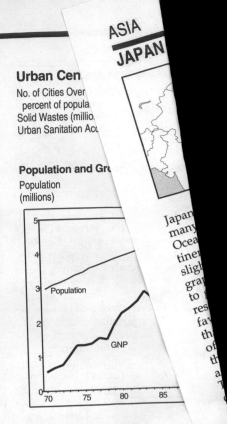

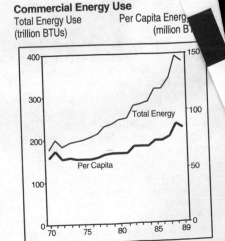

Quality of Life

Life Expectancy (years)	78.3
Infant Mortality (per 1000)	5.0
Population Under 15 Years	17.0%
Population Over 65 Years	10.1%

Land Use and Habitats

Cropland (sq. miles):	17,903
per capita (acres)	0.1
global rank	137
Permanent Pasture (sq. miles):	2,479
total livestock (millions)	16.6
Forest and Woodlands (sq. miles):	96,931
Wilderness Area (sq. miles)	0
Maritime Areas (EEZ, sq. miles)	14,908
Protected Areas (sq. miles):	9,276
percent of total	6.4%
No. of Threatened Species:	
mammals	5
birds	31
plants	687

Energy and Industry

Energy Production:	
solids (trillion BTUs)	249
liquids (trillion BTUs)	22
gas (trillion BTUs)	75
nuclear (gigawatt-hours)	182,871
hydroelectric (gigawatt-hours)	97,822
Energy Requirements:	
traditional fuels (trillion BTUs)	8
total (trillion BTUs)	15,707
per capita (million BTUs)	128
per capita (global rank)	29
Industrial Share of GDP	41.2%
Industrial Energy Index	5
Metal Reserve Index (world=100%)	0.4%
No. of Motor Vehicles/1000 Persons	265

Water

Renewable Supply (cubic miles)	131.3
Total Use (cubic miles):	25.9
in agriculture	49.5%
in industry	33.4%
in homes and cities	17.0%

Waste and Pollution

Urban Solid Wastes (million tons):	53.2
per capita (tons)	331.8
Hazardous Wastes (000 tons)	733.9
Sewage Treatment Plant Coverage	39.0%
SOX Emissions (000 tons)	1,391.8
NOX Emissions (000 tons)	1,542.8

Waste and Pollution (cont.)

Particulate Emissions (tons)	NA
Hydrocarbon Emissions (tons)	NA
No. of Cities Over 1 Million:	6
percent of population	27.5%

Population and Gross National Product

Population (millions) — GNP (billion $US)

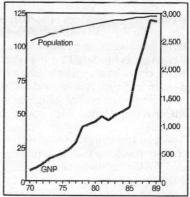

Commercial Energy Use

Total Energy Use (trillion BTUs) — Per Capita Energy Use (million BTUs)

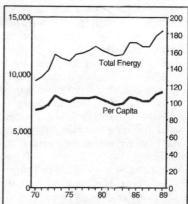

JORDAN

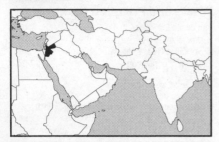

Total Area: 46,540 sq. miles
Global Rank: 91   Per Capita: 1.4 acres
Population: 21,773,000
Global Rank: 39   Growth Rate: 1.81%
Gross National Product: $4,094 m.
Global Rank: 93   Per Capita: $1,055
Greenhouse Gas Emissions
Global Share: 0.49%   Per Capita Rank: 64

The Hashemite Kingdom of Jordan is an almost landlocked country of rocky deserts, mountains, and rolling plains. The country is bordered on the north by Syria, on the east by Iraq, on the east and south by Saudi Arabia, and on the west by Israel. The port of Aqaba in the south provides Jordan with access to the Red Sea.

The predominant land feature in Jordan is the Rift Valley, which includes the Jordan River, Sea of Galilee, and the Dead Sea. About one third of Jordan's total land area can be cultivated; irrigation is widely used. Forests cover less than 0.8 percent of the country's total land area and are decreasing.

The country's limited natural resources include phosphates and potash. Jordan is a petroleum refiner and exports phosphates, fertilizer, and agricultural products.

Jordan hosts over 200 species of birds. Most species of mammals native to the country have been wiped out by overhunting. Wildlife reserves have been established to protect some remaining species, including the Arabian oryx and the Persian fallow deer.

About 70 percent of Jordan's population is urban. The largest city is the capital, Amman. Nearly one half of all Jordanians are Palestinians, including registered refugees and other displaced persons.

Major Environmental Problems

Water scarcity. Water is one of Jordan's most valuable resources, yet usage is often inefficient, and conservation efforts are lacking. Ninety percent of the country's water supply is used for agriculture. Contributing to the problem is limited rainfall and a high rate of evaporation. Demand is expected to exceed the availability of water in the near future, requiring the importation of water or the construction of desalinization plants.

Access to clean water. Drinking water in Jordan is often tainted by industrial toxins and by untreated sewage, which enters aquifers from cesspools located in its most heavily populated areas.

Land degradation. The arable land area of Jordan is rapidly decreasing, mainly due to urban expansion and desertification. Erosion is a problem in some parts of the country.

Overpopulation. Approximately 97 percent of the population lives in a 31-mile strip of land east of the Jordan River. Jordan's population is expected to increase in the next 15 years, from 4 to 7 million people, because of natural increases as well as the large number of Palestinians entering the country.

Quality of Life

Life Expectancy (years)	65.9
Infant Mortality (per 1000)	44.0
Population Under 15 Years	43.4%
Population Over 65 Years	2.4%
Literacy Rate	80.1%
Malnourished Children	NA

Land Use and Habitats

Cropland (sq. miles):	1,452
per capita (acres)	0.2
global rank	122
Permanent Pasture (sq. miles):	3,054
total livestock (millions)	1.8
Forest and Woodlands (sq. miles):	274
1985 deforestation (sq. miles)	0
Wilderness Area (sq. miles)	0
Maritime Areas (FEZ, sq. miles)	3
Protected Areas (sq. miles):	359
percent of total	1.0%
No. of Threatened Species:	
mammals	5
birds	11
plants	13

Energy and Industry

Energy Production:	
solids (trillion BTUs)	0
liquids (trillion BTUs)	1
gas (trillion BTUs)	0
nuclear (gigawatt-hours)	0
hydroelectric (gigawatt-hours)	33
Energy Requirements:	
traditional fuels (trillion BTUs)	0
total (trillion BTUs)	109
per capita (million BTUs)	28
per capita (global rank)	74
Industrial Share of GDP	28.0%
Industrial Energy Index	17
Metal Reserve Index (world=100%)	NA
No. of Motor Vehicles/1000 Persons	45

Water

Renewable Supply (cubic miles)	0.2
Total Use (cubic miles):	0.1
In agriculture	65.0%
in industry	6.0%
in homes and cities	29.0%
Access to Safe Water:	
urban population	NA
rural population	NA

Urban Centers and Waste

No. of Cities Over 1 Million:	1
percent of population	25.6%
Solid Wastes (million tons)	0.5
Urban Sanitation Access	NA

Population and Gross National Product

Population	GNP
(millions)	(billion $US)

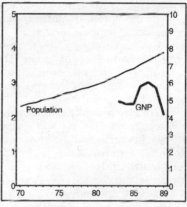

Commercial Energy Use

Total Energy Use	Per Capita Energy Use
(trillion BTUs)	(million BTUs)

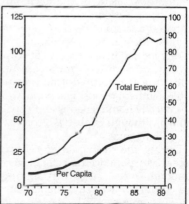

KOREA, SOUTH

Total Area: 38,231 sq. miles
  Global Rank: 100   Per Capita: 0.6 acres
Population: 42,793,000
  Global Rank: 23   Growth Rate: 0.95%
Gross National Product: $210,088 m.
  Global Rank: 15   Per Capita: $4,956
Greenhouse Gas Emissions
  Global Share: 0.77%   Per Capita Rank: 75

The Republic of Korea (South Korea) occupies the southern portion of a mountainous peninsula that abuts northeast China and separates the Yellow Sea from the Sea of Japan. The central interior and the mountainous east coast are extremely rugged and thus only lightly inhabited.

The country has only limited natural resources, including some coal, tungsten, graphite, and molybdenum. It is highly forested, with arable land found mostly in the southern plains. Farming is a major activity. A strong industrial sector provides the mainstay of the economy, however, with textiles and manufactured goods—especially automobiles and computers—among the major industries.

Because of its mountainous nature, Korea's population is very highly concentrated in a small percentage of the country. Most major population centers are located in and around the capital city of Seoul (population 10.8 million) in the northwest and on the fertile southern plains. The population is ethnically homogeneous and speaks Korean, although English is a common second language.

During the past quarter century, Korea has experienced spectacular economic and industrial growth, although at a cost of some environmental damage. Economic growth has been accompanied by a decline in population growth rates and improvement in health and literacy.

Major Environmental Problems

Water Pollution. Expansion of the water supply system has provided about 80 percent of Koreans with piped water. Despite improvements in sewage systems and industrial pollution controls, untreated discharges still contaminate many water supplies. Increased use of pesticides and fertilizers on farmland may lead to runoff of these chemicals into rivers.

Air Pollution. Rapid urbanization and industrialization have caused severe air pollution, especially in large cities. Use of low sulfur oil and other clean fuels in these cities, requirements for catalytic converters and unleaded fuel in cars, and new restrictions on industrial emissions are helping to combat the problem.

Biodiversity. More than 100 species of animals have disappeared from the rural areas. Of particular concern is the Naktong River delta, the winter home for thousands of birds. Supporters of a reforestation program have planted more than 7,500 square miles over the past two decades, reversing an earlier loss of forest habitat.

Quality of Life

Life Expectancy (years)	69.4
Infant Mortality (per 1000)	25.0
Population Under 15 Years	23.0%
Population Over 65 Years	4.1%
Literacy Rate	96.3%
Malnourished Children	NA

Land Use and Habitats

Cropland (sq. miles):	8,212
per capita (acres)	0.1
global rank	135
Permanent Pasture (sq. miles):	347
total livestock (millions)	7.0
Forest and Woodlands (sq. miles):	25,039
1985 deforestation (sq. miles)	0
Wilderness Area (sq. miles)	0
Maritime Areas (EEZ, sq. miles)	0
Protected Areas (sq. miles):	2,231
percent of total	5.8%
No. of Threatened Species:	
mammals	6
birds	22
plants	0

Energy and Industry

Energy Production:	
solids (trillion BTUs)	371
liquids (trillion BTUs)	0
gas (trillion BTUs)	0
nuclear (gigawatt-hours)	47,364
hydroelectric (gigawatt-hours)	4,559
Energy Requirements:	
traditional fuels (trillion BTUs)	41
total (trillion BTUs)	0,000
per capita (million BTUs)	71
per capita (global rank)	42
Industrial Share of GDP	44.0%
Industrial Energy Index	12
Metal Reserve Index (world=100%)	0.2%
No. of Motor Vehicles/1000 Persons	27

Water

Renewable Supply (cubic miles)	15.1
Total Use (cubic miles):	2.6
in agriculture	75.0%
in industry	14.0%
in homes and cities	11.0%
Access to Safe Water:	
urban population	91.0%
rural population	49.0%

Urban Centers and Waste

No. of Cities Over 1 Million:	6
percent of population	49.9%
Solid Wastes (million tons)	6.2
Urban Sanitation Access	99.0%

Population and Gross National Product

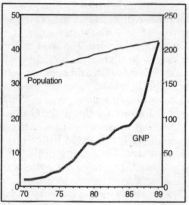

Commercial Energy Use

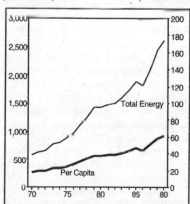

KUWAIT

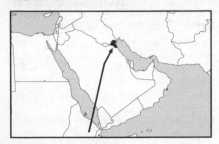

Total Area: 6,880 sq. miles
  Global Rank: 131   Per Capita: 2.2 acres
Population: 2,039,000
  Global Rank: 117   Growth Rate: 3.40%
Gross National Product: $31,855 m.
  Global Rank: 47   Per Capita: $16,164
Greenhouse Gas Emissions
  Global Share: 0.11%   Per Capita Rank: 12

Kuwait includes nine islands and a mainland region along the northwest corner of the Persian Gulf. It is bounded on the north and west by Iraq and on the south by Saudi Arabia. Kuwait is a mostly flat, arid country, with few natural resources other than oil and natural gas, which it has in abundance, and the fisheries of the Gulf.

Although agricultural production is increasing, it is limited in Kuwait by a lack of water. The fishing industry is more important, and some large-scale fishing ventures operate locally.

The country is dependent on imports of food and most other goods and equipment.

On a per capita basis, Kuwait is one of the wealthiest countries in the world, largely because it is richly endowed with oil. A considerable portion of Kuwait's wealth is also derived from investments made outside the country.

Most of the inhabitants of Kuwait are Arabic, but prior to the Persian Gulf War only about 40 percent were indigenous, because of a large number of Palestinian and other foreign workers. Native Kuwaiti citizens enjoy a greater share of the nation's prosperity than do immigrant workers. Kuwait has been ruled by an emir from the Sabah family for more than two centuries, first under the Ottoman Empire, then as a British protectorate, and then as an independent state since 1961.

Major Environmental Problems

War destruction. As a result of the Gulf War, Kuwait has become an environmental disaster, with serious degradation of its air, marine resources, and soil. Much of Kuwait's infrastructure was badly damaged, including oil wells, pipelines, and oil storage facilities. Huge lakes of oil remain to be disposed of and constitute an environmental hazard for birds and animals. Soils remain polluted with oil and soot.

Tank and troop movements also damaged Kuwait's fragile desert soils, increasing the amount of erosion caused by wind. The damage may be longlasting.

During the war, millions of barrels of oil spilled into the Gulf, threatening wildlife dependent on the Gulf ecosystem and the fisheries that provide a significant source of food for Kuwaitis. Warm Gulf temperatures are hastening the natural degradation of the spilled oil.

Water Scarcity. Kuwait is extremely arid and lacks adequate rainfall and other water resources to support agriculture on a scale large enough to make the country self-sufficient in food. Pumping of water from underground aquifers is proceeding at unsustainable rates; increasing dependence on desalinization is likely.

Quality of Life

Life Expectancy (years)	72.9
Infant Mortality (per 1000)	18.0
Population Under 15 Years	33.5%
Population Over 65 Years	1.0%
Literacy Rate	73.0%
Malnourished Children	14.0%

Land Use and Habitats

Cropland (sq. miles):	15
per capita (acres)	0.0
global rank	144
Permanent Pasture (sq. miles):	517
total livestock (millions)	0.3
Forest and Woodlands (sq. miles):	8
1985 deforestation (sq. miles)	0
Wilderness Area (sq. miles)	0
Maritime Areas (FEZ, sq. miles)	46
Protected Areas (sq. miles):	0
percent of total	0.0%
No. of Threatened Species:	
mammals	5
birds	7
plants	1

Energy and Industry

Energy Production:	
solids (trillion BTUs)	0
liquids (trillion BTUs)	3,087
gas (trillion BTUs)	201
nuclear (gigawatt-hours)	0
hydroelectric (gigawatt-hours)	0
Energy Requirements:	
traditional fuels (trillion BTUs)	0
total (trillion BTUs)	455
per capita (million BTUs)	231
per capita (global rank)	10
Industrial Share of GDP	55.6%
Industrial Energy Index	10
Metal Reserve Index (world=100%)	NA
No. of Motor Vehicles/1000 Persons	244

Water

Renewable Supply (cubic miles)	0.0
Total Use (cubic miles):	0.1
in agriculture	4.0%
in industry	32.0%
in homes and cities	64.0%
Access to Safe Water:	
urban population	100.0%
rural population	NA

Urban Centers and Waste

No. of Cities Over 1 Million:	1
percent of population	52.9%
Solid Wastes (million tons)	0.9
Urban Sanitation Access	100.0%

Population and Gross National Product

Population (millions)	GNP (billion $US)

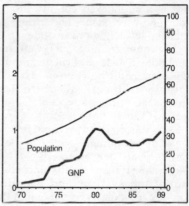

Commercial Energy Use

Total Energy Use (trillion BTUs)	Per Capita Energy Use (million BTUs)

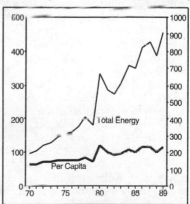

LAOS

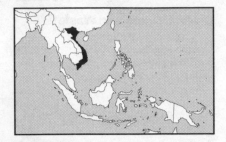

Total Area: 91,427 sq. miles
Global Rank: 76   Per Capita: 14.1 acres
Population: 4,139,000
Global Rank: 99   Growth Rate: 2.82%
Gross National Product: $614 m.
Global Rank: 133   Per Capita: $153
Greenhouse Gas Emissions
Global Share: 0.68%   Per Capita Rank: NA

Laos is a landlocked country on the Indochinese Peninsula about the size of Utah. Its neighbors include Thailand, Myanmar, China, Viet Nam, and Cambodia. Forests and rugged mountains dominate the country. The climate is tropical to subtropical monsoonal, with heavy rainfall from April to October.

Laos has had an extremely low rate of development because of more than 20 years of warfare, as well as inadequate transportation and communication systems and isolation from the sea. Nearly 85 percent of the population depends on agriculture and forestry, and 60 percent lives in the limited lowland area, which makes up only 20 percent of the country. Population growth rates are very high, adding to the pressure on the country's natural resources. Traditional methods of shifting cultivation cause loss of trees and damage to watersheds.

Laos still has substantial forest resources, but they have declined dramatically. Less than half of the country is now covered by forests because of extensive deforestation. Apart from the forest resources, Laos is believed to be rich in mineral resources that have not yet been fully exploited and surveyed. These resources include tin, potash, magnesium, coal, iron, and gypsum. The Mekong River has sub-stantial hydropower potential. Rice is the major crop.

Tin mining, coffee growing, and electricity production are the major industries, although the country's abundant hydroelectric potential has barely been tapped, and most of what hydroelectricity the country does produce is exported. Fuelwood and charcoal remain the dominant energy sources.

Major Environmental Problems

Deforestation. The country's once extensive forest resources continue to be badly degraded by uncontrolled deforestation. Poor forest management practices and slash-and-burn agriculture are major causes.

Water management. In large part because of deforestation and shifting cultivation, the country's abundant water resources have begun to deteriorate, as shown in reduced water catchment capacity, lowered water tables, flash flooding, local water shortages, and sedimentation of rivers and dams.

Habitat loss. Laos has lost approximately 70 percent of its wildlife habitat, and two thirds of its wetlands are threatened, mainly because of deforestation. Plant and animal populations have been sharply reduced.

Quality of Life

Life Expectancy (years)	48.5
Infant Mortality (per 1000)	110.0
Population Under 15 Years	44.5%
Population Over 65 Years	2.5%
Literacy Rate	NA
Malnourished Children	44.0%

Land Use and Habitats

Cropland (sq. miles):	3,479
per capita (acres)	0.6
global rank	78
Permanent Pasture (sq. miles):	3,089
total livestock (millions)	3.3
Forest and Woodlands (sq. miles):	49,421
1985 deforestation (sq. miles)	502
Wilderness Area (sq. miles)	1,688
Maritime Areas (EEZ, sq. miles)	0
Protected Areas (sq. miles):	0
percent of total	0.0%
No. of Threatened Species:	
mammals	23
birds	18
plants	3

Energy and Industry

Energy Production:	
solids (trillion BTUs)	0
liquids (trillion BTUs)	0
gas (trillion BTUs)	0
nuclear (gigawatt-hours)	0
hydroelectric (gigawatt-hours)	1,099
Energy Requirements:	
traditional fuels (trillion BTUs)	34
total (trillion BTUs)	41
per capita (million BTUs)	10
per capita (global rank)	119
Industrial Share of GDP	NA
Industrial Energy Index	NA
Metal Reserve Index (world=100%)	NA
No. of Motor Vehicles/1000 Persons	NA

Water

Renewable Supply (cubic miles)	NA
Total Use (cubic miles):	0.2
in agriculture	82.0%
in industry	10.0%
in homes and cities	8.0%
Access to Safe Water:	
urban population	61.0%
rural population	17.0%

Urban Centers and Waste

No. of Cities Over 1 Million:	0
percent of population	0.0%
Solid Wastes (million tons)	0.2
Urban Sanitation Access	NA

Population and Gross National Product

Population (millions) GNP (billion $US)

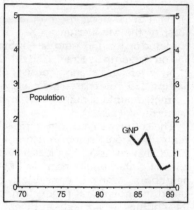

Commercial Energy Use

Total Energy Use (trillion BTUs) Per Capita Energy Use (million BTUs)

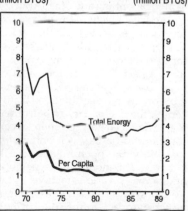

LEBANON

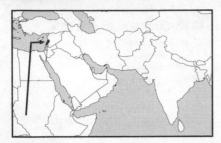

Total Area: 4,015 sq. miles
Global Rank: 136   Per Capita: 1.0 acres
Population: 2,701,000
Global Rank: 111   Growth Rate: 0.25%
Gross National Product: NA
Global Rank: NA   Per Capita: NA
Greenhouse Gas Emissions
Global Share: 0.02%   Per Capita Rank: 106

The Republic of Lebanon is located in western Asia along the northeastern coast of the Mediterranean Sea. It is bordered on the north and east by Syria and on the south by Israel. Half the size of New Jersey, Lebanon consists of a narrow, 135-mile coastal plain and two distinct mountain ranges that cradle the fertile Bekáa Valley.

The country's natural resources include limestone, some iron ore, and salt. Lebanon also has plentiful supplies of water, unlike nearly all of its neighbors. Many Lebanese are engaged in agricultural production, but the country is not self-sufficient in food. The chief crops include fruits, grains, and potatoes.

Lebanon has a higher percentage of skilled labor than any other Arab country, and 58 percent of the people live in towns larger than 10,000 inhabitants. The past few decades have seen very rapid and largely unplanned urbanization, especially along the Mediterranean coast, leading to considerable environmental degradation. Until recently, the capital city of Beirut was a major financial and commercial center for the Middle East. Chronic political instability and open military conflicts between Lebanon and its neighbors, and between various factions in Lebanon, however, have had a strong and adverse impact on the country's overall economic and environmental well-

being since 1976. A reforestation program undertaken in the 1960s was suspended, for example. After the 1982 invasion by Israel, the Ministry of the Environment ceased most of its work. Overall, the civil war has had devastating environmental results.

Major Environmental Problems

Land degradation. In recent years, Lebanon has lost much of its best agricultural land to rapid urbanization, a trend that continues unabated. The newly urbanized areas, furthermore, largely lack green areas and parks. In addition, the civil war created severe problems, including destruction of vegetation and a drop in the bird population that allowed an increase in the populations of tree-eating insects. Loss of trees has permitted erosion that damages the watershed and the region's badly needed water resources.

Water pollution. The Mediterranean Sea off the Lebanese coast has suffered severe pollution from industrial wastes, untreated sewage, and indiscriminate dumping. Other serious damage occurs because fishing techniques are destructive—fishermen frequently work by tossing dynamite into the sea and gathering up the stunned fish—and fish shortages loom.

LEBANON

Quality of Life

Life Expectancy (years)	65.1
Infant Mortality (per 1000)	48.0
Population Under 15 Years	36.0%
Population Over 65 Years	5.1%
Literacy Rate	80.1%
Malnourished Children	NA

Land Use and Habitats

Cropland (sq. miles):	1,162
per capita (acres)	0.3
global rank	112
Permanent Pasture (sq. miles):	39
total livestock (millions)	0.7
Forest and Woodlands (sq. miles):	309
1985 deforestation (sq. miles)	0
Wilderness Area (sq. miles)	0
Maritime Areas (EEZ, sq. miles)	87
Protected Areas (sq. miles):	14
percent of total	0.3%
No. of Threatened Species:	
mammals	4
birds	15
plants	6

Energy and Industry

Energy Production:	
solids (trillion BTUs)	0
liquids (trillion BTUs)	0
gas (trillion BTUs)	0
nuclear (gigawatt-hours)	0
hydroelectric (gigawatt-hours)	497
Energy Requirements:	
traditional fuels (trillion BTUs)	5
total (trillion BTUs)	116
per capita (million BTUs)	43
per capita (global rank)	60
Industrial Share of GDP	NA
Industrial Energy Index	NA
Metal Reserve Index (world=100%)	NA
No. of Motor Vehicles/1000 Persons	174

Water

Renewable Supply (cubic miles)	1.2
Total Use (cubic miles)	0.2
in agriculture	85.0%
in industry	4.0%
in homes and cities	11.0%
Access to Safe Water:	
urban population	NA
rural population	NA

Urban Centers and Waste

No. of Cities Over 1 Million:	0
percent of population	0.0%
Solid Wastes (million tons)	0.5
Urban Sanitation Access	NA

Population and Gross National Product

Population (millions)	GNP (billion $US)

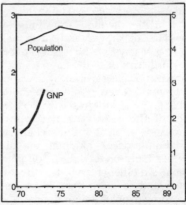

Commercial Energy Use

Total Energy Use (trillion BTUs)	Per Capita Energy Use (million BTUs)

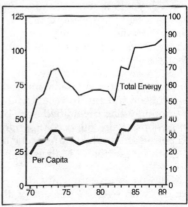

MALAYSIA

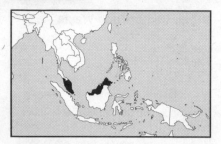

Total Area: 127,314 sq. miles
Global Rank: 61   Per Capita: 4.6 acres
Population: 17,891,000
Global Rank: 45   Growth Rate: 2.64%
Gross National Product: $35,605 m.
Global Rank: 44   Per Capita: $2,043
Greenhouse Gas Emissions
Global Share: 0.73%   Per Capita Rank: 24

Malaysia comprises two large land areas that straddle the South China Sea. The states of Sarawak and Sabah make up East Malaysia, which is located on the northern side of the large island of Borneo and consists of coastal swamps and jungle-covered hills and mountains. Tropical rainforest covers 59 percent of the country and supports thousands of plant and insect species and hundreds of mammal and bird species. Land under rubber, oil palm, cocoa, and other crops brings the total treed land to more than 75 percent, according to government figures.

In addition to its forests, the country's natural resources include deposits of tin, petroleum, copper, and iron ore. Major crops include rice, rubber, palm oil, pepper, and coconuts. East Malaysia has slightly more than one half of the nation's petroleum exports and almost three fourths of its timber exports.

The Malaysian economy was traditionally dominated by two commodities—rubber and tin. In recent years, the economy has diversified and become robust. Palm oil, cocoa, pepper, and petroleum products now make up a significant portion of Malaysia's exports.

Malaysia is an ethnically diverse country, with over 70 percent of the people living on the Malay Peninsula. The politically dominant Malays make up about one half of the country's total population.

Major Environmental Problems

Coastal degradation. Most estuaries in Malaysia are heavily silted, and a significant number are no longer productive. Coral reefs are almost absent around peninsular Malaysia, and mangroves are under threat from human exploitation in all parts of the country. The rapid decline in fish production, especially along the peninsula's west coast, is a result of overexploitation.

Water pollution. Forty percent of the rivers in peninsular Malaysia are polluted, many by discharges and runoff from tin mines. The country's coastal waters are polluted by silt and occasional oil spills. Contamination by untreated sewage is also prevalent along many coasts.

Deforestation. Although much of Malaysia is still covered by forests, more than half of the country's river basins have been seriously denuded. Logging in primary forests continues on a large scale, and this practice has prompted a growing number of protests by forest-dependent communities, particularly in Sabah and Sarawak.

MALAYSIA

Quality of Life

Life Expectancy (years)	69.5
Infant Mortality (per 1000)	24.0
Population Under 15 Years	37.6%
Population Over 65 Years	3.3%
Literacy Rate	78.4%
Malnourished Children	NA

Land Use and Habitats

Cropland (sq. miles):	18,842
per capita (acres)	0.7
global rank	66
Permanent Pasture (sq. miles):	104
total livestock (millions)	3.7
Forest and Woodlands (sq. miles):	74,672
1985 deforestation (sq. miles)	985
Wilderness Area (sq. miles)	10,981
Maritime Areas (EEZ, sq. miles)	1,836
Protected Areas (sq. miles):	4,487
percent of total	3.5%
No. of Threatened Species:	
mammals	23
birds	35
plants	NA

Energy and Industry

Energy Production:	
solids (trillion BTUs)	0
liquids (trillion BTUs)	1,125
gas (trillion BTUs)	530
nuclear (gigawatt-hours)	0
hydroelectric (gigawatt-hours)	6,260
Energy Requirements:	
traditional fuels (trillion BTUs)	80
total (trillion BTUs)	790
per capita (million BTUs)	45
per capita (global rank)	57
Industrial Share of GDP	NA
Industrial Energy Index	NA
Metal Reserve Index (world=100%)	1.3%
No. of Motor Vehicles/1000 Persons	88

Water

Renewable Supply (cubic miles)	109.4
Total Use (cubic miles):	2.3
in agriculture	47.0%
in industry	30.0%
in homes and cities	23.0%
Access to Safe Water:	
urban population	92.0%
rural population	68.0%

Urban Centers and Waste

No. of Cities Over 1 Million:	1
percent of population	9.6%
Solid Wastes (million tons)	1.5
Urban Sanitation Access	NA

Population and Gross National Product

Population	GNP
(millions)	(billion $US)

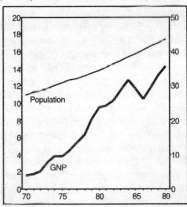

Commercial Energy Use

Total Energy Use	Per Capita Energy Use
(trillion BTUs)	(million BTUs)

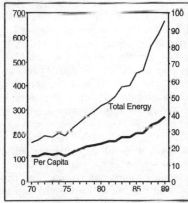

MONGOLIA

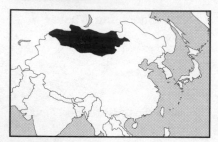

Total Area: 604,816 sq. miles
Global Rank: 17   Per Capita: 176.7 acres
Population: 2,190,000
Global Rank: 116   Growth Rate: 2.74%
Gross National Product: $3,558 m.
Global Rank: 97   Per Capita: $1,670
Greenhouse Gas Emissions
Global Share: 0.04%   Per Capita Rank: 67

The Mongolian People's Republic is a landlocked nation in northeastern Asia nestled between China and the Commonwealth of Independent States.

Almost 90 percent of Mongolia is pasture or desert; only 1 percent is arable, and the remainder is forested. The Gobi Desert in the southeast contains almost no natural vegetation. North and west of the Gobi Desert, rugged mountains rise above 13,000 feet. Salt lakes and steppes are also common.

The country's natural resources include deposits of coal, copper, molybdenum, tungsten, and phosphates. Mongolia is sparsely populated. Animal herding is the main economic activity—the country has one of the highest ratios of livestock to people in the world—and is practiced throughout the country. More than half of the adult population is engaged in herding and related agricultural activities, including growing wheat, oats, and barley. Live animals and animal products such as wool and hides account for half of Mongolia's output and nearly 90 percent of its exports; another important export is coal.

Recently, industrial development based on mineral deposits and other natural resources has been rapid. Mongolia has begun coal, copper, and molybdenum mining; grain and fodder production; manufacture of consumer goods; construction material produc-tion; and the development of a food-processing industry.

In the 1970s the country passed several laws protecting its forests, game, and water. Mongolia also has a reforestation program; its State Committee of the Council of Ministers for Science and Technical Matters is the central agency that handles environmental problems.

The 12-million-acre Big Gobi Nature Preserve is one of 13 nature preserves established to prohibit hunting, cutting of wood, and gathering of plants.

Major Environmental Problems

Desertification. Mongolia's arid climate and fragile soils in some regions make pasturelands susceptible to overgrazing. Degraded or devegetated lands are on the increase. These areas are not easy to restore, and are at risk of becoming a permanent part of the desert.

Water shortages. Mongolia's water resources are very limited, especially in regions near the Gobi Desert. Conservation measures and careful management are needed, as are efforts to keep the water from becoming polluted. Industrial development is placing new demands on the country's water resources.

Quality of Life

Life Expectancy (years)	61.3
Infant Mortality (per 1000)	68.0
Population Under 15 Years	40.2%
Population Over 65 Years	2.6%
Literacy Rate	NA
Malnourished Children	NA

Land Use and Habitats

Cropland (sq. miles):	5,309
per capita (acres)	1.6
global rank	11
Permanent Pasture (sq. miles):	479,371
total livestock (millions)	23.5
Forest and Woodlands (sq. miles):	53,726
1985 deforestation (sq. miles)	0
Wilderness Area (sq. miles)	93,171
Maritime Areas (EEZ, sq. miles)	0
Protected Areas (sq. miles):	21,691
percent of total	3.6%
No. of Threatened Species:	
mammals	9
birds	13
plants	NA

Energy and Industry

Energy Production:	
solids (trillion BTUs)	87
liquids (trillion BTUs)	0
gas (trillion BTUs)	0
nuclear (gigawatt-hours)	0
hydroelectric (gigawatt-hours)	0
Energy Requirements:	
traditional fuels (trillion BTUs)	12
total (trillion BTUs)	124
per capita (million BTUs)	58
per capita (global rank)	47
Industrial Share of GDP	NA
Industrial Energy Index	NA
Metal Reserve Index (world=100%)	0.2%
No. of Motor Vehicles/1000 Persons	NA

Water

Renewable Supply (cubic miles)	5.9
Total Use (cubic miles):	0.1
in agriculture	62.0%
in industry	27.0%
in homes and cities	11.0%
Access to Safe Water:	
urban population	78.0%
rural population	50.0%

Urban Centers and Waste

No. of Cities Over 1 Million:	0
percent of population	0.0%
Solid Wastes (million tons)	0.2
Urban Sanitation Access	100.0%

Population and Gross National Product

Population (millions)	GNP (billion $US)

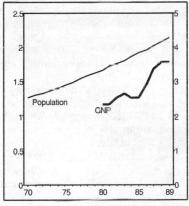

Commercial Energy Use

Total Energy Use (trillion BTUs)	Per Capita Energy Use (million BTUs)

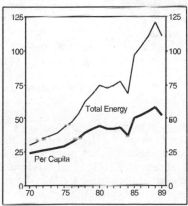

MYANMAR

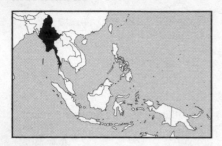

Total Area: 261,212 sq. miles
Global Rank: 38   Per Capita: 4.0 acres
Population: 41,675,000
Global Rank: 24   Growth Rate: 2.09%
Gross National Product: $16,330 m.
Global Rank: 61   Per Capita: $400
Greenhouse Gas Emissions
Global Share: 1.14%   Per Capita Rank: 45

Myanmar (Burma) is the largest country on the southeast Asian mainland. Facing the Bay of Bengal and the Andaman Sea on the west and south, it shares borders with Thailand, Laos, China, India, and Bangladesh. The country has a tropical monsoon climate. Mountain ranges with elevations up to 14,990 feet above sea level are located along the northern, eastern, and western borders.

Traditionally, Myanmar has been an agricultural economy that has relied heavily on rice cultivation and timber exploitation. In addition to its forests and rivers, the country also has a wealth of mineral and energy resources that remain largely untapped; these include oil, tin, copper, and tungsten. The country is also a major source of illegal opium and cannabis.

Myanmar's population consists of the people from the plains and a variety of tribes, some of which are struggling for autonomy. The country has one of the strongest Buddhist cultures in Asia.

Other than the degradation of its forests, Myanmar has relatively few environmental problems because of the absence of both urban and rural population pressures, a relatively unintensive agricultural system, and a very small mining, processing, and manufacturing sector. Natural ecosystems have therefore not undergone as much transformation or degradation as they have in many other developing countries.

Major Environmental Problems

Deforestation. The rapidly increasing illegal exploitation of forests for timber, shifting cultivation, and natural fires have destroyed more than two thirds of Myanmar's moist tropical forests, including its teak forests. Because deforestation facilitates erosion, removes soil nutrients, permits weed infestation, diverts runoff, and reduces water infiltration and percolation, the damage affects the entire watershed.

Natural disasters. Myanmar lies in a climatic zone that is frequently subjected to heavy precipitation, river flooding, and occasional cyclones. Flooding causes a reduction in agricultural production, erosion and sediment loading, and the spreading of infectious diseases. Earthquakes are also common and occasionally devastating in this region.

Internal disorder and isolationism. Political disorder and repression within Myanmar have steered attention away from solving environmental problems.

MYANMAR

Quality of Life

Life Expectancy (years)	60.0
Infant Mortality (per 1000)	70.0
Population Under 15 Years	36.0%
Population Over 65 Years	3.4%
Literacy Rate	80.6%
Malnourished Children	75.0%

Land Use and Habitats

Cropland (sq. miles):	38,741
per capita (acres)	0.6
global rank	72
Permanent Pasture (sq. miles):	1,394
total livestock (millions)	15.8
Forest and Woodlands (sq. miles):	125,166
1985 deforestation (sq. miles)	405
Wilderness Area (sq. miles)	9,833
Maritime Areas (EEZ, sq. miles)	1,967
Protected Areas (sq. miles):	669
percent of total	0.3%
No. of Threatened Species:	
mammals	23
birds	42
plants	23

Energy and Industry

Energy Production:	
solids (trillion BTUs)	1
liquids (trillion BTUs)	35
gas (trillion BTUs)	40
nuclear (gigawatt-hours)	0
hydroelectric (gigawatt-hours)	0
Energy Requirements:	
traditional fuels (trillion BTUs)	175
total (trillion BTUs)	254
per capita (million BTUs)	6
per capita (global rank)	139
Industrial Share of GDP	NA
Industrial Energy Index	NA
Metal Reserve Index (world=100%)	0.1%
No. of Motor Vehicles/1000 Persons	NA

Water

Renewable Supply (cubic miles)	259.6
Total Use (cubic miles):	1.0
in agriculture	90.0%
in industry	3.0%
in homes and cities	7.0%
Access to Safe Water:	
urban population	38.0%
rural population	28.0%

Urban Centers and Waste

No. of Cities Over 1 Million:	1
percent of population	7.9%
Solid Wastes (million tons)	2.1
Urban Sanitation Access	35.0%

Population and Gross National Product

Population (millions) — GNP (billion $US)

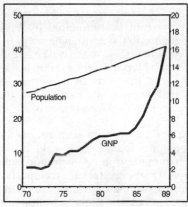

Commercial Energy Use

Total Energy Use (trillion BTUs) — Per Capita Energy Use (million BTUs)

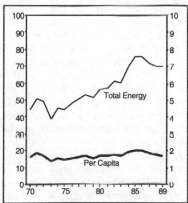

NEPAL

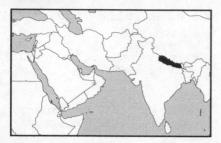

Total Area: 54,362 sq. miles
  Global Rank: 87   Per Capita: 1.8 acres
Population: 19,143,000
  Global Rank: 42   Growth Rate: 2.48%
Gross National Product: $3,071 m.
  Global Rank: 102   Per Capita: $164
Greenhouse Gas Emissions
  Global Share: 0.15%   Per Capita Rank: 112

Situated between China and India, Nepal's terrain is dominated by high mountains in the north, where 8 of the world's 10 highest peaks can be found. Central Nepal harbors the lower ranges of the Himalayas, which are drained by mountain rivers, while the south offers a lowland region of arable land.

The climate varies as sharply as the geography: from bitterly cold in the high mountain areas to humid subtropical in the central valley. Nepal has a corresponding diversity of flora and fauna, in habitats ranging from dense tropical monsoon forests to highly productive paddy fields and from deciduous forests to subalpine and alpine pastures.

Nepal ranks among the least developed and poorest countries; its major economic resources are hydropower and its natural scenic beauty, which supports tourism. Other natural resources include timber and water. Most of the population is engaged in agriculture. The chief crops include rice, maize, wheat, sugar cane, tobacco, herbs, and oilseeds.

A rapidly growing population has begun to put pressure on natural resources. The population is composed of many different ethnic groups. More than a dozen different languages are spoken.

Major Environmental Problems

Deforestation. The forests in Nepal are cleared for several reasons. Population growth increases the need for agricultural land. Ninety percent of Nepalese fuel needs are met with firewood obtained from forests. Living trees are stripped of branches and leaves to serve as fodder for livestock, reducing the reproductive ability of trees, while saplings are grazed by feeding animals. Contracts are sold to cut the forests to support the timber industry, with little effort made toward reforestation.

Land degradation. A result of deforestation, natural development of the unstable Himalayas, and human activities such as road and bridge construction, land degradation causes the loss of millions of cubic feet of topsoil every year, severely affecting agriculture. Erosion could be better controlled through soil and water conservation measures, limiting deforestation, and practicing better farming methods such as contour plowing or planting crops in strips on hillsides.

Unsafe drinking water. Untreated sewage is dumped into rivers, and drinking water is not treated. The result is endemic waterborne diseases.

Quality of Life

Life Expectancy (years)	50.9
Infant Mortality (per 1000)	128.0
Population Under 15 Years	41.4%
Population Over 65 Years	2.7%
Literacy Rate	25.6%
Malnourished Children	68.6%

Land Use and Habitats

Cropland (sq. miles):	10,197
per capita (acres)	0.3
global rank	105
Permanent Pasture (sq. miles):	7,722
total livestock (millions)	16.0
Forest and Woodlands (sq. miles):	9,575
1985 deforestation (sq. miles)	324
Wilderness Area (sq. miles)	0
Maritime Areas (EEZ, sq. miles)	0
Protected Areas (sq. miles):	3,701
percent of total	6.8%
No. of Threatened Species:	
mammals	22
birds	20
plants	21

Energy and Industry

Energy Production:	
solids (trillion BTUs)	0
liquids (trillion BTUs)	0
gas (trillion BTUs)	0
nuclear (gigawatt-hours)	0
hydroelectric (gigawatt-hours)	545
Energy Requirements:	
traditional fuels (trillion BTUs)	198
total (trillion BTUs)	215
per capita (million BTUs)	11
per capita (global rank)	111
Industrial Share of GDP	15.0%
Industrial Energy Index	8
Metal Reserve Index (world=100%)	NA
No. of Motor Vehicles/1000 Persons	NA

Water

Renewable Supply (cubic miles)	10.8
Total Use (cubic miles):	0.6
in agriculture	95.0%
in industry	1.0%
in homes and cities	4.0%
Access to Safe Water:	
urban population	66.0%
rural population	33.0%

Urban Centers and Waste

No. of Cities Over 1 Million:	0
percent of population	0.0%
Solid Wastes (million tons)	0.4
Urban Sanitation Access	NA

Population and Gross National Product

Population (millions) — GNP (billion $US)

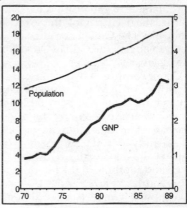

Commercial Energy Use

Total Energy Use (trillion BTUs) — Per Capita Energy Use (million BTUs)

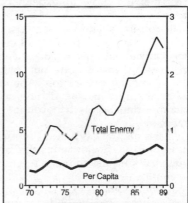

OMAN

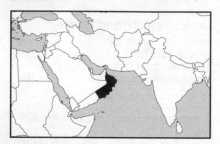

Total Area: 82,029 sq. miles
Global Rank: 79   Per Capita: 35.0 acres
Population: 1,502,000
Global Rank: 123   Growth Rate: 3.79%
Gross National Product: $7,625 m.
Global Rank: 73   Per Capita: $5,273
Greenhouse Gas Emissions
Global Share: 0.04%   Per Capita Rank: 58

The Sultanate of Oman is located at the southeastern corner of the Arabian Peninsula. The Omani coastline abuts the Arabian Sea and Gulf of Oman and extends over 1,000 miles.

Oman comprises two inhabited regions, the northern area along the Gulf of Oman and the southern region of Dhufar, that are separated by a vast expanse of uninhabited desert. Besides sandy deserts and plains, the country has a northern mountain range and foothills in the interior and in the south.

Although Oman is an arid country, it supports a rich and varied bird population. The country is home to at least 372 bird species, of which 74 are resident breeders. Sixty-three species of butterflies have also been recorded.

The country's natural resources include oil, asbestos, copper, and limestone. Only about 1 percent of Oman's surface area is under cultivation, with dates being the major crop. Animal husbandry and marine fishing are other important factors in the country's rural economy.

Oil and natural gas production and refining are the major industries, although banking and shipping services also employ some people; oil provides 95 percent of Oman's exports. Oman's oil was discovered in 1964 and first exported in 1967. Oil revenues have

begun to transform a totally undeveloped, traditional kingdom into a state equipped with health care, education, modern infrastructure and communications, and even environmental protection agencies. The growing demands of this rapidly changing society threaten to outstrip the country's water resources.

Major Environmental Problems

Water scarcity. Vast areas of Oman lack water resources. Rainfall is often insufficient to support dryland agriculture. Irrigation water is usually drawn from shallow aquifers, and recurrent droughts affect the overall supply. The introduction of modern water pumps has also allowed water to be drawn at rates faster than natural recharge, threatening depletion of aquifers.

Soil salinity. Extensive pumping in the northern coastal area has resulted in seawater intrusion into the region's shallow aquifers. In the interior, pumps draw water of higher salinity than can be used in traditional farming methods.

Oil pollution. Accidental spills and intentional discharges from the many oil tankers in the Gulf of Oman and the Strait of Hormuz have polluted many beaches.

Quality of Life

Life Expectancy (years)	63.9
Infant Mortality (per 1000)	40.0
Population Under 15 Years	47.2%
Population Over 65 Years	2.1%
Literacy Rate	NA
Malnourished Children	NA

Land Use and Habitats

Cropland (sq. miles):	185
per capita (acres)	0.1
global rank	139
Permanent Pasture (sq. miles):	3,861
total livestock (millions)	1.2
Forest and Woodlands (sq. miles):	0
1985 deforestation (sq. miles)	NA
Wilderness Area (sq. miles)	18,413
Maritime Areas (EEZ, sq. miles)	2,169
Protected Areas (sq. miles):	208
percent of total	0.3%
No. of Threatened Species:	
mammals	5
birds	8
plants	2

Energy and Industry

Energy Production:	
solids (trillion BTUs)	0
liquids (trillion BTUs)	1,274
gas (trillion BTUs)	86
nuclear (gigawatt-hours)	0
hydroelectric (gigawatt-hours)	0
Energy Requirements:	
traditional fuels (trillion BTUs)	0
total (trillion BTUs)	138
per capita (million BTUs)	95
per capita (global rank)	35
Industrial Share of GDP	NA
Industrial Energy Index	4
Metal Reserve Index (world=100%)	0.0%
No. of Motor Vehicles/1000 Persons	NA

Water

Renewable Supply (cubic miles)	0.5
Total Use (cubic miles):	0.1
in agriculture	94.0%
in industry	3.0%
in homes and cities	3.0%
Access to Safe Water:	
urban population	87.0%
rural population	42.0%

Urban Centers and Waste

No. of Cities Over 1 Million:	0
percent of population	0.0%
Solid Wastes (million tons)	0.1
Urban Sanitation Access	100.0%

Population and Gross National Product

Population (millions)

GNP (billion $US)

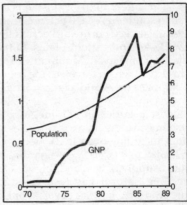

Commercial Energy Use

Total Energy Use (trillion BTUs)

Per Capita Energy Use (million BTUs)

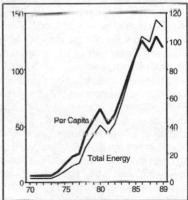

PAKISTAN

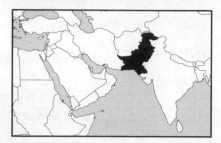

Total Area: 307,369 sq. miles
Global Rank: 34   Per Capita: 1.6 acres
Population: 122,626,000
Global Rank: 8   Growth Rate: 3.44%
Gross National Product: $39,457 m.
Global Rank: 42   Per Capita: $333
Greenhouse Gas Emissions
Global Share: 0.47%   Per Capita Rank: 139

The Islamic Republic of Pakistan is located in southern Asia. It extends from the Arabian Sea, northward across the Thar Desert and eastern plains, to the majestic Himalayan Mountains. The Indus River, which traverses the country, supplies the world's largest irrigation system.

Pakistan is rich in wildlife, and is also home to more than 6,000 species of plants, including over 2,000 species of medicinal plants. The country has a limited supply of coal and oil, but has extensive natural gas reserves and some iron ore. Forests cover about 5 percent of the total land area. Arable land encompasses about 36 percent of the total land area.

Crops include wheat, rice, and cotton as well as opium and cannabis grown for the illegal international drug trade. Textiles are a major export. Most of the nation's remaining land is either mountainous terrain or is devoted to livestock grazing.

Pakistan has a very high population growth rate, exceeding 3 percent, which is stretching both land and water resources to their limits and exacerbating environmental problems. Most of the population lives in rural areas, but urban centers, such as Karachi, Lahore, and Islamabad, are growing quickly. Large numbers of young people are also migrating out of the country in search of work.

Major Environmental Problems

Water pollution. Barely one half of the population has access to safe water, and only two cities have sewage treatment plants. Water quality is deteriorating still further in many areas because of inadequate sewage facilities, industrial wastes, and agricultural runoff.

Water scarcity. Water is scarce in most parts of the country because of inadequate rainfall, high rates of evaporation, and increasing salinity in the available water supply as a result of irrigation. The construction of dams also restricts the flow of fresh water into the coastal region.

Land degradation. The country's huge population creates enormous pressures on a finite amount of arable land. Poor management practices, including overgrazing and overharvesting, as well as erosion caused by water and wind, are among the most immediate causes.

Deforestation. Pakistan's already limited forest resources are shrinking by more than 1 percent each year. Indiscriminate cutting for household fuelwood and timber needs and clearing for agricultural purposes are the major causes.

Quality of Life

Life Expectancy (years)	56.5
Infant Mortality (per 1000)	109.0
Population Under 15 Years	46.4%
Population Over 65 Years	2.3%
Literacy Rate	34.8%
Malnourished Children	42.0%

Land Use and Habitats

Cropland (sq. miles):	80,039
per capita (acres)	0.4
global rank	95
Permanent Pasture (sq. miles):	19,305
total livestock (millions)	98.9
Forest and Woodlands (sq. miles):	13,514
1985 deforestation (sq. miles)	35
Wilderness Area (sq. miles)	10,569
Maritime Areas (EEZ, sq. miles)	1,230
Protected Areas (sq. miles):	14,112
percent of total	4.6%
No. of Threatened Species:	
mammals	15
birds	25
plants	8

Energy and Industry

Energy Production:	
solids (trillion BTUs)	49
liquids (trillion BTUs)	91
gas (trillion BTUs)	370
nuclear (gigawatt-hours)	33
hydroelectric (gigawatt-hours)	16,974
Energy Requirements:	
traditional fuels (trillion BTUs)	263
total (trillion BTUs)	1,261
per capita (million BTUs)	11
per capita (global rank)	116
Industrial Share of GDP	23.9%
Industrial Energy Index	34
Metal Reserve Index (world=100%)	0.0%
No. of Motor Vehicles/1000 Persons	5

Water

Renewable Supply (cubic miles)	71.5
Total Use (cubic miles):	36.8
in agriculture	98.0%
in industry	1.0%
in homes and cities	1.0%
Access to Safe Water:	
urban population	99.0%
rural population	35.0%

Urban Centers and Waste

No. of Cities Over 1 Million:	6
percent of population	13.4%
Solid Wastes (million tons)	7.9
Urban Sanitation Access	40.0%

Population and Gross National Product

Population (millions)	GNP (billion $US)

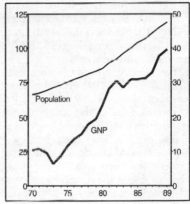

Commercial Energy Use

Total Energy Use (trillion BTUs)	Per Capita Energy Use (million BTUs)

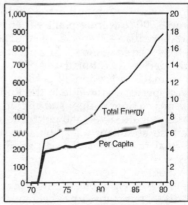

PHILIPPINES

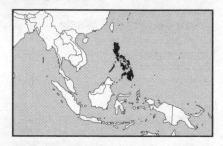

Total Area: 115,828 sq. miles
  Global Rank: 66   Per Capita: 1.2 acres
Population: 62,413,000
  Global Rank: 14   Growth Rate: 2.49%
Gross National Product: $44,252 m.
  Global Rank: 38   Per Capita: $727
Greenhouse Gas Emissions
  Global Share: 0.78%   Per Capita Rank: 86

The Republic of the Philippines comprises 7,107 islands located between the Pacific Ocean and the South China Sea. It is the second largest archipelagic nation in the world.

The country suffers frequent natural disasters. The 1991 eruption of Mt. Pinatubo destroyed 650,000 jobs and 300 square miles of the country's best agricultural land and also forced 250,000 people from their homes. A 1990 earthquake devastated the city of Baquio in northern Luzon. On average, 19 typhoons hit the country each year, and three major droughts struck during the 1980s.

The Philippines are endowed with many natural resources, including forests, minerals, wildlife, fisheries, and rich soils. The country has a very high degree of biodiversity, with some 9,000 flowering plant varieties and more than 450 species of coral as well as a large number of lizard and bird species. An estimated 44 percent of animal species and 43 percent of plant species are unique to the Philippines. Mineral deposits include nickel, cobalt, silver, and gold. There are also abundant unexploited geothermal resources and small oil deposits.

About 60 percent of the large and rapidly growing population lives in rural areas, but many urban centers are experiencing rapid growth. A comparatively weak national economy has been unable to absorb the population growth, so unemployment and poverty are widespread.

Major Environmental Problems

Deforestation and land degradation. At the end of World War II more than half of the Philippines were covered by forests. Today forests cover less than one fifth of the country. The main causes are indiscriminate—and often illegal—logging, as well as increasing population and agricultural pressures. Deforestation contributes to soil erosion, siltation, flooding, and drought; it also degrades habitats rich in biodiversity.

Coastal degradation. Much of the widespread coastal damage results from natural causes such as excessive rainfall and tropical storms. The most serious destruction is from silt eroded from deforested or upland agricultural areas, destructive fishing methods, and coral mining.

Pollution. Air and soil pollution poses an increasing health hazard, particularly in urban areas. Disposal of industrial and other toxic wastes has also created a serious problem, with at least 38 river systems severely polluted.

Quality of Life

Life Expectancy (years)	63.5
Infant Mortality (per 1000)	45.0
Population Under 15 Years	38.4%
Population Over 65 Years	3.0%
Literacy Rate	89.7%
Malnourished Children	42.0%

Land Use and Habitats

Cropland (sq. miles):	30,772
per capita (acres)	0.3
global rank	107
Permanent Pasture (sq. miles):	4,788
total livestock (millions)	14.8
Forest and Woodlands (sq. miles):	40,734
1985 deforestation (sq. miles)	355
Wilderness Area (sq. miles)	0
Maritime Areas (EEZ, sq. miles)	6,896
Protected Areas (sq. miles):	2,255
percent of total	1.9%
No. of Threatened Species:	
mammals	12
birds	39
plants	106

Energy and Industry

Energy Production:	
solids (trillion BTUs)	26
liquids (trillion BTUs)	11
gas (trillion BTUs)	0
nuclear (gigawatt-hours)	0
hydroelectric (gigawatt-hours)	6,545
Energy Requirements:	
traditional fuels (trillion BTUs)	351
total (trillion BTUs)	001
per capita (million BTUs)	15
per capita (global rank)	101
Industrial Share of GDP	33.3%
Industrial Energy Index	9
Metal Reserve Index (world=100%)	0.3%
No. of Motor Vehicles/1000 Persons	6

Water

Renewable Supply (cubic miles)	77.5
Total Use (cubic miles):	7.1
in agriculture	61.0%
in industry	21.0%
in homes and cities	18.0%
Access to Safe Water:	
urban population	100.0%
rural population	75.0%

Urban Centers and Waste

No. of Cities Over 1 Million:	1
percent of population	13.6%
Solid Wastes (million tons)	5.4
Urban Sanitation Access	98.0%

Population and Gross National Product

Population (millions)	GNP (billion $US)

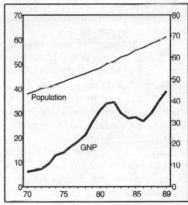

Commercial Energy Use

Total Energy Use (trillion BTUs)	Per Capita Energy Use (million BTUs)

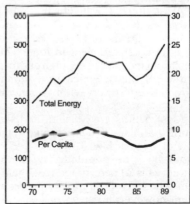

SAUDI ARABIA

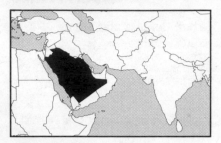

Total Area: 829,982 sq. miles
Global Rank: 12   Per Capita: 37.6 acres
Population: 14,134,000
Global Rank: 53   Growth Rate: 3.96%
Gross National Product: $85,842 m.
Global Rank: 27   Per Capita: $6,319
Greenhouse Gas Emissions
Global Share: 0.59%   Per Capita Rank: 26

The Kingdom of Saudi Arabia occupies about 80 percent of the Arabian Peninsula and is approximately the size of the United States east of the Mississippi River. Saudi Arabia is the 12th largest country in the world and is mostly desert. Rugged mountain ranges by the Red Sea in the southwest slope eastward to the Persian Gulf. The capital of Saudi Arabia, Riyadh, has a population of about 1.25 million.

Saudi Arabia is the world's third largest producer of petroleum products, as well as the largest holder of proven oil reserves. Oil exports account for 88 percent of the country's exports by value and about 60 percent of all government revenues. In addition, the country has deposits of natural gas, iron, gold, and copper.

Agriculture is limited by the lack of arable land and water. Dates and grains are the major crops. The country is not self-sufficient in food. The per capita income is very high because of the oil fields, which have transformed Saudi society within a generation.

Most Saudis are Muslim, and the country adheres to a strict interpretation of Islamic law. Until the 1960s, about half the population was nomadic, as is 20 percent today. Urbanization has advanced rapidly in recent years, however; 56 percent of the population lives in cities or towns, another

23 percent in villages. Nearly one third of Saudi Arabia's population is made up of resident foreigners, who make up a large share of the work force.

Major Environmental Problems

Coastal pollution. Saudi Arabia has 1,560 miles of coastline, where most of its oil trading occurs. Heavy oil tanker traffic in the Persian Gulf and spillage from a large number of coastal refineries have resulted in many oil spills. Damage to coastal resources, especially to fisheries and wildlife, has been severe. In addition, the environmental damage to the Gulf because of the Persian Gulf War was extremely severe.

Desertification. The encroachment of the desert is proceeding at a rate of about 30 feet per year in some areas of the country. There have been attempts to thwart continued desertification by tree planting, particularly in the largest oasis, Al-Hasa, where more than 6 million trees were planted.

Water depletion. Agriculture is largely irrigated, but water is pumped from aquifers at rates faster than they can be replenished. The U.S. Department of Agriculture estimates that Saudi Arabia's aquifers could be dry within the next 10 to 20 years.

Quality of Life

Life Expectancy (years)	63.3
Infant Mortality (per 1000)	71.0
Population Under 15 Years	45.3%
Population Over 65 Years	2.2%
Literacy Rate	62.4%
Malnourished Children	NA

Land Use and Habitats

Cropland (sq. miles):	4,575
per capita (acres)	0.2
global rank	129
Permanent Pasture (sq. miles):	328,185
total livestock (millions)	12.2
Forest and Woodlands (sq. miles):	4,633
1985 deforestation (sq. miles)	0
Wilderness Area (sq. miles)	262,118
Maritime Areas (EEZ, sq. miles)	719
Protected Areas (sq. miles):	21,697
percent of total	2.6%
No. of Threatened Species:	
mammals	9
birds	12
plants	1

Energy and Industry

Energy Production:	
solids (trillion BTUs)	0
liquids (trillion BTUs)	10,598
gas (trillion BTUs)	988
nuclear (gigawatt-hours)	0
hydroelectric (gigawatt-hours)	0
Energy Requirements:	
traditional fuels (trillion BTUs)	0
total (trillion BTUs)	2,403
per capita (million BTUs)	177
per capita (global rank)	19
Industrial Share of GDP	42.8%
Industrial Energy Index	16
Metal Reserve Index (world=100%)	0.0%
No. of Motor Vehicles/1000 Persons	173

Water

Renewable Supply (cubic miles)	0.5
Total Use (cubic miles):	0.0
in agriculture	47.0%
in industry	8.0%
in homes and cities	45.0%
Access to Safe Water:	
urban population	100.0%
rural population	74.0%

Urban Centers and Waste

No. of Cities Over 1 Million:	2
percent of population	22.6%
Solid Wastes (million tons)	4.8
Urban Sanitation Access	100.0%

Population and Gross National Product

Population (millions) GNP (billion $US)

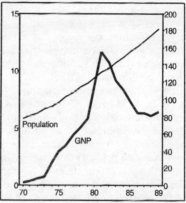

Commercial Energy Use

Total Energy Use (trillion BTUs) Per Capita Energy Use (million BTUs)

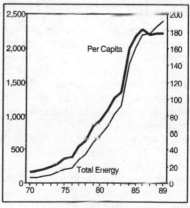

SINGAPORE

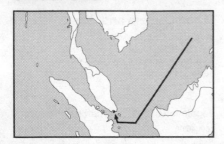

Total Area: 239 sq. miles
Global Rank: 144   Per Capita: 0.1 acres
Population: 2,723,000
Global Rank: 110   Growth Rate: 1.25%
Gross National Product: $28,888 m.
Global Rank: 50   Per Capita: $10,742
Greenhouse Gas Emissions
Global Share: 0.11%   Per Capita Rank: 25

The Republic of Singapore is a city-state located at the southern tip of the Malay Peninsula. Because of its promontory location between the Indian and Pacific oceans, Singapore has been called "the Gibraltar of the East."

The highest point on Singapore Island is only 533 feet above sea level. The "urban jungle" of high-rise buildings that dominates the island has replaced Singapore's natural forests. The remaining primary and mangrove forests cover fewer than 3 square miles. Some limited intensive agriculture is also practiced, but much of the country's food supply must be imported.

Singapore is one of the most densely populated countries of the world. About 75 percent of the population is Chinese, 15 percent is Malay, and 7 percent is Indian. Approximately 86 percent of Singapore's inhabitants live in high-rise condominiums and apartments. During several decades of intense economic development, however, the country has striven to protect its environment. Almost 5 million trees and shrubs have been planted since the government began a Garden City campaign in 1967.

An important international trading center, Singapore is also a major manufacturer and exporter of garments, electronics, machinery, and telecommunications equipment. Singapore has the highest per capita gross national product of any country in Asia except Japan.

Since 1972, Singapore has had a Ministry of the Environment, which has concentrated its efforts on water conservation, legislation, and the enforcement of existing environmental laws.

Major Environmental Problems

Industrial pollution. Singapore is a major petroleum refiner and also has a significant manufacturing industry. Rapid but not always careful industrialization has led to pollution problems, which are made worse by the lack of land, an inadequate water supply, and the growth of the urban area in close proximity to industrial operations.

Urbanization. The rapid growth of the city means that congestion, pollution, and noise from automobiles have become more serious problems, as has waste disposal; both are exacerbated by the lack of land and the limited water supply. A very small percentage of its people are employed in agriculture, and these farmers practice intensive cultivation. The country has only small natural forests or other natural areas remaining and, consequently, little wildlife.

Quality of Life

Life Expectancy (years)	73.5
Infant Mortality (per 1000)	8.0
Population Under 15 Years	23.2%
Population Over 65 Years	4.9%
Literacy Rate	NA
Malnourished Children	11.0%

Land Use and Habitats

Cropland (sq. miles):	4
per capita (acres)	0.0
global rank	146
Permanent Pasture (sq. miles):	0
total livestock (millions)	0.4
Forest and Woodlands (sq. miles):	12
1985 deforestation (sq. miles)	0
Wilderness Area (sq. miles)	0
Maritime Areas (EEZ, sq. miles)	1
Protected Areas (sq. miles):	10
percent of total	4.4%
No. of Threatened Species:	
mammals	NA
birds	NA
plants	16

Energy and Industry

Energy Production:	
solids (trillion BTUs)	0
liquids (trillion BTUs)	0
gas (trillion BTUs)	0
nuclear (gigawatt-hours)	0
hydroelectric (gigawatt-hours)	0
Energy Requirements:	
traditional fuels (trillion BTUs)	0
total (trillion BTUs)	372
per capita (million BTUs)	138
per capita (global rank)	26
Industrial Share of GDP	37.1%
Industrial Energy Index	8
Metal Reserve Index (world=100%)	NA
No. of Motor Vehicles/1000 Persons	88

Water

Renewable Supply (cubic miles)	0.1
Total Use (cubic miles):	0.0
in agriculture	4.0%
in industry	51.0%
in homes and cities	45.0%
Access to Safe Water:	
urban population	100.0%
rural population	NA

Urban Centers and Waste

No. of Cities Over 1 Million:	1
percent of population	100.0%
Solid Wastes (million tons)	0.9
Urban Sanitation Access	97.0%

Population and Gross National Product

Population	GNP
(millions)	(billion $US)

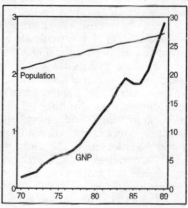

Commercial Energy Use

Total Energy Use	Per Capita Energy Use
(trillion BTUs)	(million BTUs)

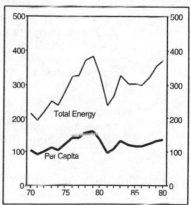

SRI LANKA

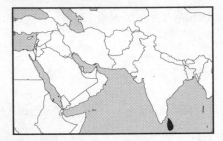

Total Area: 25,332 sq. miles
Global Rank: 109   Per Capita: 0.9 acres
Population: 17,217,000
Global Rank: 46   Growth Rate: 1.33%
Gross National Product: $6,938 m.
Global Rank: 75   Per Capita: $408
Greenhouse Gas Emissions
Global Share: 0.11%   Per Capita Rank: 126

The Democratic Socialist Republic of Sri Lanka is a tropical island nation in the Indian Ocean. It has two main terrestrial features: a mountainous area and a lowland plain. Arable land accounts for 34 percent of the island.

The country's natural resources include limestone, graphite, mineral sands, gemstones, and phosphates. Rice, tea, rubber, and coconuts are among the chief crops. The country is a petroleum refiner and also processes tea, rubber, and other agricultural commodities.

Sri Lanka is richly endowed with more than 700 indigenous species of wildlife. The country has a long and proud tradition of natural resource conservation dating back over 23 centuries.

Today, over 12 percent of the total land area is under "protected" status. Though home to a highly literate population and an ancient civilization, Sri Lanka has seen deterioration in environmental quality and living standards and grave ethnic strife in recent decades. The conflicts and rapid population growth between 1960 and 1980 have contributed to environmental problems.

Major Environmental Problems

Deforestation. Rapid loss of forest cover is a serious problem, especially in the wet zone. Most of the wet-zone forests have been removed for timber exportation, to make way for commercial crop plantations, for firewood collection, or for small-scale agricultural expansion. Denuded slopes cannot hold water, causing floods, erosion, and landslides.

Coastal degradation. The mining of coral from reefs for the production of lime is one of the most destructive causes of coastal degradation; in addition, the rapid development of tourism has contributed to increased pollution levels. Siltation arising from agricultural development in upland areas also damages coastal mangroves, coral reefs, and estuaries.

Water pollution. Industrial waste water, improper disposal of sewage runoff, and poorly managed irrigation systems, accompanied by occasional droughts, worsen the quality and lower the amount of Sri Lanka's dwindling freshwater resources.

Wildlife destruction. Wildlife populations are coming under severe pressure. The primary causes are agricultural encroachment on wildlife habitats, poaching, and tourism. The pesticides and other chemicals that enter water supplies have also adversely affected wildlife.

Quality of Life

Life Expectancy (years)	70.3
Infant Mortality (per 1000)	28.0
Population Under 15 Years	30.3%
Population Over 65 Years	4.4%
Literacy Rate	88.4%
Malnourished Children	34.0%

Land Use and Habitats

Cropland (sq. miles):	7,340
per capita (acres)	0.3
global rank	113
Permanent Pasture (sq. miles):	1,695
total livestock (millions)	3.4
Forest and Woodlands (sq. miles):	6,745
1985 deforestation (sq. miles)	224
Wilderness Area (sq. miles)	0
Maritime Areas (EEZ, sq. miles)	1,998
Protected Areas (sq. miles):	3,026
percent of total	11.9%
No. of Threatened Species:	
mammals	7
birds	8
plants	209

Energy and Industry

Energy Production:	
solids (trillion BTUs)	0
liquids (trillion BTUs)	0
gas (trillion BTUs)	0
nuclear (gigawatt-hours)	0
hydroelectric (gigawatt-hours)	2,654
Energy Requirements:	
traditional fuels (trillion BTUs)	75
total (trillion BTUs)	145
per capita (million BTUs)	9
per capita (global rank)	127
Industrial Share of GDP	26.8%
Industrial Energy Index	4
Metal Reserve Index (world=100%)	0.1%
No. of Motor Vehicles/1000 Persons	9

Water

Renewable Supply (cubic miles)	10.4
Total Use (cubic miles).	1.5
in agriculture	96.0%
in industry	2.0%
in homes and cities	2.0%
Access to Safe Water:	
urban population	87.0%
rural population	40.0%

Urban Centers and Waste

No. of Cities Over 1 Million:	0
percent of population	0.0%
Solid Wastes (million tons)	0.6
Urban Sanitation Access	74.0%

Population and Gross National Product

Population	GNP
(millions)	(billion $US)

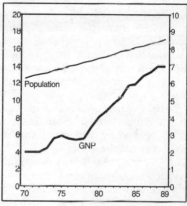

Commercial Energy Use

Total Energy Use	Per Capita Energy Use
(trillion BTUs)	(million BTUs)

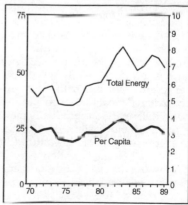

SYRIA

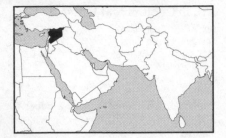

Total Area: 71,497 sq. miles
Global Rank: 81   Per Capita: 3.7 acres
Population: 12,530,000
Global Rank: 55   Growth Rate: 3.61%
Gross National Product: $11,050 m.
Global Rank: 63   Per Capita: $914
Greenhouse Gas Emissions
Global Share: 0.10%   Per Capita Rank: 113

The Syrian Arab Republic is located at the northeastern corner of the Mediterranean Sea. Slightly larger than North Dakota, much of the country is mountainous and semidesert. It shares borders with Turkey, Iraq, Jordan, Lebanon, and Israel.

There is a narrow coastal plain in Syria near the Mediterranean Sea. The plain is backed by a mountainous region that spans the entire length of the country in the west. East of the mountains are several plains, where most of Syria's cities are located and where its major crops are grown. The bulk of the country is dominated by the Syrian Desert in the southeast.

The country's natural resources include oil, phosphates, chrome, manganese, and iron ore. About 31 percent of the land area is arable, and only 4 percent is covered by forests. The more productive soils in Syria's western region, which have been cultivated for centuries, produce chiefly wheat and other grains, cotton, fruits, and tobacco. Animal meats and wool are also produced. Irrigation is gradually making more of the eastern part of the country productive for agriculture, but at some cost in land degradation.

Oil production is a major industry, as are mining and light manufacturing, but most of the work force is employed in agriculture or in herding animals, in service jobs, or as semi-skilled labor. The major exports are oil, textiles, fruits and vegetables, and phosphates.

Arabs make up over 90 percent of Syria's population. Arabic is the official language, but many others are spoken. Most Syrians adhere to the Muslim religion. Over one half of the population is urban, with most city dwellers living in Damascus—the capital, with a population of about 1.3 million—and a few other cities.

Major Environmental Problems

Water pollution. Many of the water supplies in Syria are unsafe for drinking. The causes of water pollution include the lack of adequate sewage systems and dumping of untreated wastes from petroleum processing and other industries.

Land degradation. Much of the irrigated land in Syria is seriously affected by salinity and waterlogging, the result of improper or excessive irrigation. Annual crop losses from salinization exceed $300 million. Overgrazing in some parts of the country is leading to increased desertification.

Coastal pollution. The Syrian coast along the Mediterranean has been damaged by oil pollution.

Quality of Life

Life Expectancy (years)	65.0
Infant Mortality (per 1000)	48.0
Population Under 15 Years	47.7%
Population Over 65 Years	2.3%
Literacy Rate	64.5%
Malnourished Children	NA

Land Use and Habitats

Cropland (sq. miles):	21,247
per capita (acres)	1.1
global rank	31
Permanent Pasture (sq. miles):	30,846
total livestock (millions)	16.1
Forest and Woodlands (sq. miles):	2,772
1985 deforestation (sq. miles)	0
Wilderness Area (sq. miles)	0
Maritime Areas (EEZ, sq. miles)	40
Protected Areas (sq. miles):	0
percent of total	0.0%
No. of Threatened Species:	
mammals	4
birds	15
plants	13

Energy and Industry

Energy Production:	
solids (trillion BTUs)	0
liquids (trillion BTUs)	727
gas (trillion BTUs)	9
nuclear (gigawatt-hours)	0
hydroelectric (gigawatt-hours)	4,705
Energy Requirements:	
traditional fuels (trillion BTUs)	0
total (trillion BTUs)	354
per capita (million BTUs)	29
per capita (global rank)	71
Industrial Share of GDP	16.0%
Industrial Energy Index	33
Metal Reserve Index (world=100%)	NA
No. of Motor Vehicles/1000 Persons	NA

Water

Renewable Supply (cubic miles)	1.8
Total Use (cubic miles).	0.8
in agriculture	83.0%
in industry	10.0%
in homes and cities	7.0%
Access to Safe Water:	
urban population	91.0%
rural population	68.0%

Urban Centers and Waste

No. of Cities Over 1 Million:	2
percent of population	30.1%
Solid Wastes (million tons)	1.3
Urban Sanitation Access	72.0%

Population and Gross National Product

Population (millions)   GNP (billion $US)

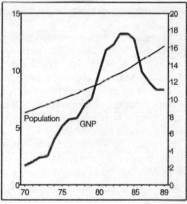

Commercial Energy Use

Total Energy Use (trillion BTUs)   Per Capita Energy Use (million BTUs)

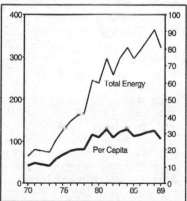

THAILAND

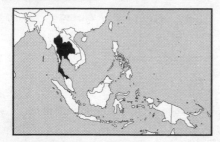

Total Area: 198,112 sq. miles
  Global Rank: 47   Per Capita: 2.3 acres
Population: 55,702,000
  Global Rank: 19   Growth Rate: 1.53%
Gross National Product: $68,766 m.
  Global Rank: 30   Per Capita: $1,254
Greenhouse Gas Emissions
  Global Share: 1.49%   Per Capita Rank: 53

The Kingdom of Thailand is located in the middle of the Indochinese Peninsula. The country straddles two mountain systems, with large alluvial plains between them. Southern Thailand is part of the Malay Peninsula and has long coastlines bordering the Gulf of Thailand and the Andaman Sea. The country shares borders with Myanmar, Laos, Cambodia, and Malaysia.

The country's natural resources include timber, rubber, natural gas, and some mineral deposits—tin, tungsten, and tantalum. Thailand is also richly endowed with flora and fauna. Estimates of the number of flowering plant species range as high as 15,000; mammals include 92 species of bats.

Most Thais live in rural areas and earn their livelihoods from agricultural activities. Nearly one half of the country's total land mass is cultivated. Chief crops include rice, sugar, and manioc, as well as opium and cannabis for the illegal drug trade.

Thailand is rapidly urbanizing and industrializing. Over 10 percent of the country's population already lives in the Bangkok metropolitan area, which contains 75 percent of the manufacturing industries. The industrial sector of the economy quadrupled in the 20 years from 1970 to 1990. This represents growth from a few hundred factories to over 50,000, with their attendant problems of air and water pollution and waste disposal.

Major Environmental Problems

Deforestation. According to government figures, 28 percent of Thailand remains forested, but the country is rapidly being denuded. The primary causes are logging (which was banned in 1989) and encroachment by farmers.

Wildlife destruction. As Thailand's forests shrink, natural habitats for wildlife also disappear. Hunters exacerbate the problem. As a result, many species are either endangered or extremely vulnerable.

Water scarcity. Thailand is confronted by a growing water shortage, as well as related problems of flooding, inadequate water control, and deteriorating water quality. The primary causes include the destruction of forested watersheds, poor management of irrigation systems, and inefficient water use.

Urban environmental quality. The ongoing deterioration of environmental quality in Bangkok is directly related to rapid urbanization. Industrial pollution, air pollution, an inadequate sewage system, and traffic congestion are serious problems.

Quality of Life

Life Expectancy (years)	65.0
Infant Mortality (per 1000)	28.0
Population Under 15 Years	29.3%
Population Over 65 Years	3.4%
Literacy Rate	93.0%
Malnourished Children	28.0%

Land Use and Habitats

Cropland (sq. miles):	85,429
per capita (acres)	1.0
global rank	36
Permanent Pasture (sq. miles):	2,973
total livestock (millions)	15.9
Forest and Woodlands (sq. miles):	54,981
1985 deforestation (sq. miles)	1,463
Wilderness Area (sq. miles)	10,847
Maritime Areas (EEZ, sq. miles)	331
Protected Areas (sq. miles):	19,713
percent of total	10.0%
No. of Threatened Species:	
mammals	26
birds	34
plants	63

Energy and Industry

Energy Production:	
solids (trillion BTUs)	92
liquids (trillion BTUs)	92
gas (trillion BTUs)	191
nuclear (gigawatt-hours)	0
hydroelectric (gigawatt-hours)	5,568
Energy Requirements:	
traditional fuels (trillion BTUs)	532
total (trillion BTUs)	1,546
per capita (million BTUs)	28
per capita (global rank)	73
Industrial Share of GDP	35.1%
Industrial Energy Index	7
Metal Reserve Index (world=100%)	0.5%
No. of Motor Vehicles/1000 Persons	12

Water

Renewable Supply (cubic miles)	26.4
Total Use (cubic miles):	7.7
in agriculture	90.0%
in industry	6.0%
in homes and cities	4.0%
Access to Safe Water:	
urban population	67.0%
rural population	76.0%

Urban Centers and Waste

No. of Cities Over 1 Million:	1
percent of population	12.8%
Solid Wastes (million tons)	2.5
Urban Sanitation Access	84.0%

Population and Gross National Product

Population	GNP
(millions)	(billion $US)

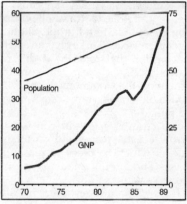

Commercial Energy Use

Total Energy Use	Per Capita Energy Use
(trillion BTUs)	(million BTUs)

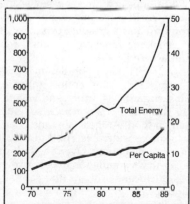

TURKEY

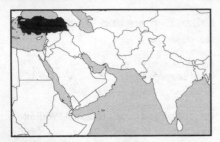

Total Area: 300,941 sq. miles
Global Rank: 35   Per Capita: 3.4 acres
Population: 55,868,000
Global Rank: 18   Growth Rate: 2.08%
Gross National Product: $77,283 m.
Global Rank: 28   Per Capita: $1,412
Greenhouse Gas Emissions
Global Share: 0.42%   Per Capita Rank: 117

The Republic of Turkey is located in west-central Asia, with a small portion lying in southeastern Europe. Slightly larger than Texas, Turkey has an extensive coastline that fronts the Mediterranean and Black seas. The country borders on the Commonwealth of Independent States, Iran, Iraq, Greece, and Bulgaria.

The country's terrain consists of narrow coastal plains and an inland plateau, which becomes increasingly rugged and mountainous as it progresses east and south.

Turkey's natural resources include extensive deposits of coal and chromium, as well as deposits of antimony, copper, and mercury. Mining and a growing industrial sector are important economic activities; Turkey is one of the world's leading exporters of chromium and a growing producer of iron, steel, machinery, electronics, and manufactured goods.

Much of Turkey's population works on farms, producing cotton, tobacco, grains, sugar beets, fruits, and vegetables. The country is normally self-sufficient in food. At the same time, there has been considerable rural-to-urban migration in Turkey. Over one half of the country's population lives in urban areas, including Ankara (the capital), Istanbul, and Izmir. Employment in the manufacturing and industrial sectors is growing. Over a million Turks

also work abroad, especially in western Europe. Recent improvements in infrastructure have resulted in nationwide electrification and telephone connections in every village.

Although the country is officially secular, nearly all Turks are Muslim. It has been estimated that about 10 million Turks are of Kurdish origin. The former center of the Ottoman Empire, Turkey is a popular tourist attraction.

Major Environmental Problems

Air and water pollution. Modernization has put pressure on the country's natural resources, and the major cities have problems with air and water pollution. High levels of sulfur dioxide and lead pollution are found in Istanbul's air, and mercury pollution has been discovered in the nearby Sea of Marmara. Mercury, chemicals, and detergents that have been dumped into the country's rivers have led to a dangerous water pollution problem.

Deforestation. Turkey's forests are declining. Some forestland is converted to farmland annually, more is converted to grazing lands, and forest fires set by humans destroy several thousand acres each year. The result is reduced water retention.

Quality of Life

Life Expectancy (years)	64.1
Infant Mortality (per 1000)	76.0
Population Under 15 Years	33.7%
Population Over 65 Years	3.8%

Land Use and Habitats

Cropland (sq. miles):	107,664
per capita (acres)	1.3
global rank	21
Permanent Pasture (sq. miles):	33,205
total livestock (millions)	62.9
Forest and Woodlands (sq. miles):	77,988
Wilderness Area (sq. miles)	0
Maritime Areas (EEZ, sq. miles)	914
Protected Areas (sq. miles):	1,039
percent of total	0.3%
No. of Threatened Species:	
mammals	5
birds	18
plants	1,952

Energy and Industry

Energy Production:	
solids (trillion BTUs)	427
liquids (trillion BTUs)	114
gas (trillion DTUs)	6
nuclear (gigawatt-hours)	0
hydroelectric (gigawatt-hours)	17,943
Energy Requirements:	
traditional fuels (trillion BTUs)	90
total (trillion BTUs)	1,674
per capita (million BTUs)	31
per capita (global rank)	67
Industrial Share of GDP	35.6%
Industrial Energy Index	21
Metal Reserve Index (world=100%)	0.3%
No. of Motor Vehicles/1000 Persons	26

Water

Renewable Supply (cubic miles)	47.0
Total Use (cubic miles):	3.7
in agriculture	57.0%
in industry	19.0%
in homes and cities	24.0%

Waste and Pollution

Urban Solid Wastes (million tons):	21.5
per capita (tons)	236.0
Hazardous Wastes (000 tons)	NA
Sewage Treatment Plant Coverage	0.8%
SOX Emissions (000 tons)	390.1
NOX Emissions (000 tons)	192.9

Waste and Pollution (cont.)

Particulate Emissions (tons)	NA
Hydrocarbon Emissions (tons)	771.4
No. of Cities Over 1 Million:	4
percent of population	21.6%

Population and Gross National Product

Population (millions) — GNP (billion $US)

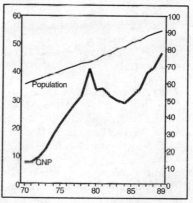

Commercial Energy Use

Total Energy Use (trillion BTUs) — Per Capita Energy Use (million BTUs)

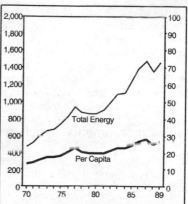

VIET NAM

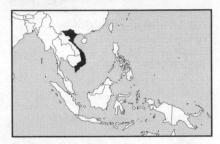

Total Area: 128,063 sq. miles
Global Rank: 60   Per Capita: 1.2 acres
Population: 66,693,000
Global Rank: 13   Growth Rate: 2.15%
Gross National Product: $6,880 m.
Global Rank: 76   Per Capita: $105
Greenhouse Gas Emissions
Global Share: 0.70%   Per Capita Rank: 97

Viet Nam is located in southeastern Asia and borders China, Laos, Cambodia, and the South China Sea. The climate is humid, with monsoon rains during both the hot summer and relatively cool winter.

The southern part of Viet Nam constitutes the estuary of the Mekong River and is consequently low, flat, and marshy. Rich soil and abundant water make this area extremely fertile for rice cultivation, but a rapidly growing population makes it very crowded.

The economy here is mainly agricultural. The northern lowlands are also heavily populated and intensely cultivated. The rugged northern highlands areas are covered by tropical forests.

The country's natural resources include deposits of such minerals as coal, phosphates, manganese, and bauxite. Agriculture and mining are the mainstays of the economy. Viet Nam has developed slowly, in part because of the effects of the Viet Nam War and the subsequent U.S.-led embargo.

Major Environmental Problems

Deforestation. Forests once covered approximately two thirds of the country, but over the past 50 years, more than half of these forests have been lost. The loss can be attributed to war damage, including defoliation by American forces, agriculture, legal and illegal cutting for firewood and construction material, and accidental fires and other causes. Damage is particularly severe in the northern part of the country.

Soil degradation. Viet Nam has very little cultivated land per capita, which leads to overcultivation. In addition, intense precipitation speeds soil erosion on cleared lands, leading to rapid impoverishment of the soil, a loss of stored nutrients, acidification of the land, and pollution of waterways.

Water resources. The distribution of Viet Nam's water resources is highly uneven in time and space, causing flooding of low river basins and destruction of agricultural crops, property, and sometimes human lives. Decreasing amounts of water runoff in the dry season cause shortages for agricultural production and domestic use. Flooding, pollution of surface water by industrial and domestic wastes, and sediments in rivers are growing problems.

Marine degradation. Pollution from oil spills and other sources, along with overfishing, are depleting the onceplentiful sea life of Viet Nam's coastal waters.

Quality of Life

Life Expectancy (years)	61.5
Infant Mortality (per 1000)	64.0
Population Under 15 Years	37.6%
Population Over 65 Years	4.0%
Literacy Rate	87.6%
Malnourished Children	60.0%

Land Use and Habitats

Cropland (sq. miles):	25,483
per capita (acres)	0.2
global rank	118
Permanent Pasture (sq. miles):	1,293
total livestock (millions)	18.4
Forest and Woodlands (sq. miles):	37,838
1985 deforestation (sq. miles)	251
Wilderness Area (sq. miles)	0
Maritime Areas (EEZ, sq. miles)	2,788
Protected Areas (sq. miles):	3,444
percent of total	2.7%
No. of Threatened Species:	
mammals	28
birds	34
plants	388

Energy and Industry

Energy Production:	
solids (trillion BTUs)	150
liquids (trillion BTUs)	18
gas (trillion BTUs)	0
nuclear (gigawatt-hours)	0
hydroelectric (gigawatt-hours)	2,247
Energy Requirements:	
traditional fuels (trillion BTUs)	226
total (trillion BTUs)	441
per capita (million BTUs)	7
per capita (global rank)	136
Industrial Share of GDP	NA
Industrial Energy Index	NA
Metal Reserve Index (world=100%)	0.0%
No. of Motor Vehicles/1000 Persons	NA

Water

Renewable Supply (cubic miles)	90.2
Total Use (cubic miles):	1.2
in agriculture	78.0%
in industry	9.0%
in homes and cities	13.0%
Access to Safe Water:	
urban population	48.0%
rural population	45.0%

Urban Centers and Waste

No. of Cities Over 1 Million:	2
percent of population	6.5%
Solid Wastes (million tons)	2.9
Urban Sanitation Access	48.0%

Population and Gross National Product

Population (millions)	GNP (billion $US)

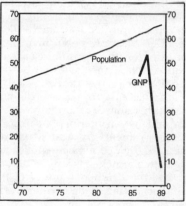

Commercial Energy Use

Total Energy Use (trillion BTUs)	Per Capita Energy Use (million BTUs)

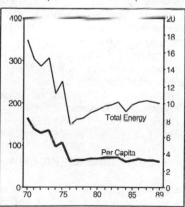

YEMEN

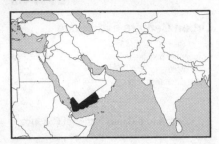

Total Area: 203,846 sq. miles
  Global Rank: 46   Per Capita: 11.2 acres
Population: 11,687,000
  Global Rank: 59   Growth Rate: 3.67%
Gross National Product: $9,207 m.
  Global Rank: 68   Per Capita: $817
Greenhouse Gas Emissions
  Global Share: 0.04%   Per Capita Rank: 115

The Republic of Yemen was established in May 1991 with the merger of the Yemen Arab Republic and the People's Democratic Republic of Yemen. Bordered on the north and east by Saudi Arabia, Yemen's western border faces Ethiopia across the Red Sea. The country has a narrow coastal plain in the south, rising to a mountainous region and then an interior plateau.

Most Yemenis are Arab Muslims. They are divided almost equally between two principal Islamic religious groups: the Zaidi community of the Shi'a sect, found in the northern, central, and eastern portions of the country, and the Shafa'i community of the Sunni sect in the south and southwest.

Unlike many other Arabs, Yemenis are almost completely sedentary and live in small villages scattered throughout the country.

The country's natural resources are limited to petroleum, which is the major export. Although Yemen grows grains, fruits, and dates and raises cattle and sheep, it imports the majority of its commodities and foodstuffs. There is little domestic industry.

Major Environmental Problems

Potable water. Safe drinking water is a serious problem in both urban and rural areas throughout the country. The major part of the potable water comes from wells and is easily contaminated. The problem is exacerbated by the lack of sewage and waste disposal systems in urban and rural areas.

Water scarcity. Yemen has little rainfall and little surface water. Therefore, groundwater is the major source of household water. The increase in groundwater use and in groundwater irrigation is quickly lowering the water table in many areas.

Land degradation. *Wadi* (which means valley, river, or dry river bed) areas receive unexpectedly severe floods that can demolish irrigation systems and wash away soil. As workers leave the rural areas and terraces deteriorate, erosion has become a serious concern in the highland areas as well. The depletion of plant cover in many rangeland and woodland areas has made erosion a problem even in nonagricultural areas.

Soil degradation. Tihama, a hot, sandy, semidesert that separates the Red Sea coast from the generally less arid mountainous areas of the interior, is particularly affected by soil salinization. This is due to the improper use of groundwater, which can be extremely saline in this area, for irrigation of crops.

Quality of Life

Life Expectancy (years)	50.2
Infant Mortality (per 1000)	120.0
Population Under 15 Years	49.5%
Population Over 65 Years	2.4%
Literacy Rate	38.6%
Malnourished Children	61.0%

Land Use and Habitats

Cropland (sq. miles):	5,718
per capita (acres)	0.3
global rank	108
Permanent Pasture (sq. miles):	62,027
total livestock (millions)	5.8
Forest and Woodlands (sq. miles):	12,008
1985 deforestation (sq. miles)	NA
Wilderness Area (sq. miles)	45,200
Maritime Areas (EEZ, sq. miles)	2,256
Protected Areas (sq. miles):	0
percent of total	0.0%
No. of Threatened Species:	
mammals	NA
birds	NA
plants	3

Energy and Industry

Energy Production:	
solids (trillion BTUs)	0
liquids (trillion BTUs)	670
gas (trillion BTUs)	0
nuclear (gigawatt-hours)	0
hydroelectric (gigawatt-hours)	0
Energy Requirements:	
traditional fuels (trillion BTUs)	3
total (trillion BTUs)	110
per capita (million BTUs)	10
per capita (global rank)	122
Industrial Share of GDP	0.1%
Industrial Energy Index	NA
Metal Reserve Index (world=100%)	NA
No. of Motor Vehicles/1000 Persons	NA

Water

Renewable Supply (cubic miles)	0.6
Total Use (cubic miles):	0.8
in agriculture	93.4%
in industry	2.0%
in homes and cities	4.6%
Access to Safe Water:	
urban population	100.0%
rural population	48.0%

Urban Centers and Waste

No. of Cities Over 1 Million:	0
percent of population	0.0%
Solid Wastes (million tons)	NA
Urban Sanitation Access	66.0%

Population and Gross National Product

Population (millions) GNP (billion $US)

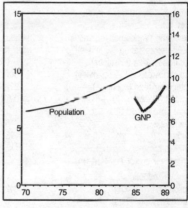

Commercial Energy Use

Total Energy Use (trillion BTUs) Per Capita Energy Use (million BTUs)

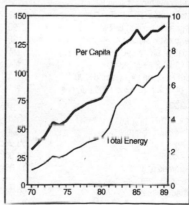

KOREA, NORTH

Quality of Life

Life Expectancy (years)	69.8
Infant Mortality (per 1000)	28.0
Population Under 15 Years	29.3%
Population Over 65 Years	3.5%
Literacy Rate	NA
Malnourished Children	NA

Land Use and Habitats

Cropland (sq. miles):	7,722
per capita (acres)	0.2
global rank	124
Permanent Pasture (sq. miles):	193
total livestock (millions)	5.1
Forest and Woodlands (sq. miles):	34,633
1985 deforestation (sq. miles)	0
Wilderness Area (sq. miles)	0
Maritime Areas (EEZ, sq. miles)	500
Protected Areas (sq. miles):	224
percent of total	0.5%
No. of Threatened Species:	
mammals	5
birds	25
plants	NA

Energy and Industry

Energy Production:	
solids (trillion BTUs)	1,342
liquids (trillion BTUs)	0
gas (trillion BTUs)	0
nuclear (gigawatt-hours)	0
hydroelectric (gigawatt-hours)	31,750
Energy Requirements:	
traditional fuels (trillion BTUs)	38
total (trillion BTUs)	1,919
per capita (million BTUs)	90
per capita (global rank)	38
Industrial Share of GDP	NA
Industrial Energy Index	NA
Metal Reserve Index (world=100%)	NA
No. of Motor Vehicles/1000 Persons	NA

Water

Renewable Supply (cubic miles)	16.1
Total Use (cubic miles):	3.4
in agriculture	73.0%
in industry	16.0%
in homes and cities	11.0%
Access to Safe Water:	
urban population	100.0%
rural population	100.0%

Urban Centers and Waste

No. of Cities Over 1 Million:	1
percent of population	10.2%
Solid Wastes (million tons)	2.6
Urban Sanitation Access	100.0%

Population

Population
(millions)

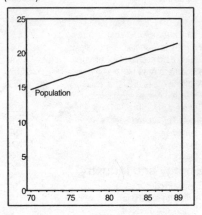

Commercial Energy Use

Total Energy Use   Per Capita Energy Use
(trillion BTUs)   (million BTUs)

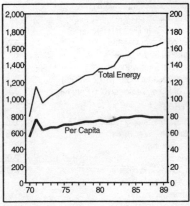

UNITED ARAB EMIRATES

Quality of Life

Life Expectancy (years)	69.9
Infant Mortality (per 1000)	26.0
Population Under 15 Years	28.6%
Population Over 65 Years	1.3%
Literacy Rate	NA
Malnourished Children	NA

Land Use and Habitats

Cropland (sq. miles):	151
per capita (acres)	0.1
global rank	141
Permanent Pasture (sq. miles):	772
total livestock (millions)	1.0
Forest and Woodlands (sq. miles):	12
1985 deforestation (sq. miles)	NA
Wilderness Area (sq. miles)	7,481
Maritime Areas (EEZ, sq. miles)	229
Protected Areas (sq. miles):	0
percent of total	0.0%
No. of Threatened Species:	
mammals	4
birds	7
plants	NA

Energy and Industry

Energy Production:	
solids (trillion BTUs)	0
liquids (trillion BTUs)	3,745
gas (trillion BTUs)	723
nuclear (gigawatt hours)	0
hydroelectric (gigawatt-hours)	0
Energy Requirements:	
traditional fuels (trillion BTUs)	0
total (trillion BTUs)	850
per capita (million BTUs)	553
per capita (global rank)	2
Industrial Share of GDP	55.4%
Industrial Energy Index	3
Metal Reserve Index (world=100%)	NA
No. of Motor Vehicles/1000 Persons	NA

Water

Renewable Supply (cubic miles)	0.1
Total Use (cubic miles):	0.2
in agriculture	80.0%
in industry	9.0%
in homes and cities	11.0%
Access to Safe Water:	
urban population	100.0%
rural population	100.0%

Urban Centers and Waste

No. of Cities Over 1 Million:	NA
percent of population	NA
Solid Wastes (million tons)	0.5
Urban Sanitation Access	100.0%

Population and Gross National Product

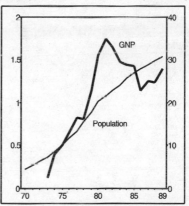

Population (millions)	GNP (billion $US)

Commercial Energy Use

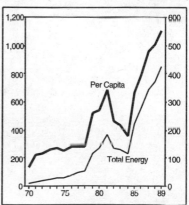

Total Energy Use (trillion BTUs)	Per Capita Energy Use (million BTUs)

513

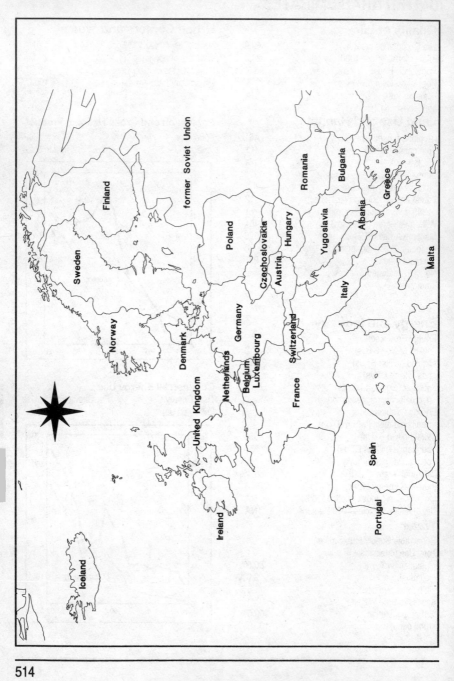

Europe

This chapter contains environmental profiles for the European countries listed. Data for the (former) Soviet Union are given, but additional data and short descriptions of environmental problems are given for each Republic separately. The continuing civil war in the former Yugoslavia (treated here as a whole) is rapidly worsening environmental and human conditions in that region. Technical notes and data sources are given beginning on page 641.

AUSTRIA

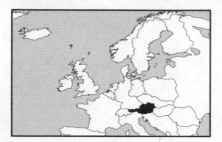

Total Area: 32,374 sq. miles
Global Rank: 104   Per Capita: 2.7 acres
Population: 7,583,000
Global Rank: 78   Growth Rate: 0.07%
Gross National Product: $125,486 m.
Global Rank: 21   Per Capita: $16,559
Greenhouse Gas Emissions
Global Share: 0.22%   Per Capita Rank: 44

Austria is blessed with superb mountains and forests that attract visitors from around the world. The country is primarily mountainous, with the Alps and their approaches dominating the western and southern provinces. The eastern provinces and Vienna are located in the Danube River basin.

Austria has a social market economy, with the government operating various state monopolies, utilities, and services. Many large corporations are state-owned but operate as private businesses. Small, scattered farms provide about 60 percent of domestic food requirements.

Forests cover about 39 percent of Austria's territory, while another 18 percent is cultivated cropland. There are 129 protected areas or nature reserves covering almost 20 percent of the country; 302 plant species and 108 animal species are protected by law.

Austrian government officials appreciate the value of their natural resources and are taking steps to protect them. In Vienna, for example, anyone who cuts down a tree must replace it. The use of deicing salts on mountain roads has been limited to cut down on runoff that harms trees. In 1985, the country introduced the most stringent exhaust standards for cars in Europe.

Industry has recycled raw materials since 1973, but now municipalities are becoming involved in recycling solid waste. Special procedures exist for disposal of batteries.

Coal and oil-fired power stations and industrial plants account for the great majority of Austria's sulfur dioxide emissions, a major ingredient in tree-killing acid rain. The country has imposed emission controls and limited the sulfur content of fuel. Sulfur dioxide emissions have been reduced by two thirds over the period from 1980 to 1988; further reductions are planned.

Major Environmental Problems

Forest degradation. Forest damage is caused by a combination of air and soil pollution. Nitrogen oxides and sulfur dioxide are the main culprits in the air, while in the soil agricultural chemicals also play a role. Estimates of forest defoliation indicate that about 25 percent of the country's forests have suffered some damage.

New protected areas. With the end of the Cold War, the former "no-man's-lands" along Austria's borders with Czechoslovakia and Hungary present new opportunities for parks and protected areas. For example, conservationists from Austria, Hungary, and Czechoslovakia are urging the creation of a trilateral national park along the floodplain areas of the Danube, Thaya, and March rivers.

AUSTRIA

Quality of Life

Life Expectancy (years)	74.4
Infant Mortality (per 1000)	11.0
Population Under 15 Years	17.4%
Population Over 65 Years	14.3%

Land Use and Habitats

Cropland (sq. miles):	5,919
per capita (acres)	0.5
global rank	84
Permanent Pasture (sq. miles):	7,780
total livestock (millions)	6.8
Forest and Woodlands (sq. miles):	12,355
Wilderness Area (sq. miles)	0
Maritime Areas (EEZ, sq. miles)	0
Protected Areas (sq. miles):	6,154
percent of total	19.0%
No. of Threatened Species:	
mammals	2
birds	13
plants	25

Energy and Industry

Energy Production:	
solids (trillion BTUs)	22
liquids (trillion BTUs)	48
gas (trillion BTUs)	44
nuclear (gigawatt-hours)	0
hydroelectric (gigawatt-hours)	36,138
Energy Requirements:	
traditional fuels (trillion BTUs)	16
total (trillion BTUs)	1,092
per capita (million BTUs)	144
per capita (global rank)	25
Industrial Share of GDP	37.0%
Industrial Energy Index	5
Metal Reserve Index (world–100%)	0.0%
No. of Motor Vehicles/1000 Persons	381

Water

Renewable Supply (cubic miles)	13.5
Total Use (cubic miles):	0.8
in agriculture	8.0%
in Industry	73.0%
in homes and cities	19.0%

Waste and Pollution

Urban Solid Wastes (million tons).	3.0
per capita (tons)	229.0
Hazardous Wastes (000 tons)	440.8
Sewage Treatment Plant Coverage	72.0%
SOX Emissions (000 tons)	136.6
NOX Emissions (000 tons)	232.5

Waste and Pollution (cont.)

Particulate Emissions (tons)	43.0
Hydrocarbon Emissions (tons)	513.5
No. of Cities Over 1 Million:	1
percent of population	27.6%

Population and Gross National Product

Population (millions)	GNP (billion $US)

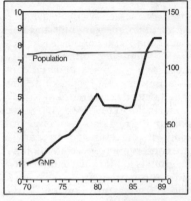

Commercial Energy Use

Total Energy Use (trillion BTUs)	Per Capita Energy Use (million BTUs)

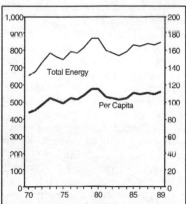

BELGIUM

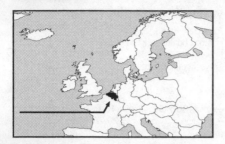

Total Area: 12,780 sq. miles
  Global Rank: 118   Per Capita: 0.8 acres
Population: 9,845,000
  Global Rank: 66   Growth Rate: −0.03%
Gross National Product: $154,907 m.
  Global Rank: 19   Per Capita: $15,730
Greenhouse Gas Emissions
  Global Share: 0.37%   Per Capita Rank: 32

Belgium is characterized by a fertile maritime plain, pleasant hills and valleys, and the mountainous Ardennes Forest. The densely populated country contains two regions with significant political powers: Dutch-speaking Flanders in the north and French-speaking Wallonia in the south. The regions have responsibility for land planning, but overlap with the central government in nature conservation and water policy.

Belgium is in the midst of one of the world's foremost industrial centers. Within 100 miles are London, Paris, and the Ruhr Valley. With a highly skilled work force, the country exports heavily. Its products range from steel to lace, which has been made since the 16th century. Its major natural resource is deposits of coal.

Belgium is headquarters to most of the institutions of the European Community, yet it has a relatively poor record in applying European Community environmental legislation within its borders. Wallonia and Flanders tightened laws on the transport and disposal of toxic wastes after the discovery in 1983 of thousands of illegal hazardous waste dumps.

Belgium's energy use has changed considerably over the past two decades. The use of coal and oil has declined since 1970, while the use of natural gas has increased. Nuclear energy provided none of the country's energy needs in 1970, but by 1988 it provided 9 percent of the country's energy, somewhat higher than the average in industrialized countries.

Major Environmental Problems

Water pollution. Water protection laws in effect since 1971 have not stopped factories in steel-making regions from releasing wastes into the Meuse. The Meuse supplies drinking water to 5 million people, yet it is highly polluted. Fines are so low that companies would rather pay them than treat their effluents adequately.

Pollution from agricultural sources—animal manures and excess fertilizers—has increased the concentrations of nitrates in many rivers, which in turn has increased algal growth in surface waters. In the Escaut-Doel River, for instance, nitrate concentrations rose about 67 percent from 1970 to the late 1980s.

Air pollution. Belgium is the home of a number of smokestack industries that contribute to Europe's air pollution. The acidic particles carried aloft have caused acid rain problems in other countries. There are some signs of progress, however. By the late 1980s in Brussels, for example, average concentrations of sulfur dioxide had declined to about one third of the 1975 level.

BELGIUM

Quality of Life

Life Expectancy (years)	74.8
Infant Mortality (per 1000)	10.0
Population Under 15 Years	17.6%
Population Over 65 Years	14.0%

Land Use and Habitats

Cropland (sq. miles):	3,174
per capita (acres)	NA
global rank	130
Permanent Pasture (sq. miles):	2,367
total livestock (millions)	9.5
Forest and Woodlands (sq. miles):	2,364
Wilderness Area (sq. miles)	0
Maritime Areas (EEZ, sq. miles)	10
Protected Areas (sq. miles):	277
percent of total	2.4%
No. of Threatened Species:	
mammals	2
birds	13
plants	11

Energy and Industry

Energy Production:	
solids (trillion BTUs)	92
liquids (trillion BTUs)	0
gas (trillion BTUs)	0
nuclear (gigawatt-hours)	41,218
hydroelectric (gigawatt-hours)	366
Energy Requirements:	
traditional fuels (trillion BTUs)	6
total (trillion BTUs)	1,861
per capita (million BTUs)	189
per capita (global rank)	14
Industrial Share of GDP	30.8%
Industrial Energy Index	12
Metal Reserve Index (world=100%)	NA
No. of Motor Vehicles/1000 Persons	366

Water

Renewable Supply (cubic miles)	2.0
Total Use (cubic miles):	2.2
in agriculture	4.0%
in industry	85.0%
in homes and cities	11.0%

Waste and Pollution

Urban Solid Wastes (million tons):	3.8
per capita (tons)	376.5
Hazardous Wastes (000 tons)	1,008.3
Sewage Treatment Plant Coverage	22.9%
SOX Emissions (000 tons)	456.2
NOX Emissions (000 tons)	327.3

Waste and Pollution (cont.)

Particulate Emissions (tons)	NA
Hydrocarbon Emissions (tons)	412.1
No. of Cities Over 1 Million:	0
percent of population	0.0%

Population and Gross National Product

Population   GNP
(millions)   (billion $US)

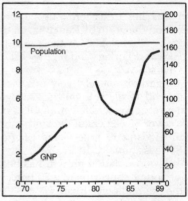

Commercial Energy Use

Total Energy Use   Per Capita Energy Use
(trillion BTUs)   (million BTUs)

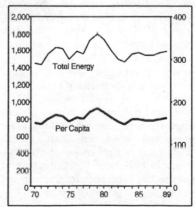

BULGARIA

Total Area: 42,822 sq. miles
Global Rank: 96   Per Capita: 3.0 acres
Population: 9,010,000
Global Rank: 70   Growth Rate: 0.11%
Gross National Product: $21,097 m.
Global Rank: 58   Per Capita: $2,344
Greenhouse Gas Emissions
Global Share: 0.33%   Per Capita Rank: 31

Bulgaria lies in eastern Europe, bordered on the north by Romania, on the west by Yugoslavia, on the south by Greece and Turkey, and on the east by the Black Sea.

Bulgaria has a relatively warm climate and fertile soil, but has meager water resources and few minerals. Forests cover 34 percent of the land; more than 115 square miles were planted with trees annually during the last two decades. Population growth has been slow; today approximately 70 percent of the population is urban.

Along with its eastern European neighbors, Bulgaria followed the Soviet economic development pattern after World War II, which emphasized heavy industries, such as chemical, metallurgical, and electrical. About 90 percent of farm acreage has been collectivized and linked into 300 large complexes. Private farming has been responsible for a large share of the production of key crops, such as potatoes, vegetables, fruit, meat, and honey.

Oil and natural gas, nearly all imported from the former Soviet Union, represented more than half of Bulgaria's total energy consumption. Beginning in 1991, however, Bulgaria had to pay in hard currency for this energy, creating shortages and economic hardships. Approximately 9 percent of the country's electricity has been generated by nuclear power stations, but these are now reported as being partially shut down.

Major Environmental Problems

Land contamination. About 115 square miles of land that are next to metallurgical plants are polluted with heavy metals. Soils have also been degraded by mining operations and by the dumping of industrial, domestic, and agricultural wastes.

Water pollution. Raw sewage, heavy metals, nitrates, oil derivatives, and detergents have created severe pollution in the middle and lower reaches of virtually all of Bulgaria's large rivers. Bulgaria is a heavy contributor of the industrial pollution and raw sewage that flows into the Black Sea.

Air pollution. Cities, such as the capital Sofia, as well as Ruse, Bruges, Varian, and Plovdivd, all experience severe air pollution. Industrial emissions are the primary source of the pollutants. Chlorine emissions in Ruse—from a Romanian plant just across the Danube—sparked protests in early 1987.

Threatened forests. Air pollution has damaged—moderately to severely—approximately one quarter of Bulgaria's forests.

Quality of Life

Life Expectancy (years)	72.0
Infant Mortality (per 1000)	16.0
Population Under 15 Years	18.7%
Population Over 65 Years	11.3%
Literacy Rate	NA
Malnourished Children	NA

Land Use and Habitats

Cropland (sq. miles):	16,008
per capita (acres)	1.1
global rank	29
Permanent Pasture (sq. miles):	7,807
total livestock (millions)	15.3
Forest and Woodlands (sq. miles):	14,934
1985 deforestation (sq. miles)	0
Wilderness Area (sq. miles)	0
Maritime Areas (EEZ, sq. miles)	127
Protected Areas (sq. miles):	499
percent of total	1.2%
No. of Threatened Species:	
mammals	3
birds	15
plants	89

Energy and Industry

Energy Production:	
solids (trillion BTUs)	479
liquids (trillion BTUs)	3
gas (trillion BTUs)	0
nuclear (gigawatt-hours)	2,695
hydroelectric (gigawatt-hours)	2,687
Energy Requirements:	
traditional fuels (trillion BTUs)	17
total (trillion BTUs)	1,309
per capita (million BTUs)	145
per capita (global rank)	24
Industrial Share of GDP	NA
Industrial Energy Index	26
Metal Reserve Index (world=100%)	0.3%
No. of Motor Vehicles/1000 Persons	137

Water

Renewable Supply (cubic miles)	4.3
Total Use (cubic miles):	3.4
in agriculture	55.0%
in industry	38.0%
in homes and cities	7.0%
Access to Safe Water:	
urban population	100.0%
rural population	96.0%

Urban Centers and Waste

No. of Cities Over 1 Million:	1
percent of population	13.2%
Solid Wastes (million tons)	1.5
Urban Sanitation Access	100.0%

Population and Gross National Product

Population (millions) — GNP (billion $US)

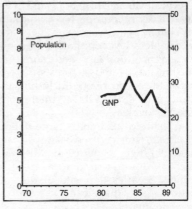

Commercial Energy Use

Total Energy Use (trillion BTUs) — Per Capita Energy Use (million BTUs)

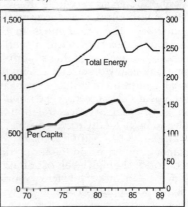

CZECHOSLOVAKIA

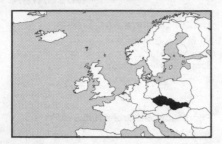

Total Area: 49,370 sq. miles
Global Rank: 90   Per Capita: 2.0 acres
Population: 15,667,000
Global Rank: 49   Growth Rate: 0.21%
Gross National Product: $50,379 m.
Global Rank: 35   Per Capita: $3,222
Greenhouse Gas Emissions
Global Share: 0.74%   Per Capita Rank: 16

Czechoslovakia, which is located in the heart of central Europe, has a continental climate with warm summers and cold winters. Over one half of the country is agricultural land and more than one third is covered by forests. Several major European rivers, including the Danube, Elbe, and Vltava, run through Czechoslovakia.

Czechoslovakia holds large deposits of coal, which is used as the primary fuel in power generation. Minerals such as uranium and iron are also mined. Smaller deposits of oil and natural gas, which can be found at great depths, have not been exploited.

In 1989, the country changed from a centralized socialist regime, which had emphasized heavy industry and collectivization and paid very little attention to the environment, to a representative democracy. The economy is in the throes of transformation to a market economy. Czechoslovakia's population is ethnically diverse: the main national groups are Czechs (63 percent) and Slovaks (32 percent). The population is increasingly concentrated in urban and highly industrialized areas.

Life expectancy in Czechoslovakia is among the lowest in the industrialized world. The high levels of pollution seem to be an important factor contributing to poor public health, along with other factors such as diet, high rates of smoking, and work-related stress.

Major Environmental Problems

Air pollution. Air pollution is a severe problem throughout Czechoslovakia. Sulfur dioxide from power generation seriously impairs the health of citizens, especially children. Carbon dioxide, fly ash, heavy metals, and other noxious emissions from power, steel, chemical, and metallurgical plants also cause extensive damage.

Air pollution has destroyed or damaged extensive areas of forest in Czechoslovakia. About three fourths of all trees show some signs of defoliation, and 33 percent are moderately to severely damaged.

Water pollution. Water pollution is also severe in many communities. Industry, mining, and agriculture all generate pollution that threatens the quality of both groundwater and surface water supplies. Most wastewater is not adequately treated; many towns have contaminated water supplies.

Land degradation. Mining and agricultural activities have left the land susceptible to erosion and compaction. Acid rain (and other factors) has acidified much of the soil. The loss of trees as a result of air pollution has further impoverished soils. These factors have contributed to a rise in the number of endangered species.

CZECHOSLOVAKIA

Quality of Life

Life Expectancy (years)	71.2
Infant Mortality (per 1000)	15.0
Population Under 15 Years	21.0%
Population Over 65 Years	10.9%
Literacy Rate	NA
Malnourished Children	NA

Land Use and Habitats

Cropland (sq. miles):	19,722
per capita (acres)	0.8
global rank	55
Permanent Pasture (sq. miles):	6,336
total livestock (millions)	13.6
Forest and Woodlands (sq. miles):	17,819
1985 deforestation (sq. miles)	0
Wilderness Area (sq. miles)	0
Maritime Areas (EEZ, sq. miles)	0
Protected Areas (sq. miles):	7,582
percent of total	15.4%
No. of Threatened Species:	
mammals	2
birds	18
plants	29

Energy and Industry

Energy Production:	
solids (trillion BTUs)	1,643
liquids (trillion BTUs)	6
gas (trillion BTUs)	26
nuclear (gigawatt-hours)	24,578
hydroelectric (gigawatt-hours)	4,274
Energy Requirements:	
traditional fuels (trillion BTUs)	14
total (trillion BTUs)	2,819
per capita (million BTUs)	180
per capita (global rank)	17
Industrial Share of GDP	NA
Industrial Energy Index	40
Metal Reserve Index (world=100%)	0.0%
No. of Motor Vehicles/1000 Persons	200

Water

Renewable Supply (cubic miles)	6.7
Total Use (cubic miles):	1.4
in agriculture	9.0%
in industry	68.0%
in homes and cities	23.0%
Access to Safe Water:	
urban population	100.0%
rural population	100.0%

Urban Centers and Waste

No. of Cities Over 1 Million:	1
percent of population	8.3%
Solid Wastes (million tons)	2.9
Urban Sanitation Access	100.0%

Population and Gross National Product

Population (millions) — GNP (billion $US)

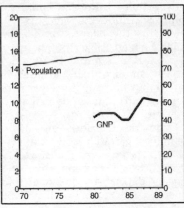

Commercial Energy Use

Total Energy Use (trillion BTUs) — Per Capita Energy Use (million BTUs)

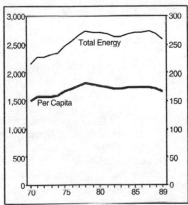

DENMARK

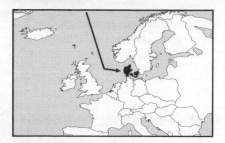

Total Area: 16,629 sq. miles
Global Rank: 114   Per Capita: 2.1 acres
Population: 5,143,000
Global Rank: 90   Growth Rate: 0.08%
Gross National Product: $100,384 m.
Global Rank: 23   Per Capita: $19,535
Greenhouse Gas Emissions
Global Share: 0.18%   Per Capita Rank: 33

The northern European country of Denmark includes the peninsula of Jutland plus the islands of Zealand, Funen, Lolland, Falster, Bornholm, and 401 smaller islands. Denmark is slightly smaller than Vermont and New Hampshire combined. About one fourth of the country's population lives in the city of Copenhagen.

Denmark's terrain is low and flat; the highest elevation in the country is 568 feet. The economy is characterized by industrial expansion, diversification, and dependence on foreign trade, which accounts for more than 50 percent of gross domestic product. Agricultural exports, which dominated until the end of the 1950s, now account for only about 20 percent of total exports.

Shocked by rising international oil prices, Denmark embarked on an energy self-sufficiency program during the 1970s. Oil production in the Danish North Sea began in 1972; by 1989 domestic oil and gas production provided half of domestic energy requirements, and the government hopes to increase this ratio in the 1990s.

Denmark also has significantly reduced its energy consumption, which fell about 22 percent from 1979 to 1989. The government has taken advantage of falling oil prices by imposing higher energy taxes to encourage greater conservation.

Denmark has been a leader in environmental pollution controls. About 98 percent of its population is served by wastewater treatment plants. By the late 1980s, concentrations of sulfur dioxide in Copenhagen had dropped to about 40 percent of the 1978 level.

Major Environmental Problems

North Sea pollution. Pollution of the North Sea is increasing, especially nitrogen and phosphorus pollution that comes from rivers in central and western Europe. Nutrient levels in the coastal belt from the Netherlands to the north of Denmark have generally doubled, leading to severe algal blooms over the past few decades.

Hazardous waste sites. Like most other western industrial societies, Denmark allowed millions of tons of hazardous wastes to be dumped with few precautions; 3,115 old sites that are thought to contain chemical wastes have been identified. Funds have been earmarked to begin to clean up these sites.

Pollution from animal manures. Livestock farms produce a concentrated source of animal manures. The nitrogen in these manures is a prime cause of increased nitrate concentrations in surface and drinking waters.

DENMARK

Quality of Life

Life Expectancy (years)	75.4
Infant Mortality (per 1000)	7.0
Population Under 15 Years	16.4%
Population Over 65 Years	14.9%

Land Use and Habitats

Cropland (sq. miles):	9,865
per capita (acres)	1.2
global rank	22
Permanent Pasture (sq. miles):	846
total livestock (millions)	11.5
Forest and Woodlands (sq. miles):	1,903
Wilderness Area (sq. miles)	0
Maritime Areas (EEZ, sq. miles)	5,653
Protected Areas (sq. miles):	1,631
percent of total	9.8%
No. of Threatened Species:	
mammals	1
birds	16
plants	7

Energy and Industry

Energy Production:	
solids (trillion BTUs)	0
liquids (trillion BTUs)	219
gas (trillion BTUs)	99
nuclear (gigawatt-hours)	0
hydroelectric (gigawatt-hours)	24
Energy Requirements:	
traditional fuels (trillion BTUs)	11
total (trillion BTUs)	708
per capita (million BTUs)	138
per capita (global rank)	27
Industrial Share of GDP	28.9%
Industrial Energy Index	4
Metal Reserve Index (world=100%)	NA
No. of Motor Vehicles/1000 Persons	323

Water

Renewable Supply (cubic miles)	2.6
Total Use (cubic miles):	0.4
in agriculture	43.0%
in industry	27.0%
in homes and cities	30.0%

Waste and Pollution

Urban Solid Wastes (million tons):	2.6
per capita (tons)	447.3
Hazardous Wastes (000 tons)	123.4
Sewage Treatment Plant Coverage	98.0%
SOX Emissions (000 tons)	266.7
NOX Emissions (000 tons)	294.2

Waste and Pollution (cont.)

Particulate Emissions (tons)	NA
Hydrocarbon Emissions (tons)	160.9
No. of Cities Over 1 Million:	1
percent of population	26.9%

Population and Gross National Product

Population   GNP
(millions)   (billion $US)

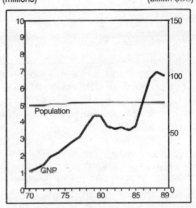

Commercial Energy Use

Total Energy Use   Per Capita Energy Use
(trillion BTUs)   (million BTUs)

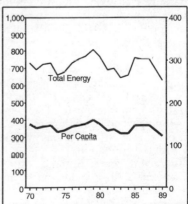

FINLAND

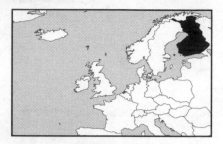

Total Area: 130,550 sq. miles
  Global Rank: 59   Per Capita: 16.8 acres
Population: 4,975,000
  Global Rank: 92   Growth Rate: 0.30%
Gross National Product: $112,945 m.
  Global Rank: 22   Per Capita: $22,770
Greenhouse Gas Emissions
  Global Share: 0.17%   Per Capita Rank: 34

Finland shares its eastern border with the former Soviet Union and its northern and northwestern borders with Norway and Sweden. The Baltic Sea on the west and south washes up on a 620-mile coastline with over 20,000 islands. Finland has at least 60,000 lakes. One fourth of the country lies above the Arctic Circle.

Forest covers about 70 percent of Finland's territory. Timber is the most important natural resource—the country ranks seventh in world timber production. In the north, native Lapps graze reindeer on lichen in a fragile, alpine ecosystem.

About 68 percent of Finland's population lives in the larger coastal cities, especially Helsinki. Domestic energy sources include hydroelectric power, peat, and wood, but the population relies heavily on imported oil, nuclear power, coal, and natural gas.

In 1989, the two-year-old Finnish Commission on Environment and Development released a report stating the country's commitment to sustainable development and its willingness to adjust consumption levels, energy pricing, and transportation.

In recent years, Finland signed agreements with Poland, the former Soviet Union, and with central European and other Baltic states to work at reducing the serious levels of air and water pollution in the region.

Major Environmental Problems

Air pollution and acid rain. Manufacturing and power plants cause serious air pollution in cities. Sulfur emissions from wood pulp plants and other sources have increased soil acidity. Lakes are shallow and highly susceptible to acid rain. While acid precipitation levels are lower in Finland than they are in central Europe, Finland's distinctive bedrock and climate make its environment especially vulnerable. Over 50 percent of the sulfur in Finland's precipitation comes from other countries. Thus regional agreements will be necessary to significantly reduce the damage.

Water pollution. Finland is working to reduce the output of wastes from its own factories and from those of bordering nations into the Baltic Sea. Wastes are dumped from paper and pulp mills and from mining and other industries. Chemical runoff from farmland and other diffuse sources has also added to the problem.

Endangered species. Some 1,011 species of Finland's 40,000 known species of plants, animals, and birds are considered endangered. Most have been affected by changes to their natural habitats. Since 1950, 22 percent of Finland's wetlands have been destroyed.

Quality of Life

Life Expectancy (years)	75.0
Infant Mortality (per 1000)	6.0
Population Under 15 Years	18.4%
Population Over 65 Years	12.3%

Land Use and Habitats

Cropland (sq. miles):	9,471
per capita (acres)	1.2
global rank	24
Permanent Pasture (sq. miles):	475
total livestock (millions)	2.8
Forest and Woodlands (sq. miles):	89,660
Wilderness Area (sq. miles)	11,349
Maritime Areas (EEZ, sq. miles)	379
Protected Areas (sq. miles):	3,117
percent of total	2.4%
No. of Threatened Species:	
mammals	3
birds	12
plants	7

Energy and Industry

Energy Production:	
solids (trillion BTUs)	53
liquids (trillion BTUs)	0
gas (trillion BTUs)	0
nuclear (gigawatt-hours)	19,091
hydroelectric (gigawatt-hours)	12,952
Energy Requirements:	
traditional fuels (trillion BTUs)	28
total (trillion BTUs)	1,103
per capita (million BTUs)	222
per capita (global rank)	11
Industrial Share of GDP	35.4%
Industrial Energy Index	11
Metal Reserve Index (world=100%)	0.3%
No. of Motor Vehicles/1000 Persons	382

Water

Renewable Supply (cubic miles)	26.4
Total Use (cubic miles):	0.9
in agriculture	3.0%
in industry	85.0%
in homes and cities	12.0%

Waste and Pollution

Urban Solid Wastes (million tons):	2.0
per capita (tons)	330.7
Hazardous Wastes (000 tons)	253.5
Sewage Treatment Plant Coverage	75.0%
SOX Emissions (000 tons)	350.4
NOX Emissions (000 tons)	281.0

Waste and Pollution (cont.)

Particulate Emissions (tons)	NA
Hydrocarbon Emissions (tons)	199.5
No. of Cities Over 1 Million:	1
percent of population	20.3%

Population and Gross National Product

Population (millions)	GNP (billion $US)

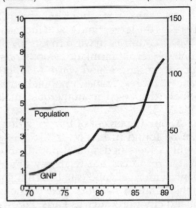

Commercial Energy Use

Total Energy Use (trillion BTUs)	Per Capita Energy Use (million BTUs)

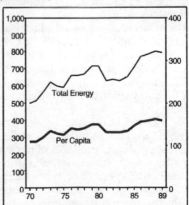

FRANCE

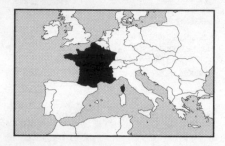

Total Area: 212,931 sq. miles
Global Rank: 45   Per Capita: 2.4 acres
Population: 56,138,000
Global Rank: 17   Growth Rate: 0.35%
Gross National Product: $953,916 m.
Global Rank: 5   Per Capita: $17,052
Greenhouse Gas Emissions
Global Share: 1.53%   Per Capita Rank: 49

France, which is about the size of Texas, is the largest and one of the most diverse countries in western Europe. It contains fertile farmland, woodlands, mountain ranges, and warm Mediterranean shores. France's population is widely dispersed in numerous small cities.

About 40 percent of Europe's flora can be found in France. It also has a highly diversified animal population. Water resources are relatively abundant, with rivers and canals forming a transportation network that includes inland city ports such as Paris. Forests and woodlands cover about 27 percent of the country's land area; about 57 percent is used for agriculture. About 8 percent of the country is protected natural areas.

Both farming and agro-industry are successful and widespread. Wheat, sugar beets, maize, and barley are France's principal crops. The chalky hillsides found in many regions make for the production of highly acclaimed wines.

France has limited reserves of coal, natural gas, and oil but is the world's highest per capita producer of nuclear power, which supplies the country with about 75 percent of its electricity. Hydropower resources also contribute to electricity production. Imported oil or gas still accounts for a large share of the country's energy supply.

Major Environmental Problems

Water pollution. Industrial pollution, nitrates from agricultural activities, and urban wastes make many French rivers badly polluted. Concentrations of nitrates, mainly from the runoff of animal manures and fertilizers from farms, have increased in the Loire River and are still very high in the Seine River.

The country has launched several major efforts to improve water quality. The portion of the population served by wastewater treatment plants has increased from 19 percent in 1970 to 52 percent in the late 1980s, but France still lags well behind most other countries in western Europe.

Air pollution. Air pollution remains a significant problem, especially in the major cities, where traffic congestion is also a major problem. Automobile exhausts and industrial combustion of fossil fuels are the major sources. France has set yearly goals for reducing the main air pollutants, such as sulfur oxides, nitrogen oxides, and carbon.

Forest damage. Damage to forests from acid rain and other pollutants has been moderate in France. About 6 percent of trees have been moderately to severely damaged; about 20 percent have suffered some damage.

FRANCE

Quality of Life

Life Expectancy (years)	75.9
Infant Mortality (per 1000)	8.0
Population Under 15 Years	19.8%
Population Over 65 Years	12.7%

Land Use and Habitats

Cropland (sq. miles):	73,819
per capita (acres)	0.8
global rank	51
Permanent Pasture (sq. miles):	44,780
total livestock (millions)	47.6
Forest and Woodlands (sq. miles):	57,073
Wilderness Area (sq. miles)	0
Maritime Areas (EEZ, sq. miles)	13,487
Protected Areas (sq. miles):	18,454
percent of total	8.7%
No. of Threatened Species:	
mammals	6
birds	21
plants	112

Energy and Industry

Energy Production:	
solids (trillion BTUs)	365
liquids (trillion BTUs)	145
gas (trillion BTUs)	115
nuclear (gigawatt-hours)	303,928
hydroelectric (gigawatt-hours)	51,158
Energy Requirements:	
traditional fuels (trillion BTUs)	97
total (trillion BTUs)	8,355
per capita (million BTUs)	149
per capita (global rank)	23
Industrial Share of GDP	29.3%
Industrial Energy Index	7
Metal Reserve Index (world=100%)	0.2%
No. of Motor Vehicles/1000 Persons	410

Water

Renewable Supply (cubic miles)	40.8
Total Use (cubic miles):	9.6
in agriculture	15.0%
in industry	69.0%
in homes and cities	16.0%

Waste and Pollution

Urban Solid Wastes (million tons):	30.2
per capita (tons)	399.3
Hazardous Wastes (000 tons)	3,306.0
Sewage Treatment Plant Coverage	52.0%
SOX Emissions (000 tons)	1,675.0
NOX Emissions (000 tons)	1,860.2

Waste and Pollution (cont.)

Particulate Emissions (tons)	328.4
Hydrocarbon Emissions (tons)	2,068.5
No. of Cities Over 1 Million:	3
percent of population	19.2%

Population and Gross National Product

Population (millions)	GNP (billion $US)

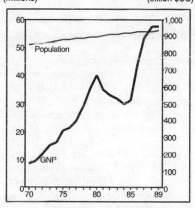

Commercial Energy Use

Total Energy Use (trillion BTUs)	Per Capita Energy Use (million BTUs)

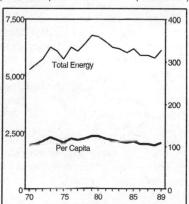

GERMANY

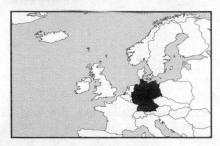

Total Area: 137,801 sq. miles
  Global Rank: 57   Per Capita: 1.1 acres
Population: 77,573,000
  Global Rank: 12   Growth Rate: -0.02%
Gross National Product: $1,202,789 m.
  Global Rank: 4   Per Capita: $19,633
Greenhouse Gas Emissions
  Global Share: 3.44%   Per Capita Rank: 21

October 3, 1990, marked the end of one of the most dramatic vestiges of World War II. On that date, the democratic government of West Germany and the collapsed communist government of East Germany were reunified into a single German nation.

The former West Germany is modern, urbanized, and industrialized. Like most other western market economies, western Germany has substantially improved its energy efficiency and made major investments to control air and water pollution. Although it is still dependent on imported oil and gas, the government is emphasizing energy conservation with programs to improve space-heating efficiency and upgrade insulation in buildings.

The former East Germany, in contrast, built an economy based on heavy industry that relied on domestic resources such as brown coal, or lignite. Industries such as steelmaking tended to use older, less efficient, heavily polluting technologies. Industrial plants were generally not well maintained, adding to pollution.

With the change to a market economy, many uncompetitive eastern German companies are expected to close, which should reduce emissions of air and water pollutants.

East Germany became subject to the environmental laws of West Germany and the European Community (EC)

when it formally joined West Germany in 1990. The EC's waste management, water quality, and air pollution provisions will be enforced in eastern Germany in 1996.

Major Environmental Problems

Air pollution. The southern part of eastern Germany has been devastated by air pollution from coal-burning utilities and industries. On a per capita basis, emissions of sulfur dioxide in eastern Germany are about 15 times greater than emissions in western Germany. These emissions contribute to acid rain problems. Industries and power plants also emit massive amounts of particulates. Most cars use leaded gasoline, which spews hazardous lead emissions into the air.

Water pollution. Raw sewage and industrial effluents laced with heavy metals and toxic chemicals have devastated the rivers in eastern Germany. Many of these pollutants are carried into the Baltic Sea, which is heavily polluted.

Forest damage. Forest damage from acid rain and other pollutants is a concern in both eastern and western Germany. In both sections of the country, as much as 50 percent of the trees are reported to have been damaged.

Quality of Life

Life Expectancy (years)	74.8
Infant Mortality (per 1000)	9.0
Population Under 15 Years	16.4%
Population Over 65 Years	15.5%

Land Use and Habitats

Cropland (sq. miles):	47,842
per capita (acres)	0.4
global rank	98
Permanent Pasture (sq. miles):	21,873
total livestock (millions)	60.2
Forest and Woodlands (sq. miles):	40,093
Wilderness Area (sq. miles)	0
Maritime Areas (EEZ, sq. miles)	195
Protected Areas (sq. miles):	19,128
percent of total	13.9%
No. of Threatened Species:	
mammals (former W.Germany)	2
birds (former W. Germany)	17
plants (former W. Germany)	16

Energy and Industry

Energy Production:	
solids (trillion BTUs)	5,392
liquids (trillion BTUs)	216
gas (trillion BTUs)	530
nuclear (gigawatt-hours)	161,281
hydroelectric (gigawatt-hours)	18,570
Energy Requirements:	
traditional fuels (trillion BTUs)	42
total (trillion BTUs)	10,001
per capita (million BTUs)	179
per capita (global rank)	18
Industrial Share of GDP	NA
Industrial Energy Index	NA
Metal Reserve Index (world=100%)	0.1%
No. of Motor Vehicles/1000 Persons	NA

Water

Renewable Supply (cubic miles)	23.0
Total Use (cubic miles):	12.1
in agriculture	19.6%
in industry	69.6%
in homes and cities	10.7%

Waste and Pollution

Urban Solid Wastes (million tons):	21
per capita (tons)	45.1
Hazardous Wastes (000 tons) (FDR)	15,659
Sewage Treatment Coverage (FDR)	90%
SOX Emissions (000 tons)	7,394
NOX Emissions (000 tons)	4,086

Waste and Pollution (cont.)

Particulate Emissions (tons) (FDR)	295
Hydrocarbon Emissions (tons)	3,498
No. of Cities Over 1 Million:	6
percent of population	11.9%

Population and Gross National Product

Population (millions)	GNP (billion $US)

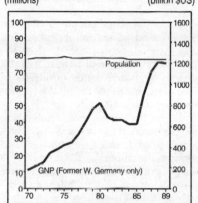

Commercial Energy Use

Total Energy Use (trillion BTUs)	Per Capita Energy Use (million BTUs)

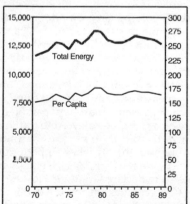

GREECE

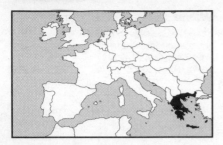

Total Area: 50,961 sq. miles
Global Rank: 88   Per Capita: 3.2 acres
Population: 10,047,000
Global Rank: 64   Growth Rate: 0.23%
Gross National Product: $52,927 m.
Global Rank: 34   Per Capita: $5,280
Greenhouse Gas Emissions
Global Share: 0.29%   Per Capita Rank: 42

Nephos is the name people have given to the cloud of air pollution hanging over Athens, where one third of the nation's population of 10 million lives. Nephos regularly sends hundreds of Greek citizens to the hospital with respiratory and heart complaints. It is the result of the rapid industrialization that occurred in the 1970s. Growth was heaviest in textiles, chemicals, and nonmetallic minerals, all of which are heavy polluters. Other sources are power stations, automobiles, and the high-sulfur oil used in central heating.

One component of the smog is sulfur dioxide, which degrades marble and other stone into gypsum that can wash away in the rain. This potent chemical reaction has already pocked and discolored Greece's priceless outdoor monuments and statues. Because more than 8 million tourists visit Greece each year, the damage poses a serious threat to the nation's economy.

The government has instituted control measures. Only a limited number of cars may enter the central part of the city on a given weekday. Auto traffic is limited and trucks are banned throughout the city when air pollution indices are too high; 19 such emergencies were declared from 1982 to 1989.

Greece relies on imported oil for about two thirds of its energy supply. The government is trying to encourage the replacement of oil with indigenous resources such as lignite and hydropower. Alternative energy sources such as solar and wind power also are increasingly being used. Greece has the largest area of solar collectors installed in Europe, and installations are increasing at a rate of about 10 percent a year. Photovoltaic and wind power stations have been installed on a number of the country's islands.

Major Environmental Problems

Air pollution. Pollution monitoring stations are in place throughout greater Athens, the major industrial area, and in 11 other Greek cities. Motor vehicles must now comply with emissions standards. Pollution levels in Athens, however, are still high.

Water pollution. Severe problems exist in some gulfs, notably Saronikos, where 50 percent of the country's industry is located, and Thermaikos. Industrial effluents are discharged untreated, and oil tankers and ships spill oil or empty bilges into water. Saronikos is a receptacle for all the municipal wastewater of greater Athens and for untreated sewage.

Runoff from farmlands can also be an important source of pollution. Since 1970 Greek farmers have doubled the amount of nitrogenous fertilizers that they apply to their land.

Quality of Life

Life Expectancy (years)	75.7
Infant Mortality (per 1000)	17.0
Population Under 15 Years	18.2%
Population Over 65 Years	13.1%

Land Use and Habitats

Cropland (sq. miles):	15,151
per capita (acres)	1.0
global rank	38
Permanent Pasture (sq. miles):	20,290
total livestock (millions)	18.6
Forest and Woodlands (sq. miles):	10,116
Wilderness Area (sq. miles)	0
Maritime Areas (EEZ, sq. miles)	1,950
Protected Areas (sq. miles):	400
percent of total	0.8%
No. of Threatened Species:	
mammals	4
birds	19
plants	531

Energy and Industry

Energy Production:	
solids (trillion BTUs)	268
liquids (trillion BTUs)	37
gas (trillion BTUs)	5
nuclear (gigawatt-hours)	0
hydroelectric (gigawatt-hours)	2,149
Energy Requirements:	
traditional fuels (trillion BTUs)	21
total (trillion BTUs)	909
per capita (million BTUs)	91
per capita (global rank)	37
Industrial Share of GDP	29.2%
Industrial Energy Index	15
Metal Reserve Index (world=100%)	0.3%
No. of Motor Vehicles/1000 Persons	127

Water

Renewable Supply (cubic miles)	10.8
Total Use (cubic miles):	1.7
in agriculture	63.0%
in industry	29.0%
in homes and cities	8.0%

Waste and Pollution

Urban Solid Wastes (million tons):	3.5
per capita (tons)	215.6
Hazardous Wastes (000 tons)	466.1
Sewage Treatment Plant Coverage	0.5%
SOX Emissions (000 tons)	396.7
NOX Emissions (000 tons)	105.3

Waste and Pollution (cont.)

Particulate Emissions (tons)	NA
Hydrocarbon Emissions (tons)	286.5
No. of Cities Over 1 Million:	1
percent of population	34.2%

Population and Gross National Product

Population	GNP
(millions)	(billion $US)

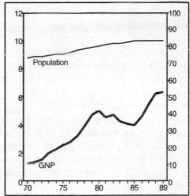

Commercial Energy Use

Total Energy Use	Per Capita Energy Use
(trillion BTUs)	(million BTUs)

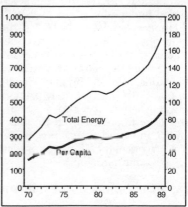

HUNGARY

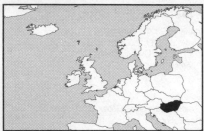

Total Area: 35,918 sq. miles
Global Rank: 101   Per Capita: 2.2 acres
Population: 10,552,000
Global Rank: 62   Growth Rate: -0.18%
Gross National Product: $27,656 m.
Global Rank: 53   Per Capita: $2,616
Greenhouse Gas Emissions
Global Share: 0.25%   Per Capita Rank: 61

Considered by some to be the most westernized nation in eastern Europe, Hungary is moving rapidly to a market economy. About 90 percent of all households possess televisions, washing machines, and refrigerators; automobile ownership is increasing, and food consumption has risen.

However, other things are not so bright: life expectancy is low for an industrialized country. Environmental pollution is thought to have played a significant role in shortening life spans; for example, an increasing number of children living in Hungary's industrial areas have developed chronic respiratory diseases. Pollution is considered most serious in the industrial regions, particularly in the northeast and around Budapest.

Hungary's relative lack of natural resources, such as coal, may have been a blessing in disguise for its environmental welfare. Coal provides only about one fifth of Hungary's energy supply, with the rest split primarily between natural gas and oil, both of which are imported from the former Soviet Union, and nuclear power. Hard currency prices for oil and gas are causing economic hardship.

Major Environmental Problems

Air pollution. The air is cleaner than in some neighboring countries, but it is still a significant problem in many urban and industrial areas. About 4.3 million people—41 percent of the population—are exposed to high levels of sulfur and nitrogen oxides; about 3.4 million people must cope with excessive particulate pollution. The sulfur dioxide emissions per square mile are much greater than those in many of the western European countries.

Water quality. While water quality is improving, it still remains a significant problem in many areas. Only about 20 percent of waste water is correctly treated; adequate sewerage facilities exist for only about 46 percent of the population. Out of approximately 3,000 settlements in Hungary, some 740—25 percent—do not have safe supplies of drinking water because of high levels of nitrate and arsenic pollution.

Lake pollution. Lake Balaton, one of the largest freshwater lakes in central Europe and an important recreational area in Hungary, has been threatened by sharply increased levels of industrial and municipal pollutants. Government efforts to improve water quality, which began in 1983, have helped; after updating 10 sewage treatment plants, the total amount of phosphorus entering the lake has been halved.

HUNGARY

Quality of Life

Life Expectancy (years)	70.2
Infant Mortality (per 1000)	20.0
Population Under 15 Years	17.8%
Population Over 65 Years	12.5%
Literacy Rate	NA
Malnourished Children	NA

Land Use and Habitats

Cropland (sq. miles):	20,413
per capita (acres)	1.2
global rank	20
Permanent Pasture (sq. miles):	4,622
total livestock (millions)	12.0
Forest and Woodlands (sq. miles):	6,517
1985 deforestation (sq. miles)	0
Wilderness Area (sq. miles)	0
Maritime Areas (EEZ, sq. miles)	0
Protected Areas (sq. miles):	1,974
percent of total	5.5%
No. of Threatened Species:	
mammals	2
birds	16
plants	21

Energy and Industry

Energy Production:	
solids (trillion BTUs)	211
liquids (trillion BTUs)	98
gas (trillion BTUs)	220
nuclear (gigawatt-hours)	13,889
hydroelectric (gigawatt-hours)	155
Energy Requirements:	
traditional fuels (trillion BTUs)	26
total (trillion BTUs)	1,274
per capita (million BTUs)	121
per capita (global rank)	31
Industrial Share of GDP	36.9%
Industrial Energy Index	34
Metal Reserve Index (world=100%)	0.1%
No. of Motor Vehicles/1000 Persons	169

Water

Renewable Supply (cubic miles)	1.4
Total Use (cubic miles):	1.3
in agriculture	30.0%
in industry	55.0%
in homes and cities	9.0%
Access to Safe Water:	
urban population	100.0%
rural population	95.0%

Urban Centers and Waste

No. of Cities Over 1 Million:	1
percent of population	20.0%
Solid Wastes (million tons)	1.9
Urban Sanitation Access	100.0%

Population and Gross National Product

Population (millions)	GNP (billion $US)

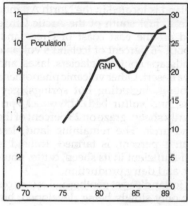

Commercial Energy Use

Total Energy Use (trillion BTUs)	Per Capita Energy Use (million BTUs)

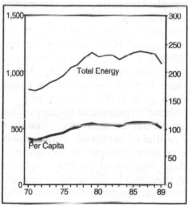

IRELAND

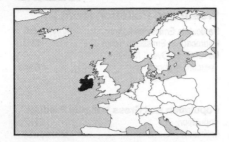

Total Area: 27,135 sq. miles
  Global Rank: 108   Per Capita: 4.7 acres
Population: 3,720,000
  Global Rank: 103   Growth Rate: 0.92%
Gross National Product: $29,590 m.
  Global Rank: 49   Per Capita: $8,028
Greenhouse Gas Emissions
  Global Share: 0.13%   Per Capita Rank: 30

Ireland is predominantly rural. Most of its area (82 percent) is used for agriculture, including peatlands (17 percent). Forests cover another 5 percent.

The country's resources include zinc, lead, and some oil and natural gas. Principal crops include turnips, potatoes, and barley. The country is not self-sufficient in food.

Traditional images of a countryside of thatched cottages are challenged by accelerating urbanization, farm development schemes, and energy demands. Environmental estimates foresee significant alterations in the Irish landscape within a generation.

Ireland's population is concentrated in three regions: Dublin/Dun Laoghaire, Cork/Cobh, and Shannon/Limerick. Today, over 40 percent of the Irish reside within 60 miles of the capital city.

Major Environmental Problems

Land use. In the south central region, between Shannon and the urbanized coast, farms are being consolidated—the average farm holding is now more than 100 acres. The use of fertilizers and pesticides on croplands has risen rapidly, adding to runoff problems. Hedgerow losses have been estimated at 14 percent since the mid-1970s, with negative consequences for wildlife habitat and plant diversity.

Forests. Ireland implemented a tree planting policy in 1947, creating many acres of new spruce and pine forest each year. However, these coniferous plantations create extensive tracts without much plant and animal diversity, and needle litter acidifies the soil. Ireland's broadleaf forests were nearly eliminated prior to World War II; they now account for less than 1 percent of the country's area. Half of these woodlands are in private hands.

Water. Only 2 percent of river channels have been classified as seriously polluted. However, an examination of 39 lakes since 1974 found excessive nutrient levels in 25 of them as a result of agricultural runoff.

Fossil fuel. Ireland's turf bogs are a unique ecological resource. Some raised bogs in the central region are as much as 23 feet deep and represent centuries of growth, but none are completely protected. Milled peat ranks third as a component of energy production, fueling 14 specialized electricity generating stations. Turf sods remain an important household fuel. Peat silt accumulates in lakes, however, introducing excessive amounts of suspended solids. Current stocks are estimated to last another 30 years, after which time the use of cleared bog lands is uncertain.

Quality of Life

Life Expectancy (years)	74.1
Infant Mortality (per 1000)	9.0
Population Under 15 Years	26.0%
Population Over 65 Years	10.1%

Land Use and Habitats

Cropland (sq. miles):	3,680
per capita (acres)	0.6
global rank	69
Permanent Pasture (sq. miles):	18,108
total livestock (millions)	11.8
Forest and Woodlands (sq. miles):	1,317
Wilderness Area (sq. miles)	0
Maritime Areas (EEZ, sq. miles)	1,468
Protected Areas (sq. miles):	104
percent of total	0.4%
No. of Threatened Species:	
mammals	0
birds	10
plants	4

Energy and Industry

Energy Production:	
solids (trillion BTUs)	47
liquids (trillion BTUs)	0
gas (trillion BTUs)	81
nuclear (gigawatt-hours)	0
hydroelectric (gigawatt-hours)	993
Energy Requirements:	
traditional fuels (trillion BTUs)	0
total (trillion BTUs)	379
per capita (million BTUs)	103
per capita (global rank)	34
Industrial Share of GDP	37.4%
Industrial Energy Index	34
Metal Reserve Index (world=100%)	0.3%
No. of Motor Vehicles/1000 Persons	263

Water

Renewable Supply (cubic miles)	12.0
Total Use (cubic miles):	0.2
in agriculture	10.0%
in industry	74.0%
in homes and cities	16.0%

Waste and Pollution

Urban Solid Wastes (million tons):	1.2
per capita (tons)	186.0
Hazardous Wastes (000 tons)	22.0
Sewage Treatment Plant Coverage	11.2%
SOX Emissions (000 tons)	163.1
NOX Emissions (000 tons)	84.9

Waste and Pollution (cont.)

Particulate Emissions (tons)	128.9
Hydrocarbon Emissions (tons)	70.5
No. of Cities Over 1 Million:	0
percent of population	0.0%

Population and Gross National Product

Population (millions)	GNP (billion $US)

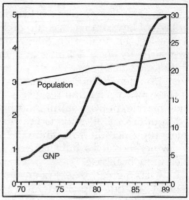

Commercial Energy Use

Total Energy Use (trillion BTUs)	Per Capita Energy Use (million BTUs)

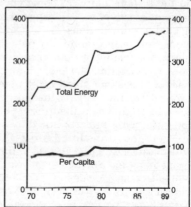

ITALY

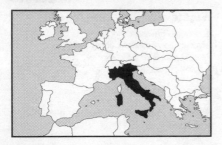

Total Area: 116,318 sq. miles
Global Rank: 65   Per Capita: 1.3 acres
Population: 57,061,000
Global Rank: 16   Growth Rate: -0.03%
Gross National Product: $858,018 m.
Global Rank: 6   Per Capita: $15,033
Greenhouse Gas Emissions
Global Share: 1.60%   Per Capita Rank: 47

Italy has given the western world a rich heritage of law, drama, art, and architecture. Yet the boot of Europe, which gave birth to ancient Rome and the Renaissance, has been slow to protect its environment in modern times.

The country's natural resources include marble, potash, sulfur, and limited supplies of oil and natural gas. Chief crops include fruits and vegetables, wine, and olives. Italy has a diversified industrial base.

Italy has a great variety of environmental laws, but implementation and enforcement have been slow. There are several explanations: the recession in the 1980s forced the government to defer expenses such as pollution control; and the responsibility for some environmental matters was transferred to regional administrations. As a result, among European Community nations Italy has a relatively poor record of applying environmental legislation.

There are some signs of change, however. Treatment plants that are designed to cut down on all forms of pollution are being built. Sulfur dioxide emissions have declined since the 1970s because of wider use of sulfur-free methane and a switch to the use of fossil fuels with a lower sulfur content. Political groups, such as the Italia Nostra and Green parties, have increased the level of environmental awareness among citizens.

At the national level there are some efforts to document the country's environmental problems. In 1986, Italy established a Ministry of Environment.

Maintaining Italy's heritage is important not only for historical reasons but for economic ones as well. Tourism is an important force in the economy. In 1990, 50 million tourists visited Italy.

Major Environmental Problems

Air pollution. Sulfur dioxide from industry and home heating is a threat to stone monuments. Acidic particles cause darkening of indoor artworks. Sulfur dioxide emissions have declined, but nitrogen oxide emissions remain high.

Water pollution. Coastal waters and inland rivers contain heavy loads of industrial and agricultural pollution. Acid rain has polluted lakes in the north. Industrial solvents dumped on land threaten to contaminate some local water supplies. Most lakes and rivers are too polluted for swimming. In the lagoon of Venice and along much of the Adriatic coast, the high phosphorus and nitrogen content is stimulating algal growth, which in turn depletes marine life. The Po, Adige, and Reno rivers are seriously contaminated with industrial, agricultural, and municipal effluents.

Quality of Life

Life Expectancy (years)	75.7
Infant Mortality (per 1000)	11.0
Population Under 15 Years	15.5%
Population Over 65 Years	12.8%

Land Use and Habitats

Cropland (sq. miles):	46,459
per capita (acres)	0.5
global rank	79
Permanent Pasture (sq. miles):	18,830
total livestock (millions)	31.4
Forest and Woodlands (sq. miles):	26,012
Wilderness Area (sq. miles)	0
Maritime Areas (EEZ, sq. miles)	2,132
Protected Areas (sq. miles):	5,021
percent of total	4.3%
No. of Threatened Species:	
mammals	3
birds	19
plants	151

Energy and Industry

Energy Production:	
solids (trillion BTUs)	12
liquids (trillion BTUs)	187
gas (trillion BTUs)	563
nuclear (gigawatt-hours)	0
hydroelectric (gigawatt-hours)	34,184
Energy Requirements:	
traditional fuels (trillion BTUs)	44
total (trillion BTUs)	6,579
per capita (million BTUs)	115
per capita (global rank)	32
Industrial Share of GDP	33.7%
Industrial Energy Index	6
Metal Reserve Index (world=100%)	0.1%
No. of Motor Vehicles/1000 Persons	424

Water

Renewable Supply (cubic miles)	43.0
Total Use (cubic miles):	13.5
in agriculture	59.0%
in industry	27.0%
in homes and cities	14.0%

Waste and Pollution

Urban Solid Wastes (million tons):	19.1
per capita (tons)	230.3
Hazardous Wastes (000 tons)	4,011.3
Sewage Treatment Plant Coverage	59.8%
SOX Emissions (000 tons)	2,655.8
NOX Emissions (000 tons)	1,873.4

Waste and Pollution (cont.)

Particulate Emissions (tons)	498.1
Hydrocarbon Emissions (tons)	911.4
No. of Cities Over 1 Million:	5
percent of population	25.4%

Population and Gross National Product

Population (millions)	GNP (billion $US)

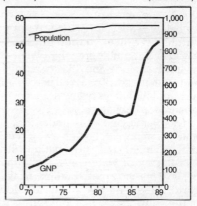

Commercial Energy Use

Total Energy Use (trillion BTUs)	Per Capita Energy Use (million BTUs)

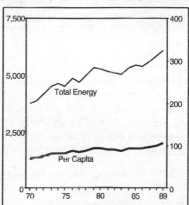

NETHERLANDS

Total Area: 14,413 sq. miles
 Global Rank: 116   Per Capita: 0.6 acres
Population: 14,951,000
 Global Rank: 52   Growth Rate: 0.63%
Gross National Product: $221,036 m.
 Global Rank: 14   Per Capita: $14,878
Greenhouse Gas Emissions
 Global Share: 0.52%   Per Capita Rank: 35

About 30 percent of the Netherlands lies below sea level. For centuries, the Dutch have been using pumps—driven by windmills until the advent of the steam engine—and dikes to reclaim land from the sea. Today, 60 percent of the population lives below sea level in a manmade habitat.

The Netherlands has undergone a rapid transformation from an agricultural to a highly industrial nation with a vast array of waterways, including major rivers and canals. Rotterdam, the world's largest port, is also the location of the world's largest oil refinery. Natural gas is the country's main natural resource.

The Netherlands is the most densely populated country in Europe and one of the most severely polluted countries in the world. About half the pollution in the Netherlands comes from other countries, including roughly 80 percent of the country's surface water pollution, 50 percent of its smog, and 60 percent of its acid rain. Pollution has taken a heavy toll on the environment. A third of the trees are dying, wildlife populations are dropping, and a number of species have become extinct.

The Netherlands is the first country in the world to adopt an explicit policy—the National Environmental Policy Plan—designed to create a sustainable society.

Major Environmental Problems

Water pollution. Three of Europe's industry-choked rivers (the Rhine, the Meuse, and the Schelde) converge on this small country and the North Sea. The rivers and the sea carry enormous quantities of pollution in the form of heavy metals, organic compounds, and nutrients such as nitrates and phosphates.

Air pollution. Even though the bicycle is still the most popular mode of transport, Dutch people drive the most cars per square mile and burn the most fossil fuel per person in Europe, creating levels of air pollution high enough to cause concern for human health, crops, and forests. Industrial activities such as refining also contribute to this problem. Emissions of sulfur dioxide have declined from about 490,000 tons in 1980 to about 240,000 tons in 1990, nearly fulfilling the country's commitment to cut emission levels by 50 percent from 1980 to 1995.

Drinking water contamination. Dutch farmers are among the most intense users of chemical fertilizers in the world. In addition, more and more animal manure is being put on the land. As a result, the groundwater is increasingly contaminated with high levels of nitrates.

NETHERLANDS

Quality of Life

Life Expectancy (years)	76.9
Infant Mortality (per 1000)	8.0
Population Under 15 Years	18.4%
Population Over 65 Years	11.7%

Land Use and Habitats

Cropland (sq. miles):	3,606
per capita (acres)	0.2
global rank	133
Permanent Pasture (sq. miles):	4,131
total livestock (millions)	20.0
Forest and Woodlands (sq. miles):	1,158
Wilderness Area (sq. miles)	0
Maritime Areas (EEZ, sq. miles)	327
Protected Areas (sq. miles):	1,371
percent of total	9.5%
No. of Threatened Species:	
mammals	2
birds	13
plants	7

Energy and Industry

Energy Production:	
solids (trillion BTUs)	0
liquids (trillion BTUs)	153
gas (trillion BTUs)	2,146
nuclear (gigawatt-hours)	4,022
hydroelectric (gigawatt-hours)	41
Energy Requirements:	
traditional fuels (trillion BTUs)	2
total (trillion BTUs)	2,803
per capita (million BTUs)	189
per capita (global rank)	15
Industrial Share of GDP	30.7%
Industrial Energy Index	12
Metal Reserve Index (world=100%)	NA
No. of Motor Vehicles/1000 Persons	362

Water

Renewable Supply (cubic miles)	2.4
Total Use (cubic miles):	3.5
in agriculture	34.0%
in industry	61.0%
in homes and cities	5.0%

Waste and Pollution

Urban Solid Wastes (million tons):	7.6
per capita (tons)	450.3
Hazardous Wastes (000 tons)	1,653.0
Sewage Treatment Plant Coverage	92.0%
SOX Emissions (000 tons)	319.6
NOX Emissions (000 tons)	622.6

Waste and Pollution (cont.)

Particulate Emissions (tons)	83.8
Hydrocarbon Emissions (tons)	439.7
No. of Cities Over 1 Million:	2
percent of population	14.0%

Population and Gross National Product

Population	GNP
(millions)	(billion $US)

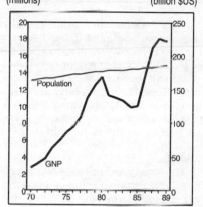

Commercial Energy Use

Total Energy Use	Per Capita Energy Use
(trillion BTUs)	(million BTUs)

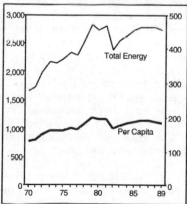

NORWAY

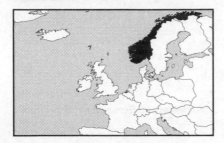

Total Area: 125,056 sq. miles
Global Rank: 62   Per Capita: 19.0 acres
Population: 4,212,000
Global Rank: 97   Growth Rate: 0.28%
Gross National Product: $92,425 m.
Global Rank: 24   Per Capita: $22,005
Greenhouse Gas Emissions
Global Share: 0.21%   Per Capita Rank: 13

No other country in Europe has such large areas of almost untouched wilderness as Norway. Only 3 to 4 percent of the country is arable or developed. Within its borders are 250,000 lakes, large forests, high plateaus, steep fjords, mountains, and valleys. The Nature Conservation Act protects about 4.4 percent of the country in national parks, forests, wetlands, and seabird colonies.

The long coastline has encouraged a venerable fishing tradition that continues today. During the past two decades, however, the importance of fishing to the Norwegian economy has declined.

Norway became a major producer of oil and gas beginning in the 1970s. By 1987, oil and gas exports accounted for about 12 percent of its gross national product. The country also has deposits of copper and nickel.

Hydropower provides nearly all the nation's electricity; nearly 75 percent of the economically exploitable water resources have been harnessed. Two thirds of the electricity produced is used by industries, including the aluminum and steel industries.

Industrial development has brought with it environmental problems common to most developed countries. In addition, pollution from sources outside Norway—especially the more heavily industrialized regions of central Europe and the United Kingdom—is a serious concern. Sulfur dioxide and nitrogen oxide emissions from other countries are carried to Norway, contributing about 90 percent of the acid rain, which has caused acidification of forests, rivers and lakes.

The government is intensely committed to reducing Norway's pollution and to working with other nations to curb regional and global problems. Protected natural areas constitute 15 percent of the country.

Major Environmental Problems

Acid rain. Lakes across almost 7,000 square miles in southern Norway have become so acidified that they no longer support fish. Forests are showing damage too. The country has reduced its own sulfur dioxide emissions by 60 percent over the past 10 years, and aims to halve the remaining emissions by 1993.

Air pollution. Since 1970 an increase in road traffic has led to a 40 percent increase in emissions of carbon dioxide, a greenhouse gas. Annual nitrogen oxide emissions increased from about 194,000 tons in 1975 to about 234,000 tons in 1990. Although emissions are low compared with those in other countries, they are becoming a problem within cities and industrial areas.

Quality of Life

Life Expectancy (years)	76.8
Infant Mortality (per 1000)	7.0
Population Under 15 Years	18.4%
Population Over 65 Years	15.3%

Land Use and Habitats

Cropland (sq. miles):	3,390
per capita (acres)	0.5
global rank	80
Permanent Pasture (sq. miles):	429
total livestock (millions)	4.0
Forest and Woodlands (sq. miles)	32,162
Wilderness Area (sq. miles)	21,724
Maritime Areas (EEZ, sq. miles)	7,818
Protected Areas (sq. miles):	18,407
percent of total	14.7%
No. of Threatened Species:	
mammals	3
birds	8
plants	12

Energy and Industry

Energy Production:	
solids (trillion BTUs)	10
liquids (trillion BTUs)	2,981
gas (trillion BTUs)	1,225
nuclear (gigawatt-hours)	0
hydroelectric (gigawatt-hours)	118,272
Energy Requirements:	
traditional fuels (trillion BTUs)	9
total (trillion BTUs)	1,553
per capita (million BTUs)	370
per capita (global rank)	6
Industrial Share of GDP	34.0%
Industrial Energy Index	9
Metal Reserve Index (world=100%)	0.8%
No. of Motor Vehicles/1000 Persons	382

Water

Renewable Supply (cubic miles)	97.2
Total Use (cubic miles):	0.5
in agriculture	8.0%
in industry	72.0%
in homes and cities	20.0%

Waste and Pollution

Urban Solid Wastes (million tons):	2.2
per capita (tons)	392.2
Hazardous Wastes (000 tons)	220.4
Sewage Treatment Plant Coverage	43.0%
SOX Emissions (000 tons)	81.5
NOX Emissions (000 tons)	242.4

Waste and Pollution (cont.)

Particulate Emissions (tons)	22.0
Hydrocarbon Emissions (tons)	270.0
No. of Cities Over 1 Million:	0
percent of population	0.0%

Population and Gross National Product

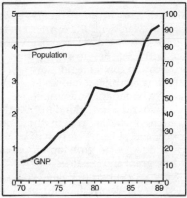

Population (millions) — GNP (billion $US)

Commercial Energy Use

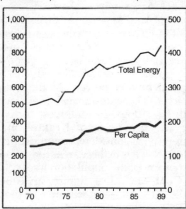

Total Energy Use (trillion BTUs) — Per Capita Energy Use (million BTUs)

POLAND

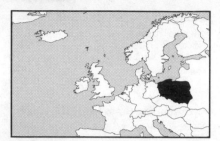

Total Area: 120,724 sq. miles
Global Rank: 64   Per Capita: 2.0 acres
Population: 38,423,000
Global Rank: 26   Growth Rate: 0.65%
Gross National Product: $64,542 m.
Global Rank: 31   Per Capita: $1,691
Greenhouse Gas Emissions
Global Share: 1.45%   Per Capita Rank: 28

Poland, whose name means *plain*, shares borders with the former Soviet Union, Germany, and Czechoslovakia. The Baltic Sea lies to its north. The northern and central regions are essentially flat. The land along Poland's southern boundary is mountainous.

The country has abundant natural resources, including coal, natural gas, copper, and silver. Nearly half of the area is devoted to growing crops, including grain and potatoes.

After World War II, Poland concentrated on an all-out drive to produce heavy industrial goods. The resulting factories use a great deal of energy and spew forth enormous amounts of air and water pollutants. The transition to a market economy is expected to improve Poland's environment, as inefficient industries will be forced to close.

Poland is one of the most polluted industrialized countries in the world. The problems are most serious in approximately 11 percent of the land, which has been designated as ecologically hazardous; the southwest, including the provinces of Krakow and Katowice, is considered the most polluted. And it is in these areas that about 35 percent of the population lives.

Coal—including lignite, an especially dirty fuel—is the source of most of Poland's energy and the culprit responsible for much of Poland's air and water pollution.

Pollution is measurably affecting human health: for example, a study of army inductees in Poland revealed that incidences of chronic bronchitis were more than three times higher in army recruitment centers in areas with high ambient sulfur dioxide levels than in those areas with cleaner air.

Major Environmental Problems

Air pollution. Poland's problems with air pollution are severe. Coal-fired power plants account for about 70 percent of Poland's emissions of sulfur dioxide and are a primary cause of respiratory ailments.

Water pollution. Over the past few decades, water pollution from industrial and municipal sources has increased dramatically. In 1983, only 6 percent of river water was considered clean enough for municipal use.

Forest damage. Poland's forests have been severely damaged, and they are considered among the worst in Europe; about three fourths of all trees in Poland show some damage from air pollution.

Hazardous Wastes. Industry generates an estimated 200,000 tons of hazardous waste annually, much of which is improperly disposed of.

POLAND

Quality of Life

Life Expectancy (years)	71.5
Infant Mortality (per 1000)	18.0
Population Under 15 Years	23.5%
Population Over 65 Years	9.1%
Literacy Rate	NA
Malnourished Children	NA

Land Use and Habitats

Cropland (sq. miles):	56,985
per capita (acres)	1.0
global rank	40
Permanent Pasture (sq. miles):	15,629
total livestock (millions)	35.0
Forest and Woodlands (sq. miles):	33,768
1985 deforestation (sq. miles)	0
Wilderness Area (sq. miles)	0
Maritime Areas (EEZ, sq. miles)	110
Protected Areas (sq. miles):	8,610
percent of total	7.1%
No. of Threatened Species:	
mammals	4
birds	16
plants	16

Energy and Industry

Energy Production:	
solids (trillion BTUs)	4,500
liquids (trillion BTUs)	8
gas (trillion BTUs)	136
nuclear (gigawatt-hours)	0
hydroelectric (gigawatt-hours)	3,761
Energy Requirements:	
traditional fuels (trillion BTUs)	29
total (trillion BTUs)	4,865
per capita (million BTUs)	127
per capita (global rank)	30
Industrial Share of GDP	NA
Industrial Energy Index	NA
Metal Reserve Index (world=100%)	0.4%
No. of Motor Vehicles/1000 Persons	128

Water

Renewable Supply (cubic miles)	11.9
Total Use (cubic miles):	4.0
in agriculture	24.0%
in industry	60.0%
in homes and cities	16.0%
Access to Safe Water:	
urban population	94.0%
rural population	82.0%

Urban Centers and Waste

No. of Cities Over 1 Million:	3
percent of population	17.5%
Solid Wastes (million tons)	57
Urban Sanitation Access	100.0%

Population and Gross National Product

Population (millions)   GNP (billion $US)

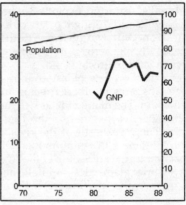

Commercial Energy Use

Total Energy Use (trillion BTUs)   Per Capita Energy Use (million BTUs)

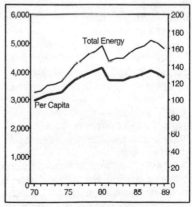

PORTUGAL

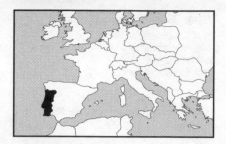

Total Area: 35,671 sq. miles
  Global Rank: 102   Per Capita: 2.2 acres
Population: 10,285,000
  Global Rank: 63   Growth Rate: 0.25%
Gross National Product: $44,145 m.
  Global Rank: 39   Per Capita: $4,303
Greenhouse Gas Emissions
  Global Share: 0.21%   Per Capita Rank: 70

Portugal's seafaring exploits shaped the New World during the Age of Exploration, but today the Atlantic breezes whisper across a much quieter, more inwardly directed land.

One of Europe's oldest countries, Portugal shares the Iberian peninsula with Spain. The mainland has two distinct regions, separated by the Tagus River. The area north of the river is mountainous, with a rainy, moderately cool climate; the area south of the river has rolling plains, less rainfall, and warmer weather, particularly in the interior.

The country's natural resources include fisheries, tungsten, iron, uranium, and marble. Almost 32 percent of the country is forested and 40 percent is cropland. Chief crops include grains, potatoes, olives, and grapes. Portugal also exports timber and timber products.

The Portuguese economy has a developing industrial sector. Major products are textiles, clothing, canned seafood, olive oil, and assembled automobiles. Portugal ranks among the world's 10 top countries in wine production and is the world's leading producer of cork.

Energy consumption has increased 68 percent during the 1980s, but it is low by European standards. The country is highly dependent on foreign energy sources.

Major Environmental Problems

Erosion. Portugal's soil is not very thick, fertile, or stable. Agricultural land, most of which is inland, has been overworked and topsoil has eroded, sometimes leaving behind bare rock. Yields per acre are about one third of the European average.

Water pollution. About 70 percent of Portugal's water pollution occurs in coastal areas. Heavy discharge is a serious threat to coastal wetlands and to underground water in some areas.

Air pollution. Portugal has air pollution problems at local and regional levels that are mainly caused by heavy concentrations of traffic or industry. This is exacerbated by adverse atmospheric conditions that prevent the normal dispersal of pollutants. The most serious pollution problems are in urban areas and in areas close to power stations and the cellulose and cement industries.

Toxic waste. Industry produces 180,000 tons of hazardous waste a year; 75 percent of it is dumped on land. Only one controlled landfill exists. The country is planning construction of a new system to properly handle this waste, which includes waste oil, cyanide, and heavy metals.

Quality of Life

Life Expectancy (years)	73.5
Infant Mortality (per 1000)	15.0
Population Under 15 Years	19.7%
Population Over 65 Years	11.8%

Land Use and Habitats

Cropland (sq. miles):	14,560
per capita (acres)	0.9
global rank	45
Permanent Pasture (sq. miles):	2,938
total livestock (millions)	10.2
Forest and Woodlands (sq. miles):	11,459
Wilderness Area (sq. miles)	0
Maritime Areas (EEZ, sq. miles)	6,850
Protected Areas (sq. miles):	1,752
percent of total	4.9%
No. of Threatened Species:	
mammals	6
birds	18
plants	90

Energy and Industry

Energy Production:	
solids (trillion BTUs)	4
liquids (trillion BTUs)	0
gas (trillion BTUs)	0
nuclear (gigawatt-hours)	0
hydroelectric (gigawatt-hours)	5,821
Energy Requirements:	
traditional fuels (trillion BTUs)	5
total (trillion BTUs)	567
per capita (million BTUs)	55
per capita (global rank)	50
Industrial Share of GDP	37.1%
Industrial Energy Index	14
Metal Reserve Index (world=100%)	0.3%
No. of Motor Vehicles/1000 Persons	155

Water

Renewable Supply (cubic miles)	8.2
Total Use (cubic miles):	2.5
in agriculture	48.0%
in industry	37.0%
in homes and cities	15.0%

Waste and Pollution

Urban Solid Wastes (million tons):	2.6
per capita (tons)	84.6
Hazardous Wastes (000 tons)	181.8
Sewage Treatment Plant Coverage	11.0%
SOX Emissions (000 tons)	224.8
NOX Emissions (000 tons)	105.8

Waste and Pollution (cont.)

Particulate Emissions (tons)	131.1
Hydrocarbon Emissions (tons)	171.9
No. of Cities Over 1 Million:	1
percent of population	15.6%

Population and Gross National Product

Population	GNP
(millions)	(billion $US)

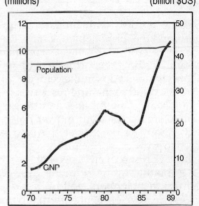

Commercial Energy Use

Total Energy Use	Per Capita Energy Use
(trillion BTUs)	(million BTUs)

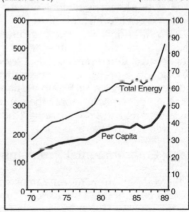

ROMANIA

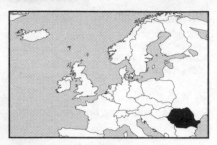

Total Area: 91,697 sq. miles
Global Rank: 75   Per Capita: 2.5 acres
Population: 23,272,000
Global Rank: 38   Growth Rate: 0.48%
Gross National Product: $53,559 m.
Global Rank: 32   Per Capita: $2,312
Greenhouse Gas Emissions
Global Share: 0.71%   Per Capita Rank: 39

Sharing borders with Bulgaria, Hungary, and the former Soviet Union, Romania is crossed by the Carpathian Mountains in the northeast and the Transylvanian Alps in the center.

The country's natural resources include coal, some oil and natural gas, timber, and some hydropower potential. About 44 percent of the land is used to grow crops, including corn and wheat. Forests cover 27 percent.

Romania, along with its Eastern European neighbors, followed a Soviet-style development pattern relying on heavy industry, especially metallurgy, oil refining, and petrochemicals. Industrial output, which appears to have stagnated since the early 1980s, also has used energy inefficiently and neglected environmental controls.

Air pollution has been less disastrous than in some neighboring countries because Romania depends less on coal, which supplies about one fourth of the country's energy. Economic hard times, however, could force the country to use its brown coal rather than imported natural gas and oil.

Major Environmental Problems

Industrial pollution. In some areas, industrial pollution is severe. For example, the town of Copsa Mica in central Romania is generally considered one of the most polluted places in Europe. Its two factories, one making black powder used in the manufacture of rubber, the other nonferrous metals, spew out about 30,000 tons of particles and soot each year on the town's 6,000 residents. Pollution controls are mostly lacking.

Water pollution. The water in about 85 percent of Romania's main rivers is not potable. In addition, some of these rivers contribute to cross-border pollution, especially pollution of the Tisza River's headwaters, which flow through Hungary's Danube River and then into the Black Sea. Much of the country's piped drinking water fails to meet health standards.

Soil erosion and degradation. About half of the country's solid domestic waste is dumped on the ground. Many industrial wastes are also disposed of in an uncontrolled manner. Important causes of soil degradation include particulate emissions from paint factories, steel yards, and metallurgical plants; mining in southern Romania; and overuse of chemical fertilizers. Approximately 30 percent of all arable land is threatened by erosion.

Disaster damage. Since 1970, the country has suffered two devastating floods, two large earthquakes that killed thousands, and the fallout of the Chernobyl nuclear accident.

Quality of Life

Life Expectancy (years)	70.2
Infant Mortality (per 1000)	22.0
Population Under 15 Years	21.8%
Population Over 65 Years	9.3%
Literacy Rate	NA
Malnourished Children	NA

Land Use and Habitats

Cropland (sq. miles):	39,961
per capita (acres)	1.1
global rank	30
Permanent Pasture (sq. miles):	17,027
total livestock (millions)	39.0
Forest and Woodlands (sq. miles):	24,602
1985 deforestation (sq. miles)	0
Wilderness Area (sq. miles)	0
Maritime Areas (EEZ, sq. miles)	123
Protected Areas (sq. miles):	2,168
percent of total	2.4%
No. of Threatened Species:	
mammals	2
birds	18
plants	68

Energy and Industry

Energy Production:	
solids (trillion BTUs)	709
liquids (trillion BTUs)	385
gas (trillion BTUs)	1,050
nuclear (gigawatt-hours)	0
hydroelectric (gigawatt-hours)	12,627
Energy Requirements:	
traditional fuels (trillion BTUs)	31
total (trillion BTUs)	3,059
per capita (million BTUs)	132
per capita (global rank)	28
Industrial Share of GDP	NA
Industrial Energy Index	NA
Metal Reserve Index (world=100%)	0.1%
No. of Motor Vehicles/1000 Persons	53

Water

Renewable Supply (cubic miles)	8.9
Total Use (cubic miles):	6.1
in agriculture	59.0%
in industry	33.0%
in homes and cities	8.0%
Access to Safe Water:	
urban population	100.0%
rural population	90.0%

Urban Centers and Waste

No. of Cities Over 1 Million:	1
percent of population	9.4%
Solid Wastes (million tons)	3.0
Urban Sanitation Access	100.0%

Population and Gross National Product

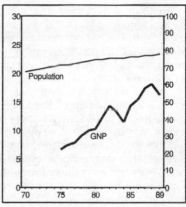

Population (millions)   GNP (billion $US)

Commercial Energy Use

Total Energy Use (trillion BTUs)   Per Capita Energy Use (million BTUs)

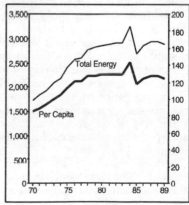

SOVIET UNION, FORMER

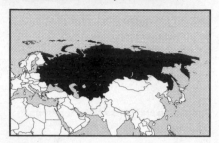

Total Area: 8,649,349 sq. miles
Global Rank: 1   Per Capita: 19.2 acres
Population: 288,595,000
Global Rank: 3   Growth Rate: 0.78%
Gross National Product: $2,659,500 m.
Global Rank: 3   Per Capita: $9,288
Greenhouse Gas Emissions
Global Share: 13.57%   Per Capita Rank: 15

The breakup of the former Union into 15 independent states revealed the extent of the environmental damage permitted and produced under the communist regime. Although information available on the individual republics remains sketchy, it is clear that the vast and varied terrain of the former U.S.S.R. has suffered from a variety of serious environmental problems, which have been passed on to new governments still struggling to establish frameworks and procedures for political and economic life. In a number of countries, however, environmental protests played a prominent role in the political movements that led to independence. Reflecting a strong new environmental consciousness of the people, care for the environment has high priority among the reforms pushed by many of the new states.

The republics, taken together, have abundant natural resources, including 30 percent of the world's reserves of iron ore and manganese, 20 percent of the standing timber, and about 25 percent of the energy resources, including petroleum, coal, oil, and natural gas. These resources are unevenly distributed among the republics.

The former Soviet policies of rapid industrialization were based on heavy industry without environmental controls, inefficient agriculture heavily dependent on toxic chemicals, and an inadequately monitored nuclear program. These practices have produced widespread and severe air, soil, and water pollution, soil degradation, deforestation, and desertification. The Aral Sea, once comparable to the largest of the Great Lakes, has dropped in size by 40 percent since the 1960s, exposing a saline sea bottom whose salt and sand have spread over surrounding territories in dust storms. In addition, the Chernobyl disaster and other instances of nuclear contamination continue to exact a high price in elevated rates of cancer and other diseases. These environmental problems are also unevenly distributed among the various republics.

Armenia

Total Area: 11,500 sq. miles
Population: 3,376,000

During the 1980s, two environmental disasters adversely affected Armenia. In 1986, fallout from the Chernobyl accident spread radioactivity over the country. In 1988, a major earthquake killed 55,000 people; a tremendous shortage of relief supplies hampered rescue efforts and increased the death toll. Soil pollution from toxic chemicals such as DDT is widespread. Polluted water is not treated. An environmental movement, which ultimately merged into the independence movement, began in the late 1980s around the issue of air pollution in the capital Yerevan.

Azerbaijan
Total Area: 33,400 sq. miles
Population: 7,137,000

Bordering on the polluted Caspian sea, Azerbaijan shares with neighboring Armenia such problems as soil pollution from the use of DDT. This pesticide, though technically banned in 1970, continued in widespread use during the 1970s and 1980s. Highly toxic defoliants were also extensively used in the monoculture of irrigated cotton. Water pollution is also a significant problem. About half of the townships lack sewers, and only about one quarter of polluted water receives proper treatment. Azerbaijan possesses extensive energy resources, including petroleum.

Belarus
Total Area: 80,100 sq. miles
Population: 10,260,000

Lying directly downwind of Chernobyl, which sits just over the border in neighboring Ukraine, Belarus received a heavy and widespread dose of radiation in the 1986 nuclear plant disaster. Chemical pollution of the soil is also widespread, with one quarter of soil samples showing excess levels of pesticides. Only 14 percent of the collective farm homes have piped hot water.

Estonia
Total Area: 17,400 sq. miles
Population: 1,582,000

Estonia has the smallest population of the new republics. It shares many of the problems of its neighbors bordering on the Baltic Sea, which is polluted by wastes both from industry and from the inadequate sewage treatment systems of the capital, Tallinn, and other cities. Although not severely polluted in comparison with some of the other states, the air contains a number of pollutants in excess of standards. As in the other Baltic states, environmental protests contributed to the movement that resulted in independence.

Georgia
Total Area: 26,900 sq. miles
Population: 5,464,000

Water pollution is a serious problem in Georgia, from the polluted Black Sea on which the country borders to the surface water, 70 percent of which is contaminated with bacteria. Digestive diseases are double the average of all the Baltics. Only 18 percent of the wastewater in the main port of Batumi receives proper treatment. Throughout the country, three fourths of polluted water is untreated. Overuse of pesticides has left almost half of the soil samples showing an excess of these toxic chemicals.

Kazakhstan
Total Area: 1,048,900 sq. miles
Population: 16,793,000

Two major man-made ecological catastrophes have despoiled large areas of Kazakhstan, seriously affecting both the people's health and the country's present and future prosperity. Nuclear pollution persists from hundreds of above- and below-ground atomic tests; the people of eastern Kazakhstan are reputed to have received larger doses of radiation than those of any other

SOVIET UNION, FORMER

country. In addition, local people blame animal and human diseases on radiation leaks from a military site used for dismantling nuclear weapons. Kazakhstan's 1990 declaration of sovereignty outlawed nuclear testing.

Waterways to the Aral Sea have been diverted for irrigation, with a devastating effect on Kazakhstan. Its once-thriving fishery has been destroyed and neighboring farmlands ruined by windblown salt and sand. The climate has become much more severe with the loss of the Aral's moderating influence. In addition, the irrigated lands, which have increased by 70 percent since 1960, are becoming increasingly saline. Overuse of agricultural chemicals is also widespread. In 1992, the country signed an agreement with an American oil company to develop its massive Tengiz oilfield.

Kyrgyzstan (formerly Kirgizia)

Total Area: 76,600 sq. miles
Population: 4,422,000

Like other Central Asian countries that grow irrigated cotton in arid soil, Kyrgyzstan has experienced increasing soil salinity. Water pollution is a serious problem, with one third of the people getting their water directly from streams and wells. In a given year, one quarter of the people suffer serious waterborne diseases, resulting in about 1,500 deaths a year, half of them babies less than one year old. On the collective farms, only 20 percent of homes have piped water. During the 1980s, however, the amount of land in forest reserves has increased. The Republic is also turning away from cotton monoculture and beginning to diversify its agriculture.

Latvia

Total Area: 24,900 sq. miles
Population: 2,681,000

Environmental protests about the pollution from a paper mill at Jurmala, a beach resort, helped spark the drive for Latvian independence in 1989. Air and water pollution are problems elsewhere in Latvia as well. The capital of Riga has an antiquated water treatment plant. Throughout the country, almost half the surface water is contaminated with bacteria. Auto exhaust from cars built without environmental controls account for 80 percent of the air pollution in Riga.

Lithuania

Total Area: 25,200 sq. miles
Population: 3,728,000

An increase in childhood diseases in the capital of Vilnius during the 1980s indicated a declining environment. More than one third of the country's surface water is contaminated with bacteria. In addition, the country depends heavily on the Ignalina nuclear reactor, which is of the dangerous design used at Chernobyl. Ignalina provides 70 percent of the country's electricity, as well as a major portion of its export earnings, through sales of electricity to Latvia and Belarus.

Moldova (formerly Moldavia)

Total Area: 13,000 sq. miles
Population: 4,367,000

High rates of disease and infant mortality result in part from excessive use of pesticides and fertilizers—six times the quantities per acre typically used in California—in the country's important fruit and vegetable growing industry, as well as bacterial contamination. Water pollution is widespread, with 40 percent of the groundwater showing bacterial contamination and 45 percent of the ponds and streams showing chemical contamination.

Russia

Total Area: 6,591,100 sq. miles
Population: 148,543,000

By far the largest of the new republics, Russia contains vast and varied natural resources as well as a variety of severe environmental problems. Chelyabinsk, a city in the southern Ural Mountains, may be the most radioactive place on Earth because of wastes and spills from its plutonium plant. Industries also threaten to pollute giant Lake Baikal, the world's deepest. Contributing to serious pollution of major rivers, urban air, and the soil are Russia's heavy industries and mines, built without environmental controls; its heavy dependence on coal-fired electric plants and ill-designed nuclear reactors; its antiquated urban infrastructure; and its excessive use of agricultural chemicals. Deforestation and soil erosion threaten some areas. Between 1970 and 1990, the life expectancy of Moscow dwellers dropped by 10 years. A 20 percent drop in soil humus occurred in many areas during the same period. However, investment in the environment plays an important part in current reforms.

Tajikistan (formerly Tadzhikistan)

Total Area: 55,200 sq. miles
Population: 5,358,000

Since the 1960s, irrigated land in Tajikistan has increased by 50 percent,

bringing with it the increasing soil salinity that also afflicts other Central Asian states practicing cotton monoculture. The Republic is beginning to diversify its agriculture, however, as farmers break away from Soviet-enforced emphasis on cotton. Sanitary facilities are inadequate, with only 15 percent of the collective farm homes possessing piped water. Tajikistan has the second highest infant mortality rate (43.2 per 1,000) among the new republics.

Turkmenistan (formerly Turkmenia)

Total Area: 188,400 sq. miles
Population: 3,714,000

Turkmenistan has been severely damaged by the former Soviet program of growing irrigated cotton in arid land. The amount of land under irrigation has increased 140 percent since the 1960s, bringing with it the salinization of the soil, overuse of agricultural chemicals, and pollution of local water supplies that have afflicted other Central Asian states as well. Turkmenistan also suffers from desertification and disease brought on by the salts and sand blown from the dried-up Aral Sea in neighboring Kazakhstan. With much of the land devoted to cotton, food supplies are inadequate and rates of disease very high. Infrastructure is inadequate, with about half the townships lacking sewers and piped water reaching only about 2 percent of collective farm homes. As a result, waterborne diseases cause about one quarter of infant deaths. In addition, the country borders on the polluted Caspian Sea. Turkmenistan has the lowest life expectancy (65.2 years) and the highest

SOVIET UNION, FORMER

infant mortality rate (54.7 per 1,000) among the new republics.

Ukraine

Total Area: 233,000 sq. miles
Population: 51,944,000

Home of Chernobyl, the Ukraine suffered enormous exposure to radiation following the accident. One tenth of the republic was contaminated, and many thousands of persons still live on, farm, and eat the produce of lands whose levels of background radiation are unsafe. Although the Chernobyl reactors have been ordered closed, the country depends on reactors of similar design for 40 percent of its power. Other types of pollution are also quite severe. Industrial pollution is particularly bad at Krivoy Rog in the southeast. The city of Odessa takes its drinking water from the extremely polluted Dniestr River. The city's cancer rate rose 27 percent in the 15 years after 1975, possibly because of this pollution. Kiev also has inadequate water treatment, and dioxins have been found in its water supply. In 1990, excessive fertilization and decay was noted in the Bay of Odessa on the Black Sea.

Uzbekistan

Total Area: 172,700 sq. miles
Population: 20,708,000

With a 50 percent increase in irrigated land since the 1960s, Uzbekistan has, like its Central Asian neighbors, suffered the effects of cotton monoculture, including soil salinization, water pollution, and excessive application of agricultural chemicals, including DDT, which contaminates some soil. The republic is now reducing its crop area devoted to cotton. Industrial wastes also pollute much of the country's water, and water treatment is inadequate. Less than 30 percent of polluted water is treated. Fewer than half the townships have sewers, and fewer than one quarter of the collective farm homes have piped water. Waterborne diseases cause about 20 percent of infant deaths. In addition, the country is heavily affected by the sand and salt blown from the dried-up Aral Sea, causing desertification and disease. Forest reserves have also decreased during the 1980s.

Source for Total Area and Population figures for the former Soviet Union given in the data notes at the end of the country profiles differ from the source for the same categories given in text for individual republics. For this reason, totals do not correspond. See Data Notes on Country Profiles for source of Population and Total Area figures.

SOVIET UNION, FORMER

Quality of Life

Life Expectancy (years)	70.0
Infant Mortality (per 1000)	24.0
Population Under 15 Years	24.8%
Population Over 65 Years	9.2%
Literacy Rate	NA
Malnourished Children	NA

Land Use and Habitats

Cropland (sq. miles):	890,463
per capita (acres)	2.0
global rank	6
Permanent Pasture (sq. miles):	1,432,819
total livestock (millions)	349.4
Forest and Woodlands (sq. miles):	3,652,510
1985 deforestation (sq. miles)	0
Wilderness Area (sq. miles)	2,903,559
Maritime Areas (EEZ, sq. miles)	17,337
Protected Areas (sq. miles):	92,949
percent of total	1.1%
No. of Threatened Species:	
mammals	20
birds	38
plants	531

Energy and Industry

Energy Production:	
solids (trillion BTUs)	14,299
liquids (trillion BTUs)	24,139
gas (trillion BTUs)	25,541
nuclear (gigawatt-hours)	213,001
hydroelectric (gigawatt-hours)	222,803
Energy Requirements:	
traditional fuels (trillion BTUs)	742
total (trillion BTUs)	55,540
per capita (million BTUs)	194
per capita (global rank)	13
Industrial Share of GDP	NA
Industrial Energy Index	NA
Metal Reserve Index (world=100%)	14.8%
No. of Motor Vehicles/1000 Persons	51

Water

Renewable Supply (cubic miles)	1051.9
Total Use (cubic miles):	84.7
in agriculture	65.0%
in industry	29.0%
in homes and cities	6.0%
Access to Safe Water:	
urban population	100.0%
rural population	100.0%

Urban Centers and Waste

No. of Cities Over 1 Million:	24.0
percent of population	15.3%
Solid Wastes (million tons)	45.8
Urban Sanitation Access	100.0%

Population

Population
(millions)

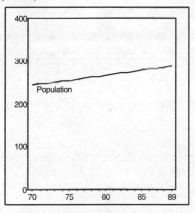

Commercial Energy Use

Total Energy Use
(trillion BTUs)

Per Capita Energy Use
(million BTUs)

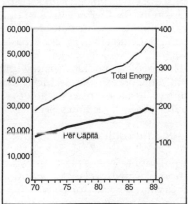

SPAIN

Total Area: 194,892 sq. miles
Global Rank: 48   Per Capita: 3.2 acres
Population: 39,187,000
Global Rank: 25   Growth Rate: 0.30%
Gross National Product: $376,075 m.
Global Rank: 11   Per Capita: $9,626
Greenhouse Gas Emissions
Global Share: 0.93%   Per Capita Rank: 60

Spain, the second largest country in Europe, has a varied climate. The north is wet, the south is relatively rainy, and the central plains are arid. Approximately 5 percent of Spain's land area is protected.

The country's natural resources include coal, some oil and gas, iron, uranium, and mercury. About 40 percent of the country is cropland.

In the past 30 years, the portion of Spain's population that is urban has increased from 56 to 78 percent. The largest concentration is in Madrid, the capital, which has a population of 3 million. The economy has changed from mainly agricultural to a mix of industry and services. Tourism is an important source of income but is also a source of environmental stress, especially on the Mediterranean coast during the summer. About half of Spain's urban population lives in large coastal cities.

Hydropower provides Spain with a significant portion of its electricity. The country's 10 nuclear reactors, however, provide nearly three times as much.

Major Environmental Problems

Air pollution. Spain's major cities suffer from elevated levels of air pollution. Per capita emissions of conventional pollutants are generally above the average for western Europe.

Water pollution. Poor sewage and water treatment facilities, as well as offshore oil and gas production, contribute to severe pollution in the Mediterranean. The population served by wastewater treatment facilities has increased dramatically, from 14 percent in 1975 to 48 percent in the late 1980s, but Spain still lags behind many of its European neighbors.

Farmers have nearly doubled their applications of nitrogen fertilizers since 1970. This has put added pressure on river water quality. For example, nitrate concentrations in the Guadalquivir are up about 25 percent since 1975.

Land degradation. Agricultural productivity is low by European standards because of poor soils, irregular rainfall, and inefficient farming practices. While a state-directed reforestation plan to increase wood production and contain soil erosion is under way, much of the new planting has been offset by recent losses from forest fires. In addition, monoculture plantations, notably eucalyptus, do not support biodiversity.

Forest damage. Tree damage is relatively light compared to that in most European countries; about 22 percent of Spain's forests have suffered some defoliation.

Quality of Life

Life Expectancy (years)	76.7
Infant Mortality (per 1000)	10.0
Population Under 15 Years	18.5%
Population Over 65 Years	12.0%

Land Use and Habitats

Cropland (sq. miles):	78,552
per capita (acres)	1.3
global rank	18
Permanent Pasture (sq. miles):	39,421
total livestock (millions)	51.1
Forest and Woodlands (sq. miles):	60,425
Wilderness Area (sq. miles)	0
Maritime Areas (EEZ, sq. miles)	4,708
Protected Areas (sq. miles):	13,556
percent of total	7.0%
No. of Threatened Species:	
mammals	6
birds	23
plants	449

Energy and Industry

Energy Production:	
solids (trillion BTUs)	452
liquids (trillion BTUs)	41
gas (trillion BTUs)	58
nuclear (gigawatt-hours)	56,124
hydroelectric (gigawatt-hours)	19,530
Energy Requirements:	
traditional fuels (trillion BTUs)	20
total (trillion BTUs)	3,221
per capita (million BTUs)	82
per capita (global rank)	40
Industrial Share of GDP	36.8%
Industrial Energy Index	27
Metal Reserve Index (world=100%)	0.5%
No. of Motor Vehicles/1000 Persons	295

Water

Renewable Supply (cubic miles)	26.5
Total Use (cubic miles):	10.9
in agriculture	62.0%
in industry	26.0%
in homes and cities	12.0%

Waste and Pollution

Urban Solid Wastes (million tons):	10.0
per capita (tons)	276.6
Hazardous Wastes (000 tons)	1,882.2
Sewage Treatment Plant Coverage	48.0%
SOX Emissions (000 tons)	3,581.5
NOX Emissions (000 tons)	1,046.9

Waste and Pollution (cont.)

Particulate Emissions (tons)	NA
Hydrocarbon Emissions (tons)	929.0
No. of Cities Over 1 Million:	2
percent of population	22.1%

Population and Gross National Product

Population (millions) | GNP (billion $US)

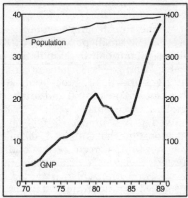

Commercial Energy Use

Total Energy Use (trillion BTUs) | Per Capita Energy Use (million BTUs)

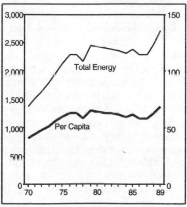

SWEDEN

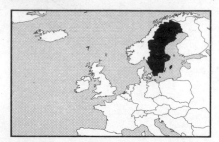

Total Area: 173,727 sq. miles
  Global Rank: 51   Per Capita: 13.2 acres
Population: 8,444,000
  Global Rank: 74   Growth Rate: 0.22%
Gross National Product: $184,999 m.
  Global Rank: 17   Per Capita: $21,958
Greenhouse Gas Emissions
  Global Share: 0.22%   Per Capita Rank: 55

Sweden, lying in the heart of Scandinavia, is the fourth largest country in Europe. The small population of 8.4 million—about half the population of greater London—is 85 percent urban and lives mostly in Stockholm and other cities in the central and southern region of the country.

Sweden has almost 100,000 lakes and a coastline that is about 4,700 miles long. About 62 percent of the land is forested. Sweden is rich in minerals such as iron ore, which is mined in central Sweden and from vast deposits in Lapland. Manufacturing has gradually evolved from the traditional production of timber and minerals to advanced industries, such as the production of special steels.

Sweden's main source of energy is electricity generated either by hydro-electric or nuclear plants. A 1980 referendum included a recommendation that all nuclear power be phased out by the year 2010. Substantial nuclear fallout hit the country from the Chernobyl accident in the former Soviet Union, causing the government to restrict freshwater fishing, mushroom picking, hunting, and reindeer farming in some areas. Following that disaster, the government decided to speed up the phaseout; two reactors will be closed in 1995 and 1996, respectively. To replace its nuclear power, Sweden expects to import more natural gas and coal.

Sweden has an ambitious environmental protection program. About 84 percent of the population is now served by advanced wastewater-treatment technology. Sulfur dioxide emissions have decreased by more than two thirds from the peak figures of the early 1970s and are now among the lowest in Europe.

Major Environmental Problems

Soil and water acidification. Sweden has made great strides in reducing sources of acid rain in its own country. In fact, only about 12 percent of all sulfur in acid deposition in Sweden comes from Swedish sources, with the rest coming from nearby countries, such as Poland and Germany. Soil tests in southern Sweden have found 3- to 30-fold increases in the acidity of the soil over the past 60 years. In southern Sweden, deposition is about 3 to 8 times above the level most soils can absorb without damage. Similarly, acidification has seriously affected about 16,000 lakes.

Pollution in the North and Baltic seas. Both seas have shown alarming signs of environmental stress, primarily as a result of farm runoffs of nitrogen. A massive bloom of planktonic algae in the North Sea in early 1988 caused a major fish kill off Sweden and Norway.

SWEDEN

Quality of Life

Life Expectancy (years)	77.1
Infant Mortality (per 1000)	6.0
Population Under 15 Years	17.7%
Population Over 65 Years	17.7%

Land Use and Habitats

Cropland (sq. miles):	11,015
per capita (acres)	0.8
global rank	52
Permanent Pasture (sq. miles):	2,154
total livestock (millions)	4.4
Forest and Woodlands (sq. miles):	108,185
Wilderness Area (sq. miles)	8,937
Maritime Areas (EEZ, sq. miles)	600
Protected Areas (sq. miles):	6,789
percent of total	3.9%
No. of Threatened Species:	
mammals	1
birds	14
plants	9

Energy and Industry

Energy Production:	
solids (trillion BTUs)	0
liquids (trillion BTUs)	0
gas (trillion BTUs)	0
nuclear (gigawatt-hours)	65,885
hydroelectric (gigawatt-hours)	72,105
Energy Requirements:	
traditional fuels (trillion BTUs)	113
total (trillion BTUs)	2,240
per capita (million BTUs)	266
per capita (global rank)	9
Industrial Share of GDP	34.8%
Industrial Energy Index	10
Metal Reserve Index (world=100%)	0.3%
No. of Motor Vehicles/1000 Persons	421

Water

Renewable Supply (cubic miles)	42.2
Total Use (cubic miles):	1.0
in agriculture	9.0%
in industry	55.0%
in homes and cities	36.0%

Waste and Pollution

Urban Solid Wastes (million tons).	2.9
per capita (tons)	290.5
Hazardous Wastes (000 tons)	551.0
Sewage Treatment Plant Coverage	95.0%
SOX Emissions (000 tons)	242.4
NOX Emissions (000 tons)	331.7

Waste and Pollution (cont.)

Particulate Emissions (tons)	187.3
Hydrocarbon Emissions (tons)	484.9
No. of Cities Over 1 Million:	1
percent of population	19.7%

Population and Gross National Product

Population (millions)	GNP (billion $US)

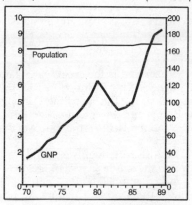

Commercial Energy Use

Total Energy Use (trillion BTUs)	Per Capita Energy Use (million BTUs)

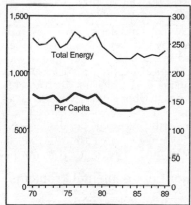

SWITZERLAND

Total Area: 15,942 sq. miles
Global Rank: 115   Per Capita: 1.5 acres
Population: 6,609,000
Global Rank: 84   Growth Rate: 0.42%
Gross National Product: $184,389 m.
Global Rank: 18   Per Capita: $28,019
Greenhouse Gas Emissions
Global Share: 0.16%   Per Capita Rank: 59

Tiny and pristine, green and mountainous, Switzerland hardly seems a likely site for environmental problems. Yet they exist.

Switzerland is the great watershed of Europe. The Rhine flows to the North Sea, the Inn feeds the Danube, the Rhone empties into the Mediterranean, and the Ticino is the source of the River Po.

The Alps run roughly east and west through the southern part of the country and constitute about 60 percent of Switzerland's area. The Jura Mountains stretch from southwest to northwest and occupy 10 percent of the territory. The remaining 30 percent is plateau, where the nation's larger cities and industrial sections are concentrated.

Switzerland lacks raw materials other than timber but is a well-developed manufacturing and finance center. Typical export products such as watches and precision instruments carry high labor value. Switzerland depends on the world economy for its prosperity; its small population—6.6 million—consumes only a fraction of what it produces.

Major Environmental Problems

Air pollution. Vehicles are the prime source of air pollution in Switzerland, so it has established emissions ceilings

well below the limits set by the European Community. The federal government has prohibited the import or refinery production of leaded gasoline.

Solid waste. More than 3.1 million tons of solid waste is collected from cities each year. About 80 percent of the waste is incinerated in more than 40 different installations, and more than half of those recycle the heat that is produced. During combustion, the chloride in polyvinyl chloride transforms itself into chlorhydric acid, which contributes to acid rain. Solid waste also includes harmful heavy metals such as mercury and cadmium.

Water pollution. Switzerland is among the leaders in Europe in treating municipal wastewater; about 90 percent of its population is served by wastewater treatment plants.

Pollution from agricultural sources, however, appears to be increasing. Swiss farmers have increased applications of nitrogen fertilizers by 86 percent since 1970, which is polluting rivers with nitrates. Nitrate concentrations in the Aare, for example, are up about 96 percent since 1975.

Biodiversity. A high percentage of Switzerland's plant and animal life is vulnerable to habitat destruction and pollution.

SWITZERLAND

Quality of Life

Life Expectancy (years)	77.1
Infant Mortality (per 1000)	7.0
Population Under 15 Years	16.4%
Population Over 65 Years	14.3%

Land Use and Habitats

Cropland (sq. miles):	1,591
per capita (acres)	0.2
global rank	134
Permanent Pasture (sq. miles):	6,212
total livestock (millions)	4.2
Forest and Woodlands (sq. miles):	4,062
Wilderness Area (sq. miles)	0
Maritime Areas (EEZ, sq. miles)	0
Protected Areas (sq. miles):	429
percent of total	2.7%
No. of Threatened Species:	
mammals	2
birds	15
plants	19

Energy and Industry

Energy Production:	
solids (trillion BTUs)	NA
liquids (trillion BTUs)	NA
gas (trillion BTUs)	0
nuclear (gigawatt-hours)	22,836
hydroelectric (gigawatt-hours)	29,772
Energy Requirements:	
traditional fuels (trillion BTUs)	8
total (trillion BTUs)	1,023
per capita (million BTUs)	155
per capita (global rank)	21
Industrial Share of GDP	NA
Industrial Energy Index	NA
Metal Reserve Index (world=100%)	NA
No. of Motor Vehicles/1000 Persons	439

Water

Renewable Supply (cubic miles)	10.2
Total Use (cubic miles):	0.8
in agriculture	4.0%
in industry	73.0%
in homes and cities	23.0%

Waste and Pollution

Urban Solid Wastes (million tons):	3.1
per capita (tons)	284.6
Hazardous Wastes (000 tons)	440.8
Sewage Treatment Plant Coverage	90.0%
SOX Emissions (000 tons)	81.5
NOX Emissions (000 tons)	213.8

Waste and Pollution (cont.)

Particulate Emissions (tons)	23.1
Hydrocarbon Emissions (tons)	335.0
No. of Cities Over 1 Million:	0
percent of population	0.0%

Population and Gross National Product

Population (millions)	GNP (billion $US)

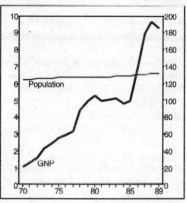

Commercial Energy Use

Total Energy Use (trillion BTUs)	Per Capita Energy Use (million BTUs)

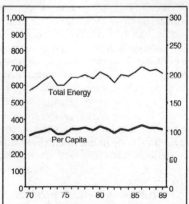

UNITED KINGDOM

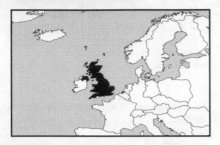

Total Area: 94,547 sq. miles
Global Rank: 73   Per Capita: 1.1 acres
Population: 57,237,000
Global Rank: 15   Growth Rate: 0.22%
Gross National Product: $837,778 m.
Global Rank: 7   Per Capita: $14,669
Greenhouse Gas Emissions
Global Share: 2.20%   Per Capita Rank: 27

The United Kingdom occupies the major part of the British Isles. Its terrain includes green hills and plains that slope to chalk cliffs and the sea. Densely populated in parts, it still considers its countryside and seacoast—the longest in Europe—important elements of national identity.

The country's natural resources include coal, North Sea oil and gas, tin, and limestone. Only 9.5 percent of the land is still forested, and 28 percent is devoted to cropland. Wheat, barley, and dairy products are the chief crops.

The United Kingdom was the cradle of the Industrial Revolution. "Fog everywhere," Dickens wrote about Victorian London, for London's industry and its hearths burned coal. The air of London is clear now, and even the Thames has been cleaned up to the point where salmon have returned. The United Kingdom has a complex environmental legal and regulatory structure, which covers land use, resource management, and pollution control. While it previously refused to limit sulfur dioxide emissions, it is now heavily involved in European Community deliberations and actions to limit emissions of greenhouse gases and other pollutants.

The United Kingdom produces a wide variety of products, everything from jets and sleek automobiles to traditional crumpets and woolens.

Major Environmental Problems

Air pollution. Even with emissions controls, the United Kingdom is responsible for 9 to 12 percent of the sulfur (the active ingredient in acid rain) deposited in Norway. Over 70 percent of the United Kingdom's sulfur dioxide emissions come from power stations. Nitrogen oxides are emitted from large combustion plants and vehicles.

Water pollution. Rivers are generally of good quality, but in some areas pollution from farm waste remains a major problem. In 1988, half of all serious water pollution incidents reported were caused by pollution from farms. The United Kingdom disposes of 17 percent of its sewage by dumping it into the sea; in 1989, 24 percent of the country's beaches reported water contaminated beyond the standards of the European Community. The United Kingdom is also considered one of the most significant polluters of the North Sea.

Radon. This colorless, odorless gas produces almost half the total radiation received by humans in the United Kingdom. It is estimated that about 75,000 houses may require remedial work because of excessive radon concentrations.

UNITED KINGDOM

Quality of Life

Life Expectancy (years)	75.3
Infant Mortality (per 1000)	9.0
Population Under 15 Years	19.6%
Population Over 65 Years	15.0%

Land Use and Habitats

Cropland (sq. miles):	26,008
per capita (acres)	0.3
global rank	110
Permanent Pasture (sq. miles):	43,232
total livestock (millions)	48.5
Forest and Woodlands (sq. miles):	9,127
Wilderness Area (sq. miles)	0
Maritime Areas (EEZ, sq. miles)	6,893
Protected Areas (sq. miles):	17,912
percent of total	18.9%
No. of Threatened Species:	
mammals	2
birds	22
plants	22

Energy and Industry

Energy Production:	
solids (trillion BTUs)	2,247
liquids (trillion BTUs)	3,657
gas (trillion BTUs)	1,634
nuclear (gigawatt-hours)	64,599
hydroelectric (gigawatt-hours)	6,969
Energy Requirements:	
traditional fuels (trillion BTUs)	3
total (trillion BTUs)	8,575
per capita (million BTUs)	150
per capita (global rank)	22
Industrial Share of GDP	37.9%
Industrial Energy Index	7
Metal Reserve Index (world=100%)	0.1%
No. of Motor Vehicles/1000 Persons	337

Water

Renewable Supply (cubic miles)	28.8
Total Use (cubic miles):	6.8
in agriculture	3.0%
in industry	77.0%
in homes and cities	20.0%

Waste and Pollution

Urban Solid Wastes (million tons):	22.0
per capita (tons)	343.0
Hazardous Wastes (000 tons)	2,424.4
Sewage Treatment Plant Coverage	84.0%
SOX Emissions (000 tons)	3,914.3
NOX Emissions (000 tons)	2,769.3

Waste and Pollution (cont.)

Particulate Emissions (tons)	564.2
Hydrocarbon Emissions (tons)	2,276.7
No. of Cities Over 1 Million:	4
percent of population	23.4%

Population and Gross National Product

Population	GNP
(millions)	(billion $US)

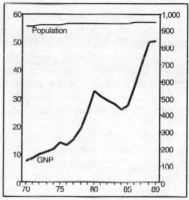

Commercial Energy Use

Total Energy Use	Per Capita Energy Use
(trillion BTUs)	(million BTUs)

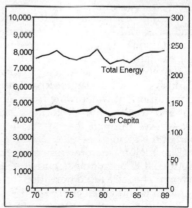

YUGOSLAVIA

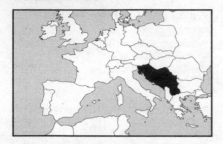

Total Area: 98,763 sq. miles
  Global Rank: 71   Per Capita: 2.7 acres
Population: 23,807,000
  Global Rank: 37   Growth Rate: 0.58%
Gross National Product: $76,825 m.
  Global Rank: 29   Per Capita: $3,296
Greenhouse Gas Emissions
  Global Share: 0.48%   Per Capita Rank: 68

Yugoslavia was formed in 1918 from the former kingdoms of Serbia and Montenegro plus parts of the Turkish and Austro-Hungarian empires. Of the region's 24 million people, about 8 million are Serbian and 4.5 million are Croatian. Other groups include Slovenians, Macedonians, and Montenegrans.

The country's political history has been turbulent. In 1991, that turbulence overflowed. Fighting broke out as the country splintered into ethnic fragments. Several declared independence, only to be attacked by the Serbian-dominated army. Armed ethnic groups continued to wage war in 1992, disrupting food supplies and destroying cities.

The region's terrain is one third lowland hills and plains and two thirds mountainous. It controls the most important land routes from central and western Europe to the Aegean Sea and Turkish straits. The Danube River—the most important water route from central and western Europe to the Black Sea—flows through the northeastern part of the region.

The region's natural resources include coal, copper, timber, and iron. Its economy began a rapid transition from agrarian to industrial after World War II. But little attention was paid to the replacement of old, polluting technologies with newer, cleaner ones. The problem was compounded by reliance on heavily polluting lignite (brown coal). Thermal power plants are the biggest contributors to air and water pollution.

Many towns and cities are seriously polluted, particularly in winter, when particles and fumes from coal mingle with exhaust from the chemical, plastics, and cement industries.

Major Environmental Problems

Air pollution. Mortality from respiratory diseases is twice as high in large cities as in small ones, and it is three times higher in large cities than it is in rural areas. Air pollution has also damaged the region's forests; in Slovenia, for example, nearly one fourth of the trees are moderately to severely defoliated.

Water pollution. Only half the country's total stream flow is clean enough for swimming, fishing, or, with purification, drinking. The most polluted river is the Sava, which deteriorated from having drinkable water to water that requires treatment even before industrial use.

Soil erosion. A high proportion of the country is subject to erosion because of deforestation and improper soil cultivation on steep land.

YUGOSLAVIA

Quality of Life

Life Expectancy (years)	72.1
Infant Mortality (per 1000)	25.0
Population Under 15 Years	21.1%
Population Over 65 Years	8.2%

Land Use and Habitats

Cropland (sq. miles):	29,985
per capita (acres)	0.8
global rank	54
Permanent Pasture (sq. miles):	24,525
total livestock (millions)	20.5
Forest and Woodlands (sq. miles):	36,039
Wilderness Area (sq. miles)	0
Maritime Areas (EEZ, sq. miles)	203
Protected Areas (sq. miles):	3,055
percent of total	3.1%
No. of Threatened Species:	
mammals	3
birds	17
plants	191

Energy and Industry

Energy Production:	
solids (trillion BTUs)	658
liquids (trillion BTUs)	155
gas (trillion BTUs)	81
nuclear (gigawatt-hours)	4,689
hydroelectric (gigawatt-hours)	23,731
Energy Requirements:	
traditional fuels (trillion BTUs)	34
total (trillion BTUs)	1,927
per capita (million BTUs)	81
per capita (global rank)	41
Industrial Share of GDP	49.4%
Industrial Energy Index	15
Metal Reserve Index (world=100%)	0.5%
No. of Motor Vehicles/1000 Persons	131

Water

Renewable Supply (cubic miles)	36.0
Total Use (cubic miles):	2.1
in agriculture	12.0%
in industry	72.0%
in homes and cities	16.0%

Waste and Pollution

Urban Solid Wastes (million tons):	2.7
per capita (tons)	63.3
Hazardous Wastes (000 tons)	NA
Sewage Treatment Plant Coverage	NA
SOX Emissions (000 tons)	1,818.3
NOX Emissions (000 tons)	209.4

Waste and Pollution (cont.)

Particulate Emissions (tons)	NA
Hydrocarbon Emissions (tons)	661.2
No. of Cities Over 1 Million:	1
percent of population	6.6%

Population and Gross National Product

Population (millions)	GNP (billion $US)

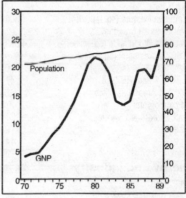

Commercial Energy Use

Total Energy Use (trillion BTUs)	Per Capita Energy Use (million BTUs)

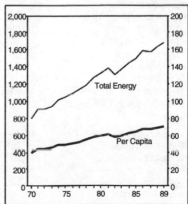

ALBANIA

Quality of Life

Life Expectancy (years)	71.6
Infant Mortality (per 1000)	39.0
Population Under 15 Years	30.3%
Population Over 65 Years	4.8%
Literacy Rate	NA
Malnourished Children	NA

Land Use and Habitats

Cropland (sq. miles):	2,730
per capita (acres)	0.5
global rank	77
Permanent Pasture (sq. miles):	1,556
total livestock (millions)	3.8
Forest and Woodlands (sq. miles):	4,039
1985 deforestation (sq. miles)	0
Wilderness Area (sq. miles)	0
Maritime Areas (EEZ, sq. miles)	47
Protected Areas (sq. miles):	210
percent of total	1.9%
No. of Threatened Species:	
mammals	2
birds	14
plants	76

Energy and Industry

Energy Production:	
solids (trillion BTUs)	33
liquids (trillion BTUs)	115
gas (trillion BTUs)	15
nuclear (gigawatt-hours)	0
hydroelectric (gigawatt-hours)	3,598
Energy Requirements:	
traditional fuels (trillion BTUs)	15
total (trillion BTUs)	148
per capita (million BTUs)	47
per capita (global rank)	56
Industrial Share of GDP	NA
Industrial Energy Index	X
Metal Reserve Index (world=100%)	0.1%
No. of Motor Vehicles/1000 Persons	NA

Water

Renewable Supply (cubic miles)	2.4
Total Use (cubic miles):	0.0
in agriculture	76.0%
in industry	18.0%
in homes and cities	6.0%
Access to Safe Water:	
urban population	100.0%
rural population	95.0%

Urban Centers and Waste

No. of Cities Over 1 Million:	0
percent of population	0.0%
Solid Wastes (million tons)	0.3
Urban Sanitation Access	100.0%

Population

Population
(millions)

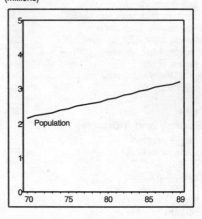

Commercial Energy Use

Total Energy Use (trillion BTUs)   Per Capita Energy Use (million BTUs)

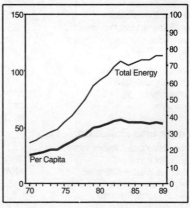

LUXEMBOURG

Quality of Life

Life Expectancy (years)	74.4
Infant Mortality (per 1000)	10.0
Population Under 15 Years	17.3%
Population Over 65 Years	12.9%

Land Use and Habitats

Cropland (sq. miles):	NA
per capita (acres)	NA
global rank	0
Permanent Pasture (sq. miles):	266
total livestock (millions)	NA
Forest and Woodlands (sq. miles):	335
Wilderness Area (sq. miles)	0
Maritime Areas (EEZ, sq. miles)	NA
Protected Areas (sq. miles):	0
percent of total	0.0%
No. of Threatened Species:	
mammals	1
birds	8
plants	2

Energy and Industry

Energy Production:	
solids (trillion BTUs)	NA
liquids (trillion BTUs)	NA
gas (trillion BTUs)	NA
nuclear (gigawatt-hours)	NA
hydroelectric (gigawatt-hours)	822
Energy Requirements:	
traditional fuels (trillion BTUs)	0
total (trillion BTUs)	161
per capita (million BTUs)	433
per capita (global rank)	4
Industrial Share of GDP	35.2%
Industrial Energy Index	X
Metal Reserve Index (world=100%)	NA
No. of Motor Vehicles/1000 Persons	470

Water

Renewable Supply (cubic miles)	0.2
Total Use (cubic miles):	0.0
in agriculture	13.0%
in industry	45.0%
in homes and cities	42.0%

Waste and Pollution

Urban Solid Wastes (million tons):	0.2
per capita (tons)	422.8
Hazardous Wastes (000 tons)	817.7
Sewage Treatment Plant Coverage	91.0%
SOX Emissions (000 tons)	13.2
NOX Emissions (000 tons)	20.9

Waste and Pollution (cont.)

Particulate Emissions (tons)	3.3
Hydrocarbon Emissions (tons)	22.0
No. of Cities Over 1 Million:	NA
percent of population	NA

Population and Gross National Product

Population (millions)   GNP (billion $US)

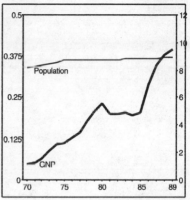

Commercial Energy Use

Total Energy Use (trillion BTUs)   Per Capita Energy Use (million BTUs)

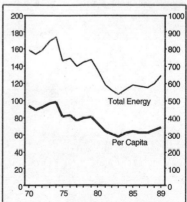

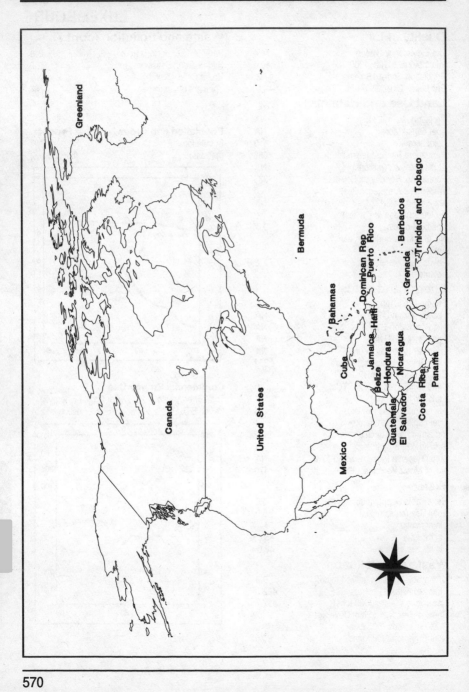

North America

This chapter contains environmental profiles for the North American countries listed, including those in Central America and the Caribbean. Technical notes and data sources are given beginning on page 641.

BARBADOS

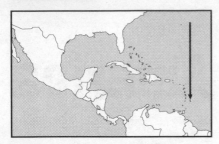

Total Area: 166 sq. miles
Global Rank: 145   Per Capita: 0.4 acres
Population: 255,000
Global Rank: 144   Growth Rate: 0.16%
Gross National Product: $1,669 m.
Global Rank: 117   Per Capita: $6,555
Greenhouse Gas Emissions
Global Share: 0.00%   Per Capita Rank: 85

Pear-shaped Barbados is the most easterly island in the Caribbean. Before it was settled in the 17th century, this island was covered by tropical forest. Within a century, British settlers had cleared all but a few remnants of woodland to plant sugar cane and other crops. Less than half of one percent of the land mass remains forested today. The island remained under British rule until it adopted a constitution and became independent in 1966.

Sugar, once the island's economic mainstay, is still a major export, but less than 5 percent of the population is currently employed in agricultural production. Since 1950, the amount of land under cultivation has fallen by a third, much of it going for housing.

Barbados is one of the most densely populated countries in the world. Each year the numbers of both long-stay tourists and cruise ship passengers substantially surpass the number of permanent inhabitants. Nonetheless, residents enjoy a fairly high standard of living, mostly from tourism and light manufacturing.

Barbados's main natural resources are its pleasant climate, its beaches, and its natural beauty. Coral reefs surround most of the island, habitat for fish that support an important local fishing industry. In 1980 the government established a marine reserve to protect 617 acres of coastline and reef.

Four other marine and coastal areas are being considered for protection.

Major Environmental Problems

Soil erosion. Although all of Barbados is prone to erosion because of shallow soils and lack of vegetative cover, erosion is particularly a problem in the hilly northeastern region of the island, which suffers periodic landslides and rock falls. In addition, mechanization of the sugar industry has increased erosion because growers make less use of the cane-hole system of planting. This effective soil conservation method developed in Barbados as a result of centuries of experience.

Coastal pollution. Oil slicks, apparently discharged as waste from passing ships, are a threat to the island's reefs and fishing industry. Flying fish, which are surface spawners, are particularly at risk.

Solid waste disposal. Barbados accepts and then incinerates wastes from ships calling at the port of Bridgetown. Open-air burning raises health hazards. Local waste is placed in sanitary landfills; identifying appropriate sites is becoming increasingly difficult. In addition, illegal garbage disposal pollutes gullies and old quarries and threatens to contaminate aquifers.

BARBADOS

Quality of Life

Life Expectancy (years)	74.6
Infant Mortality (per 1000)	11.0
Population Under 15 Years	23.6%
Population Over 65 Years	11.4%
Literacy Rate	NA
Malnourished Children	7.4%

Land Use and Habitats

Cropland (sq. miles):	127
per capita (acres)	0.3
global rank	106
Permanent Pasture (sq. miles):	15
total livestock (millions)	0.2
Forest and Woodlands (sq. miles):	0
1985 deforestation (sq. miles)	0
Wilderness Area (sq. miles)	0
Maritime Areas (EEZ, sq. miles)	646
Protected Areas (sq. miles):	0
percent of total	0.0%
No. of Threatened Species:	
mammals	1
birds	1
plants	1

Energy and Industry

Energy Production:	
solids (trillion BTUs)	0
liquids (trillion BTUs)	2
gas (trillion BTUs)	1
nuclear (gigawatt-hours)	0
hydroelectric (gigawatt-hours)	0
Energy Requirements:	
traditional fuels (trillion BTUs)	2
total (trillion BTUs)	13
per capita (million BTUs)	51
per capita (global rank)	54
Industrial Share of GDP	20.9%
Industrial Energy Index	NA
Metal Reserve Index (world=100%)	NA
No. of Motor Vehicles/1000 Persons	NA

Water

Renewable Supply (cubic miles)	0.0
Total Use (cubic miles):	0.0
in agriculture	7.0%
in industry	41.0%
in homes and cities	52.0%
Access to Safe Water:	
urban population	100.0%
rural population	100.0%

Urban Centers and Waste

No. of Cities Over 1 Million:	0
percent of population	0.0%
Solid Wastes (million tons)	0.0
Urban Sanitation Access	100.0%

Population and Gross National Product

Population (millions) — GNP (billion $US)

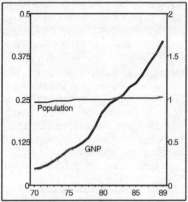

Commercial Energy Use

Total Energy Use (trillion BTUs) — Per Capita Energy Use (million BTUs)

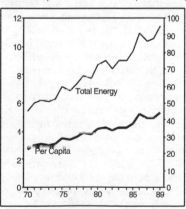

BELIZE

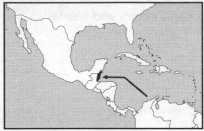

Total Area: 8,865 sq. miles
  Global Rank: 127   Per Capita: 30.3 acres
Population: 187,000
  Global Rank: 146   Growth Rate: 2.39%
Gross National Product: $313 m.
  Global Rank: 135   Per Capita: $1,717
Greenhouse Gas Emissions
  Global Share: 0.00%   Per Capita Rank: 147

Belize, a small English-speaking country with a spectacular barrier reef, nestles at the northern end of Central America on the Caribbean Sea. Formerly called British Honduras, the country gained independence in 1981.

Belize has the largest coral reef in the Western Hemisphere and the second largest in the world after Australia's Great Barrier Reef. An extremely rich ecosystem of coastal lagoons, mangrove swamps, and sea grass beds accompanies the reef and supports highly diverse sea life.

Forests, many of them managed and protected, cover 93 percent of the country and support highly diverse plant and animal life.

The country has a small population of less than 200,000 and a low population density of 18 persons per square mile. Although the population's natural rate of increase is 4 percent a year, heavy emigration drops the effective annual growth rate to 2.4 percent.

During its colonial period, Belize depended on timber and other forest products for its chief exports. Sugar cane was the leading agricultural export crop, but citrus fruit now holds that position. Tourism and construction are booming. The state promotes ecotourism in the reefs and forests.

Belize has no heavy industry and no energy source other than wood. Sugar cane, citrus processing, and banana packing are major light industries. Oil is imported from other Caribbean nations.

Because Belize still has a small population and is not heavily developed, it has few serious environmental problems. While its government appears committed to managing the forests and protecting the reefs, it often lacks the personnel and resources for effective management.

Major Environmental Problems

Water pollution. Near cities, surface water that is polluted with sewage, sugar cane processing effluent, and industrial wastes causes public health problems and damages the fish population. Only the capital city, Belmopan, is fully sewered.

Endangered species. Because of its expanse of rainforest, Belize has excellent wildlife populations. However, 55 of its species are threatened or endangered, including the green turtle, iguana, harpy eagle, spoonbill, wood stork, and certain hawks and parrots. The Belize Audubon Society is a strong advocate for wildlife protection.

Agricultural chemicals. Runoff of fertilizers, pesticides, and silt from the sugar cane fields in the north threatens the country's outstanding coral reefs.

Quality of Life

Life Expectancy (years)	NA
Infant Mortality (per 1000)	NA
Population Under 15 Years	NA
Population Over 65 Years	NA
Literacy Rate	NA
Malnourished Children	36.0%

Land Use and Habitats

Cropland (sq. miles):	216
per capita (acres)	NA
global rank	NA
Permanent Pasture (sq. miles):	185
total livestock (millions)	NA
Forest and Woodlands (sq. miles):	3,907
1985 deforestation (sq. miles)	35
Wilderness Area (sq. miles)	0
Maritime Areas (EEZ, sq. miles)	0
Protected Areas (sq. miles):	287
percent of total	3.2%
No. of Threatened Species:	
mammals	8
birds	4
plants	38

Energy and Industry

Energy Production:	
solids (trillion BTUs)	0
liquids (trillion BTUs)	0
gas (trillion BTUs)	0
nuclear (gigawatt-hours)	0
hydroelectric (gigawatt-hours)	0
Energy Requirements:	
traditional fuels (trillion BTUs)	3
total (trillion BTUs)	5
per capita (million BTUs)	NA
per capita (global rank)	NA
Industrial Share of GDP	22.6%
Industrial Energy Index	NA
Metal Reserve Index (world=100%)	NA
No. of Motor Vehicles/1000 Persons	NA

Water

Renewable Supply (cubic miles)	3.8
Total Use (cubic miles):	0.0
in agriculture	90.0%
in industry	0.0%
in homes and cities	10.0%
Access to Safe Water:	
urban population	94.0%
rural population	44.0%

Urban Centers and Waste

No. of Cities Over 1 Million:	0
percent of population	0.0%
Solid Wastes (million tons)	NA
Urban Sanitation Access	94.0%

Commercial Energy Use
Total Energy Use
(trillion BTUs)

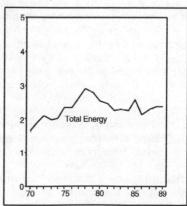

CANADA

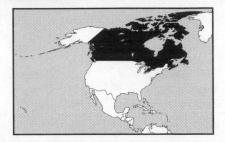

Total Area: 3,851,725 sq. miles
  Global Rank: 2   Per Capita: 92.9 acres
Population: 26,521,000
  Global Rank: 32   Growth Rate: 0.88%
Gross National Product: $531,647 m.
  Global Rank: 8   Per Capita: $20,224
Greenhouse Gas Emissions
  Global Share: 1.68%   Per Capita Rank: 8

Canada is the second largest country in the world, yet it is one of the least densely populated. Close to 90 percent of its inhabitants are concentrated in the region near the United States/Canada border. The remaining land is either sparsely populated or completely deserted.

Canada has abundant mineral resources and produces a wide range of metals and minerals, including nickel, zinc, asbestos, potash, copper, lead, and iron ore. It also has abundant energy resources, including uranium, oil, natural gas, and coal. The country's hydroelectric potential is enormous and currently accounts for two thirds of the electricity generated.

Canada also has huge timber resources, although they are being destroyed by improper timbering in some areas. Forests cover 36 percent of the country, and forestry was a $44 billion industry in 1987. Canada is the world's largest exporter of timber, pulp, and newsprint. Canada is also a major grain producer and an exporter of wheat.

The Atlantic provinces of Nova Scotia, Newfoundland, New Brunswick, and Prince Edward Island and the west-central provinces of Saskatchewan and Manitoba have a primarily agricultural economic base. Ontario and Quebec in the center of the country and British Columbia and Alberta in the west are the industrial centers of

Canada. Alberta is the principal oil and gas producer, British Columbia is the main lumber producer, and Quebec and Ontario are the largest producers of hydroelectricity.

As part of Canada's National Green Plan, the country is seeking to set aside 12 percent of its land as protected space. Only 5 percent is currently protected.

Major Environmental Problems

Acid rain. Acid rain, much of it of U.S. origin, has severely affected 150,000 Canadian lakes and has strained relations between the United States and Canada. Metal smelting in eastern Canada, coal-burning utilities in Canada and the United States, and vehicle emissions on both sides of the border have degraded the productivity of Canadian forests, with negative consequences for tourism and agriculture.

Marine habitat degradation. Canada is the world's largest exporter of fish, including cod, flounder, scallops, lobster, herring, and salmon. Fish habitats are being damaged by agriculture, mining, forestry, urban development, and industry. Almost one half of the shellfish-growing areas in Nova Scotia and 192 square miles in British Columbia are closed because of contaminated waters.

Quality of Life

Life Expectancy (years)	76.7
Infant Mortality (per 1000)	7.0
Population Under 15 Years	20.0%
Population Over 65 Years	10.0%

Land Use and Habitats

Cropland (sq. miles):	177,452
per capita (acres)	4.3
global rank	3
Permanent Pasture (sq. miles):	127,413
total livestock (millions)	24.1
Forest and Woodlands (sq. miles):	1,382,239
Wilderness Area (sq. miles)	2,473,308
Maritime Areas (EEZ, sq. miles)	11,349
Protected Areas (sq. miles):	190,935
percent of total	5.0%
No. of Threatened Species:	
mammals	5
birds	6
plants	13

Energy and Industry

Energy Production:	
solids (trillion BTUs)	1,628
liquids (trillion BTUs)	3,596
gas (trillion BTUs)	3,774
nuclear (gigawatt-hours)	79,871
hydroelectric (gigawatt-hours)	291,448
Energy Requirements:	
traditional fuels (trillion BTUs)	63
total (trillion BTUs)	10,509
per capita (million BTUs)	400
per capita (global rank)	5
Industrial Share of GDP	34.8%
Industrial Energy Index	15
Metal Reserve Index (world=100%)	6.1%
No. of Motor Vehicles/1000 Persons	457

Water

Renewable Supply (cubic miles)	696.1
Total Use (cubic miles):	10.1
in agriculture	8.4%
in industry	80.4%
in homes and cities	11.2%

Waste and Pollution

Urban Solid Wastes (million tons):	10.1
per capita (tons)	525.7
Hazardous Wastes (000 tons)	3,625.6
Sewage Treatment Plant Coverage	66.0%
SOX Emissions (000 tons)	4,081.8
NOX Emissions (000 tons)	2,141.2

Waste and Pollution (cont.)

Particulate Emissions (tons)	1,883.3
Hydrocarbon Emissions (tons)	2,486.1
No. of Cities Over 1 Million:	3
percent of population	29.8%

Population and Gross National Product

Population (millions)	GNP (billion $US)

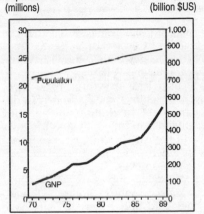

Commercial Energy Use

Total Energy Use (trillion BTUs)	Per Capita Energy Use (million BTUs)

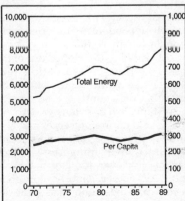

COSTA RICA

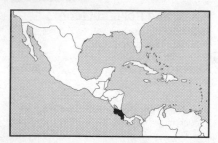

Total Area: 19,729 sq. miles
Global Rank: 111   Per Capita: 4.2 acres
Population: 3,015,000
Global Rank: 109   Growth Rate: 2.64%
Gross National Product: $4,884 m.
Global Rank: 84   Per Capita: $1,663
Greenhouse Gas Emissions
Global Share: 0.08%   Per Capita Rank: 41

One of the smallest Central American republics, Costa Rica is located in a narrow section of the isthmus between Nicaragua and Panama.

Costa Rica has three major geographic regions: the flat, open Caribbean coast lowlands, the interior highlands, and the hilly and irregular Pacific coast. The country is endowed with a rich variety of physical and biological resources.

Mineral resources are neither abundant nor widely exploited, although some gold and silver deposits have been mined. The country does have significant hydropower potential, and hydropower generates nearly 99 percent of the country's electricity; Costa Rica also exports electricity to neighboring countries. However, Costa Rica is largely dependent on imported fuels, particularly petroleum.

Costa Rica has developed one of the most ambitious conservation programs in the world, with a focus on preserving the country's biodiversity. It has established an extensive network of parks and nature preserves and also protects by law a significant portion of the country's remaining forests, much of which, however, remains in private hands. Altogether, slightly more than one fourth of the country has some degree of protection.

Although some species are threatened or endangered, the country remains rich in biodiversity. Increasing numbers of wildlife specialists are being trained to preserve this resource. The country recently set a precedent by licensing a major drug company to explore its fauna and flora for pharmaceutical purposes. A portion of the license fees and possible future royalties will be used to help preserve biodiversity.

Major Environmental Problems

Deforestation. Forests once covered almost all of Costa Rica. But these forests have largely been cleared for agriculture, and reforestation efforts have been limited. Since 1986, however, there has been some development of forest plantations and of agroforestry—combinations of trees and pasture. Deforestation has also been brought under better control in recent years. Experts estimate that without more substantial reforestation efforts, however, Costa Rica may have to import most of its wood before the end of the century.

Soil erosion. Deforestation has also led to land degradation. Forestland has been converted to pasture in areas with low-fertility soils on steep hillsides where heavy rainfall is common. This has resulted in serious soil erosion and poor productivity.

COSTA RICA

Quality of Life

Life Expectancy (years)	74.7
Infant Mortality (per 1000)	18.0
Population Under 15 Years	34.5%
Population Over 65 Years	3.4%
Literacy Rate	92.8%
Malnourished Children	8.0%

Land Use and Habitats

Cropland (sq. miles):	2,039
per capita (acres)	0.4
global rank	93
Permanent Pasture (sq. miles):	8,958
total livestock (millions)	2.1
Forest and Woodlands (sq. miles):	6,332
1985 deforestation (sq. miles)	251
Wilderness Area (sq. miles)	0
Maritime Areas (EEZ, sq. miles)	1,000
Protected Areas (sq. miles):	2,340
percent of total	11.9%
No. of Threatened Species:	
mammals	10
birds	14
plants	456

Energy and Industry

Energy Production:	
solids (trillion BTUs)	0
liquids (trillion BTUs)	0
gas (trillion BTUs)	0
nuclear (gigawatt-hours)	0
hydroelectric (gigawatt-hours)	3,330
Energy Requirements:	
traditional fuels (trillion BTUs)	32
total (trillion BTUs)	96
per capita (million BTUs)	33
per capita (global rank)	64
Industrial Share of GDP	26.7%
Industrial Energy Index	NA
Metal Reserve Index (world=100%)	0.0%
No. of Motor Vehicles/1000 Persons	53

Water

Renewable Supply (cubic miles)	22.8
Total Use (cubic miles):	0.3
in agriculture	89.0%
in industry	7.0%
in homes and cities	4.0%
Access to Safe Water:	
urban population	100.0%
rural population	84.0%

Urban Centers and Waste

No. of Cities Over 1 Million:	1
percent of population	33.7%
Solid Wastes (million tons)	0.3
Urban Sanitation Access	100.0%

Population and Gross National Product

Population
(millions)

GNP
(billion $US)

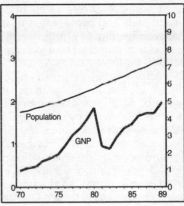

Commercial Energy Use

Total Energy Use
(trillion BTUs)

Per Capita Energy Use
(million BTUs)

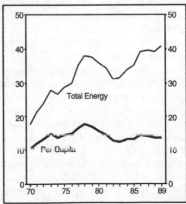

CUBA

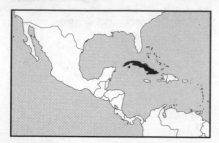

Total Area: 42,802 sq. miles
Global Rank: 97   Per Capita: 2.6 acres
Population: 10,608,000
Global Rank: 60   Growth Rate: 1.03%
Gross National Product: $20,900 m.
Global Rank: 59   Per Capita: $1,991
Greenhouse Gas Emissions
Global Share: 0.13%   Per Capita Rank: 92

The Republic of Cuba consists of numerous islets and cays located in the Caribbean Sea about 140 miles south of the Florida peninsula. The main island of Cuba is the largest in the West Indies and comprises flat or gently rolling plains, hills, and mountains that reach heights of 6,000 feet. The subtropical climate is moderated by trade winds.

Cuba's natural resources include cobalt, iron ore, copper, manganese, salt, timber, and the world's fourth largest deposits of nickel. Nickel is exported. Agricultural production includes citrus fruits, tobacco, coffee, rice, and beans. The country also is an exporter of shellfish. Cuba is a major exporter of sugar, planting 40 percent of its cultivated land with sugar cane. In the early 1980s, Cuba began burning bagasse—waste derived from the sugar cane production process—in place of oil in its sugar mills. Most other fuel must be imported.

Cuba has the greatest species diversity in the West Indies and the highest degree of endemic, or unique, species. With its expanse of wetlands and mangrove forests, Cuba plays host to the most diverse marine life of all the Antillean islands.

Cuba was the longest-held Spanish possession in the Americas, and Spanish is the principal language. Since the 1959 revolution, the government nationalized virtually all industry.

Health care and living standards for many Cubans have improved. However, the country's inefficient planned economy, coupled with a long-standing conflict with the United States that has barred Cuban sugar and tobacco exports from that market, has led to economic hardships and shortages or rationing of many commodities and virtually all luxuries. The country's relationship with Russia, on which it is dependent for oil, is changing rapidly.

Major Environmental Problems

Deforestation. In 1812, over 90 percent of Cuba was forested. By 1900, half of the forests had been removed, and in 1959 only 14 percent of the land was forested. After the 1959 revolution, however, reforestation efforts have protected watersheds and helped to prevent soil erosion. Shortages of lumber and other construction materials have also encouraged campaigns against waste. Cuba now has the lowest deforestation rate of any Latin American country.

Endangered wildlife. Records show that since 1800, over 100 vertebrate species have become extinct in Cuba. Human modifications of natural habitats, overhunting, and the introduction of exotic plants and animals have endangered additional species.

CUBA

Quality of Life

Life Expectancy (years)	75.2
Infant Mortality (per 1000)	15.0
Population Under 15 Years	23.2%
Population Over 65 Years	7.9%
Literacy Rate	94.0%
Malnourished Children	NA

Land Use and Habitats

Cropland (sq. miles):	12,853
per capita (acres)	0.8
global rank	57
Permanent Pasture (sq. miles):	11,471
total livestock (millions)	7.9
Forest and Woodlands (sq. miles):	10,637
1985 deforestation (sq. miles)	8
Wilderness Area (sq. miles)	0
Maritime Areas (EEZ, sq. miles)	1,401
Protected Areas (sq. miles):	2,758
percent of total	6.4%
No. of Threatened Species:	
mammals	2
birds	15
plants	874

Energy and Industry

Energy Production:	
solids (trillion BTUs)	0
liquids (trillion BTUs)	28
gas (trillion BTUs)	1
nuclear (gigawatt-hours)	0
hydroelectric (gigawatt-hours)	81
Energy Requirements:	
traditional fuels (trillion BTUs)	169
total (trillion BTUs)	616
per capita (million BTUs)	59
per capita (global rank)	46
Industrial Share of GDP	NA
Industrial Energy Index	X
Metal Reserve Index (world=100%)	4.6%
No. of Motor Vehicles/1000 Persons	NA

Water

Renewable Supply (cubic miles)	8.3
Total Use (cubic miles):	1.9
in agriculture	89.0%
in industry	2.0%
in homes and cities	9.0%
Access to Safe Water:	
urban population	NA
rural population	NA

Urban Centers and Waste

No. of Cities Over 1 Million:	1
percent of population	19.8%
Solid Wastes (million tons)	1.6
Urban Sanitation Access	NA

Population

Population
(millions)

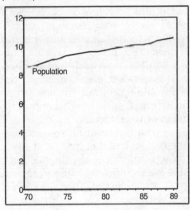

Commercial Energy Use

Total Energy Use   Per Capita Energy Use
(trillion BTUs)   (million BTUs)

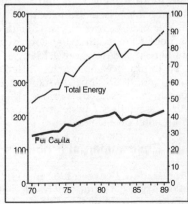

DOMINICAN REPUBLIC

Total Area: 18,814 sq. miles
  Global Rank: 112   Per Capita: 1.7 acres
Population: 7,170,000
  Global Rank: 83   Growth Rate: 2.22%
Gross National Product: $6,351 m.
  Global Rank: 78   Per Capita: $906
Greenhouse Gas Emissions
  Global Share: 0.04%   Per Capita Rank: 131

The Dominican Republic occupies the eastern section of the island of Hispaniola, which it shares with Haiti. It has close to 800 miles of coastline along the Atlantic Ocean and the Caribbean Sea. It is divided lengthwise by a central mountain range of volcanic origin, Cordillera Central, which reaches heights of 10,000 feet.

The country's natural resources include nickel, bauxite, gold, and silver. Although mining and minerals processing is a significant industry, agriculture is the major economic activity, along with tourism and other service-related industries and fisheries. The major crops include sugar cane, coffee, and cocoa.

As the Dominican Republic has become more urban, its resource consumption has risen dramatically. At the same time, a growing class of landless poor is exploiting the country's natural resources to survive. Many are forced to practice subsistence agriculture on mountain slopes or migrate to urban areas in search of scarce wage labor. The result is a wide array of environmental problems.

Major Environmental Problems

Deforestation. Between 1962 and 1980 the country lost a significant fraction of its forests. Laws now prohibit logging or woodcutting operations, but the clearing of forestlands for crop production, tourism development, or hydroelectric dams has been promoted with subsidies and tax shelters. Although an adequate legal and institutional framework exists for environmental management, the responsible agencies are plagued by conflicting mandates, understaffing, and little political clout. An illegal charcoal and fuelwood market provides a high proportion of urban energy needs. Little incentive exists for forest management or reforestation.

Water shortages. Deforestation undermines attempts at water resource management. Without forest cover to retain water after rains, rivers become raging torrents after tropical storms and recede to a trickle afterwards. The rivers and springs that provide water to the urban centers and the Cibao Valley's irrigation system are drying up. In the capital of Santo Domingo, water is one of the top commodities sold in sidewalk markets.

Soil erosion and marine degradation. Subsistence farming on mountain slopes and heavy rains on deforested terrain both result in rapid erosion of valuable topsoil. So large is the volume of topsoil carried by rivers to the sea that it chokes coral reefs, degrading habitats for aquatic life and reducing fishery stocks.

DOMINICAN REPUBLIC

Quality of Life

Life Expectancy (years)	65.8
Infant Mortality (per 1000)	65.0
Population Under 15 Years	36.3%
Population Over 65 Years	2.9%
Literacy Rate	83.3%
Malnourished Children	26.0%

Land Use and Habitats

Cropland (sq. miles):	5,583
per capita (acres)	0.5
global rank	85
Permanent Pasture (sq. miles):	8,077
total livestock (millions)	3.9
Forest and Woodlands (sq. miles):	2,382
1985 deforestation (sq. miles)	15
Wilderness Area (sq. miles)	0
Maritime Areas (EEZ, sq. miles)	1,038
Protected Areas (sq. miles):	26
percent of total	0.1%
No. of Threatened Species:	
mammals	1
birds	5
plants	NA

Energy and Industry

Energy Production:	
solids (trillion BTUs)	0
liquids (trillion BTUs)	0
gas (trillion BTUs)	0
nuclear (gigawatt-hours)	0
hydroelectric (gigawatt-hours)	952
Energy Requirements:	
traditional fuels (trillion BTUs)	26
total (trillion BTUs)	109
per capita (million BTUs)	16
per capita (global rank)	99
Industrial Share of GDP	25.5%
Industrial Energy Index	NA
Metal Reserve Index (world=100%)	0.1%
No. of Motor Vehicles/1000 Persons	17

Water

Renewable Supply (cubic miles)	4.8
Total Use (cubic miles):	0.7
in agriculture	89.0%
in industry	6.0%
in homes and cities	5.0%
Access to Safe Water:	
urban population	86.0%
rural population	28.0%

Urban Centers and Waste

No. of Cities Over 1 Million:	1
percent of population	30.7%
Solid Wastes (million tons)	0.9
Urban Sanitation Access	77.0%

Population and Gross National Product

Population (millions) — GNP (billion $US)

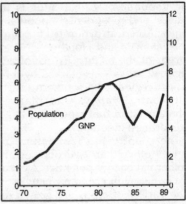

Commercial Energy Use

Total Energy Use (trillion BTUs) — Per Capita Energy Use (million BTUs)

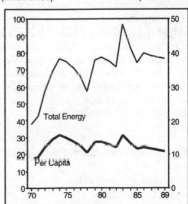

EL SALVADOR

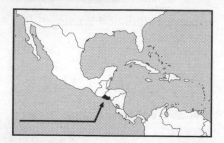

Total Area: 8,123 sq. miles
Global Rank: 128   Per Capita: 1.0 acres
Population: 5,252,000
Global Rank: 89   Growth Rate: 1.93%
Gross National Product: $5,634 m.
Global Rank: 82   Per Capita: $1,094
Greenhouse Gas Emissions
Global Share: 0.02%   Per Capita Rank: 145

The Republic of El Salvador is the smallest and most densely populated Central American nation. It is bordered by Guatemala and Honduras. Ninety percent of the country is of volcanic origin. El Salvador is marked by three distinct regions: the southern coastal belt, central valleys and plateaus (where most of the population lives), and northern mountains.

The country has few natural resources other than hydropower and geothermal energy potential. Agriculture is the main economic activity. A wide variety of crops are grown, including coffee, cotton, rice, beans, corn, and other grains. Agricultural products—especially coffee—are the country's principal exports. Industrial activities include the manufacture of textiles and clothing.

Most of El Salvador's land has been converted from forestland to farmland. Rapid population growth coupled with a greater use of the most productive lands for cash export crops displaced subsistence farmers and reduced production of basic foods such as maize, rice, and beans.

Major Environmental Problems

Deforestation. Today, less than 15 percent of the original forest cover remains, and most of this is highly degraded. Deforestation not only rep-resents the loss of a major natural resource but also leads to many other serious environmental problems.

Soil degradation. A major consequence of deforestation, soil loss or damage has been accelerated by the fragility of soils, steep terrain, and improper cultivation methods. Soil erosion has reached levels believed to be a serious threat to economic recovery of the agricultural sector.

Loss of water quality. Deforestation, soil erosion, and environmental pollution contribute to this already serious environmental problem. River water pollution threatens drinking water supplies. Lack of watershed management and deforestation leads to uncontrolled flooding and depleted groundwater supplies.

Loss of biodiversity. The loss of native plants and animals is very substantial. Most of the economically important species are now extinct, and little hope exists for successful reintroduction of these species because the environment has become so degraded.

Toxic wastes. There are few controls over the use and disposal of toxic chemicals. Buildup of chemicals in soil, livestock, food chains, and humans is a serious concern.

EL SALVADOR

Quality of Life

Life Expectancy (years)	62.2
Infant Mortality (per 1000)	64.0
Population Under 15 Years	42.5%
Population Over 65 Years	3.1%
Literacy Rate	73.0%
Malnourished Children	NA

Land Use and Habitats

Cropland (sq. miles):	2,830
per capita (acres)	0.4
global rank	102
Permanent Pasture (sq. miles):	2,355
total livestock (millions)	1.8
Forest and Woodlands (sq. miles):	402
1985 deforestation (sq. miles)	19
Wilderness Area (sq. miles)	0
Maritime Areas (EEZ, sq. miles)	355
Protected Areas (sq. miles):	101
percent of total	1.2%
No. of Threatened Species:	
mammals	6
birds	2
plants	24

Energy and Industry

Energy Production:	
solids (trillion BTUs)	0
liquids (trillion BTUs)	0
gas (trillion BTUs)	0
nuclear (gigawatt-hours)	0
hydroelectric (gigawatt-hours)	1,449
Energy Requirements:	
traditional fuels (trillion BTUs)	38
total (trillion BTUs)	83
per capita (million BTUs)	16
per capita (global rank)	98
Industrial Share of GDP	23.1%
Industrial Energy Index	NA
Metal Reserve Index (world=100%)	NA
No. of Motor Vehicles/1000 Persons	28

Water

Renewable Supply (cubic miles)	4.5
Total Use (cubic miles):	0.2
in agriculture	89.0%
in industry	4.0%
in homes and cities	7.0%
Access to Safe Water:	
urban population	76.0%
rural population	10.0%

Urban Centers and Waste

No. of Cities Over 1 Million:	0
percent of population	0.0%
Solid Wastes (million tons)	0.5
Urban Sanitation Access	86.0%

Population and Gross National Product

Population	GNP
(millions)	(billion $US)

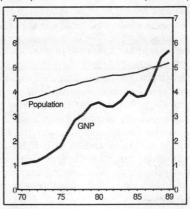

Commercial Energy Use

Total Energy Use	Per Capita Energy Use
(trillion BTUs)	(million BTUs)

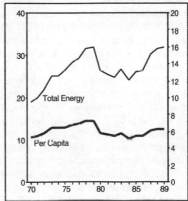

GUATEMALA

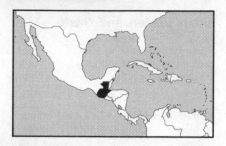

Total Area: 42,042 sq. miles
Global Rank: 98   Per Capita: 2.9 acres
Population: 9,197,000
Global Rank: 69   Growth Rate: 2.88%
Gross National Product: $7,980 m.
Global Rank: 71   Per Capita: $893
Greenhouse Gas Emissions
Global Share: 0.15%   Per Capita Rank: 76

Guatemala is a country with a rich cultural and biological heritage that has provided the country with strong tourism potential. Archeological ruins of the Olmec and Mayan cultures are scattered throughout the country. Guatemala also exhibits a startling array of natural environments. The country is divided into four major geographic regions: the Pacific coastal plain, the Pacific mountain chain, the interior highlands, and the Peten-Caribbean lowlands.

Guatemala is also a land deeply divided along political, cultural, and economic lines. Although the population is mostly rural, the largest city, Guatemala City, has a population of just under 1 million and is growing rapidly. About 45 percent of the population maintain indigenous lifestyles.

Guatemala's natural resources include nickel, tropical woods, some crude oil, and fisheries. Most energy supplies other than wood are imported. The economy is highly dependent on agricultural production, which accounts for virtually all of the country's exports. Chief crops include coffee, cotton, sugar cane, and bananas. The government has placed emphasis on the production of export crops at the expense of staple foods, necessitating increased food imports.

Agricultural land distribution in Guatemala is highly skewed, both in location and in size. Approximately 3 percent of landowners possess 65 percent of the land. The most fertile agricultural lands, those along the Atlantic and Pacific coasts, are dedicated to the large-scale production of export crops. Landless peasants are increasingly forced to farm severely sloped lands or to migrate to the northern lowlands.

Major Environmental Problems

Deforestation. Guatemala still has substantial forests covering more than one third of the country, but deforestation is proceeding at alarming rates. All over the country, forested lands are being cleared and converted to farming and ranching and to provide wood for household needs. An estimated three fourths of all households use fuelwood for domestic energy needs. The deforestation contributes to accelerated erosion and soil loss.

Biodiversity. Guatemala's natural environments, though relatively small, are exceptionally diverse. These ecosystems harbor a wide variety of the plant and animal species on which a large part of the population depends for its sustenance and economic well-being. Deforestation and other changes in land use are accelerating the rate of species extinction and thus reducing the country's biodiversity.

GUATEMALA

Quality of Life

Life Expectancy (years)	62.0
Infant Mortality (per 1000)	59.0
Population Under 15 Years	44.3%
Population Over 65 Years	2.5%
Literacy Rate	55.1%
Malnourished Children	68.0%

Land Use and Habitats

Cropland (sq. miles):	7,239
per capita (acres)	0.5
global rank	83
Permanent Pasture (sq. miles):	5,367
total livestock (millions)	3.6
Forest and Woodlands (sq. miles):	14,788
1985 deforestation (sq. miles)	347
Wilderness Area (sq. miles)	0
Maritime Areas (EEZ, sq. miles)	383
Protected Areas (sq. miles):	341
percent of total	0.8%
No. of Threatened Species:	
mammals	10
birds	10
plants	305

Energy and Industry

Energy Production:	
solids (trillion BTUs)	0
liquids (trillion BTUs)	7
gas (trillion BTUs)	0
nuclear (gigawatt-hours)	0
hydroelectric (gigawatt-hours)	2,092
Energy Requirements:	
traditional fuels (trillion BTUs)	84
total (trillion BTUs)	147
per capita (million BTUs)	17
per capita (global rank)	94
Industrial Share of GDP	NA
Industrial Energy Index	2
Metal Reserve Index (world=100%)	NA
No. of Motor Vehicles/1000 Persons	NA

Water

Renewable Supply (cubic miles)	27.8
Total Use (cubic miles):	0.2
in agriculture	74.0%
in industry	17.0%
in homes and cities	9.0%
Access to Safe Water:	
urban population	91.0%
rural population	41.0%

Urban Centers and Waste

No. of Cities Over 1 Million:	0
percent of population	0.0%
Solid Wastes (million tons)	0.7
Urban Sanitation Access	72.0%

Population and Gross National Product

Population
(millions)

GNP
(billion $US)

Commercial Energy Use

Total Energy Use
(trillion BTUs)

Per Capita Energy Use
(million BTUs)

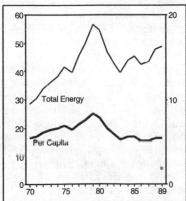

HAITI

Total Area: 10,714 sq. miles
Global Rank: 124   Per Capita: 1.1 acres
Population: 6,513,000
Global Rank: 85   Growth Rate: 2.01%
Gross National Product: $2,325 m.
Global Rank: 107   Per Capita: $364
Greenhouse Gas Emissions
Global Share: 0.01%   Per Capita Rank: 158

Haiti is a country in the West Indies that occupies the western third of the island of Hispaniola, which it shares with the Dominican Republic. Nearly 85 percent of the terrain is mountainous (the name Haiti comes from the Indian word meaning high ground). Although Haiti's climate is classified as tropical, rainfall is irregular, and extremes marked by droughts and hurricanes are not uncommon.

Haiti is the poorest country in the Western Hemisphere. Its natural resources are limited to bauxite, the ore from which aluminum is refined. Other than sugar refining and textile production, there is little industry. Most of the population is employed in subsistence agriculture and farming. Chief crops include coffee, sugar cane, cocoa, and sisal. Unemployment runs high, and many Haitians work abroad. Widespread poverty has exacerbated environmental problems.

After 40 years of dictatorship followed by a period of political instability, Haiti held democratic elections and installed a popularly elected government. Overthrow of this elected government, however, has led to an economic embargo, creating great hardship for Haitians. The crisis has hastened the devastation of forests through cutting for charcoal, often the only source of income available to people who are unemployed.

Major Environmental Problems

Deforestation. The extensive cutting of trees and shrubs for firewood and charcoal, Haiti's primary fuel sources, have devastated Haiti's forests. Less than 2 percent of the country remains forested. Cutting of the remaining trees is most severe in the impoverished rural areas. Cooking fuel is already in short supply in some areas.

Land degradation. Soil erosion, already severe, is accelerating as the pressure to expand food crops grows. Farmers seeking land are forced to move further up mountain slopes or into other marginal areas. Deforestation is adding to the problem as trees are cut down for fuel and agricultural practices increasingly focus on greater numbers of subsistence crops (cereal and corn) and fewer tree crops (coffee and cocoa). Exacerbating the condition are cultivation techniques that disregard soil conservation.

Water pollution. Although groundwater is plentiful in Haiti, safe drinking water is scarce. Sewage systems and sewage treatment are nonexistent. Outside the capital city of Port-au-Prince, less than 40 percent of the population has access to a safe water supply. As a result, waterborne diseases are widespread.

Quality of Life

Life Expectancy (years)	54.8
Infant Mortality (per 1000)	97.0
Population Under 15 Years	40.2%
Population Over 65 Years	3.9%
Literacy Rate	53.0%
Malnourished Children	51.0%

Land Use and Habitats

Cropland (sq. miles):	3,494
per capita (acres)	0.4
global rank	103
Permanent Pasture (sq. miles):	1,351
total livestock (millions)	4.6
Forest and Woodlands (sq. miles):	154
1985 deforestation (sq. miles)	8
Wilderness Area (sq. miles)	0
Maritime Areas (EEZ, sq. miles)	620
Protected Areas (sq. miles):	30
percent of total	0.3%
No. of Threatened Species:	
mammals	1
birds	4
plants	NA

Energy and Industry

Energy Production:	
solids (trillion BTUs)	0
liquids (trillion BTUs)	0
gas (trillion BTUs)	0
nuclear (gigawatt-hours)	0
hydroelectric (gigawatt-hours)	317
Energy Requirements:	
traditional fuels (trillion BTUs)	52
total (trillion BTUs)	63
per capita (million BTUs)	10
per capita (global rank)	120
Industrial Share of GDP	38.0%
Industrial Energy Index	NA
Metal Reserve Index (world=100%)	0.0%
No. of Motor Vehicles/1000 Persons	NA

Water

Renewable Supply (cubic miles)	2.6
Total Use (cubic miles):	0.0
in agriculture	68.0%
in industry	8.0%
in homes and cities	24.0%
Access to Safe Water:	
urban population	55.0%
rural population	36.0%

Urban Centers and Waste

No. of Cities Over 1 Million:	1
percent of population	15.8%
Solid Wastes (million tons)	0.4
Urban Sanitation Access	NA

Population and Gross National Product

Population (millions) GNP (billion $US)

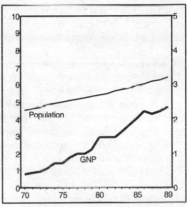

Commercial Energy Use

Total Energy Use (trillion BTUs) Per Capita Energy Use (million BTUs)

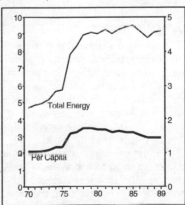

HONDURAS

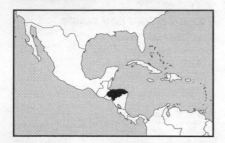

Total Area: 43,277 sq. miles
  Global Rank: 94   Per Capita: 5.4 acres
Population: 5,138,000
  Global Rank: 91   Growth Rate: 3.18%
Gross National Product: $4,628 m.
  Global Rank: 87   Per Capita: $930
Greenhouse Gas Emissions
  Global Share: 0.13%   Per Capita Rank: 57

Honduras is located in the middle of the Central American isthmus, bounded by Nicaragua, El Salvador, and Guatemala.

Honduras is economically the poorest Central American country and one of the poorest in the Western Hemisphere, but it is rich in renewable natural resources. The country has fertile coastal regions, which comprise 20 percent of the land. The remaining 80 percent is mountainous.

Biologically and climatologically, the country is located in a transition zone where tropical and temperate species can be found in reef, pine forest, savanna, and rainforest ecosystems. The reefs of the Caribbean coast, the cloud forests in central Honduras, and the Mayan archeological ruins of Copan are unique, albeit threatened, treasures.

The country's natural resources include timber and numerous minerals, among them gold, silver, copper, and lead. The Honduran economy is largely based on natural resources, which are being progressively degraded. Mining, textile production, and agriculture are important.

The country has a high birth rate, and immigration to urban areas is also rising rapidly. In consequence, urban populations are outgrowing the capacity of health, sanitation, education, and social institutions. Population growth

is also increasing pressure on natural resources as farmers seek more land to grow food.

Major Environmental Problems

Deforestation. Logging of pine and hardwoods, largely for export, is a major cause of deforestation, in large part because of improper logging practices. Deforestation is also aggravated by small farmers clearing land to grow subsistence crops.

Land degradation. Deforestation, uncontrolled development, and improper land use all contribute to land degradation. Farming on steep slopes and other marginal lands has led to widespread loss of soil and degradation of watersheds, bringing long-term decreases in agricultural productivity. Conflicts between large landholders and subsistence farmers have increased pressure on the landless, who are forced to continue to practice slash-and-burn agriculture on the hillsides.

Water pollution. The 34-square-mile Yojoa Lake, the country's largest freshwater source and a major source of fish, is threatened with contamination by heavy metals from a nearby mine. A number of rivers and streams are also at risk of poisoning by chemicals used in mining processes.

Quality of Life

Life Expectancy (years)	63.9
Infant Mortality (per 1000)	69.0
Population Under 15 Years	43.2%
Population Over 65 Years	2.8%
Literacy Rate	73.1%
Malnourished Children	34.0%

Land Use and Habitats

Cropland (sq. miles):	6,988
per capita (acres)	0.9
global rank	48
Permanent Pasture (sq. miles):	9,846
total livestock (millions)	3.2
Forest and Woodlands (sq. miles):	12,896
1985 deforestation (sq. miles)	347
Wilderness Area (sq. miles)	4,347
Maritime Areas (EEZ, sq. miles)	776
Protected Areas (sq. miles):	2,739
percent of total	6.3%
No. of Threatened Species:	
mammals	7
birds	11
plants	48

Energy and Industry

Energy Production:	
solids (trillion BTUs)	0
liquids (trillion BTUs)	0
gas (trillion BTUs)	0
nuclear (gigawatt-hours)	0
hydroelectric (gigawatt-hours)	879
Energy Requirements:	
traditional fuels (trillion BTUs)	52
total (trillion BTUs)	84
per capita (million BTUs)	17
per capita (global rank)	92
Industrial Share of GDP	25.1%
Industrial Energy Index	NA
Metal Reserve Index (world=100%)	0.0%
No. of Motor Vehicles/1000 Persons	9

Water

Renewable Supply (cubic miles)	24.5
Total Use (cubic miles):	0.3
in agriculture	91.0%
in industry	5.0%
in homes and cities	4.0%
Access to Safe Water:	
urban population	89.0%
rural population	60.0%

Urban Centers and Waste

No. of Cities Over 1 Million:	0
percent of population	0.0%
Solid Wastes (million tons)	0.5
Urban Sanitation Access	88.0%

Population and Gross National Product

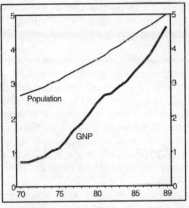

Population (millions) — GNP (billion $US)

Commercial Energy Use

Total Energy Use (trillion BTUs) — Per Capita Energy Use (million BTUs)

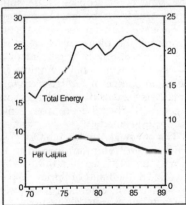

JAMAICA

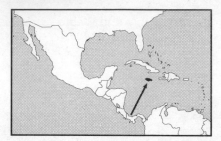

Total Area: 4,243 sq. miles
  Global Rank: 135   Per Capita: 1.1 acres
Population: 2,456,000
  Global Rank: 113   Growth Rate: 1.21%
Gross National Product: $3,507 m.
  Global Rank: 98   Per Capita: $1,445
Greenhouse Gas Emissions
  Global Share: 0.03%   Per Capita Rank: 98

The third largest island in the Caribbean, Jamaica is approximately 150 miles long and 20 to 50 miles wide. The island harbors a wide variety of landforms and habitats, ranging from sandy beaches and mangrove swamps to the rugged limestone terrain of the Cockpit Country and the crests of the Blue Mountains, which rise to more than 7,400 feet. It is home to many endemic animal and plant species: 27 birds, 20 lizards, 82 ferns, and 784 flowering plants are found nowhere else in the world.

The country's natural resources include bauxite, gypsum, and limestone, as well as local fisheries, a favorable climate, and recreational opportunities that make the island a tourist destination. The chief crops include sugar cane, citrus fruits, bananas, coffee, and cocoa as well as cannabis, which is produced for the illegal drug trade. Jamaica imports over 95 percent of its energy. Tourism, a major employer, is the main source of foreign exchange. Jamaica is the world's third largest producer of the bauxite ore from which aluminum is made.

The Arawaks, who inhabited Jamaica when Columbus landed on its shores in 1494, called their home Xayamaca, the Land of Springs. Spanish and British colonial rule brought the decimation of the Arawaks. Today, three fourths of the population is of African and European origin. Jamaica gained its independence in 1962.

Major Environmental Problems

Land degradation. Livestock grazing and subsistence crop cultivation, often on steep slopes, are destroying forests and causing erosion. Only about 17 percent of the country remains covered by forests, and these are threatened by conversion to timber and coffee plantations. The country's annual soil loss is estimated at 80 million tons. As the habitats for endemic animals and plants are destroyed, some of these species face extinction.

Water pollution. In the Kingston metropolitan area, which houses one third of Jamaica's population, discharge of sewage and industrial effluent has contaminated groundwater. Rapid growth of this urban area exacerbates the problem. The drastic pollution of the Kingston Harbor and urban expansion have severely reduced local fisheries. Untreated sewage has also caused instances when north coast beaches are polluted to levels higher than are acceptable for recreational swimming.

Mining pollution. Bauxite mining disturbs large tracts of land. Waste from the processing of bauxite and alumina has polluted air and groundwater.

Quality of Life

Life Expectancy (years)	72.5
Infant Mortality (per 1000)	17.0
Population Under 15 Years	30.9%
Population Over 65 Years	6.6%
Literacy Rate	98.4%
Malnourished Children	7.0%

Land Use and Habitats

Cropland (sq. miles):	1,039
per capita (acres)	0.3
global rank	114
Permanent Pasture (sq. miles):	734
total livestock (millions)	1.0
Forest and Woodlands (sq. miles):	718
1985 deforestation (sq. miles)	8
Wilderness Area (sq. miles)	0
Maritime Areas (EEZ, sq. miles)	1,149
Protected Areas (sq. miles):	0
percent of total	0.0%
No. of Threatened Species:	
mammals	6
birds	2
plants	8

Energy and Industry

Energy Production:	
solids (trillion BTUs)	0
liquids (trillion BTUs)	0
gas (trillion BTUs)	0
nuclear (gigawatt-hours)	0
hydroelectric (gigawatt-hours)	114
Energy Requirements:	
traditional fuels (trillion BTUs)	5
total (trillion BTUs)	63
per capita (million BTUs)	26
per capita (global rank)	77
Industrial Share of GDP	42.0%
Industrial Energy Index	13
Metal Reserve Index (world=100%)	0.6%
No. of Motor Vehicles/1000 Persons	18

Water

Renewable Supply (cubic miles)	2.0
Total Use (cubic miles):	0.1
in agriculture	86.0%
in industry	7.0%
in homes and cities	7.0%
Access to Safe Water:	
urban population	95.0%
rural population	46.0%

Urban Centers and Waste

No. of Cities Over 1 Million:	0
percent of population	0.0%
Solid Wastes (million tons)	0.3
Urban Sanitation Access	14.0%

Population and Gross National Product

Population (millions)	GNP (billion $US)

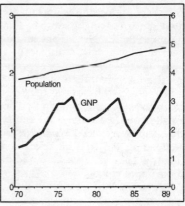

Commercial Energy Use

Total Energy Use (trillion BTUs)	Per Capita Energy Use (million BTUs)

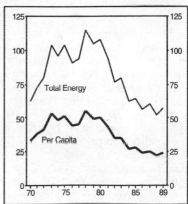

MEXICO

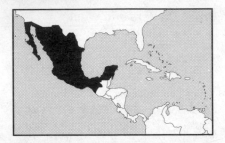

Total Area: 756,049 sq. miles
Global Rank: 13   Per Capita: 5.5 acres
Population: 88,598,000
Global Rank: 11   Growth Rate: 2.20%
Gross National Product: $202,132 m.
Global Rank: 16   Per Capita: $2,332
Greenhouse Gas Emissions
Global Share: 2.01%   Per Capita Rank: 62

Mexico is bounded on the north by the United States and on the south by Guatemala and Belize. Dry steppe and desert terrain cover most of the northern half, while the southern part is in a tropical zone. Several tropical forests are located in the southern region, some in the state of Quintana Roo and the Valley of Mexico. Average rainfall in the south can exceed 120 inches per year, feeding the five biggest rivers, including the Grijalva-Usumacinta and the Papaloapan.

More than half of the country's crops are grown on arid or semiarid lands, which make up approximately three fourths of the country. Much of this land is also at elevations above 4,200 feet in the northern and central plateaus.

The country has important natural resources, including oil, gold, silver, copper, and lead. Mexico is an oil exporter. Despite rapidly growing industrial and service sectors, agriculture remains a major activity. The principal crops include corn, cotton, wheat, coffee, and sugar cane.

Mexico's population is growing rapidly, although the growth is slowing. The country is also becoming more urban. Mexico City, the capital, has a population of more than 20 million. The concentration of people and industry in the Mexico City area has led to very severe environmental hazards.

Major Environmental Problems

Pollution. Air, water, and land pollution is severe around industrial areas. Mexico City and the surrounding region, in particular, suffer from atmospheric inversions that trap severe smog and high levels of lead and other toxic materials in the air. There are few controls on industrial facilities, although the government has begun to impose stricter regulations and recently shut down a state-owned refinery for environmental reasons. Controls on auto emissions have recently been established. Lack of adequate sewage treatment and industrial effluents also pollute rivers, especially in urban areas and in the industrial zone along the Mexico-U.S. border.

Deforestation. Mexican forests are being cut down and cleared at a substantial rate, estimated at about 2,375 square miles per year. The principal causes include the needs of a growing population for land to farm and the expanding development of the industrial sector.

Water scarcity. More than half of Mexico's population and industry and much of its cropland lies at altitudes above 1,600 feet; most water resources are lower. The result is a crucial need in much of the country for water.

Quality of Life

Life Expectancy (years)	68.9
Infant Mortality (per 1000)	43.0
Population Under 15 Years	35.0%
Population Over 65 Years	3.2%
Literacy Rate	87.3%
Malnourished Children	NA

Land Use and Habitats

Cropland (sq. miles):	95,405
per capita (acres)	0.7
global rank	64
Permanent Pasture (sq. miles):	287,641
total livestock (millions)	74.6
Forest and Woodlands (sq. miles):	166,023
1985 deforestation (sq. miles)	2,375
Wilderness Area (sq. miles)	11,777
Maritime Areas (EEZ, sq. miles)	11,008
Protected Areas (sq. miles):	36,369
percent of total	4.8%
No. of Threatened Species:	
mammals	26
birds	35
plants	1,111

Energy and Industry

Energy Production:	
solids (trillion BTUs)	210
liquids (trillion BTUs)	5,731
gas (trillion BTUs)	933
nuclear (gigawatt-hours)	0
hydroelectric (gigawatt-hours)	22,949
Energy Requirements:	
traditional fuels (trillion BTUs)	226
total (trillion BTUs)	4,474
per capita (million BTUs)	52
per capita (global rank)	52
Industrial Share of GDP	32.2%
Industrial Energy Index	23
Metal Reserve Index (world=100%)	1.0%
No. of Motor Vehicles/1000 Persons	71

Water

Renewable Supply (cubic miles)	85.8
Total Use (cubic miles):	13.0
in agriculture	86.0%
in industry	8.0%
in homes and cities	6.0%
Access to Safe Water:	
urban population	79.0%
rural population	49.0%

Urban Centers and Waste

No. of Cities Over 1 Million:	5
percent of population	32.5%
Solid Wastes (million tons)	12.9
Urban Sanitation Access	100.0%

Population and Gross National Product

Population (millions)	GNP (billion $US)

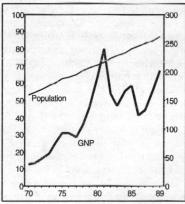

Commercial Energy Use

Total Energy Use (trillion BTUs)	Per Capita Energy Use (million BTUs)

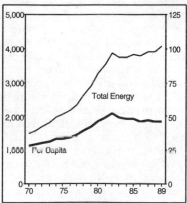

NICARAGUA

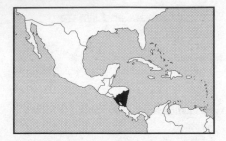

Total Area: 50,192 sq. miles
  Global Rank: 89   Per Capita: 8.3 acres
Population: 3,871,000
  Global Rank: 102   Growth Rate: 3.36%
Gross National Product: $3,183 m.
  Global Rank: 101   Per Capita: $910
Greenhouse Gas Emissions
  Global Share: 0.17%   Per Capita Rank: 17

Nicaragua is the largest of the Central American republics, bordering Costa Rica to the south and Honduras to the north. Nearly 60 percent of the population resides in the Pacific coastal region, which contains an active coastal volcanic chain, the region's largest bodies of water, and only 15 percent of the country's land area; the climate in this region is relatively dry. The mountainous central highlands gradually join with the largely uninhabited, humid Caribbean lowlands in the east.

Timber, arable land, and fisheries are among Nicaragua's main natural resources. The country also has deposits of gold, silver, copper, and lead. The area's main agricultural crops are corn, cotton, coffee, and sugar, and it is the largest exporter of beef in Central America.

Nicaragua's tropical climate is home to over 44 species of birds, 45 species of fish, and over 10,000 known species of plants. The country has the most extensive area of remaining forests in Central America, which are estimated to cover more than 25 percent of the region (virtually all of which is located in the eastern areas).

The western part of the country is one of the world's most active earthquake regions, with major quakes occurring periodically. This has caused major environmental problems, including pollution, erosion, and damage to water supply and sewage systems. For much of the past decade, civil war disrupted the country and prevented environmental protection.

Major Environmental Problems

Deforestation. There are no undisturbed natural forests remaining in western Nicaragua. Use of wood and charcoal for fuel is one cause; more important causes are logging and clearing of land for raising cattle. Almost 40 percent of the land has been affected by the resulting changes in hydrology, soils, and biology.

Land degradation. Soil erosion is rampant throughout most of western Nicaragua. This is a consequence of deforestation and of unrestricted expansion of farming onto steeply sloped areas. Subsistence farming on such lands has led to poor yields and to a deterioration of soil and water quality.

Pesticide use. Over the past 20 years, pesticide use has risen dramatically in Nicaragua. Although heavy pesticide use began on large commercial farms, this practice has now spread to all areas of the agricultural sector. The effects include the rise of new and harmful species, runoff of pesticides into the water supply, and the incorporation of pesticides into the food chain.

AND TOBAGO

Total Area: 1,981 sq. miles
Global Rank: 138   Per Capita: 1.0 acres
Population: 1,281,000
Global Rank: 125   Growth Rate: 1.68%
Gross National Product: $3,949 m.
Global Rank: 95   Per Capita: $3,135
Greenhouse Gas Emissions
Global Share: 0.08%   Per Capita Rank: 9

idad and Tobago, the southern-
st island country of the Lesser An-
s in the Caribbean Sea, comprises
islands 18 miles apart. Like its
ghbors, it was set up as an agricul-
l colony worked by African slaves.
owing the end of slavery in 1834,
orted labor from India and China
e the islands a diverse ethnic
eup. In 1962, the country gained its
ependence.

The islands support a rich diversity
ora, fauna, and sea life, including
nsive coral reefs. Trinidad and To-
o, 60 percent of whose land area
ains forests or swamp, boasts one
e world's few examples of sustain-
forestry projects, the 3,800-acre
a Rerve, which has been suc-
full managed since 1927. The
trys 13 wildlife sanctuaries.

in resources include oil, natu-
as, asphalt. The country has a
ped industrial sector, in-
oleum refining and chemi-
turing. Agriculture plays a
ole in the economy, al-
sland exports sugar and
The country is not self-
ood.

and Tobago provides a
human services including
ducation, safe water, and
ith proven oil reserves
only about another dec-
empting to diversify its
economy into light manufacturing and
tourism.

Major Environmental Problems

Land degradation. The boom years
saw the loss of good agricultural land
to residential, commercial, and industrial development. In addition, removal of vegetation, especially from
sloping land, whether for farming, for
squatter housing, or by forest fires has
led to erosion and flooding.

Oil pollution. Because Trinidad and
Tobago lies near a major shipping
route from the Caribbean and Gulf of
Mexico to the Atlantic, tar balls and
other oil pollution often foul the island's beaches.

Water pollution. Pollution of both inland and marine waters by runoff and
sediment, agricultural chemicals, industrial waste, and sewage from inadequately managed plants constitutes a
growing problem.

Tourism damage. Like other Caribbean island states, Trinidad and Tobago suffers localized damage from
tourism, which includes the release of
untreated sewage from hotels, degradation of coral reefs by boat anchors
and divers, and overfishing of shellfish.

Quality of Life

Life Expectancy (years)	63.3
Infant Mortality (per 1000)	62.0
Population Under 15 Years	44.6%
Population Over 65 Years	2.1%
Literacy Rate	NA
Malnourished Children	22.0%

Land Use and Habitats

Cropland (sq. miles):	4,915
per capita (acres)	0.8
global rank	53
Permanent Pasture (sq. miles):	20,656
total livestock (millions)	2.7
Forest and Woodlands (sq. miles):	13,475
1985 deforestation (sq. miles)	467
Wilderness Area (sq. miles)	5,873
Maritime Areas (EEZ, sq. miles)	617
Protected Areas (sq. miles):	167
percent of total	0.3%
No. of Threatened Species:	
mammals	8
birds	7
plants	72

Energy and Industry

Energy Production:	
solids (trillion BTUs)	0
liquids (trillion BTUs)	0
gas (trillion BTUs)	0
nuclear (gigawatt-hours)	0
hydroelectric (gigawatt-hours)	269
Energy Requirements:	
traditional fuels (trillion BTUs)	33
total (trillion BTUs)	67
per capita (million BTUs)	18
per capita (global rank)	90
Industrial Share of GDP	NA
Industrial Energy Index	NA
Metal Reserve Index (world=100%)	NA
No. of Motor Vehicles/1000 Persons	14

Water

Renewable Supply (cubic miles)	42.0
Total Use (cubic miles):	0.2
in agriculture	54.0%
in industry	21.0%
in homes and cities	25.0%
Access to Safe Water:	
urban population	78.0%
rural population	19.0%

Urban Centers and Waste

No. of Cities Over 1 Million:	1
percent of population	26.1%
Solid Wastes (million tons)	0.5
Urban Sanitation Access	32.0%

Population and Gross National Product

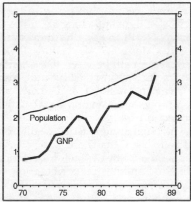

Commercial Energy Use

Total Energy Use   Per Capita Energy Use
(trillion BTUs)   (million BTUs)

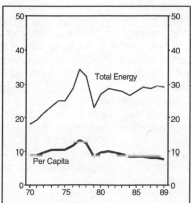

PANAMA

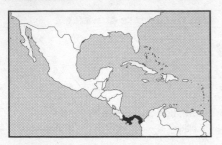

Total Area: 29,760 sq. miles
Global Rank: 106   Per Capita: 7.9 acres
Population: 2,418,000
Global Rank: 114   Growth Rate: 2.07%
Gross National Product: $4,071 m.
Global Rank: 94   Per Capita: $1,719
Greenhouse Gas Emissions
Global Share: 0.06%   Per Capita Rank: 51

Panama's geographic position on a narrow isthmus stretching 375 miles to connect North and South America has largely determined its destiny. It has provided a path between the Atlantic and Pacific Oceans, first by trail, then by river and railroad, and finally via the 52-mile-long Panama Canal, which opened in 1914.

The canal brought a degree of prosperity to the Canal Zone and to Panama's larger cities, which boast good sanitation and health services. Few of these services are available in squatter settlements or in rural areas, where nearly half the population lives.

With a spine of 11,000-foot mountains, Panama has a variety of habitats, including tropical rainforests, upland forests, savannas, and coastal mangroves. Such diverse habitats result in a high degree of biodiversity. However, many of these habitats are being destroyed by colonization projects in forest and wetland areas intended to accommodate the country's rapid population growth.

Agricultural land is expanding to produce exports such as bananas, coffee, and sugar. Pastureland is expanding to raise cattle for domestic consumption. Mangrove forests are being cut to make way for shrimp ponds, which produce shrimp for export. Other major exports include timber and copper ore.

Major Environmental Problems

Deforestation. During the 1980s Panama lost about 139 square miles of tropical rainforest a year to colonization projects in which rural people cleared the land for farms and pasture. The government encouraged colonization—in one case the National Guard recruited volunteers to clear a forest—but did little to channel the efforts into sustainable projects such as agroforestry or sustainable timber cutting.

Land degradation. As a result of the widespread loss of forest cover, Panama is losing about 2,000 tons of topsoil per year as heavy tropical rains wash it down the rivers to the coasts, where it destroys coastal fishery habitats. Much of the colonization occurred on the Caribbean coast, where the soil is poor and unsuited to agriculture. Within a few years, soil fertility was exhausted and farmers were forced to clear new areas.

Destruction of marine habitats. Panama's fishery resources are an important source of food domestically as well as a major export commodity. The coastal mud flats and mangrove forests that sustain these resources face many threats, including agricultural runoff, construction of commercial shrimp ponds, and recreational development.

Quality of Life

Life Expectancy (years)	72.0
Infant Mortality (per 1000)	23.0
Population Under 15 Years	33.1%
Population Over 65 Years	4.1%
Literacy Rate	88.1%
Malnourished Children	24.0%

Land Use and Habitats

Cropland (sq. miles):	2,228
per capita (acres)	0.6
global rank	73
Permanent Pasture (sq. miles):	5,985
total livestock (millions)	1.8
Forest and Woodlands (sq. miles):	12,896
1985 deforestation (sq. miles)	139
Wilderness Area (sq. miles)	0
Maritime Areas (EEZ, sq. miles)	1,183
Protected Areas (sq. miles):	5,120
percent of total	17.2%
No. of Threatened Species:	
mammals	13
birds	14
plants	344

Energy and Industry

Energy Production:	
solids (trillion BTUs)	0
liquids (trillion BTUs)	0
gas (trillion BTUs)	0
nuclear (gigawatt-hours)	0
hydroelectric (gigawatt-hours)	2,182
Energy Requirements:	
traditional fuels (trillion BTUs)	18
total (trillion BTUs)	72
per capita (million BTUs)	30
per capita (global rank)	68
Industrial Share of GDP	14.9%
Industrial Energy Index	10
Metal Reserve Index (world=100%)	0.0%
No. of Motor Vehicles/1000 Persons	NA

Water

Renewable Supply (cubic miles)	34.6
Total Use (cubic miles):	0.3
in agriculture	77.0%
in industry	11.0%
in homes and cities	12.0%
Access to Safe Water:	
urban population	100.0%
rural population	66.0%

Urban Center

No. of Cities Over 1 M	
percent of population	
Solid Wastes (million to	
Urban Sanitation Access	

Population and Gross

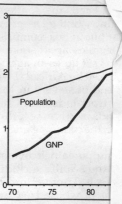

Population
(millions)

Population

GNP

Commercial Energy Us

Total Energy Use
(trillion BTUs)

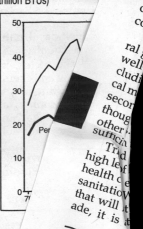

TRINIDAD AND TOBAGO

Quality of Life

Life Expectancy (years)	70.9
Infant Mortality (per 1000)	16.0
Population Under 15 Years	33.3%
Population Over 65 Years	5.1%
Literacy Rate	NA
Malnourished Children	4.0%

Land Use and Habitats

Cropland (sq. miles):	463
per capita (acres)	0.2
global rank	123
Permanent Pasture (sq. miles):	42
total livestock (millions)	0.2
Forest and Woodlands (sq. miles):	853
1985 deforestation (sq. miles)	3
Wilderness Area (sq. miles)	0
Maritime Areas (EEZ, sq. miles)	297
Protected Areas (sq. miles):	59
percent of total	3.0%
No. of Threatened Species:	
mammals	1
birds	3
plants	4

Energy and Industry

Energy Production:	
solids (trillion BTUs)	0
liquids (trillion BTUs)	306
gas (trillion BTUs)	140
nuclear (gigawatt-hours)	0
hydroelectric (gigawatt-hours)	0
Energy Requirements:	
traditional fuels (trillion BTUs)	3
total (trillion BTUs)	201
per capita (million BTUs)	159
per capita (global rank)	20
Industrial Share of GDP	39.7%
Industrial Energy Index	54
Metal Reserve Index (world=100%)	NA
No. of Motor Vehicles/1000 Persons	205

Water

Renewable Supply (cubic miles)	1.2
Total Use (cubic miles):	0.0
in agriculture	35.0%
in industry	38.0%
in homes and cities	27.0%
Access to Safe Water:	
urban population	100.0%
rural population	87.0%

Urban Centers and Waste

No. of Cities Over 1 Million:	0
percent of population	0.0%
Solid Wastes (million tons)	0.2
Urban Sanitation Access	100.0%

Population and Gross National Product

Population (millions)	GNP (billion $US)

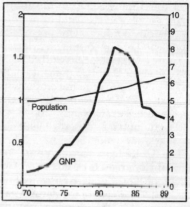

Commercial Energy Use

Total Energy Use (trillion BTUs)	Per Capita Energy Use (million BTUs)

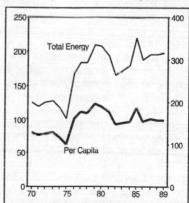

UNITED STATES

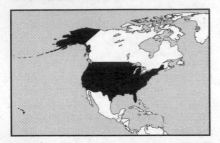

Total Area: 3,618,706 sq. miles
Global Rank: 4   Per Capita: 9.3 acres
Population: 249,224,000
Global Rank: 4   Growth Rate: 0.81%
Gross National Product: $5,200,840 m.
Global Rank: 1   Per Capita: $21,039
Greenhouse Gas Emissions
Global Share: 17.81%   Per Capita Rank: 6

The United States is the world's fourth largest country in area and in population. Sharing borders on the north with Canada and on the south with Mexico, the country is geologically and ecologically diverse. About 20 percent of the land is devoted to growing crops, with the rest split approximately equally among forests, rangelands, and other lands—mountains, deserts, wetlands and lakes, and wilderness.

The United States has abundant mineral resources. It produces 15 percent of the world's oil, 20 percent of the coal, and 25 percent of the natural gas. It is also the leading producer of nuclear power and the second largest producer of hydropower. The country is a major producer of several metals, including iron, steel, copper, cadmium, and lead. With the world's largest economy, the country consumes even more natural resources than it produces, especially on a per capita basis. It is the world's largest consumer of energy and the largest or second largest consumer of nine metals.

The country has fertile soils and an extremely productive agricultural sector. It is the world's largest producer and exporter of grains and maintains the third largest herd of cattle. It is also the second largest user of pesticides, after the former Soviet Union, and operates more than twice as much farm machinery as any other country.

The United States pioneered the idea of national parks and wilderness reserves and now has 396 protected areas totaling over 10 percent of the land area.

Major Environmental Problems

Air pollution. The United States has led the way in efforts to control urban air pollution and recently tightened its regulations. Although air quality is generally improving, many urban areas do not meet national standards for smog. U.S. emissions contribute substantially to the acid rain that falls on parts of the United States and Canada.

Water pollution. Controls on industrial and municipal effluents into rivers and lakes have improved water quality in much of the nation. However, runoff of excess pesticides and fertilizers from farms remains a serious threat to lakes and estuaries, where pesticides and other toxic materials can accumulate in shellfish and where excess nutrients can cause algal blooms, degrading water quality.

Global warming contribution. The United States is the largest single emitter of greenhouse gases. More than 20 percent of the carbon dioxide released from burning fossil fuels worldwide comes from the United States.

Quality of Life

Life Expectancy (years)	75.5
Infant Mortality (per 1000)	10.0
Population Under 15 Years	21.2%
Population Over 65 Years	11.4%

Land Use and Habitats

Cropland (sq. miles):	733,263
per capita (acres)	1.9
global rank	7
Permanent Pasture (sq. miles):	932,305
total livestock (millions)	171.6
Forest and Woodlands (sq. miles):	1,134,749
Wilderness Area (sq. miles)	170,108
Maritime Areas (EEZ, sq. miles)	37,496
Protected Areas (sq. miles):	379,698
percent of total	10.5%
No. of Threatened Species:	
mammals	21
birds	43
plants	2,476

Energy and Industry

Energy Production:	
solids (trillion BTUs)	20,736
liquids (trillion BTUs)	17,297
gas (trillion BTUs)	16,280
nuclear (gigawatt-hours)	529,352
hydroelectric (gigawatt-hours)	272,023
Energy Requirements.	
traditional fuels (trillion BTUs)	1,150
total (trillion BTUs)	76,355
per capita (million BTUs)	309
per capita (global rank)	7
Industrial Share of GDP	29.3%
Industrial Energy Index	12
Metal Reserve Index (world-100%)	8.7%
No. of Motor Vehicles/1000 Persons	573

Water

Renewable Supply (cubic miles)	594.6
Total Use (cubic miles)	112.1
in agriculture	42.0%
in industry	46.0%
in homes and cities	12.0%

Waste and Pollution

Urban Solid Wastes (million tons).	230.1
per capita (tons)	692.0
Hazardous Wastes (000 tons)	262,636.4
Sewage Treatment Plant Coverage	74.0%
SOX Emissions (000 tons)	22,811.4
NOX Emissions (000 tons)	21,819.6

Waste and Pollution (cont.)

Particulate Emissions (tons)	7,603.8
Hydrocarbon Emissions (tons)	20,387.0
No. of Cities Over 1 Million:	30
percent of population	36.3%

Population and Gross National Product

Population	GNP
(millions)	(billion $US)

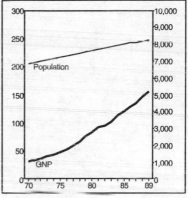

Commercial Energy Use

Total Energy Use	Per Capita Energy Use
(trillion BTUs)	(million BTUs)

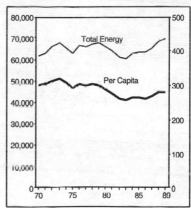

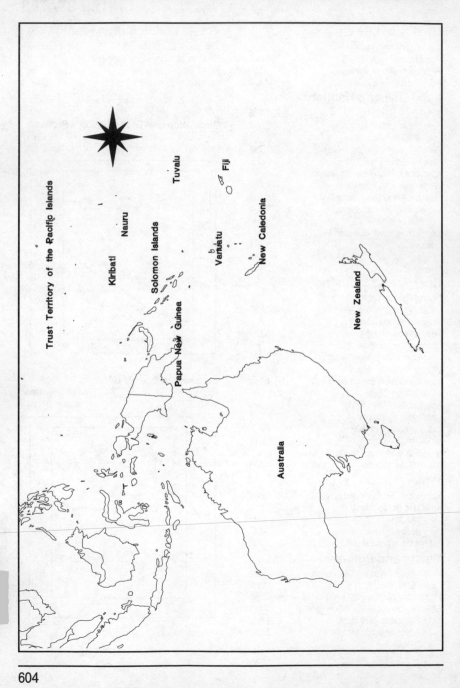

Oceania

This chapter contains environmental profiles for the countries listed within Oceania. Technical notes and data sources are given beginning on page 641.

AUSTRALIA

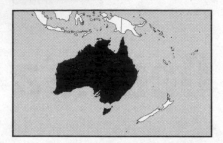

Total Area: 2,967,845 sq. miles
Global Rank: 6   Per Capita: 112.6 acres
Population: 16,873,000
Global Rank: 47   Growth Rate: 1.37%
Gross National Product: $269,503 m.
Global Rank: 12   Per Capita: $16,192
Greenhouse Gas Emissions
Global Share: 1.13%   Per Capita Rank: 7

The island continent of Australia is surrounded by a wealth of water: the Tasman Sea, the Coral Sea, the Arafura Sea, the Timor Sea, and the Indian Ocean.

Australia is both a geographic concept and a political entity. The western two thirds of the continent range from hyperarid to semiarid, and the bulk of the population lives along the relatively well-watered eastern and southeastern coasts. While it is about the size of the continental United States, Australia has only about 7 percent of the U.S. population. Australia, once a British penal colony, is a well-developed country with a well-educated work force and a democratic government.

Australia is rich in mineral and biological resources. Because of its huge size and physical isolation, it contains an assemblage of plants and animals found nowhere else on Earth. The native mammals of Australia are the marsupials (pouched mammals) and monotremes (egg-laying mammals) that underwent eons of independent development. The habitat zones of Australia are as diverse as any continent, ranging from hot arid desert to rainforest and alpine meadows to temperate grassland. The Great Barrier Reef, off the northeast coast, is the largest coral reef in the world.

Australia's economy is diverse and, in many ways, self-sufficient. While it has a well-developed agricultural sector—Australia is the world's largest producer of wool and is a major wheat exporter—Australia also has a large industrial sector, which includes manufacturing and the mining of coal, iron, precious metals, and fossil fuels.

Major Environmental Problems

Land degradation. Soil erosion due to inappropriate land use is widespread. Soil salinity has become a problem because of the use of poor-quality water. The loss of native vegetation from agriculture, overgrazing, development, and urbanization has contributed to soil salinity.

Endangered species. Many unique plants, mammals, birds, and fish are at risk of extinction in Australia primarily because of the loss of natural habitat. In South Australia alone, for example, fully 80 percent of natural vegetation in the agricultural areas has been cleared. Of 102 native mammals there, 28 percent are extinct and another 40 percent are either endangered, vulnerable, or rare. Competition, or predation, from feral introduced species (such as rabbits, horses, camels, goats, deer, foxes, cats, starlings, pigeons, sparrows, and hundreds of plants) further threatens the continued existence of native plants and animals.

AUSTRALIA

Quality of Life

Life Expectancy (years)	76.1
Infant Mortality (per 1000)	8.0
Population Under 15 Years	21.5%
Population Over 65 Years	9.5%

Land Use and Habitats

Cropland (sq. miles):	188,934
per capita (acres)	7.3
global rank	2
Permanent Pasture (sq. miles):	1,613,869
total livestock (millions)	186.6
Forest and Woodlands (sq. miles):	409,266
Wilderness Area (sq. miles)	885,835
Maritime Areas (EEZ, sq. miles)	17,360
Protected Areas (sq. miles):	176,272
percent of total	5.9%
No. of Threatened Species:	
mammals	35
birds	39
plants	2,133

Energy and Industry

Energy Production:	
solids (trillion BTUs)	3,739
liquids (trillion BTUs)	981
gas (trillion BTUs)	589
nuclear (gigawatt-hours)	0
hydroelectric (gigawatt-hours)	14,499
Energy Requirements:	
traditional fuels (trillion BTUs)	118
total (trillion BTUs)	3,573
per capita (million BTUs)	215
per capita (global rank)	12
Industrial Share of GDP	31.5%
Industrial Energy Index	10
Metal Reserve Index (world=100%)	7.6%
No. of Motor Vehicles/1000 Persons	500

Water

Renewable Supply (cubic miles)	82.3
Total Use (cubic miles):	4.3
in agriculture	33.0%
in industry	2.0%
in homes and cities	65.0%

Waste and Pollution

Urban Solid Wastes (million tons):	11.0
per capita (tons)	558.2
Hazardous Wastes (000 tons)	NA
Sewage Treatment Plant Coverage	NA
SOX Emissions (000 tons)	NA
NOX Emissions (000 tons)	NA

Waste and Pollution (cont.)

Particulate Emissions (tons)	NA
Hydrocarbon Emissions (tons)	NA
No. of Cities Over 1 Million:	4
percent of population	50.6%

Population and Gross National Product

Population (millions)	GNP (billion $US)

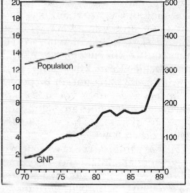

Commercial Energy Use

Total Energy Use (trillion BTUs)	Per Capita Energy Use (million BTUs)

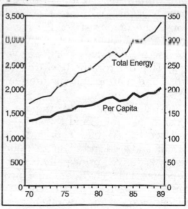

FIJI

Total Area: 7,054 sq. miles
  Global Rank: 130   Per Capita: 5.9 acres
Population: 764,000
  Global Rank: 132   Growth Rate: 1.78%
Gross National Product: $1,171 m.
  Global Rank: 122   Per Capita: $1,560
Greenhouse Gas Emissions
  Global Share: 0.00%   Per Capita Rank: 122

The Republic of Fiji is an archipelago consisting of the two main islands of Viti Levu and Vanu Levu and 300 smaller islets. It is located about 1,200 miles south of the equator in the southwest Pacific Ocean. The main islands, which together account for 87 percent of the land area, are of volcanic origin, while the smaller ones are mainly low-lying coral reefs. The people live mainly on Viti Levu.

Fiji has a tropical ocean climate with a high annual rainfall, and it is vulnerable to severe storms since it lies within the Pacific typhoon belt. Earthquakes are not unusual.

The two main islands are rich in species and ecosystems. Habitats include rainforests, savannas, marshes, rivers, streams, lakes, reefs, and lagoons. The rainforests of Fiji have a remarkable diversity of plants, yet the number of mammal species is very small. The coral reefs harbor a diversity of fish and marine animals unique to the South Pacific.

Agriculture and food preparation —including fishing and forestry—are the largest industries. Tourism is important, and gold and silver are mined. Energy is derived principally from hydropower. Fiji's environmental problems are not severe, given the country's rich endowment and low rate of population growth. But the clustering of all towns and most villages, industries, and people in the coastal zone means that careful planning will be necessary to preserve this zone's special resources of mangroves, reefs, sea life, water, and great natural beauty.

Major Environmental Problems

Deforestation. Between 1969 and 1988 there was more than a 30 percent reduction in Fiji's forest resources, mainly from the impact of logging. The loss of forest cover threatens the highly diverse flora as well as the few species of mammals.

Land degradation. Soil erosion is caused by inadequate farming practices on sloped land and poorly managed logging operations. Soil transported into coastal ecosystems smothers coral reefs, chokes mangroves, and reduces the local fish population.

Pollution. Coral sand extraction, oil and gas exploration, sewage and waste disposal, and overfishing pose a serious threat to the marine environment. Toxic waste, sewage, and air pollution related to development projects persist in urban areas while the widespread use of pesticides, fertilizer run-off, and slumping and salinization of ground water contribute to pollution in rural areas.

Quality of Life

Life Expectancy (years)	63.7
Infant Mortality (per 1000)	27.0
Population Under 15 Years	34.0%
Population Over 65 Years	2.7%
Literacy Rate	NA
Malnourished Children	NA

Land Use and Habitats

Cropland (sq. miles):	927
per capita (acres)	0.8
global rank	56
Permanent Pasture (sq. miles):	232
total livestock (millions)	0.3
Forest and Woodlands (sq. miles):	4,575
1985 deforestation (sq. miles)	8
Wilderness Area (sq. miles)	0
Maritime Areas (FFZ, sq. miles)	4,383
Protected Areas (sq. miles):	21
percent of total	0.3%
No. of Threatened Species:	
mammals	1
birds	5
plants	25

Energy and Industry

Energy Production:	
solids (trillion BTUs)	0
liquids (trillion BTUs)	0
gas (trillion BTUs)	0
nuclear (gigawatt-hours)	0
hydroelectric (gigawatt-hours)	334
Energy Requirements:	
traditional fuels (trillion BTUs)	11
total (trillion BTUs)	24
per capita (million BTUs)	32
per capita (global rank)	65
Industrial Share of GDP	20.9%
Industrial Energy Index	NA
Metal Reserve Index (world=100%)	NA
No. of Motor Vehicles/1000 Persons	39

Water

Renewable Supply (cubic miles)	6.9
Total Use (cubic miles):	0.0
in agriculture	60.0%
in industry	20.0%
in homes and cities	20.0%
Access to Safe Water:	
urban population	95.0%
rural population	68.0%

Urban Centers and Waste

No. of Cities Over 1 Million:	0
percent of population	0.0%
Solid Wastes (million tons)	0.1
Urban Sanitation Access	90.0%

Population and Gross National Product

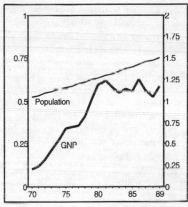

Population (millions)   GNP (billion \$US)

Commercial Energy Use

Total Energy Use (trillion BTUs)   Per Capita Energy Use (million BTUs)

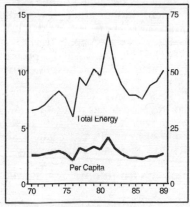

NEW ZEALAND

Total Area: 104,628 sq. miles
Global Rank: 69   Per Capita: 19.7 acres
Population: 3,392,000
Global Rank: 105   Growth Rate: 0.87%
Gross National Product: $39,670 m.
Global Rank: 41   Per Capita: $11,798
Greenhouse Gas Emissions
Global Share: 0.15%   Per Capita Rank: 19

Located in the southwest Pacific, New Zealand comprises two main islands and a number of smaller ones. The country has abundant water, hydroelectric, and fossil energy resources, and a temperate climate for highly productive pastoral and forestry industries. The country claims the fifth largest fishery in the world. A remarkable 30 percent of the land is in publicly owned national parks, forest parks, and protected reserves.

New Zealand is sparsely populated. Out of 3.4 million people in the country, 80 percent live in cities, most of which have fewer than 100,000 people. One exception, however, is Auckland, home to 25 percent of the population.

Since the 1880s, New Zealand's economy has depended on the export of agricultural products, especially mutton, wool, beef, and dairy products. Recently the economy has broadened to include tourism and exports of fish, timber, and some manufactured goods.

In 1991, New Zealand completed major revisions of its natural resource management laws. Now, with the exception of minerals management, the aim is to achieve sustainable use.

Major Environmental Problems

Impacts of introduced species. After centuries of separation from other land masses, evolution has created ecosystems unique to the islands. But plants, animals, and insects brought by settlers are having a severe impact. For example, the Australian opossum is damaging large areas in New Zealand forests. Waternet weed threatens to clog lakes on North Island. Control and eradication is costly.

Bird species in New Zealand also have been hard-hit by predation by and competition with introduced animals. Intensive conservation work has kept some species, such as the Chatham Islands black robin (which at one time had only five members), from extinction.

Ownership of natural resources. The Treaty of the Waitangi (1840) between the British Crown and Maori chiefs provided for Maori "exclusive and undisturbed possession" of the land and its resources. Maori claims to large tracts of land, fisheries, forests, and geothermal resources are under discussion, giving rise to major uncertainties about property rights and natural resource and environmental management authority.

Deforestation. As a result of extensive clearing for pastureland, only one third of New Zealand's indigenous forest remains, although commercial forest stocks are growing.

Quality of Life

Life Expectancy (years)	74.8
Infant Mortality (per 1000)	11.0
Population Under 15 Years	22.4%
Population Over 65 Years	10.0%

Land Use and Habitats

Cropland (sq. miles):	1,958
per capita (acres)	0.4
global rank	100
Permanent Pasture (sq. miles):	52,807
total livestock (millions)	70.9
Forest and Woodlands (sq. miles):	28,263
Wilderness Area (sq. miles)	14,373
Maritime Areas (EEZ, sq. miles)	18,661
Protected Areas (sq. miles):	10,962
percent of total	10.5%
No. of Threatened Species:	
mammals	1
birds	26
plants	254

Energy and Industry

Energy Production:	
solids (trillion BTUs)	59
liquids (trillion BTUs)	72
gas (trillion BTUs)	177
nuclear (gigawatt hours)	0
hydroelectric (gigawatt-hours)	21,999
Energy Requirements:	
traditional fuels (trillion BTUs)	0
total (trillion BTUs)	631
per capita (million BTUs)	188
per capita (global rank)	16
Industrial Share of GDP	28.0%
Industrial Energy Index	13
Metal Reserve Index (world=100%)	0.0%
No. of Motor Vehicles/1000 Persons	485

Water

Renewable Supply (cubic miles)	95.3
Total Use (cubic miles):	0.3
in agriculture	44.0%
in Industry	10.0%
in homes and cities	46.0%

Waste and Pollution

Urban Solid Wastes (million tons):	2.1
per capita (tons)	510.4
Hazardous Wastes (000 tons)	NA
Sewage Treatment Plant Coverage	88.0%
SOX Emissions (000 tons)	NA
NOX Emissions (000 tons)	NA

Waste and Pollution (cont.)

Particulate Emissions (tons)	NA
Hydrocarbon Emissions (tons)	NA
No. of Cities Over 1 Million:	0
percent of population	0.0%

Population and Gross National Product

Population	GNP
(millions)	(billion $US)

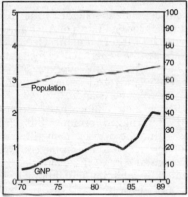

Commercial Energy Use

Total Energy Use	Per Capita Energy Use
(trillion BTUs)	(million BTUs)

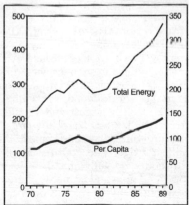

PAPUA NEW GUINEA

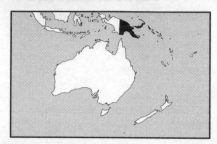

Total Area: 178,700 sq. miles
Global Rank: 50   Per Capita: 29.5 acres
Population: 3,874,000
Global Rank: 101   Growth Rate: 2.26%
Gross National Product: $3,387 m.
Global Rank: 99   Per Capita: $894
Greenhouse Gas Emissions
Global Share: 0.02%   Per Capita Rank: 128

The independent state of Papua New Guinea is located north of Australia in the southwestern Pacific Ocean. It comprises the eastern half of the island of New Guinea (the world's second largest island) and several smaller, mostly volcanic, islands.

Papua New Guinea has a diverse and often rugged terrain. Although it lies within the tropics, many different climates can be found in the country. The central core of the main island is formed by a high mountain range. To the north lies a great depression, which includes three large river basins and a series of smaller ranges. To the southwest are alluvial swamps and plains that are crossed by large rivers. Papua New Guinea has 14 active volcanoes.

The country is extremely rich in fauna and flora. There are over 11,000 plant species alone, including 2,000 ferns. Over 85 percent of the land mass remains under forest cover, including some of the least disturbed tropical forests in the world. Papua New Guinea has the world's largest and smallest parrots, the largest lizard, the largest doves and butterflies, and some of the smallest frogs. The country is also richly endowed with large deposits of copper and gold and immense, though unexploited, hydroelectric potential. Production of petroleum for export will begin in late 1992. Major natural gas fields have also been found.

Papua New Guinea remains essentially untouched by urbanization and industrialization. The population remains overwhelmingly rural and widely scattered, with the largest concentrations in the highland provinces where 40 percent of the people live. Some 85 percent of the people live in subsistence economy. Thus far, exploitation of the country's resources has been for export rather than domestic consumption.

Major Environmental Problems

Deforestation. Many of Papua New Guinea's forests are being unsustainably logged, and areas rich in biodiversity are being destroyed. Poor management, insufficient involvement of local landowners in land use decisions, too little government oversight, corruption, and inefficiency contribute to the problem.

Mining Damage. Open-pit mining in Papua New Guinea has caused serious environmental damage in many areas. Environmental and social damage caused by the Bougainville copper mine, the country's largest, prompted a public outcry by local people, and in 1990 the government ordered the mine to be closed. Several other large-scale mining projects, however, are continuing to operate and to pollute the area.

PAPUA NEW GUINEA

Quality of Life

Life Expectancy (years)	53.9
Infant Mortality (per 1000)	59.0
Population Under 15 Years	40.0%
Population Over 65 Years	1.9%
Literacy Rate	52.0%
Malnourished Children	NA

Land Use and Habitats

Cropland (sq. miles):	1,498
per capita (acres)	0.3
global rank	117
Permanent Pasture (sq. miles):	324
total livestock (millions)	1.9
Forest and Woodlands (sq. miles):	147,606
1985 deforestation (sq. miles)	89
Wilderness Area (sq. miles)	15,069
Maritime Areas (EEZ, sq. miles)	9,137
Protected Areas (sq. miles):	112
percent of total	0.1%
No. of Threatened Species:	
mammals	4
birds	25
plants	68

Energy and Industry

Energy Production:	
solids (trillion BTUs)	0
liquids (trillion BTUs)	0
gas (trillion BTUs)	0
nuclear (gigawatt-hours)	0
hydroelectric (gigawatt-hours)	456
Energy Requirements:	
traditional fuels (trillion BTUs)	52
total (trillion BTUs)	86
per capita (million BTUs)	23
per capita (global rank)	82
Industrial Share of GDP	30.6%
Industrial Energy Index	NA
Metal Reserve Index (world=100%)	0.2%
No. of Motor Vehicles/1000 Persons	5

Water

Renewable Supply (cubic miles)	192.2
Total Use (cubic miles):	0.0
in agriculture	49.0%
in industry	22.0%
in homes and cities	29.0%
Access to Safe Water:	
urban population	93.0%
rural population	23.0%

Urban Centers and Waste

No. of Cities Over 1 Million:	0
percent of population	0.0%
Solid Wastes (million tons)	0.1
Urban Sanitation Access	54.0%

Population and Gross National Product

Population	GNP
(millions)	(billion $US)

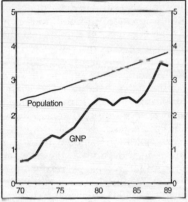

Commercial Energy Use

Total Energy Use	Per Capita Energy Use
(trillion BTUs)	(million BTUs)

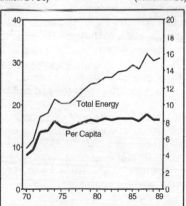

SOLOMON ISLANDS

Total Area: 11,158 sq. miles
Global Rank: 120   Per Capita: 22.3 acres
Population: 320,000
Global Rank: 143   Growth Rate: 3.28%
Gross National Product: $176 m.
Global Rank: 141   Per Capita: $568
Greenhouse Gas Emissions
Global Share: 0.00%   Per Capita Rank: 156

This sparsely populated archipelago of densely forested, mountainous tropical islands is located about 1,000 miles northeast of Australia in the Pacific Ocean. It is perhaps best known for Guadalcanal, scene of one of World War II's fiercest battles. The island's 320,000 inhabitants are mostly Melanesian and speak more than 120 indigenous languages.

The Solomon Islands' natural resources include timber, fisheries, and some mineral ores. A recent agreement, the Wellington Convention, prohibits tuna fleets from using drift nets throughout the South Pacific. In the past, some of these nets stretched as wide as 35 miles, catching in their clutches dolphins and porpoises. Organizations such as Greenpeace, which orchestrated the fight against drift nets, have concluded that the Wellington Convention is working. For the Solomons, a signatory to the convention, the agreement will help to ensure that tuna—its leading export—are not depleted.

Market activity notwithstanding, most islanders work only intermittently for money. About 85 percent of the population engages to some extent in subsistence agriculture. Most live in small, widely scattered settlements along the coasts.

Little of these tropical islands' prehistory is known, yet excavations indicate a hunter-gatherer people lived there as early as 1000 B.C. Some islanders are descendants of ancient peoples who migrated to the area from Southeast Asia.

Official action on environmental concerns has been slow to take hold. A 1970 regulation prohibits pollution of any body of water, stream, or river, as well as beaches, shores, and harbors. Enforcement is difficult, however, and relatively rare, especially for sources of eroded soil, the most common water pollutant.

Major Environmental Problems

Deforestation. Careless logging operations are damaging or destroying large areas of forests, one of the country's prime natural resources. Policing of logging operations remains deficient, and reforestation does not yet match the rate of logging in natural forests. A 38-square-mile plantation forest is being developed.

Erosion. Heavy rains make exposed soils vulnerable to erosion. Soil erosion is widespread on agricultural lands, particularly when farming is done on steep slopes and in cleared forest areas. The supply of arable land is limited, thus adding pressure to farm areas more susceptible to erosion. Deforestation is also a major cause of erosion.

SOLOMON ISLANDS

Quality of Life

Life Expectancy (years)	NA
Infant Mortality (per 1000)	NA
Population Under 15 Years	NA
Population Over 65 Years	NA
Literacy Rate	NA
Malnourished Children	34.0%

Land Use and Habitats

Cropland (sq. miles):	220
per capita (acres)	NA
global rank	NA
Permanent Pasture (sq. miles):	66
total livestock (millions)	NA
Forest and Woodlands (sq. miles):	9,884
1985 deforestation (sq. miles)	4
Wilderness Area (sq. miles)	0
Maritime Areas (EEZ, sq. miles)	5,174
Protected Areas (sq. miles):	0
percent of total	0.0%
No. of Threatened Species:	
mammals	2
birds	20
plants	3

Energy and Industry

Energy Production:	
solids (trillion BTUs)	0
liquids (trillion BTUs)	0
gas (trillion BTUs)	0
nuclear (gigawatt-hours)	0
hydroelectric (gigawatt-hours)	0
Energy Requirements:	
traditional fuels (trillion BTUs)	1
total (trillion BTUs)	3
per capita (million BTUs)	NA
per capita (global rank)	NA
Industrial Share of GDP	NA
Industrial Energy Index	NA
Metal Reserve Index (world=100%)	0.0%
No. of Motor Vehicles/1000 Persons	NA

Water

Renewable Supply (cubic miles)	10.7
Total Use (cubic miles):	0.0
in agriculture	40.0%
in industry	20.0%
in homes and cities	40.0%
Access to Safe Water:	
urban population	82.0%
rural population	68.0%

Urban Centers and Waste

No. of Cities Over 1 Million:	0
percent of population	0.0%
Solid Wastes (million tons)	NA
Urban Sanitation Access	56.0%

Commercial Energy Use
Total Energy Use
(trillion BTUs)

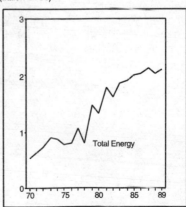

Total Energy

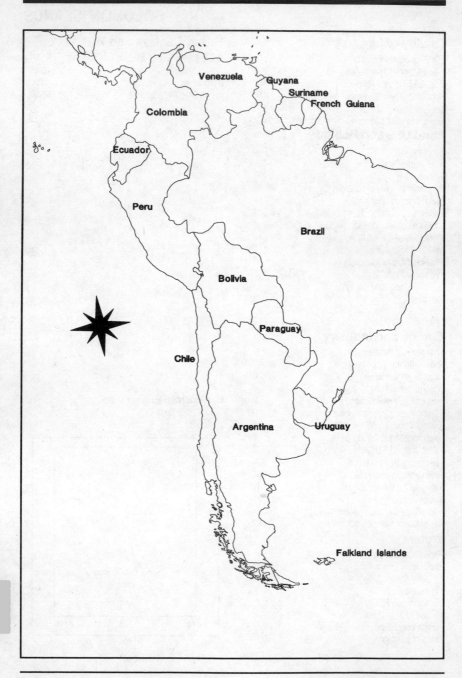

South America

This chapter contains environmental profiles for the South American countries listed. Technical notes and data sources are given beginning on page 641.

ARGENTINA

Total Area: 1,068,279 sq. miles
Global Rank: 8   Per Capita: 21.2 acres
Population: 32,322,000
Global Rank: 30   Growth Rate: 1.27%
Gross National Product: $53,324 m.
Global Rank: 33   Per Capita: $1,671
Greenhouse Gas Emissions
Global Share: 0.59%   Per Capita Rank: 73

Argentina is the second largest country in South America; it also claims nearly 0.5 million square miles of island and antarctic territories. The variety of climates and topography of the country yields a wide diversity of ecosystems. From the northern border with Bolivia, the high, barren, arid Andean plateau extends southward along the Chilean/Argentine border. The southernmost tip of the continent is subantarctic, with harsh winds sweeping across the Patagonian steppes. In sharp contrast, the northern Gran Chaco region is tropical and subtropical. In between are spectacular mountainous areas with glacial valleys, rich farming areas on the pampas, and the littoral, which includes the drainages of the Paraná, Iguazú, and Uruguay rivers. These three rivers converge to form the immense estuary of the Río de la Plata, where the capital city of Buenos Aires is located.

Argentina's economy has traditionally been largely based on agriculture, but with substantial industrial activities as well. Major products include grains, oilseeds, livestock (beef), motor vehicles, textiles, petroleum, and steel. In recent years, rapid inflation and related difficulties have brought the economy to the edge of collapse. Much of the manufacture and virtually all of the international trade movement take place in Buenos Aires, the capital and

largest city, where nearly half of the population resides.

Major Environmental Problems

Air and water pollution. In spite of its large land mass, Argentina's population is heavily concentrated in urban areas, especially in Buenos Aires. These concentrations have led to air pollution in Buenos Aires and other major cities as well as to widespread water pollution. Increased pesticide and fertilizer use in farming areas has also polluted rivers.

Waste disposal. Environmental concerns are slowly getting the public's attention, but laws have yet to be passed concerning such questions as disposal of hazardous waste and disposal of nuclear waste. Also needed are proper management and clear jurisdictional authority over environmental threats to public health.

Soil erosion. Heavy flooding is a problem in both urban and rural areas near rivers. Adequate flood controls do not exist; improper land use practices also contribute to erosion. The result is that much of the fertile soil ends up in the Río de la Plata or other rivers. The more severe flooding is in the northern part of the country, but southern lakes are also experiencing problems.

ARGENTINA

Quality of Life

Life Expectancy (years)	70.6
Infant Mortality (per 1000)	32.0
Population Under 15 Years	28.3%
Population Over 65 Years	8.1%
Literacy Rate	95.3%
Malnourished Children	NA

Land Use and Habitats

Cropland (sq. miles):	138,031
per capita (acres)	2.8
global rank	4
Permanent Pasture (sq. miles):	549,421
total livestock (millions)	90.4
Forest and Woodlands (sq. miles):	228,958
1985 deforestation (sq. miles)	405
Wilderness Area (sq. miles)	57,823
Maritime Areas (EEZ, sq. miles)	4,496
Protected Areas (sq. miles):	48,798
percent of total	4.6%
No. of Threatened Species:	
mammals	25
birds	53
plants	157

Energy and Industry

Energy Production:	
solids (trillion BTUs)	12
liquids (trillion BTUs)	978
gas (trillion BTUs)	744
nuclear (gigawatt-hours)	5,552
hydroelectric (gigawatt-hours)	15,150
Energy Requirements:	
traditional fuels (trillion BTUs)	100
total (trillion BTUs)	1,962
per capita (million BTUs)	61
per capita (global rank)	44
Industrial Share of GDP	32.7%
Industrial Energy Index	18
Metal Reserve Index (world=100%)	0.1%
No. of Motor Vehicles/1000 Persons	127

Water

Renewable Supply (cubic miles)	166.5
Total Use (cubic miles):	6.6
in agriculture	73.0%
in industry	18.0%
in homes and cities	9.0%
Access to Safe Water:	
urban population	73.0%
rural population	17.0%

Urban Centers and Waste

No. of Cities Over 1 Million:	3
percent of population	42.5%
Solid Wastes (million tons)	5.6
Urban Sanitation Access	100.0%

Population and Gross National Product

Population
(millions)

GNP
(billion $US)

Commercial Energy Use

Total Energy Use
(trillion BTUs)

Per Capita Energy Use
(million BTUs)

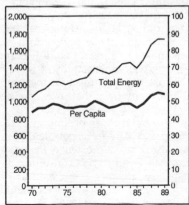

BOLIVIA

Total Area: 424,155 sq. miles
Global Rank: 26   Per Capita: 37.1 acres
Population: 7,314,000
Global Rank: 81   Growth Rate: 2.76%
Gross National Product: $4,269 m.
Global Rank: 91   Per Capita: $600
Greenhouse Gas Emissions
Global Share: 0.14%   Per Capita Rank: 71

Bolivia is the fifth largest country in South America; it is almost as large as Texas and California combined. Within its landlocked borders are found very diverse regions, including plains, Amazonian rainforests, and Andean peaks. While the eastern half of the country is the site of extensive pastures and forests as well as the world's highest navigable body of water, Lake Titicaca, two thirds of the population lives on a barren plateau in the Andes, where temperatures average about 45° F.

Bolivia is able to draw from an abundant supply of natural resources. The eastern lowlands offer sizable stretches of land suitable for crop and livestock production. Agriculture employs almost half of the working population in the production of coffee, sugar, and soybeans. Along with beef and cowhides, these agricultural exports make up almost one fifth of the country's economic activity.

Industry, exploiting tin, zinc, gold, and antimony from the richest ore deposits in South America, is the second largest economic sector. Energy is derived principally from petroleum and natural gas, and almost all of the crude petroleum produced is consumed domestically. Despite these natural resources, Bolivia provides its people with one of the lowest levels of income in South America.

Major Environmental Problems

Natural resource management. The most pressing environmental issue in Bolivia concerns the responsible development of the abundant natural resources in the eastern lowlands. While the area holds much potential for growth, rapid development occurring in parts of the area has resulted in the wasteful exploitation of forests and other renewable natural resources. Indiscriminate land clearing, poor land use, and road construction may soon deplete the area of these valuable resources.

Loss of biodiversity. As a consequence of deforestation and unguided land settlement, Bolivia's rich natural habitats are under siege. Animal species, in addition, are in danger of extinction from illegal traffic in hides and skins. The expansion of economic activity has created conflicts between new settlers and the relatively small but increasingly vocal indigenous population.

Water pollution. Water pollution is a problem, especially in arid and semiarid regions, where water is scarce. Pollutants discharged by industry and as a result of illegal cocaine production are contaminating irrigation and drinking water. Urban pollution is also a concern.

Quality of Life

Life Expectancy (years)	53.1
Infant Mortality (per 1000)	110.0
Population Under 15 Years	43.9%
Population Over 65 Years	2.8%
Literacy Rate	77.5%
Malnourished Children	51.0%

Land Use and Habitats

Cropland (sq. miles):	13,359
per capita (acres)	1.2
global rank	26
Permanent Pasture (sq. miles):	102,896
total livestock (millions)	23.4
Forest and Woodlands (sq. miles):	214,865
1985 deforestation (sq. miles)	452
Wilderness Area (sq. miles)	68,764
Maritime Areas (EEZ, sq. miles)	0
Protected Areas (sq. miles):	26,155
percent of total	6.2%
No. of Threatened Species:	
mammals	21
birds	34
plants	31

Energy and Industry

Energy Production:	
solids (trillion BTUs)	0
liquids (trillion BTUs)	43
gas (trillion BTUs)	108
nuclear (gigawatt-hours)	0
hydroelectric (gigawatt-hours)	1,270
Energy Requirements:	
traditional fuels (trillion BTUs)	16
total (trillion BTUs)	100
per capita (million BTUs)	14
per capita (global rank)	104
Industrial Share of GDP	27.0%
Industrial Energy Index	8
Metal Reserve Index (world=100%)	0.4%
No. of Motor Vehicles/1000 Persons	18

Water

Renewable Supply (cubic miles)	72.0
Total Use (cubic miles):	0.3
in agriculture	85.0%
in industry	5.0%
in homes and cities	10.0%
Access to Safe Water:	
urban population	77.0%
rural population	15.0%

Urban Centers and Waste

No. of Cities Over 1 Million:	1
percent of population	16.9%
Solid Wastes (million tons)	0.8
Urban Sanitation Access	55.0%

Population and Gross National Product

Population	GNP
(millions)	(billion $US)

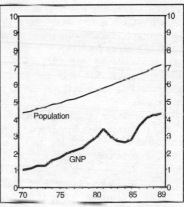

Commercial Energy Use

Total Energy Use	Per Capita Energy Use
(trillion BTUs)	(million BTUs)

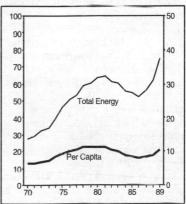

BRAZIL

Total Area: 3,286,418 sq. miles
Global Rank: 5   Per Capita: 14.0 acres
Population: 150,368,000
Global Rank: 6   Growth Rate: 2.07%
Gross National Product: $ 434,715m.
Global Rank: 9   Per Capita: $2,952
Greenhouse Gas Emissions
Global Share: 3.93%   Per Capita Rank: 54

Brazil covers nearly half the land area of South America. It is home to much of the Amazon Basin, which is drained by the Amazon, the world's largest river, and is covered by the largest remaining tropical forest in the world. Nearly one third of Brazil is covered by tropical forest.

Brazil is richly endowed with animal and plant species. The tropical forest provides a habitat for the most diverse assemblage of species on the planet.

Brazil has large deposits of many minerals, including iron; gold and gemstones are actively mined. The country has enormous hydroelectric resources, and its rivers contain more than one fifth of the world's fresh water. Exports include industrial products as well as agricultural goods.

Brazil's large population is concentrated in the eastern part of the country, which includes the major cities of Rio de Janeiro and São Paulo. Inequality of land distribution is a major socioeconomic problem, with one third of the population living on 6 percent of the land area. Lack of opportunity in the countryside has forced millions of poor Brazilians into cities that cannot provide them with adequate services.

As a federation, Brazil lacks uniform environmental controls across the country. Nonetheless, recent years have seen some environmental progress. With 70 percent of the cars burning pure alcohol and the rest a mixture of alcohol and gasoline, air quality has improved in many areas. And the coastal forests in southern Brazil, which had largely disappeared, are expanding by natural regeneration.

Major Environmental Problems

Deforestation. Clearing of land results in the loss of millions of acres of tropical forest every year. The cutting and burning accelerated during the middle part of the 1980s but is now being brought under better control. Along with the forests, habitats for many species are being destroyed, resulting in concerns about species extinction and the loss of biodiversity.

Water pollution. Serious pollution of rivers near large and medium-sized cities is common. Dumping of untreated sewage and industrial wastes into streams in urban areas and mercury in gold-mining areas create locally serious water contamination.

Land degradation. Very poor soils underlie much of the Amazon region, and they often wash away when trees are cut. In other areas, shortages of available land have pushed poor farmers onto marginal or steeply sloping lands that erode easily.

Quality of Life

Life Expectancy (years)	64.9
Infant Mortality (per 1000)	63.0
Population Under 15 Years	33.7%
Population Over 65 Years	3.9%
Literacy Rate	81.1%
Malnourished Children	31.0%

Land Use and Habitats

Cropland (sq. miles):	303,668
per capita (acres)	1.3
global rank	17
Permanent Pasture (sq. miles):	656,371
total livestock (millions)	214.0
Forest and Woodlands (sq. miles):	2,135,637
1985 deforestation (sq. miles)	9,768
Wilderness Area (sq. miles)	780,158
Maritime Areas (EEZ, sq. miles)	12,233
Protected Areas (sq. miles):	79,248
percent of total	2.4%
No. of Threatened Species:	
mammals	24
birds	123
plants	240

Energy and Industry

Energy Production:	
solids (trillion BTUs)	120
liquids (trillion BTUs)	1,215
gas (trillion BTUs)	126
nuclear (gigawatt-hours)	1,832
hydroelectric (gigawatt-hours)	214,239
Energy Requirements:	
traditional fuels (trillion BTUs)	2,088
total (trillion BTUs)	6,977
per capita (million BTUs)	47
per capita (global rank)	55
Industrial Share of GDP	42.9%
Industrial Energy Index	10
Metal Reserve Index (world=100%)	5.0%
No. of Motor Vehicles/1000 Persons	104

Water

Renewable Supply (cubic miles)	1245.3
Total Use (cubic miles):	8.4
in agriculture	40.0%
in industry	17.0%
in homes and cities	43.0%
Access to Safe Water:	
urban population	100.0%
rural population	86.0%

Urban Centers and Waste

No. of Cities Over 1 Million:	14
percent of population	35.2%
Solid Wastes (million tons)	22.7
Urban Sanitation Access	89.0%

Population and Gross National Product

Population   GNP
(millions)   (billion $US)

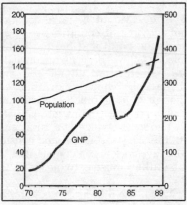

Commercial Energy Use

Total Energy Use   Per Capita Energy Use
(trillion BTUs)   (million BTUs)

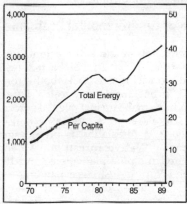

CHILE

Total Area: 292,254 sq. miles
Global Rank: 2   Per Capita: 14.2 acres
Population: 13,173,000
Global Rank: 54   Growth Rate: 1.66%
Gross National Product: $23,424 m.
Global Rank: 55   Per Capita: $1,808
Greenhouse Gas Emissions
Global Share: 0.11%   Per Capita Rank: 108

Chile is a narrow strip of land west of the Andes Mountains. It is isolated from neighboring countries by the desert in the north and by the Andes. Chile has three diverse regions: the north, which is agricultural, arid, and hot; the center, which is industrialized, although with a significant agricultural sector, and has a temperate climate; and the south, which is a rural area with forests, lakes, farms, and considerable livestock and a climate that, at the southernmost extreme, is quite cold.

Chile is the fifth largest country in fishery production. Energy and mining are also strong industries in Chile. However, there have been neither environmental impact studies nor a uniform environmental policy.

Major Environmental Problems

Deforestation and soil erosion. Chile has a terrain that is favorable to forests and a forest industry that is both strong and important economically. Forest products make up just over 10 percent of Chile's exports, and as a consequence, deforestation is progressing rapidly. Native forests have been cleared for pine plantations, and the wood chips industry is expanding.

This misuse of the forests also is leading to soil erosion, biodiversity loss, and water pollution. However, incentives for reforestation that may help offset the economic drive toward clear-cutting have been developed.

Water pollution. Competition for water among agricultural, mining, and urban users is increasing and beginning to pose a serious environmental threat. This is exacerbated by steadily increasing watershed degradation and by the pollution of the rivers and other water sources. Watershed degradation also contributes to erosion, floods, and sediment problems. In the summer, farmers create a serious health threat by using sewage water for irrigation.

Urban pollution. Much of Chile's population is urban, and the environmental quality of the capital city of Santiago has been steadily deteriorating. Air pollution stems from uncontrolled industrial pollution and vehicular exhausts, resulting in a thick smog that covers the city; emergency conditions are becoming frequent. Water pollution is especially bad as a result of untreated sewage. Environmental policies exist, although enforcement is weak.

Overfishing. Chile's productive fishery is in danger of being destroyed, because this resource is being exploited at a rate that exceeds a sustainable yield. Without controls, the fish catch is likely to decline precipitously.

Quality of Life

Life Expectancy (years)	71.5
Infant Mortality (per 1000)	20.0
Population Under 15 Years	30.4%
Population Over 65 Years	5.4%
Literacy Rate	93.4%
Malnourished Children	10.0%

Land Use and Habitats

Cropland (sq. miles):	17,471
per capita (acres)	0.9
global rank	50
Permanent Pasture (sq. miles):	51,931
total livestock (millions)	12.5
Forest and Woodlands (sq. miles):	33,977
1985 deforestation (sq. miles)	193
Wilderness Area (sq. miles)	89,136
Maritime Areas (EEZ, sq. miles)	8,835
Protected Areas (sq. miles):	52,702
percent of total	18.0%
No. of Threatened Species:	
mammals	9
birds	18
plants	192

Energy and Industry

Energy Production:	
solids (trillion BTUs)	54
liquids (trillion BTUs)	55
gas (trillion BTUs)	63
nuclear (gigawatt-hours)	0
hydroelectric (gigawatt-hours)	9,606
Energy Requirements:	
traditional fuels (trillion BTUs)	67
total (trillion BTUs)	567
per capita (million BTUs)	44
per capita (global rank)	59
Industrial Share of GDP	NA
Industrial Energy Index	NA
Metal Reserve Index (world=100%)	7.0%
No. of Motor Vehicles/1000 Persons	53

Water

Renewable Supply (cubic miles)	112.3
Total Use (cubic miles):	4.0
in agriculture	89.0%
in industry	5.0%
in homes and cities	6.0%
Access to Safe Water:	
urban population	100.0%
rural population	21.0%

Urban Centers and Waste

No. of Cities Over 1 Million:	1
percent of population	35.9%
Solid Wastes (million tons)	2.3
Urban Sanitation Access	100.0%

Population and Gross National Product

Population (millions)	GNP (billion $US)

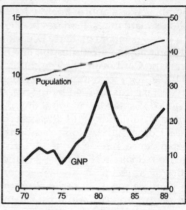

Commercial Energy Use

Total Energy Use (trillion BTUs)	Per Capita Energy Use (million BTUs)

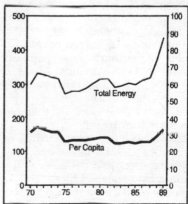

COLOMBIA

Total Area: 439,726 sq. miles
Global Rank: 25   Per Capita: 8.5 acres
Population: 32,978,000
Global Rank: 29   Growth Rate: 1.97%
Gross National Product: $37,470 m.
Global Rank: 43   Per Capita: $1,159
Greenhouse Gas Emissions
Global Share: 1.40%   Per Capita Rank: 23

Colombia covers approximately half a million square miles. It shares borders with Venezuela, Brazil, Peru, Ecuador, and Panama and straddles the Pacific Ocean and Caribbean Sea. The country has three main topographical regions: flat coastal areas divided by the Sierra Nevada de Santa Marta Mountains, the Central Highlands, and the eastern plains. Colombia has a long tradition of independence, having gained its freedom from Spain in 1821. It has a democratic government.

Colombia's climate varies from the heat of the tropical rainforest on the coast and eastern plains to temperate conditions on the plateau, which has frequent light rain. The mountain areas have permanent snow cover. Because of its varied climatic conditions, a variety of crops, from coffee to rice to tobacco, can be grown.

With almost 33 million people, Colombia is the fourth most populous country in Latin America. About 70 percent of the population lives in cities; the rest of the country is sparsely populated, with a density of less than two persons per square mile.

Colombia has many natural resources. Its exports include oil, coal, coffee, bananas, and cut flowers. It is also a major center of illegal cocaine processing and distribution, which has contributed both to a climate of violence and corruption and to environ-

mental degradation in some parts of the country.

Major Environmental Problems

Land degradation. Because large regions have been cleared for cattle raising, coffee production, and mining, soil erosion is a particular concern. Heavy rains on cleared areas often wash soil away, clogging streams. Poor logging practices have also led to advanced stages of land degradation.

Deforestation. Over the years there has been an increasing trend toward deforestation of the nation's biologically diverse woodlands and forests. Tropical hardwoods, pines, and eucalyptus are harvested from its forests. Because these massive timber resources are currently being overexploited, they are dwindling rapidly. In some parts of the country, the presence of cocaine traffickers makes protection of the forests impossible.

Endangered species. Colombia's Choco region, which extends along the Pacific watershed, has one of the world's largest numbers of endemic bird species and extremely varied plant communities. As the forest is cut back, however, habitats disappear. Two thirds of Colombia's endemic bird species are endangered.

Quality of Life

Life Expectancy (years)	68.3
Infant Mortality (per 1000)	40.0
Population Under 15 Years	34.1%
Population Over 65 Years	3.5%
Literacy Rate	86.7%
Malnourished Children	27.0%

Land Use and Habitats

Cropland (sq. miles):	20,772
per capita (acres)	0.4
global rank	96
Permanent Pasture (sq. miles):	155,598
total livestock (millions)	34.0
Forest and Woodlands (sq. miles):	195,367
1985 deforestation (sq. miles)	3,436
Wilderness Area (sq. miles)	58,519
Maritime Areas (EEZ, sq. miles)	2,329
Protected Areas (sq. miles):	35,914
percent of total	8.2%
No. of Threatened Species:	
mammals	25
birds	69
plants	316

Energy and Industry

Energy Production:	
solids (trillion BTUs)	489
liquids (trillion BTUs)	815
gas (trillion BTUs)	164
nuclear (gigawatt-hours)	0
hydroelectric (gigawatt-hours)	29,877
Energy Requirements:	
traditional fuels (trillion BTUs)	197
total (trillion BTUs)	1,136
per capita (million BTUs)	35
per capita (global rank)	63
Industrial Share of GDP	36.4%
Industrial Energy Index	14
Metal Reserve Index (world=100%)	0.1%
No. of Motor Vehicles/1000 Persons	28

Water

Renewable Supply (cubic miles)	256.7
Total Use (cubic miles):	1.3
in agriculture	43.0%
in industry	16.0%
in homes and cities	41.0%
Access to Safe Water:	
urban population	88.0%
rural population	87.0%

Urban Centers and Waste

No. of Cities Over 1 Million:	4
percent of population	27.3%
Solid Wastes (million tons)	5.0
Urban Sanitation Access	85.0%

Population and Gross National Product

Population (millions)	GNP (billion $US)

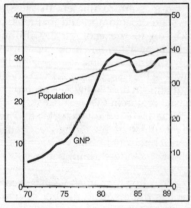

Commercial Energy Use

Total Energy Use (trillion BTUs)	Per Capita Energy Use (million BTUs)

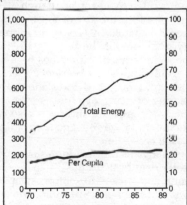

ECUADOR

Total Area: 109,481 sq. miles
 Global Rank: 67   Per Capita: 6.6 acres
Population: 10,587,000
 Global Rank: 61   Growth Rate: 2.56%
Gross National Product: $9,668 m.
 Global Rank: 65   Per Capita: $937
Greenhouse Gas Emissions
 Global Share: 0.49%   Per Capita Rank: 14

Ecuador is approximately the size of the state of Colorado and includes, in addition to the ecologically unique Galápagos Islands, three geographically distinct regions: the Amazonian jungle in the east (Oriente), the Andean highlands in the center (Sierra), and the coastal region in the west (Costa).

Ecuador is an oil exporter and receives most of its foreign exchange from its petroleum sales. Other major exports include shrimp, bananas, and flowers.

According to many botanists, Ecuador has the greatest number of plant species of any South American country—more than twice that of the entire continental United States. The Oriente contains 70 percent of all species found in Brazilian Amazonia, though it is only one fifth the size. The Costa has been designated by ecologist Norman Myers as one of the world's 10 "hot spots" in terms of extinctions because of its high number of endemic species and rapid rate of deforestation. The clearing of mangrove forests to make ponds for growing shrimp is also reducing biodiversity and degrading coastal ecosystems.

Positive factors include a successful ecotourism trade in the Galápagos Islands and a debt-for-nature swap in 1987 that channeled $10 million toward environmental protection organizations and activities.

Major Environmental Problems

Deforestation. In the Costa region, approximately 95 percent of the forests have been cut down, and the remaining forests will disappear within 10 to 15 years if the rate of destruction continues unabated. The Sierra is already almost completely devoid of natural forest cover. It is estimated that all the Oriente's forest cover will be gone within about 40 years if destruction continues.

Land degradation. A direct result of Ecuador's high deforestation rate is land degradation. The damage includes soil erosion, flooding, devegetation, and desertification. In the past 25 years, land degradation has increased about 30 percent, and the trend continues. Demographic pressures from rapid population growth have pushed people into previously uninhabited areas, leading to more intensive use of lands and to overgrazing. Government policies encourage timber felling and colonization.

Industrial and urban pollution. Other significant ecological problems facing Ecuador include inadequate water and sewage facilities in urban areas and contamination caused by oil spills in the Oriente and by improper mining practices in the Costa.

ECUADOR

Quality of Life

Life Expectancy (years)	65.4
Infant Mortality (per 1000)	63.0
Population Under 15 Years	37.7%
Population Over 65 Years	3.3%
Literacy Rate	85.8%
Malnourished Children	39.0%

Land Use and Habitats

Cropland (sq. miles):	10,243
per capita (acres)	0.6
global rank	70
Permanent Pasture (sq. miles):	19,691
total livestock (millions)	10.8
Forest and Woodlands (sq. miles):	43,243
1985 deforestation (sq. miles)	1,310
Wilderness Area (sq. miles)	0
Maritime Areas (EEZ, sq. miles)	4,475
Protected Areas (sq. miles):	41,257
percent of total	37.7%
No. of Threatened Species:	
mammals	21
birds	64
plants	121

Energy and Industry

Energy Production:	
solids (trillion BTUs)	0
liquids (trillion BTUs)	580
gas (trillion BTUs)	4
nuclear (gigawatt-hours)	0
hydroelectric (gigawatt-hours)	4,917
Energy Requirements:	
traditional fuels (trillion BTUs)	69
total (trillion BTUs)	292
per capita (million BTUs)	28
per capita (global rank)	72
Industrial Share of GDP	NA
Industrial Energy Index	8
Metal Reserve Index (world=100%)	NA
No. of Motor Vehicles/1000 Persons	28

Water

Renewable Supply (cubic miles)	75.0
Total Use (cubic miles):	1.3
in agriculture	90.0%
in industry	3.0%
in homes and cities	7.0%
Access to Safe Water:	
urban population	75.0%
rural population	37.0%

Urban Centers and Waste

No. of Cities Over 1 Million:	2
percent of population	27.5%
Solid Wastes (million tons)	1.2
Urban Sanitation Access	75.0%

Population and Gross National Product

Population (millions) GNP (billion $US)

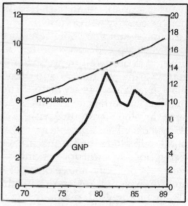

Commercial Energy Use

Total Energy Use (trillion BTUs) Per Capita Energy Use (million BTUs)

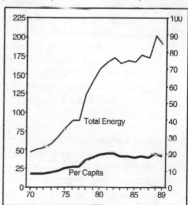

GUYANA

Total Area: 82,999 sq. miles
Global Rank: 78   Per Capita: 66.7 acres
Population: 796,000
Global Rank: 130   Growth Rate: 0.15%
Gross National Product: $271 m.
Global Rank: 137   Per Capita: $341
Greenhouse Gas Emissions
Global Share: 0.01%   Per Capita Rank: 123

Guyana is a small, resource-rich South American country with a variety of ethnic groups, a complex political history, and a vast store of unexploited resources. It is bordered by the Atlantic Ocean, Suriname, Brazil, and Venezuela. Guyana is a country on the brink of making important decisions about how to develop its resource base.

Guyana's inhabitants live mainly in a small strip along the Caribbean Sea. The interior—tropical forests and savannas—is not only unexploited, it is largely unexplored. Yet it is rich in minerals, including gold, diamonds, copper, uranium, iron ore, and perhaps the world's largest deposits of bauxite, which is used in making aluminum.

The economy is a mix of government-owned industries (sugar and bauxite mining), private enterprise (rice farming), and cooperative farms. Although mainly agricultural, Guyana has a number of small manufacturing plants that assemble garments, stoves, and refrigerators. The economy has never boomed; it declined during the 1980s, leaving Guyana deeply in debt.

Now, however, the economy appears poised for further development, which the government recognizes will significantly affect the still largely unspoiled environment. Where development has already occurred, the expected environmental problems have resulted. The government is now working to develop the institutions and legislation needed for sustainable development.

Major Environmental Problems

Water quality and management. Most of Guyana's water for domestic, agricultural, and industrial use is taken from artesian wells near the coast. Overuse of these wells is causing a drop in the water table, which could lead to contamination by saline water from the ocean. Alternative sources of surface waters are available for development.

Soil protection. The fragile inland soils require a protective forest cover. In some areas forests have not regenerated after clear-cutting, and the soils have eroded.

Sewage and solid waste disposal. Inadequate and malfunctioning sewerage systems and pit latrines, along with dumping of solid waste into drainage canals, threaten public health. Because parts of Guyana's coast lie below sea level, breaches of its sea defenses permit sea water to flood latrines and septic tanks, contaminating drinking water in poorly maintained water mains. The country lacks sufficient trained personnel to control these problems.

Quality of Life

Life Expectancy (years)	63.2
Infant Mortality (per 1000)	56.0
Population Under 15 Years	31.8%
Population Over 65 Years	3.8%
Literacy Rate	96.4%
Malnourished Children	20.7%

Land Use and Habitats

Cropland (sq. miles):	1,911
per capita (acres)	1.5
global rank	13
Permanent Pasture (sq. miles):	4,749
total livestock (millions)	0.6
Forest and Woodlands (sq. miles):	63,201
1985 deforestation (sq. miles)	12
Wilderness Area (sq. miles)	47,121
Maritime Areas (EEZ, sq. miles)	503
Protected Areas (sq. miles):	45
percent of total	0.1%
No. of Threatened Species:	
mammals	12
birds	9
plants	68

Energy and Industry

Energy Production:	
solids (trillion BTUs)	0
liquids (trillion BTUs)	0
gas (trillion BTUs)	0
nuclear (gigawatt-hours)	0
hydroelectric (gigawatt-hours)	8
Energy Requirements:	
traditional fuels (trillion BTUs)	4
total (trillion BTUs)	13
per capita (million BTUs)	16
per capita (global rank)	96
Industrial Share of GDP	31.2%
Industrial Energy Index	NA
Metal Reserve Index (world=100%)	0.2%
No. of Motor Vehicles/1000 Persons	NA

Water

Renewable Supply (cubic miles)	57.8
Total Use (cubic miles):	1.3
in agriculture	99.0%
in industry	0.0%
in homes and cities	1.0%
Access to Safe Water:	
urban population	94.0%
rural population	74.0%

Urban Centers and Waste

No. of Cities Over 1 Million:	0
percent of population	0.0%
Solid Wastes (million tons)	0.1
Urban Sanitation Access	85.0%

Population and Gross National Product

Population (millions)   GNP (billion $US)

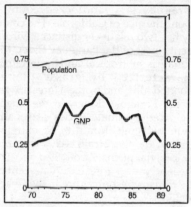

Commercial Energy Use

Total Energy Use (trillion BTUs)   Per Capita Energy Use (million BTUs)

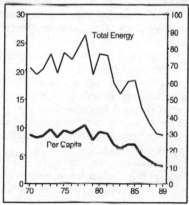

PARAGUAY

Total Area: 157,044 sq. miles
  Global Rank: 54   Per Capita: 23.5 acres
Population: 4,277,000
  Global Rank: 96   Growth Rate: 2.93%
Gross National Product: $4,096 m.
  Global Rank: 92   Per Capita: $986
Greenhouse Gas Emissions
  Global Share: 0.19%   Per Capita Rank: 18

Paraguay is a landlocked country about the size of California. The country has two relatively distinct environments: east of the Paraguay River, the climate is subtropical, and the terrain is characterized by grassy plains, wooded hills, and tropical forests; west of the Paraguay River, in the Chaco region, the climate varies seasonally from extreme humidity to extreme aridity, and the terrain is characterized by low, flat plains. About 39 percent of the land area is forested; 70 percent of the forestry resources are in the Chaco region.

Paraguay's economy relies primarily on agriculture. About half the land area is used for pasture, and about 5 percent is used for crops. Cotton and soybeans account for roughly 35 percent of the country's agricultural output; livestock also is an important component.

Paraguay has reduced its dependence on imported oil by developing hydroelectric resources and an alcohol fuel industry based on sugar cane. Fuelwood and bagasse (the residue left from sugar cane processing) account for about 60 percent of total energy requirements.

The massive Itaipu hydroelectric plant on the Parana River, which was jointly developed by Paraguay and Brazil, has a generating capacity of 12,600 megawatts; at present, Para-

guay sells most of its share of the power to Brazil.

Major Environmental Problems

Deforestation. During the 1980s, large areas of forest were lost. Paraguay embarked on a national reforestation program, but the program was badly hurt by the 1982–83 recession and little reforestation has taken place. At the current rate of deforestation, few forests will remain by the year 2010.

The primary cause of deforestation in Paraguay is the clearing of land for agriculture. In the process, farmers generally slash and burn 70 to 80 percent of the useful wood and 90 to 95 percent of the biomass, a process that releases carbon dioxide into the atmosphere. Clearing also may greatly increase soil erosion.

Water pollution. In Asuncion, the capital, many creeks are seriously polluted. Pollution sources include food industries, sewage drainage systems, and the leather and alcohol industries.

Solid waste collection. Asuncion's solid waste is dumped in a natural depression that is a source of unsanitary conditions affecting 10,000 or more people. Most other cities either use open-air dumps or have no waste services at all.

Quality of Life

Life Expectancy (years)	66.9
Infant Mortality (per 1000)	42.0
Population Under 15 Years	39.6%
Population Over 65 Years	3.0%
Literacy Rate	90.1%
Malnourished Children	NA

Land Use and Habitats

Cropland (sq. miles):	8,556
per capita (acres)	1.3
global rank	19
Permanent Pasture (sq. miles):	80,309
total livestock (millions)	11.3
Forest and Woodlands (sq. miles):	55,405
1985 deforestation (sq. miles)	819
Wilderness Area (sq. miles)	29,831
Maritime Areas (EEZ, sq. miles)	0
Protected Areas (sq. miles):	4,578
percent of total	2.9%
No. of Threatened Species:	
mammals	14
birds	24
plants	12

Energy and Industry

Energy Production:	
solids (trillion BTUs)	0
liquids (trillion BTUs)	0
gas (trillion BTUs)	0
nuclear (gigawatt-hours)	0
hydroelectric (gigawatt-hours)	2,784
Energy Requirements:	
traditional fuels (trillion BTUs)	52
total (trillion BTUs)	88
per capita (million BTUs)	21
per capita (global rank)	85
Industrial Share of GDP	22.4%
Industrial Energy Index	5
Metal Reserve Index (world=100%)	NA
No. of Motor Vehicles/1000 Persons	NA

Water

Renewable Supply (cubic miles)	22.6
Total Use (cubic miles).	0.1
in agriculture	78.0%
in industry	7.0%
in homes and cities	15.0%
Access to Safe Water:	
urban population	65.0%
rural population	7.0%

Urban Centers and Waste

No. of Cities Over 1 Million:	0
percent of population	0.0%
Solid Wastes (million tons)	0.4
Urban Sanitation Access	55.0%

Population and Gross National Product

Population (millions)	GNP (billion $US)

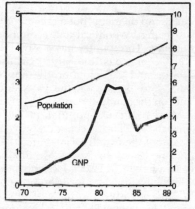

Commercial Energy Use

Total Energy Use (trillion BTUs)	Per Capita Energy Use (million BTUs)

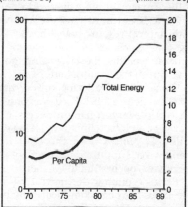

PERU

Total Area: 496,215 sq. miles
  Global Rank: 18   Per Capita: 14.7 acres
Population: 21,550,000
  Global Rank: 40   Growth Rate: 2.08%
Gross National Product: $32,608 m.
  Global Rank: 46   Per Capita: $1,545
Greenhouse Gas Emissions
  Global Share: 0.47%   Per Capita Rank: 65

Peru is a country of breathtaking beauty and diversity, but it is currently hamstrung by political and economic problems. The country has a long Pacific Ocean coastline, and borders Ecuador and Colombia on the north, Brazil and Bolivia on the east, and Chile on the south.

Most of Peru's population lives along the dry Pacific coast, on only 10 percent of the country's land area. Behind the coast, the Andes Mountains reach a height of 22,000 feet and provide the headwaters for tributaries of the Amazon River. To the east of the mountains begins the tropical rainforest, which covers 60 percent of the country and which stretches from Peru clear across the continent to the mouth of the Amazon at the Atlantic Ocean.

Peru is extraordinarily endowed with natural resource wealth, including forests, fisheries, and legendary mineral wealth—the silver and gold that lured the conquistadors in the 1500s, as well as lead, zinc, copper, and iron ore. Before 1982, Peru was one of the world's largest fish producers, but that year a global climatological event called *El Niño* stifled the cold upwelling that supported huge schools of anchovies, decimating the fishery.

Peru's economic decline during the late 1980s has been complicated by the presence of two Marxist terrorist groups. Much of Peru's infrastructure

has become dysfunctional. In 1990, cholera, a potentially fatal disease spread through poor-quality water and a lack of sanitation, broke out in a coastal Peruvian town and spread to other countries in Latin America.

Peru is fortunate to have environmental legislation, active environmentalist groups, and university researchers. However, their concerns are currently overshadowed by economic decline and political unrest.

Major Environmental Problems

Soil degradation. Except for the areas along its rivers, most of Peru's land—both mountain drylands and that underlying the tropical forests—contains poor-quality soil that is easily degraded. Centuries of grazing plus recent logging in forests threaten soil productivity and increased erosion.

Overfishing and marine pollution. Overfishing by Peruvian and foreign fleets has slowed the recovery of the anchovy fishery. An additional and growing threat to the fishery is the pollution of coastal waters by industrial and municipal wastes and poisonous mine tailings. Sewage treatment facilities and controls on industrial pollution and disposal of mine wastes will be needed if the fishery is to be sustained.

Quality of Life

Life Expectancy (years)	61.4
Infant Mortality (per 1000)	88.0
Population Under 15 Years	35.5%
Population Over 65 Years	3.3%
Literacy Rate	85.1%
Malnourished Children	43.0%

Land Use and Habitats

Cropland (sq. miles):	14,402
per capita (acres)	0.4
global rank	94
Permanent Pasture (sq. miles):	104,710
total livestock (millions)	22.3
Forest and Woodlands (sq. miles):	265,058
1985 deforestation (sq. miles)	1,042
Wilderness Area (sq. miles)	141,544
Maritime Areas (EEZ, sq. miles)	3,965
Protected Areas (sq. miles):	21,304
percent of total	4.3%
No. of Threatened Species:	
mammals	29
birds	65
plants	353

Energy and Industry

Energy Production:	
solids (trillion BTUs)	3
liquids (trillion BTUs)	278
gas (trillion BTUs)	19
nuclear (gigawatt-hours)	0
hydroelectric (gigawatt-hours)	10,518
Energy Requirements:	
traditional fuels (trillion BTUs)	92
total (trillion BTUs)	459
per capita (million BTUs)	22
per capita (global rank)	84
Industrial Share of GDP	30.5%
Industrial Energy Index	12
Metal Reserve Index (world=100%)	0.9%
No. of Motor Vehicles/1000 Persons	NA

Water

Renewable Supply (cubic miles)	9.6
Total Use (cubic miles):	1.5
in agriculture	72.0%
in industry	9.0%
in homes and cities	19.0%
Access to Safe Water:	
urban population	78.0%
rural population	22.0%

Urban Centers and Waste

No. of Cities Over 1 Million:	1
percent of population	29.0%
Solid Wastes (million tons)	3.0
Urban Sanitation Access	71.0%

Population and Gross National Product

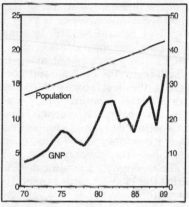

Population (millions) — GNP (billion $US)

Commercial Energy Use

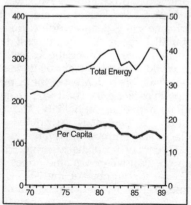

Total Energy Use (trillion BTUs) — Per Capita Energy Use (million BTUs)

SURINAME

Total Area: 63,038 sq. miles
  Global Rank: 85   Per Capita: 95.6 acres
Population: 422,000
  Global Rank: 136   Growth Rate: 1.94%
Gross National Product: $1,320 m.
  Global Rank: 120   Per Capita: $3,188
Greenhouse Gas Emissions
  Global Share: 0.01%   Per Capita Rank: 72

Suriname, on the tropical Atlantic coast of northern South America, is a land of unspoiled natural beauty. Its small population and most of its economic activities are concentrated along the coast. Inland, Amerindians and Bushnegroes, the descendants of escaped African slaves, continue their traditional ways of life. The recent civil war and continued internal conflict have limited economic development and destabilized the economy.

The economy of Suriname declined during the 1980s. It earns foreign currency from exports of rice, assorted other agricultural products, shrimp, and—its most important products—bauxite, alumina, and aluminum. Suriname produces 3.3 percent of the world's total production of bauxite.

Because of its lack of development, Suriname's forests and wildlife are as yet undisturbed—the rate of forest destruction there is among the lowest in the world. Ninety percent of its land area is still forested. Most of the population lives along the coast, 70 percent in Paramaribo, its capital city. The remaining 10 percent is distributed in villages along three main rivers.

As part of its plans to protect its natural resources, Suriname hopes to increase the number of tourists who come to enjoy its undisturbed wilderness. For its size, Suriname contains an amazing diversity of flora and fauna.

At present, little of it is threatened within the country. Suriname has 670 species of birds, 184 species of mammals, 152 species of reptiles, 95 species of amphibians, and more than 300 species of fish. Nesting beaches for four species of sea turtles are found on the coast.

Major Environmental Problems

Unspoiled environment. Suriname has few of the environmental problems that plague other countries. The coastal mangroves and swamps have escaped harm, as they are economically unattractive for many development projects. These habitats, however, nourish a productive fishery and attract bird watchers and game hunters.

The country's small population has left much of the country nearly primeval. The undisturbed neotropical Amazonian forest that covers much of the interior of Suriname is a major biodiversity resource and an opportunity for conservation. Protected areas cover at least 5 percent of the land surface.

Farming the swamps. Freshwater swamps being converted into rice paddies, to which pesticides and agrochemicals are applied, will require strict regulation of irrigation and drainage to avoid polluting the estuarine zone.

Quality of Life

Life Expectancy (years)	68.8
Infant Mortality (per 1000)	33.0
Population Under 15 Years	33.7%
Population Over 65 Years	3.8%
Literacy Rate	94.9%
Malnourished Children	NA

Land Use and Habitats

Cropland (sq. miles):	263
per capita (acres)	0.4
global rank	97
Permanent Pasture (sq. miles):	77
total livestock (millions)	0.1
Forest and Woodlands (sq. miles):	57,355
1985 deforestation (sq. miles)	12
Wilderness Area (sq. miles)	42,778
Maritime Areas (EEZ, sq. miles)	391
Protected Areas (sq. miles):	2,946
percent of total	4.7%
No. of Threatened Species:	
mammals	11
birds	6
plants	68

Energy and Industry

Energy Production:	
solids (trillion BTUs)	0
liquids (trillion BTUs)	9
gas (trillion BTUs)	0
nuclear (gigawatt-hours)	0
hydroelectric (gigawatt-hours)	912
Energy Requirements:	
traditional fuels (trillion BTUs)	0
total (trillion BTUs)	21
per capita (million BTUs)	51
per capita (global rank)	53
Industrial Share of GDP	25.8%
Industrial Energy Index	NA
Metal Reserve Index (world=100%)	0.2%
No. of Motor Vehicles/1000 Persons	86

Water

Renewable Supply (cubic miles)	48.0
Total Use (cubic miles):	0.1
in agriculture	89.0%
in industry	5.0%
in homes and cities	6.0%
Access to Safe Water:	
urban population	82.0%
rural population	56.0%

Urban Centers and Waste

No. of Cities Over 1 Million:	0
percent of population	0.0%
Solid Wastes (million tons)	0.0
Urban Sanitation Access	64.0%

Population and Gross National Product

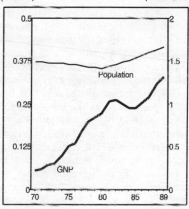

Population (millions) — GNP (billion $US)

Commercial Energy Use

Total Energy Use (trillion BTUs) — Per Capita Energy Use (million BTUs)

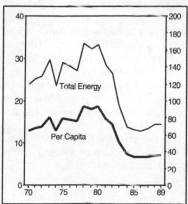

VENEZUELA

Total Area: 352,137 sq. miles
Global Rank: 31   Per Capita: 11.4 acres
Population: 19,735,000
Global Rank: 41   Growth Rate: 2.61%
Gross National Product: $41,459 m.
Global Rank: 40   Per Capita: $2,156
Greenhouse Gas Emissions
Global Share: 0.54%   Per Capita Rank: 46

Venezuela is a country about twice the size of California with vast energy, mineral, and other natural resources, an educated population, and a high standard of living. It is located on the northern coast of South America, along the Caribbean Sea. Venezuela was liberated from Spain by the heroic Simon Bolivar in 1830, but it was then run by a series of dictators until 1958. It is now considered one of the most stable democracies in South America. Most of the population is clustered along the coast and in major cities; the interior is largely undeveloped *llanos* (flat grasslands) and rainforest.

Flush with revenue from its substantial oil reserves, Venezuela developed rapidly during the 1970s into a modern urban country. Oil, iron ore, and bauxite, along with agricultural products, are its main exports. However, waste, corruption, and falling oil prices brought an economic decline over the 1980s. In 1989 urban residents rioted when the government removed subsidies from food, gasoline, and bus fares to meet the economic requirements of its foreign lenders. Despite such problems, Venezuela has a relatively high per capita income among South American countries.

In addition to oil reserves, Venezuela has one of the largest undeveloped coal fields in Latin America, as well as bauxite, iron ore, and gold. It is

researching methods of converting its enormous reserve of 1,200 billion barrels of bitumen, a very heavy hydrocarbon, into an inexpensive fuel.

Major Environmental Problems

Deforestation and soil degradation. Venezuela lost an average of 1,000 square miles of forest per year during the 1980s. It has a respectable 17,374 square miles in protected areas. The *llanos* are being overgrazed and degraded, leading to erosion and soil compaction.

Urban and industrial pollution. This pollution is most intense along the Caribbean coast, where most of the population is concentrated. Sewage treatment is scarce, and industrial pollution controls are few and poorly enforced.

Freshwater pollution. Both of Venezuela's major lakes are significantly polluted. After freshwater inflows to Lake Valencia were diverted for irrigation, urban sewage was the only water left going into the lake. Oil and urban pollution in Lake Maracaibo, which is dotted with oil rigs, has killed most of the fish and closed shoreline resorts. In the Guiana highlands, the impacts of gold and diamond mining cause severe river pollution.

Quality of Life

Life Expectancy (years)	69.6
Infant Mortality (per 1000)	36.0
Population Under 15 Years	36.6%
Population Over 65 Years	3.0%
Literacy Rate	88.1%
Malnourished Children	7.0%

Land Use and Habitats

Cropland (sq. miles):	15,039
per capita (acres)	0.5
global rank	88
Permanent Pasture (sq. miles):	68,147
total livestock (millions)	19.2
Forest and Woodlands (sq. miles):	117,625
1985 deforestation (sq. miles)	946
Wilderness Area (sq. miles)	114,835
Maritime Areas (EEZ, sq. miles)	1,405
Protected Areas (sq. miles):	78,245
percent of total	22.2%
No. of Threatened Species:	
mammals	19
birds	34
plants	105

Energy and Industry

Energy Production:	
solids (trillion BTUs)	58
liquids (trillion BTUs)	4,122
gas (trillion BTUs)	750
nuclear (gigawatt-hours)	0
hydroelectric (gigawatt hours)	34,200
Energy Requirements:	
traditional fuels (trillion BTUs)	20
total (trillion BTUs)	1,763
per capita (million BTUs)	92
per capita (global rank)	36
Industrial Share of GDP	45.8%
Industrial Energy Index	21
Metal Reserve Index (world=100%)	0.2%
No. of Motor Vehicles/1000 Persons	129

Water

Renewable Supply (cubic miles)	205.4
Total Use (cubic miles):	1.0
in agriculture	46.0%
in industry	11.0%
in homes and cities	43.0%
Access to Safe Water:	
urban population	89.0%
rural population	89.0%

Urban Centers and Waste

No. of Cities Over 1 Million:	2
percent of population	26.6%
Solid Wastes (million tons)	3.6
Urban Sanitation Access	97.0%

Population and Gross National Product

Population (millions) — GNP (billion $US)

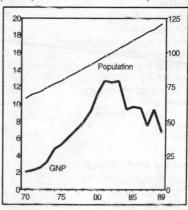

Commercial Energy Use

Total Energy Use (trillion BTUs) — Per Capita Energy Use (million BTUs)

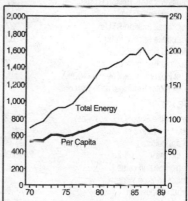

URUGUAY

Quality of Life

Life Expectancy (years)	72.0
Infant Mortality (per 1000)	24.0
Population Under 15 Years	24.4%
Population Over 65 Years	10.6%
Literacy Rate	96.2%
Malnourished Children	16.0%

Land Use and Habitats

Cropland (sq. miles):	5,035
per capita (acres)	1.0
global rank	33
Permanent Pasture (sq. miles):	52,189
total livestock (millions)	35.1
Forest and Woodlands (sq. miles):	2,583
1985 deforestation (sq. miles)	0
Wilderness Area (sq. miles)	0
Maritime Areas (EEZ, sq. miles)	461
Protected Areas (sq. miles):	122
percent of total	0.2%
No. of Threatened Species:	
mammals	5
birds	11
plants	11

Energy and Industry

Energy Production:	
solids (trillion BTUs)	0
liquids (trillion BTUs)	0
gas (trillion BTUs)	0
nuclear (gigawatt-hours)	0
hydroelectric (gigawatt-hours)	3,900
Energy Requirements:	
traditional fuels (trillion BTUs)	27
total (trillion BTUs)	112
per capita (million BTUs)	37
per capita (global rank)	62
Industrial Share of GDP	28.2%
Industrial Energy Index	7
Metal Reserve Index (world=100%)	NA
No. of Motor Vehicles/1000 Persons	96

Water

Renewable Supply (cubic miles)	14.2
Total Use (cubic miles):	0.2
in agriculture	91.0%
in industry	3.0%
in homes and cities	6.0%
Access to Safe Water:	
urban population	85.0%
rural population	5.0%

Urban Centers and Waste

No. of Cities Over 1 Million:	1
percent of population	38.7%
Solid Wastes (million tons)	0.5
Urban Sanitation Access	60.0%

Population and Gross National Product

Population (millions)   GNP (billion $US)

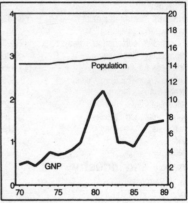

Commercial Energy Use

Total Energy Use (trillion BTUs)   Per Capita Energy Use (million BTUs)

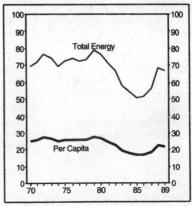

Zero means zero or less than half of the unit used (e.g., for Water, Total Use = 0.0 cubic miles; this is zero or less than 0.05 cubic miles). NA means that information is not available.

Total Area (1989) includes both land and water areas within a country's borders; data are from the Food and Agriculture Organisation of the United Nations (FAO). Countries are ranked from largest (1) to smallest by area. **Population** is based on 1990 estimates from the United Nations Population Division; countries are again ranked from largest to smallest. (**NOTE:** For each of the former Soviet republics, **Total Area** (including land and water areas) and **Population** (as of January 1, 1991) data are from the Center for International Research, U.S. Bureau of the Census. The **Growth Rate** is the annual rate of natural increase in population.) The **Gross National Product** (GNP) is a measure of the value of goods and services produced by a national economy. Countries are ranked from largest to smallest. GNP estimates are generally from the World Bank, although some are extracted from publications of the U.S. Central Intelligence Agency. The GNP for Germany is for the former West Germany only. Estimates for GNP are not available for some centrally planned economies. **Greenhouse Gas Emissions** are calculated by the World Resources Institute, using data from a variety of sources, and the **Global Share** is based on each country's emissions of carbon dioxide, methane, and chlorofluorocarbons—weighted by these gases' respective heating effects and lifetimes; countries are ranked from largest to smallest **per capita** emitters. Only countries for which data are available are included in rankings.

Country Data Pages

The set of data presented for industrial countries that are members of the Organisation for Economic Cooperation and Development (OECD) differs slightly from that of other countries, especially developing countries. OECD members have different environmental problems than do many developing countries (e.g., industrial pollution instead of malnutrition), and greater availability of information on these topics.

Data appearing only for OECD countries is preceded in these notes by an asterisk (*).

Quality of Life

Life Expectancy (years): 1990 life expectancy at birth is the average number of years a newborn baby can expect to live if current age-specific mortality rates remain the same throughout its life (U.N. Population Division).

Infant Mortality (per 1,000): 1990 number of babies dying before one year of age divided by the number of live births in that year, multiplied by 1,000 (U.N. Population Division).

Population Under 15 Years, Population Over 65 Years: Estimate of 1995 population in each of these dependent age groups (U.N. Population Division).

Literacy Rate: 1990 percentage of adults over 15 years of age who can read and write. Illiterates are those who cannot read with understanding and write a short and simple statement on his or her ordinary life. The interpretation of this definition varies widely and actual definitions of literacy are not strictly comparable between countries (United Nations Educational, Scientific and Cultural Organization [UNESCO]).

Malnourished Children: From single-year studies ranging from 1980–89, this is a measure of chronic undernutrition between the ages of 24 months and 59 months where children's height is less than 77 percent of the median for their age, also called stunting (United Nations Children's Fund [UNICEF], United Nations Development Programme [UNDP]).

Land Use and Habitats

Cropland: 1989 area of temporary and permanent crops, gardens, temporary meadows, and temporary fallow. Cropland data under Belgium are for Belgium and Luxembourg combined. 1989 **per capita** values; **global rank** excludes countries for which either cropland or population data are not available (FAO).

Permanent pasture: 1989 area used for five years or more for forage, including natural and cultivated crops. (Data for Belgium are from the OECD.) 1989 **total livestock** includes cattle, sheep, goats, pigs, equines, buffalo, and camels (FAO).

Forest and Woodlands: 1989 natural or planted stands of trees as well as logged areas that will be reforested in the near future. (Forest and Woodlands data for Belgium are from the OECD.) **1985 deforestation** is the most recent estimate available for deforestation in each country, the majority of which data is from a 1988 interim report by the United Nations Food and Agriculture Organization. Estimates for selected countries cover more recent time periods. Deforestation includes areas estimated to be permanently converted to nonforest uses that year and explicitly does not include logged areas if natural or artificial reseeding is planned (*World Resources 1992–93* [Oxford University Press, New York, 1992], by the World Resources Institute in collaboration with the United Nations Environment Programme and the United Nations Development Programme).

Wilderness Area: Areas of at least 1,544 square miles showing no evidence of human development on aeronautical navigation charts published by the U.S. Defense Mapping Agency during the early to mid-1980s (published by J. Michael McCloskey and Heather Spalding in the journal *AMBIO*, Vol. 18, No. 5, 1989). No land area is excluded so that this estimate includes mountains, deserts, tundra, forests, and glaciers.

Maritime Areas: The Exclusive Economic Zone (**EEZ**) is a claim by a maritime nation to all the resources in an area up to 200 nautical miles off its shores. The areas shown here are the potential EEZ areas, not the actual areas. Landlocked countries are shown with a maritime area of zero (0). Only half the countries have established a full EEZ (United Nations Office of Ocean Affairs and the Law of the Sea).

Protected Areas: 1991 land area of protected areas (over 2,540 acres) under national protection in one of five World Conservation Union (IUCN) categories and where access is at least partially restricted: scientific reserves and strict nature reserves, national and provincial parks, natural monuments and natural landmarks, managed nature reserves and wildlife sanctuaries, and protected landscapes and seascapes; **percent of**

total is calculated on the basis of total land area (World Conservation Monitoring Centre, Cambridge, United Kingdom).

Number of Threatened Species: Lists the number of **mammal, bird**, and **plant** species that are endangered, vulnerable, rare, or indeterminate (the risk of extinction is acknowledged but the exact degree is unknown). Data on mammals excludes whales and porpoises, and threatened birds are listed for countries where they breed or winter (variety of sources, primarily the World Conservation Union and the World Conservation Monitoring Centre).

Energy and Industry

All energy data are derived from the database prepared for the United Nations Statistical Office, *1989 Energy Statistics Yearbook* (New York, 1991). Solid, liquid, and gas production is reported in British thermal units (BTUs).

Energy Production: Solids are defined as coals, lignite, peat coke, oil shale, and bituminous sands; **liquids** are defined as crude petroleum and natural gas liquids (obtained in the processing of natural gas); **gas** is defined as natural gas, methane recovered from coal mines and sewage plants, coke oven gas, and blast furnace gas; **nuclear** is electricity produced by existing plants (gigawatt-hours); and **hydroelectric** is electricity produced by water power, except that pumped storage units are excluded (gigawatt-hours).

Energy Requirements: Estimate of the total energy requirements or consumption of a country, in conventional fuel equivalents. It includes traditional fuels and values electricity by the amount of fossil fuels that would be required for its generation. **Traditional fuels** include fuelwood, charcoal, bagasse, and animal and vegetal wastes; **total** requirements include traditional fuels and all solid, liquid, gas, and electricity; **per capita** requirements (or consumption) is calculated using the 1989 mid-year population; and **global rank** is calculated only for those countries with both energy requirement and population data.

Industrial Share of GDP: Recent, generally 1989, data on the amount of gross domestic product generated by industrial activities, including manufacturing (World Bank).

Industrial Energy Index: 1989 measure of energy intensity, and therefore energy efficiency, defined as megajoules of energy used in industrial activities divided by the value (in dollars) of the amount of the gross domestic product generated by industrial activity. This index ranges from 1 (Congo) to 66 (China); the United States has a score of 12 (World Bank and International Energy Administration). High scores show poor energy efficiency while low scores show high efficiency. Very low scores, such as for the Congo, could obscure the energy inefficiency of industry if that industry is very labor intensive and thus dependent on human energy, or if it uses traditional fuels.

Metal Reserve Index: The mean of its share of world reserves of each of 15 globally important metals. Shares shown as 0.0 percent are not zero but are less than 0.05 percent.

Number of Motor Vehicles/1,000 Persons: From each country's most recent census year, this refers generally to privately owned vehicles with four or more wheels used for noncommercial purposes, although some countries include taxis and rental cars in their reports (International Road Federation).

Water

Data on water supply and demand are from Chapter 22, "Freshwater," of *World Resources 1992–93* (Oxford University Press, New York, 1992), by the World Resources Institute in collaboration with the United Nations Environment Programme and the United Nations Development Programme.

Renewable Supply: The renewable supply of fresh water is the average annual flow of rivers and aquifers generated by rainfall within each country. River flows from neighboring countries are sometimes counted.

Total Use: The total use of water is that withdrawn from surface or underground sources for any use; **in agriculture** includes use of water for irrigation and the raising of livestock; **in industry** includes use of water for industrial processes, including that used to cool thermoelectric plants; **in homes and cities** includes drinking water and water for

use in commercial establishments, public services, and municipalities.

Access to Safe Water: Figures are supplied to the World Health Organization (WHO) by national governments and may represent optimistic assessments; **urban populations'** access to safe drinking water for urban populations is defined as access to piped water or to a public standpipe within 650 feet of a dwelling or housing unit; **rural populations'** access to safe drinking water is defined as treated surface water or untreated water from protected springs, boreholes, and sanitary wells located such that a family member need not spend a disproportionate amount of the day fetching water (WHO).

Urban Centers and Waste; Waste and Pollution

Number of Cities Over 1 Million: The number of cities in 1990 estimated to have a population of at least 1 million people; **percent of population** is the share of the country's total population that lives in these large cities (U.N. Population Division).

Solid Wastes, *Urban Solid Wastes: The estimated amount of waste generated in 1990 by the urban population of a country that would require incineration or landfill for disposal; ***per capita** is the amount generated by the average urban resident (OECD).

*Hazardous Wastes: Recent reports of waste known to contain harmful substances. Exact definitions vary among countries (OECD).

*Sewage Treatment Plant Coverage: Includes the percentage of the national population served by wastewater treatment plants for the most recent year that information is available. It can represent those served by only primary treatment or by secondary or tertiary treatment as well (OECD).

Urban Sanitation Access: Figures are supplied to WHO by national governments and may represent optimistic assessments. Access to sanitation services is defined as connections to public sewers or household systems (e.g., septic tanks, community toilets, pit privies, and pour-flush latrines) (WHO).

*SOx Emissions: Emissions of sulfur in the form of sulfur oxides contribute, in the form of sulfuric acid, to acid rain, which affects agriculture, forests, lakes and rivers, and the weathering of buildings. Different countries use differing methods for estimating these emissions. High concentrations of sulfur dioxide have important adverse health effects for the elderly, young children, and people with respiratory illness (OECD and the Cooperative Programme for Monitoring and Evaluation of the Long Range Transmission of Air Pollutants in Europe [EMEP]).

*NOx Emissions: Emissions of nitrogen in the form of nitrogen oxides contribute, in the form of nitric acid, to acid rain, which affects agriculture, forests, lakes and rivers, and the weathering of buildings. Different countries use differing methods for estimating these emissions. Nitrogen oxides contribute to photochemical smog and the production of tropospheric ozone, which has important adverse health effects for the elderly, young children, and people with respiratory illness (OECD, EMEP).

*Particulate Emissions: The health effects of suspended particulate matter depend on the biological and chemical makeup of the particles. Heavy metals condensed onto dust particles can be particularly toxic (OECD).

*Hydrocarbon Emissions: Hydrocarbons, in the presence of sunlight and along with nitrogen oxides, are responsible for photochemical smog. Hydrocarbons arise from the escape, evaporation, or incomplete combustion of fuels, lubricants, and solvents, as well as the incomplete combustion of biomass (OECD, EMEP).

changes in countries' economic health or variable currency exchange rates.

Population: Given in millions, population figures are derived from the database of the the U.N. Population Division published in *World Population Prospects as Assessed in 1990* (1991).

Gross National Product (GNP): The gross national product, given in billions of U.S. dollars, is a measure of the total goods and services produced in a country. These data are not adjusted for inflation (World Bank).

Commercial Energy Use

Derived from the database prepared for the United Nations Statistical Office, *1989 Energy Statistics Yearbook* (New York, 1991). Does not include energy from traditional (i.e., biomass) fuels. Occasional spikes or dips in the time series for energy use (consumption) are true reflections of the underlying data held in international data systems, but might result from a transcription error by the reporting country or international institution.

Total Energy Use: Reports on the total energy content of energy consumed from solid, liquid, and gaseous fuels, as well as nuclear, hydroelectric, geothermal, and wind-generated electric power. In contrast to *energy requirements* in the accompanying data (previously described), commercial energy use does not include traditional fuels and converts primary electricity to its BTU equivalent.

Per Capita Energy Use: Apportions annual commercial energy use by each country's mid-year population.

Line Graphs

These time-series data are from 1970–89 where available.

Population and Gross National Product

Occasional spikes and dips in the time series on gross national product can reflect sudden

Further information on data and sources is contained in World Resources 1992–93 *(Oxford University Press, New York, 1992), by the World Resources Institute in collaboration with the United Nations Environment Programme and United Nations Development Programme.*

Index

INDEX